DOING DATA SCIENCE IN R

DOING DATA SCIENCE IN R

An Introduction for Social Scientists

Mark Andrews

Los Angeles | London | New Delhi
Singapore | Washington DC | Melbourne

Los Angeles | London | New Delhi
Singapore | Washington DC | Melbourne

SAGE Publications Ltd
1 Oliver's Yard
55 City Road
London EC1Y 1SP

SAGE Publications Inc.
2455 Teller Road
Thousand Oaks, California 91320

SAGE Publications India Pvt Ltd
B 1/I 1 Mohan Cooperative Industrial Area
Mathura Road
New Delhi 110 044

SAGE Publications Asia-Pacific Pte Ltd
3 Church Street
#10-04 Samsung Hub
Singapore 049483

Editor: Aly Owen
Assistant editor: Lauren Jacobs
Production editor: Ian Antcliff
Copyeditor: QuADS Prepress Pvt Ltd
Proofreader: Neville Hankins
Marketing manager: Ben Griffin-Sherwood
Cover design: Shaun Mercier
Typeset by: C&M Digitals (P) Ltd, Chennai, India
Printed in the UK

Library of Congress Control Number: 2020945072

British Library Cataloguing in Publication data

A catalogue record for this book is available from
the British Library

ISBN 978-1-5264-8676-9
ISBN 978-1-5264-8677-6 (pbk)

At SAGE we take sustainability seriously. Most of our products are printed in the UK using responsibly sourced
papers and boards. When we print overseas we ensure sustainable papers are used as measured by the PREPS
grading system. We undertake an annual audit to monitor our sustainability.

CONTENTS

ABOUT THE AUTHOR

Mark Andrews (PhD) is Senior Lecturer in the Department of Psychology at Nottingham Trent University. There, he specializes in teaching statistics and data science at all levels from undergraduate to PhD level. Currently, he is the Chair of the British Psychological Society's Mathematics, Statistics, and Computing section. Between 2015 and 2018, Dr Andrews was funded by the UK's Economic and Social Research Council (ESRC) to provide advanced training workshops on Bayesian data analysis to UK-based researchers at PhD level and beyond in the social sciences. Dr Andrews' background is in computational cognitive science, particularly focused Bayesian models of human cognition. He has a PhD in Cognitive Science from Cornell University, and was a postdoctoral researcher in the Gatsby Computational Neuroscience Unit in UCL and also in the Department of Psychology in UCL.

ONLINE RESOURCES

Lecturers can visit https://study.sagepub.com/andrews to find a range of additional resources to support teaching and aid your students' study.

Instructor resources

- **PowerPoint slides** covering key themes and topics from every chapter, which are available for you to download and tailor in support of your teaching.
- An **instructor's manual**, providing a guide to using the book in teaching and resources for teaching, including ideas for student activities and assessments.
- **Datasets** for you to share with your students in class or for assignments, which will support their mastery of data science techniques.

1

Data Analysis and Data Science

Introduction

This book is about statistical data analysis of real-world data using modern tools. It is aimed at those who are currently engaged in, or planning to be engaged in, analysis of statistical data of the kind that might arise at or beyond PhD level scientific research, especially in the social sciences. The data in these fields is complex. There are many variables and complex relationship between them. Analysing this data almost always requires data wrangling, exploration, and visualization. Above all, it involves modelling the data using flexible probabilistic models. These models are then used to reason and make predictions about the scientific phenomenon being studied. This book aims to address all of these topics. The term we use for these topics and their corresponding methods and tools is *data science*.

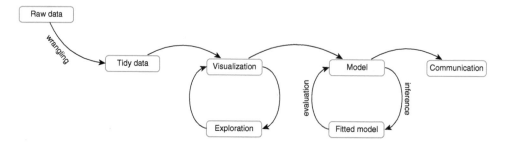

Figure 1.1 The data science workflow. Raw data is usually messy and not yet amenable to analysis of any kind. Data wrangling takes the raw data and transforms it into a new tidy format. This data is then explored and visualized in an iterative manner, which may also include some further wrangling. This eventually leads to probabilistic modelling, which itself involves an iterative process of statistical inference and model evaluation. Finally, we communicate our results in articles, presentations, webpages, etc.

As we use the term throughout this book, *data science* is a set of interrelated computational or mathematical methods and tools that are used in the general data analysis workflow that we outline in Figure 1.1. This workflow begins with data in its nascent and raw form. Raw data is usually impossible or extremely difficult to work with, even casually or informally. The process of transforming the data so that it amenable to further analysis is *data wrangling*, and the resulting data sets are said to be *tidy*. This data can then be explored and visualized. We view data exploration and data visualization as ultimately accomplishing the same thing. One usually involves quantitative descriptive analysis, while the other involves graphical analysis, but both aim to discover potentially interesting patterns and behaviours in the data. The exploratory analysis stage then leads us to posit a tentative probabilistic model of the data. Put more precisely, it leads us to posit a tentative probabilistic model of the phenomenon that generated the data. Inevitably, this model involves unknown variables that must be inferred using statistical inference. This leads to a fitted model, which may be then evaluated and possibly extended and modified, thus leading to further inference. Eventually, we communicate our results in reports, presentations, webpages, etc.

Each of the stages of this data science workflow involves computational and mathematical concepts and methods. In fact, it is this combination of the computational and the mathematical or statistical that is a defining feature or key characteristic of data science as we conceive of it. Without using computers, and thus performing any stages of the workflow manually in some manner, only practically trivial types of analysis could be accomplished, and even then the analysis would be laborious and error prone. By contrast, the more proficient we are with the relevant computational tools, the more efficient and sophisticated our analyses can be. In this sense, computing skills, specifically reading and writing code, are integral and vital parts of modern data analysis. These cannot be generally sidestepped or avoided by using graphical user interfaces (GUIs) to statistics programs. While programs like these are sometimes suitable for novices or for casual use, they are profoundly limited and inefficient in comparison to writing code in a high-level programming language.

In addition to computing tools, many of the stages of the data science workflow involve mathematical and statistical concepts and methods. This is especially true of the statistical modelling stage, which requires a proper understanding of mathematical and probabilistic models, and related topics such as statistical inference. Simply being able to perform a statistical analysis computationally, accompanied by a vague and impressionistic understanding of what the analysis is doing and why it is doing it, will not generally be sufficient. Without a deeper and theoretical understanding of probabilistic models, statistical inference, and related concepts, we will not be able to make principled and informed choices concerning which models to use for any given problem. Nor would we be able to understand the meaning of the results of the inference, and we would be limited or mistaken in the practical and scientific conclusions that we make when we use these models for explanation or prediction. Moreover, statistical models of the kind that we cover in this book should not be seen as a list of independent tools in a big toolbox, each one designed for a different task or application, and each with its own rules and principles. Rather, more generally, we should view statistical modelling as a systematic framework, or even a language, for building mathematical models of scientific phenomena using observed data. While we may talk about normal linear models, or zero-inflated Poisson models, etc., these are just examples of the infinitely many models that we can build to model the scientific problem at hand. Being aware of statistical modelling as a flexible and systematic framework that is based on pragmatic and theoretical principles allows us to more competently and confidently perform statistical analysis, and also greatly increases the range and scope of the analyses that are readily available to us.

What is data science?

Even if we accept the nature and the value of the data analysis workflow that we've just outlined, it is reasonable to ask whether it should properly be called 'data science'. Is this not just using a new word, even a buzzword, in place of much more established terms like 'statistics' or 'statistical data analysis'? We are using the term 'data science' rather than 'statistics' *per se* or some variant thereof because data analysis as we've outlined it arguably goes beyond the usual focus of statistics, at least as it is traditionally understood. Mathematical statistics as a scientific or mathematical discipline has focused largely on the statistical modelling component of the programme we outlined above. As we've hopefully made clear, this component is of profound importance, and in fact we would argue that it is the single most important part and even ultimate goal of data analysis. Nonetheless, in practice, data wrangling alone occupies far more of our time and effort in any analysis, and exploration and visualization should be seen as necessary precursors to, and even continuous with, the statistical modelling itself. Likewise, traditional statistics often marginalizes the practical matter of computing tools. In statistics textbooks, even excellent ones, for example, code examples may not be provided for all analyses, and the code may not be integrated tightly with the coverage of the statistical methods. In this sense, traditional statistics does not thoroughly deal with all the parts of the data analysis workflow that we have outlined. This is not a criticism of statistics, but just a recognition of its particular focus.

This general point about real-world data analysis being more than just the traditional focus of mathematical statistics was actually made decades ago by Tukey (1962). There, Tukey, who was one of the most influential statisticians of the twentieth century and a pioneer of exploratory data analysis and data visualization, preferred the term *data analysis* as the general term for what he and other statistical analysts actually do in practice. For Tukey, inferential statistics and statistical modelling were necessary and vital, but only as a component of a much bigger and multifaceted undertaking, which he called 'data analysis'.

While the general spirit of the argument about the breadth and scope of data analysis that Tukey (1962) outlined is very much in keeping with the perspective we follow here, modern data analysis has a character that goes beyond Tukey's vision, however broad and comprehensive it was. This is due to the computing revolution. For example, when Tukey was writing in the early 1960s, the world's fastest computers[1] were capable of around 1 million calculations per second. Approximately 60 years later in 2020, the world's fastest computer[2] is capable of around 500 quadrillion (5×10^{17}) calculations per second, and a typical consumer desktop can perform hundreds of billions of calculations per second. This revolution has transformed all aspects of data analysis, and now computing is as vital and integral a part of data analysis as are mathematics and statistics. It was largely the recognition of the vital and transformative role of computing that lead Cleveland (2001) to coin the term 'data science'. As we use the term, therefore, data science is the blend of computational and statistical methods applied to all the aspects of data analysis.

Even if we accept that the defining feature of data science is generally the combined application of computational tools and statistical methods to data analysis, the term 'data science' has some popular connotations that are somewhat at odds with the more general understanding of the term that we are following in this book. In particular, for some people, data science is all about concepts like predictive analytics, big data, machine learning, deep learning, data mining of massive unstructured data sets including natural language corpora. It is seen as largely a branch of computer science and engineering, and is something that is done in the big tech companies like Google, Amazon, Facebook, Apple, Netflix and Twitter. It is absolutely true that data science, particularly as it is practised in industry, heavily avails tools like machine learning and big data analysis software, and is applied to the analysis of massive unstructured data sets. As real and important as these activities are, we see them here as just one application of data science as we generally understand the term. Also, in this particular application of data science, some topics and issues take precedence over or dominate others. For example, in these contexts, the software and hardware problems of being able to analyse data that is on such a large scale are the major practical issues. Likewise, for some applications, being able to perform successful predictions using statistical methods is the only goal,

---

[1] https://en.wikipedia.org/wiki/Atlas_(computer)

[2] https://en.wikipedia.org/wiki/Fugaku_(supercomputer)

and so the assumed statistical models on which these predictions are based are less important or even irrelevant (see Breiman, 2001, for a well-known early discussion of these two different general 'cultures' of using statistical methods).

In summary, in this book, we use the term 'data science' as the general term for modern data analysis, which is something that always involves a tight integration of computational and statistical methods and tools. In this, we are hopefully faithfully following the broad and general understanding of what real-world data analysis entails as described by Tukey (1962), albeit with the additional vital feature of intensive use of computational tools. In some contexts, data science has a more particular focus on big data, data mining, machine learning and related concepts. That particular focus is not the focus of this book, and so this book is probably not ideal for anyone keen to learn more about data science in just this sense of the term.

 Why R, not Python?

We have stated repeatedly that computational methods and tools are vital for doing data science. In this book, the computing language and environment that we use is the *R Project for Statistical Computing*, simply known as R. More specifically, we use the modern incarnation of R that is based on the so-called *tidyverse*. In Chapter 2 we provide a proper introduction to R. Here, we wish to just outline why R is our choice of language and environment, what the alternatives are, and what this entails in terms of the our conception of what data science is and how it is practised.

Given our conception of the data science workflow that we outlined in Figure 1.1, R is an inevitable choice. We believe that R is simply the best option for performing all the major components that we outline there. For example, for the data wrangling component, which can be extremely laborious, R packages that are part of the tidyverse such as `readr`, `dplyr` and `tidyr`, which we cover in Chapter 3, make data wrangling fast and efficient and even pleasurable. For data visualization, the `ggplot2` package provides us with essentially a high-level and expressive language for data visualization. For the statistical modelling loop, which we cover in all the chapters of Part II of this book, R provides a huge treasure trove of packages for virtually every conceivable type of statistical methods and models. Also, R is the dominant environment, using packages like `rstan` and `brms`, for doing Bayesian probabilistic modelling using the Stan probabilistic programming language. We cover Bayesian models throughout the chapters of Part II. For communication, R provides us with the ability to produce reproducible data analysis reports using RMarkdown, Knitr and other tools, which we describe in Chapter 7.

Everything we cover in this book could be done using another programming language, or possibly using some set of different languages. Chief among these alternatives is Python. Python is close to being the most widely used general-purpose programming language of any kind. It has been very popular for almost two decades, and its dominance and popularity have been increasing in recent years. Moreover, one of Python's major domains of application is data science, with some arguing that it should preferred over R for data science generally. For the big data, big tech, data mining, machine learning sense of data science that we mentioned above, Python certainly ought to be the dominant choice over R. This is for multiple reasons. First, Python is now the principal computing language for doing machine learning, deep learning and related activities. Also, because Python is a general-purpose programming language and one that is widely used on the back end of web applications, this makes integrating data science tools with the 'production' web server software much easier and scalable. Likewise, Python is a very powerful and well-designed general-purpose programming language, which means that it is easier to write complex highly structured software applications in Python than in a specialized language like R. This again facilitates the integration of Python data science tools with production- or enterprise-level software applications. Nonetheless, for the more general conception of data science that we are following in this book, Python is more limited than R. For example, for data wrangling of typical rectangular data structures, Python's `pandas` package, as excellent as it is, is not as high level and expressive as R's tidyverse-based packages like `dplyr` and `tidyr`. This entails that wrangling data into shape in R can be easier and involve less lower-level procedural and imperative code than when using Python. Likewise for data visualization, Python's `matplotlib` package is very powerful but is also lower-level than `ggplot2`. This entails that relatively complex visualization requires considerably more procedural or imperative code, which is harder and slower to read and write than using the more expressive high-level code of `ggplot2`. The higher-level counterpart of `matplotlib` is `seaborn`, which is excellent, but `seaborn` is less powerful and extensive in terms of its features than `ggplot`. For statistical modelling, at the moment, there frankly is no competition between R and Python. Even though Python has excellent statistics packages like `statsmodels`, these provide only a fraction of the statistical models and methods that are available from R packages. Finally, although dynamic notebooks like Jupyter[3] are widely used by Python users, and are excellent too, it is not as easy to create reproducible reports, for example for publication in scientific journals, using Jupyter as it is using RMarkdown and knitr. In fact, currently the easiest way to write a Python-based reproducible manuscript is to use Python *within* R using the `reticulate` package.

 Who is this book for?

As mentioned at the start of this chapter, the prototypical audience at whom this book is aimed are those engaged in data analysis in scientific research, specifically research at or beyond PhD level. In scientific research, statistics obviously plays a vital role, and specifically this is based on using data to build and interpret statistical or probabilistic models of the scientific phenomenon being studied. This book is heavily focused on this particular kind of statistical data analysis. As we've mentioned, in data science as it is practised in industry and business, often the other 'culture' of statistics (see Breiman, 2001), namely predictive analytics and algorithms, is the dominant one, and so this book is not ideal for those whose primary data science interests are of that kind.

We've explicitly stated that this book is intended for those doing research in the social sciences, but this also requires some explanation. The explicit targeting of the social sciences is largely just to keep some focus and limits to the sets of examples that are used throughout the book. However, beyond the example data sets that are used, there is little about this content that is of relevance to only those doing research in social science disciplines. All the

---

[3]https://jupyter.org/

content on data wrangling, exploration and visualization, statistical modelling, etc., is hopefully just as relevant to someone doing research in some field of biology as it is to someone doing research in the social sciences. The nature of the data in terms of its complexity, and the nature of the analysis of this data using complex statistical models, are traditionally very similar in biology and social sciences. In fact, the statistics practised in all of these fields has all arisen from a common original source, particularly the early twentieth-century pioneering work of R. A. Fisher (e.g. Fisher, 1925).

We assume that the readers of this book will already be familiar with statistics to an extent. For example, we assume that they've taken undergraduate-level courses introducing statistics as it is used and applied in some discipline of science. We will present the statistical methods that we cover from a foundational perspective, and so not assume that readers are already confident and familiar with the fundamental principles of statistical inference and modelling. However, we do assume that they will have already had an introduction to statistics so that concepts like the 'normal distribution', 'linear regression' and 'confidence intervals' will be relatively familiar, even if they don't have a very precise grasp of their technical meaning. On the other hand, we do not assume any familiarity with any computing methods, nor R in particular. In fact, we assume that many readers will be brand new to R.

The style and structure of this book

Apart from this brief introductory chapter, all the remainder of the book is a blend of expository text, R code, mathematical equations, diagrams and R-based plots. It is intended that people will read this book while using R to execute all the code examples and so produce all the results that are presented either as R output or as figures. Of course, if readers wish to read first and then run the code later, perhaps on a second reading, that is entirely a matter of preference. However, all the code that we present throughout this book is ready to run, and does not require anything other than the R packages that are explicitly mentioned in the code and the relevant data sets, which are all available on the website that accompanies the book.

The book is divided into three parts. Part I is all about the parts of the data science workflow shown in Figure 1.1 except for the statistical modelling loop part. Thus, in Part I we provide a comprehensive general introduction to R, a chapter on data wrangling using `dplyr`, `tidyr`, etc., a chapter on data visualization, and another on data exploration. We then go into more detail about programming in R, and conclude Part I with a chapter on doing reproducible data analysis using tools like RMarkdown and Git. Part II of the book, which is the largest part, is all about the statistical modelling loop part of the data science workflow. There, we provide a general introduction to statistical inference, and then cover all the major types of regression models, specifically normal linear regression, generalized linear models, multilevel models, nonlinear regression, and path analysis and related models. In Part III, which is the shortest part, we cover some specialized topics that are not necessarily part of the statistical modelling topics, but not general or introductory either. Specifically, in Part III, we provide an introduction to using R for high-performance computing, making interactive graphics web apps using Shiny, and a general introduction to Bayesian probabilistic programming using Stan.

PART I

FUNDAMENTALS OF DATA ANALYSIS AND DATA SCIENCE

Part I Contents

2

Introduction to R

What is R, and why should we use it?

While there are many ways of defining what R is, for most practical purposes, it is sufficient to describe R simply as a program for doing statistics and data analysis. If you've done any kind of statistics or data analyses, the chances are extremely high that you've used some computer program to do so. The range of such programs is large. They include SPSS, SAS, Stata, Minitab, Python, Matlab, Maple, Mathematica, Tableau, Excel, SQL, and many others. These do not all do the same thing, and so are not necessarily interchangeable. Some, like Python, are general-purpose programming languages that have become widely used for data science. Others, like SQL, are database language. SPSS is primarily a GUI program for statistics, originally targeted at researchers in the social sciences. R can be seen as just another program in this large and heterogeneous list. The advantages of R, however, which set it apart from many other programs, boil down to three interrelated factors: it is immensely powerful, it is open source, and it very (and increasingly) widely used. Let us now consider each of these three points further.

A power tool for data analysis

The range and depth of statistical analyses and general data analyses that can be accomplished with R are immense:

- Built into R's standard set of packages is virtually the entire repertoire of widely known and used statistical methods. These include general and generalized linear regression analyses (which themselves include analyses of variance, t-tests and correlations), descriptive statistical methods and nonparametric methods.
- Also built into R is an extensive graphics library (see the `graphics` package, which is usually termed the 'base R' plotting package) for doing virtually the entire repertoire of statistical plots and graphics, and these graphics tools can be combined programmatically to lead to any desired plot or visualization.
- In addition to its built-in tools, R has a vast set of add-on or contributed packages. There are presently over 16,000 additional contributed packages (to be precise, there are 16,105 packages as of 12 August 2020). While they differ in size, each one will usually provide at least dozens of additional tools and methods for statistics, data manipulation and processing, or graphics. Some of these packages could be described as almost mini-languages in themselves. For example, and as we'll see below, the package `ggplot2` is effectively a mini-language for data visualization, while packages like `dplyr` and `tidyr` are effectively mini-languages for data wrangling and manipulation. In addition, because R is the *de facto* standard computing platform for the discipline of statistics, almost every new or existing statistical technique developed by statisticians is made available as a package in R. With all of these packages, we are hard pressed to find anything at all related to statistics and data analysis, including data graphics and visualization, that is not currently available in R.
- As large as the set of R packages is, the capabilities of R do not stop here. R is a high-level and expressive programming language that is specialized to efficiently manipulate and perform calculations or analyses on data. This entails that R can be used programmatically to greatly increase the speed and efficiency of any data analysis. More importantly, R can be extended by writing custom programs and functions, which may then be packaged and distributed for others to use. While writing large or complex extension packages would require

some programming skill and experience, programming in R on a smaller and simpler scale is in fact relatively easy, and basics can be mastered quickly. Given that R is a programming language, there is then effectively no real limit on its capabilities.

- The R programming language itself can be extended by interfacing with other programming languages like C, C++, Fortran and Python. In particular, the popular Rcpp package greatly simplifies integrating R with C++, thus allowing fast and efficient C++ code to be used seamlessly within R. Likewise, R can be easily interfaced with high-performance computing or big data tools like Hadoop, Spark, SQL, parallel computing libraries, cluster computing, and so on.

Taken together, these points entail that R is an extremely powerful and extensible environment for doing any kind of statistical computing or data analysis.

Open source software

R is free and open source software, distributed according to the GNU public licence. Likewise, virtually all of the 16,000 or so contributed R packages are free and open source software, with over 99% of them being distributed in accordance with one of the major open source licences, such as GNU, MIT, BSD, Apache, Creative Commons or Artistic. It is important to emphasize the distinctions in practice and in principle between free and open source software, on the one hand, and freeware, on the other. Freeware is proprietary software that is distributed, usually only in binary form and with certain restrictions and conditions, at no monetary cost to the user. While it can be used in a limited sense at no cost, it cannot be extended or developed, its source code cannot be viewed, and its non-monetary cost can be revoked at any time. Free and open source software, on the other hand, is licensed so that anyone can use it and develop it in any manner, including and especially by viewing and extending its source code. Free and open source software is defined by four essential freedoms:[1]

- The freedom to run the program in any manner and for any purpose
- The freedom to study and modify the source code
- The freedom to distribute copies of the original code
- The freedom to distribute modified versions of the code.

In practical terms, the most obvious consequence of R's free and open source nature is that it is freely available for everyone to use, on more or less any device they choose. It is mostly widely used on Windows, Macs, and Linux, but because it is available in open source it can in principle be compiled for any platform, and can be used on Android, iOS, Chrome OS, and many others. This means that anyone can use R at any time anywhere and always at no cost. And because of its licence, this will always be the case.

Open source software always has the potential to 'go viral' and develop a large self-sustaining community of user/developers. This is precisely what has happened in the case of R. Users are drawn in initially because it is available at no cost, can be used on any platform, and

---

[1]https://www.gnu.org/philosophy/free-sw.html

has a large number of built-in or add-on tools. Because R is an open platform, developers such as academic statisticians or data scientists who want to reach a large audience write further add-on packages and make them publicly available. This draws in more users. The users themselves may write blogs, books, articles, or teach with R, thus attracting still more users, and so on.

Popularity

The *Journal of Statistical Software*[2] is the most widely used academic journal describing advances and developments in software for statistics. While it accepts articles describing methods implemented in a wide variety of languages, it is overwhelmingly dominated by programs written in R. This fact illustrates that when it comes to the computational implementation of modern statistical methods, R is the *de facto* standard.

In an extensive analysis of general data science software (Muenchen, 2019), R is ranked as one of the five most popular data science programs in jobs for data scientists, and in multiple surveys of data scientists, it is often ranked as the first or second mostly widely used data science tool, and among the most widely 'followed' topics on Quora and LinkedIn. Likewise, despite being a domain-specific language, according to many rankings of widely used programming and scripting languages worldwide, R is currently highly ranked. Indeed, R is currently very highly ranked according to many rankings of widely used programming languages of any kind. For example, the latest RedMonk ratings[3] place R at rank 13; the latest TIOBE ratings[4] place R at rank 8; and the latest PYPL ratings[5] place R at rank 7.

 Installing R and RStudio

Installing R is usually a painless process, but it also usually involves two, or maybe three, separate steps. First, R itself must be installed. This will install the R interpreter and also what we will call R's standard library. The interpreter is the means by which all our R commands are converted into machine code that is then executed on our machine. The standard library is the set of built-in packages mentioned above that provide all the basic or most widely used tools for doing statistics, analysis and visualization. With that, we will have a fully functioning R environment. However, by stopping here, the interface through which we'll interact with R will be very minimal and lacking many features that would make our use of R more pleasant and efficient. As such, the second installation step will be to install the *RStudio Desktop* environment. This is a very popular interface to R that will greatly transform the ease and efficiency with which we work with R. Throughout the remainder of this book, we'll assume that we're always working with the RStudio Desktop. The third

---

[2]https://www.jstatsoft.org

[3]https://redmonk.com/sogrady/2020/07/27/language-rankings-6-20/

[4]https://www.tiobe.com/tiobe-index

[5]http://pypl.github.io/PYPL.html

installation step is the installation of extra R packages. As mentioned above, R has over 16,000 add-on packages. Users can install them on demand from within R in a manner just like installing apps on a mobile device. When first installing R, it's often a good idea to also install a minimal set of must-have packages. After that, additional R packages can be installed as and when they are needed.

We will now describe how to install R and the RStudio Desktop, and then, after we say more about how to use R and RStudio, we will look at installing R packages in a separate section.

Installing R

To install the latest version of R on Windows, go to:

```
https://cran.r-project.org/bin/windows/base/
```

For the installer for the latest version of R for Macs, go to:

```
https://cran.r-project.org/bin/macosx/
```

For Windows, the installer is an executable file (with an `.exe` extension). For Macs, it is the installer file ending with the `.pkg` extension. In either case, always go for the installer of the latest R version (which, as of August 2020, is 4.0.2). We install R with these installers just as we would install any other program on Windows or Macs.

If we're using Linux, we can follow steps similar to the above to get a installer. However, it is likely that everything will be simpler if we just use our Linux distribution's own package manager and install R with that. For example, with Debian- and Ubuntu-based distributions, we can use the apt-get package manager, or use the pacman installer on Arch Linux.

Installing RStudio Desktop

The RStudio Desktop is one of the software products created by the company RStudio. Although RStudio is a private commercial company, it releases its software under a free and open source licence (namely the GNU Affero General Public License). It also sells technical support for these products, but this is aimed at companies and organizations rather than individuals. Simply put, we can use RStudio software just as we use all R software: at no cost, and according to a free and open source licence. Any prices that are listed for RStudio software are for commercial support.

The webpage

```
https://www.rstudio.com/products/rstudio/download/
```

provides us with the necessary links to the Windows, Mac, and Linux installers. Choose the *RStudio Desktop: Free* option, which we will see is listed as under an open source licence. The latest version (as of August 2020) is 1.3.1056. We use the installers here just as we would use any Windows and Mac installers. For Linux users, there are versions for popular Linux distributions such as Ubuntu and Fedora.

Guided Tour of RStudio Desktop

Having installed R and the RStudio Desktop, we can now effectively forget about R. It is fully installed, and it will be doing all the computing whenever we use RStudio Desktop, but it runs in the background and we don't have to use it directly. For all practical purposes, it will seem like we are just using a single standalone desktop application.

A note on terminology. Strictly speaking, *RStudio* is the company that created and maintains the *RStudio Desktop* software, among other pieces of software. In practice, almost everyone, including those who work for RStudio itself, refer to RStudio Desktop simply as RStudio, and we'll do so here as well. Another product made by RStudio, the RStudio Server, which we'll describe below, is also sometimes called RStudio, but we'll usually explicitly refer to that as the RStudio Server.

We open RStudio just as we would any other desktop application (e.g. double-clicking an icon, or typing its name in a launcher), and when we do so, we will be greeted by something that should look exactly like Figure 2.1.

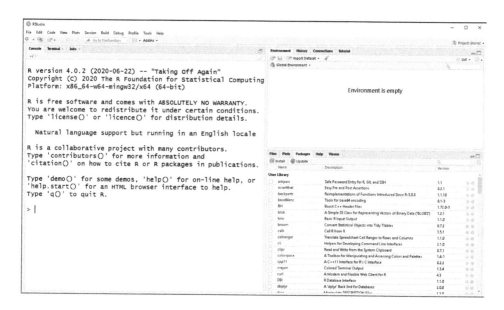

Figure 2.1 The typical layout of the RStudio Desktop when it is first opened

We will see three main windows, which we will describe in more detail below. For now, we see that to the left, occupying about half the screen by default, is a window with the *console* pane. To the right, there are two other windows arranged vertically. Usually (in fact almost always) we also have two windows on the left. On top of the window with the console pane, we usually have a script editor. If it is not present, it can be brought up by the key command Ctrl+Shift+N (Cmd+Shift+N on Macs), or by going to the File menu at the top of the screen and choosing *New File > R Script*. Doing so will create a blank and untitled R script in the script editor window, which will now occupy the upper left quadrant of the screen. Our screen should now look like Figure 2.2.

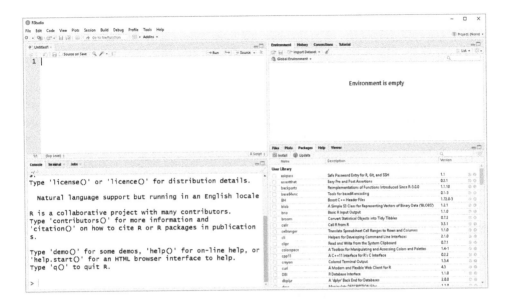

Figure 2.2 RStudio Desktop with R script editor window in upper left quadrant

We'll now look in more detail at each of these four windows.

Console window The console window usually occupies about half of the left-hand side of the screen. Like all windows, it can be resized with the mouse, or with the window resize buttons to the upper right of each window. In the console window, by default, there are tabs for three panes: the Console, the Terminal, and Jobs. The tab for the console is usually the active one. This is where we type R commands, followed by Enter, and get all our results and output. It is the single most important part of the RStudio Desktop. We will use it extensively, beginning with our introduction to R commands in the next section. The next tab is the Terminal, and this is the command line interface to our computer's operating system. So, on Windows, this is usually the DOS command line. On Macs and Linux, it is the Unix shell, such as the bash shell. Unlike the console, the terminal is not as widely used. It may in fact never be used, and is only necessary when we need a command line interface to our operating system. The Jobs pane is also not as widely used. It is for running scripts asynchronously.

Script editor window The script editor is where we write scripts of R commands. We use scripts whenever we want to save our R commands for later reuse, or whenever the R commands are becoming relatively long and complex. We write here just as we would write in any text file editor (e.g. Notepad), and we can save these files on our computer's file system as normal. As we'll see below, we can execute or *run* the commands we write in any script either line by line or region by region or by executing the whole script at once. If we run individual lines or regions, the R code effectively gets copied to the console followed by Enter just as if we copied and pasted from the editor to the console. We can run the whole script at once, as we'll see below, by using the *source* command, for which there is a button on the upper right of the editor window.

Environment, History, etc., window In the upper right pane, there are tabs for the Environment, History, and Connections panes. Sometimes there are other tabs, such as for Build and Git. Of these, Environment and History are the more commonly used. As we'll see as soon as we start using R commands and creating variables, the details of the variables and data structures that are in our current R session are listed in the Environment. We will have the option of clearing or deleting any or all of these whenever we wish. Likewise, we may save all of these objects to file, and reload them later. The Environment window also provides us with a convenient means of importing data files. The History window provides a list of all the R commands that we have typed. This is a particularly useful feature, as we will see. It allows us to review everything we have typed in our R session, and allows us to extract and rerun any commands we want. We may also save our command history to file at any time. The other tabs available in this window are not usually used as often. Connections is used for connecting with databases or clusters, and we will see it again later in the book. Build, which may not be listed at all, is for building packages or compiling code. Git, which likewise may not exist, is for version control of our code using Git. We will talk about using Git for version control in Chapter 6.

Files, Plots, Packages, Help, Viewer window The lower right window provides tabs for browsing files, viewing plots, managing R packages, reading help files, and for viewing html documents. The Files window is a regular file browser, where we can view, create, delete, etc., files and directories. The Plots window is where all figures created during our R session are shown. If we produce many figures, they are placed in a stack and we can move forwards and backwards between them. The Packages window, which we will return to in more detail in the next section, lists all our installed R packages. From here, we can also activate packages for our current R session, as well as install new packages. The Help window displays help pages for any R command or package. We can browse through these pages, but a particularly useful feature is how we can jump straight to a needed help page for a command or package directly from the R command line or script editor. We will return to this feature in one of the next sections. The Viewer window is where we can view html pages that are created in RStudio. These could include Shiny web apps or the html pages produced by RMarkdown documents. These are topics to which we will return in later chapters.

RStudio menus

At the top of the RStudio Desktop there is the following set of menus.

File The File menu is primarily for the opening, closing and saving of files. Often, these files will be R scripts that open in the script editor. But they could also be R data files, RMarkdown documents, Shiny apps, etc. Here, we can also open and close RStudio *projects*, which is a very useful organizing feature to which we will return below.

Edit The Edit menu primarily provides tools for standard file editing operations such as copy, cut, paste, search and replace, and undo and redo. It also provides code folding features, which is very useful for reducing clutter when editing relatively large R scripts.

Code The Code menu provides many useful tools for making editing and running code considerably easier and more efficient. We will explore these features in more depth in subsequent sections, but they include adding and removing code comments, reformatting code, jumping to functions within and between scripts, and creating code regions that can then be run independently.

View The View menu primarily provides options to move around RStudio quickly. These options are all bound to key combinations, as are many other RStudio features, and learning these key combinations is certainly worthwhile because of the eventual speed and efficiency gains that they provide.

Plots The Plots menu primarily provides features that are also available in the Plots window itself.

Session The Session menu allows us to start new separate RStudio sessions. These then run independently of one another. Also in the Session menu, we can restart the R session in the background, which is a useful feature. Remember that RStudio itself is just a front to an R session that runs in the background. Sometimes it is a good idea to restart the R session so as to start in a clean and fresh state. This can be done through the Session menu *Restart R* option, which is also bound to the key combination Ctrl+Shift+F10. Also in Session are options to set R's *working directory*. The concept of a working directory is a simple but important one, and we will cover it below.

Build The Build menu provides features for running scripts for *software builds*. This is particularly used for creating R packages.

Debug The Debug menu provides tools for debugging our R code. Debugging usually only becomes a necessity when R programming *per se*, and not something that is usually required when writing individual commands or scripts of commands.

Profile The Profile menu provides tools for profiling the running and efficiency of our R code. Code efficiency is certainly not something that those new to R need to worry about, but when writing relatively complex code, profiling can identify bottlenecks.

Tools The Tools menu provides miscellaneous tools such as for working with version control using Git, accessing the computer operating system's command line interface, installing and updating packages (as could also be done in the Package window), and viewing and modifying keyboard shortcuts. Here, we can also access the *Global Options* and *Project Options*. Global Options is where all the general R and RStudio settings are set. One immediately useful setting here is the *Appearance* setting, which can allow us to change the font, font size, and colour theme of RStudio to suit our preference. Project Options are for the RStudio project-specific settings. We will return to these below.

Help The Help menu provides much the same information as can be found in the Help window. It also provides some additional links to online resources, such as RStudio's cheat sheets,[6] which are excellent concise guides to many different R and RStudio topics. Also available in the Help menu are tools to access RStudio internal diagnostics. This is only needed if RStudio seems to be malfunctioning.

 First steps in R

R is very a powerful tool. While it is unquestionably a wonderful thing that everyone can have access to this powerful tool at no monetary cost, now or ever, R's power can also be intimidating and off-putting at the beginning. People who wish to learn R may simply not know where to begin. Worse still, some people dive in too deep at the beginning, tackling complex analyses before they have a good handle on the basics, and find things difficult and frustrating, and may then even abandon trying to learn R at all.

To learn R, it is best to learn the fundamentals first. In what follows, we have provided a sequence of steps that cover many of these. With each step, we'll introduce some fundamental concepts or tools, and these concepts and tools can build on one another and be

---

[6]https://www.rstudio.com/resources/cheatsheets/

combined to lead to yet more concepts and tools. What we will not cover in these steps are the major topics like data wrangling, data visualization and statistical analyses. These will be covered in depth in subsequent chapters, and build upon a knowledge of the fundamentals that we cover here.

Step 0: Using the R console

R is a command-based system. We type commands, R translates them into machine instructions, which our computer then executes, and then we often, but not necessarily, get back some output. The commands can be typed into the R console, or else they can be put into a script and run as a batch. When learning R, it is usually best to start with typing commands in the R console.

When we initially open RStudio, our console will usually look something like this:

```
R version 4.0.2 (2020-06-22) -- "Taking Off Again"
Copyright (C) 2020 The R Foundation for Statistical Computing
Platform: x86_64-pc-linux-gnu (64-bit)

R is free software and comes with ABSOLUTELY NO WARRANTY.
You are welcome to redistribute it under certain conditions.
Type 'license()' or 'licence()' for distribution details.

R is a collaborative project with many contributors.
Type 'contributors()' for more information and
'citation()' on how to cite R or R packages in publications.

Type 'demo()' for some demos, 'help()' for on-line help, or
'help.start()' for an HTML browser interface to help.
Type 'q()' to quit R.

>
```

Notice that, at the bottom, there is a single line beginning with >. This is the R console's command prompt, and it is where we type our commands. We then press Enter, and our command is executed. The output of the command, if any, is displayed on the next line or lines, and then a new > prompt appears.

Step 1: Using R as a calculator

A useful way to think about R, and not an inaccurate one either, is that it is simply a calculator. It is useful therefore to learn R by first treating it just like an ordinary handheld calculator, and then learning the ways it extends or goes beyond the capabilities of a calculator. Just as we would with a calculator, we can start using R by doing arithmetic – adding, subtracting, multiplying, dividing, and so on.

So, let's start by adding 2 and 2. We do this by typing `2 + 2` at the command prompt, and then pressing Enter. What we see should look exactly[7] as follows:

```
> 2 + 2
#> [1] 4
```

Notice that the result of the calculation is displayed on the line following the command. That line begins with a `[1]`, and we will return to what this means below but for now it can be ignored.

Now let's do some more. Each time, we'll type the command, press Enter, get the result, and then a new > prompt occurs, and we type the next command and so on. So calculating the sum of 3 and 3, and of 10, 17 and 5, will lead to the following:

```
> 3 + 3
#> [1] 6
> 10 + 17 + 5
#> [1] 32
```

Using history. Before we proceed, take a look at our *History* window. It should look like this:

```
2 + 2
3 + 3
10 + 17 + 5
```

In other words, it is a list of everything we've just typed. If we click on any line here, we will select it. If we then click on To Console, this line will be copied to the console, and we can press Enter to re-execute. More usefully, we can move through our history with the up and down arrow keys on our keyboard. Repeatedly pressing the up arrow key will bring up the list of each command we just typed, and repeatedly pressing the down arrow key will bring us back down. At any point as we go through the list, we can press Enter to rerun that command, which then adds that command onto the end of the History.

Let's look at some more arithmetic. For *subtraction*, we use the - symbol:

```
> 5 - 3
#> [1] 2
> 8 - 1
#> [1] 7
```

Multiplication uses the asterisk symbol *:

```
> 5 * 5
#> [1] 25
```

---

[7]In this book, each line of the console's output begins with #>, which will not appear in the actual console. We use the #> just to make it easier to read and to distinguish between the commands that we input into the console and the output that is then displayed.

```
> 2 * 4
#> [1] 8
```

Division uses the / symbol:

```
> 1 / 2
#> [1] 0.5
> 2 / 7
#> [1] 0.2857143
```

Exponents (i.e. raising a number to the power of another number) are accomplished with the caret symbol ^:

```
> 2 ^ 8
#> [1] 256
> 10 ^ 3
#> [1] 1000
```

Exponents also work if we use **, but this is less common:

```
> 2 ** 8
#> [1] 256
> 10 ** 3
#> [1] 1000
```

Just like on a calculator, we can combine the +, -, *, /, ^ operators in any commands:

```
> 2 + 3 - 6 / 2
#> [1] 2
> 10 * 2 - 3 / 5 ^ 2
#> [1] 19.88
```

Note that precedence order of operations will be ^ followed by * or / followed by + or -, and just like on a calculator, we can use parentheses to control the order of operations:

```
> 2 / (3 * 2)
#> [1] 0.3333333
> (2 / 3) * 2
#> [1] 1.333333
```

In the above, we were always dealing with positive values. However, we can always precede any number with a - to get its negative value:

```
> -2 * 3
#> [1] -6
> 10 ^ -3
#> [1] 0.001
```

Notice that throughout all the above commands, we put a space around the +, -, *, /, ^ operators. This is a matter of recommended style to improve readability, not a requirement. In other words, the following all work in exactly the same way:

```
> 2+3
#> [1] 5
```

```
> 2+     3
#> [1] 5
> 2  +   3
#> [1] 5
```

It is just recommended to use the 2 + 3 version. On the other hand, while it is also possible to have spaces after the - sign that we use to negate a value, the recommended style is to not do so, and so we use 3 / -2 and not 3 / - 3, though both will do the same thing.

Step 2: Variables and assignment

A major step forward in using R, and a major step beyond the capabilities of a handheld calculator, is the use of variables and the assignment of values to variables. In effect, this simply allows us to store the values of calculations for later use, but that in fact is a very powerful thing.

Consider what happens when we type the following at the command prompt and then press Enter:

```
> (12 / 3.5) ^ 2 + (1 / 2.5) ^ 3 + (1 + 2 + 3) ^ 0.33
#> [1] 13.6254
```

All the constituent numbers are stored in our computer's memory, calculations are done on them, and then the result is stored in memory. This is then displayed as the output on our screen, and because nothing further needs to be done with it, it is removed from memory. We can, however, keep this value stored in memory by *assigning* it to a variable. We do this with the *assignment operator* <-, which is a < symbol followed directly by a - symbol. The <- can be typed by key combination Alt+- (i.e. Alt key and minus key together) or Option+- on the Mac. So if we want to assign the value of the above calculation to a variable named x, we would type

```
> x <- (12 / 3.5) ^ 2 + (1 / 2.5) ^ 3 + (1 + 2 + 3) ^ 0.33
```

Notice that on pressing Enter here, there is no output on screen. The calculation is done as normal but rather than outputting it to the screen, the value is assigned to the variable named x. If we now type the name x at the prompt, its value will be displayed:

```
> x
#> [1] 13.6254
```

We can then do calculations with this variable just like we would with any other number:

```
> x ^ 2
#> [1] 185.6516
> x * 3.6
#> [1] 49.05145
```

And we can assign any of these values to new variables:

```
> y <- x ^ 2
> y <- x * 3.6
```

In general, the assignment rule is

```
name <- expression
```

The `expression` is any R code that returns some value. This could be the result of a calculation, as in the above examples, but it could also be the 'output', or result, of some complex statistical analysis, which is something we will see repeatedly in later sections and chapters. In the simplest case, it could also be just a single numeric or other value, such as

```
> x <- 42
```

The `name` has to follow certain naming conventions. In all the above examples, we used a single lowercase letter, but in general it can consist of multiple characters. Specifically, it can consist of letters, which can be either lowercase or uppercase, numbers, dots, and underscores. It must, however, begin with a letter or a dot that is not followed by a number. So all of the following are acceptable:

```
x123
.x
x_y_z
xXx_123
```

But all of the following are *not* acceptable:

```
_x
.2x
x-y-z
```

Although many names like `x123` etc. are valid names, the recommendation is to use names that are meaningful, relatively short, without dots (using the underscore _ instead for punctuation), and primarily consisting of lowercase characters. Examples like the following are recommended:

```
> age <- 29
> income <- 38575.65
> is_married <- TRUE
> years_married <- 7
```

Step 3: Vectors

Up to now, all the values we've been dealing with have been single values. In general, we can have variables in R that refer to collections of values. These are known as *data structures*. There are many different types of data structures in R, but the two that we encounter most often are *vectors* and *data frames*. Data frames are probably the single most important data structure in R and are the default form for representing data sets for statistical analyses. But data frames are themselves collections of vectors, and so vectors are a very important fundamental data structure in R. In fact, as we will see, single values, like all those used above, are actually vectors with exactly one element.

Vectors are one-dimensional sequences of values. While they will often be created for us by the R functions that we use, such as by some data analysis functions, we can also create vectors ourselves using the `c()` function. For example, if we want to create a vector of the first 10 prime numbers, we could type the following:

```
> primes <- c(2, 3, 5, 7, 11, 13, 17, 19, 23, 29)
```

To use the `c()` function, where c stands for *combine*, we simply put within it a set of values with commas between them.

Vector operations

We can now perform operations, like those we saw above, on the `primes` vector just as we would on a single-valued variable. For example, we can do arithmetic operations:

```
> primes + 1
#>  [1]  3  4  6  8 12 14 18 20 24 30
> primes / 2
#>  [1]  1.0  1.5  2.5  3.5  5.5  6.5  8.5  9.5 11.5 14.5
> primes ^ 2
#>  [1]  4  9 25 49 121 169 289 361 529 841
```

In these cases, the operations are applied to each element of the vector.

Indexing

For any vector, we can refer to individual elements using indexing operations. For example, to get the first or fifth elements of `primes`, we would use square brackets as follows:

```
> primes[1]
#> [1] 2
> primes[5]
#> [1] 11
```

If we want to index sets of elements, rather than just individual elements, we can use vectors (made with the `c()` function) inside the indexing square brackets. For example, if we want to extract the seventh, fifth and third elements, in that order, we can type the following:

```
> primes[c(7, 5, 3)]
#> [1] 17 11  5
```

If we want to refer to a consecutive set of elements, such as the second to the fifth elements, we can type the following:

```
> primes[2:5]
#> [1]  3  5  7 11
```

In R, the expression n:m, where n and m are integers, gives us the vector of integers from n to m. So, for example, 2:5 means the same thing as c(2, 3, 4, 5).

If we use a negative-valued index, we can refer to all elements *except* one. For example, all elements of primes except the first element, or except the second element, can be obtained as follows:

```
> primes[-1]
#> [1]  3  5  7 11 13 17 19 23 29
> primes[-2]
#> [1]  2  5  7 11 13 17 19 23 29
```

If we precede a vector of indices by a minus, we'll return all elements except those in the index vector. For example, we can get all elements except the seventh, fifth and third elements as follows:

```
> primes[-c(7, 5, 3)]
#> [1]  2  3  7 13 19 23 29
```

Single-valued vectors

Unlike some other programming languages, R does not represent single values as elementary data types. Single values are in fact just vectors with only one element, and so can be indexed, and so on, just like any other vector:

```
> x <- 42
> x[1]
#> [1] 42
```

Character vectors

Our primes vector is a sequences of decimal numbers. We can verify this by applying the class function to the vector and seeing that it is a numeric vector:

```
> class(primes)
#> [1] "numeric"
```

We can, however, have many other types of vectors. For example, we can have character strings, which are string of characters that are surrounded by quotation marks. These are, in fact, very widely used in R. For example, here's a vector of the names of the six nations taking part in an annual rugby union tournament:

```
> nation <- c('ireland', 'england', 'scotland', 'wales', 'france', 'italy')
```

This vector is of type `character`, which we can verify as follows:

```
> class(nation)
#> [1] "character"
```

Note that we can use single or double quotation marks for each string, as in the following example:

```
> nation <- c("ireland", 'england', "scotland", 'wales', 'france', 'italy')
```

Just like numeric vectors, we can index character vectors:

```
> nation[1]
#> [1] "ireland"
> nation[-2]
#> [1] "ireland"  "scotland" "wales"    "france"   "italy"
> nation[4:6]
#> [1] "wales"   "france" "italy"
```

We cannot, however, perform arithmetic functions on character vectors. We will obtain an error if we try:

```
> # does not work
> nation + 2
#> Error in nation + 2: non-numeric argument to binary operator
> nation * 2
#> Error in nation * 2: non-numeric argument to binary operator
```

Logical vectors

Another widely used type of vector is a logical or Boolean vector. A Boolean variable is a binary variable that takes on values of true or false. In R, these values are represented using TRUE or T for true, and FALSE or F for false. For example, a vector of values representing whether each of a set of five people is male could be as follows:

```
> is_male <- c(TRUE, FALSE, TRUE, TRUE, FALSE)
```

This could also be created more succinctly as follows:

```
> is_male <- c(T, F, T, T, F)
```

Using `class`, we can verify that this vector is a logical vector:

```
> class(is_male)
#> [1] "logical"
```

We can index logical vectors just like numeric or character vectors:

```
> is_male[2]
#> [1] FALSE
> is_male[c(1, 2)]
#> [1]  TRUE FALSE
```

Arithmetic operations on logical vectors can be applied to logical vectors, but only by first converting TRUE and FALSE to the numbers 1 and 0, respectively:

```
> is_male * 2
#> [1] 2 0 2 2 0
> is_male - 2
#> [1] -1 -2 -1 -1 -2
```

The vector returned by operations like this is a numeric vector:

```
> result <- is_male * 2
> class(result)
#> [1] "numeric"
```

We can also apply Boolean or logical operations to logical vectors. These logical operations are AND, OR, and NOT. The AND operator tests if two logical values are both true. In R, it is represented by &:

```
> TRUE & FALSE
#> [1] FALSE
> TRUE & TRUE
#> [1] TRUE
```

In these examples, we have a single Boolean variables on either side of the &, but given that a single value is a vector of one element, we could also apply the & to vectors of multiple elements:

```
> c(T, F, T) & c(T, T, F)
#> [1]  TRUE FALSE FALSE
```

In this case, the & operation is individually applied to the first, second, and third elements of both vectors.

The OR operator tests if one or the other is true, and is represented by the | character:

```
> TRUE | FALSE
#> [1] TRUE
> TRUE | TRUE
#> [1] TRUE
```

We can negate a logical value by using the ! operator:

```
> !TRUE
#> [1] FALSE
```

```
> !FALSE
#> [1] TRUE
```

Just as we can combine arithmetic operations, so too can we combine logical operations, using parentheses to control the order of operations if necessary:

```
> (TRUE | !TRUE) & FALSE
#> [1] FALSE
> (TRUE | !TRUE) & !FALSE
#> [1] TRUE
```

Equality/inequality operations

Equality and inequality operations can be applied to different types of vectors, and also return logical vectors. For example, we can test if each value of a vector of numbers, such as primes, is equal to a specific value as follows:

```
> primes == 7
#>  [1] FALSE FALSE FALSE  TRUE FALSE FALSE FALSE FALSE FALSE FALSE
```

Again, given that a single value is a vector of one element, we can also apply this operator to individual values:

```
> 12 == (6 * 2)
#> [1] TRUE
```

And we can test if values are not equal with !=, as in the following examples:

```
> 12 != (6 * 2)
#> [1] FALSE
> primes != 3
#>  [1]  TRUE FALSE  TRUE  TRUE  TRUE  TRUE  TRUE  TRUE  TRUE  TRUE
```

We can test if numbers are less than, or greater than, another number with the < and > operators, respectively:

```
> primes < 5
#>  [1]  TRUE  TRUE FALSE FALSE FALSE FALSE FALSE FALSE FALSE FALSE
> primes > 8
#>  [1] FALSE FALSE FALSE FALSE  TRUE  TRUE  TRUE  TRUE  TRUE  TRUE
```

We can test if numbers are less than or equal to, or greater than or equal to, another number with the <= and >= operators, respectively:

```
> primes <= 7
#>  [1]  TRUE  TRUE  TRUE  TRUE FALSE FALSE FALSE FALSE FALSE FALSE
> primes >= 3
#>  [1] FALSE  TRUE  TRUE  TRUE  TRUE  TRUE  TRUE  TRUE  TRUE  TRUE
```

We can also apply equality or inequality operations to character vectors:

```
> nation == 'england'
#> [1] FALSE   TRUE FALSE FALSE FALSE FALSE
> nation != 'england'
#> [1]   TRUE FALSE   TRUE   TRUE   TRUE   TRUE
```

The meaning of some inequality operations, such as the following, may be initially unclear:

```
> nation >= 'italy'
#> [1] FALSE FALSE   TRUE   TRUE FALSE   TRUE
```

In this case, greater than or less than is defined by alphabetical order, and so `nation >= 'italy'` is evaluating whether each listed nation is alphabetically after, or the same as, the string `italy`.

Coercing vectors

An important property of all vectors is that they are homogeneous, in that all their elements must be of the same data type. For example, we can't have a vector with some numbers, some logical values, and some characters. If we try to make a heterogeneous vector like this, some of our elements will be *coerced* into other types. If we, for example, try to combine some logical values with some numbers, the logical values will be coerced into numbers (TRUE will be converted to 1, FALSE will be converted to 0):

```
> c(TRUE, FALSE, 3, 2, -1, TRUE)
#> [1]   1   0   3   2 -1   1
```

If we try to combine numbers of logical values with character strings, they will all be coerced into strings, as in the following example:

```
> c(2.75, 11.3, TRUE, FALSE, 'dog', 'cat')
#> [1] "2.75"   "11.3"   "TRUE"   "FALSE" "dog"   "cat"
```

Combining vectors

Just as we combined numbers or other single values into vectors using the `c()` function, so too can we combine vectors with `c()`. For example, to combine the `primes` vector, with the vectors that are the squares and cubes of `primes`, we would do the following:

```
> c(primes, primes^2, primes^3)
#>  [1]     2     3     5     7    11    13    17    19    23    29     4     9
#> [13]    25    49   121   169   289   361   529   841     8    27   125   343
#> [25]  1331  2197  4913  6859 12167 24389
```

In this case we have produced a vector of 30 elements. These don't all fit on one line and so are wrapped over three lines. The first row displays elements 1 to 12. The second row begins with the 13th element, and the third row begins with the 25th element. Now we can see the meaning of the [1] on the output that we encountered in all of the above examples. The [1] is merely the index of the first element of the vector shown on the corresponding line.

Named vectors

The elements of a vector can be named. For example, we could provide names to our elements when we create the vector as in the following example:

```
> ages <- c(bob = 27, bill = 19, charles = 24)
> ages
#>     bob    bill charles
#>      27      19      24
```

We can access the vector's values now by their names as well as by an index as before:

```
> ages['bob']
#> bob
#>  27
> ages['bill']
#> bill
#>   19
```

If we have an already existing vector, we can add names using the names function as in the following example:

```
> ages <- c(27, 19, 24)
> names(ages) <- c('bob', 'bill', 'charles')
> ages
#>     bob    bill charles
#>      27      19      24
```

Missing values

In any vector, regardless of its type, there can be missing values. In R, missing values are denoted by NA, which can be inserted explicitly into any vector as in the following examples:

```
> x <- c(1, 2, NA, 4, 5)
> x
#> [1]  1  2 NA  4  5
> y <- c('be', NA, 'afeard')
> y
#> [1] "be"      NA        "afeard"
```

The NA here is not a character or a string. It is a special symbol with a special meaning in R. In other words, there is an important difference between the following two vectors:

```
> c(1, 2, NA, 4, 5)     # this is a numeric vector, but with a missing value
#> [1]  1  2 NA  4  5
> c(1, 2, 'NA', 4, 5)   # the "NA" coerces this to be a character vector
#> [1] "1"  "2"  "NA" "4"  "5"
```

Step 4: Data frames

The data frame is probably the most important data structure in R. As mentioned, data frames are how we almost always represent real-world data sets in R, and most statistical analysis commands, especially modern ones, assume data is provided in the form of data frames. We will provide a much more comprehensive coverage of data frames in subsequent chapters, but for now we'll just describe some of their essential features.

Data frames are rectangular data structures: they have a certain number of columns, and each column has the same number of rows. Each column is in fact a vector, and so data frames are essentially collections of equal-length vectors.

Usually, data frames are created when we read in the contents of a data file, such as a .csv or .xlsx file. However, for the purposes of introduction, we can produce them on the command line with the data.frame() function as in the following example:

```
> data_df <- data.frame(name = c('billy', 'joe', 'bob'), age = c(21, 29, 23))
> data_df
#>    name age
#> 1 billy  21
#> 2   joe  29
#> 3   bob  23
```

As we can see, this creates a data frame with three rows and two columns. The columns are variables, and the rows are the observations of these variables.

We can refer to the elements of a data frame in different ways. The simplest is to use double indices, one for the rows, one for the columns. For example, to refer to the element in the third row of the second column,

```
> data_df[3, 2]
#> [1] 23
```

We can refer to the first and third row of the second column by using a vector of indices for the rows:

```
> data_df[c(1, 3), 2]
#> [1] 21 23
```

We can refer to all the elements of the third row, by leaving the second index blank:

```
> data_df[3, ]
#>    name age
#> 3   bob  23
```

We have more options available if we want to refer to one or more columns. We could, for example, use the double indices, but leaving the first index blank to refer to all rows. For example, to refer to the second column, we would do the following:

```
> data_df[,2]
#> [1] 21 29 23
```

On the other hand, we could also refer to the column by name. To do so, we could use the following $ notation:

```
> data_df$age
#> [1] 21 29 23
```

Here, age can be seen as a property of data_df, and so data_df$age accesses this property. An alternative syntax that accomplishes the same thing is to use *double* square brackets as follows:

```
> data_df[['age']]
#> [1] 21 29 23
```

If, on the other hand, we were to use *single* square brackets, we would obtain the following:

```
> data_df['age']
#>    age
#> 1   21
#> 2   29
#> 3   23
```

This is a subset of data_df that is itself a data frame.

Step 5: Other data structures

So far we have met vectors and data frames. These are probably the most commonly encountered data structures in R, but there are others. Here is a brief overview.

Lists

Lists in R allow for the storage of multiple heterogeneous data structures. As an example, the list in the following example contains three vectors of different types, and with different numbers of elements:

```
> example_list <- list(A = TRUE, B = c(1, 2, 3), C = c('cat', 'dog'))
> example_list
#> $A
#> [1] TRUE
#>
#> $B
#> [1] 1 2 3
#>
#> $C
#> [1] "cat" "dog"
```

We can refer to the elements of the list just as we would refer to the variables of a data frame, which is not surprising given that in fact data frames are ultimately lists of vectors of the same length:

```
> example_list[['B']]
#> [1] 1 2 3
> example_list$B
#> [1] 1 2 3
> example_list[[1]]
#> [1] TRUE
```

Matrices

Matrices are equivalent to two-dimensional vectors. They contain homogeneous data types and are arranged in a rectangular $n \times m$ format, where each of the n rows has exactly m columns, and each of the m columns has exactly n rows. In the following example, we put the first 10 primes in a matrix of 2 rows and 5 columns:

```
> matrix(c(2, 3, 5, 7, 11, 13, 17, 19, 23, 29), nrow=2, ncol=5)
#>      [,1] [,2] [,3] [,4] [,5]
#> [1,]   2    5   11   17   23
#> [2,]   3    7   13   19   29
```

Notice how the elements are arranged by columns first (i.e. the first `primes` element is in the first row and first column, the second element is in the second row of the first column, etc.). Alternatively, we can arrange the elements by rows as follows:

```
> matrix(c(2, 3, 5, 7, 11, 13, 17, 19, 23, 29), byrow = T, nrow=2, ncol=5)
#>      [,1] [,2] [,3] [,4] [,5]
#> [1,]   2    3    5    7   11
#> [2,]  13   17   19   23   29
```

We may also create matrices by *binding* vectors by rows or columns. For example, we may stack vectors as rows on top of one another by an `rbind` operation as follows:

```
> rbind(c(1, 2), c(3, 4))
#>      [,1] [,2]
#> [1,]   1    2
#> [2,]   3    4
```

Alternatively, we may stack them as columns side by side, using `cbind`:

```
> cbind(c(1, 2), c(3, 4))
#>      [,1] [,2]
#> [1,]   1    3
#> [2,]   2    4
```

We can index the elements, rows, and columns in a matrix similarly to how we did so in the case of data frames:

```
> primes_m <- matrix(c(2, 3, 5, 7, 11, 13, 17, 19, 23, 29), byrow = T, nrow=2, ncol=5)
> primes_m
```

```
#>        [,1] [,2] [,3] [,4] [,5]
#> [1,]    2    3    5    7   11
#> [2,]   13   17   19   23   29
```

Here, we index a single element, all elements of a row, or all elements of column, respectively:

```
> primes_m[1, 3]    # row 1, column 3
#> [1] 5
> primes_m[2, ]     # row 2, all cols
#> [1] 13 17 19 23 29
> primes_m[, 3]     # column 3, all rows
#> [1]  5 19
```

Matrix algebra operations, such as matrix inverse and inner or outer products, may be applied to R matrices. We will not discuss these operations further here but will return to them as we encounter them in later chapters.

Arrays

Arrays are *n*-dimensional generalizations of matrices, which are strictly two-dimensional data structures. We can create an array in a similar manner to how we created matrices, as in the following examples:

```
> example_array <- array(c(1, 2, 3, 4, 5, 6, 7, 8), dim=c(2,2,2))
> example_array
#> , , 1
#>
#>        [,1] [,2]
#> [1,]    1    3
#> [2,]    2    4
#>
#> , , 2
#>
#>        [,1] [,2]
#> [1,]    5    7
#> [2,]    6    8
```

We can index arrays just as we did with matrices, but now with three indices, as in the following examples:

```
> example_array[1,2,]
#> [1] 3 7
> example_array[,1,]
#>        [,1] [,2]
#> [1,]    1    5
#> [2,]    2    6
```

Step 6: Functions

While data structures hold data in R, functions are used to do things to or with the data. In almost all functions, we put data structures in, calculations are done to or using this data, and new data structures, perhaps just a single value, are then returned. So far, we have seen two functions: `c()`, which combines vectors, and `data.frame()`, which creates data frames. Altogether, across all R packages and R's standard library, there are at least tens of thousands of functions available in R, and probably many more. That, of course, is an overwhelmingly large list, but at the start all we need to know is a relatively small set, and we then learn more gradually as we continue to use R.

To explore some functions, we'll use our primes vector above. We can count the number of elements in the vector as follows:

```
> length(primes)
#> [1] 10
```

We can get the sum, mean, median, standard deviation and variance as follows:

```
> sum(primes)
#> [1] 129
> mean(primes)
#> [1] 12.9
> median(primes)
#> [1] 12
> sd(primes)
#> [1] 9.024042
> var(primes)
#> [1] 81.43333
```

Nested functions

We can nest functions as in the following example:

```
> round(sqrt(mean(primes)))
#> [1] 4
```

Here, we first calculate the mean of `primes`, then get its square root using `sqrt`, and then round the result using `round`.

Optional arguments

In all above the above examples, the functions take a single vector of any length as their input *argument*, and return a single value (vector of length 1) as its output. In some cases, functions might take additional arguments, which if left unspecified are given default values. For example, `mean()` takes an additional `trim` argument, which trims out a certain proportion of the extreme values of the vector, and then calculates the mean. By default, the value of `trim` is 0, meaning that no trimming is done by default. If, on the other hand, we want to trim out 10% of the highest and lowest values, we would set `trim` to `0.1` as follows:

```
> mean(primes, trim=0.1)
#> [1] 12.25
```

Function help pages

Knowing that `mean()` takes an additional optional argument `trim`, and what `trim` does and what is its default value is, can be discovered from the help page for `mean()`. In fact, all functions will have a help page, which will usually tell us exactly what should go into the function, what the function does and what comes out, and it usually also provides examples of its use. We can always access the help page of a function by preceding the function's name with `?` and pressing Enter:

```
> ?mean
```

This is equivalent to typing `help()` with the function's name inside:

```
> help("mean")
```

Another alternative is to press the F1 key when our cursor is on the function's name on the console.

Custom functions

R makes it easy to create new functions. We will return to making custom functions in Chapter 6, but for now here is an example of a function that calculates the arithmetic mean:

```
> my_mean <- function(x){ sum(x)/length(x) }
```

Of course, the function `mean` already exists so there is little need for a custom function that does the same thing. However, it serves as a simple example of how to make a function. As can be easily surmised, `my_mean` takes a vector as input and divides its sum by the number of elements in it. It then returns this value. The `x` is a placeholder for whatever variable we input into the function. We would use it just as we would use `mean`:

```
> my_mean(primes)
#> [1] 12.9
```

Step 7: Scripts

Scripts are files where we write R commands, which can be then saved for later use. We can bring up RStudio's script editor with Ctrl+Shift+N, or go to *File > New File > R script*, or click on the 🔲 icon on the left of the taskbar below the menu and choose R script.

Executing code in scripts

In the script in the editor, we can write any R commands that could be written and executed in the console. Unlike in the console, when we press Enter after a command we have typed in the editor, the command is not executed. All Enter does is move the cursor onto the next line in the script, just as would happen in any text or code editor. If we want to run a command, we place the cursor anywhere on the line, and click the ⇥ Run icon. This will copy the line to the console and run it there. We can achieve the exact same effect by pressing Ctrl+Enter. That is, we place the cursor anywhere on the line, press Ctrl+Enter, and it will be copied to the console and executed.

In a script, we can have as many lines of code as we wish, and there can be as many blank lines as we wish. For example, our script could consist of the following lines:

```
1 composites <- c(4, 6, 8, 9, 10, 12, 14, 15, 16, 18)
2
3 composites_plus_one <- composites + 1
4
5 composites_minus_one <- composites - 1
```

If we place the cursor on line 1, we can then click the ⇥ Run icon, or press Ctrl+Enter. The line is then copied to the console and executed, and then the cursor jumps to the next line of code (line 3). We can then click ⇥ Run or press Ctrl+Enter again, which copies line 3 to the console and executes it, and then the cursor moves to line 5. This way, we can step through a long list of commands, executing them one by one, by just repeatedly clicking the ⇥ Run icon, or repeatedly pressing Ctrl+Enter.

In addition to running the commands in our script line by line, we can select multiple lines with our mouse and again press the ⇥ Run icon, or press Ctrl+Enter.

We may also run the entire script at once. This is known as *sourcing* the script. We may accomplish this by pressing the ⇥ Source icon on the left of the editor's taskbar. This then runs a `source()` command on the console with the name (or temporary name) of our script.

Multiline commands

One reason why writings in scripts are very practically valuable, even if we don't wish to save the scripts, is when we write long and complex commands. For example, let's say we are creating a data frame with more than a few variables and more than a few observations per variable. In this case, we can split the command over multiple lines as in the following example:

```
1 Df <- data.frame(name = c('jane', 'joe', 'billy', 'bob', 'jim'),
2                  age = c(23, 27, 24, 32, 19),
3                  sex = c('female', 'male', 'male', 'male', 'male'),
4                  occupation = c('doctor', 'tinker', 'tailor', 'soldier', 'spy')
5 )
```

We can execute this command as if it was on a single line by placing the cursor anywhere on any line and pressing the ⇥ Run icon, or repeatedly pressing Ctrl+Enter.

When writing multiline commands, it is advisable that we use consistent indentation to increase readability. The following multiline command will work perfectly, but it is more difficult to read, and perhaps to edit too:

```
1 Df <- data.frame(name = c('jane', 'joe', 'billy', 'bob', 'jim'),
2 age = c(23, 27, 24, 32, 19),
3                            sex = c('female', 'male', 'male', 'male',
'male'),
4               occupation = c('doctor', 'tinker', 'tailor', 'soldier', 'spy')
5 )
```

We can always get improved and consistent indentation by highlighting all our lines and then going to the Code menu and selecting *Reindent Lines*. More efficiently, we can accomplish the same thing by highlighting the lines and then pressing Ctrl+I.

Comments

An almost universal feature of programming language is the option to write *comments* in the code files. A comment allows us to write notes or comments around the code that are then skipped over when the script or the code lines are being executed. This is particularly useful for writing explanatory notes to ourselves or to others. In R, anything following the # symbol on any line is treated as a comment. Any line starting with # will be ignored completely when the code is being run, and we can place a # at any point on a line, and anything written after it is also ignored. The following code shows some examples of the use of comments:

```
1 # Here is a data frame with four variables.
2 # The variables are name, age, sex, occupation.
3 Df <- data.frame(name = c('jane', 'joe', 'billy', 'bob', 'jim'),
4                  # This line is a comment too.
5                  age = c(23, 27, 24, 32, 19), # Another comment.
6                  sex = c('female', 'male', 'male', 'male', 'male'),
7                  occupation = c('doctor', 'tinker', 'tailor', 'soldier', 'spy')
8 )
```

Code sections

We can use comments to divide up a script into sections as in the following example:

```
1 # Create vectors -------------------------------------------------------------
2
3 primes <- c(2, 3, 5, 7, 11, 13, 17, 19, 23, 29)
4 composites <- c(4, 6, 8, 9, 10, 12, 14, 15, 16, 18)
5
6
7 # Some calculations ----------------------------------------------------------
8
9 primes_plus_one <- primes + 1
```

```
10 composites_squared <- composites ^ 2
11
12
13 # Some more calculations  -----------------------------------------------
14
15 primes_lt_20 <- primes[primes < 20] # prime numbers less than 20
```

In this example, we have created three code sections, each one defined by the section header that begins with # and ends with a sequence of dashes ----. We can always create a new section with *Code > Insert Section*, or the key command Ctrl+Shift+R. In general, however, for the RStudio editor, a code section is demarcated by any line beginning with # and any with at least four dashes ----, equal signs ====, or hashes ####.

On the one hand, a section is nothing but a set of lines preceded by a commented line that reads like a section header. This, of course, helps to make the code readable. However, RStudio recognizes these sections as distinct units of the script. For starters, we can jump between sections by selecting the name of the section listed when we press the ⊞ icon, which appears at the bottom left of the editor when sections are used in the script. We can also bring up the list of sections by Alt+Shift+J. In addition, the ☰ icon in the top right corner of the editor provides a list of our sections, which we can jump to by clicking. For short scripts, jumping between sections does not offer much in terms of efficiency, but this feature is particularly useful for moving between sections in longer scripts.

We may also collapse or expand any of our sections. For example, if our cursor is within the Some calculations section above, we can select *Edit > Folding > Collapse* to hide the contents of this section. This can also be accomplished with the keyboard shortcut Alt+L. We can expand or uncollapse the section with *Edit > Folding > Expand*, which can also be done with Alt+Shift+L. We can collapse all sections simultaneously with *Edit > Folding > Collapse All*, or Alt+O, and expand all sections simultaneously with *Edit > Folding > Expand All*, Alt+Shift+O.

Another particularly useful feature of code sections is that we may also run all the code in a section with *Code > Run Region > Run Code Section*, or else with a Ctrl+Alt+T shortcut.

Saving a script

We save a script just like we would save any other file. We can use the 🖫 button at the top left of the Editor window. Likewise, we can select *File > Save*, which is mapped to the Ctrl+S keyboard shortcut. The resulting file is just a text file, and not some special format that can only be read by R or RStudio. In can be opened in any of the countless programs that can open text files. In principle, it can be named anything we like. However, it is recommended that we only use lowercase letters, numbers, and underscores — so no spaces or hyphens or dots — and that it should always end with the file extension .R. The .R file extension is automatically included if it is not already there when we save a script using RStudio.

Step 8: Installing and loading packages

As mentioned above, there are over 16,000 add-on R packages as of August 2020. These are installed on demand, just as one installs apps on a mobile device. The easiest way to install packages is from the *Packages* pane, which is in the lower right window (see Figure 2.3(a)).

There we will see a listing of all the R packages that are currently installed on our system. In the top right of the window, there is the ⟳ button. This refreshes the listing to make sure that any very recently installed packages are also shown. The packages are always listed alphabetically, so we can browse through the list to see if what we want is already there. There is also a search box, which is at the top right. If we start typing the name of any package there, the package listing will be filtered to match what we type.

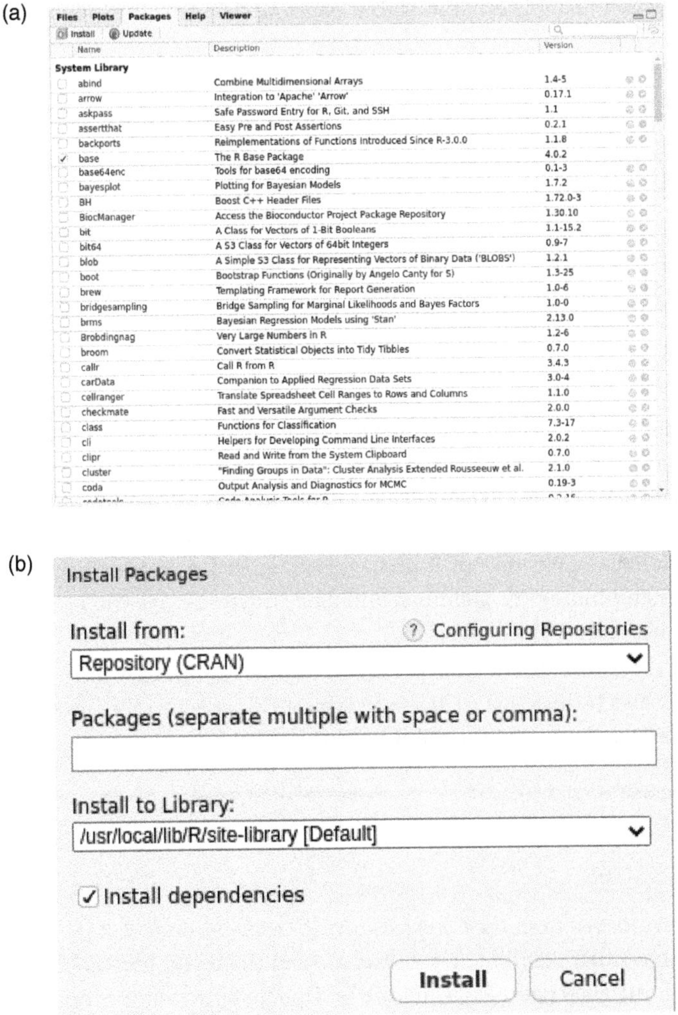

Figure 2.3 (a) The packages pane in the RStudio Desktop, which is by default in the lower right-hand quadrant window. (b) The Install Packages dialog box that appears when we press the Install button in the upper left of the packages pane

To install a package, click the ⊙ Install button on the top left. This will bring up a dialog box (see Figure 2.3(b)) where we can type in the packages that we want. As soon as we start typing in the box for the package names, packages matching the characters we've typed will be shown. From this, we can select what we want. We can type the names of multiple packages into the Install Packages dialog box, separating them with a space or a comma. When we click on Install, we will notice that commands are run in our console. For example, if we install the package `dplyr`, we will see the following command appear in our console, which will then automatically execute:

```
> install.packages ("dplyr")
```

If we select multiple packages to install (e.g. `dplyr`, `tidyr`, and `ggplot2`) then the same `install.packages` command is run, but with a vector of names as the input argument:

```
> install.packages (c ("dplyr", "tidyr", "ggplot2"))
```

Given that the Install Packages dialog box just runs these commands, we can always type them directly into the console ourselves.

As soon as these commands are executed, we will see the progress of the installation in the R console. There, in the top left, a 🛑 will be shown when the installation is occurring and we will see activity happening in the console. When the installation is complete, the stop sign will disappear and the normal > command prompt will return to the console.

Which packages to install?

A common question, especially when learning R initially, concerns which packages we should install. There is no general answer to this question because it heavily depends on the type of analyses we need to do or the type of data we will be working with. However, we highly recommend always installing the `tidyverse` collection of packages. The tidyverse describes itself as 'an opinionated collection of R packages designed for data science ... (that) share an underlying design philosophy, grammar, and data structures'. We will use these packages extensively from now on in this book.

Although `tidyverse` is a collection of packages, and these packages can be individually installed, they can also be installed *en masse* by typing *tidyverse* into the Install Packages dialog box, or alternatively by typing the following in the console:

```
> install.packages ('tidyverse')
```

Updating packages

R packages are downloaded from the *Comprehensive R Archive Network* (CRAN), which is a network of mirror servers that distribute R software around the world. We can always check for any updates to our installed packages using the 🔄 Update button at the top of our Packages window. This will list any packages with versions that are more recent than those you have installed. We can then update some or all of these packages. It is generally a good idea to periodically check for updates and update all packages if necessary.

Loading packages

Having installed any package, it is now available for use in any R session. However, it needs to be activated or loaded for this to happen. In other words, our installed packages can only be used when they are loaded into our R session. We can load them by clicking on the tick box next to the package name in the Packages listing. Unticking the package will deactivate or unload it. We will notice that when we tick or untick this box, a `library()` command is run on the console. This can always be typed directly, rather than clicking on the tick box. For example, to load all the `tidyverse` packages, type

```
> library("tidyverse")
```

Throughout the remainder of this book, we will be using many packages, and we will always load them from a `library()` command run on the console.

Package masking

When we load a package, we are often greeted with messages like the following:

```
> library("dplyr")
Attaching package: 'dplyr'

The following objects are masked from 'package:stats':

    filter, lag

The following objects are masked from 'package:base':

    intersect, setdiff, setequal, union
```

What this means is that the `dplyr` package has loaded up two functions, `filter` and `lag`, that were previously loaded by the `stats` package, and four other functions, `intersect`, `setdiff`, `setequal`, and `union`, that were loaded previously by the `base` package. Both the `stats` and the `base` packages are loaded by default in any R session. If we now try to use, for example, `filter`, we will be given the `filter` function of `dplyr` rather than the `filter` function of `stats`. In general, R searches for functions according to its *search path*, which we can see with the following command:

```
> search()
#>  [1] ".GlobalEnv"          "package:forcats"    "package:stringr"
#>  [4] "package:dplyr"       "package:purrr"      "package:readr"
#>  [7] "package:tidyr"       "package:tibble"     "package:ggplot2"
#> [10] "package:tidyverse"   "package:stats"      "package:graphics"
#> [13] "package:grDevices"   "package:utils"      "package:datasets"
#> [16] "package:methods"     "Autoloads"          "package:base"
```

So, for example, if we search for a function named `filter`, we will find the `filter` in `dplyr` first, because `dplyr` is nearer the start of the search path than the `stats` package. This does not mean that the masked functions are unavailable. We can access them directly using the `<package name>::<function name>` syntax as in the following examples:

```
> stats::filter()      # The `filter` function in the `stats` package.
> base::intersect()    # The `intersect` function in the `base` package.
```

Step 9: Reading in and viewing data

We mentioned that when we are dealing with real data sets in R, we almost always read them into R from files. R allows us to import data from a very large variety of data file types, including from other statistics programs such as SPSS, Stata, SAS, Minitab, and common file formats like .xlsx and .csv. Here, we'll just look at the example of importing .csv files, which is a particularly common scenario anyway, and the procedure we follow for importing the other file formats is similar.

When learning R initially, the easiest way to import data is using the 🖳 Import Dataset button in the *Environment* pane. This will give us options to import from a number of different file types. If we are importing .csv, we can choose either *From Text (base)...* or *From Text (readr)...*. The former option imports the .csv file using the function `read.csv()`, which is part of the *base R* set of packages. The latter option uses the `read_csv()` function from the readr package, which is part of the `tidyverse` package collection. Throughout this book, we recommend always using `tidyverse` over base R functions whenever the options are available, and so we will always use the *From Text (readr)...* option for importing .csv files.

Upon choosing the *From Text (readr)...* option, if the readr package is not yet installed, we will be asked if to install it. However, it will already be available for us if we installed `tidyverse`, as described in the previous step. We will then be given a typical file import dialog box, just as we would encounter in many other programs (see Figure 2.4). There we choose the file we want to use using a file browser. At the bottom left of the dialog box, there are various options for parsing the .csv file. Often we can just leave these at their default values. However, it is often a good idea to explicitly choose a new *Name* for the data frame into which the contents of the .csv will be read. By default, the name of the data frame will be the file name, but often it is preferable to have a shorter name. In this book, we usually end the name of the data frame with _df (e.g. `data_df`, `scores_df`). The _df ending makes it clear that the object is a data frame.

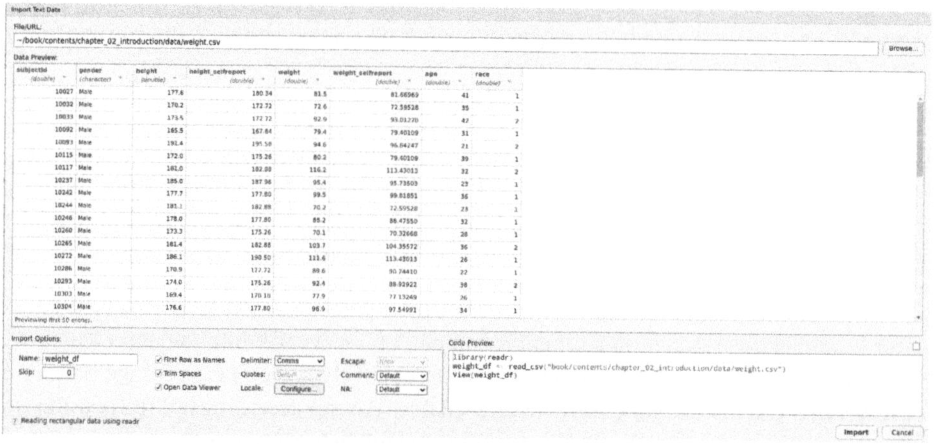

Figure 2.4 The `read_csv`-based dialog box for reading csv files using readr, which is part of `tidyverse`

We will also notice that, at bottom right, there is a *Code Preview* of the code that will be run in the console once we click the Import button. What this shows us is that the *Import Dataset* dialog box is just a means to create a few lines of code that will then be run in the console. We can always write this code, or at least its essential parts, explicitly in the console or in a script. In fact, we strongly advise doing so because it is ultimately much quicker and efficient than going through a GUI dialog box. However, to do this in a reusable way, and without having to remember or type long file paths, it is necessary to first understand the concept of the R session's working directory, which we will deal with below.

Let's say the .csv file that we wish to import is named `weight.csv` and exists in our personal `Downloads` directory on a Windows device. If we choose the name `weight_df` for the imported data, rather than the default, we should see the following code and output in the console:

```
library(readr)
weight_df <- read_csv("C:/Users/andrews/Downloads/weight.csv")
View(weight_df)
#> Parsed with column specification:
#> cols(
#> subjectid = col_double(),
#> gender = col_character(),
#> height = col_double(),
#> height_selfreport = col_double(),
#> weight = col_double(),
#> weight_selfreport = col_double(),
#> age = col_double(),
#> race = col_double()
#> )
```

The message displayed after the `read_csv()` command is run (i.e. `Parsed with column specification` ...) tells us how many variables have been created in the resulting data frame, and of which data types these variables are. As can be seen, we have eight variables (`subjectid`, `gender`, ..., `race`), and corresponding to each one is either `col_double()` or, in the case of `gender`, `col_character()`. The `col_double()` indicates that the corresponding variable is a normal numerical variable ('double' refers to double floating point number, which is a decimal number represented by 8 bytes of memory). The `col_character` indicates that the `gender` variable is a character vector.

The last line of the code that was run above is `View(weight_df)`. This brings up a data frame viewer that looks like a spreadsheet. With this, we may obviously browse through the variables and observations, we may sort according to any variable, and using the ▽ Filter icon, we can filter the data set according to selected ranges of values of the variables. Although `View` is certainly a useful tool, we can in fact view, sort, select and filter the data much more efficiently using command line tools like `dplyr`. This is something to which we will return in depth in the next chapter, under the topic of *data wrangling*. For now, we will just provide an introduction to viewing the data in the data frame.

Certainly the easiest way to look at a data frame in R is simply to type its name in the console as follows:

```
> weight_df
#> # A tibble: 6,068 x 8
#>    subjectid gender height height_selfreport weight weight_selfrepo~  age  race
#>        <dbl> <chr>   <dbl>             <dbl>  <dbl>            <dbl> <dbl> <dbl>
#>  1     10027 Male     178.              180.   81.5             81.7   41     1
#>  2     10032 Male     170.              173.   72.6             72.6   35     1
#>  3     10033 Male     174.              173.   92.9             93.0   42     2
#>  4     10092 Male     166.              168.   79.4             79.4   31     1
#>  5     10093 Male     191.              196.   94.6             96.6   21     2
#>  6     10115 Male     172               175.   80.2             79.4   39     1
#>  7     10117 Male     181               183.  116.             113.    32     2
#>  8     10237 Male     185               188.   95.4             95.7   23     1
#>  9     10242 Male     178.              178.   99.5             99.8   36     1
#> 10     10244 Male     181.              183.   70.2             72.6   23     1
#> # ... with 6,058 more rows
```

There is a lot to see here. We see that there are 6068 rows and eight variables. We see the first 10 values of all 8 variables, and see that there is also one additional variable, `race`, whose values are not shown. We also see the corresponding data type of each of the variables. At the top of the listing, we see that the data frame is a tibble. A *tibble* is simply a `tidyverse`-flavoured data frame. It is a regular data frame but with some relatively minor additional features.

The number of observations, variables, and even the number of significant digits that are shown can be controlled using the `options()` function. For example, by default, 10 observations will be shown. If we want, say, up to 15 observations to be shown by default, we can type

```
> options(tibble.print_max = 15, tibble.print_min = 15)
```

The `tibble.print_max` and `tibble.print_min` values need not be equal. For example, we can set them as follows:

```
> options(tibble.print_max = 15, tibble.print_min = 5)
```

In this case, any tibble with up to 15 observations will be shown in full, but if it has over 15 observations, then only the first 5 observations will be shown. The number of displayed variables, on the other hand, is set with the `tibble.width` option. If we always wish to see all rows of all tibble data frames, we can set the following options:

```
> options(tibble.print_max = Inf)
```

For an individual tibble data frame such as `weight_df`, we can show all rows as follows:

```
> print(weight_df, n = Inf)
```

By default, only the number of columns that can fit on the console will be displayed. This means, of course, that when we widen our console, we may always fit in more variables, and if we're using a narrower console, fewer variables are shown. If we always want all variables to be displayed, wrapping them if necessary to fit, then we set `tibble.width` to `Inf`:

```
> options(tibble.width = Inf)
```

We may set `tibble.print_max`, `tibble.print_min` and `tibble.width` back to their default behaviour as follows:

```
> options(tibble.print_max = NULL, tibble.print_min = NULL, tibble.width = NULL)
```

We can control the number of significant digits that are displayed by the `pillar.sigfig` option:

```
> options(pillar.sigfig = 5)
```

Step 10: Working directory, RStudio projects, and clean workspaces

Every R session has a *working directory*, which we can think of as the directory (or folder) on the computer's file system in which the R session is running. In other words, we can think of the R session as belonging to, or running inside, some directory somewhere on the system. By default, this is often the user's home directory. We can always list our session's working directory with `getwd()`. On Windows, this will appear something like the following:

```
> getwd()
> #> [1] "C:/Users/andrews"
```

On Macs, it will appear something like the following:

```
> getwd()
> #> /Users/andrews/
```

The practical importance of the working directory is that it is the default location from which files are read and to which files are written whenever we are using *relative* rather than *absolute* path names. The use of relative paths is necessary to allow our R scripts to be usable either by others or by ourselves on different devices.

An absolute path name gives the exact location of the file on the file system by specifying the file's name, the directory it is in, the directory in which its directory is located, and so on, up to the root of the file system. For example, on a Windows machine, an absolute path name for a file might be `C:/Users/andrews/Downloads/data/data.csv`. From this we see that the file `data.csv` is a directory named `data` that is in `Downloads` in `andrews` in `Users` on the `C` drive. We could read this file into R with the following command:

```
data_df <- read_csv("C:/Users/andrews/Downloads/data/data.csv")
```

This command will always work (assuming the file and directories exist) regardless of what the R session's working directory is. A relative path name, on the other hand, might be `data/`

data.csv. This specifies that data.csv is in a directory called data, but it does not explicitly tell us the location of data. In these situations, the location is always assumed to be the R session's working directory. Consider the following commands:

```
data_1_df <- read_csv("data.csv")
data_2_df <- read_csv("data/data.csv")
```

The first would read in the file data.csv from the working directory, while the second would read in the file data.csv from the data subdirectory in the working directory. Likewise, the command

```
write_csv(data_df, 'my_new_data.csv')
```

will write the data to the file my_new_data.csv in the current working directory.

In general, R scripts that use absolute path names are not usable either by others or by ourselves on different machines. For example, if I had the following script, it would only be usable by me on a particular device:

```
data_df <- read_csv("C:/Users/andrews/Downloads/data/data.csv")
some_function(data_df)
```

If I wanted to share this code with others, or use it myself on another device, then it would be better to use relative paths as follows:

```
data_df <- read_csv("data.csv")
some_function(data_df)
```

Assuming that data.csv is the session's working directory, this code will now work everywhere for anyone.

The working directory for the R session can always be changed by going to *Session > Set Working Directory > Choose Directory*, which can be obtained by the key command Ctrl+Shift+H. This allows us to set the working directory to be any directory of our choice.

RStudio projects

When we are working on a particular data analysis task, one that might involve multiple interrelated data files and scripts, it is usually a good idea to set the working directory to be the directory where all these scripts and data files are located. For example, let's say the directory where we kept our scripts and data was data_analysis and was organized as follows:

```
data_analysis/
  -- script_1.R
  -- script_2.R
  -- data/
        -- data_1.csv
        -- data_2.csv
```

In this case, it would be advisable to set the working directory to be the location of data_analysis whenever we are working on these files. Inside the script_1.R or script_2.R, we would then be able to include command code such as the following:

```
data_1_df <- read_csv('data/data_1.csv')
```

Having set the working directory to the location of data_analysis, whenever these scripts are run, they would always refer to the appropriate data files.

To facilitate this, RStudio allows us to set our data_analysis directory as an *RStudio project*. To do so, we go to *File > New Project* and choose *Existing Directory* and then choose the data_analysis directory. Likewise, if we have other directories with their own sets of inter-related files and scripts, we can set these as separate projects too. Having set up these projects, whenever we start RStudio, we can open a project, and then switch between projects. Whenever we open a project, or switch between projects, our working directory is then automatically switched to the project's directory. As such, our working will always be set to the appropriate directories for whichever files we are working on and it need never be set manually.

RStudio projects also allow us to have project-specific settings for our command history. In other words, all the commands used whenever we are working on a particular project will be saved to a history file specific to that project which can be loaded automatically every time we open or switch to that project. We can ensure that our history is always saved by setting the *Always save history* option in *Tools > Project Options*.

Clean workspaces

In general, R allows us to always save the contents of our *workspace* to a file, usually named .RData, when terminating our session. Our workspace contains the collection of objects (e.g. data sets and other variables) we've created and that exists in our R session. This collection can be viewed in the Environment window. If we save these objects to file, they can be automatically loaded the next time we start R.

This saving and loading of the workspace may seem like a very useful feature. For example, if during the course of a long session we have created multiple new data frames and other data structures, it may seem particularly useful to be able to save them all to file, and then reload them back into our session when we start again. However, despite appearances, this may be counterproductive. We may end up with a cluttered workspace that is full of objects, many of which were intended to be only temporary. Even if there are some we do wish to keep, we may not be sure where they came from or how they were created. It is much better practice to always write code that creates the variables and data structures that we need. For example, rather than saving many data frames that we have derived from processing some raw data that we initially imported, it is far better to have a single script that reads the raw data and then runs a series of commands on this data, thus creating, or re-creating, all the derived data frames.

RStudio projects also give us the option of always saving or never saving our workspace, and always or never loading the workspace file at startup. These options are available in

Tools > Project Options. We recommend that these options are always set to *never* save or load the contents of the workspace. This ensures that we always have, or can have, a clean workspace whose contents we are in control of.

At any point during our RStudio session, we can restart R itself through *Session > Restart R*. Doing so prior to running any script is good practice because it ensures that our script will not have any hidden dependencies, and that any data structures or functions it does depend on are contained in the code itself.

3

Data Wrangling

Introduction

Traditional statistics textbooks and courses routinely assume that the data is ready for analysis. Their starting point for any analysis is usually a neat table of rows and columns, with all and only the relevant variables, each with meaningful names, and often accompanied with a useful description or summary of what each variable signifies or measures. In reality, the starting point of any analysis is almost always a very messy, unstructured or ill-formatted data set, or even multiple separate data sets, that must first be cleaned up and modified before any further analysis can begin. Throughout this book, we will use the term *data wrangling* to describe the process of taking data in its unstructured, messy, or complicated original form and converting it into a clean and tidy format that allows data exploration, visualization, and eventually statistical modelling and analysis to proceed efficiently and relatively effortlessly. Other terms for data wrangling include *data munging*, *data cleaning*, *data pre-processing*, and *data preparation*.

The central role of data wrangling in any type of data analysis should not be underestimated. Part of the lore of modern data science is the belief that up to 80% of all data science activities involve data wrangling (see, for example, Lohr, 2014), and this 80% figure is backed up by surveys of what data scientists do (see, for example, CrowdFlower, 2016, 2017). Even if this number is not accurate, data wrangling is a necessary and potentially very time-consuming and laborious activity for any data analysis. As such, developing data wrangling skills is essential for doing data analysis efficiently.

Data wrangling tools in R

There are many tools in R for doing data wrangling. Here, we will focus on a core set of interrelated `tidyverse` tools. These include the commands available in the `dplyr` package, particularly its so-called *verbs* such as the following:

- `select`
- `rename`
- `slice`
- `filter`
- `mutate`
- `arrange`
- `group_by`
- `summarize`.

In addition, `dplyr` provides tools for merging and joining data sets such as the following:

- `inner_join`
- `left_join`
- `right_join`
- `full_join`.

Next, there are the tools in the `tidyr` package, particularly the following:

- `pivot_longer`
- `pivot_wider`.

These and other tools can then be combined together using the `%>%` pipe operator for efficient data analysis *pipelines*.

Most of these tools can be loaded into R by loading the `tidyverse` package of packages:

```
library(tidyverse)
```

 ## Reading text file data into a data frame

In principle, raw data can exist in any format in any type of file. In practice, it is common to have data in a roughly rectangular format (i.e. with rows and columns), in text files such as .csv, .tsv, or .txt. The `readr` package, which is loaded when we load `tidyverse`, allows us to efficiently import data that is in such files. It has many commands for importing data in many different text file formats. The most commonly used include:

- `read_csv` for files where the values on each line are separated by commas
- `read_tsv` for files where the values are separated by tabs
- `read_delim` for files where the values are separated by arbitrary delimiters such as |, :, ; (both `read_csv` and `read_tsv` are special cases of the more general `read_delim` command)
- `read_table` for files where the values are separated by one or more, and possible inconsistently many, white spaces.

These commands usually read from files stored locally on the computer on which R is running. For example, if we have a .csv file named `data.csv` that is inside a directory called `data` that was in our working directory, we would read this by default as follows:

```
read_csv('data/data.csv')
```

However, these commands can also read from files on the internet. In this case, we provide a URL for the file. These commands can also read compressed files if they are compressed in the .xz, .bz2, .gz, or .zip compression formats.

As an example data set, we will use the data contained in the file `blp-trials-short.txt`. We will read it into a data frame named `blp_df` as follows:

```
blp_df <- read_csv("data/blp-trials-short.txt")
blp_df
#> # A tibble: 1,000 x 7
#>    participant lex   spell   resp     rt prev.rt rt.raw
#>          <dbl> <chr> <chr>   <chr> <dbl>   <dbl>  <dbl>
#>  1          20 N     staud   N       977     511    977
```

```
#>  2           9 N     dinbuss  N      565     765     565
#>  3          47 N     snilling N      562     496     562
#>  4         103 N     gancens  N      572     656     572
#>  5          45 W     filled   W      659     981     659
#>  6          73 W     journals W      538    1505     538
#>  7          24 W     apache   W      626     546     626
#>  8          11 W     flake    W      566     717     566
#>  9          32 W     reliefs  W      922    1471     922
#> 10          96 N     sarves   N      555     806     555
#> # … with 990 more rows
```

We can use the `dplyr` command `glimpse` to look at the resulting data frame:

```
glimpse(blp_df)
#> Rows: 1,000
#> Columns: 7
#> $ participant <dbl> 20, 9, 47, 103, 45, 73, 24, 11, 32, 96, 82, 37, 52, 96, 9…
#> $ lex         <chr> "N", "N", "N", "N", "W", "W", "W", "W", "W", "N", "W", "W…
#> $ spell       <chr> "staud", "dinbuss", "snilling", "gancens", "filled", "jou…
#> $ resp        <chr> "N", "N", "N", "N", "W", "W", "W", "W", "W", "N", "W", "N…
#> $ rt          <dbl> 977, 565, 562, 572, 659, 538, 626, 566, 922, 555, 657, NA…
#> $ prev.rt     <dbl> 511, 765, 496, 656, 981, 1505, 546, 717, 1471, 806, 728, …
#> $ rt.raw      <dbl> 977, 565, 562, 572, 659, 538, 626, 566, 922, 555, 657, 71…
```

As we can see, there are 1000 rows and seven variables. This data frame gives the trial-by-trial results from a type of cognitive psychology experiment known as a *lexical decision task*. In a lexical decision task, participants are shown a string of characters and they have to indicate, with a key press, whether that string of characters is a word in their language. On each row of the data frame, among other things, we have an identifier of the participant, what string of characters they were shown, what key they pressed, what their reaction time was, and so on.

 ## Manipulating data frames using `dplyr`

The `dplyr` package provides a set of versatile interrelated commands for manipulating data frames. Chief among these commands are `dplyr`'s *verbs* listed above. Here, we will look at each one.

Selecting variables with `select`

In our `blp_df` data frames we have seven variables. Let's say, as is often the case when processing raw data, that we only need some of these. The `dplyr` command `select` allows us to select those we want. For example, if we just want the participant's id, whether the displayed string was an English word or not, what their key press response was, what their reaction time was, then we would do the following:

```
select(blp_df, participant, lex, resp, rt)
#> # A tibble: 1,000 x 4
#>    participant lex   resp     rt
#>          <dbl> <chr> <chr> <dbl>
#>  1          20 N     N       977
#>  2           9 N     N       565
#>  3          47 N     N       562
#>  4         103 N     N       572
#>  5          45 W     W       659
#>  6          73 W     W       538
#>  7          24 W     W       626
#>  8          11 W     W       566
#>  9          32 W     W       922
#> 10          96 N     N       555
#> # ... with 990 more rows
```

Importantly, select returns a *new* data frame with the selected variables. In other words, the original blp_df data frame is still left fully intact. This feature of returning a new data frame and not altering the original data frame is true of all of the dplyr verbs and many other wrangling commands that we'll meet below.

We can select a range of variables by specifying the first and last variables in the range with a : between them as follows:

```
select(blp_df, spell:prev.rt)
#> # A tibble: 1,000 x 4
#>    spell    resp     rt prev.rt
#>    <chr>    <chr> <dbl>   <dbl>
#>  1 staud    N       977     511
#>  2 dinbuss  N       565     765
#>  3 snilling N       562     496
#>  4 gancens  N       572     656
#>  5 filled   W       659     981
#>  6 journals W       538    1505
#>  7 apache   W       626     546
#>  8 flake    W       566     717
#>  9 reliefs  W       922    1471
#> 10 sarves   N       555     806
#> # ... with 990 more rows
```

We can also select a range of variables using indices as in the following example:

```
select(blp_df, 2:5) # columns 2 to 5
#> # A tibble: 1,000 x 4
#>    lex   spell    resp     rt
#>    <chr> <chr>    <chr> <dbl>
#>  1 N     staud    N       977
#>  2 N     dinbuss  N       565
```

```
#>  3 N      snilling N           562
#>  4 N      gancens   N          572
#>  5 W      filled    W          659
#>  6 W      journals W           538
#>  7 W      apache    W          626
#>  8 W      flake     W          566
#>  9 W      reliefs   W          922
#> 10 N      sarves    N          555
#> # … with 990 more rows
```

We can select variables according to the character or characters that they begin with. For example, we select all variables that being with p as follows:

```
select(blp_df, starts_with('p'))
#> # A tibble: 1,000 x 2
#>     participant prev.rt
#>           <dbl>    <dbl>
#>  1           20      511
#>  2            9      765
#>  3           47      496
#>  4          103      656
#>  5           45      981
#>  6           73     1505
#>  7           24      546
#>  8           11      717
#>  9           32     1471
#> 10           96      806
#> # … with 990 more rows
```

Or we can select variables by the characters they end with:

```
select(blp_df, ends_with('t'))
#> # A tibble: 1,000 x 3
#>     participant     rt prev.rt
#>           <dbl> <dbl>    <dbl>
#>  1           20   977      511
#>  2            9   565      765
#>  3           47   562      496
#>  4          103   572      656
#>  5           45   659      981
#>  6           73   538     1505
#>  7           24   626      546
#>  8           11   566      717
#>  9           32   922     1471
#> 10           96   555      806
#> # … with 990 more rows
```

We can select variables that contain a certain set of characters in any position. For example, the following selects variables whose names contain the string `rt`:

```
select(blp_df, contains('rt'))
#> # A tibble: 1,000 x 4
#>    participant    rt prev.rt rt.raw
#>          <dbl> <dbl>   <dbl>  <dbl>
#> 1           20   977     511    977
#> 2            9   565     765    565
#> 3           47   562     496    562
#> 4          103   572     656    572
#> 5           45   659     981    659
#> 6           73   538    1505    538
#> 7           24   626     546    626
#> 8           11   566     717    566
#> 9           32   922    1471    922
#> 10          96   555     806    555
#> # ... with 990 more rows
```

The previous example selected the variable `participant` because it contained the string `rt`. However, if we had wanted to select only those variables that contained `rt` where it clearly meant reaction time, we could use a *regular expression* match. For example, the regular expression `^rt|rt$` will match the `rt` if it begins or ends a string. Therefore, we can select the variables that contain `rt`, where the string `rt` means reaction time, as follows:

```
select(blp_df, matches('^rt|rt$'))
#> # A tibble: 1,000 x 3
#>       rt prev.rt rt.raw
#>    <dbl>   <dbl>  <dbl>
#> 1    977     511    977
#> 2    565     765    565
#> 3    562     496    562
#> 4    572     656    572
#> 5    659     981    659
#> 6    538    1505    538
#> 7    626     546    626
#> 8    566     717    566
#> 9    922    1471    922
#> 10   555     806    555
#> # ... with 990 more rows
```

Removing variables. We can use `select` to *remove* variables as well as select them. To remove a variable, we precede its name with a minus sign:

```
select(blp_df, -participant) # remove `participant`
#> # A tibble: 1,000 x 6
```

```
#>     lex   spell     resp      rt prev.rt rt.raw
#>    <chr> <chr>    <chr> <dbl>    <dbl>   <dbl>
#>  1 N     staud    N       977      511     977
#>  2 N     dinbuss  N       565      765     565
#>  3 N     snilling N       562      496     562
#>  4 N     gancens  N       572      656     572
#>  5 W     filled   W       659      981     659
#>  6 W     journals W       538     1505     538
#>  7 W     apache   W       626      546     626
#>  8 W     flake    W       566      717     566
#>  9 W     reliefs  W       922     1471     922
#> 10 N     sarves   N       555      806     555
#> # ... with 990 more rows
```

Just as we selected ranges or sets of variables above, we can remove them by preceding their selection functions with minus signs. For example, to remove variables indexed 2 to 6, we would type the following:

```
select(blp_df, -(2:6))
#> # A tibble: 1,000 x 2
#>    participant rt.raw
#>          <dbl>  <dbl>
#>  1          20    977
#>  2           9    565
#>  3          47    562
#>  4         103    572
#>  5          45    659
#>  6          73    538
#>  7          24    626
#>  8          11    566
#>  9          32    922
#> 10          96    555
#> # ... with 990 more rows
```

Or, as another example, we can remove the variables that contain the string `rt` as follows:

```
select(blp_df, -contains('rt'))
#> # A tibble: 1,000 x 3
#>     lex   spell     resp
#>    <chr> <chr>    <chr>
#>  1 N     staud    N
#>  2 N     dinbuss  N
#>  3 N     snilling N
#>  4 N     gancens  N
#>  5 W     filled   W
#>  6 W     journals W
#>  7 W     apache   W
```

```
#>  8 W       flake    W
#>  9 W       reliefs  W
#> 10 N       sarves   N
#> # … with 990 more rows
```

Reordering variables. When we select variables with `select`, we control their order in the resulting data frame. For example, if we select `spell`, `participant`, `res`, the resulting data frame will have them in their selected order:

```
select(blp_df, spell, participant, resp)
#> # A tibble: 1,000 x 3
#>    spell     participant resp
#>    <chr>           <dbl> <chr>
#>  1 staud              20 N
#>  2 dinbuss             9 N
#>  3 snilling           47 N
#>  4 gancens           103 N
#>  5 filled             45 W
#>  6 journals           73 W
#>  7 apache             24 W
#>  8 flake              11 W
#>  9 reliefs            32 W
#> 10 sarves             96 N
#> # … with 990 more rows
```

However, clearly the resulting data frame only returned those variables that we selected. We can, however, include all remaining variables after those we explicitly selected by using `everything()` as follows:

```
select(blp_df, spell, participant, resp, everything())
#> # A tibble: 1,000 x 7
#>    spell     participant resp  lex      rt prev.rt rt.raw
#>    <chr>           <dbl> <chr> <chr> <dbl>   <dbl>  <dbl>
#>  1 staud              20 N     N       977     511    977
#>  2 dinbuss             9 N     N       565     765    565
#>  3 snilling           47 N     N       562     496    562
#>  4 gancens           103 N     N       572     656    572
#>  5 filled             45 W     W       659     981    659
#>  6 journals           73 W     W       538    1505    538
#>  7 apache             24 W     W       626     546    626
#>  8 flake              11 W     W       566     717    566
#>  9 reliefs            32 W     W       922    1471    922
#> 10 sarves             96 N     N       555     806    555
#> # … with 990 more rows
```

We can also use `everything` to move some variables to the start of the list, and some to the end, and have the remaining variables in the middle. For example, we can move **resp** to the start of the list of variables, move `participant` to the end, and then have everything else in between as follows:

```
select(blp_df, resp, everything(), -participant, participant)
#> # A tibble: 1,000 x 7
#>    resp  lex   spell         rt prev.rt rt.raw participant
#>    <chr> <chr> <chr>      <dbl>   <dbl>  <dbl>       <dbl>
#>  1 N     N     staud        977     511    977          20
#>  2 N     N     dinbuss      565     765    565           9
#>  3 N     N     snilling     562     496    562          47
#>  4 N     N     gancens      572     656    572         103
#>  5 W     W     filled       659     981    659          45
#>  6 W     W     journals     538    1505    538          73
#>  7 W     W     apache       626     546    626          24
#>  8 W     W     flake        566     717    566          11
#>  9 W     W     reliefs      922    1471    922          32
#> 10 N     N     sarves       555     806    555          96
#> # ... with 990 more rows
```

In this example, we essentially move `resp` to the front of the list, followed by all remaining variables. Then we remove `participant` using -participant and then reinsert it at the end of the list of the remaining variables.

Selecting by condition with `select_if`. Thus far, we have selected variables according to properties of their names or by their indices. The `select_if` function is a powerful function that allows us to select variables according to properties of their values. For example, the function `is.character` will verify whether a vector is a character vector or not, and `is.numeric` will verify if a vector is a numeric vector, as in the following:

```
x <- c(1, 42, 3)
y <- c('good', 'dogs', 'brent')
is.numeric(x)
#> [1] TRUE
is.numeric(y)
#> [1] FALSE
is.character(x)
#> [1] FALSE
is.character(y)
#> [1] TRUE
```

We can use the function `is.character` to select the variables that are character vectors as follows:

```
select_if(blp_df, is.character)
#> # A tibble: 1,000 x 3
#>    lex   spell     resp
#>    <chr> <chr>    <chr>
#>  1 N     staud    N
```

```
#>    2 N      dinbuss  N
#>    3 N      snilling N
#>    4 N      gancens  N
#>    5 W      filled   W
#>    6 W      journals W
#>    7 W      apache   W
#>    8 W      flake    W
#>    9 W      reliefs  W
#>   10 N      sarves   N
#> # … with 990 more rows
```

Note that in this command, we use the function itself, `is.character`. We do not use the function call, `is.character()`. In the following example, we select the numeric variables in `blp_df`:

```
select_if(blp_df, is.numeric)
#> # A tibble: 1,000 x 4
#>     participant     rt prev.rt rt.raw
#>           <dbl> <dbl>   <dbl>  <dbl>
#>   1          20   977     511    977
#>   2           9   565     765    565
#>   3          47   562     496    562
#>   4         103   572     656    572
#>   5          45   659     981    659
#>   6          73   538    1505    538
#>   7          24   626     546    626
#>   8          11   566     717    566
#>   9          32   922    1471    922
#> 10          96   555     806    555
#> # … with 990 more rows
```

We can use custom functions with `select_if`. In Chapter 2, we briefly described how to create custom functions in R. This is a topic to which we will return in more depth in Chapter 6. Now, and throughout the remainder of this chapter, we will create some custom functions to use with data wrangling, but we will not delve too deep into the details of how they work.

As an example, the following function will return TRUE if the variable is a numeric variable with a mean that is less than 700:

```
has_low_mean <- function(x){
   is.numeric(x) && (mean(x, na.rm = T) < 700)
}
```

Now, we can select variables that meet this criterion as follows:

```
select_if(blp_df, has_low_mean)
#> # A tibble: 1,000 x 3
#>     participant     rt prev.rt
```

```
#>                <dbl> <dbl>   <dbl>
#>   1               20   977     511
#>   2                9   565     765
#>   3               47   562     496
#>   4              103   572     656
#>   5               45   659     981
#>   6               73   538    1505
#>   7               24   626     546
#>   8               11   566     717
#>   9               32   922    1471
#>  10               96   555     806
#> # ... with 990 more rows
```

We can also use an *anonymous* function within `select_if`. An anonymous function is a function without a name, and its use is primarily for situations where functions are used in a one-off manner, and so there is no need to save them. As an example, the anonymous version of `has_low_mean` is simply the following:

```
function(x){ is.numeric(x) && (mean(x, na.rm = T) < 700) }
```

We can put this anonymous function inside `select_if` as follows:

```
select_if(blp_df, function(x){ is.numeric(x) && (mean(x, na.rm = T) < 700) })
#> # A tibble: 1,000 x 3
#>     participant      rt prev.rt
#>           <dbl> <dbl>   <dbl>
#>   1          20   977     511
#>   2           9   565     765
#>   3          47   562     496
#>   4         103   572     656
#>   5          45   659     981
#>   6          73   538    1505
#>   7          24   626     546
#>   8          11   566     717
#>   9          32   922    1471
#>  10          96   555     806
#> # ... with 990 more rows
```

We can make a less verbose version of this anonymous function using a syntactic shortcut that is part of the `purrr` package, which is loaded when we load `tidyverse`, as follows:

```
select_if(blp_df, ~is.numeric(.) && (mean(., na.rm = T) < 700))
#> # A tibble: 1,000 x 3
#>     participant      rt prev.rt
#>           <dbl> <dbl>   <dbl>
#>   1          20   977     511
#>   2           9   565     765
```

```
#>   3             47   562      496
#>   4            103   572      656
#>   5             45   659      981
#>   6             73   538     1505
#>   7             24   626      546
#>   8             11   566      717
#>   9             32   922     1471
#>  10             96   555      806
#> # … with 990 more rows
```

Renaming variables with `rename`

When we select individual variables with `select`, we can rename them too, as in the following example:

```
select(blp_df, subject=participant, reaction_time=rt)
#> # A tibble: 1,000 x 2
#>    subject reaction_time
#>      <dbl>         <dbl>
#>  1      20           977
#>  2       9           565
#>  3      47           562
#>  4     103           572
#>  5      45           659
#>  6      73           538
#>  7      24           626
#>  8      11           566
#>  9      32           922
#> 10      96           555
#> # … with 990 more rows
```

While this is useful, the data frame that is returned just contains the selected variables. If we want to rename some variables, and get a data frame with all variables, including the renamed ones, we should use `rename`:

```
rename(blp_df, subject=participant, reaction_time=rt)
#> # A tibble: 1,000 x 7
#>    subject lex   spell    resp  reaction_time prev.rt rt.raw
#>      <dbl> <chr> <chr>    <chr>         <dbl>   <dbl>  <dbl>
#>  1      20 N     staud    N               977     511    977
#>  2       9 N     dinbuss  N               565     765    565
#>  3      47 N     snilling N               562     496    562
#>  4     103 N     gancens  N               572     656    572
#>  5      45 W     filled   W               659     981    659
#>  6      73 W     journals W               538    1505    538
#>  7      24 W     apache   W               626     546    626
#>  8      11 W     flake    W               566     717    566
```

```
#>  9       32 W      reliefs  W                922    1471    922
#> 10       96 N       sarves  N                555     806    555
#> # ... with 990 more rows
```

Useful variants of rename include rename_all, rename_at, and rename_if. The rename_all function allows us, as the name implies, to rename all the variables using some renaming function, that is a function that takes a string as input and returns another as output. As an example of such a function, here is a purrr-style anonymous function, using the str_replace_all function from the stringr package, that replaces any dot in the variable name with an underscore:

```
rename_all(blp_df, ~str_replace_all(., '\\.', '_'))
#> # A tibble: 1,000 x 7
#>    participant lex   spell     resp      rt prev_rt rt_raw
#>          <dbl> <chr> <chr>     <chr> <dbl>   <dbl>  <dbl>
#>  1          20 N     staud     N       977     511    977
#>  2           9 N     dinbuss   N       565     765    565
#>  3          47 N     snilling  N       562     496    562
#>  4         103 N     gancens   N       572     656    572
#>  5          45 W     filled    W       659     981    659
#>  6          73 W     journals  W       538    1505    538
#>  7          24 W     apache    W       626     546    626
#>  8          11 W     flake     W       566     717    566
#>  9          32 W     reliefs   W       922    1471    922
#> 10          96 N     sarves    N       555     806    555
#> # ... with 990 more rows
```

In this example, because str_replace_all uses regular expressions for text pattern matching, and in a regular expression a '.' character means 'any character', we have to use \\. to refer to a literal dot.

The rename_at function allows us to select certain variables, and then apply a renaming function just to these selected variables. We can use selection functions like contains or matches that we used above, but it is necessary to surround these functions with the vars function. In the following example, we select all variables whose names contain rt at their start or end, and then replace their occurrences of rt with reaction_time:

```
rename_at(blp_df,
          vars(matches('^rt|rt$')),
          ~str_replace_all(., 'rt', 'reaction_time'))
#> # A tibble: 1,000 x 7
#>    participant lex   spell resp  reaction_time prev.reaction_t~ reaction_time.r~
#>          <dbl> <chr> <chr> <chr>         <dbl>            <dbl>            <dbl>
#>  1          20 N     staud N               977              511              977
#>  2           9 N     dinb~ N               565              765              565
#>  3          47 N     snil~ N               562              496              562
#>  4         103 N     ganc~ N               572              656              572
```

```
#>  5       45 W     fill~ W          659              981            659
#>  6       73 W     jour~ W          538             1505            538
#>  7       24 W     apac~ W          626              546            626
#>  8       11 W     flake W          566              717            566
#>  9       32 W     reli~ W          922             1471            922
#> 10       96 N     sarv~ N          555              806            555
#> # ... with 990 more rows
```

Similarly to how we used `select_if`, `rename_if` can be used to rename variables whose values match certain criteria. For example, if we wanted to capitalize the names of those variables that are character variables, we could type the following:

```
rename_if(blp_df, is.character, str_to_upper)
#> # A tibble: 1,000 x 7
#>    participant LEX   SPELL     RESP    rt prev.rt rt.raw
#>          <dbl> <chr> <chr>     <chr> <dbl>   <dbl>  <dbl>
#>  1          20 N     staud     N       977     511    977
#>  2           9 N     dinbuss   N       565     765    565
#>  3          47 N     snilling  N       562     496    562
#>  4         103 N     gancens   N       572     656    572
#>  5          45 W     filled    W       659     981    659
#>  6          73 W     journals  W       538    1505    538
#>  7          24 W     apache    W       626     546    626
#>  8          11 W     flake     W       566     717    566
#>  9          32 W     reliefs   W       922    1471    922
#> 10          96 N     sarves    N       555     806    555
#> # ... with 990 more rows
```

In this example, we use `str_to_upper` from the package `stringr`, which is also loaded by `tidyverse`, to convert the names of the selected variables to uppercase.

Selecting observations with `slice` and `filter`

With `select` and `rename`, we were selecting or removing variables. The commands `slice` and `filter` allow us to select or remove observations. We use `slice` to select observations by their indices. For example, to select rows 10, 20, 50, 100, 500, we would simply type the following:

```
slice(blp_df, c(10, 20, 50, 100, 500))
#> # A tibble: 5 x 7
#>   participant lex   spell  resp    rt prev.rt rt.raw
#>         <dbl> <chr> <chr>  <chr> <dbl>   <dbl>  <dbl>
#> 1          96 N     sarves N       555     806    555
#> 2          46 W     mirage W       778     571    778
#> 3          72 N     gright N       430     675    430
#> 4           3 W     gleam  W       361     370    361
#> 5          92 W     coaxes W       699     990    699
```

Given that, for example, `10:100` would list the integers 10 to 100 inclusive, we can select just these observations as follows:

```
slice(blp_df, 10:100)
#> # A tibble: 91 x 7
#>    participant lex   spell        resp     rt prev.rt rt.raw
#>          <dbl> <chr> <chr>        <chr> <dbl>   <dbl>  <dbl>
#>  1          96 N     sarves       N       555     806    555
#>  2          82 W     deceits      W       657     728    657
#>  3          37 W     nothings     N        NA     552    712
#>  4          52 N     chuespies    N       427     539    427
#>  5          96 N     mowny        N      1352    1020   1352
#>  6          96 N     cranned      N       907     573    907
#>  7          89 N     flud         N       742     834    742
#>  8           3 N     bromble      N       523     502    523
#>  9           7 N     trubbles     N       782     458    782
#> 10          35 N     playfound    N       643     663    643
#> # ... with 81 more rows
```

Just as we did with `select`, we can precede the indices with a minus sign to drop the corresponding observations. Thus, for example, we can drop the first 10 observations as follows:

```
slice(blp_df, -(1:10))
#> # A tibble: 990 x 7
#>    participant lex   spell        resp     rt prev.rt rt.raw
#>          <dbl> <chr> <chr>        <chr> <dbl>   <dbl>  <dbl>
#>  1          82 W     deceits      W       657     728    657
#>  2          37 W     nothings     N        NA     552    712
#>  3          52 N     chuespies    N       427     539    427
#>  4          96 N     mowny        N      1352    1020   1352
#>  5          96 N     cranned      N       907     573    907
#>  6          89 N     flud         N       742     834    742
#>  7           3 N     bromble      N       523     502    523
#>  8           7 N     trubbles     N       782     458    782
#>  9          35 N     playfound    N       643     663    643
#> 10          46 W     mirage       W       778     571    778
#> # ... with 980 more rows
```

A useful `dplyr` function that can be used in `slice` and elsewhere is `n()`, which gives the number of observations in the data frame. Using this, we can, for example, list the observations from index 600 to the end as follows:

```
slice(blp_df, 600:n())
#> # A tibble: 401 x 7
#>    participant lex   spell        resp     rt prev.rt rt.raw
#>          <dbl> <chr> <chr>        <chr> <dbl>   <dbl>  <dbl>
#>  1          16 W     earthworms   W       767     659    767
#>  2          50 W     markers      W       664     852    664
```

```
#>  3           35 N    spoton     N      522      721    522
#>  4           88 W    tawny      N       NA      535    856
#>  5           51 N    gember     N      562      598    562
#>  6           63 W    classed    W      706      429    706
#>  7           63 N    clallers   N      401      495    401
#>  8            8 W    pauper     W      734     1126    734
#>  9            2 W    badges     W      485      498    485
#> 10           97 N    foarded    N      802      464    802
#> # … with 391 more rows
```

Likewise, we could list the last 11 rows as follows:

```
slice(blp_df, (n()-10):n())
#> # A tibble: 11 x 7
#>     participant lex   spell      resp      rt prev.rt rt.raw
#>           <dbl> <chr> <chr>      <chr> <dbl>    <dbl>  <dbl>
#>  1           29 N     khandles   N       511      777    511
#>  2           88 N     ixcurs     N       504      552    504
#>  3           50 N     homply     N       518      583    518
#>  4          103 W     baste      W       683      454    683
#>  5           67 W     tall       W       476      572    476
#>  6           45 W     gardens    W       586     1023    586
#>  7          105 W     goldfinch  N        NA      903    775
#>  8           72 W     varmint    N        NA      507    653
#>  9            3 W     lurked     W       537      520    537
#> 10            3 W     village    W       538      522    538
#> 11           17 W     fudge      W       410      437    410
```

The `filter` command is a powerful means to filter observations according to their values. Note that when we say that `filter` filters observations, we mean it filters them *in*, or keeps them, rather than filters them *out*, or removes them. For example, we can select all the observations where the `lex` variable is N as follows:

```
filter(blp_df, lex == 'N')
#> # A tibble: 502 x 7
#>     participant lex   spell      resp      rt prev.rt rt.raw
#>           <dbl> <chr> <chr>      <chr> <dbl>    <dbl>  <dbl>
#>  1           20 N     staud      N       977      511    977
#>  2            9 N     dinbuss    N       565      765    565
#>  3           47 N     snilling   N       562      496    562
#>  4          103 N     gancens    N       572      656    572
#>  5           96 N     sarves     N       555      806    555
#>  6           52 N     chuespies  N       427      539    427
#>  7           96 N     mowny      N      1352     1020   1352
#>  8           96 N     cranned    N       907      573    907
#>  9           89 N     flud       N       742      834    742
#> 10            3 N     bromble    N       523      502    523
#> # … with 492 more rows
```

Notice that here we must use the == equality operator. We can also filter by multiple conditions by listing each one with commas between them. For example, the following gives us the observations where lex has the value of N and resp has the value of W:

```
filter(blp_df, lex == 'N', resp=='W')
#> # A tibble: 35 x 7
#>    participant lex   spell    resp      rt prev.rt rt.raw
#>          <dbl> <chr> <chr>    <chr> <dbl>    <dbl>  <dbl>
#>  1          73 N     bunding  W        NA      978   1279
#>  2          63 N     gallays  W        NA      589    923
#>  3          50 N     droper   W        NA      741    573
#>  4           6 N     flooder  W        NA      524    557
#>  5          73 N     khantum  W        NA      623   1355
#>  6          81 N     seaped   W        NA      765    691
#>  7          43 N     gafers   W        NA      556    812
#>  8         101 N     winchers W        NA      632    852
#>  9          81 N     flaged   W        NA      674    609
#> 10          11 N     frocker  W        NA      653    665
#> # … with 25 more rows
```

The following gives us those observations where lex has the value of N, resp has the value of W and rt.raw is less than or equal to 500:

```
filter(blp_df, lex == 'N', resp=='W', rt.raw <= 500)
#> # A tibble: 5 x 7
#>   participant lex   spell    resp      rt prev.rt rt.raw
#>         <dbl> <chr> <chr>    <chr> <dbl>    <dbl>  <dbl>
#> 1          28 N     cown     W        NA      680    498
#> 2          17 N     beeched  W        NA      450    469
#> 3          29 N     conforn  W        NA      495    497
#> 4          35 N     blear    W        NA      592    461
#> 5          89 N     stumming W        NA      571    442
```

This command is equivalent to making a conjunction of conditions using & as follows:

```
filter(blp_df, lex == 'N' & resp=='W' & rt.raw <= 500)
#> # A tibble: 5 x 7
#>   participant lex   spell    resp      rt prev.rt rt.raw
#>         <dbl> <chr> <chr>    <chr> <dbl>    <dbl>  <dbl>
#> 1          28 N     cown     W        NA      680    498
#> 2          17 N     beeched  W        NA      450    469
#> 3          29 N     conforn  W        NA      495    497
#> 4          35 N     blear    W        NA      592    461
#> 5          89 N     stumming W        NA      571    442
```

We can make a *disjunction* of conditions for filtering using the logical OR symbol |. For example, to filter observations where rt.raw was either less than 500 or greater than 1000, we can type the following:

```
filter(blp_df, rt.raw < 500 | rt.raw > 1000)
#> # A tibble: 296 x 7
#>    participant lex   spell       resp      rt prev.rt rt.raw
#>          <dbl> <chr> <chr>       <chr> <dbl>   <dbl>  <dbl>
#>  1          52 N     chuespies   N       427     539    427
#>  2          96 N     mowny       N      1352    1020   1352
#>  3          28 W     stelae      N        NA     678    497
#>  4          85 W     forewarned  N        NA     525    350
#>  5          24 W     owl         W       470     535    470
#>  6          97 W     soda        W       436     447    436
#>  7          81 N     fugate      N       425     403    425
#>  8         105 N     pamps       N        NA     884   1494
#>  9          27 W     outgrowth   N        NA     633   1014
#> 10          82 W     kitty       W       431     476    431
#> # … with 286 more rows
```

If we want to filter by observations whose values of certain variables are in a set, we can use the %in% operator. For example, here we filter observations where values of rt.raw are in the set of integers from 500 to 510:

```
filter(blp_df, rt.raw %in% 500:510)
#> # A tibble: 26 x 7
#>    participant lex   spell        resp     rt prev.rt rt.raw
#>          <dbl> <chr> <chr>        <chr> <dbl>   <dbl>  <dbl>
#>  1          44 W     subscribed   W       509     475    509
#>  2          89 W     snatcher     W       506    1004    506
#>  3           2 N     tronculling  N       508     490    508
#>  4          43 N     trabnate     N       510     542    510
#>  5          75 N     dousleens    N       508     924    508
#>  6          94 W     strangeness  W       508     522    508
#>  7          68 W     greed        W       505     653    505
#>  8          32 N     krifo        N       508     607    508
#>  9           2 W     tweaks       W       508     474    508
#> 10          85 N     waffs        N       506     471    506
#> # … with 16 more rows
```

In general, we may filter the observations by creating any complex Boolean conditional using combinations of logical AND &, logical OR |, logical NOT !, and other operators. For example, here we filter observations where lex is w, the length of the spell is less than 5, and either resp is not equal to lex or rt.raw is greater than 900:

```
filter(blp_df,
       lex == 'W',
       str_length(spell) < 5 & (resp != lex | rt.raw > 900))
#> # A tibble: 14 x 7
#>    participant lex   spell resp     rt prev.rt rt.raw
#>          <dbl> <chr> <chr> <chr> <dbl>   <dbl>  <dbl>
#>  1          21 W     bosk  N        NA     608   1532
```

```
#>  2              68 W    wily   N         NA     723    636
#>  3              30 W    sew    N         NA     473    524
#>  4              34 W    jibs   N         NA     781    756
#>  5              85 W    rote   N         NA     505    458
#>  6              13 W    oofs   N         NA     560    654
#>  7              72 W    awed   N         NA    1203   1801
#>  8              14 W    yids   N         NA     625    620
#>  9              68 W    oho    N         NA     633    630
#> 10             103 W    carl   N         NA    1046   1042
#> 11              46 W    brae   N         NA     644    720
#> 12              81 W    bloc   N         NA     759    575
#> 13              75 W    kind   W        903    1067    903
#> 14              67 W    irk    N         NA     605    570
```

The `filter` command has the variants `filter_all`, `filter_at`, and `filter_if`. In these com-mands, filtering is applied on the basis of the values of selected sets of variables. For example, using `filter_all`, we can filter rows that contain at least one NA value:

```
filter_all(blp_df, any_vars(is.na(.)))
#> # A tibble: 179 x 7
#>      participant lex    spell        resp     rt prev.rt rt.raw
#>            <dbl> <chr> <chr>        <chr> <dbl>   <dbl>  <dbl>
#>  1            37 W     nothings     N        NA     552    712
#>  2            28 W     stelae       N        NA     678    497
#>  3            85 W     forewarned   N        NA     525    350
#>  4           105 N     pamps        N        NA     884   1494
#>  5            27 W     outgrowth    N        NA     633   1014
#>  6            89 W     chards       N        NA     545    754
#>  7            63 N     shrudule     N        NA       0   2553
#>  8            73 W     chiggers     N        NA     726    654
#>  9            73 N     bunding      W        NA     978   1279
#> 10            22 W     aitches      N        NA     521    665
#> # … with 169 more rows
```

In this case, the . signifies the variables that are selected, which in the case of `filter_all` is all variables. Thus, this command is filtering observations where any variable contains an NA. On the other hand, to apply the filtering rules to a selected set of variables we can use `filter_at`. For example, the following filters all observations where the values of all variables that start or end with `rt` are greater than 500:

```
filter_at(blp_df, vars(matches('^rt|rt$')), all_vars(. > 500))
#> # A tibble: 530 x 7
#>      participant lex    spell        resp     rt prev.rt rt.raw
#>            <dbl> <chr> <chr>        <chr> <dbl>   <dbl>  <dbl>
#>  1            20 N     staud        N       977     511    977
#>  2             9 N     dinbuss      N       565     765    565
#>  3           103 N     gancens      N       572     656    572
#>  4            45 W     filled       W       659     981    659
```

```
#>  5          73 W      journals W       538     1505    538
#>  6          24 W      apache    W      626      546    626
#>  7          11 W      flake     W      566      717    566
#>  8          32 W      reliefs   W      922     1471    922
#>  9          96 N      sarves    N      555      806    555
#> 10          82 W      deceits   W      657      728    657
#> # … with 520 more rows
```

As another example, the following filters all observations where all variables that start or end with rt have values that are less than the median values of those values. In other words, all filtered observations have values of the rt variables that are lower than the medians of these variables:

```
filter_at(blp_df,
          vars(matches('^rt|rt$')),
          all_vars(. < median(., na.rm=T)))
#> # A tibble: 251 x 7
#>    participant lex   spell      resp    rt prev.rt rt.raw
#>          <dbl> <chr> <chr>     <chr> <dbl>   <dbl>  <dbl>
#> 1           47 N     snilling  N       562     496    562
#> 2           52 N     chuespies N       427     539    427
#> 3            3 N     bromble   N       523     502    523
#> 4           36 W     outposts  W       560     461    560
#> 5           24 W     owl       W       470     535    470
#> 6           97 W     soda      W       436     447    436
#> 7           18 N     tesslier  N       560     477    560
#> 8           81 N     fugate    N       425     403    425
#> 9           29 N     placker   N       542     558    542
#> 10          82 W     kitty     W       431     476    431
#> # … with 241 more rows
```

The filter_if variant of filter, like select_if or rename_if, allows us to select variables according to their properties, rather than their names, and then apply filtering commands to the selected variables. For example, we can select the numeric variables in the data frames and then filter the observations where all the values of the selected variables are less than the median value of these variables:

```
filter_if(blp_df,
          is.numeric,
          all_vars(. < median(., na.rm=T)))
#> # A tibble: 138 x 7
#>    participant lex   spell      resp    rt prev.rt rt.raw
#>          <dbl> <chr> <chr>     <chr> <dbl>   <dbl>  <dbl>
#> 1            3 N     bromble   N       523     502    523
#> 2           36 W     outposts  W       560     461    560
#> 3           24 W     owl       W       470     535    470
#> 4           18 N     tesslier  N       560     477    560
#> 5           29 N     placker   N       542     558    542
```

```
#>  6              6 N    checsons N     491    555    491
#>  7             19 N    jontage  N     413    471    413
#>  8             44 W    snows    W     437    432    437
#>  9             13 N    lavo     N     479    510    479
#> 10             17 N    basyl    N     413    508    413
#> # … with 128 more rows
```

Changing variables and values with `mutate`

The `mutate` command is a very powerful tool in the `dplyr` toolbox. It allows us to create new variables and alter the values of existing ones.

As an example, we can create a new variable `acc` that takes the value TRUE whenever `lex` and `resp` have the same value as follows:

```
mutate(blp_df, acc = lex == resp)
#> # A tibble: 1,000 x 8
#>    participant lex   spell      resp    rt prev.rt rt.raw acc
#>          <dbl> <chr> <chr>      <chr> <dbl>   <dbl>  <dbl> <lgl>
#>  1          20 N     staud      N       977     511    977 TRUE
#>  2           9 N     dinbuss    N       565     765    565 TRUE
#>  3          47 N     snilling   N       562     496    562 TRUE
#>  4         103 N     gancens    N       572     656    572 TRUE
#>  5          45 W     filled     W       659     981    659 TRUE
#>  6          73 W     journals   W       538    1505    538 TRUE
#>  7          24 W     apache     W       626     546    626 TRUE
#>  8          11 W     flake      W       566     717    566 TRUE
#>  9          32 W     reliefs    W       922    1471    922 TRUE
#> 10          96 N     sarves     N       555     806    555 TRUE
#> # … with 990 more rows
```

As another example, we can create a new variable that gives the length of the word given by the `spell` variable:

```
mutate(blp_df, len = str_length(spell))
#> # A tibble: 1,000 x 8
#>    participant lex   spell      resp    rt prev.rt rt.raw   len
#>          <dbl> <chr> <chr>      <chr> <dbl>   <dbl>  <dbl> <int>
#>  1          20 N     staud      N       977     511    977     5
#>  2           9 N     dinbuss    N       565     765    565     7
#>  3          47 N     snilling   N       562     496    562     8
#>  4         103 N     gancens    N       572     656    572     7
#>  5          45 W     filled     W       659     981    659     6
#>  6          73 W     journals   W       538    1505    538     8
#>  7          24 W     apache     W       626     546    626     6
#>  8          11 W     flake      W       566     717    566     5
#>  9          32 W     reliefs    W       922    1471    922     7
```

```
#> 10              96 N     sarves    N       555     806    555    6
#> # … with 990 more rows
```

We can also create multiple new variables at the same time as in the following example:

```
mutate(blp_df,
       acc = lex == resp,
       fast = rt.raw < mean(rt.raw, na.rm=TRUE))
#> # A tibble: 1,000 x 9
#>     participant lex   spell     resp   rt prev.rt rt.raw acc    fast
#>           <dbl> <chr> <chr>     <chr> <dbl>   <dbl>  <dbl> <lgl> <lgl>
#>  1           20 N     staud     N       977     511    977 TRUE  FALSE
#>  2            9 N     dinbuss   N       565     765    565 TRUE  TRUE
#>  3           47 N     snilling  N       562     496    562 TRUE  TRUE
#>  4          103 N     gancens   N       572     656    572 TRUE  TRUE
#>  5           45 W     filled    W       659     981    659 TRUE  TRUE
#>  6           73 W     journals  W       538    1505    538 TRUE  TRUE
#>  7           24 W     apache    W       626     546    626 TRUE  TRUE
#>  8           11 W     flake     W       566     717    566 TRUE  TRUE
#>  9           32 W     reliefs   W       922    1471    922 TRUE  FALSE
#> 10           96 N     sarves    N       555     806    555 TRUE  TRUE
#> # … with 990 more rows
```

As with other `dplyr` verbs, `mutate` has `mutate_all`, `mutate_at`, `mutate_if` variants. The `mutate_all` variant will apply a transformation function to all variables in the data frame, and then replace the original values of all variables with the results of the function. For example, the following will apply the `as.character` function, which converts any vector into a character vector, to all the variables in `blp_df`:

```
mutate_all(blp_df, as.character)
#> # A tibble: 1,000 x 7
#>     participant lex   spell     resp  rt    prev.rt rt.raw
#>     <chr>       <chr> <chr>     <chr> <chr> <chr>   <chr>
#>  1 20          N     staud     N     977   511     977
#>  2 9           N     dinbuss   N     565   765     565
#>  3 47          N     snilling  N     562   496     562
#>  4 103         N     gancens   N     572   656     572
#>  5 45          W     filled    W     659   981     659
#>  6 73          W     journals  W     538   1505    538
#>  7 24          W     apache    W     626   546     626
#>  8 11          W     flake     W     566   717     566
#>  9 32          W     reliefs   W     922   1471    922
#> 10 96          N     sarves    N     555   806     555
#> # … with 990 more rows
```

The `mutate_at` variant allows us to apply a function to selected variables. For example, we could apply a log transform to all the `rt` variables as follows:

```
mutate_at(blp_df, vars(matches('^rt|rt$')), log)
#> # A tibble: 1,000 x 7
#>    participant lex   spell    resp    rt prev.rt rt.raw
#>          <dbl> <chr> <chr>    <chr> <dbl>   <dbl>  <dbl>
#>  1          20 N     staud    N      6.88    6.24   6.88
#>  2           9 N     dinbuss  N      6.34    6.64   6.34
#>  3          47 N     snilling N      6.33    6.21   6.33
#>  4         103 N     gancens  N      6.35    6.49   6.35
#>  5          45 W     filled   W      6.49    6.89   6.49
#>  6          73 W     journals W      6.29    7.32   6.29
#>  7          24 W     apache   W      6.44    6.30   6.44
#>  8          11 W     flake    W      6.34    6.58   6.34
#>  9          32 W     reliefs  W      6.83    7.29   6.83
#> 10          96 N     sarves   N      6.32    6.69   6.32
#> # ... with 990 more rows
```

The `mutate_if` variant selects variables by their properties and then applies a function to the selected variables. In the following example, we select all variables that are character vectors and convert them to a *factor*, which is a categorical variable vector with a defined set of values or 'levels', using the `as.factor` function:

```
mutate_if(blp_df, is.character, as.factor)
#> # A tibble: 1,000 x 7
#>    participant lex   spell    resp    rt prev.rt rt.raw
#>          <dbl> <fct> <fct>    <fct> <dbl>   <dbl>  <dbl>
#>  1          20 N     staud    N       977     511    977
#>  2           9 N     dinbuss  N       565     765    565
#>  3          47 N     snilling N       562     496    562
#>  4         103 N     gancens  N       572     656    572
#>  5          45 W     filled   W       659     981    659
#>  6          73 W     journals W       538    1505    538
#>  7          24 W     apache   W       626     546    626
#>  8          11 W     flake    W       566     717    566
#>  9          32 W     reliefs  W       922    1471    922
#> 10          96 N     sarves   N       555     806    555
#> # ... with 990 more rows
```

Recoding. We have a number of options to use with `mutate` and its variants for recoding the values of variables. Perhaps the simplest option is `if_else`. This evaluates a condition for each value of a variable. If the result is TRUE, it returns one value, otherwise it returns another. As an example, the following code creates a new variable `speed` that takes the value `fast` if `rt.raw` is less than 750, and takes the value `slow` otherwise,

```
mutate(blp_df,
       speed = if_else(rt.raw < 750,
                       'fast',
                       'slow'))
)
```

```
#> # A tibble: 1,000 x 8
#>    participant lex   spell     resp     rt prev.rt rt.raw speed
#>          <dbl> <chr> <chr>     <chr> <dbl>   <dbl>  <dbl> <chr>
#>  1          20 N     staud     N       977     511    977 slow
#>  2           9 N     dinbuss   N       565     765    565 fast
#>  3          47 N     snilling  N       562     496    562 fast
#>  4         103 N     gancens   N       572     656    572 fast
#>  5          45 W     filled    W       659     981    659 fast
#>  6          73 W     journals  W       538    1505    538 fast
#>  7          24 W     apache    W       626     546    626 fast
#>  8          11 W     flake     W       566     717    566 fast
#>  9          32 W     reliefs   W       922    1471    922 slow
#> 10          96 N     sarves    N       555     806    555 fast
#> # … with 990 more rows
```

Another widely used recoding method is `recode`. For example, to replace the `lex` variable's values `W` and `N` with `word` and `nonword`, we would do the following:

```
mutate(blp_df,
       lex = recode(lex, 'W'='word', 'N'='nonword')
)
#> # A tibble: 1,000 x 7
#>    participant lex     spell     resp     rt prev.rt rt.raw
#>          <dbl> <chr>   <chr>     <chr> <dbl>   <dbl>  <dbl>
#>  1          20 nonword staud     N       977     511    977
#>  2           9 nonword dinbuss   N       565     765    565
#>  3          47 nonword snilling  N       562     496    562
#>  4         103 nonword gancens   N       572     656    572
#>  5          45 word    filled    W       659     981    659
#>  6          73 word    journals  W       538    1505    538
#>  7          24 word    apache    W       626     546    626
#>  8          11 word    flake     W       566     717    566
#>  9          32 word    reliefs   W       922    1471    922
#> 10          96 nonword sarves    N       555     806    555
#> # … with 990 more rows
```

Given that both `lex` and `resp` are coded identically, we can apply the same recoding rule to both using `mutate_at` as in the following example:

```
mutate_at(blp_df,
          vars(lex, resp),
          ~recode(., 'W'="word", 'N'="nonword")
)
#> # A tibble: 1,000 x 7
#>    participant lex     spell     resp       rt prev.rt rt.raw
#>          <dbl> <chr>   <chr>     <chr>   <dbl>   <dbl>  <dbl>
#>  1          20 nonword staud     nonword   977     511    977
#>  2           9 nonword dinbuss   nonword   565     765    565
```

```
#>  3            47 nonword snilling nonword    562     496     562
#>  4           103 nonword gancens  nonword    572     656     572
#>  5            45 word    filled   word       659     981     659
#>  6            73 word    journals word       538    1505     538
#>  7            24 word    apache   word       626     546     626
#>  8            11 word    flake    word       566     717     566
#>  9            32 word    reliefs  word       922    1471     922
#> 10            96 nonword sarves   nonword    555     806     555
#> # ... with 990 more rows
```

When we are recoding numeric vales using `recode`, we must surround the values we would like to transform using backticks as in the following example:

```
mutate(blp_df, rt = recode(rt, `977` = 1000, `562` = 100))
#> # A tibble: 1,000 x 7
#>    participant lex   spell     resp    rt prev.rt rt.raw
#>          <dbl> <chr> <chr>     <chr> <dbl>   <dbl>  <dbl>
#>  1          20 N     staud     N      1000     511    977
#>  2           9 N     dinbuss   N       565     765    565
#>  3          47 N     snilling  N       100     496    562
#>  4         103 N     gancens   N       572     656    572
#>  5          45 W     filled    W       659     981    659
#>  6          73 W     journals  W       538    1505    538
#>  7          24 W     apache    W       626     546    626
#>  8          11 W     flake     W       566     717    566
#>  9          32 W     reliefs   W       922    1471    922
#> 10          96 N     sarves    N       555     806    555
#> # ... with 990 more rows
```

For more complex recoding operations we can use the `case_when` function. For example, we could use `case_when` to convert values of `prev.rt` that are below 500 to `fast`, and those above 1500 to `slow`, and those between 500 and 1500 to `medium`:

```
mutate(blp_df,
       prev.rt = case_when(
                 prev.rt < 500 ~ 'fast',
                 prev.rt > 1500 ~ 'slow',
                 TRUE ~ 'medium'
       )
)
#> # A tibble: 1,000 x 7
#>    participant lex   spell     resp    rt prev.rt rt.raw
#>          <dbl> <chr> <chr>     <chr> <dbl> <chr>    <dbl>
#>  1          20 N     staud     N       977 medium     977
#>  2           9 N     dinbuss   N       565 medium     565
#>  3          47 N     snilling  N       562 fast       562
#>  4         103 N     gancens   N       572 medium     572
```

```
#>  5           45 W      filled    W       659 medium      659
#>  6           73 W      journals  W       538 slow        538
#>  7           24 W      apache    W       626 medium      626
#>  8           11 W      flake     W       566 medium      566
#>  9           32 W      reliefs   W       922 medium      922
#> 10           96 N      sarves    N       555 medium      555
#> # … with 990 more rows
```

On each line of case_when we have a ~. To the left of ~, we have a condition. To the right, we have the replacement value for those values for which the condition is true. Whichever condition first evaluates as true will determine which replacement value is used. For example, in the following example, values lower than 500 are classified as extra-fast and values lower than 550 are classified as fast. Clearly, any value that is less than 550 is also less than 500, but whichever condition first evaluates to TRUE will determine the replacement value. As such, in the following example, values lower than 500 will be replaced by extra-fast:

```
mutate(blp_df,
        prev.rt = case_when(
                prev.rt < 500 ~ 'extra-fast',
                prev.rt < 550 ~ 'fast',
                TRUE ~ 'not-fast'

        )

)
#> # A tibble: 1,000 x 7
#>     participant lex   spell     resp     rt prev.rt      rt.raw
#>           <dbl> <chr> <chr>     <chr> <dbl> <chr>         <dbl>
#>  1           20 N     staud     N       977 fast            977
#>  2            9 N     dinbuss   N       565 not-fast        565
#>  3           47 N     snilling  N       562 extra-fast      562
#>  4          103 N     gancens   N       572 not-fast        572
#>  5           45 W     filled    W       659 not-fast        659
#>  6           73 W     journals  W       538 not-fast        538
#>  7           24 W     apache    W       626 fast            626
#>  8           11 W     flake     W       566 not-fast        566
#>  9           32 W     reliefs   W       922 not-fast        922
#> 10           96 N     sarves    N       555 not-fast        555
#> # … with 990 more rows
```

On the other hand, in the following example, values lower than 500 will be listed as fast, rather than extra-fast:

```
mutate(blp_df,
        prev.rt = case_when(
                prev.rt < 550 ~ 'fast',
                prev.rt < 500 ~ 'extra-fast',
                TRUE ~ 'not-fast'

        )
```

```
)
#> # A tibble: 1,000 x 7
#>    participant lex   spell      resp     rt prev.rt  rt.raw
#>         <dbl> <chr> <chr>      <chr> <dbl> <chr>      <dbl>
#>  1          20 N     staud      N       977 fast        977
#>  2           9 N     dinbuss    N       565 not-fast    565
#>  3          47 N     snilling   N       562 fast        562
#>  4         103 N     gancens    N       572 not-fast    572
#>  5          45 W     filled     W       659 not-fast    659
#>  6          73 W     journals   W       538 not-fast    538
#>  7          24 W     apache     W       626 fast        626
#>  8          11 W     flake      W       566 not-fast    566
#>  9          32 W     reliefs    W       922 not-fast    922
#> 10          96 N     sarves     N       555 not-fast    555
#> # ... with 990 more rows
```

The final line in the case_when above has TRUE in place of a condition. This ensures that if any value does not meet any of the previous conditions, it will be assigned the corresponding replacement value in this final line. Had we left this final line out, then any values not meeting the previous conditions would have been replaced by NA, as seen in the following example:

```
mutate(blp_df,
        prev.rt = case_when(
                prev.rt < 550 ~ 'fast',
                prev.rt < 500 ~ 'extra-fast'
        )
)
#> # A tibble: 1,000 x 7
#>    participant lex   spell      resp     rt prev.rt rt.raw
#>         <dbl> <chr> <chr>      <chr> <dbl> <chr>     <dbl>
#>  1          20 N     staud      N       977 fast       977
#>  2           9 N     dinbuss    N       565 <NA>       565
#>  3          47 N     snilling   N       562 fast       562
#>  4         103 N     gancens    N       572 <NA>       572
#>  5          45 W     filled     W       659 <NA>       659
#>  6          73 W     journals   W       538 <NA>       538
#>  7          24 W     apache     W       626 fast       626
#>  8          11 W     flake      W       566 <NA>       566
#>  9          32 W     reliefs    W       922 <NA>       922
#> 10          96 N     sarves     N       555 <NA>       555
#> # ... with 990 more rows
```

Another useful recoding function is mapvalues, which is part of the plyr package. With this, we use two vectors of the same length and that are named from and to. Any value that matches a value in from is mapped to its corresponding value in to. As an example, if we wanted to map the range of integers from 500 to 1000 to the reverse of this range (i.e. 1000, 999, ..., 500), we could do the following:

```
mutate(blp_df,
         rt_reverse = plyr::mapvalues(rt, from=500:1000, to=1000:500)
)
#> # A tibble: 1,000 x 8
#>    participant lex   spell      resp    rt prev.rt rt.raw rt_reverse
#>          <dbl> <chr> <chr>      <chr> <dbl>   <dbl>  <dbl>      <dbl>
#>  1           20 N     staud      N       977     511    977        523
#>  2            9 N     dinbuss    N       565     765    565        935
#>  3           47 N     snilling   N       562     496    562        938
#>  4          103 N     gancens    N       572     656    572        928
#>  5           45 W     filled     W       659     981    659        841
#>  6           73 W     journals   W       538    1505    538        962
#>  7           24 W     apache     W       626     546    626        874
#>  8           11 W     flake      W       566     717    566        934
#>  9           32 W     reliefs    W       922    1471    922        578
#> 10           96 N     sarves     N       555     806    555        945
#> # ... with 990 more rows
```

Transmuting. A variant of mutate is transmute, which has the _all, _at, and _if variants too. The transmute function works like mutate except that it only returns the newly created variables, and so drops all the original variables. For example, in the following code, we create two new variables and only these are returned by the transmute function:

```
transmute(blp_df,
           speed = rt.raw / 1000,
           accuracy = lex == resp)
#> # A tibble: 1,000 x 2
#>     speed accuracy
#>     <dbl> <lgl>
#>  1 0.977 TRUE
#>  2 0.565 TRUE
#>  3 0.562 TRUE
#>  4 0.572 TRUE
#>  5 0.659 TRUE
#>  6 0.538 TRUE
#>  7 0.626 TRUE
#>  8 0.566 TRUE
#>  9 0.922 TRUE
#> 10 0.555 TRUE
#> # ... with 990 more rows
```

Sorting observations with arrange

Sorting observations in a data frame is easily accomplished with arrange. For example, to sort by participant and then by spell, we would do the following:

```
arrange(blp_df, participant, spell)
#> # A tibble: 1,000 x 7
#>    participant lex   spell      resp       rt prev.rt rt.raw
#>          <dbl> <chr> <chr>      <chr> <dbl>   <dbl>  <dbl>
#>  1           1 W     abyss      W       629     683    629
#>  2           1 N     baisees    N       524     574    524
#>  3           1 W     carport    W       779     605    779
#>  4           1 N     cellies    N       792     652    792
#>  5           1 W     chafing    W       601     720    601
#>  6           1 N     dametails  N       694     635    694
#>  7           1 N     foother    N       789     566    789
#>  8           1 W     gantries   W       644     581    644
#>  9           1 N     hogtush    N       679     568    679
#> 10           1 N     lisedess   N       679     619    679
#> # ... with 990 more rows
```

We can sort by the reverse order of any variable by using the desc command on the variable. In the following example, we sort by participant, and then by spell in reverse order:

```
arrange(blp_df, participant, desc(spell))
#> # A tibble: 1,000 x 7
#>    participant lex   spell      resp       rt prev.rt rt.raw
#>          <dbl> <chr> <chr>      <chr> <dbl>   <dbl>  <dbl>
#>  1           1 N     wintes     N       545     629    545
#>  2           1 N     treeps     N       607     610    607
#>  3           1 W     squashes   W       494     491    494
#>  4           1 N     sinkhicks  N       536     519    536
#>  5           1 W     shafting   W       553     571    553
#>  6           1 W     month      W       500     498    500
#>  7           1 N     lisedess   N       679     619    679
#>  8           1 N     hogtush    N       679     568    679
#>  9           1 W     gantries   W       644     581    644
#> 10           1 N     foother    N       789     566    789
#> # ... with 990 more rows
```

Subsampling data frames

The dplyr package provides two methods to sample from a data frame. The sample_frac allows us to sample a specified proportion of observations. In the following example, we randomly sample 10% of the data frame:

```
sample_frac(blp_df, 0.1)
#> # A tibble: 100 x 7
#>    participant lex   spell      resp    rt prev.rt rt.raw
#>          <dbl> <chr> <chr>      <chr> <dbl>  <dbl>  <dbl>
#>  1          32 N     griteings  N       496    577    496
#>  2          30 W     ligged     N       701    658    701
```

```
#>    3           47 N      bowtin      N      634     821     634
#>    4           10 W      restowed    W      686     493     686
#>    5           97 W      soda        W      436     447     436
#>    6           13 N      cothes      N      543     426     543
#>    7          101 W      tauter      W       NA     456     668
#>    8           42 W      harepare    W      803    1163     803
#>    9           36 N      platefuls   N       NA     506     508
#> 10            31 N      dodgers     N      536     636     536
#> # … with 90 more rows
```

By default, the sampling will occur without replacement, which we can override as follows:

```
sample_frac(blp_df, 0.1, replace=FALSE)
#> # A tibble: 100 x 7
#>    participant lex   spell       resp     rt prev.rt rt.raw
#>          <dbl> <chr> <chr>      <chr> <dbl>   <dbl>  <dbl>
#>  1          21 N     ditted      N      719     644    719
#>  2          63 N     fealt       N      518     450    518
#>  3          71 W     clockwork   W      513     478    513
#>  4          36 N     eadlarks    N      506     604    506
#>  5          79 N     bipeds      W      754     897    754
#>  6          52 W     reject      W      528     812    528
#>  7          75 N     rudely      W      599     501    599
#>  8          64 N     seemstone   N      732    1006    732
#>  9          20 W     inlit       N     1007     560   1007
#> 10          64 N     gleeking    N      941    1475    941
#> # … with 90 more rows
```

We may also sample a specified number of observations, as in the following example, where we randomly sample 15 observations:

```
sample_n(blp_df, 15)
#> # A tibble: 15 x 7
#>    participant lex   spell       resp     rt prev.rt rt.raw
#>          <dbl> <chr> <chr>      <chr> <dbl>   <dbl>  <dbl>
#>  1         105 N     fondism     N      827     541    827
#>  2          68 N     counties    W      493     491    493
#>  3          37 N     neers       N      412     439    412
#>  4           7 N     cupbils     N      565     699    565
#>  5          75 W     attain      W     1004     658   1004
#>  6          21 N     endays      N      561     547    561
#>  7          71 N     seiss       N      764     590    764
#>  8          68 N     howned      N       NA     522   2891
#>  9          20 W     whole       W      544     628    544
#> 10          18 W     quota       W      669     575    669
#> 11          21 W     baytime     N     1437    1511   1437
#> 12          88 W     stateless   N       NA     505    778
```

#> 13	14 N	daftness	W	685	607	685
#> 14	67 W	kide	N	717	459	431
#> 15	45 N	burnished	N	732	691	732

We may also sample the top or bottom observations according to some variable. For example, here we select the top 15 observations by their rt.raw values:

```
top_n(blp_df, 15, rt.raw)
#> # A tibble: 15 x 7
#>     participant lex   spell       resp    rt prev.rt rt.raw
#>           <dbl> <chr> <chr>       <chr> <dbl>  <dbl>  <dbl>
#>  1          63 N     shrudule    N        NA      0   2553
#>  2          51 W     trumping    W        NA    670   2777
#>  3          73 W     plank       N        NA    631   1939
#>  4          65 W     savers      N        NA   1168   5815
#>  5          70 N     ashdess     N        NA    510   2256
#>  6          68 N     howned      N        NA    522   2891
#>  7          85 W     twitted     W        NA   1029.  2625
#>  8          65 W     forenames   W        NA    471   4537
#>  9          78 N     gassolled   N        NA    755   2362
#> 10          12 W     coursed     N        NA   1054   3434
#> 11          54 W     puffer      N        NA    582   1972
#> 12         105 N     fragrents   N        NA   1090   2554
#> 13          10 W     clung       W        NA   1835   9925
#> 14          90 N     clate       N        NA   1051   2199
#> 15          66 W     submersed   W        NA   2199   3029
```

Reducing data with summarize and group_by

The dplyr package has a function summarize (or, equivalently, summarise) that applies summarizing functions to variables. A summarizing function is essentially any function that takes a vector and reduces it to single values. The summarize function is vital for exploratory data analysis and we will use it extensively in Chapter 5. However, for now, especially when used with the group_by function, it is an essential tool for data wrangling.

To see how summarize works, we may calculate some summary statistics of the particular variables as in the following example:

```
summarize(blp_df,
          mean_rt = mean(rt, na.rm = T),
          median_rt = median(rt, na.rm = T),
          sd_rt.raw = sd(rt.raw, na.rm = T)
)
#> # A tibble: 1 x 3
#>   mean_rt median_rt sd_rt.raw
#>     <dbl>     <dbl>     <dbl>
#> 1    638.       588      474.
```

(Note that here it is necessary to use na.rm = T to remove the NA values in the variables.)

We can use the `summarize_all` variant of `summarize` to apply a summarization function to all variables, as in the following example:

```
summarize_all(blp_df, n_distinct)
#> # A tibble: 1 x 7
#>    participant    lex spell  resp    rt prev.rt rt.raw
#>          <int> <int> <int> <int> <int>   <int>  <int>
#> 1           78     2   990     2   421     493    516
```

Here, `n_distinct` returns the number of unique values in each variable. The `summarize_at` will apply a summary function to selected variables. In the following example, we calculate the mean of all the reaction time variables:

```
summarize_at(blp_df, vars(matches('^rt|rt$')), ~mean(., na.rm=T))
#> # A tibble: 1 x 3
#>      rt prev.rt rt.raw
#>   <dbl>   <dbl>  <dbl>
#> 1  638.    660.   708.
```

The `summarize_if` function will apply the summary function to variables selected by their properties, such as whether they are numeric variables, as in the following example:

```
summarize_if(blp_df, is.numeric, ~mean(., na.rm=T))
#> # A tibble: 1 x 4
#>    participant    rt prev.rt rt.raw
#>          <dbl> <dbl>   <dbl>  <dbl>
#> 1         49.5  638.    660.   708.
```

Using the `_all`, `_at`, `_if` variants, we can also apply multiple summary functions simultaneously. In the following example, we calculate three summary statistics for `rt` alone:

```
summarise_at(blp_df,
             vars(rt),
             list(mean = ~mean(., na.rm=T),
                  median = ~median(., na.rm=T),
                  sd = ~sd(., na.rm=T)
                 )
            )
#> # A tibble: 1 x 3
#>    mean median    sd
#>   <dbl>  <dbl> <dbl>
#> 1  638.    588   191.
```

In the following, we calculate the same three summary statistics for two variables:

```
summarise_at(blp_df,
             vars(rt, rt.raw),
             list(mean = ~mean(., na.rm=T),
```

```
      median = ~median(., na.rm=T),
      sd = ~sd(., na.rm=T)

   )

)
#> # A tibble: 1 x 6
#>   rt_mean rt.raw_mean rt_median rt.raw_median rt_sd rt.raw_sd
#>     <dbl>       <dbl>     <dbl>         <dbl> <dbl>     <dbl>
#> 1    638.        708.       588           605  191.      474.
```

In this case, the name of the summary value is appended to the name of each variable.

The `summarize` command, and its variants, become considerably more powerful when combined with the `group_by` command. Effectively, `group_by` groups the observations within a data frame according to the values of specified variables. For example, the following command groups `blp_df` into groups of observations according to value of the `lex` variable:

```
blp_by_lex <- group_by(blp_df, lex)
```

If we view the resulting grouped data frame, it appears more or less as normal:

```
blp_by_lex
#> # A tibble: 1,000 x 7
#> # Groups:   lex [2]
#>    participant lex   spell    resp     rt prev.rt rt.raw
#>          <dbl> <chr> <chr>    <chr> <dbl>   <dbl>  <dbl>
#>  1          20 N     staud    N       977     511    977
#>  2           9 N     dinbuss  N       565     765    565
#>  3          47 N     snilling N       562     496    562
#>  4         103 N     gancens  N       572     656    572
#>  5          45 W     filled   W       659     981    659
#>  6          73 W     journals W       538    1505    538
#>  7          24 W     apache   W       626     546    626
#>  8          11 W     flake    W       566     717    566
#>  9          32 W     reliefs  W       922    1471    922
#> 10          96 N     sarves   N       555     806    555
#> # ... with 990 more rows
```

Like `blp_df`, it has 1000 observations and seven variables. However, in addition, it is composed of two groups that are defined by the values of the `lex` variable. We see this from the second line of the output, i.e. `Groups: lex [2]`.

If we now apply `summarize` to this grouped data frame, we will obtain summary statistics for each group, as in the following example:

```
summarize(blp_by_lex, mean = mean(rt, na.rm=T))
#> # A tibble: 2 x 2
#>   lex    mean
#>   <chr> <dbl>
#> 1 N      638.
#> 2 W      637.
```

We may also apply the _all, _at, _if variants as before:

```
summarize_at(blp_by_lex,
             vars(rt),
             list(mean = ~mean(., na.rm=T),
                  median = ~median(., na.rm=T),
                  sd = ~sd(., na.rm=T)
                 )
)
#> # A tibble: 2 x 4
#>   lex    mean median    sd
#>   <chr> <dbl>  <dbl> <dbl>
#> 1 N      638.    585  198.
#> 2 W      637.    588  183.
```

Using group_by and summarize together is a powerful way to create new (reduced) data frames. For example, in blp_df, there are 78 unique participants. For each participant, and for each of the two stimuli types (i.e. the N and W values of lex), we can calculate the number of stimuli they were shown (using the dplyr command n(), which calculates the number of observations for each group), their number of accurate responses and their average response reaction time:

```
summarize(group_by(blp_df, participant, lex),
          n_stimuli = n(),
          correct_resp = sum(resp == lex, na.rm=T),
          reaction_time = mean(rt.raw, na.rm=T))
#> # A tibble: 156 x 5
#> # Groups:   participant [78]
#>    participant lex   n_stimuli correct_resp reaction_time
#>          <dbl> <chr>     <int>        <int>         <dbl>
#>  1           1 N             9            9          649.
#>  2           1 W             7            7          600
#>  3           2 N             7            6          625.
#>  4           2 W             6            5          477.
#>  5           3 N             4            4          540.
#>  6           3 W             8            7          529
#>  7           4 N             5            5          589.
#>  8           4 W             5            4          465.
#>  9           5 N             1            1          495
#> 10           5 W             3            2          571
#> # ... with 146 more rows
```

The data frame thus produced has 156 observations: two for each of the 78 participants. Finally, any grouped data frame can be ungrouped by the ungroup command, as in the following example:

```
ungroup(blp_by_lex)
#> # A tibble: 1,000 x 7
```

```
#>    participant lex   spell     resp     rt prev.rt rt.raw
#>            <dbl> <chr> <chr>    <chr> <dbl>   <dbl>  <dbl>
#>  1          20 N     staud     N       977     511    977
#>  2           9 N     dinbuss   N       565     765    565
#>  3          47 N     snilling  N       562     496    562
#>  4         103 N     gancens   N       572     656    572
#>  5          45 W     filled    W       659     981    659
#>  6          73 W     journals  W       538    1505    538
#>  7          24 W     apache    W       626     546    626
#>  8          11 W     flake     W       566     717    566
#>  9          32 W     reliefs   W       922    1471    922
#> 10          96 N     sarves    N       555     806    555
#> # … with 990 more rows
```

 ## The %>% operator

The %>% operator in R is known as the *pipe*. It was introduced relatively recently to R, and is a simple yet major innovation. It allows us to create sequences of functions, sometimes known as *pipelines*, that avoid the use of repeated nested functions or temporary data structures. The result is usually very clean, readable and uncluttered code.

The %>% pipe, and related operators like %<>% and %$%, are part of the magrittr package. The pipe itself is, however, automatically loaded by the dplyr package, as well as by tidyverse. In RStudio, the keyboard shortcut Ctrl+Shift+M types %>%.

To understand pipes, let us begin with a very simple example. The following primes variable is a vector of the first 10 prime numbers:

```
primes <- c(2, 3, 5, 7, 11, 13, 17, 19, 23, 29)
```

We can calculate the sum of primes as follows:

```
sum(primes)
#> [1] 129
```

We may then calculate the square root of this sum:

```
sqrt(sum(primes))
#> [1] 11.35782
```

We may then calculate the logarithm of this square root:

```
log(sqrt(sum(primes)))
#> [1] 2.429906
```

The final calculation is a triple nested function. In this example, it is not particularly difficult to read, but often when there is excessive nesting, the result appears cluttered and unreadable. Consider the following example where we combine primes with a vector of three NA values, subsample five values with replacement, sum the result, removing missing values, then calculate the logarithm to base 2 of the square root:

```
log(sqrt(sum(sample(c(primes, rep(NA, 3)), size=5, replace=T), na.rm=T)),
base=2)
#> [1] 2.660964
```

We may try to improve the readability of this code by breaking the function over multiple lines:

```
log(
  sqrt(
    sum(
      sample(
        c(primes, rep(NA, 3)),
        size=5,
        replace=T),
      na.rm=T)),
  base=2)
#> [1] 2.564642
```

It is questionable whether this improves readability at all. An alternative approach to improve readability is to create intermediate variables as in the following code:

```
primes_appended <- c(primes, rep(NA, 3))
primes_subsample <- sample(primes_appended, size=5, replace=T)
primes_subsample_sum <- sum(primes_subsample, na.rm=T)
sqrt_primes_subsample_sum <- sqrt(primes_subsample_sum)
log(sqrt_primes_subsample_sum, base=2)
#> [1] 2.377444
```

Or, alternatively, we could reuse the same temporary variable for the intermediate calculations:

```
tmpvar <- c(primes, rep(NA, 3))
tmpvar <- sample(tmpvar, size=5, replace=T)
tmpvar <- sum(tmpvar, na.rm=T)
tmpvar <- sqrt(tmpvar)
log(tmpvar, base=2)
#> [1] 2.229716
```

In either case, the resulting code is relatively cluttered, and creates some unnecessary temporary variables.

The %>% is *syntactic sugar* (code that is designed to replace other code in a way that is simpler, more elegant, or easier to read or write) that re-expresses nested functions as sequences. It is a binary operator that takes the value of its left-hand side and places it inside the function on the right-hand side. This is best understood by example. If we have a variable x and a function f(), we can apply the function to the variable with f(x). This is equivalent to the following:

```
x %>% f()    # equivalent to f(x)
```

On the other hand, the nested application of a set of functions `f()`, `g()`, and `h()` would be equivalent to the following:

```
x %>% f() %>% g() %>% h()    # equivalent to h(g(f(x)))
```

Returning to some of our examples above, we will see how they can be rewritten with pipes. In each case, we will precede the piped version with a comment showing its original version:

```
# sum(primes)
primes %>% sum()
#> [1] 129
# sum(primes, na.rm=T)
primes %>% sum(na.rm=T)
#> [1] 129
# log(sqrt(sum(primes)))
primes %>% sum() %>% sqrt() %>% log()
#> [1] 2.429906
# log(sqrt(sum(primes, na.rm=T)), base=2)
primes %>%
   sum(na.rm=T) %>%
   sqrt() %>%
   log(base=2)
#> [1] 3.505614
# log(sqrt(sum(sample(c(primes, rep(NA, 3)), size=5, replace=T), na.rm=T)),
base=2)
primes %>%
   c(rep(NA, 3)) %>%
   sample(size=5, replace=T) %>%
   sum(na.rm=T) %>%
   sqrt() %>%
   log(base=2)
#> [1] 3.022197
```

In each case, we can view the pipeline as beginning with some variable or expression, sending that to a function, the output of which is sent as input to the next function in the pipeline, and so on.

When used with the `dplyr` wrangling tools, as well as other tools that we will meet shortly, we then have a veritable mini-language for data wrangling. For example, in the following code we create some new variables, select, rename and reorder some of the variables, and sort by `participant` and then by `speed`:

```
blp_df %>%
   mutate(accuracy = resp == lex,
          stimulus = recode(lex, 'W'='word', 'N'='nonword')
   ) %>%
   select(participant, stimulus, item=spell, accuracy, speed=rt.raw) %>%
   arrange(participant, speed)
```

```
#> # A tibble: 1,000 x 5
#>    participant stimulus item       accuracy speed
#>          <dbl> <chr>    <chr>      <lgl>    <dbl>
#>  1            1 word     squashes   TRUE       494
#>  2            1 word     month      TRUE       500
#>  3            1 nonword  baisees    TRUE       524
#>  4            1 nonword  sinkhicks  TRUE       536
#>  5            1 nonword  wintes     TRUE       545
#>  6            1 word     shafting   TRUE       553
#>  7            1 word     chafing    TRUE       601
#>  8            1 nonword  treeps     TRUE       607
#>  9            1 word     abyss      TRUE       629
#> 10            1 word     gantries   TRUE       644
#> # ... with 990 more rows
```

As another example, in the following code, we filter the data frame by keeping only observations where `lex` takes the value `w`, then we calculate the word length and the accuracy of the response, rename the `rt.raw` variable, group by word length, calculate the average accuracy and reaction time, select some key variables and sort the result:

```
blp_df %>%
  filter(lex == 'W') %>%
  mutate(word_length = str_length(spell),
         accuracy = resp == lex) %>%
  rename(speed = rt.raw) %>%
  group_by(word_length) %>%
  summarize_at(vars(accuracy, speed), ~mean(., na.rm=T)) %>%
  ungroup() %>%
  select(word_length, accuracy, speed) %>%
  arrange(word_length, accuracy, speed)
#> # A tibble: 9 x 3
#>    word_length accuracy speed
#>          <int>    <dbl> <dbl>
#> 1            3    0.7    551.
#> 2            4    0.744  649.
#> 3            5    0.718  825.
#> 4            6    0.807  723.
#> 5            7    0.821  704.
#> 6            8    0.835  678.
#> 7            9    0.595  914.
#> 8           10    0.714  670.
#> 9           11    0.5    700.
```

Combining data frames

There are at least three major ways to combine data frames. They are what we'll call *binds*, *joins*, and *set operations*.

Combining data frames with binds

A *bind* operation is a simple operation that either vertically stacks data frames that share common variables, or horizontally stacks data frames that have the same number of observations.

To illustrate, we will create three small data frames. Here, we use `tibble` to create the data frame. This is very similar to using `data.frame` to create a data frame, as we saw in Chapter 2, but will create a tibble-flavoured data frame, which is the common type of data frame in the tidyverse:

```
Df_1 <- tibble(x = c(1, 2, 3),
               y = c(2, 7, 1),
               z = c(0, 2, 7))

Df_2 <- tibble(y = c(5, 7),
               z = c(6, 7),
               x = c(1, 2))

Df_3 <- tibble(a = c(5, 6, 1),
               b = c('a', 'b', 'c'),
               c = c(T, T, F))
```

The `Df_1` and `Df_2` data frames share common variable names. They can be vertically stacked using a `bind_rows` operation:

```
bind_rows(Df_1, Df_2)
#> # A tibble: 5 x 3
#>       x     y     z
#>   <dbl> <dbl> <dbl>
#> 1     1     2     0
#> 2     2     7     2
#> 3     3     1     7
#> 4     1     5     6
#> 5     2     7     7
```

Note that the variables, which are in different orders in the two data frames, are aligned properly when bound together. Any number of compatible data frames can be combined using `bind_rows`, as in the following example:

```
bind_rows(Df_1, Df_2, Df_2, Df_1)
#> # A tibble: 10 x 3
#>       x     y     z
#>   <dbl> <dbl> <dbl>
#> 1     1     2     0
#> 2     2     7     2
#> 3     3     1     7
#> 4     1     5     6
```

```
#> 5    2    7    7
#> 6    1    5    6
#> 7    2    7    7
#> 8    1    2    0
#> 9    2    7    2
#> 10   3    1    7
```

The Df_1 and Df_3 data frames have the same number of observations and so can be stacked side by side with a bind_cols operation:

```
bind_cols(Df_1, Df_3)
#> # A tibble: 3 x 6
#>       x     y     z     a b     c
#>   <dbl> <dbl> <dbl> <dbl> <chr> <lgl>
#> 1     1     2     0     5 a     TRUE
#> 2     2     7     2     6 b     TRUE
#> 3     3     1     7     1 c     FALSE
```

As with bind_rows, bind_cols will bind any number of compatible data frames:

```
bind_cols(Df_1, Df_3, Df_3, Df_1)
#> # A tibble: 3 x 12
#>   x...1 y...2 z...3 a...4 b...5 c...6 a...7 b...8 c...9 x...10 y...11 z...12
#>   <dbl> <dbl> <dbl> <dbl> <chr> <lgl> <dbl> <chr> <lgl>  <dbl>  <dbl>  <dbl>
#> 1     1     2     0     5 a     TRUE      5 a     TRUE       1      2      0
#> 2     2     7     2     6 b     TRUE      6 b     TRUE       2      7      2
#> 3     3     1     7     1 c     FALSE     1 c     FALSE      3      1      7
```

In this case, the variable names are appended with digits to make them unique.

Combining data frames by joins

A *join* operation is a common operation in relational databases using SQL. It allows us to join separate tables according to shared keys. As an example of a join operation on data frames using dplyr, consider the blp_df data frame. It has a variable spell that gives the identity of the stimulus shown on each trial of the lexical decision experiment. In a separate file, the blp_stimuli.csv file, we have three additional variables for these stimuli:

```
stimuli <- read_csv('data/blp_stimuli.csv')
stimuli
#> # A tibble: 55,865 x 4
#>   spell  old20   bnc subtlex
#>   <chr>  <dbl> <dbl>   <dbl>
#> 1 a/c     1.95    14       0
#> 2 aas     1.55     9       1
#> 3 aback   1.85   327      15
#> 4 abaft   2        8       2
```

```
#>   5 aband    1.95      0        0
#>   6 abase    1.7       6        2
#>   7 abased   1.75      6        0
#>   8 abashed  1.85     57        0
#>   9 abate    1.75     69        5
#> 10 abates    1.75      9        2
#> # ... with 55,855 more rows
```

As can be seen, there are four variables in `stimuli`: the `spell` variable that denotes the stimulus string and three others, `old20`, `bnc`, and `subtlex`, that describe properties of that stimulus string.

We can join these two data frames with `inner_join`. An `inner_join` operation, like all the `_join` operations we consider here, always operates on two data frames, which we will refer to as the left and right data frames. It searches through the values of variables that are shared by the two data frames in order to find matching values. In `blp_df` and `stimuli`, there is just one shared variable, namely `spell`. Thus, an `inner_join` of `blp_df` and `stimuli` will find values of `spell` on the left data frame that occur as values of `spell` on the right-hand side. It will then join the corresponding observations of both data frames:

```
inner_join(blp_df, stimuli)
#> # A tibble: 1,000 x 10
```

	participant	lex	spell	resp	rt	prev.rt	rt.raw	old20	bnc	subtlex
#>	<dbl>	<chr>	<chr>	<chr>	<dbl>	<dbl>	<dbl>	<dbl>	<dbl>	<dbl>
#> 1	20	N	staud	N	977	511	977	1.85	0	0
#> 2	9	N	dinbuss	N	565	765	565	2.9	0	0
#> 3	47	N	snilling	N	562	496	562	1.8	0	0
#> 4	103	N	gancens	N	572	656	572	2.3	0	0
#> 5	45	W	filled	W	659	981	659	1.45	5340	1336
#> 6	73	W	journals	W	538	1505	538	2.7	1030	83
#> 7	24	W	apache	W	626	546	626	2.45	130	17
#> 8	11	W	flake	W	566	717	566	1.5	274	84
#> 9	32	W	reliefs	W	922	1471	922	2.25	185	1
#> 10	96	N	sarves	N	555	806	555	1.65	0	0

```
#> # ... with 990 more rows
```

In general, in an `inner_join`, if the left data frame has no values on the shared variables that match those on the right data frame, the observations from the left data frame are dropped. In addition, all observations on the right data frame that do not have matching observations on the left always get dropped too.

In the example above, all observations of `blp_df` had values of `spell` that matched values of `spell` in `stimuli`. However, consider the following two data frames:

```
Df_a <- tibble(x = c(1, 2, 3),
               y = c('a', 'b', 'c'))
Df_b <- tibble(x = c(2, 3, 4),
               z = c('d', 'e', 'f'))
```

In this case, the first value of x in Df_a does not match any value of x in Df_b, and so the corresponding observation is dropped in an inner_join:

```
inner_join(Df_a, Df_b)
#> # A tibble: 2 x 3
#>       x y     z
#>   <dbl> <chr> <chr>
#> 1     2 b     d
#> 2     3 c     e
```

A left_join, on the other hand, will preserve all values on the left and put NA as the corresponding values of the variables on the right if there are no matching values:

```
left_join(Df_a, Df_b)
#> # A tibble: 3 x 3
#>       x y     z
#>   <dbl> <chr> <chr>
#> 1     1 a     <NA>
#> 2     2 b     d
#> 3     3 c     e
```

A right_join preserves all observations from the right, and places NA as the corresponding values of variables from the left that are not matched:

```
right_join(Df_a, Df_b)
#> # A tibble: 3 x 3
#>       x y     z
#>   <dbl> <chr> <chr>
#> 1     2 b     d
#> 2     3 c     e
#> 3     4 <NA>  f
```

With blp_df and stimuli, because all observations of spell in blp_df match values of spell in stimuli, the inner_join and left_join are identical, which we can verify as follows (using all_equal):

```
all_equal(inner_join(blp_df, stimuli),
          left_join(blp_df, stimuli)
)
#> [1] TRUE
```

On the other hand, there are many values of spell in stimuli that do not match any values of spell in blp_df. As such, a right_join leads to a large number of observations with NA values:

```
right_join(blp_df, stimuli)
#> # A tibble: 55,875 x 10
#>   participant lex   spell   resp    rt prev.rt rt.raw old20  bnc subtlex
```

```
#>                <dbl> <chr> <chr>   <chr> <dbl>   <dbl>   <dbl> <dbl> <dbl>    <dbl>
#>   1               20 N     staud   N       977     511     977  1.85     0        0
#>   2                9 N     dinbuss N       565     765     565  2.9      0        0
#>   3               47 N     snilling N      562     496     562  1.8      0        0
#>   4              103 N     gancens N       572     656     572  2.3      0        0
#>   5               45 W     filled  W       659     981     659  1.45  5340     1336
#>   6               73 W     journals W      538    1505     538  2.7   1030       83
#>   7               24 W     apache  W       626     546     626  2.45   130       17
#>   8               11 W     flake   W       566     717     566  1.5    274       84
#>   9               32 W     reliefs W       922    1471     922  2.25   185        1
#>  10               96 N     sarves  N       555     806     555  1.65     0        0
#> # ... with 55,865 more rows
```

A `full_join` keeps all observations in both the left and right data frames. If used with `blp_df` and `stimuli`, the result is identical to a `right_join`, as we can verify as follows:

```
all_equal(full_join(blp_df, stimuli),
          right_join(blp_df, stimuli)
)
#> [1] TRUE
```

For the case of `Df_a` and `Df_b`, where observations in both the left and right data frames do not have matches, a `full_join` is as follows:

```
full_join(Df_a, Df_b)
#> # A tibble: 4 x 3
#>       x y     z
#>   <dbl> <chr> <chr>
#> 1     1 a     <NA>
#> 2     2 b     d
#> 3     3 c     e
#> 4     4 <NA>  f
```

In all of the above examples, the data frames shared only one common variable. Consider the following cases:

```
Df_4 <- tibble(x = c(1, 2, 3),
               y = c(2, 7, 1),
               z = c(0, 2, 7))

Df_5 <- tibble(a = c(1, 1, 7),
               b = c(2, 3, 7),
               c = c('a', 'b', 'c'))
```

`Df_4` and `Df_5` do not share any common variables. In this case, we need to specify pairs of variables to match on. We have multiple options for how to do this. In the following example, we look for matches between `x` on the left and `a` on the right:

```
inner_join(Df_4, Df_5, by=c('x' = 'a'))
#> # A tibble: 2 x 5
#>       x      y      z      b c
#>   <dbl> <dbl> <dbl> <dbl> <chr>
#> 1     1     2     0     2 a
#> 2     1     2     0     3 b
```

On the other hand, in the following example, we look for matches between x and y on the left and a and b on the right:

```
inner_join(Df_4, Df_5, by=c('x' = 'a', 'y' = 'b'))
#> # A tibble: 1 x 4
#>       x      y      z c
#>   <dbl> <dbl> <dbl> <chr>
#> 1     1     2     0 a
```

Combining data frames by set operations

In dplyr, the functions intersect, union, etc., allow us to combine data frames *that have identical variables* using set operations.

Consider the following data frames:

```
Df_6 <- tibble(x = c(1, 2, 3),
               y = c(4, 5, 6),
               z = c(7, 8, 9))



Df_7 <- tibble(y = c(6, 7),
               z = c(9, 10),
               x = c(3, 4))
```

Both data frames have the same variables and happen to share a row of observations, even if the variables are in different orders. As such, their intersection and union are as follows:

```
intersect(Df_6, Df_7)
#> # A tibble: 1 x 3
#>       x      y      z
#>   <dbl> <dbl> <dbl>
#> 1     3     6     9
union(Df_6, Df_7)
#> # A tibble: 4 x 3
#>       x      y      z
#>   <dbl> <dbl> <dbl>
#> 1     1     4     7
#> 2     2     5     8
#> 3     3     6     9
#> 4     4     7    10
```

We may also calculate the set differences between `Df_6` and `Df_7`:

```
setdiff(Df_6, Df_7) # Rows in Df_6 not in Df_7
#> # A tibble: 2 x 3
#>       x     y     z
#>   <dbl> <dbl> <dbl>
#> 1     1     4     7
#> 2     2     5     8
setdiff(Df_7, Df_6) # Rows in Df_7 not in Df_6
#> # A tibble: 1 x 3
#>       y     z     x
#>   <dbl> <dbl> <dbl>
#> 1     7    10     4
```

3●7 Reshaping with `pivot_longer` and `pivot_wider`

A so-called *tidy* data set, at least according to its widespread usage in the context of data analysis using R, is a data set where all rows are observations, all columns are variables, and each variable is a single value. Although what exactly counts as an observation may in fact vary from situation to situation, usually whether a data set is *tidy* or not is immediately quite clear. For example, consider the following data frame:

```
recall_df <- read_csv('data/repeated_measured_a.csv')
recall_df
#> # A tibble: 5 x 4
#>   Subject   Neg   Neu   Pos
#>   <chr>   <dbl> <dbl> <dbl>
#> 1 Faye       26    12    42
#> 2 Jason      29     8    35
#> 3 Jim        32    15    45
#> 4 Ron        22    10    38
#> 5 Victor     30    13    40
```

In this data frame, for each subject, we have three values, which are their scores on a memory test in three different conditions of an experiment. The conditions are `Neg` (negative), `Neu` (neutral), `Pos` (positive). Arguably, we could describe each row as an observation, namely the observation of all memory scores from a particular subject. However, each column is not a variable. The `Neg`, `Neu`, `Pos` are, in fact, *values* of a variable, namely the condition of the experiment. Therefore, to tidy this data frame, we need a variable for the subject, another for the experiment's condition, and another for the memory score for the corresponding subject in the corresponding condition. To achieve this, we perform what is sometimes known as a *wide to long* transformation. The `tidyr` package has a function `pivot_longer` for this transformation.

To use `pivot_longer`, we must specify the variables (using the `cols` argument) that we want to pivot from wide to long. In our case, it is the variables `Neg`, `Neu`, `Pos`, and we can select these by `cols = -Subject`, which means all variables except `Subject`. Next, using the argument names_to, we must provide a name for the column that will indicate the experimental condition. We will do this with names_to = 'condition'. The values of this condition variable will consist of the values Neg, Neu, Pos. Finally, using the argument values_to, we must provide a name for the column that will indicate the memory scores. We will do this with values_to = 'score'. The values of this score variable will consist of the values of the original Neg, Neu, Pos columns. Altogether, we have the following:

```
recall_long <- pivot_longer(recall_df,
                            cols = -Subject,
                            names_to = 'condition',
                            values_to = 'score')
recall_long
#> # A tibble: 15 x 3
#>    Subject condition score
#>    <chr>   <chr>     <dbl>
#>  1 Faye    Neg          26
#>  2 Faye    Neu          12
#>  3 Faye    Pos          42
#>  4 Jason   Neg          29
#>  5 Jason   Neu           8
#>  6 Jason   Pos          35
#>  7 Jim     Neg          32
#>  8 Jim     Neu          15
#>  9 Jim     Pos          45
#> 10 Ron     Neg          22
#> 11 Ron     Neu          10
#> 12 Ron     Pos          38
#> 13 Victor  Neg          30
#> 14 Victor  Neu          13
#> 15 Victor  Pos          40
```

Now each row is an observation providing the memory score for the given subject in the given condition, and each column is a variable.

Once the data frame is in this format, other operations, such as those using the dplyr functions, become much easier. For example, to calculate some summary statistics on the memory score per condition, we would do the following:

```
recall_long %>%
  group_by(condition) %>%
  summarize_at('score', list(median=median,
                             mean=mean,
                             min=min,
                             max=max)
  )
#> # A tibble: 3 x 5
#>   condition median mean  min   max
#>   <chr>     <dbl>  <dbl> <dbl> <dbl>
```

```
#> 1 Neg          29   27.8    22    32
#> 2 Neu          12   11.6     8    15
#> 3 Pos          40   40      35    45
```

The inverse of `pivot_longer` is `pivot_wider`. It is very similar to `pivot_longer` and we use `names_from` and `values_from` in the opposite sense to `names_to` and `values_to`:

```
pivot_wider(recall_long, names_from = 'condition', values_from = 'score')
#> # A tibble: 5 x 4
#>    Subject   Neg    Neu    Pos
#>    <chr>     <dbl> <dbl> <dbl>
#> 1 Faye        26    12    42
#> 2 Jason       29     8    35
#> 3 Jim         32    15    45
#> 4 Ron         22    10    38
#> 5 Victor      30    13    40
```

Some `pivot_longer` operations are not as simple as the one just described. Consider the following data:

```
recall_2_df <- read_csv('data/repeated_measured_b.csv')
recall_2_df
#> # A tibble: 5 x 7
#>   Subject Cued_Neg Cued_Neu Cued_Pos Free_Neg Free_Neu Free_Pos
#>   <chr>      <dbl>    <dbl>    <dbl>    <dbl>    <dbl>    <dbl>
#> 1 Faye         15       16       14       13       13       12
#> 2 Jason         4        9       10        6        7        9
#> 3 Jim           7        9       10        8        9        5
#> 4 Ron          17       18       20       12       14       15
#> 5 Victor       16       13       14       12       13       14
```

In this data frame, we have six columns that are the values of a combination of two experimental variables. One variable is a binary variable that indicates whether the experimental condition was Cued or Free (i.e. whether the subject's memory recall was cued by some stimuli or was a free recall). The other variable is the condition as in the `recall_df` data frame. If we perform a `pivot_longer` as we did before we obtain the following:

```
pivot_longer(recall_2_df,
             cols = -Subject,
             names_to = 'condition',
             values_to = 'score')
#> # A tibble: 30 x 3
#>    Subject condition score
#>    <chr>   <chr>     <dbl>
#>  1 Faye    Cued_Neg    15
#>  2 Faye    Cued_Neu    16
#>  3 Faye    Cued_Pos    14
#>  4 Faye    Free_Neg    13
```

```
#>  5 Faye      Free_Neu      13
#>  6 Faye      Free_Pos      12
#>  7 Jason     Cued_Neg       4
#>  8 Jason     Cued_Neu       9
#>  9 Jason     Cued_Pos      10
#> 10 Jason     Free_Neg       6
#> # … with 20 more rows
```

Here, the condition is not exactly a variable, but a combination of variables. To pivot_
longer into two variables, we use two names in names_to, and use names_pattern to indicate
how to split the names Cued_Neg, Cued_Neu, etc.:

```
recall_2_long <- pivot_longer(recall_2_df,
                              cols = -Subject,
                              names_to = c('cue', 'emotion'),
                              names_pattern = '(Cued|Free)_(Neg|Pos|Neu)',
                              values_to = 'score')
recall_2_long
#> # A tibble: 30 x 4
#>    Subject cue    emotion score
#>    <chr>   <chr>  <chr>   <dbl>
#>  1 Faye    Cued   Neg        15
#>  2 Faye    Cued   Neu        16
#>  3 Faye    Cued   Pos        14
#>  4 Faye    Free   Neg        13
#>  5 Faye    Free   Neu        13
#>  6 Faye    Free   Pos        12
#>  7 Jason   Cued   Neg         4
#>  8 Jason   Cued   Neu         9
#>  9 Jason   Cued   Pos        10
#> 10 Jason   Free   Neg         6
#> # … with 20 more rows
```

To perform the inverse of the above pivot_longer, we primarily just need to indicate two
columns to take the names from:

```
pivot_wider(recall_2_long,
            names_from = c('cue', 'emotion'),
            values_from = 'score')
#> # A tibble: 5 x 7
#>    Subject Cued_Neg Cued_Neu Cued_Pos Free_Neg Free_Neu Free_Pos
#>    <chr>      <dbl>    <dbl>    <dbl>    <dbl>    <dbl>    <dbl>
#> 1 Faye          15       16       14       13       13       12
#> 2 Jason          4        9       10        6        7        9
#> 3 Jim            7        9       10        8        9        5
#> 4 Ron           17       18       20       12       14       15
#> 5 Victor        16       13       14       12       13       14
```

4

Data Visualization

Introduction

Data visualization is a major part of data analysis. Far from being just a means to add some eye candy or ornamentation to otherwise dull reports or presentation slides, visualization allows us explore data and find patterns that would easily be missed were we to rely only on numerical summary statistics. A classic example that vividly illustrates this point is known as *Anscombe's quartet* (Anscombe, 1973). In this example, there are four separate data sets, each with two variables labelled x and y. The means and standard deviations of both the x and y variables are identical across all four data sets. Likewise, the Pearson's correlation coefficient between the x and y is also identical across the data sets. These summary statistics are shown in the following table.

set	mean(x)	mean(y)	sd(x)	sd(y)	cor(x, y)
I	9	7.5	3.32	2.03	0.82
II	9	7.5	3.32	2.03	0.82
III	9	7.5	3.32	2.03	0.82
IV	9	7.5	3.32	2.03	0.82

On the basis of these numbers, the four data sets seem to be identical, or at least it seems likely that they will be highly similar. However, when we visualize the scatterplots of x and y variables for each case, it is evident that they differ from one another in substantial ways (see Figure 4.1). A key characteristic of data visualization, therefore, is that 'it forces us to notice what we never expected to see' (Tukey, 1977). In other words, data visualization is not simply a means to graphically illustrate what we already know, but to reveal patterns and structures in the data.

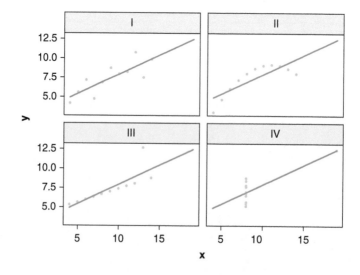

Figure 4.1 Anscombe's quartet. Across all of the four data sets shown here, the means and standard deviations of the x and y variables are identical, as is the correlation between x and y

There is no strict formula or procedure that we must always follow when visualizing data. Any data set can be visualized in many ways; some of these will be informative and provide insight, others will not. Generally, we should aim to fully explore the data and maximize what can be learned from it. To do so, we should always try to look at the data in different ways, from different perspectives, and at coarser and finer levels. This process is iterative in that we may start with something very simple and then progressively refine it. Sometimes we need to work by trial and error, starting with some visualization technique that then needs to be abandoned in favour of another. In general, we should keep in mind some guiding principles. For example, Hartwig and Dearing (1979), when describing exploratory data analysis generally, state that we should be guided by principles of *scepticism* and *openness*. We ought to be sceptical as to the possibility that any visualization may obscure or misrepresent our data, and we should be open to the possibility of patterns and structures that we were not expecting. Some guiding principles for visualization mentioned by Edward R. Tufte in his *Visual Display of Quantitative Information* (Tufte, 1983) are the following:

* Above all else show the data.
* Avoid distorting what the data have to say.
* Present many numbers in a small space.
* Encourage the eye to compare different pieces of data.
* Reveal the data at several levels of detail, from a broad overview to the fine structure.

Just as we have guiding principles, so too are there major visualization tools or techniques that should generally be known. The major tools that we will consider here primarily include the following:

* *Histograms, density plots, barplots.* These are used to display the distribution of values of continuous and discrete variables.
* *Boxplots.* Like histograms and density plots, boxplots (or box-and-whisker plots) display the distribution of values of continuous variables. However, they are more closely tied to robust statistical descriptions and so deserve to be treated as a class in themselves.
* *Scatterplots.* Scatterplots and their variants such as *bubbleplots* are used to display bivariate data, or the relationships between two variables. Usually, scatterplots are used in cases where both variables are continuous, but may also be used, though perhaps with additional modification, when one variable is discrete.

There are, however, many other important types of data visualization methods. For example, heatmaps are used to display large rectangular grids of data, and geospatial maps display data superimposed on maps of physical space such as a country. As important as these methods are, we have not included them in order to keep this chapter to a manageable size. There are many goods books that delve much deeper into data visualization using ggplot. Highly recommended is Healy (2019).

Plotting in R with ggplot

In R, there are two major sets of tools for visualization. These are usually known as the *base R* and the *ggplot* plotting systems. The base R plotting system is part of the default, or base, installation of R. Its principal command is `plot`. The ggplot system is provided by the `ggplot2` package (see Wickham, 2016), which is part of the tidyverse, and its principal command is `ggplot`. The *gg* in its name refers to the *grammar of graphics* (Wilkinson, 2005; Wickham, 2010), which is a system of rules for mapping variables in a data set to properties (e.g. shape, size, colour, position) of a plot. While the base R plotting system is powerful and not to be dismissed or seen as obsolete, here will exclusively use ggplot. The reason for this is that ggplot is a higher-level plotting system, meaning that it allows us to create complex visualizations with a minimal amount of code. The same visualizations can almost always be produced using the base plot as well, but doing so usually involves much more code and much more fine-tuning.

To use the ggplot plotting system, we must first load the `ggplot2` package. This can be loaded directly as follows:

```
library(ggplot2)
```

Alternatively, we can just load `tidyverse`, which then loads `ggplot2`:

```
library(tidyverse)
```

There are three key pieces of information that we specify with the `ggplot` command:

1. The data set containing all the data. This is almost always a single data frame, but sometimes it is multiple data frames.
2. A set of *aesthetic mappings*. This is where we map variables in the data frame to properties like shape, size, colour, and position of the graphic.
3. A set of *layers* that render the aesthetic mappings, usually according to prespecified *geoms* or geometric objects such as lines, points and bars.

The best way to understand these components and how `ggplot` works is to work with some very simple examples. To begin, we'll create a very simple tribble data frame using the `tribble` command, which allows us to create a tibble in an easy to read row-by-row layout:

```
simple_df <- tribble(
   ~var1, ~var2, ~var3,
   1,    4,   'a',
   3,   10,  'a',
   7,   40,  'b',
   10,  90,  'b'
)
```

Let's say that we want to create a simple scatterplot where the values of `var1` specify the position of points along the *x*-axis and the values of `var2` specify the positions of points along the *y*-axis. To do so, we would start by specifying the data frame we're using as `simple_df` and then specify the aesthetic mapping we want as in the following command:

```
ggplot(simple_df,
        mapping = aes(x = var1, y = var2)
)
```

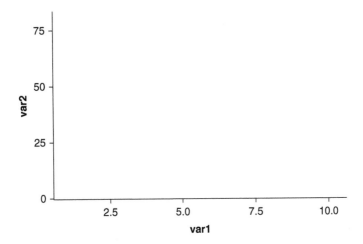

As can be seen, in itself, this did not produce much. It essentially created a blank canvas with the var1 and var2 mapped to the *x*-axis and *y*-axis, respectively. To see the points, we need to add a layer that tells ggplot how to render the graphic using the mapping we have set up. Because we want a scatterplot, we use the geom_point geom function as follows:

```
ggplot(simple_df,
        mapping = aes(x = var1, y = var2)
) + geom_point()
```

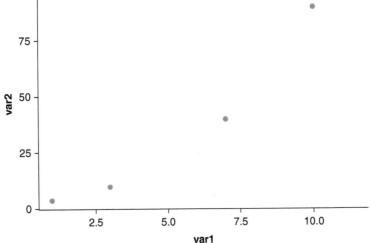

If we now prefer to display this same data using a line plot, we can exchange geom_point() for geom_line():

```
ggplot(simple_df,
        mapping = aes(x = var1, y = var2)
) + geom_line()
```

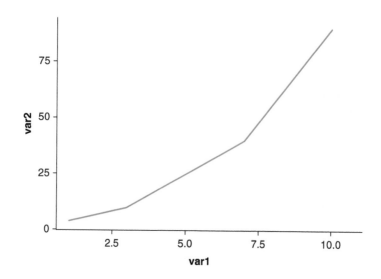

We could extend the original scatterplot by adding an additional aesthetic mapping by using var3. Because this is a discrete variable, it could be mapped to a discrete property of the points, such as their shape. This is very simple to do. We need only add shape = var3 to the aes function, and then when we render with geom_point, the points will have shapes according to their values of var3:

```
ggplot(simple_df,
       mapping = aes(x = var1, y = var2, shape = var3)
) + geom_point()
```

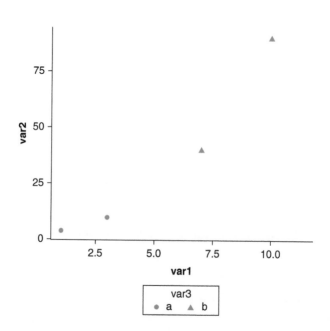

Or if we prefer to represent `var3` with colours, we could use `colour = var3` (we could also use `color = var3`, if you prefer American English spelling, or even just `col = var3`):

```
ggplot(simple_df,
        mapping = aes(x = var1, y = var2, colour = var3)
) + geom_point()
```

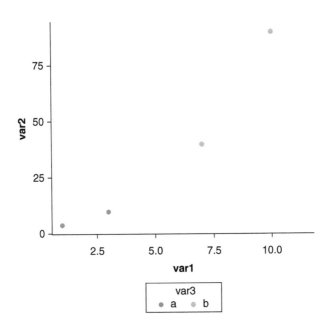

These examples just scratch the surface of what `ggplot` is capable of, but they do illustrate its general functionality. In the following sections, we will provide much more depth and explore many more features of `ggplot`. Before we proceed, we should note that in all the above examples, we were using somewhat verbose commands. For example, the second argument to `ggplot` is always assumed to be the `aes` mapping (the first argument is always the name of the data frame), so we could drop `mapping =`, as in the following example:

```
ggplot(simple_df,
        aes(x = var1, y = var2)
) + geom_point()
```

Likewise, because the first and second argument to `aes` are assumed to be the x and y axis mapping, we could drop the `x =` and `y =`, as in the following example:

```
ggplot(simple_df,
        aes(var1, var2)
) + geom_point()
```

In what follows, we will usually keep the more verbose style, but you may prefer to drop it as you get more used to how `ggplot` works.

Histograms, density plots, barplots, etc.

Histograms and related visualization methods like frequency polygons, area plots, density plots, and barplots are simple but still highly effective tools to visualize the distribution of values of continuous variables.

Histograms

Histograms are one of the simplest and generally most useful ways of visualizing distributions of the values of individual variables. To illustrate them, we'll use the weight data frame, from which we will subsample 1000 points in order to reduce the number of data points:

```
weight_df <- read_csv("data/weight.csv") %>%
  sample_n(1000)
```

If we want to display the distribution of the height variable, we would proceed as follows:

```
ggplot(weight_df,
       mapping = aes(x = height)
) + geom_histogram()
```

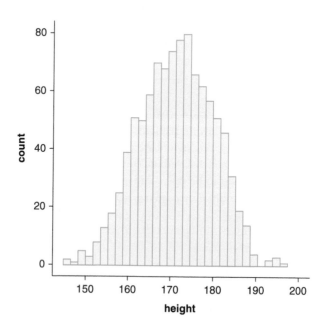

By default, the histogram will have 30 bins. It is usually good to override this either by specifying another value for bins, or by specifying the binwidth. Given that the height variable is measured in centimetres, we can specify that each bin should be 2.54 cm, or 1 inch, as follows:

```
ggplot(weight_df,
       mapping = aes(x = height)
) + geom_histogram(binwidth = 2.54)
```

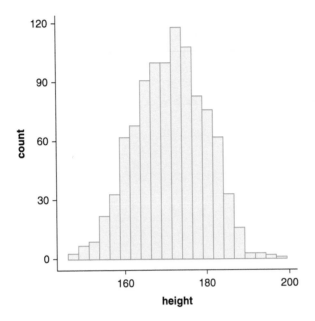

Any histogram consists of a set of bars, and each bar has a colour for its interior and another for its border. The interior colour is its `fill` colour, while `colour` specifies the colour of its border. If, for example, we wanted a histogram with dark blue interior and white border, which may help to distinguish between consecutive bars, we would type the following:

```
ggplot(weight_df,
       mapping = aes(x = height)
) + geom_histogram(binwidth = 2.54, colour = 'white', fill = 'darkblue')
```

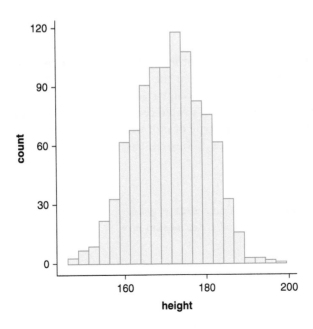

If, in the aes mapping, we specify that either colour or fill, or both, should be mapped to some another variable with discrete values, we obtain a *stacked* histogram. In the following example, we set the fill values to vary by the gender variable:

```
ggplot(weight_df,
        mapping = aes(x = height, fill = gender)
) + geom_histogram(binwidth = 2.54)
```

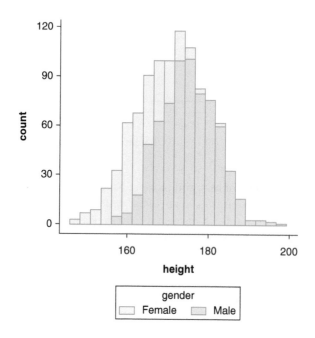

In a stacked histogram, the colour within each bin codes the proportion of that bin's values that correspond to each value of the discrete variable. A variant of the stacked histogram above is where each bar occupies 100% of the plot's height so that what is shown is the proportion of the bin's value corresponding to each value of the grouping variable. We can obtain this type of plot with by setting position to fill within geom_histogram (by default, geom_histogram has position = stack), as in the following example:

```
ggplot(weight_df,
        mapping = aes(x = height, fill = gender)
) + geom_histogram(binwidth = 2.54, position = 'fill')
```

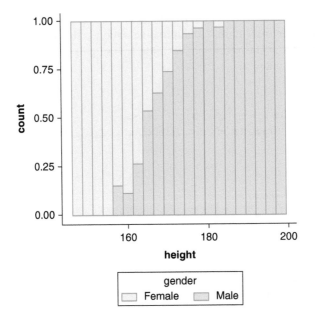

If, rather than a stacked histogram, we want two separate histograms, one for males and another for females, we can use other options. One option is to specify position = 'dodge' within geom_histogram as follows:

```
ggplot(weight_df,
       mapping = aes(x = height, fill = gender)
) + geom_histogram(binwidth = 2.54, position = 'dodge')
```

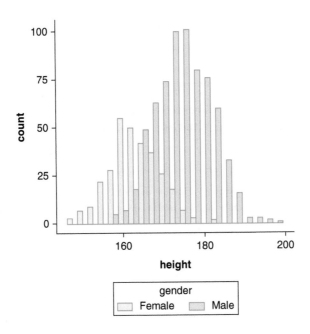

This option uses the same bins as before but puts two non-overlapping bars at each bin, one for males and one for females. An alternative option is to place the bars corresponding to males and females at the exact same location by using `position = 'identity'` within `geom_histogram` as follows:

```
ggplot(weight_df,
        mapping = aes(x = height, fill = gender)
) + geom_histogram(binwidth = 2.54, position = 'identity')
```

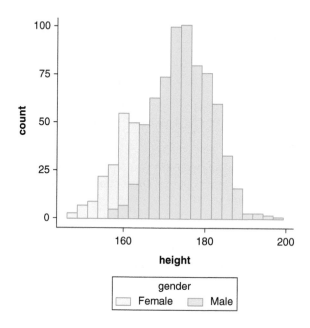

Notice that when using this `position = 'identity'` option, the second group, which in this case corresponds to the males, occludes the first one. We can avoid complete occlusion by setting the `alpha`, or opacity, level of the bars to be a value less than 1.0 as in the following example:

```
ggplot(weight_df,
        mapping = aes(x = height, fill = gender)
) + geom_histogram(binwidth = 2.54, position = 'identity', alpha = 0.75)
```

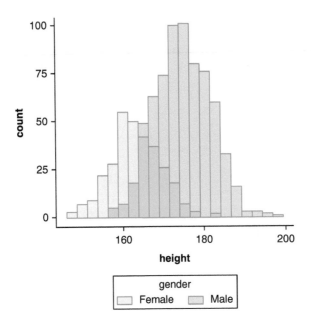

Another option to deal with occlusion is to map `gender` to `colour` rather than `fill`, and set `fill` to be white

```
ggplot(weight_df,
        mapping = aes(x = height, colour = gender)
) + geom_histogram(binwidth = 2.54, fill = 'white', position = 'identity', alpha= 0.5)
```

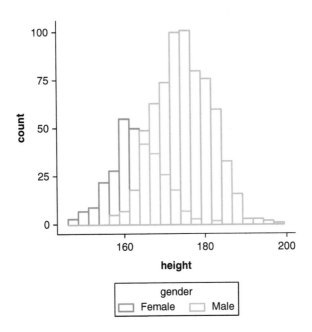

Frequency polygons

A frequency polygon is similar to a histogram but instead of using bars to display the number of values in each bin, it uses connected lines. The following plot displays the number of
`height` values in each bin of width 2.54 cm:

```
ggplot(weight_df,
        mapping = aes(x = height)
) + geom_freqpoly(binwidth = 2.54, colour = 'steelblue')
```

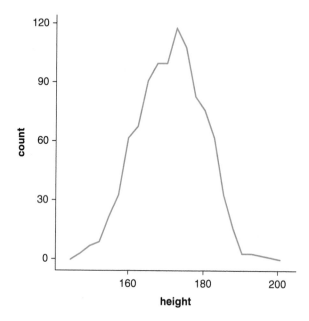

If we map `gender` to `colour`, we produce two overlaid lines. This is the frequency polygon
equivalent of the histogram using `position = 'identity'`:

```
ggplot(weight_df,
        mapping = aes(x = height, colour = gender)
) + geom_freqpoly(binwidth = 2.54) # `position = 'identity'` is the default
```

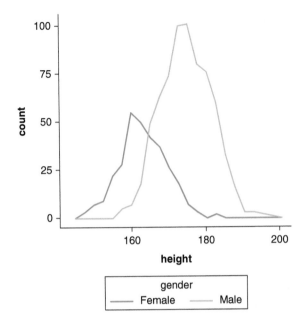

If we prefer a *stacked* frequency polygon, we use `position = 'stack'`:

```
ggplot(weight_df,
        mapping = aes(x = height, colour = gender)
) + geom_freqpoly(binwidth = 2.54, position = 'stack')
```

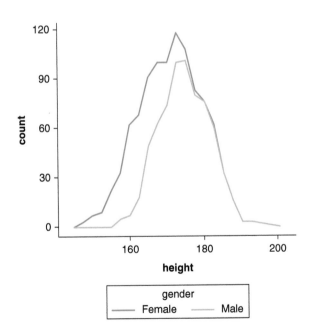

A related option is an *area plot*. To get the equivalent of the overlaid histograms, but with filled interiors, instead of using `geom_freqpoly`, we can use `geom_area`:

```
ggplot(weight_df,
        mapping = aes(x = height, fill = gender)
) + geom_area(binwidth = 2.54, stat = "bin", position = 'identity', alpha = 0.5)
```

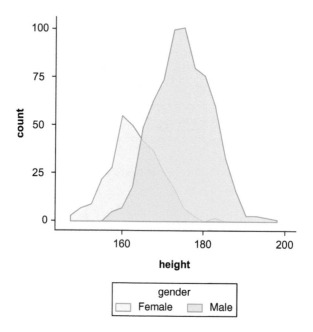

To obtain a stacked area plot, change `position` to have the value of `'stack'`:

```
ggplot(weight_df,
        mapping = aes(x = height, fill = gender)
) + geom_area(binwidth = 2.54, stat = "bin", position = 'stack')
```

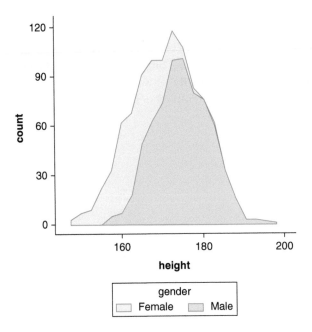

We also have the option of setting `position` to have the value of `'fill'`:

```
ggplot(weight_df,
       mapping = aes(x = height, fill = gender)
) + geom_area(binwidth = 2.54, stat = "bin", position = 'fill')
```

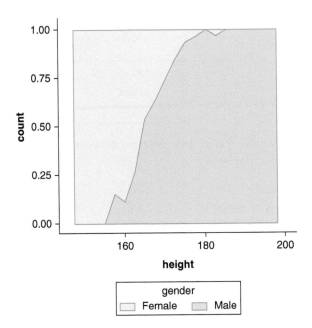

Density plots

Histograms work by dividing the range of values of a variable into equal-sized bins and simply counting the number of values in each bin. *Density plots,* on the other hand, use *kernel
density estimation* to estimate a probability density over the variable. In practical terms, we
can see this as the moving average smoothing of histograms. The default density plot of the
height variable is obtained as follows:

```
ggplot(weight_df,
        mapping = aes(x = height)
) + geom_density()
```

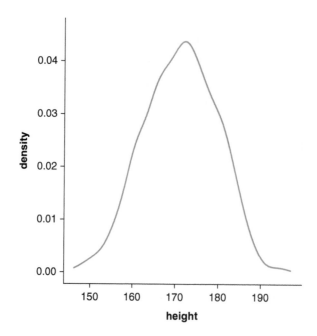

As with the histogram, we may change the colour of the border and the interior of the density
plot with colour and fill, respectively

```
ggplot(weight_df,
        mapping = aes(x = height)
) + geom_density(colour = 'white', fill = 'darkblue')
```

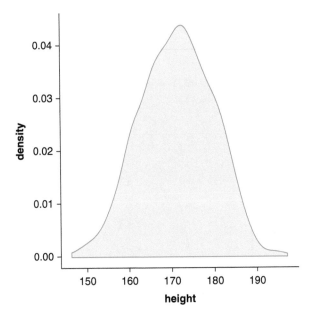

If we set `fill` or `colour`, or both, to map to `gender`, then the default result is the density plot equivalent of overlaid histograms above. As seen in the following example, we avoid complete occlusion of one density plot by the other by use of the `alpha` parameter:

```
ggplot(weight_df,
       mapping = aes(x = height, fill = gender, colour = gender)
) + geom_density(alpha = 0.5)
```

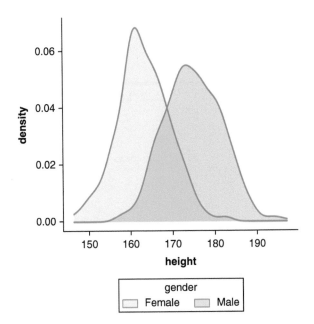

To accomplish the density plot equivalent of the stacked histogram, we set `position =` `'stack'`:

```
ggplot(weight_df,
       mapping = aes(x = height, fill = gender, colour = gender)
) + geom_density(position = 'stack')
```

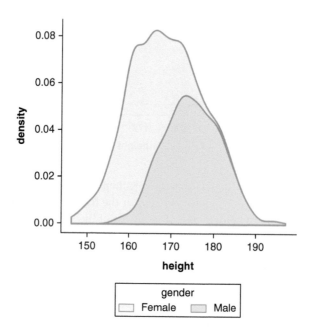

The density plot equivalent of the filled stack histogram is accomplished with `position =` `'fill'`:

```
ggplot(weight_df,
       mapping = aes(x = height, fill = gender, colour = gender)
) + geom_density(position = 'fill')
```

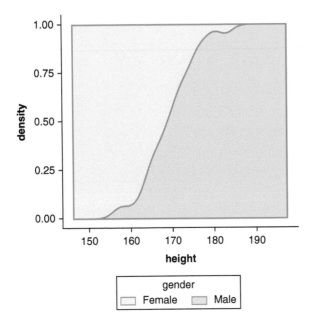

Barplots

Both histograms and density plots assume that the variables are continuous. For discrete variables, their counterpart is a *barplot*. For each value of the discrete variable, the barplot displays the number of observed instances of that value in the data. As an example, the following titanic data frame tells us, for each of the 1309 passengers on the RMS *Titanic* on its fateful maiden voyage in 1912, their sex, age, and passenger class, and whether they survived or not:

```
titanic_df <- read_csv('data/TitanicSurvival.csv') %>% select(-X1)
glimpse(titanic_df)
#> Rows: 1,309
#> Columns: 4
#> $ survived       <chr> "yes", "yes", "no", "no", "no", "yes", "yes", "no", …
#> $ sex            <chr> "female", "male", "female", "male", "female", "male", …
#> $ age            <dbl> 29.0000, 0.9167, 2.0000, 30.0000, 25.0000, 48.0000, …
#> $ passengerClass <chr> "1st", "1st", "1st", "1st", "1st", "1st", "1st", "1s …
```

The number of passengers in each passenger class is given by the following barplot:

```
ggplot(titanic_df,
       mapping = aes(x = passengerClass)
) + geom_bar()
```

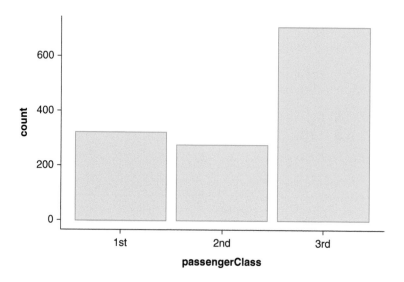

If we map the `fill` property to the variable `survived`, we may see the number of passengers in each class who survived or not:

```
ggplot(titanic_df,
        mapping = aes(x = passengerClass, fill = survived)
) + geom_bar()
```

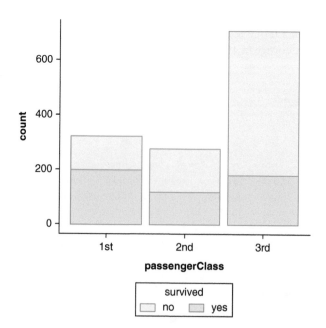

We may display the same information using side-by-side bars, one for those who survived and other for those who did not, as follows:

```
ggplot(titanic_df,
        mapping = aes(x = passengerClass, fill = survived)
) + geom_bar(position = 'dodge')
```

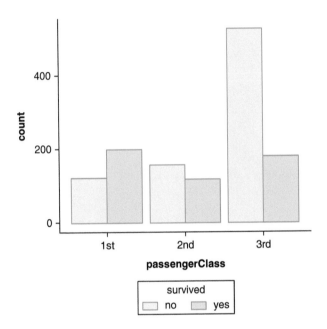

Sometimes we wish to draw a barplot where the heights of the bars are given by the value of a variable in the data set. Consider the following small data set:

```
carprices <- read_csv('data/carprice.csv') %>%
  group_by(Type) %>%
  summarise(price = mean(Price))
carprices
#> # A tibble: 6 x 2
#>    Type     price
#>    <chr>    <dbl>
#> 1 Compact   12.8
#> 2 Large     24.3
#> 3 Midsize   21.8
#> 4 Small     10.0
#> 5 Sporty    19.4
#> 6 Van       18.3
```

In this, we have two variables: `Type`, which indicates the type of vehicle; and `price`, which gives the average price of each vehicle type. We can plot this data by mapping the `y` attribute to `price` and indicate `stat = 'identity'` in `geom_bar`:

```
ggplot(carprices,
        mapping = aes(x = Type, y = price)
) + geom_bar(stat = 'identity')
```

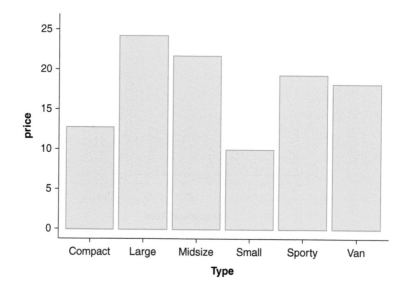

Mapping the `fill` variable allows us to display values for two discrete variables:

```
fat_rats <- read_csv('data/FatRats.csv') %>%
  group_by(Protein, Source) %>%
  summarize(gain = mean(Gain), se = sd(Gain)/sqrt(n()))

ggplot(fat_rats,
        mapping = aes(x = Source, y = gain, fill = Protein)
) + geom_bar(stat = 'identity', position = 'dodge')
```

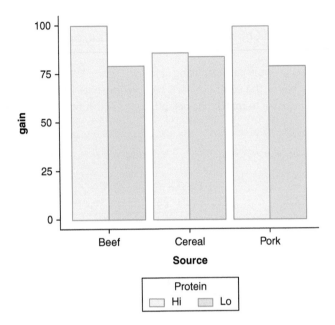

In this example we see that the bars corresponding to `Hi` and `Lo` values of `Protein` are touching one another, while there is a gap between the pair of bars corresponding to the `Beef`, `Cereal`, `Pork` values of `Source`. How close the `Hi` and `Lo` bars are is determined by the `width` parameter of `dodge`, which defaults to 0.9 in this case. If we wish to change this parameter, for example to a width of 1.0, we need to use `position = position_dodge(width = 1.0)` (the statement `position = 'dodge'` is a shortcut to `position = position_dodge()`):

```
ggplot(fat_rats,
        mapping = aes(x = Source, y = gain, fill = Protein)
) + geom_bar(stat = 'identity', position = position_dodge(width = 1.0))
```

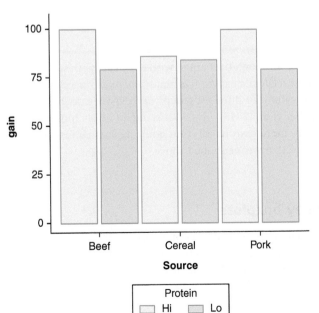

Notice that when the `width` of the position dodge is set to 1.0, the distance between all bars in the plot is the same. Thus, by setting `width` lower than 1.0, we push the two bars in each pair closer together.

We may add error bars to these barplots using `geom_errorbar`. With `geom_errorbar`, in order to position the error bar at the centre of each bar, we must set the `width` of the `position_dodge` of the `geom_errorbar` to match the default dodge width of the bars, which is 0.9:

```
ggplot(fat_rats,
         mapping = aes(x = Source, y = gain, fill = Protein, ymin = gain - se,
ymax = gain + se)
) + geom_bar(stat = 'identity', position = 'dodge') +
  geom_errorbar(width = 0.2, position = position_dodge(width = 0.9))
```

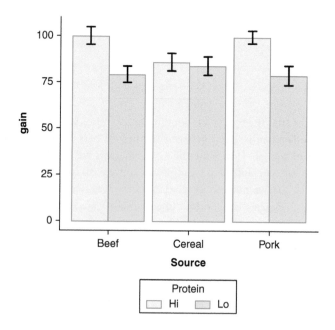

As a word of warning, although the barplot with error bars with standard errors has been and still is widely used in academic papers, it is highly *not* recommended as a means of displaying the distribution of values for different groups or categories. As has been made clear in, for example, Weissgerber et al. (2015), bars with standard errors hide the raw data and tend to conceal and obscure more than reveal, thus going against almost all the guiding principles for data visualization that we mentioned above.

Tukey boxplots

Boxplots, also known as box-and-whisker plots, are used to display the distribution of values of a variable. One subtype of boxplot is the *Tukey boxplot* (Tukey, 1977). These are in fact the most common subtype and are the default type implemented in `ggplot2` using the `geom_boxplot` function.

For some of the following examples, we'll use the R built-in `swiss` data set that provides data on fertility rates in 47 Swiss provinces in 1888. One predictor variable, `Examination`, gives the proportion of army draftees in each province who received the highest mark in an army examination. Another, `Catholic`, gives the proportion in each province who are Catholic. Because each province has either a clear majority of Catholics or a clear majority of Protestants, we will create a new logical variable, `catholic`, that indicates if the province's Catholic proportion is greater than 0.5 or not. The data frame also has the name of the province as its row name, and we will create a new variable with these names:

```
swiss_df <- swiss %>% rownames_to_column('province') %>%
  mutate(catholic = Catholic > 50)
```

In the following plot, we use a Tukey boxplot to display the distribution of the `Fertility` variable in the `swiss` data set:

```
ggplot(swiss_df,
       mapping = aes(y = Fertility)
) + geom_boxplot()
```

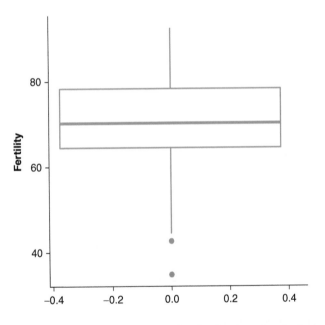

Notice that in this case, where we are displaying the distribution of a single variable only, we only set the y attribute in the `aes` mapping. The boxplot extends along the y-axis, is centred at 0 on the x-axis, and the left and right edges of the box are positioned at $x \approx -0.4$ and $x \approx 0.4$. This default style for a single boxplot can be improved by indicating that the x-axis variable is discrete by setting `x = ''` within the `aes` mapping, and then changing the width of the boxplot:

```
ggplot(swiss_df,
       mapping = aes(x = '', y = Fertility)
) + geom_boxplot(width = 0.25)
```

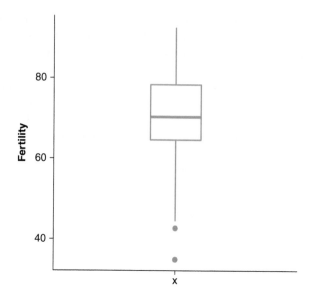

We may convert this vertically extended boxplot to a horizontal one using `coord_flip()`:

```
ggplot(swiss_df,
        mapping = aes(x = '', y = Fertility)
) + geom_boxplot(width = 0.25) +
    coord_flip()
```

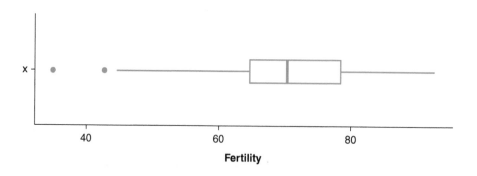

Tukey boxplots are defined as follows:

1. The *box* extends from the 25th to the 75th percentile.
2. The line or band within the box is the median value, which is also the 50th percentile.
3. The *whiskers* extend to the furthest points above the 75th percentile, or below the 25th percentile, that are within 1.5 times the interquartile range (the range from the 25th to the 75th percentile).
4. Any value beyond 1.5 times the interquartile range above the 75th percentile or below the 25th percentile is represented by a point and is classed as an *outlier*.

From a Tukey boxplot, we obtain robust measures both of central tendency, given by the band within the box, and of the scale, given by the width of the box. We may also see whether and to what extent the distribution is skewed, by both the relative position of the band within the box and the relative lengths of the two whiskers. We may also obtain a sense of kurtosis from the Tukey boxplot, which we will describe in more detail below. However, clearly we are not showing all the available data, and visual summaries, however robust and efficient, can always conceal or obscure some important information. It is generally a good idea, therefore, to supplement the boxplot with visualizations of the individual data points. One possibility is to provide a *rug plot*, which displays the location of every data point using a short line, as we see in the following example:

```
ggplot(swiss_df,
       mapping = aes(x = '', y = Fertility)
) + geom_boxplot(width = 0.25) +
   coord_flip() +
   geom_rug(sides ='l')
```

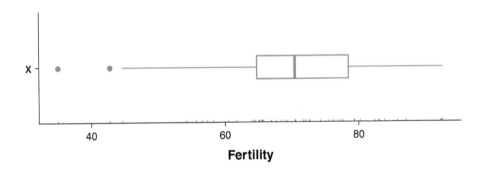

Note that we specify `sides = 'l'` in the `geom_rug` function to indicate that the rug should only be shown on the left axis, which is the bottom when the axis is flipped.

Another option for displaying all the data, which can also be used in combination with the rug plot, is to provide a *jitter* plot as follows:

```
ggplot(swiss_df,
       mapping = aes(x = '', y = Fertility)
) + geom_boxplot(width = 0.25) +
   geom_rug(sides = 'l') +
   geom_jitter() +
   coord_flip()
```

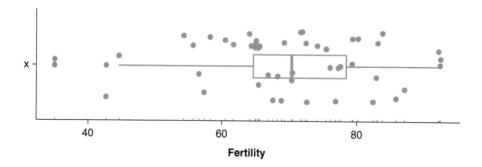

A jitter plot is like a scatterplot but where each point is randomly perturbed, which is useful if points tend to occur in identical or very close locations. The jitter plot just shown, however, may be tidied up by reducing the spread of the points along the vertical axis so that they are within the width of the box on that axis (using the width parameter of the geom_jitter function), and by reducing their size (using the size parameter). In addition, the outlier points no longer need to be displayed because all points will now be displayed by the jitter plot. We now display the outlier points by setting outlier.shape = NA within the geom_boxplot function:

```
ggplot(swiss_df,
       mapping = aes(x = '', y = Fertility)
) + geom_boxplot(width = 0.25, outlier.shape = NA) +
  geom_rug(sides = 'l') +
  geom_jitter(width = 0.1, size = 0.75) +
  coord_flip()
```

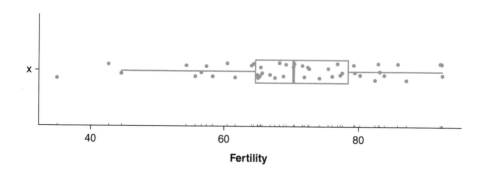

By mapping the x property to a third variable, we may display multiple boxplots side by side:

```
ggplot(swiss_df,
       mapping = aes(x = catholic, y = Fertility)
) + geom_boxplot(width = 0.25, outlier.shape = NA) +
  geom_jitter(width = 0.1, size = 0.75)
```

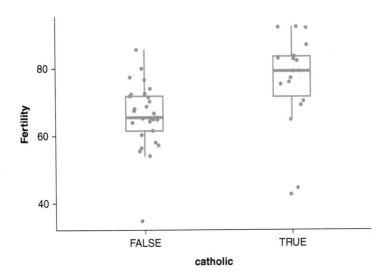

When comparing boxplots, one convention is to scale the width of the box with the square root of the sample size, which we may do by setting varwidth to TRUE. In addition, we may set notch to TRUE to provide a measure of the uncertainty concerning the true value of the median (calculated as 1.58 times the interquartile range divided by the square root of the sample size):

```
ggplot(swiss_df,
       mapping = aes(x = catholic, y = Fertility)
) + geom_boxplot(width = 0.25, outlier.shape = NA, varwidth = T, notch = T) +
   geom_jitter(width = 0.1, size = 0.75)
```

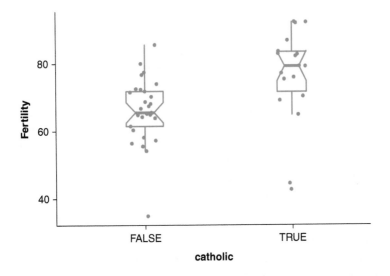

Note, however, that when the median band is close to either the 25th or 75th percentile, the notch may not display properly and so is not generally useful.

It may be helpful to colour-code the different boxplots using `colour` or `fill`, or both. In this case, because the legend will be superfluous (given that the boxplots will be labelled by the x-axis), we may remove the legend by setting `legend.position = 'none'` in the `theme` function:

```
morley %>%
  mutate(Expt = as.factor(Expt)) %>%
  ggplot(
    mapping = aes(x = Expt, y = Speed, fill = Expt)
  ) + geom_boxplot(width = 0.25, outlier.shape = NA, varwidth = T) +
  geom_jitter(aes(colour = Expt), alpha = 0.5, width = 0.1, size = 0.75) +
  theme(legend.position = 'none')
```

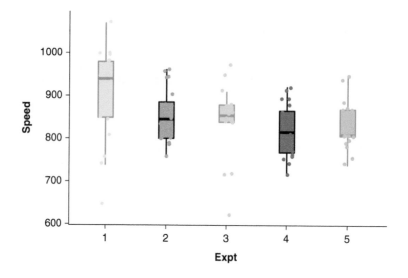

Finally, we may use another variable, other than that used for the x-axis, as the `colour` variable, thus displaying boxplots for each combination of the values of the two grouping variables. For example, in the following plot, using the data set `ToothGrowth`, which is built into R, we display one boxplot for the length (`len`) of tooth growth for each combination of the three levels of a `dose` variable and two different methods of supply `supp`. In this case, if we want to use jitters in addition to the boxplots, we need to position the jitters using `position_jitterdodge`:

```
ToothGrowth %>%
  mutate(dose = as.factor(dose)) %>%
  ggplot(mapping = aes(x = dose, y = len, colour = supp)
  ) + geom_boxplot(outlier.shape = NA, varwidth = T) +
  geom_jitter(position = position_jitterdodge(0.5), size = 0.75)
```

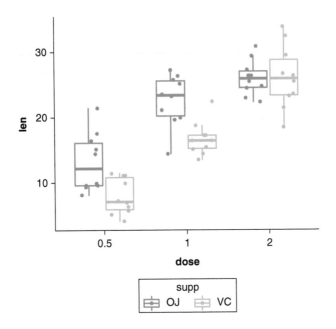

4.5 Scatterplots

We've already seen some simple scatterplots. Here, we'll provide more in-depth coverage using the `weight_df` data frame. The following code will display a scatterplot of `weight` as a function of `height`:

```
ggplot(weight_df,
       mapping = aes(x=height, y=weight)
) + geom_point()
```

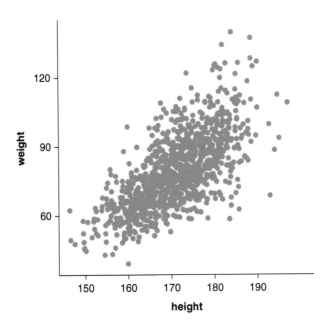

In this example, the values of `height` and `weight` determine the x and y coordinates of the points, respectively. Other attributes of the points, like their shape and size, are not determined by the data, and so are set to their default values, which in this case corresponds to filled dots of unit size. In general, however, we change those attributes that are not determined by the data from their default values by specifying `size`, `shape`, etc., values within the geoms. For example, we change the previous plots to have points that are 0.5 the size of the original and are triangles as follows:

```
ggplot(weight_df,
        mapping = aes(x=height, y=weight)
) + geom_point(size = 0.5, shape='triangle')
```

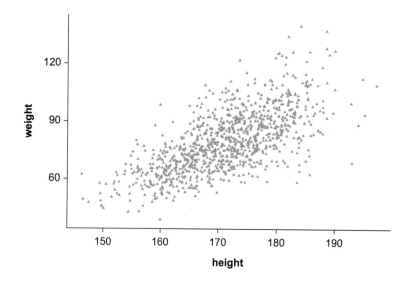

As in histograms, density plots, barplots, etc., scatterplots can also have the colour of the points determined by another variable. In the following example, we colour-code the points according to whether the observation corresponds to a male or a female:

```
ggplot(weight_df,
        mapping = aes(x=height, y=weight, colour = gender)
) + geom_point(size = 0.5)
```

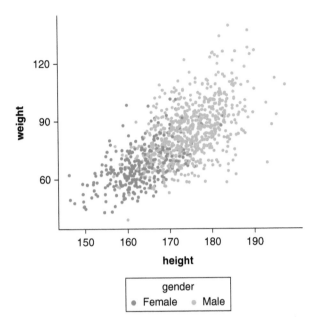

Adding marginal distributions

Scatterplots display pairs of values as points in two-dimensional space. It is often also useful to simultaneously see the distribution of the values over the individual variables. There are a few different options to do so. A common choice is to use a rug plot, as we saw above in the case of boxplots, which displays values on each dimension as short lines. In the following example, we'll change the `alpha` transparency value and the line width (using `size`) to make the rug plot less cluttered:

```
ggplot(weight_df,
       mapping = aes(x=height, y=weight, colour=gender)
) +
  geom_point(size = 0.5) +
  geom_rug(alpha = 0.5, size = 1/10)
```

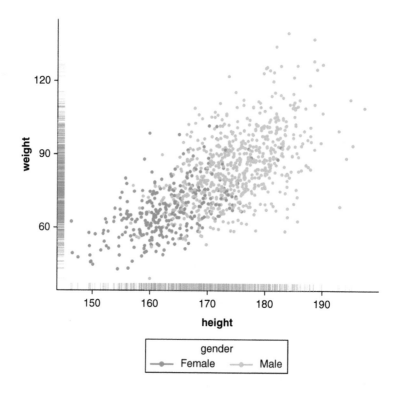

A wider set of options for marginal distributions in scatterplots is available with the `ggMarginal` function that is part of the `ggExtra` package:

```
library("ggExtra")
```

To use `ggMarginal`, we need to first assign the plot object to a named variable such as `p`:

```
p <- ggplot(weight_df,
       mapping = aes(x=height, y=weight, colour=gender)
) + geom_point(size = 0.5)
```

Notice that in this case nothing is displayed. The `ggplot` function creates the scatterplot as before, but assigns it to `p` rather than displaying it. We may now display the scatterplot with its marginal distributions as follows:

```
ggMarginal(p)
```

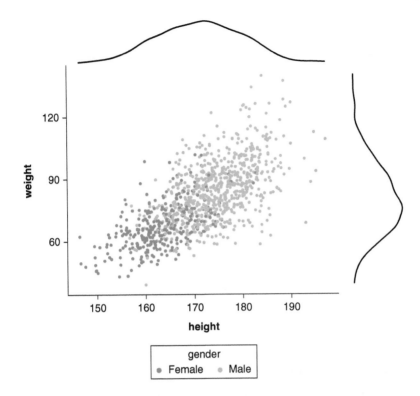

As can be seen, by default, density functions for the `height` and `weight` variables are displayed along the top and right sides, respectively. In addition, by default, the grouping colour is not shown. We can override these defaults. For example, to produce a marginal histogram, rather than a density plot, that uses the `aes` colour mapping, we may do the following:

```
ggMarginal(p, type = 'histogram', groupColour = T, groupFill = T,
           position = 'identity', alpha = 0.5)
```

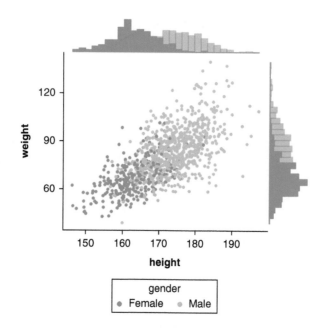

Adding a smoothing function

A *loess* (locally estimated scatterplot smoothing) smoother aims to capture the trends in a scatterplot by fitting a locally weighted regression function, usually a low-degree polynomial, at evenly spaced values along the range of values of the predictor or explanatory variable. Its local weighting feature weights data points closer to the central point more than those further away. The loess smoother is the default smoother for use with scatterplots and can be obtained using geom_smooth().

In the following plot, we display a scatterplot of the fertility rate against the Examination score of each province:

```
ggplot(swiss_df,
       mapping = aes(x = Examination, y = Fertility)
) + geom_point() + geom_smooth()
```

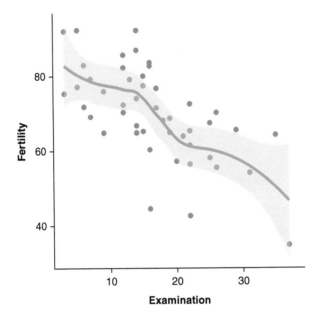

By default, the loess smoother uses 80 evenly spaced points in the range of the predictor variable, and uses a linear regression at each point. We can change the number of evaluation points and the regression function to be used by specifying the value of n and `formula`, respectively, in `geom_smooth`. For example, in the following example, we evaluate the linear regression at five points:

```
ggplot(swiss_df,
        mapping = aes(x = Examination, y = Fertility)
) + geom_point() + geom_smooth(n = 5, formula = y ~ x)
```

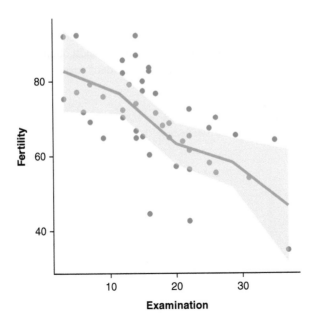

We can produce a linear fit to the scatterplot by setting method = 'lm' in geom_smooth() as in the following plot:

```
ggplot(swiss_df,
        mapping = aes(x = Examination, y = Fertility)
) + geom_point() + geom_smooth(method = 'lm')
```

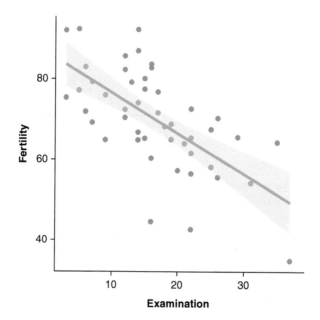

This will display the least squares line of best fit that we would obtain from a standard linear regression analysis. Note that we may turn off the standard error shading by setting se = F:

```
ggplot(swiss_df,
        mapping = aes(x = Examination, y = Fertility)
) + geom_point() + geom_smooth(method = 'lm', se = F)
```

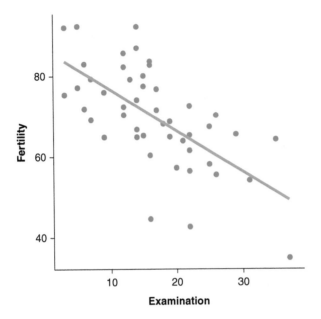

If we map `colour` to `catholic`, as we've seen, each point will colour-code whether the corresponding province is Catholic or Protestant:

```
ggplot(swiss_df,
        mapping = aes(x = Examination, y = Fertility, colour = catholic)
) + geom_point()
```

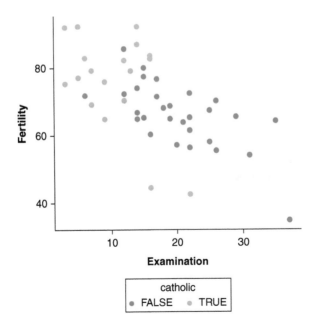

If, in addition, we were to add a smoothing curve or line of best fit, we would produce one for each of the two sets of points defined by the `catholic` variable:

```
ggplot(swiss_df,
       mapping = aes(x = Examination, y = Fertility, colour = catholic)
) + geom_point() + geom_smooth(method = 'lm', se = F)
```

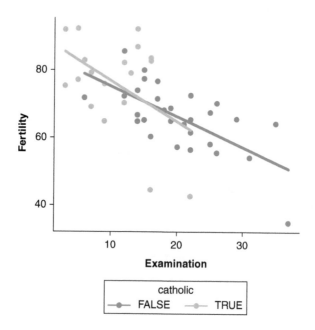

As can be seen, each line extends only over the range of its subset of points. However, we extend each line to full range of values by setting `fullrange` to `TRUE`:

```
ggplot(swiss_df,
       mapping = aes(x = Examination, y = Fertility, colour = catholic)
) + geom_point() + geom_smooth(method = 'lm', se = F, fullrange = T)
```

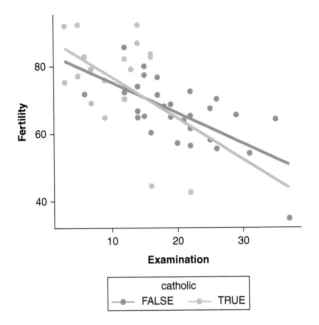

It may be that we would prefer to have a single line of best fit to all the points in the scatterplot while still keeping the points colour-coded by a third variable. To do so, we need to restrict the `colour = catholic` aesthetic mapping to `geom_point()` as in the following example. As can be seen, each line extends only over the range of its subset of points. However, we extend each line to the full range of values by setting `fullrange` to TRUE:

```
ggplot(swiss_df,
       mapping = aes(x = Examination, y = Fertility)
) + geom_point(mapping = aes(colour = catholic)) +
  geom_smooth(method = 'lm', se = F, fullrange = T)
```

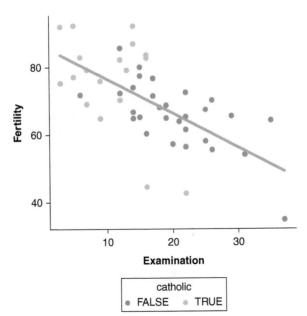

In the above example, both `geom_point` and `geom_smooth` inherited the global `aes` mapping. Then `geom_point` added the additional mapping of `colour = catholic`.

Adding labels

We may use labels instead of, or in addition to, points in the scatterplot by setting the `label` mapping and using `geom_text`:

```
swiss_df %>%
ggplot(
        mapping = aes(x = Examination, y = Fertility, label = province, colour = catholic)
) + geom_point(size = 0.5) +
    geom_text(size = 2)
```

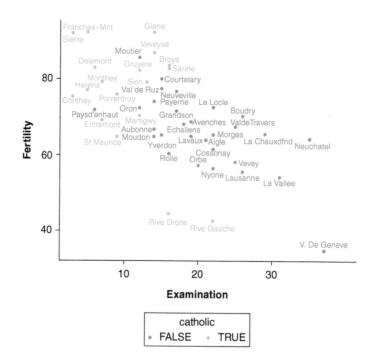

In some cases, some labels overlap one another, and in all cases, the labels lie over the points. Using the `geom_text_repel` from the `ggrepel` package in place of `geom_text` can overcome, or at least minimize, some of these problems:

```
library(ggrepel)
```

```
swiss_df %>%
ggplot(
        mapping = aes(x = Examination, y = Fertility, label = province, colour = catholic)
) + geom_point(size = 0.5) +
    geom_text_repel(size = 2, segment.alpha = 0.5)
```

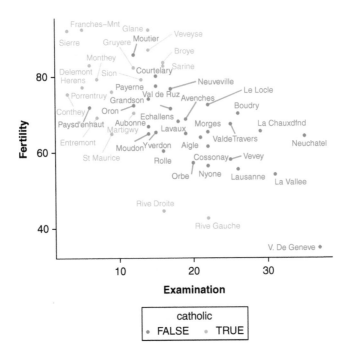

For scatterplots with a relatively large number of points, labelling all points may lead more to clutter than to clarity. However, if we are selective as to which plots we label, then this may be very useful to draw attention to certain points, as in the following example, where we only label those provinces where fertility rates were very high or very low:

```
swiss_df %>%
  mutate(extreme = ifelse(Fertility < 50 | Fertility > 90, province, '')) %>%
ggplot(
      mapping = aes(x = Examination, y = Fertility, label = extreme,
      colour = catholic)
) + geom_point(size = 0.5) +
    geom_text_repel(size = 2)
```

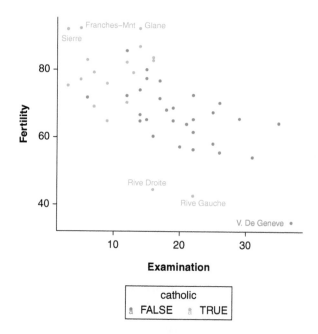

As an alternative to geom_text or geom_text_repel, we could use geom_label or geom_label_repel:

```
swiss_df %>%
  mutate(extreme = ifelse(Fertility < 50 | Fertility > 90, province, '')) %>%
  ggplot(mapping = aes(x = Examination, y = Fertility, label = extreme, colour
= catholic)
         ) +
  geom_point(size = 0.5) +
  geom_label_repel(size = 2)
```

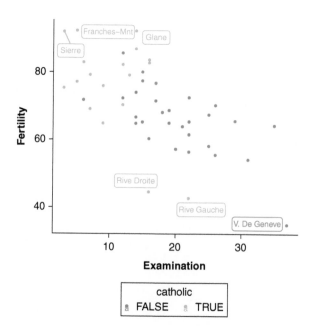

Bubbleplots

Bubbleplots are scatterplots where the size of the point is determined by the value of a third variable. In the following, using the `midwest` data set from `ggplot2`, we plot the percentage of professional workers against the percentage of university-educated people in different counties in the US Mid West. We then scale the size of the point with the population:

```
midwest %>%
    ggplot(mapping = aes(x = percollege, y = percprof, size = poptotal)
        ) +
    geom_point(alpha = 0.5)
```

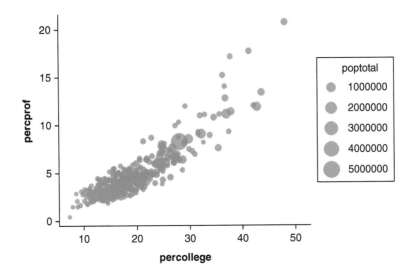

While any continuous variable could be mapped to `size`, because larger 'bubbles' visually imply that the observation to which the point corresponds is also larger in some physical sense, it is perhaps generally advisable that `size` should map to a variable describing size in some sense, such as population or area.

 Facet plots

Facet plots allow us to produce multiple related subplots, where each subplot displays some subset of the data. As an example, in the following we plot the barplot of survival or not by both passenger class and by the sex of the passenger on the *Titanic*:

```
ggplot(titanic_df,
        mapping = aes(x = passengerClass, fill = survived)
    ) + geom_bar(position = 'dodge') +
    facet_wrap(~sex)
```

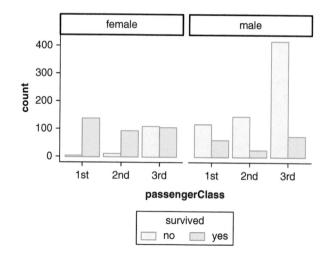

In this case, we simply added `facet_wrap(~sex)` as an additional statement at the end of the plot that produced the barplot of survival rates by passenger class.

In cases where there are multiple subplots, `facet_wrap` will *wrap* the subplots. For example, in the following plot we produce one scatterplot with line of best fit for each of 18 subjects in an experiment. This data, available in `sleepstudy.csv`, was originally derived from a data set in the package `lme4`:

```
sleepstudy_df <- read_csv("data/sleepstudy.csv")

ggplot(sleepstudy_df,
          mapping = aes(x = Days, y = Reaction, colour = Subject)
) + geom_point() +
   geom_smooth(method = 'lm', se = F) +
   facet_wrap(~Subject) +
   theme_minimal() +
   theme(legend.position = 'none')
```

With `facet_wrap`, we may use `nrow` to specify the number of rows to use:

```
ggplot(sleepstudy_df,
          mapping = aes(x = Days, y = Reaction, colour = Subject)
) + geom_point() +
   geom_smooth(method = 'lm', se = F) +
   facet_wrap(~Subject, nrow = 3) +
   theme_minimal() +
   theme(legend.position = 'none')
```

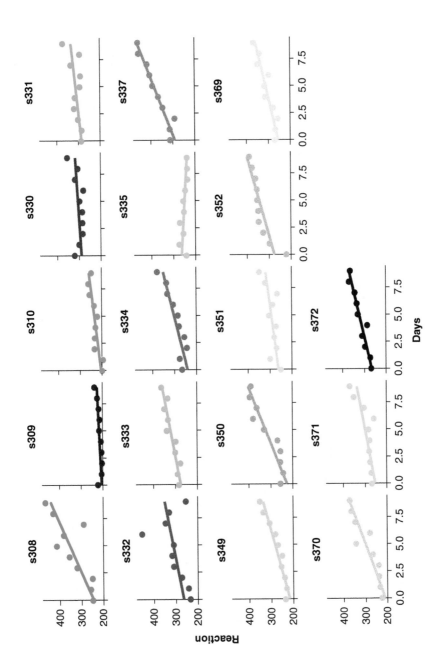

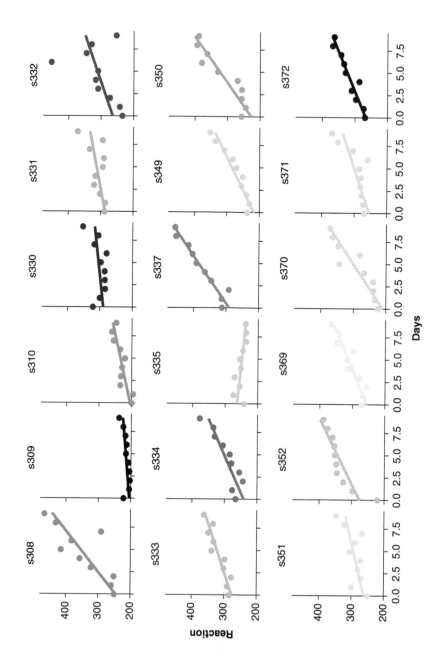

We may facet by two, or more, discrete variables simultaneously using `facet_grid`, which will produce a grid with the columns signifying the values of one of the faceting variables and the rows signifying the other. In the following example, we show histograms of weight for males and females who are either young (defined as below the median age) or not, and in one of two different racial categories:

```
weight_df %>%
    filter(race %in% c(1, 2)) %>%
    mutate(young = age < median(age),
           race = as.factor(race)) %>%
    ggplot(mapping = aes(x = weight, fill = gender)) +
    geom_histogram(binwidth = 10, position = 'dodge', alpha = 0.75) +
    facet_grid(young ~ race, labeller = label_both)
```

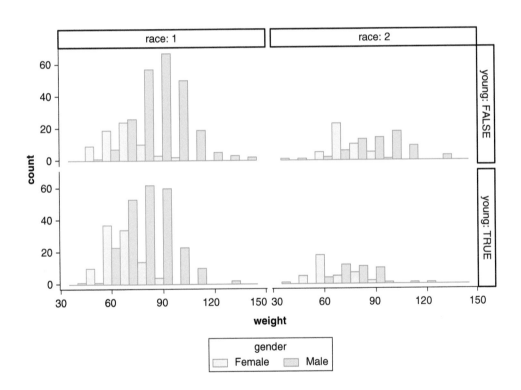

5

Exploratory Data Analysis

Introduction

In his famous book *Exploratory Data Analysis*, John Tukey (1977) describes exploratory data analysis as detective work. He likens data analysts to police investigators who look for and meticulously collect vital evidence from a crime scene. By contrast, he describes the task undertaken within the courts system of making a prosecution case and evaluating evidence for or against the case as analogous to confirmatory data analysis. In confirmatory data analysis, we propose models of the data and then evaluate these models. This is almost always the ultimate goal of data analysis, but just as good detective work is necessary for the successful operation of the judicial system, so exploratory data analysis is a vital first step prior to confirmatory data analysis and data modelling generally. As Tukey (1977, p. v) puts it: 'It is important to understand what you can do before you learn to measure how well you seem to have done it.' Similar perspectives are to be found in Hartwig and Dearing (1979, p. 9) who argue that the more we understand our data, the 'more effectively data can be used to develop, test, and refine theory'.

In this book we are wholly committed to the idea that probabilistic modelling is the ultimate goal and even the *raison d'être* of data analysis. Part II is devoted to covering this topic in depth. However, and in line with the advice of Tukey (1977), Hartwig and Dearing (1979), and others, this probabilistic modelling can only be done thoroughly and well if we understand our data. In particular, understanding the data allows us to select suitable and customized models for the data, rather than naively choosing familiar off-the-shelf models that may be either limited or inappropriate.

 Univariate data

In this chapter, we describe quantitative and graphical methods for exploratory data analysis by focusing on *univariate data*. Univariate data is data concerning a single variable. For example, if we record the estimated market value of each house in a sample of houses and record nothing other than this value, then our data set would be a univariate one. Put like this, it is rare indeed for real-world data sets to be truly univariate. In any data set, however small, we almost always have values concerning more than one variable. Nonetheless, understanding univariate data has a fundamental role in data analysis. First of all, even when we do have data concerning dozens or even hundreds of variables, we often need to understand individual variables in isolation. In other words, we often first explore or analyse our many variables individually before examining the possible relationships between them. More important, however, is that often our ultimate goal when analysing data is to perform *conditionally univariate* analyses. In other words, we are often interested in understanding how the distribution of one variable changes given, or conditioned upon, the values of one or many other variables. For example, to use our house price example, we may be ultimately interested in understanding house prices, and all the other variables that we collect (when the house was first built, how many bedrooms it has, where it is located, whether it is detached, semi-detached or terraced, etc.), are used to understand how the distribution of prices varies. Conditionally univariate analysis of this kind is, in fact, what is being done in all regression analyses that consider a single outcome variable at a time. This encompasses virtually all the well-known types of regression analyses, whether based on linear, generalized linear, or multi-level models. Almost all of the many examples of regression analyses that we consider in Part II of this book are examples of this kind. Conditionally univariate analysis is also a major part of exploratory data analysis: we are often interested in exploring, whether by visualizations or using summary statistics, how one variable is distributed when other variables are held constant. In fact, many cases of what we might term 'bivariate' or 'multivariate' exploratory analysis may be more accurately described as conditionally univariate exploratory analyses.

Types of univariate data

In a famous paper, Stevens (1946) defined four (univariate) data types that are characterized by whether their so-called *level of measurement* is *nominal, ordinal, interval,* or *ratio*. Roughly speaking, according to this account, nominal data consists of values that are names or labels. Ordinal data consists of values that have some natural ordering or rank. The interval and ratio data types are types of continuous variables. Ratio are distinguished from interval scales by whether they have a non-arbitrary, or true, zero or not, respectively. Although this typology is still seen as definitive in psychology and some other social science fields, it is not one that we will use here because is not widely endorsed, or even widely known, in statistics and data analysis generally. In fact, almost since its inception, it has been criticized as overly strict, limited, and likely to lead to poor data analysis practice (see, for example, Velleman and Wilkinson, 1993, and references therein). In general, in statistics and data science, there is no single definitive taxonomy of data types. Different, though often related, categorizations abound, with each one having finer or coarser data type distinctions. Nonetheless, it is worthwhile to make these typological distinctions because different types of data are often best described, visualized, and eventually statistically modelled using different approaches and techniques. For example, when and why to use the different types of regression analyses described in Part II of this book are often based solely on what type of data we are trying to model. The following data types are based on distinctions that are very widely or almost universally held. In each case, however, their definitions are rather informal, and whether any given data is best classified as one type or another is not always clear or uncontroversial.

Continuous data *Continuous data* represents the values or observations of variable that can take any value in a continuous metric space such as the real line or some interval thereof. Informally speaking, we'll say that a variable is continuous if its values can be ordered, and that between any two values there exists another value and hence an infinite number of other values. A person's height, weight, or even age are usually taken to be continuous variables, as are variables like speed, time, and distance. All these examples take only positive values, but others like a bank account's balance or temperature (on the Celsius or Fahrenheit scale, for example) can also take negative values. Another important subtype of the continuous variables are proportions, percentages, and probabilities. These exist strictly on the interval of the real line between 0 and 1. In their data typology, Mosteller and Tukey (1977) consider these as part of a special data type in itself, but here, we'll just treat them as a subtype of the continuous data variables.

Categorical data *Categorical data* is where each value takes one of a (usually, but not necessarily) finite number of values that are categorically distinct and so are not ordered, and do not exist as points on some interval or metric space. Examples include a person's nationality, country of residence, and occupation. Likewise, subjects or participants in an experiment or study are assigned categorically distinct identifiers, and could be assigned to categorically distinct experimental conditions, such as a control group or treatment group. Values of categorical variables cannot naturally or uncontroversially be placed in order, nor is there is any natural or uncontroversial sense of distance between them. The values of a categorical variable are usually names or labels, and hence *nominal data* is another widely used term for categorical data. A categorical variable that can only take one of two possible values (control versus treatment, correct versus incorrect, etc.) is usually referred to simply as a 'binary' or 'dichotomous' variable. Categorical variables taking on more than two variables are sometimes called 'polychotomous'.

Ordinal data *Ordinal data* represents values of a variable that can be ordered but have no natural or uncontroversial sense of distance between them. First, second, third, and so on, are values with a natural order, but there is no general sense of distance between them. For example, knowing that three students scored in first, second and third place, respectively, on an exam tells us nothing about how far apart their scores were. All we generally know is that the student who came first had a higher score than the student who came second, who had a higher score than the student who came third. Ordinal variables may be represented by numbers: for example, first, second and third place could be represented by the numbers 1, 2 and 3. These numbers have a natural order (i.e. $1 < 2 < 3$) but do not exist in metric space.

Count data *Count data* is tallies of the number of times something has happened or some value of a variable has occurred. The number of cars stopped at a traffic light, the number of people in a building, the number of questions answered correctly in an exam, are all counts. In each case, the values take non-negative integer values. In general, they have a lower bound of zero, but do not necessarily have an upper bound. In some cases, like the number of questions answered correctly on an exam with 100 questions, there is also an upper bound. In other cases, like the number of shark attacks at Bondi Beach in any given year, there is no defined upper value. The values of a count variable are obviously ordered, but also have a true sense of distance. For example, a score of 87 correct answers on an exam is as far from a score of 90 as a score of 97 is from 100.

Characterizing univariate distributions

We can describe any univariate distribution in terms of three major features: *location, spread,* and *shape*. We will explore each of these in detail below through examples, but they can be defined roughly as follows:

Location The *location* or *central tendency* of a distribution describes, in general, where the mass of the distribution is located on an interval or along a range of possible values. More specifically, it describes the typical or central values that characterize the distribution. Adding a constant to all values of a distribution will change the location of the distribution, by essentially shifting the distribution rigidly to left or to the right.

Dispersion The *dispersion, scale,* or *spread* of a distribution tells us how dispersed or spread out the distribution is. It tells us roughly how much variation there is in the distribution's values, or how far apart the values are from one another on average.

Shape The shape of a distribution is roughly anything that is described by neither the location nor spread. Two of the most important shape characteristics are *skewness* and *kurtosis*. Skewness tells us how much asymmetry there is in the distribution. A left or negative skew means that the tail on the left (that which points in the negative direction) is longer than that on the right, and this entails that the centre of mass is more to the right and in the positive direction. Right or positive skew is defined by a long tail to the right, or in the positive direction, and hence the distribution is more massed to the left. Kurtosis is a measure of how much mass is in the centre versus the tails of the distribution.

 ## Measures of central tendency

Let us assume that we have a sample of n univariate values denoted by $x_1, x_2, \ldots, x_i, \ldots, x_n$. Three commonly used measures of central tendency, at least in introductory approaches to statistics, are the arithmetic mean, the median, and the mode. Let us examine each in turn.

Arithmetic mean

The arithmetic mean, or usually known as simply *the mean*, is defined as follows:

$$\bar{x} = \frac{1}{n} \sum_{i=1}^{n} x_i.$$

It can be seen as the centre of gravity of the set of values in the sample. This is not simply a metaphor to guide our intuition. For example, if we had n point masses, each of equal mass, positioned at points $\omega_1, \omega_2, \ldots, \omega_n$ along some linear continuum, then $\Omega = \frac{1}{n} \sum_{i=1}^{n} \omega_i$ is their centre of gravity.

The arithmetic mean is also the finite-sample counterpart of the *mathematical expectation* or *expected value* of a random variable. If X is a continuous random variable with probability distribution P(X), then the expected value of X is defined as

$$\langle X \rangle = \int_{-\infty}^{\infty} x P(X = x) \, dx.$$

On the other hand, if X takes on K discrete values, then its expected value is

$$\langle X \rangle = \sum_{k=1}^{K} x_k P(X = x_k).$$

A finite sample of points $x_1, x_2, \ldots, x_i, \ldots, x_n$ can be represented as a discrete probability distribution of a random variable X with a finite number of values such that $P(X = x_i) = 1/n$. Therefore,

$$\langle X \rangle = \sum_{i=1}^{n} x_i P(X = x_i) = \frac{1}{n} \sum_{i=1}^{n} x_i = \bar{x}.$$

As we will discuss in more detail below, the mean is highly sensitive to outliers, which we will define for now as simply highly atypical values. As an example, consider the following human reaction time (in milliseconds) data:

```
rt_data <- c(567, 1823,  517,  583,  317,  367,  250,  503,
             317,  567,  583,  517,  650,  567,  450,  350)
```

The mean of this data is

```
mean(rt_data)
#> [1] 558
```

This value is depicted by the red dot in Figure 5.1. However, here there is an undue influence of the relatively high second value. If we remove this value, the mean becomes much lower:

```
rt_data[-2] %>% mean()
#> [1] 473.6667
```

This new mean is shown by the large, pale red dot in Figure 5.1.

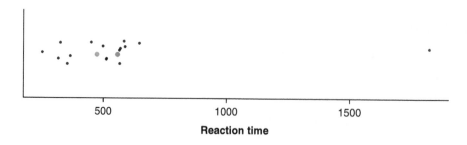

Figure 5.1 The red dot shows the mean value of the set of points in black. In this case, there is an undue influence of the one relatively large value. The dark red dot displays the mean of the sample after that one large value is removed

Median

The median of a finite sample is defined as the middle point in the sorted list of its values. If there is an odd number of values, there is exactly one point in the middle of the sorted list of values. If there is an even number of values, there are two points in the middle of the sorted list. In this case, the median is the arithmetic mean of these two points. In the rt_data data set, the median is as follows:

```
median(rt_data)
#> [1] 517
```

The sample median just defined is the finite-sample counterpart of the median of a random variable. Again, if X is a random variable with probability distribution $P(X)$, then its median is defined as the value m that satisfies

$$\int_{-\infty}^{m} P(X=x)\,dx = \frac{1}{2}.$$

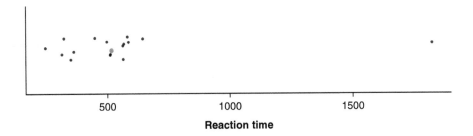

Reaction time

Figure 5.2 The red dot shows the median value of the set of points in black. In this case, unlike with the mean, there is no undue influence of the one relatively large value

Unlike the mean, the median is robust to outliers. In Figure 5.2, we see how the median is not unduly influenced by the presence of the one extreme value. In fact, if this point were removed, the median would be unaffected.

Mode

The sample mode is the value with the highest frequency. When dealing with random variables, the mode is clearly defined as the value that has the highest probability mass or density. For example, if X is a continuous variable, then the mode is given as follows:

$$\text{mode} = \underset{x}{\text{argmax}}\, P(X = x),$$

which is the value of x for which the density $P(X = x)$ is at its maximum. For a discrete variable, the mode is similarly defined:

$$\text{mode} = \underset{x_k}{\text{argmax}}\, P(X = x_k).$$

While the mode is clearly defined for random variables, for finite samples it is in fact not a simple matter. For example, using our `rt_data` data above, we can calculate the frequency of occurrence of all values as follows:

```
table(rt_data)
#> rt_data
#>  250  317  350  367  450  503  517  567  583  650 1823
#>    1    2    1    1    1    1    2    3    2    1    1
```

Clearly, in this case, most values occur exactly once. We can identify the value that occurs most often as follows:

```
which.max(table(rt_data)) %>% names()
#> [1] "567"
```

In practice, it often occurs that all values in the data set occur exactly once. This is especially the case when values can be anything in a wide range of values. In these cases, there is essentially no mode, or the mode can be said to be undefined. One strategy to deal with these situations is to bin the data first. To illustrate this, let us sample 10,000 values from a normal distribution with a mean of 100 and standard deviation of 50:

```
N <- 10000
x <- rnorm(N, mean = 100, sd = 50)
```

We know that the mode of this normal distribution is 100. However, because the values generated by rnorm are specified with many decimal digits, we are astronomically unlikely to get any more than one occurrence per each unique value. We can confirm this easily:

```
length(unique(x)) == N
#> [1] TRUE
```

One possibility in this case would be to bin these values into, say, 50 equal-sized bins, and then find the middle value of the bin with the highest frequency. We may do this using the hist function. This is usually used for plotting, but also can return counts of values that are binned, and we can suppress the plot with plot = F:

```
H <- hist(x, 50, plot=F)
```

We can use which.max applied to the counts property of the object that hist returns. This will give us the index of the bin with the highest frequency, and then we can use the mids property to get the mid-point of that bin. We can put this in a function as follows:

```
sample_mode <- function(x, n_bins=10){
  h <- hist(x, breaks = n_bins, plot = F)
  h$mids[which.max(h$counts)]
}

sample_mode(x)
#> [1] 75
sample_mode(x, n_bins = 50)
#> [1] 95
sample_mode(x, n_bins = 100)
#> [1] 97.5
```

Robust measures of central tendency

We've seen that the mean is unduly influenced by outliers. More technically, the mean has a low *breakdown* point. The breakdown point of a statistic is the proportion of values in a sample that can be arbitrarily large before the statistic becomes arbitrarily large. The mean has a breakdown point of zero. By making just one value arbitrarily large, the mean becomes arbitrarily large. By contrast, the median has a very high breakdown point. In fact up to 50% of the values of a sample can be arbitrarily large before the median becomes arbitrarily large.

The median, therefore, is said to be a very robust statistic, and the mean is a particularly unrobust statistic.

There are versions of the standard arithmetic mean that are specifically designed to be robust. The *trimmed mean* removes a certain percentage of values from each extreme of the distribution before calculating the mean as normal. The following code, for example, removes 10% of values from the high and low extremes of rt_data:

```
mean(rt_data, trim = 0.10)
#> [1] 489.6429
```

The trimmed mean can be calculated using the following function:

```
trimmed_mean <- function(x, trim = 0.1){
  n <- length(x)
  lo <- floor(n * trim) + 1
  hi <- n + 1 - lo
  sort(x)[lo:hi] %>%
    mean()
}
```

Thus, we see that in the case of rt_data, where $n = 16$, the trimmed mean is based on elements 2 to 15 of rt_data when it is sorted.

A particular type of trimmed mean is the *interquartile mean*. This is where the bottom and top quartiles are discarded, and the mean is based on the remaining elements:

```
iqr_mean <- function(x){
  q1 <- quantile(x, probs = 0.25)
  q3 <- quantile(x, probs = 0.75)
  x[x > q1 & x < q3] %>%
    mean()
}
```

```
iqr_mean(rt_data)
#> [1] 506.875
```

An alternative to the trimmed mean, which discards elements, is the *winsorized mean,* which replaces values at the extremes of the distributions with values at the thresholds of these extremes. For example, we could replace elements below the 10th percentile by the value of the 10th percentile, and likewise replace elements above the 90th percentile by the value of the 90th percentile. The following code implements a winsorized mean function:

```
winsorized_mean <- function(x, trim = 0.1){
  low <- quantile(x, probs = trim) #
  high <- quantile(x, probs = 1 - trim)
  x[x < low] <- low
  x[x > high] <- high
```

```
   mean (x)
}
```

```
winsorized_mean(rt_data, trim = 0.1)
#> [1] 484.6875
```

Another robust measure of central tendency is the *midhinge*, which is the centre point between the first and third quartiles. This is equivalent to the arithmetic mean of these two values:

```
midhinge <- function(x){
   quantile(x, probs = c(0.25, 0.75)) %>%
      mean ()
}
```

```
midhinge(rt_data)
#> [1] 466.875
```

The midhinge is a more robust measure of the central tendency than the *midrange*, which is the centre of the full range of the distribution and so equivalent to the arithmetic mean of its minimum and the maximum values:

```
midrange <- function(x){
   range(x) %>% mean ()
}
```

```
midrange(rt_data)
#> [1] 1036.5
```

A related robust measure is the *trimean*, which is defined as the average of the median and the midhinge. Given that the midhinge is

$$\text{midhinge} = \frac{Q_1 + Q_3}{2},$$

where Q_1 and Q_3 are the first and third quartiles, the *trimean* is defined as

$$\text{trimean} = \frac{Q_2 + (Q_1 + Q_3)/2}{2} = \frac{Q_1 + 2Q_2 + Q_3}{4}.$$

As such, we can see the trimean as a weighted average of the first, second, and third quartiles:

```
trimean <- function(x){
   c(midhinge(x), median(x)) %>%
      mean ()
}
```

```
trimean(rt_data)
#> [1] 491.9375
```

Measures of dispersion

Variance and standard deviation

Just as the mean is usually the default choice, for good or ill, as a measure of central tendency, the standard measure of the dispersion of distribution is the *variance* or *standard deviation*. These two measures should be seen as essentially one measure, given that the standard deviation is simply the square root of the variance.

For a continuous random variable X the variance is defined as

$$\text{variance} = \int (x-\bar{x})^2\, P(X=x)\,dx,$$

while for a discrete random variable X it is defined as

$$\text{variance} = \sum_{k=1}^{K}(x_k-\bar{x})^2\, P(X=x_k).$$

From this, we can see that the variance of a random variable is defined as the expected value of the squared difference of values from the mean. In other words, we could state the variance as follows:

$$\text{variance} = \langle d^2 \rangle, \quad \text{where } d = x - \bar{x}.$$

As we saw in the case of the mean, a finite sample of values $x_1, x_2, ..., x_n$ can be seen as a discrete probability distribution defined at points $x_1, x_2, ..., x_n$ and each with probability $1/n$. From this, for a finite sample, the variance is defined as

$$\text{variance} = \sum_{i=1}^{n}(x_i-\bar{x})^2\, P(X=x_i) = \sum_{i=1}^{n}(x_i-\bar{x})^2\, \frac{1}{n} = \frac{1}{n}\sum_{i=1}^{n}(x_i-\bar{x})^2.$$

This is exactly the mean of the squared differences from the mean. Though R has a built-in function for the sample variance, as we will soon see, the sample variance as we have just defined it can be calculated with the following function:

```
variance <- function(x) {
  mean((x - mean(x))^2)
}
```

One issue with the sample variance as just defined is that it is a *biased* estimator of the variance of the probability distribution of which $x_1, x_2, ..., x_n$ are assumed to be a sample. An unbiased estimator of the population's variance is defined as follows:

$$\text{variance} = \frac{1}{n-1}\sum_{i=1}^{n}(x_i-\bar{x})^2.$$

This is what is calculated by R's built-in variance function var. Applied to our rt_data data, the variance is

```
var(rt_data)
#> [1] 127933.6
```

The standard deviation is the square root of this number, which is calculated by R's `sd` function, as we see in the following code:

```
var(rt_data) %>% sqrt()
#> [1] 357.6781
sd(rt_data)
#> [1] 357.6781
```

Given that the variance is exactly, or close to exactly, the average of the squared distances of the values from the mean, to intuitively understand the value of a variance we must think in terms of squared distances from the mean. Because the standard deviation is the square root of the variance, its value will be approximately the average distance of all points from the mean. For this reason, the standard deviation may be easier to intuitively understand than the variance. In addition, the standard deviation affords some valuable rules of thumb to understand the distribution of the values of a variable. For example, for any approximately normally distributed values, approximately 70% of values are within 1 standard deviation from the mean, approximately 95% of values are within 2 standard deviations from the mean, and approximately 99% of values are within 2.5 standard deviations from the mean. For other kinds distributions, these rules of thumb may be over- or underestimates of the distribution of values. However, *Chebyshev's inequality* ensures that no more than $1/k^2$ of the distribution's values will be more than k standard deviations from the mean. And so, even in the most extreme cases, 75% of values will always be within 2 standard deviations from the mean, and approximately 90% of cases will be within 3 standard deviations from the mean.

Trimmed and winsorized estimates of variance and standard deviation

The variance and standard deviation are doubly or triply susceptible to outliers. They are based on the value of the mean, which is itself prone to the influence of outliers. They are based on squared differences from the mean, which will increase the influence of large differences. They are based on a further arithmetic mean operation, which again is unduly influenced by large values.

Just as with the mean, however, we may trim or winsorize the values before calculating the variance or standard deviation The following code creates a function that will trim values from the extremes of a sample, as described previously, before applying a descriptive statistic function. By default, it uses `mean`, but we can replace this with any function:

```
trimmed_descriptive <- function(x, trim = 0.1, descriptive = mean) {
  n <- length(x)
  lo <- floor(n * trim) + 1
  hi <- n + 1 - lo
  sort(x)[lo:hi] %>%
    descriptive()
}
```

```
trimmed_descriptive(rt_data, descriptive = var)
#> [1] 12192.09
trimmed_descriptive(rt_data, descriptive = sd)
#> [1] 110.4178
```

We can also define a winsorizing function that can be used with any descriptive statistic:

```
winsorized_descriptive <- function(x, trim = 0.1, descriptive = mean){
  low <- quantile(x, probs = trim) #
  high <- quantile(x, probs = 1 - trim)
  x[x < low] <- low
  x[x > high] <- high
  descriptive(x)
}
```

```
winsorized_descriptive(rt_data, trim = 0.1, var)
#> [1] 12958.73
winsorized_descriptive(rt_data, trim = 0.1, sd)
#> [1] 113.8364
```

Median absolute deviation

A much more robust alternative to the variance and standard deviation is the *median absolute deviation from the median* (MAD). As the name implies, it is the median of the absolute differences of all values from the median, and so is defined as follows:

$$\text{MAD} = \text{median}(|x_i - m|).$$

We can code this in R as follows:

```
sample_mad <- function(x){
  median(abs(x - median(x)))
}
```

```
sample_mad(rt_data)
#> [1] 66.5
```

The MAD is very straightforward to understand. For example, we know immediately that exactly half of all values are less than the value of the MAD.

In the case of the normal distribution, $\text{MAD} \approx \sigma / 1.48$, where σ is the distribution's standard deviation. Given this, the MAD is often scaled by approximately 1.48 so as to act as a robust estimator of the standard deviation. In R, the built-in command (part of the stats package) for calculating the MAD is mad and this is by default calculated as follows:

$$\text{mad} = 1.4826 \times \text{median}(|x_i - m|).$$

We can verify this in the following code:

```
1.4826 * sample_mad(rt_data)
#> [1] 98.5929
mad(rt_data)
#> [1] 98.5929
```

Note how much lower the MAD is than the sample standard deviation, which is 357.68.

Range estimates of dispersion

By far the simplest measure of the dispersion of a set of values is the *range*, which is the difference between the maximum and minimum values. In R, the command `range` returns the minimum and the maximum values *per se*, rather than their difference, but we can calculate the range easily as in the following example:

```
max(rt_data) - min(rt_data)
#> [1] 1573
```

Although the range is informative, it is also obviously extremely prone to the undue influence of outliers given that is defined in terms of the extremities of the set of values. More robust alternative estimates of the dispersion are based on quantiles. The following function returns the difference between some specified upper and lower quantile value:

```
quantile_range <- function(x, lower, upper){
  quantile(x, probs = c(lower, upper)) %>%
    unname() %>%
    diff()
}
```

Given that the minimum and maximum values of a set of numbers are the 0th and the 100th percentiles, respectively, this function can be used to return the standard defined range, as in the following example:

```
quantile_range(rt_data, lower = 0.0, upper = 1.0)
#> [1] 1573
```

This is obviously the 100% inner range of the values. The 90% inner range of rt_data is as follows:

```
quantile_range(rt_data, lower = 0.05, upper = 0.95)
#> [1] 643
```

The range from the 10th to the 90th percentile, which gives the 80% inner range, is as follows:

```
quantile_range(rt_data, lower = 0.1, upper = 0.9)
#> [1] 299.5
```

This range is known as the *interdecile range*. On the other hand, the range from the 25th to the 75th percentile, which gives the 50% inner range, is as follows:

```
quantile_range(rt_data, lower = 0.25, upper = 0.75)
#> [1] 208.25
```

This range is known as the *interquartile range* (IQR), which can also be calculated using the built-in IQR command in R:

```
IQR(rt_data)
#> [1] 208.25
```

Just as with MAD, in normal distributions, there is a constant relationship between the IQR and the standard deviation. Specifically, IQR ≈ 1.349σ, and so IQR/1.349 is a robust estimator of the standard deviation:

```
IQR(rt_data) / 1.349
#> [1] 154.3736
```

 Measure of skewness

Skewness is a measure of the asymmetry of a distribution of numbers. For a random variable X, the skewness is the *third standardized moment* defined as follows:

$$\text{skew} = \frac{\left\langle (X-\mu)^3 \right\rangle}{\left\langle (X-\mu)^2 \right\rangle^{3/2}} = \frac{\left\langle (X-\mu)^3 \right\rangle}{\sigma^3}.$$

The numerator is the expected value of the *third central moment*, which is the expected value of the cube of the difference of the variable from the mean,

$$\left\langle (X-\mu)^3 \right\rangle = \int (x-\mu)^3 \, P(X=x) \, dx.$$

The denominator is the cube of the standard deviation, given that the standard deviation σ is the square root of the second central moment $\left\langle (X-\mu)^2 \right\rangle$.

Whenever there is a longer tail to the right of the distribution, the skewness takes a positive value. Thus, *right-skewed* or *right-tailed* distributions have *positive skew*. By contrast, whenever there is a longer tail to the left of the distribution, the skewness takes a positive value, and so *left-skewed* or *left-tailed* distributions have *negative skew*.

In a finite sample of n values, the skewness is calculated as follows:

$$\text{skew} = \frac{\frac{1}{n} \sum_{i=1}^{n} (x_i - \bar{x})^3}{s^3},$$

where x and s are the sample mean and sample standard deviation, respectively. In R, we can implement this function as follows:

```
skewness <- function(x, dof=1){
  xbar <- mean(x)
  s <- sd(x)
  mean((x - xbar)^3)/s^3
}
```

```
skewness(rt_data)
#> [1] 2.66389
```

There is no built-in function for skewness in R. However, the function just defined is also available as `skew` in the `psych` package:

```
psych::skew(rt_data)
#> [1] 2.66389
```

A slight variant is also available as `skewness` in the package `moments`:

```
moments::skewness(rt_data)
#> [1] 2.934671
```

In this version, the standard deviation is calculated based on a denominator of n rather than $n - 1$.

Trimmed and winsorized skewness

The measure of sample skewness just given is highly sensitive to outliers. This is so because it is based on sample means and standard deviations, and also because it involves cubic functions. We can, however, apply this function to trimmed or winsorized samples. We may use the above defined `trimmed_descriptive` and `winsorized_descriptive` with the `skewness` function as in the following example:

```
trimmed_descriptive(rt_data, descriptive = skewness)
#> [1] -0.4105984
winsorized_descriptive(rt_data, descriptive = skewness)
#> [1] -0.4250863
```

Notice how these measures are now both negative and with much lower absolute values.

Quantile skewness

In a symmetric distribution, the median would be in the exact centre of any quantile range. For example, in a symmetric distribution, the median would lie in the centre of the interval between the lower and upper quartiles, and likewise in the centre of the interdecile range and so on. We can use this fact to get a measure of asymmetry. If the median is closer to the lower quantile than the corresponding upper quantile, the distribution is right-tailed and so there is a positive skew. Conversely, if it is closer to the upper quantile than the corresponding lower one, the distribution is left-tailed and there is a negative skew. This leads to the following definition of *quantile skewness*:

$$\text{skew}_Q = \frac{(Q_u - m) - (m - Q_l)}{Q_u - Q_l},$$

where Q_u and Q_l are the upper and lower quantiles, respectively, and m is the median. We can implement this as follows:

```
qskewness <- function(x, p=0.25){
    Q <- quantile(x, probs = c(p, 0.5, 1 - p)) %>%
      unname()
    Q_l <- Q[1]; m <- Q[2]; Q_u <- Q[3]
    ((Q_u - m) - (m - Q_l)) / (Q_u - Q_l)
}
```

```
qskewness(rt_data) # quartile skew
#> [1] -0.4813926
qskewness(rt_data, p = 1/8) # octile skew
#> [1] -0.4578588
qskewness(rt_data, p = 1/10) # decile skew
#> [1] -0.3355593
```

Notice how these values are in line with those the trimmed and winsorized skewness measures.

Nonparametric skewness

The following function is known as the *nonparametric skewness* measure:

$$\text{skew} = \frac{\bar{x} - m}{s},$$

where $\bar{x}$ and s are the sample mean and sample standard deviation as before, and m is the same median. It will always be positive if the mean is to the right of the median, and negative if the mean is to the left of the median, and zero if the mean and median are identical. It is also bounded between -1 and 1, given that the median is always less than 1 standard deviation from the mean. It should be noted, however, that its values do not correspond to those of skewness functions defined above. It is easily implemented as follows:

```
npskew <- function(x){
    (mean(x) - median(x))/sd(x)
}
```

```
npskew(rt_data)
#> [1] 0.1146282
```

Pearson's second skewness coefficient is defined as 3 times the nonparametric skewness measure:

$$\text{skew} = 3\frac{\bar{x} - m}{s}.$$

This can be easily implemented as follows:

```
pearson_skew2 <- function(x){
  3 * npskew(x)
}
```

pearson_skew2(rt_data)
```
#> [1] 0.3438847
```

Like the nonparametric skewness measure, it will be positive if the mean is greater than the median, negative if the mean is less than the median, and zero if they are identical. It will also be bounded between −3 and 3.

Measures of kurtosis

Kurtosis is often described as measuring how *peaky* a distribution is. However, this is a misconception and kurtosis is better understood as relating to the heaviness of a distribution's tails. Westfall (2014) argues that this misconception of kurtosis as pertaining to the nature of a distribution's peak is due to Karl Pearson's suggestions that estimates of kurtosis could be based on whether a distribution is more, less, or equally *flat-topped* compared to a normal distribution. By contrast, Westfall (2014) shows that it is the mass in the tails of the distribution that primarily defines the kurtosis of a distribution.

In a random variable X, kurtosis is defined as the *fourth standardized moment*:

$$\text{kurtosis} = \frac{\langle (X-\mu)^4 \rangle}{\langle (X-\mu)^2 \rangle^2} = \frac{\langle (X-\mu)^4 \rangle}{\sigma^4}.$$

The sample kurtosis is defined analogously as follows:

$$\text{kurtosis} = \frac{\frac{1}{n}\sum_{i=1}^{n}(x_i - \bar{x})^4}{s^4},$$

where $\bar{x}$ and s are the mean and standard deviation. This simplifies to

$$\text{kurtosis} = \frac{1}{n}\sum_{i=1}^{n}z^4,$$

where $z_i = (x_i - \bar{x})/s$. This function can be implemented easily in R as follows:

```
kurtosis <- function(x){
  z <- (x - mean(x))/sd(x)
  mean(z^4)
}
```

kurtosis(rt_data)
```
#> [1] 9.851725
```

This function is also available from `moments::kurtosis`, though in that case the standard deviation is calculated with a denominator of n rather than $n − 1$.

In a normal distribution, the kurtosis, as defined above, has a value of 3. For this reason, it is conventional to subtract 3 from the kurtosis function (i.e. both the population and sample kurtosis functions). This is properly known as *excess kurtosis*, but in some implementations it is not always clearly stated that the excess kurtosis rather than kurtosis *per se* is being calculated. Here, we will explicitly distinguish between these two functions, and so the sample excess kurtosis is defined as follows:

```
excess_kurtosis <- function(x){
  kurtosis(x) - 3
}
```

```
excess_kurtosis(rt_data)
#> [1] 6.851725
```

Let us look at the excess kurtosis of a number of familiar probability distributions. Note that here we are using the `map_dbl` function from `purrr`, which is part of the `tidyverse`. Here, it will apply the excess kurtosis function to each element of `distributions`:

```
N <- 1e4
distributions <- list(normal = rnorm(N),
                      t_10 = rt(N, df = 10),
                      t_7 = rt(N, df = 7),
                      t_5 = rt(N, df = 5),
                      uniform = runif(N)
)
map_dbl(distributions, excess_kurtosis) %>%
  round(digits = 2)
#>  normal    t_10     t_7     t_5 uniform
#>   -0.07    0.90    1.80    2.59   -1.21
```

The function `rnorm` samples from a normal distribution. As we can see, the sample excess kurtosis of the normal samples is close to zero as expected. The function `rt` samples from a Student *t*-distribution. The lower the degrees of freedom, the heavier the tails. Heavy-tailed distributions have additional mass in their tails and less in their centres compared to a normal distribution. As we can see, as the tails get heavier, the corresponding sample kurtosis increases. The `runif` function samples from a uniform distribution. Uniform distributions have essentially no tails; all the mass is in the centre. As we can see, the excess kurtosis of this distribution is negative. Distributions with zero or close to zero excess kurtosis are known as *mesokurtic*. Distributions with positive excess kurtosis are known as *leptokurtic*. Distributions with negative excess kurtosis are known as *platykurtic*.

Given that kurtosis is primarily a measure of the amount of mass in the tails of the distribution relative to the mass in its centre, it is highly sensitive to the values in the extreme of a distribution. Were we to trim or winsorize the tails, as we have done above for the calculation of other descriptive statistics, we would necessarily remove values from the extremes of the sample. This could drastically distort the estimate of the kurtosis. To see this, consider the values of excess kurtosis for the five samples in the `distributions` data set above after we have trimmed and winsorized 10% of values from both extremes of each sample.

```
map_dbl(distributions,
        ~trimmed_descriptive(., descriptive = excess_kurtosis)) %>%
  round(digits = 2)
#>    normal     t_10      t_7      t_5 uniform
#>     -0.96    -0.93    -0.90    -0.88   -1.20
map_dbl(distributions,
        ~winsorized_descriptive(., descriptive = excess_kurtosis)) %>%
  round(digits = 2)
#>    normal     t_10      t_7      t_5 uniform
#>     -1.15    -1.12    -1.09    -1.08   -1.35
```

With the exception of the platykurtic uniform distribution, the estimates of the excess kurtosis of the other distributions have been distorted to such an extent that the mesokurtic and leptokurtic distributions now appear platykurtic.

This raises the question of what exactly is an outlier. Rules of thumb such as that outliers are any values beyond 1.5 times the interquartile range above the third quartile or below the first quartile would necessarily distort leptokurtic distributions if the values meeting this definition were removed. The presence of values beyond these limits may not indicate anomalous results *per se* but simply typical characteristic values of heavy-tailed distributions. What defines an outlier then can only be determined after some assumptions about the true underlying distribution have been made. For example, if we assume the distribution is mesokurtic and roughly symmetrical, then values beyond the interquartile defined limits just mentioned can be classified as anomalous. In general, then, classifying values as outliers is a challenging problem involving assumptions about the distributions and then probabilistic modelling of the data based on these assumptions. Short of taking these steps, we must be very cautious in how we define outliers, especially when calculating quantities such as kurtosis.

In the following code, we create a function to remove and winsorize outliers. The outliers are defined as any values beyond k, defaulting to k = 1.5, times the interquartile range above or below, respectively, the third and first quartiles:

```
trim_outliers <- function(x, k = 1.5){
  iqr <- IQR(x)
  limits <- quantile(x, probs = c(1, 3)/4) + c(-1, 1) * k * iqr
  x[(x > limits[1]) & (x < limits[2])]
}
```

```
winsorize_outliers <- function(x, k = 1.5){
  iqr <- IQR(x)
  limits <- quantile(x, probs = c(1, 3)/4) + c(-1, 1) * k * iqr
  outlier_index <- (x < limits[1]) | (x > limits[2])
  x[outlier_index] <- median(x)
  x
}
```

If we set k to a value greater than 1.5, we will be more stringent in our definition of outliers, and so there is considerably less distortion to the estimates of excess kurtosis:

```
map_dbl(distributions,
        ~excess_kurtosis(trim_outliers(., k = 3.0))
)
#>      normal          t_10          t_7          t_5      uniform
#> -0.06891096   0.61538989   0.87930380   1.26800749  -1.20566605
map_dbl(distributions,
        ~excess_kurtosis(winsorize_outliers(., k = 3.0))
)
#>      normal          t_10          t_7          t_5      uniform
#> -0.06891096   0.61683724   0.88825156   1.28386529  -1.20566605
```

Our rt_data has an extraordinarily high excess kurtosis value of 6.852. However, the value of 1823 is 6.01 times the interquartile range above the third quartile. When we remove this value, or replace it with the median value, the kurtosis changes dramatically:

```
excess_kurtosis(rt_data[-2])
#> [1] -1.385237
rt_replace <- rt_data
rt_replace[2] <- median(rt_data)
excess_kurtosis(rt_replace)
#> [1] -1.249404
```

Quantile-based measures of kurtosis

As with other descriptive statistics, we can use quantiles to allow us to calculate robust estimates of kurtosis. One simple procedure is to calculate the ratio of the 95% (or 99%, etc.) inner quantile interval to the interquartile range. We can denote this as follows:

$$\text{qkurtosis}_p = \frac{Q_{1-p} - Q_p}{Q_3 - Q_1},$$

where Q_1 and Q_3 are the first and third quartiles, respectively, and Q_{1-p} and Q_p are the quantiles at $1-p$ and p, respectively, where $0 \le p \le 1$. Clearly, when $p = 0.025$, qkurtosis_p is the ratio of the 95% inner quantile interval to the interquartile range.

In a normal distribution, for example, the value of $\text{qkurtosis}_{p=0.025}$ is approximately 2.91, and the value of $\text{qkurtosis}_{p=0.005}$ is approximately 3.82. In leptokurtic distributions, these values are higher. For example, in the t-distribution with $v = 5$ degrees of freedom, the values of $\text{qkurtosis}_{p=0.025}$ and $\text{qkurtosis}_{p=0.005}$ are 3.54 and 5.55, respectively. On the other hand, in platykurtic distributions, these values are lower. For example, in a uniform distribution they are 1.90 and 1.98, respectively.

It should be noted, and we see below, that the values of qkurtosis_p and of the standard kurtosis function will not be identical or even linearly related, but there will be a clear monotonic correspondence between them in most cases. Also, if we subtract 3 from the value of qkurtosis$_p$, we will get a quantile-based counterpart of excess kurtosis.

We can also extend this quantile estimate of kurtosis as follows:

$$\text{qkurtosis}_{u,p} = \frac{Q_{1-p} - Q_p}{Q_{1-u} - Q_u},$$

where $0 \leq p \leq u \leq 1$. If $u = 0.25$, then qkurtosis$_{u,p}$ is identical to qkurtosis$_p$ defined above. We can implement these functions in R as follows:

```
qkurtosis <- function(x, u=0.25, p=0.025){
  Q <- quantile(x, probs = c(p, u, 1-u, 1-p))
  diff(Q[c(1, 4)])/diff(Q[c(2, 3)])
}
```

Applying this function to the `distributions` data sets, we can investigate the effect of using different values of u and p:

```
map_dbl(distributions, qkurtosis)  - 3
#>    normal        t_10        t_7         t_5        uniform
#> -0.1247618  0.1445630  0.3278772  0.5310460 -1.1139567
map_dbl(distributions,
        ~qkurtosis(., p = 0.01/2)
) - 3
#>    normal        t_10        t_7         t_5        uniform
#>  0.6609811  1.5074351  1.7742026  2.6498583 -1.0438196
map_dbl(distributions,
        ~qkurtosis(., u=0.2, p = 0.01/2)
) - 3
#>    normal        t_10        t_7          t_5        uniform
#> -0.04845219  0.63221277  0.80167185  1.51656142 -1.36393460
```

Clearly, none of these estimates exactly match the kurtosis estimates using the standard kurtosis function. However, in all cases, there is clear correspondence between the two.

qkurtosis$_{u,p}$ is very straightforward to explain or understand. It gives the ratio of the width of the portion of the distribution containing most of the probability mass to the width of its centre. If most of the mass is near the centre, as is the case with platykurtic distributions, this ratio will be relatively low. If the tails contain a lot of mass, as is the case with leptokurtic distributions, this ratio will be relatively high.

Graphical exploration of univariate distributions

Thus far, we have used different methods for measuring characteristics of samples from univariate distributions such as their location, scale, and shape. Each of these methods provides us with valuable perspectives on the sample and consequently also provides insights into the nature of the distribution from which we assume this sample has been drawn. These are essential preliminary steps before we embark on more formal modelling of these distributions. In addition to these methods, there are valuable graphical methods for exploring univariate distributions. These ought to be seen as complementary to the quantitative methods described above. We have already seen a number of relevant methods, such as histograms and boxplots, in Chapter 4. Here, we will primarily focus on methods not covered in Chapter 4.

Stem-and-leaf plots

One of the simplest possible graphical methods for exploring a sample of univariate values is the *stem-and-leaf* plot, first proposed by Tukey (1977). In the built-in graphics package in R, the function stem produces stem-and-leaf plots. In the following code, we apply stem to a set of six example values:

```
c(12, 13, 13, 16, 21, 57) %>%
  stem()

  The decimal point is 1 digit(s) to the right of the |

  1 | 2336
  2 | 1
  3 |
  4 |
  5 | 7
```

To the left of the | are the *stems*. These are the leading digits of the set of values. To the right of the | are the *leaves*. These are the remaining digits of the values. For example, 1 | 2336 indicates that we have four values whose first digit is 1 and whose remaining digits are 2, 3, 3 and 6. In a stem-and-leaf plot, we can often display all the values in the sample, and thus there is no data loss or obscuring of the data, and yet we can still appreciate major features of the distribution such as the location, scale and shape.

The command stem.leaf from the aplpack package provides a classic Tukey-style version of the stem-and-leaf plot. In the following code, we apply the stem.leaf command to the rt_data:

```
library(aplpack)
stem.leaf(rt_data, trim.outliers = FALSE, unit=10)
1 | 2: represents 120
  leaf unit: 10
             n: 16
   1       2 | 5
   5       3 | 1156
   6       4 | 5
  (8)      5 | 01166688
   2       6 | 5
           7 |
           8 |
           9 |
```

```
10 |
11 |
12 |
13 |
14 |
15 |
16 |
17 |
1      18 | 2
```

Here, we have specified that outliers should not be trimmed and also that the order of magnitude of the leaves should be 10. As the legend indicates, rows such as 2 | 5 indicate a value of the order of 250, while 3 | 1156 indicates two values of the order of 310 (in this case, these are both the 317), one value of the order of 350 (in this case, this is 350), and one of the order of 360 (this is 367). The first column of numbers indicates the number of values as extreme as or more extreme than the values represented by the corresponding stem and leaf. For example, the 5 in the second row indicates that there are five values that are as extreme as or more extreme, relative to the median value, than the values represented by 3 | 1156. In this column, the number in parentheses, (8), indicates that the median value is in the set of values represented by 5 | 01166688.

Histograms

Stem-and-leaf plots are only useful for relatively small data sets. When the number of values becomes relatively large, the number of digits in the leaves and hence their lengths can become excessive. If we decrease the units of the plot, and thus decrease its granularity, we may end up with excessive numbers of rows – too many to display even on a single page. In this situation, it is preferable to use a histogram. We have already described how to make histograms using ggplot2 in Chapter 4. Here, we provide just a brief recap example.

For this, we will use the example of the per capita gross domestic product (GDP) in a set of different countries:

```
gdp_df <- read_csv('data/nominal_gdp_per_capita.csv')
```

As a first step, we will visualize this data with a histogram using the following code, which produces Figure 5.3:

```
gdp_df %>%
  ggplot(aes(x = gdp)) +
  geom_histogram(binwidth = 2500) +
  xlab('Per capita GDP in USD equivalents')
```

As with any histogram, we must choose a bin width or the number of bins into which we will divide all the values. Although ggplot will default to usually 30 bins in its histograms, it will raise a warning to explicitly pick a better number value. In this case, we have chosen a `binwidth` of 2500.

Even with this simple visualization, we have learned a lot. We see that most countries have per capita GDP lower than $30,000, and in fact most of these countries have incomes lower than around $15,000. The distribution is spread out from close to zero to close to $100,000, and it is highly asymmetric, with a long tail to the right.

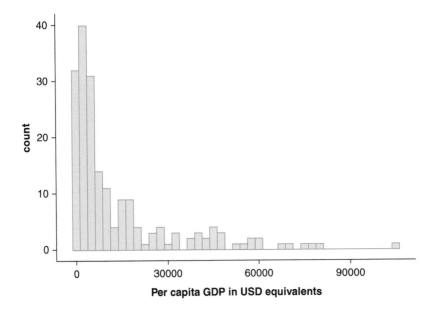

Figure 5.3 The distribution of per capita gross domestic product in a set of different countries

Boxplots

Another useful and complementary visualization method is the Tukey boxplot. Again, we have described how to make boxplots with `ggplot2` in detail in Chapter 4, and so only provide a recap here.

A horizontal Tukey boxplot with all points shown as *jittered* points, and with a *rug plot* along the horizontal axis, can be created with the following code, which produces Figure 5.4:

```
ggplot(gdp_df,
        aes(x = '', y = gdp)
) + geom_boxplot(outlier.shape = NA) +
  geom_jitter(width = 0.25, size = 0.5, alpha = 0.5) +
  geom_rug(sides = 'l') +
  coord_flip() +
  theme(aspect.ratio = 1/5) +
  xlab('')
```

As we have seen in Chapter 4, the box itself in the boxplot gives us the 25th, 50th and 75th percentiles of the data. From this, we see more clearly that 50% of the countries have per capita incomes lower than around $6000 and 75% of countries have incomes lower than around $17,000. The top 25% of the countries are spread from around $17,000 to above $100,000.

Empirical cumulative distribution functions

The *cumulative distribution function* (CDF), or just simply the *distribution function*, of a random variable X is defined as follows:

$$F(t) = P(X < t) = \int_{\infty}^{t} P(X = x)dx.$$

In other words, $F(t)$ is the probability that the random variable takes a value less than t. For a sample of values $x_1, x_2, \ldots, x_n$, we define the *empirical cumulative distribution function* (ECDF):

$$F(t) = \frac{1}{n}\sum_{i=1}^{n} I_{x_i \le t},$$

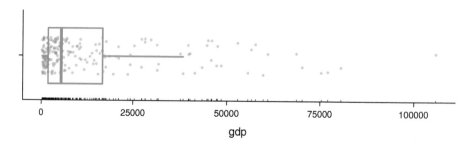

Figure 5.4 A Tukey boxplot of the distribution of per capita GDP across a set of countries

where I_A takes the value 1 if its argument A is true and takes the value 0 otherwise. We can plot the ECDF of a sample with `ggplot` as follows:

```
gdp_df %>%
  ggplot(aes(x = gdp)) +
  stat_ecdf()
```

From the ECDF in Figure 5.5, by using the percentiles on the y-axis to find the values of gdp on the x-axis that they correspond to, we can see that most of the probability mass is concentrated at low values of gdp, and that there is a long tail to the right.

Q-Q and P-P plots

Distribution functions, both theoretical and empirical, are used to make so-called quantile–quantile (Q-Q) and probability–probability (P-P) plots. Both Q-Q and P-P plots are graphical techniques that are used to essentially compare distribution functions. While both of these techniques are widely used, especially to compare a sample to a theoretical distribution, the meaning of neither technique is particularly self-evident to the untrained eye. It is necessary, therefore, to understand the technicalities of both techniques before they can be used in practice.

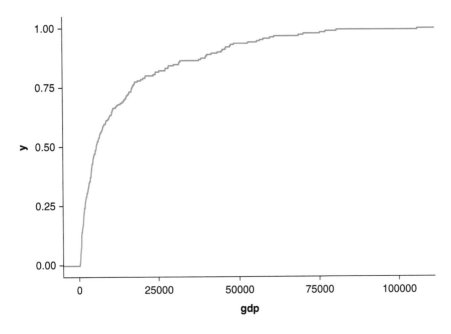

Figure 5.5 The ECDF of the per capita GDP across a set of countries

To understand both Q-Q and P-P plots, let us start with two random variables X and Y that have density functions $f(x)$ and $g(y)$, respectively, and CDFs $F(x)$ and $G(y)$, respectively. In principle, for any given quantile value $p \in (0,1)$, we can calculate $x = F^{-1}(p)$ and $y = G^{-1}(p)$, where F^{-1} and G^{-1} are the inverses of the CDFs, assuming that F^{-1} and G^{-1} exist. Therefore, the pair (x,y) are values of the random variables X and Y, respectively, that correspond to the same quantile value. If, for a range of quantile values $0 < p_1 < p_2 < ... < p_i < ... < p_n$, we calculate $x_i = F^{-1}(p_i)$ and $y_i = G^{-1}(p_i)$ and then plot each pair (x_i, y_i), we produce a Q-Q plot. If the density functions $f(x)$ and $g(y)$ are identical, then the points in the Q-Q plot will fall on the identity line, that is the line through the origin with a slope of 1. If $f(x)$ and $g(x)$ differ in their location only, that is one is a shifted version of the other, then the (x_i, y_i) will still fall on a straight line with slope equal to 1 whose intercept is no longer 0 and will represent how much the mean of Y is offset relative to that of X. If $f(x)$ and $g(x)$ have the same location but differ in their scale, then the (x_i, y_i) will again fall on a straight line with intercept 0, but the slope will not equal 1. The slope represents the ratio of standard deviation of Y to that of X. If $f(x)$ and $g(x)$ differ in both location and scale, then the (x_i, y_i) will yet again fall on a straight line, but the slope will not equal 1 and the intercept will not be 0.

These four scenarios are illustrated with normal distributions in Figure 5.6.

Whenever distributions differ only in terms of their location and scale, then their Q-Q plots will fall on a straight line and it will be possible to see how their locations and scales differ from

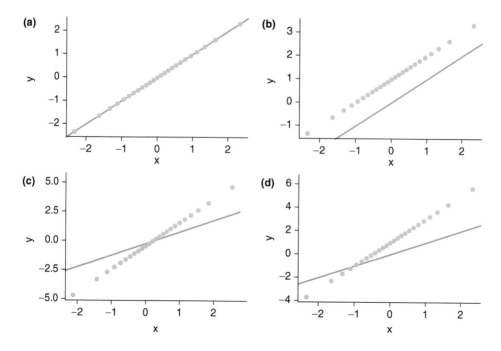

Figure 5.6 Q-Q plots corresponding to (a) two identical normal distributions, (b) two normal distributions that differ in their mean only, (c) two normal distributions that differ in their standard deviation only, and (d) two normal distributions that differ in their mean and their standard deviation

one another. Two distributions that differ in their shape will correspond to Q-Q plots where the points do not fall on straight lines. To illustrate this, in Figure 5.7, we compare standard normal distributions to t-distributions (Figures 5.7(a)–(b)), a χ^2 distribution (Figure 5.7(c)), and an exponential distribution (Figure 5.7(d)). In the case of the two t-distributions, we can see that both the left and right tails are more spread out than the corresponding tails in the normal distribution, while the centres are more similar. In the case of the χ^2 and exponential distributions, we see the left tails are far more concentrated than the left tail of the normal distribution, while the right tails are far more spread out.

We may now use Q-Q plots to compare the ECDF of a sample against the distribution function of a known probability distribution. As an example, let us again consider the rt_data data. The quantiles that these values correspond to can be found using R's ecdf function. This function returns a function that can be used to calculate the ECDF's value for any given value:

```
F <- ecdf(rt_data)
(p <- F(rt_data))
#>  [1] 0.7500 1.0000 0.5625 0.8750 0.1875 0.3125 0.0625 0.4375 0.1875 0.7500
#> [11] 0.8750 0.5625 0.9375 0.7500 0.3750 0.2500
```

Before we proceed, we see here that we have a quantile value of 1 in the p vector. This will correspond to ∞ in any normal distribution. We can avoid this by first clipping the vector of quantiles so that its minimum is $\epsilon > 0$ and its maximum is $1 - \epsilon$:

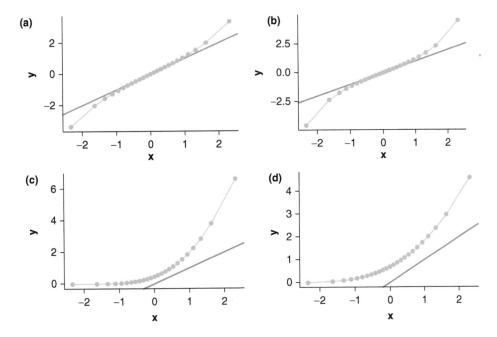

Figure 5.7 Q-Q plots comparing a normal distribution represented on the x-axis to four alternative distributions: (a) a t-distribution with $v = 5$ degrees of freedom; (b) a t-distribution with $v = 3$ degrees of freedom; (c) a χ^2 distribution with $v = 1$ degrees of freedom; (d) an exponential distribution with rate parameter $\lambda = 1$. In all cases, the straight line depicts the identity line

```
clip_vector <- function(p, epsilon=1e-3){
  pmax(pmin(p, 1-epsilon), epsilon)
}
```

```
p <- clip_vector(p)
```

We now find the values of a theoretical probability distribution that correspond to these quantiles. In this case, rather than comparing to a standard normal, we will use a normal distribution with a mean and standard deviation equal to a robust measure of the location and scale of rt_data. For this, we will use its median and MAD, respectively. We may find the theoretical quantile values by using the inverse of the CDF of that probability distribution, assuming it exists. For example, the values of a normal distribution that correspond to these quantiles can be calculated using the qnorm function:

```
qnorm(p, mean = median(rt_data), sd = mad(rt_data))
#>   [1] 583.4999 821.6750 532.5097 630.4163 429.5336 468.8101 365.7466 501.4903
#>   [9] 429.5336 583.4999 630.4163 532.5097 668.2534 583.4999 485.5844 450.5001
```

Now we can plot rt_data against qnorm(p) to produce our Q-Q plot. The code for this is below and the plot is shown in Figure 5.8:

```
tibble(y = rt_data,
       x = qnorm(p, mean = median(rt_data), sd = mad(rt_data))
```

```
) %>% ggplot(aes(x = x, y = y)) + geom_point() +
    geom_abline(intercept = 0, slope = 1, col='red')
```

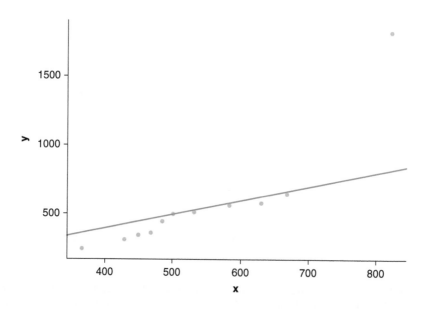

Figure 5.8 A Q-Q plot of rt_data against a normal distribution whose mean and standard deviation match its location and scale. The straight line is the identity line

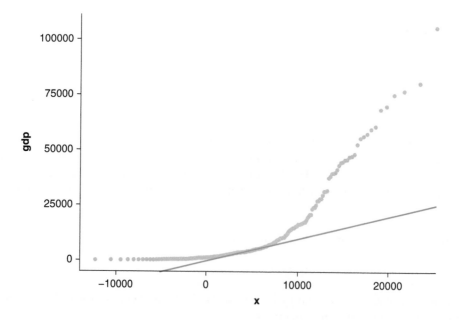

Figure 5.9 A Q-Q plot of the gdp data against a normal distribution whose mean and standard deviation match its location and scale. The straight line is the identity line "."

We can see here that points in the middle fall roughly on the identity line, but there is somewhat more spread in the left tail, and an extreme outlier in the right tail.

In Figure 5.9, we provide the Q-Q plot of the gdp values from gdp_df against a normal distribution whose mean and standard deviation roughly match the location and scale of gdp.
From this, we can see that the values on the left tail are extremely concentrated and the values on the right tail are extremely spread out.

P-P plots are related to Q-Q plots, but are less well known or widely used. To understand
them, again let us return to the case of the random variables X and Y that have density functions $f(x)$ and $g(y)$, respectively, and CDFs $F(x)$ and $G(y)$, respectively. For any value z, we may
calculate $F(z)$ and $G(z)$. If, for each value in the sequence $z_1 < z_2 < \ldots < z_i < \ldots < z_n$, we calculate
$F(z_i)$ and $G(z_i)$ and then plot each pair $(F(z_i), G(z_i))$, we produce a P-P plot.

In Figure 5.10, we provides four P-P plots, each comparing different distributions to a
normal distribution. In Figure 5.10(a), we compare the t-distribution with $v = 1$ degrees
of freedom to a standard normal distribution. Here, we see that the percentiles in the
t-distribution at or below the 10th percentile or at or above the 90th percentile correspond to close to the 0th and 100th percentiles, respectively, in a normal distribution.
This shows that the tails of the t-distribution are more spread out than those of the

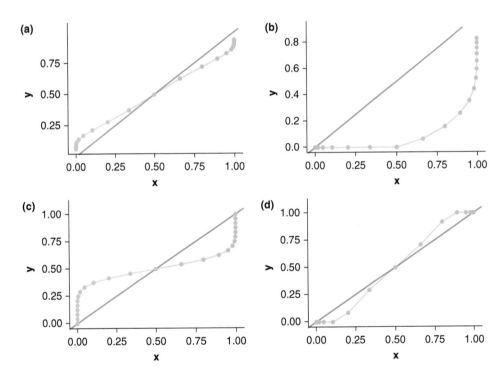

Figure 5.10 P-P plots comparing a standard normal distribution represented on
the x-axis to four alternative distributions: (a) a t-distribution with $v = 1$ degrees of
freedom; (b) a χ^2 distribution with $v = 3$ degrees of freedom; (c) a uniform distribution
from −5 to 5; (d) a uniform distribution from −1 to 1. In all cases, the straight line
depicts the identity line

normal distribution. By contrast, in Figure 5.10(d), for example, we compare a uniform distribution from −1 to 1 to a standard normal distribution. In this case, we see that the percentiles in the normal distribution at or below the 10th percentile or at or above the 90th percentile correspond to close to the 0th and 100th percentiles, respectively, in the uniform distribution. This is clearly because the uniform distribution from −1 to 1 is more compact than the normal distribution.

6

Programming in R

Introduction

When being introduced for the first time, R is often described as a programming language. This statement is technically correct, and practically very important, but it is also somewhat misleading and so ought to be put in context. While R does have all the major programming features that we expect in any programming language (functions, conditionals, iterations, etc.) and these are the reasons for R's power and extensibility, whenever we use R, especially at the beginning, we are not necessarily programming in the sense we would be if we were using C/C++, Java, etc. Certainly, whenever we use R, we are writing code and we usually put this code in scripts, which can then be executed as a batch. However, writing loops, functions, custom R objects classes, etc., is often not done until users reach a certain level of proficiency and confidence. In fact one could use R productively without engaging in programming of this kind at all. This point is meant to reassure newcomers to R that learning to use R productively does not require the same considerable initial investment as might be required when learning general-purpose programming languages. We can start with learning individual R commands, build up a repertoire of widely used commands, and eventually, after a certain level of familiarity and confidence has been achieved, we can start learning how to program in R.

In this chapter, we aim to provide an introduction to some of the major programming features of R. We'll begin with *functions* both because they can be very simple to use and because of the major role they play in programming in R generally. We will then consider *conditionals*, which allow us to execute different blocks of code depending on whether certain conditions are true. We will then turn to *iterations*, also known as *loops*. This will lead on to *functionals*, which can often take the place of traditional loops in R. As part of our consideration of functionals, we will also consider the `purrr` package that is part of the tidyverse. The aim of `purrr` is to make functionals easier and more efficient to use.

There is more to programming in R than we cover here. For example, object-oriented programming and non-standard evaluation are both practically very important features of R programming. To keep our coverage brief and introductory, we will not cover either here, but highly recommend the book by Wickham (2019) for coverage of these and other R programming topics.

Functions

Functions in R, just like in any other programming language, allow us to create custom commands to perform specific calculations or carry out specific tasks. Whenever we find ourselves repeatedly using identical or similar code statements, we can create a function to execute this code. In R, functions usually, but not necessarily, take some R objects as input and always return a new object (though this could be the `NULL` object, which signifies the absence of a defined value). We can use functions to carry out any calculations or any procedure that we could perform using any other R code.

Let's start with a numerical calculation. Let's say we have a vector of probabilities $p_1, p_2, ..., p_n$, and we want to calculate the logarithm, to a specified base, of the odds for these probabilities, that is

$$\log_b\left(\frac{p_i}{1-p_i}\right) \text{ for } i \in 1, ..., n.$$

This calculation is simple to perform using R. For example, let's say our probabilities are as follows:

```
p <- c(0.1, 0.25, 0.5, 0.75)
```

Then, the logarithm, to base 2, of the odds for the values in p is calculated as follows:

```
log(p/(1-p), base = 2)
#> [1] -3.169925 -1.584963  0.000000  1.584963
```

If, on the other hand, we wanted the logarithm to base 3 or base 5 of these odds, we would need

```
log(p/(1-p), base = 3)
#> [1] -2 -1  0  1
log(p/(1-p), base = 5)
#> [1] -1.3652124 -0.6826062  0.0000000  0.6826062
```

Likewise, if we had another vector of probabilities we could calculate the log to base 2 of the odds for these values as follows:

```
q <- c(0.33, 0.67, 0.99)
log(q/(1-q), base = 2)
#> [1] -1.021695  1.021695  6.629357
```

Clearly, in these examples, we are repeating the same or similar code statements. In general, we should avoid doing this. Not only is it tedious to repeatedly type the same code, but every time we do so, we introduce the possibility, however small, of a coding error. We can therefore create a function that takes any vector of probabilities and returns the logarithm of their odds to any desired base. We can define this function as follows:

```
log_odds <- function(p, b){
  log(p/(1-p), base = b)
}
```

To understand what is being defined here, first note that all functions in R are defined by the function keyword. The variable names within the parentheses after the function statement are the function's so-called input *arguments*. In this case, we have two arguments, named p and b. If the function took no input, then we'd simply write function() here. The code within the {} is known the function's *body*. This is otherwise normal R code, but as we will see, it is running in an informationally encapsulated environment. In this example, this code is operating on two variables, p and b, and these variables are what are we will supply as inputs whenever we call the function. The value that this code in the body calculates is then what the function returns. In general, as we will discuss below, the value of the last expression in the function's body is the value that it returns. In this case, there is obviously just one expression in the body, and the value of this expression is what is returned. In order to use a function in R, we usually (though not necessarily, as we will see) assign it to some name using the usual assignment operator. In this case, we assign the function to the name `log_odds`. We can now *call* this function to run the statements above as follows:

```
log_odds(p, 2)
#> [1] -3.169925 -1.584963  0.000000  1.584963
log_odds(p, 3)
#> [1] -2 -1  0  1
log_odds(p, 5)
#> [1] -1.3652124 -0.6826062  0.0000000  0.6826062
log_odds(q, 2)
#> [1] -1.021695  1.021695  6.629357
```

Note that although the body of the `log_odds` function lies within the `{}` braces, when a function's body contains just a single expression, we may omit the braces. For example, we could write `log_odds` as follows:

```
log_odds <- function(p, b) log(p/(1-p), base = b)
```

The braces can always be used, no matter how simple the function, but in particularly simple cases, it is not uncommon for them to be omitted.

Input arguments

Notice that in the function definition, we stated that it takes two input arguments `p` and `b`, and that the code in the body explicitly operates on `p` and `b`. As the above examples make clear, the names we use for the input argument in the function *definition* are arbitrary and do not have to correspond to the names of the variables that we use when we *call* the function. By default, whatever variable is passed in first is what the function internally defines as `p` and the second variable is what it defines as `b`. For example, consider the following code:

```
probs <- c(0.25, 0.75, 0.9)
log_base <- 2
log_odds(probs, log_base)
#> [1] -1.584963  1.584963  3.169925
```

The function `log_odds` takes the vector `probs` and the number `log_base` and internally refers to them as `p` and `b`, respectively, and then calculates and returns `log(p/(1-p), base = b)`. As we see in the following code, we may also explicitly indicate which variables are mapped to `p` and `b`:

```
log_odds(p=probs, b=log_base)
#> [1] -1.584963  1.584963  3.169925
```

When using explicit assignment like this, the order of the arguments no longer matters. Thus, we can write the above code as follows:

```
log_odds (b=log_base, p=probs)
#> [1] -1.584963   1.584963   3.169925
```

Default values for arguments

In the function we defined above, we had to explicitly provide both the probabilities and the base of the logarithms as input arguments. In some cases, however, we may prefer to allow some input arguments to take default values. For example, in this case, we may prefer the base of the logarithms to be 10 by default. We define default values in the function definition, as in the following example:

```
log_odds2 <- function (p, b=10) {
    log (p/(1-p), base = b)
}
```

We can use this function exactly as we did with the original version: that is, by providing two input arguments explicitly, as in the following examples:

```
log_odds2 (probs, log_base)
#> [1] -1.584963   1.584963   3.169925
log_odds2 (b = 3, p = probs)
#> [1] -1   1   2
```

However, if we do not include the b argument explicitly, then it will default to b=10, as in the following example:

```
log_odds2 (probs)  # here b=10
#> [1] -0.4771213   0.4771213   0.9542425
```

Optional arguments

A function can also have optional arguments indicated by ... in the arguments list in the function definition. This is often to pass arguments to functions that are called within functions. Consider the following function that calculates a polynomial function:

```
f_poly <- function (x, y, s, t) {
  x^s + y^t
}
```

Let's say that we want to create a function that returns the logarithm to some specified base of f_poly for any given values of x, y, s and t. We could do the following:

```
log_f_poly <- function (b=2, x, y, s, t) {
  log (f_poly (x, y, s, t), base = b)
}
```

However, an easier option would be the following:

```
log_f_poly <- function(..., b=2){
   log(f_poly(...), base = b)
}
```

This will capture all the arguments, other than b, in the call of log_f_poly and pass them to f_poly. We can see this in action in the following example:

```
x <- c(0.5, 1.0)
y <- c(1.0, 2.0)
s <- 2
t <- 3
log_f_poly(x, y, s, t, b=2)
#> [1] 0.3219281 3.1699250
```

Note that we may obtain the optional arguments as a list given by ... by using list(...) in the code body, as in the following trivial example function, where we return the optional argument list:

```
f <- function(...){
   list(...)
}
f(x=1, y=2, z=3)
#> $x
#> [1] 1
#>
#> $y
#> [1] 2
#>
#> $z
#> [1] 3
```

By using list(...), we can always extract and operate upon all the information provided by optional arguments.

Missing arguments

Consider the following simple function:

```
add_xy <- function(x, y, z){
   x + y
}
```

The function definition states that there will be three input arguments, x, y and z. However, in this case, it can be used without error if we only supply x and y because z is not used in the code body:

```
add_xy (5, 8)
#> [1] 13
```

In this case, we say that the z, which is explicitly stated as an input argument, is a *missing argument*. Clearly, missing arguments will not necessarily raise an error but we can always test whether any given argument is missing by using the missing function within the code body. In the following function, we test whether each of the three input arguments is missing or not:

```
is_missing_xyz <- function (x, y, z) {
  c (missing (x),
    missing (y),
    missing (z) )
}
```

```
is_missing_xyz (1, 2)
#> [1] FALSE FALSE   TRUE
is_missing_xyz (z = 1, y = 42)
#> [1]   TRUE FALSE FALSE
is_missing_xyz (5, 4, 3)
#> [1] FALSE FALSE FALSE
```

As we will see in examples later in this book, the ability to test for missing inputs provides additional flexibility in how we can use functions.

Function return values

The functions we have defined thus far have had single expressions in their bodies. The values of these expressions are what are returned by the functions. Functions, however, can have arbitrarily many statements and expressions in their body. When there are multiple statements, the value of the *last* expression is the value that is returned. To illustrate this, we can make a multi-statement version of log_odds2 as follows:

```
log_odds3 <- function (p, b=10) {
  odds <- p / (1 - p)
  log (odds, base=b)
}
log_odds3 (probs)
#> [1] -0.4771213  0.4771213  0.9542425
```

A variant of the function log_odds3 is the following:

```
log_odds4 <- function (p, b=10) {
  odds <- p / (1 - p)
  log_of_odds <- log (odds, base=b)
  log_of_odds
}
```

```
log_odds4(probs)
#> [1] -0.4771213  0.4771213  0.9542425
```

In both `log_odds3` and `log_odds4`, there are multiple code statements in their bodies. In both cases, the value returned is the value of the final expression in the body. It is also possible to have an explicit `return` statement in the function's code body:

```
log_odds5 <- function(p, b=10){
  odds <- p / (1 - p)
  log_of_odds <- log(odds, base=b)
  return(log_of_odds)
}
log_odds5(probs)
#> [1] -0.4771213  0.4771213  0.9542425
```

If a `return` statement is used, whenever it is reached, the function will immediately return its value and the remainder of the code in the body, if any, is not executed. In other words, the `return` statement allows us to *break out* of a function early, which is a useful feature that we will see below after we consider conditionals. It is conventional in R to only use explicit `return` statements for this break-out purpose, and to normally just use the final expression in the body as the function's returned value.

Function scope and environment

Consider the following function:

```
assign_x <- function(){
  x <- 17
  x
}
```

This function will takes nothing as input, and in the body assigns the value of 17 to the variable `x` and then returns this value. We can use it as follows:

```
x <- 42
assign_x() # returns 17
#> [1] 17
x           # but x is still 42
#> [1] 42
```

We see that the original value of `x` remains unchanged despite the fact that we have the statement `x <- 17` within the function's body. This is because the variable `x` within the function's body is a *local* variable, or rather it is a variable defined within a *local environment* belonging to the function. Variables in the local environment are not visible outside of that environment, which in all the examples thus far is the *global environment*, which is the top-level environment in the R session. In this sense, any function is informationally encapsulated: the variables defined by normal assignment operations within the function's local environment do not exist outside of the function, nor do normal assignment operations within the function's local environment affect variables outside the function. Here is another example of this phenomenon:

```
assign_x2 <- function(x){
  x[2] <- 42

  x

}

x <- c(2, 4, 8)

# The `x` within `assign_x2` is changed
assign_x2(x)
#> [1]  2 42  8
# The `x` in the global environment is unchanged

x
#> [1] 2 4 8
```

Although variables in the local environment are not visible or usable in the global environment, the opposite is not true. Variables in the global environment can be used in the local environment. Consider the following example:

```
increment_x <- function(){
  x + 1
}

x <- 42
increment_x()
#> [1] 43
```

The body of increment_x refers to a variable x that is not defined in the body, nor is it passed in as an input argument. When this happens, R looks for x outside the local environment. In the example above, it finds it in the global environment with a value of 42. It then increments that value by 1 and returns the result. Even in this case, however, the value of x in the global environment remains unchanged:

```
x <- 101
increment_x()
#> [1] 102
x
#> [1] 101
```

Thus far, we have mentioned a function's local environment and contrasted this with the global environment. However, functions may be nested. In that case, we have can multiple levels of environments. Consider the following example:

```
f <- function(){
  x <- 1
```

```
g <- function () {
  x + 1
}
h <- function () {
  y + 2
}
c(g(), h())
}
```

In this example, the functions g and h have their own local environment, but these environments are within the local environment of the function f, which is within the global environment. In this case, we say that the environment of f is the *parent* environment of g and h, and the global environment is the parent environment of f. This nesting of environments determines how values of variables are looked up. For example, when g is called it looks for x, which does not exist in its local environment, so it looks for it in its parent environment, which is the local environment of f. When h is called, it looks for y, which exists neither within its own local environment nor within its parent environment, so it must look for it in the global environment, which is its grandparent environment (the parent environment of its parent environment). We can see this function in action in the following example:

```
y <- 42
f()
#> [1]  2 44
```

An important feature of function environments is that they are defined by where the function is defined, not where it is called. This becomes important when a function is returned by another function. Consider the following example:

```
f <- function () {
  y <- 42
  function (x) {
    x + y
  }
}
g <- f()
```

In this example, g, which is the output of the call of f, is a function whose parent environment is the environment of f. As such, we can do the following:

```
y <- 21
g(17)
#> [1] 59
```

Note that the result here is 17 + 42 and not 17 + 21. The g function is defined as function(x) x + y, and so it must look to its parent's, or grandparent's, etc., environment to find the value of y. Although y takes the value of 21 in the global scope, it takes the value of 42 in the environment of f, which is g's parent environment.

Finally, although we mentioned that normal assignments within a local environment do not affect values in the parent, or other ancestor, environments, the special assignment operator <<- can be used to assign value in the parent environment. As a simple example, consider the following:

```
f <- function () {
  x <<- 42
}
x <- 17
f ()
x
#> [1] 42
```

In this case, we see that the assignment of the value of 42 to x has been applied to the parent environment of f, which is the global environment.

Anonymous functions

In all the functions above, the functions were assigned some name. This is not necessary. Consider the following example:

```
f <- function (x, g) {
  g (sum (x))
}
```

Here, f takes an object x and a function g and calls g (sum (x)) and returns the result. We can pass in any existing R function we wish as the value of g, as in the following examples:

```
x <- c (0.1, 1.1, 2.7)
f (x, log10)
#> [1] 0.5910646
f (x, sqrt)
#> [1] 1.974842
f (x, tanh)
#> [1] 0.9991809
```

Of course, we can also pass in any function we have defined ourselves:

```
square <- function (x) x^2
f (x, square)
#> [1] 15.21
```

However, we don't have to assign a name to our custom function and pass in that name. We can instead just pass in the unnamed, or *anonymous*, function itself, as in the following examples:

```
f (x, function (x) x^2)
#> [1] 15.21
f (x, function (x) log (x^2))
#> [1] 2.721953
```

Anonymous functions are widely used in R, as we will see when we discuss *functionals* later in this chapter.

We can create a *self-executing anonymous function* as in the following example:

```r
y <- (function (x, y, z){x + y + z}) (1, 2, 3)
y
#> [1] 6
```

Here, a function is created and called immediately and the result assigned to `y`. Given that a function like this can only be invoked once, it may seem pointless. However, it does allow us to write code in an informationally encapsulated environment, where we can possibly reuse variable names from the parent or global environment, and not interfere with variables or add clutter to those environments.

Conditionals

Conditionals allows us to execute some code based on whether some condition is true or not. Consider the following simple example:

```r
library (tidyverse)
# Make a data frame
data_df <- tibble(x = rnorm(10),
                  y = rnorm(10))
write_data <- TRUE
if (write_data) {
  write_csv(data_df, 'tmp_data.csv')
}
```

Here, we write `data_df` to a `.csv` file if and only if `write_data` is true. The conditional statement begins with the keyword `if` followed by an expression in parentheses that must evaluate to `TRUE` or `FALSE`. This is then followed by a code block delimited by `{` and `}`. Everything in this code block is executed if and only if the expression is true. Note that if the code block contains only a single expression, just as in the case of the code body of functions, the braces surrounding the code block in the conditional can be omitted, as in the following example:

```r
if (write_data) write_csv(data_df, 'tmp_data.csv')
```

`if` ... `else` **statements**

The conditional statements in the examples so far will execute some code if a condition is true, and do nothing otherwise. Sometimes, however, we want to execute one code block if the condition is true and execute an alternative code block if it is false. To do this, we use an `if` ... `else` statement, as in the following example:

```
use_new_data <- TRUE
if (use_new_data){
  data_df <- read_csv('data_new.csv')
} else {
  data_df <- read_csv('data_old.csv')
}
```

As we can see, if use_new_data is true, we read in the data from data_new.csv, otherwise we read the data in from data_old.csv.

Nesting if and if ... else statements

We may nest if and if ... else statements. In other words, we may evaluate one condition, and if it is true we may evaluate another condition, and so on. In the following example, if data_1.csv exists, we will read in its data. If it doesn't exist, then we test if data_2.csv exists. If it does, we read in its data. If not, we read in the data from data_3.csv:

```
if (file.exists('data_1.csv')) {
  data_df <- read_csv('data_1.csv')
} else if (file.exists('data_2.csv')) {
  data_df <- read_csv('data_2.csv')
} else {
  data_df <- read_csv('data_3.csv')
}
```

It should be noted that this example may not seem like nesting of if ... else statements, but rather like a chaining of these statements. However, it is exactly equivalent to the following, clearly nested, if ... else statements:

```
if (file.exists('data_1.csv')) {
  data_df <- read_csv('data_1.csv')
} else {
  if (file.exists('data_2.csv')) {
    data_df <- read_csv('data_2.csv')
  } else {
    data_df <- read_csv('data_3.csv')
  }
}
```

The only difference between these two versions is that the first version omits the (in this case, optional) {} after the first occurrence of else. As such, whether we see conditional statements like the first version as a chaining or a nesting is not meaningful.

Ultimately, nested (or chained) if and if ... else statements allow us to evaluate any binary decision tree. See Figure 6.1 for some examples.

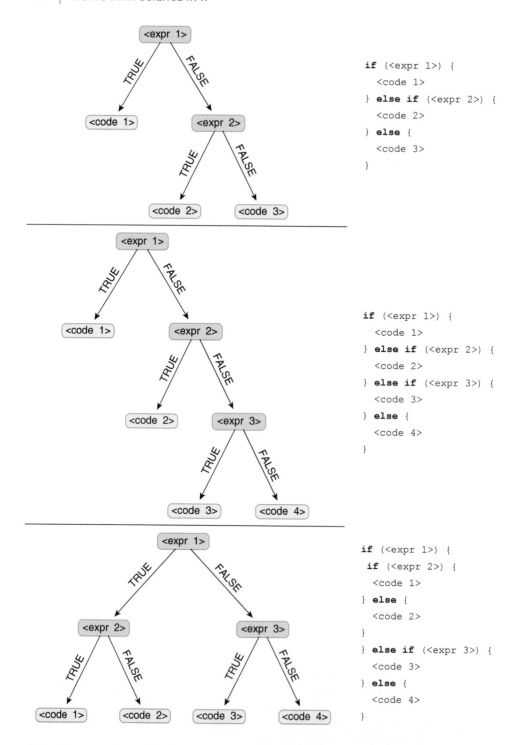

Figure 6.1 Using nested if or if ... else statements, we can create any binary decision tree where each terminal node, or leaf, of the tree is a code block and every non-terminal node is a logical expression that evaluates to true or false

Nested if and if … else statements can be used when we must choose between $K > 2$ different options. In the following example, we sample $n = 10$ random data points from one of five different distributions:

```r
n <- 10
distribution <- 'student_t'
if (distribution == 'normal') {
  y <- rnorm(n, mean = 100, sd = 15)
} else if (distribution == 'log_normal') {
  y <- log(rnorm(n, mean = 100, sd = 15))
} else if (distribution == 'student_t') {
  y <- rt(n, df = 10)
} else if (distribution == 'chisq') {
  y <- rchisq(n, df = 3)
} else if (distribution == 'uniform'){
  y <- runif(n, min = -10, 10)
}
```

switch functions

While, as we've just seen, it is possible to evaluate non-binary decisions using nested if and if … else statements, sometimes it may be natural and simpler to use a *switch* function, which executes different expressions or code blocks depending on the value of a variable. As an example, we can reimplement the previous example of random number generation using a *switch* function:

```r
distribution <- 'chisq'
y <- switch (distribution,
             normal = rnorm(n, mean = 100, sd = 15),
             log_normal = log(rnorm(n, mean = 100, sd = 15)),
             student_t = rt(n, df = 10),
             chisq = rchisq(n, df = 3),
             uniform = runif(n, min = -10, 10)
)
```

In this example, the first argument of switch is the name of a variable that takes one of five different values, namely normal, log_normal, student_t, chisq, or uniform. Based on which value is matched, it executes the code that corresponds to that value. In this example, the value of distribution is chisq and so the rchisq(n, df = 3) code is executed.

The switch function can also be used by choosing the code based on an index rather than by matching a name. In the following example, we choose the second of the five listed options by setting distribution <- 2:

```r
distribution <- 2
y <- switch (distribution,
             rnorm(n, mean = 100, sd = 15),
             log(rnorm(n, mean = 100, sd = 15)),
```

```
        rt(n, df = 10),
        rchisq(n, df = 3),
        runif(n, min = -10, 10)
)
```

In the above examples, the code that is executed is always a simple expression. However, it is possible to have an arbitrary code block instead, as in the following example:

```
distribution <- 'normal'
switch (distribution,
            'normal' = {
              mu <- runif(1, min=-10, max=10)
              sigma <- runif(1, min=0.01, max = 10)
              y <- rnorm(n, mean = mu, sd = sigma)
            },
            'student_t' = {
              mu <- runif(1, min=10, max=20)
              sigma <- runif(1, min=1.01, max = 3)
              y <- mu + rt(n, df=1) * sigma
            }
)
```

In this case, the entire code block corresponding to the value taken by `distribution` (in this case, `normal`) is executed in the global namespace.

ifelse, if_else, and case_when

If the code being executed by an `if ... else` statement is simple, such as a single expression, and optionally if we need to have the conditional vectorized, then we can use an `ifelse` function. In the following example, for each value of `reaction_time`, if it is less than 300 we return `fast`, otherwise we return `slow`:

```
reaction_time <- c(1000, 300, 200, 250, 450, 300, 250, NA)
ifelse(reaction_time < 300, 'fast', 'slow')
#> [1] "slow" "slow" "fast" "fast" "slow" "slow" "fast" NA
```

As can be seen, we obtain a vector of the same length as `reaction` with values `'fast'` and `'slow'`.

The same functionality of `ifelse` can be obtained with the `if_else` function in `dplyr`:

```
library(dplyr)
if_else(reaction_time < 300, 'fast', 'slow')
#> [1] "slow" "slow" "fast" "fast" "slow" "slow" "fast" NA
```

The `if_else` function is identical to `ifelse` but requires that the expressions corresponding to the true and false values of the logical condition are of the same type. In addition, `if_else` provides us with the option of replacing missing values with values of our choice.

The dplyr package also provides the case_when function that can be seen as a vectorized version of nested if ... else statements. It is primarily intended to be used as part of dplyr pipelines, especially within mutate functions, and we also described it in Chapter 3. As an example, we can use case_when to create a nonlinear function known as the ternary sawtooth map, which is depicted in Figure 6.2. First, consider how we could implement this function using nested if ... else statements:

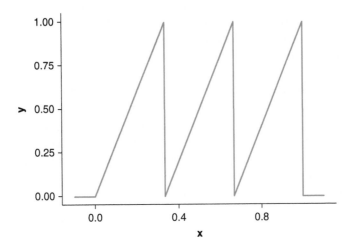

Figure 6.2 The ternary sawtooth map. This nonlinear function can be easily implemented using a case_when function

```
sawtooth <- function (x) {
  if (x < 0) {
0
} else if (x <  1/3)  {
  3 * x
} else if (x <  2/3)  {
  3 * x - 1
} else if (x <= 1) {
  3 * x - 2
} else {
  0
}
}
```

Using case_when, this function could be reimplemented as follows:

```
sawtooth2 <- function (x) {
  case_when (
    x < 0 ~ 0,
    x < 1/3 ~ 3 * x,
    x < 2/3 ~  3  * x - 1,
    x <= 1 ~ 3 * x - 2,
```

```
        TRUE  ~  0
    )
}
```

Each line within case_when (or more precisely, each comma-delimited argument) contains a *formula*, which is a statement with a ~. To the left of ~ is a logical expression, and to the right is the code that is executed if the logical expression is true. Sometimes more than one logical expression within case_when is true. That is the case here. For example, if x < 0 is true, then x < 1/3 must be true too. The case_when function proceeds through the logical expressions in order and executes the code corresponding to the first expression that is true and then stops. This means that the order of the expressions is vital to how case_when works. Note that the final statement in the example above is TRUE ~ 0. This plays the role equivalent to else in an if … else statement. Because the expression to left of ~ obviously is always true, the code to the right will be executed if and only if all other expressions are false.

The case_when function is more compact than nested if … else statements. More usefully, it is vectorized. In other words, the sawtooth function, which uses nested if … else statements, will not work properly if the input argument is a vector rather than a single value (which is, strictly speaking, a vector of length 1). By contrast, sawtooth2, which uses case_when, will work with a vector input, as in the following example:

```
x <- c(0.1, 0.3, 0.5, 0.6, 0.7, 0.9)
sawtooth2(x)
#> [1] 0.3 0.9 0.5 0.8 0.1 0.7
```

Iterations

In R, there are two types of iterations or *loops*, which we informally refer to as for loops and while loops.

for **loops**

In order to understand for loops, let us reuse the sawtooth function above. We mentioned that this function cannot be applied to vectors but only to single values. Let's say we had the following vector of 1000 elements to which we wished to apply the sawtooth function:

```
N <- 1000
x <- seq(-0.1, 1.1, length.out = N)
```

In principle, we could apply sawtooth to each element of x, one element at a time, as follows:

```
# Create a vector of 0's of same length as x
# This  can  also  be  done  with  y  <-  vector('double',  N)
y <- numeric(N)
y[1]   <- sawtooth(x[1])
```

```
y[2]   <- sawtooth(x[2])
y[3]   <- sawtooth(x[3])
...
y[N] <- sawtooth(x[N]) # where N = 1000
```

It should be obvious that we want to avoid this at all costs. Instead, we can create a `for` loop as follows:

```
for (i in 1:N) {
  y[i] <- sawtooth(x[i])
}
```

Essentially, this loop repeatedly executes the statement `y[i] <- sawtooth(x[i])`. On the first iteration, i takes the value 1. On the second iteration, i takes the value 2, and so on, until the final iteration where i takes the value of N. In other words, for each value of i from 1 to N, we execute `y[i] <- sawtooth(x[i])`.

The general form of a `for` loop is as follows:

```
for (<var> in <sequence>) {
   <code body>
}
```

The loop iteration begins with the `for` keyword followed by a expression in parentheses of the form (`<var>   in   <sequence>`) where `<var>` is what we'll call the *loop variable* and `<sequence>` is (usually) a vector or list of items. After the parentheses is some code enclosed by `{}`. For each value in the `<sequence>`, the `<var>` is set to this value and the `<code body>` is executed. We could write this in pseudo-code as follows:

```
for each  value  in  <sequence>
  set <var> equal to this value
  execute <code body>
```

In other words, the `for` loop executes the `<code body>` for each value in `<sequence>`, setting `<var>` to this value on each iteration.

Let's look at some further examples.

Example 6.1. In the following, we take a list of people's names and print a greeting to them:

```
people   <-   c('bill',   'hillary',   'donald',   'george')
for (person in people) {
  print(paste('Hello',  person))
}
#> [1] "Hello bill"
#> [1] "Hello hillary"
#> [1] "Hello donald"
#> [1] "Hello george"
```

In this example, we execute `print(paste('Hello', person))` four times. On the first iteration, the value of person takes the value of `people[1]`, which is `bill`. On the second iteration, person takes the value of `people[2]`, which is `hillary`, and so on.

Example 6.2. The `for` loop in the previous example can also be implemented as follows:

```
for (i in seq_along(people)){
 print(paste('Hello', people[i]))
}
#> [1] "Hello bill"
#> [1] "Hello hillary"
#> [1] "Hello donald"
#> [1] "Hello george"
```

Here, `seq_along(people)` gives us the sequence of integers from 1 to `length(people)`. It
is safer than doing, for example, `1:length(people)` because if people were in fact empty,
`1:length(people)` would return 1, 0, while `seq_along(people)` would return an empty vector.

Example 6.3. Here, we sum all the elements in the vector `values`:

```
values <- c(51, 45, 53, 53, 46)
s <- 0
for (value in values){ s <- s + value
}
s
#> [1] 248
```

Example 6.4. Here, we create a cumulative sum vector for `values`:

```
cumulative_values <- numeric(length(values))
for (i in seq_along (values)) {
 if (i == 1){
 cumulative_values[i] <- values[i]
}
else {
 cumulative_values[i] <- cumulative_values[i - 1] + values[i]
 }
}
cumulative_values
#> [1] 51 96 149 202 248
```

Example 6.5. In this example, we implement the famous chaotic dynamical system
described by May (1976). In this, the value of the system at time t is

$$x_t = rx_{t-1}(1 - x_{t-1}),$$

where, in its chaotic regime, r takes values approximately in the range (3.5695, 4.0), and the
initial value of the system is $x_1 \in (0, 1)$. In this example, we set $x_1 = 0.5$ and set $r = 3.75$, and
iterate for 500 iterations:

```
N <- 500
r <- 3.75
x <- numeric(N)
x[1] <- 0.5
for (t in seq(2, N)){
  x[t] <- r * x[t-1] * (1 - x[t-1])
}
```

The plot of x for each value of t is shown in Figure 6.3.

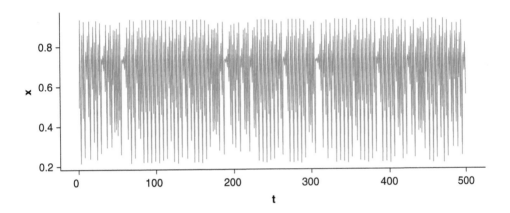

Figure 6.3 The time series of the chaotic logistic map. This time series can be obtained using a simple `for` loop

Example 6.6. The following example illustrates how we can easily automate repetitive tasks, and save ourselves a considerable amount of time otherwise spent on dull manual work. Let's say we have a large set of .csv files that we need to read in as data frames and then concatenate them into one large data frame:

```
file_names   <- c('data_1.csv',
                 'data_2.csv',
                 'data_3.csv')
# create empty list
df_list   <- vector('list', length(file_names))
# read in each file; store contents in list
for (i in seq_along(file_names)){
   df_list[[i]] <- read_csv(file_names[i])
}
# bind rows
data_df <- bind_rows(df_list)
```

In this example, there were just three files to read in and concatenated, but had there been hundreds or thousands, the required code would have been identical and the total running time might only be seconds or minutes.

`while` **loops**

Unlike `for` loops, which iterate through each value in a sequence of values, `while` loops continuously execute the code body while a condition remains true. The general form of a `while` loop is as follows:

```
while (<condition>) {
  <code body>
}
```

Here, `<condition>` is a logical expression that evaluates to TRUE or FALSE. The `while` loop will continue to execute `<code body>` as long as `<condition>` remains TRUE.

As a very simple example of a `while` loop, let's say we wish to find the largest value of k such that $2^k \leq 10^6$:

```
k <- 0
while (2^(k+1) <= 10^6) {
  k <- k + 1
}
k
#> [1] 19
```

Here, we see that we keep incrementing k by 1 until `2^(k+1)` is greater than 10^6. At that point, the condition `2^(k+1) <= 10^6` is false, and the `while` loop terminates. The final value of k is the highest of value of k such that $2^k \leq 10^6$.

Anything that can be implemented by a `for` loop can also be implemented by a `while` loop, but the converse is not true. Thus `while` loops are very powerful. As an example of a `while` loop implementing a `for` loop, let's reimplement the summation `for` loop above:

```
values <- c(51, 45, 53, 53, 46)
i <- 1
s  <- 0
while (i <= length(values))  {
 s <- s + values[i]
 i <- i + 1
}
s
#> [1] 248
```

A crucial feature of this `while` loop is the loop counter i, which is initialized to 1 and incremented by 1 on each iteration. This is a common feature of `while` loops.

Another common pattern in `while` loops is a conditional with a `break` statement. Whenever `break` occurs, the `while` loop terminates. Consider the following example where we again find the largest value of k such that $2^k \leq 10^6$:

```
k <- 0
while  (TRUE){
```

```
if (2^(k + 1) > 10^6) {
    break
}
k <- k + 1
}

k
#> [1] 19
```

Notice that in this case the `while` loop's condition is always `TRUE`, and the conditional with the `break` statement is doing the crucial work of terminating the loop.

An equivalent of `while (TRUE)` is the `repeat` statement:

```
k <- 0
repeat {

    if (2^(k + 1) > 10^6) {
        break
    }

    k <- k + 1
}
k
#> [1] 19
```

An example of a simple but non-trivial algorithm involving a `while` loop is where we sample from a discrete probability distribution. Consider the following probability distribution for a discrete random variable with six possible values:

```
p <- c(0.1, 0.2, 0.25, 0.15, 0.1, 0.2)
```

This tells us that the probability that the variable takes the value 1 is 0.1, that it takes the value 2 is 0.2, and so on. If we would like to sample from this probability distribution, we can do so using the following algorithm involving a `while` loop. First, we calculate the cumulative sum of `p`:

```
f <- cumsum(p)
f
#> [1] 0.10 0.30 0.55 0.70 0.80 1.00
```

Then we sample uniformly at random from the interval (0, 1), which we can do in R with `runif()`:

```
r <- runif(1)
```

Then we begin to step through each value of `f`, beginning with the first value, and test if `r` is less than or equal to this value. If it is, we stop. Otherwise, we move on to the next value in `f`:

```
k <- 1
while  (TRUE)  {
 if  (r <= f[k]) {
 break
 }
 k <- k + 1
}
```

This sampler could also be implemented as follows:

```
k <- 1
while (r > f[k]) {
  k <- k + 1
}
```

 Functionals

Functionals are functions that take a function and a vector as input and return a new vector. They play an important role in programming in R, often taking the place of `for` loops. There are many functionals in the base R language. Here, we will look at the most useful or widely used ones.

lapply

One of the most widely used functionals in R is the `lapply` function, which takes two required arguments, a vector or list and a function, and then applies the function to each element in the vector or list and returns a new list. As an example, instead of using a `for` loop, we could use `lapply` to apply the `sawtooth` function used above to each element of a vector `x`. Here's the original `for` loop:

```
N <- 1000
x<- seq(-0.1, 1.1, length.out = N)
y <- numeric(N)
for (i in 1:N) {
 y[i] <- sawtooth(x[i])
}
```

We can replace the preassignment of `y` (i.e. `y <- numeric(N)`) and the `for` loop entirely using `lapply` as follows:

```
y <- lapply(x, sawtooth)
```

The `lapply` function returns a list with as many elements as there are elements in `x`:

```
length(x)
#>   [1] 1000
length(y)
```

```
#> [1] 1000
class(y)
#> [1] "list"
head(y, 3) # first three elements of y
#> [[1]]
#> [1] 0
#>
#> [[2]]
#> [1] 0
#>
#> [[3]]
#>    [1] 0
```

Should we prefer y to be a vector rather than a list, we can `unlist` it:

```
y <- unlist(y)
head(y, 3)
#> [1] 0 0 0
```

There are other options too for returning a vector from a functional, as we will see shortly.

As another application of `lapply`, consider the `for` loop example above where we read in data frames from multiple files using `read_csv` and stored them in a list that was then concatenated into `data_df`:

```
file_names   <- c('data_1.csv',
                   'data_2.csv',
                   'data_3.csv')
df_list   <- vector('list', length(file_names))
for (i in seq_along(file_names)){
df_list[[i]] <- read_csv(file_names[i])
}
data_df <- bind_rows(df_list)
```

The preassignment to `df_list` and the `for` loop can be replaced with the use of `lapply`:

```
df_list <- lapply(file_names, read_csv)
```

The general form of the `lapply` function is as follows:

```
returned_list <- lapply(<vector or list>, <function>)
```

Sometimes we may need to use a function that takes arguments in `lapply`. As an example, let us imagine that we wish to calculate the trimmed mean of each vector, and also ignoring missing values, in a list of vectors. The trimmed mean, which we described in Chapter 5, is where we compute the mean after a certain proportion of the high and low elements have been trimmed. The trimmed mean of a vector, where we remove 5% of values on the upper and lower extremes of the vector, and also ignoring missing values, is as follows:

```
x   <- c(10,   20,  NA,   125,   35,   15)
mean(x, trim = 0.05, na.rm = T)
#> [1] 41
```

To use the `trim = 0.05` and `na.rm = T` arguments when we use `lapply`, we supply them as optional arguments after the function name as follows:

```
data_vectors   <- list(x = c(NA,   10,   11,   12,   1001,   -20),
                        y = c(5, 10, 7, 2500, 6),
                        z = c(2, 4, 1000, 8, 5)
)
lapply(data_vectors, mean, trim = 0.20, na.rm = T) %>%
  unlist()
#>            x          y          z
#>  11.000000   7.666667   5.666667
```

Note that because data frames (and tibbles) are essentially lists of vectors, `lapply` can be easily used to apply a function to all columns of a data frame:

```
data_df   <- tibble(x = rnorm(10),
                     y = rnorm(10),
                     z = rnorm(10))
lapply(data_df, mean) %>%
  unlist()
#>            x          y          z
#>  0.24504010  -0.43967492  -0.05399682
```

The above function accomplishes the same thing as the following `summarise_all` function, except that `summarise_all` returns a tibble:

```
summarise_all(data_df, mean)
#> # A tibble: 1 x 3
#>       x       y       z
#>    <dbl>   <dbl>   <dbl>
#> 1 0.245 -0.440 -0.0540
```

`sapply` and `vapply`

As we've seen, `lapply` always returns a list. Sometimes this returned list is a list of single values or list of vectors of the same length and type. In these cases, it would be preferable to convert these lists to vectors or matrices. We saw this in the case of using `sawtooth` with `lapply` above, where we manually converted the returned list into a vector using `unlist`. Variants of `lapply`, `sapply` and `vapply`, can facilitate doing these conversions. The `sapply` function works like `lapply` but will attempt to simplify the list as a vector or a matrix if possible. In the following example, we use `sapply` to apply `sawtooth` to each element of `x`:

```
N <- 1000
x <- seq(-0.1,  1.1,  length.out  =  N)
y <- sapply(x, sawtooth)
head(y, 5)
#> [1] 0 0 0 0 0
```

Here, because the list that would have been returned by `lapply`, had we used it here, is a list of length N of single numeric values (or numeric vectors of length 1), `sapply` can produce and return a numeric vector of length N.

If the result of `lapply` is a list of length N of numeric vectors of length 5, for example, then this list could be simplified to a matrix. In the following example, the list returned by `lapply` is a list like this:

```
data_df  <- tibble(x = rnorm(100),
                    y = rnorm(100),
                    z = rnorm(100))
lapply(data_df, quantile)
#> $x
#>          0%          25%          50%          75%          100%
#>  -2.31932737  -0.70960382  -0.05431694  0.72976278  2.13348636
#>
#> $y
#>          0%          25%          50%          75%          100%
#>  -2.82300012  -0.48106048  0.04061442  0.61636766  2.13286973
#>
#> $z
#>          0%          25%          50%          75%          100%
#>  -2.4662529  -0.6690109  -0.1111398 0.5306826      2.1873352
```

If we use `sapply` here instead, the result is a matrix:

```
sapply(data_df, quantile)
#>              x              y              z
#> 0%    -2.31932737  -2.82300012  -2.4662529
#> 25%   -0.70960382  -0.48106048  -0.6690109
#> 50%   -0.05431694   0.04061442  -0.1111398
#> 75%    0.72976278   0.61636766   0.5306826
#> 100%  2.13348636   2.13286973   2.1873352
```

In cases where the list returned by `lapply` has elements of different lengths, `sapply` cannot simplify it:

```
X <- list(x = rnorm(2),
          y = rnorm(3),
          z = rnorm(4)
)
sapply(X, function(x) x^2)
```

```
#> $x
#> [1] 0.0503656 0.1913169
#>
#> $y
#> [1] 1.7629691 0.2194715 1.7954867
#>
#> $z
#> [1] 2.7736662 0.2904671 0.9987699 0.1166150
```

The vapply function is a safer version of sapply because it specifies the nature of the returned values of each application of the function. For example, we know the default returned value of quantile will be a numeric vector of length 5. We can specify this as the FUN.VALUE argument to vapply:

```
vapply(data_df, quantile, FUN.VALUE=numeric(5))
#>                 x           y           z
#> 0%    -2.31932737  -2.82300012  -2.4662529
#> 25%   -0.70960382  -0.48106048  -0.6690109
#> 50%   -0.05431694   0.04061442  -0.1111398
#> 75%    0.72976278   0.61636766   0.5306826
#> 100%   2.13348636   2.13286973   2.1873352
```

mapply and Map

The functionals lapply, sapply, vapply take a function and apply it to each element in a vector or list. In other words, each element in the vector or list is supplied as the argument to the function. While we may, as we described above, have other arguments to the function set to fixed values for each function application, we cannot use lapply, sapply or vapply to apply functions to two or more lists or vectors at the same time. Consider the following function:

```
power <- function(x, k) x^k
```

If we had a vector of x values, and set k to 5, for example, we could do the following:

```
x <- c(2, 3, 4, 5)
sapply(x, power, k=5)
#>   [1] 32 243 1024 3125
```

However, if we had the vector of x values and a vector of k values, and wish to apply each element of x and the corresponding element of k to power, we need to use mapply, as in the following example:

```
x <- c(2, 3, 4, 5)
k <- c(2, 3, 2, 2)
mapply(power, x = x, k = k)
#> [1] 4 27 16 25
```

As we can see, for each index `i` of `x` and `k`, we calculate `power(x[i], k[i])`. This `mapply` is therefore equivalent to the following `for` loop:

```
for (i in seq_along(x)){
 power(x[i], k[i])
}
```

With `mapply`, we can iterate over any number of lists of input arguments simultaneously. As an example, the random number generator `rnorm` function takes three arguments: `n`, `mean`, and `sd`. In the following, we apply `rnorm` to each value in each of the three arguments:

```
set.seed(101)
n <- c(2, 3, 5)
mu   <- c(10,  100, 200)
sigma  <- c(1,  10, 10)
mapply(rnorm, n = n, mean = mu, sd = sigma)
#> [[1]]
#> [1] 9.673964 10.552462
#>
#> [[2]]
#> [1] 93.25056 102.14359 103.10769
#>
#> [[3]]
#> [1] 211.7397 206.1879 198.8727 209.1703 197.7674
```

As we can see, we effectively execute `rnorm(n=3, mean=10, sd=1)`, `rnorm(n=5, mean=5, sd = 10)`, and so on.

The `Map` function works just like `mapply`, with minor differences, such as never simplifying the results:

```
set.seed(101)
Map(rnorm, n = n, mean = mu, sd = sigma)
#> [[1]]
#> [1] 9.673964 10.552462
#>
#> [[2]]
#> [1] 93.25056 102.14359 103.10769
#>
#> [[3]]
#> [1] 211.7397 206.1879 198.8727 209.1703 197.7674
```

As we can see, `Map` and `mapply` are identical in their usage and in what they do. However, by default, `mapply` will attempt to simply its output like `sapply`, if possible. We saw this with the use of the `power` function with `mapply` above. However, if we replace `mapply` with `Map`, no simplification is applied, and we obtain a list as output:

```
x <- c(2, 3, 4, 5)
k <- c(2, 3, 2, 2)
```

```
Map(power, x = x, k = k)
#> [[1]]
#> [1] 4
#>
#> [[2]]
#> [1] 27
#>
#> [[3]]
#> [1] 16
#>
#> [[4]]
#> [1] 25
```

Filter, Find, and Position

The `Filter` functional takes a *predicate*, which is a function that returns a logical value, and a vector or list, and returns those elements of the list for which the predicate is true. As an example, here we have a data frame with three variables:

```
data_df  <- tibble(x = rnorm(3),
                   y = rnorm(3),
                   z = c('a',  'b',  'c')
)
```

We can select the numeric vectors of `data_df` as follows:

```
Filter(is.numeric, data_df)
#> # A tibble: 3 x 2
#>       x        y
#>    <dbl>    <dbl>
#> 1   0.526  -1.47
#> 2  -0.795  -0.237
#> 3   1.43   -0.193
```

In this example, we are doing what could otherwise be accomplished with `dplyr`'s `select_if` function:

```
select_if(data_df, is.numeric)
#> # A tibble: 3 x 2
#>       x       y
#>    <dbl>   <dbl>
#> 1   0.526 -1.47
#> 2  -0.795 -0.237
#> 3   1.43  -0.193
```

Unlike `select_if`, `Filter` can be applied to data structures other than data frames. For example, in the following, we select all elements of a random sample of 20 integers that are multiples of 3:

```
s <- sample.int(100, size=10, replace=T)
s
#>  [1] 31 79 51 14 67 42 50 43 14 25
Filter(function (x) x %% 3 == 0, s)
#> [1] 51 42
```

The `Find` function searches through a vector or list to find the first element for which a predicate is true:

```
Find(function (x) x %% 3 == 0, s)
#> [1] 51
```

If the predicate is not true of any element, then NULL is returned:

```
Find(function (x) x < 0, s)
#> NULL
```

The `Position` function is like `Find`, but returns the position of the first element for which the predicate is true:

```
Position(function (x) x %% 3 == 0, s)
#> [1] 3
```

 ## 6.6   Functionals with `purrr`

The `purrr` package in the tidyverse provides functionals like those just covered, but which are consistent with one another in terms of how they are used, and also with how other tidyverse functions are used. But `purrr` provides additional functional tools beyond those in base R. We can load `purrr` with `library(purrr)`, but it is also loaded by `library(tidyverse)`.

map

One of the main tools in `purrr` is `map` and its variants. It is very similar to `lapply`. It takes a list (or vector) and a function, and applies the function to each element of the list. To reuse an example from above, in the following we apply `read_csv` to each file name in a list of file names, and collect the data frames that are produced in a list `data_df_list`:

```
file_list    <- c('data_1.csv',
                   'data_2.csv',
                   'data_3.csv')
data_df_list <- map(file_list, read_csv)
```

As with `lapply`, we can include optional arguments for the function being applied. For example, if we wanted to read in the data files as in the previous example, but just read no more than 100 rows of data, we can include the `n_max` argument as follows:

```
data_df_list <- map(file_list, read_csv, n_max=100)
```

The `map` function has `_if` and `_at` variants, which function similarly to the `_if` and `_at` variants of the `dplyr` verbs we met earlier. For example, if we want to apply `read_csv` only if the name of the data file is not `data_2.csv`, we can use `map_if` as follows:

```
data_df_list <- map_if(file_list,
                       function(x)  x  != 'data_2.csv',
                       read_csv)
```

We could accomplish the same thing by using `map_at`, which can take positional arguments, or negative positions, to include or exclude elements of a list. For example, if we include -2 as the second argument of `map_at` it will skip the second item in `file_list`:

```
data_df_list <- map_at(file_list,
                       -2,
                       read_csv)
```

When the list that is returned by `map` or its variants can be simplified to a vector, we can use the `map_dbl`, `map_int`, `map_lgl` or `map_chr` variants of `map` to simplify the list to a vector of doubles, integers, Booleans or characters, respectively. In the following example, we apply functions that produce integers, logicals, doubles or characters, to each column of a data frame:

```
data_df <- read_csv('data_1.csv')
map_int(data_df, length)
#>    x    y    z
#> 1000 1000 1000
map_lgl(data_df, is_integer)
#>     x     y     z
#> FALSE FALSE FALSE
map_dbl(data_df, mean)
#>              x              y              z
#> -0.0259532006    0.0643665838  -0.0009872201
map_chr(data_df, class)
#>         x         y         z
#> "numeric" "numeric" "numeric"
```

There is also a `map_df` which can be used when the list contains data frames that can be concatenated together. For example, to read in all three data frames and concatenate them we can do the following:

```
data_df_all <- map_df(file_list, read_csv)
```

What is accomplished with `map_df` here is exactly what would be obtained by a combination of `map` and `dplyr`'s `bind_rows`:

```
data_df_all_2 <- map(file_list, read_csv) %>%
  bind_rows()
```

```
all_equal(data_df_all,      data_df_all_2)
#> [1] TRUE
```

The use of map_df in the above example is exactly equivalent to using map_dfr, which forces the creation of the data frame by row binding:

```
data_df_all_3 <- map_dfr(file_list, read_csv)
all_equal(data_df_all, data_df_all_3)
#> [1] TRUE
```

On the other hand, if we wanted to create a data frame by column binding, we could use map_dfc. It is possible to do this with the data frames in the previous examples because they all have equal numbers of rows:

```
data_df_all_4 <- map_dfc(file_list, read_csv)
```

The resulting data frame data_df_all_4 is of the following dimensions:

```
dim(data_df_all_4)
#> [1] 1000      9
```

Its column names are as follows:

```
names(data_df_all_4)
#> [1] "x...1" "y...2" "z...3" "x...4" "y...5" "z...6" "x...7" "y...8" "z...9"
```

purrr-style anonymous functions

We saw above that we can use anonymous functions in lapply, sapply, etc., functionals. This can be done in purrr functionals like the map family too, as we see in the following example:

```
map_dbl(data_df,
        function(x) mean(log(abs(x))))
)
#>          x          y          z
#> -0.6400092 -0.5868030 -0.5765645
```

However, purrr provides *syntactic sugar* to allow us to rewrite this as follows:

```
map_dbl(data_df,
        ~ mean(log(abs(.))))
)
#>          x          y          z
#> -0.6400092 -0.5868030 -0.5765645
```

In other words, in place of the function(x), we have ~, and in place of the anonymous function's input variable we have a dot (.).

map2 **and** pmap

When we have two or more sets of input arguments, we can use `map2` and `pmap`, respectively. Both of these functions also have the `_lgl, _int, _dbl, _chr, _df, _dfr` and `_dfc` variants that we saw with `map`.

As an example of a `map2` function, we'll use the power function with two input arguments:

```
x <- c(2, 3, 4, 5)
k <- c(2, 3, 2, 2)
map2_dbl(x, k, power)
#> [1]  4 27 16 25
```

As an example of a `pmap` function, we can reimplement the `rnorm`-based sampler that we originally wrote with `mapply`. The first argument to `pmap` is a list whose length is the number of arguments being passed to the function. If we want to iterate over different values of the n, mean and `sd` arguments for `rnorm`, as we did in the example above, we set up a list like the following:

```
args <- list(n = c(2, 3, 5),
             mean = c(10, 100, 200),
             sd = c(1, 10, 10))
```

We then use `pmap` as follows:

```
pmap(args, rnorm)
#> [[1]]
#> [1] 8.734939 9.313147 #>
#> [[2]]
#> [1] 95.54338 112.24082 103.59814 #>
#> [[3]]
#> [1] 204.0077 201.1068 194.4416 217.8691 204.9785
```

walk

The `walk` function in `purrr` is like `map` but is used with functions that are called just for their *side effects*. Put informally, a side effect of a function is an effect performed by a function other than its return value. A very common side effect of a function is writing something to a file. For example, while the `write_csv` function does return a value, it is simply the name of the file to which the content is written. The real action done by `write_csv` is in its side effect. Like `map`, `walk` has variants `walk2` and `pwalk` that are exactly analogous to `map2` and `pmap`.

As an example, let us perform the inverse of `map(file_list, read_csv)` in the following code, which takes a list of .csv files, reads in their data as data frames, and then stores them in the list `data_df_list`:

```
file_list  <- c('data_1.csv',
                'data_2.csv',
                'data_3.csv')
data_df_list <- map(file_list, read_csv)
```

The inverse should take each element in the list and write it back to the appropriately named file. For these, we can use `walk2`, which will iterate over the data frames in the list and the names in `file_list`:

```
walk2(data_df_list, file_list, write_csv)
```

keep **and** discard

The `purrr` package also provides us with functions to effectively emulate base R's `Filter`. For example, if we want to select elements from a list or vector for which some predicate is true, we can use `keep`. To select those elements for which the predicate is not true, we can use `discard`. As an example, here we select out the even numbers in a sequence of integers from 1 to 20:

```
keep(seq(20), ~ . %% 2 == 0)
#>  [1]  2  4  6  8 10 12 14 16 18 20
```

To select the odd numbers, which are obviously not the even numbers, we can use `discard` as follows:

```
discard(seq(20), ~ . %% 2 == 0)
#>  [1]  1  3  5  7  9 11 13 15 17 19
```

7

Reproducible Data Analysis

Introduction

The end product of any data analysis is usually a set of tables, figures, and the seemingly countless statistics and other quantities that specify the results of the statistical modelling or testing and that was performed. These results are then usually communicated in reports, including and especially peer-reviewed scientific articles, through talks and presentations, or through mainstream or social media. These results are the end product of an often long and arduous process, something we will call the *data analysis pipeline*, that began initially with just the raw data. For example, the original raw data might have been in the form of a set of `.xlsx` files that were downloaded from a website. These might have been wrangled and transformed repeatedly by a long series of operations, such as those described in Chapter 3, to produce various 'tidy' data sets, which themselves might then have been repeatedly and iteratively visualized and statistically analysed and modelled. It is not an exaggeration to say that this whole process might have involved hundreds or even thousands of hours of work, taking place intermittently over the course of months or even years, and involving many different people at many different stages. We can view the data analysis pipeline as akin to a factory: raw materials, in the form of the raw data, go in; these are worked on and turned into something new and valuable by the combined efforts of human labour and machines (computers); and finally, the end products are produced that are to be consumed by others.

The aim of *reproducible data analysis*, at its most general, is to make the data analysis factory or pipeline as open and transparent as possible, and to allow all others, including our future selves, to be able to exactly reproduce any of the results that were produced by it. In other words, the aim is to make it possible for anyone to determine exactly where and how any given table, figure, or statistical quantity was obtained, and to be able to reproduce any of these results exactly. If the pipeline is suitably reproducible, anyone ought to be able to take the original raw data and reproduce all the final results, or alternatively ought to be able to take the raw data and analyse it in new and different ways, thus producing new and interestingly different results.

Doing reproducible data analysis is often motivated by a general commitment to doing *open science*. Since the origin of modern science in the seventeenth century, part of its defining ethos (see Merton, 1973) has been the unrestricted sharing of the fruits of research, and also a full disclosure of all details of any research so that they may be scrutinized by others. Thus, openness and transparency are core ethical principles in all science. Recently, it has become apparent that these ethical principles, although often endorsed in principle, are not usually followed in practice, and that in fact there is a widespread culture of not sharing data (see, for example, Tenopir et al., 2011; Fecher et al., 2015; Houtkoop et al., 2018), not sharing data analysis and other computer code (see, for example, Shamir et al., 2013; Stodden et al., 2013), and that there is a widespread general lack of research transparency in science (see, for example, Iqbal et al., 2016). This has lead to repeated calls for major cultural changes related to the sharing of data and code and general research transparency under the banner of doing *open science* (see, for example, Ioannidis, 2015; Nosek et al., 2015; Gorgolewski and Poldrack, 2016; Munafò et al., 2017).

Reproducible data analysis can also be motivated simply as a means of doing higher-quality and more robust data analysis, even when this analysis is not being done as part of scientific research *per se*, such as with confidential analyses that are done in business and industry.

In these contexts, the raw data and analysis pipeline may always remain confidential and never be shared publicly. Nonetheless, doing this analysis using reproducible research practices allows for essential quality control. It allows the analysts themselves, those they do the analysis for, or future analysts who inherit the project or are brought on board later, to scrutinize and double-check every detail of the analysis and reproduce every result. These are essential measures to identify errors, increase rigour, and verify the final results and conclusions. Even, or especially, outside of academic or scientific research, there can be enormous practical and financial incentives to minimizing errors and increasing analytical rigour in data analysis. As an example, it has been argued that a lack of reproducible data analysis techniques was partly to blame for a $9 billion loss at the investment bank JPMorgan in 2012 (see Hern, 2013).

This chapter is about doing *open, transparent* and *reproducible* research using R and related software tools. In particular, we will focus on *RMarkdown* and *Knitr* for making reproducible reports, and *Git* for version control of all our files. There are other important software tools for reproducible research that we could cover, but do not do so in order to keep our coverage relatively brief and introductory. These tools include Docker for creating lightweight virtual operating systems, R packages for packaging and distributing code and data, build automation tools like GNU Make or the R package `drake` (Landau, 2018), and continuous integration tools like Jenkins[1] or Travis CI.[2]

Before we proceed, however, let us briefly discuss some terminology. The terms *open, transparent* and *reproducible* describe a set of data analysis practices. These terms are obviously not identical, but they are related. It is, however, not trivial to state the extent to which any one depends upon or requires any other. While it is not necessary to be pedantic about the definitions and scope of these terms, we will briefly outline our understanding of them.

Open Open data analysis, like open source software or open science generally, is data analysis where all the data, code, and any other required materials are fully disclosed to and shared with others, usually by being made publicly available. Being publicly available, and in an unrestricted manner, is therefore usually taken to be a defining feature of open data analysis.

Transparent Transparent data analysis is analysis where, as mentioned above, it is possible to determine exactly where and how any given table, figure, or statistical result was obtained. Making data and code and all other material open is usually a sufficient condition for the analysis to be transparent, but it is possible to conceive of situations where data and code are open and available but are poorly written and organized, or are obfuscated, or require undocumented manual intervention, and so lack transparency. Likewise, as also mentioned above, it is not necessary for data to be open, at least in the sense of publicly available, for it to be transparent.

Reproducible A reproducible data analysis is one where an independent analyst can exactly reproduce all the results. For an analysis to be reproducible it is necessary that all the data and code are available and in full working condition. Strongly implied, however, is that running the code is essentially a turnkey operation. Software tools, such as *build automation* tools like *GNU*

---

[1] https://www.jenkins.io/

[2] https://travis-ci.com/

Make, are often used, especially with larger projects. For reports and articles, and their myriad tables and figures and in-text quantities, *literate programming* tools, particularly RMarkdown with R, are used. Version control software, such as Git, is often used to organize and keep a log of the development of all the analysis code and scripts. To allow the code to be used across different operating systems and with the correct dependencies, virtual or containerized operating systems using tools such as Docker are sometimes used. Other tools, such as the `checkpoint::checkpoint()` function in R, can be used to ensure the correct versions of R package dependencies are used.

 ## Using RMarkdown for reproducible reports

As mentioned, the results of data analyses are communicated through reports such as peer-reviewed scientific articles and other manuscripts, slide or poster presentations, web-pages, and so on. For the results described in these reports to be truly reproducible, every figure, table, or any other value or quantity ought to be reproducible with minimal effort by anyone, including and especially those not directly involved in the analysis. For this, it is necessary that the data and code be made available to others. But this alone is not sufficient. Even if the necessary data and code were complete, it might still be challenging or nearly impossible for someone who was not directly involved in the analysis to identify exactly which code produced any given figure, table, or other reported quantity. This is especially the case if the results in the report were generated, as is exceedingly common, by transcribing or copying and pasting results from the output of statistical software, or inserting figures that were exported, into a word-processed document. For any given figure or table or quantity, hunting down and verifying which piece of code produced it could be very challenging and time-consuming. Moreover, there is a very high probability that the reported results will have some errors somewhere simply because they were all the product of transcription or other manual interventions. Indeed, there is no way of even categorically verifying that all the correct code and data necessary to produce the results have been made available without painstakingly finding and checking each individual piece code for each individual result.

For a report to be truly reproducible, therefore, the data, code and resulting document need to be inextricably coupled in a manner that goes beyond how documents are traditionally written. This coupling of code, data, and text is based on the concept of *literate programming* (see Knuth, 1984). In a *literate program*, the text of the documentation of a computer program and the code of that program are linked in one single file or set of files. These files can be processed by different programs to generate either the documentation manuals or the computer programs that will be compiled and executed like normal programs. While this principle has become a common means of generating documentation for computer code (see, for example, *Roxygen2* for documenting R code, *Doxygen* for documenting C++, and *Sphinx* for documenting Python), the same principle can be used to create reproducible data analysis reports, which are sometimes known as *dynamic documents* (see Xie, 2017) The most popular, and arguably the best, way of doing this using R is to use RMarkdown, or more precisely to use RMarkdown and a combination of tools including *knitr, pandoc* and others.

Before we proceed, let us briefly introduce or define a number of key concepts and tools.

RMarkdown RMarkdown itself is simply a text file format, and so an RMarkdown file is essentially a script, not unlike an R script. In fact, just like normal R scripts, we usually open, edit, and 'run' RMarkdown files inside RStudio. Unlike R scripts, which consist of just R code, possibly including comments, but nothing else, RMarkdown scripts primarily consist of a mixture of two types of code: *Markdown* code and normal R code. As we'll see, the R code in RMarkdown documents occurs in either R *chunks*, which are simply blocks of code, or *inline* R code, which is small amounts of R code inside Markdown code.

Markdown Markdown is a minimal or lightweight markup language. It was initially created by John Gruber (Gruber, 2004) primarily as means of allowing web users to create formatted posts, including links, images and lists, on online discussion forums. Markdown consists of normal text, just as you would write in an email or any other document, as well some minimal syntax that instructs how this text should be formatted when it is rendered into some output document, such as an HTML page, PDF or Microsoft Word document.

Knitr Knitr (see Xie, 2017) is a general tool for dynamic documentation generation using R. In brief and put very simply, knitr extracts R code from RMarkdown documents, runs this code, and then, by default, inserts copies of this code and the code's output into a Markdown document. Knitr then runs pandoc to create a document, such as a PDF or MS Word document, from this Markdown file.

Pandoc Pandoc (MacFarlane, 2006) is, in general, a document converter that can convert a large number of input document types to an equally large number of output document types. For present purposes, it is the means by which Markdown documents generated by knitr are converted into their final output formats such as PDF, MS Word, or ML.

LaTeX LaTeX (Lamport, 1994) is a document preparation system that is specialized for creating high-quality technical and scientific documents, especially those containing mathematical formulae and technical diagrams. It is widely used for creating academic and research manuscripts in mathematically oriented fields such as statistics, computer science and physics. LaTeX documents are created by first writing a `.tex` source code file, which is mixture of LaTeX and TeX code, markup syntax, and plain text. This `.tex` file is then usually rendered to a PDF using a LaTeX rendering engine, of which there are many, but the most widely used is the default PDFLaTeX engine.

Installation

If using RStudio, the necessary R packages, including `rmarkdown` and `knitr`, are automatically installed. Likewise, the external pandoc program is also automatically installed when `rmarkdown` is installed. While this set of tools will allow you to create HTML and MS Word documents, LaTeX must be installed to create PDF outputs. Installation and configuration of LaTeX, because it is a large external program, may not always be straightforward. It may seem, therefore, that this LaTeX installation step is not worthwhile, especially given that many people unquestionably and happily use MS Word to write their manuscripts. However, we highly recommend installing LaTeX and using the LaTeXed PDF document output over MS Word for writing manuscripts. At the very least, the typesetting quality of the resulting LaTeXed document will be considerably higher than that of the MS Word document. Moreover, by using LaTeX with RMarkdown, we can avail of all the power of LaTeX to create the final document. This includes the use of all LaTeX packages for creating and styling mathematical and technical content, including technical diagrams, fine control of figures and tables, their look and feel, and their placement, internal cross-referencing to refer to individual pages, sections, figures, etc., automatic index generation, and many more. Even if these features may seem unnecessary at first, in our opinion, it is nonetheless still worthwhile to use LaTeX with RMarkdown from the beginning, so that all these features can be used as one's experience with RMarkdown grows.

To install LaTeX for use with RMarkdown, we can install the R package `tinytex`:

```
install.packages("tinytex")
tinytex::install_tinytex()
```

This installation will take some time. After it completes, you should restart RStudio. After you restart, type the following command (note the three colons after `tinytex`):

```
tinytex:::is_tinytex()
```

After this installation completes, we can test that `rmarkdown` (which will have be installed by `tidyverse`) will render PDF documents using LaTeX with the following code:

```
writeLines("Hello $x^2$", 'test.Rmd')
rmarkdown::render("test.Rmd", output_format = "pdf_document")
```

The `writeLines` creates a tiny `.Rmd` file named `test.Rmd`. The `rmarkdown::render` command then attempts to render this as a PDF document, which will require LaTeX to be properly working. If this works as expected, we will have a PDF document named `test.pdf` in our working directory.

A minimal RMarkdown example

As just mentioned, an RMarkdown file is essentially a script containing two types of code: Markdown and normal R code. The following are the contents of a small RMarkdown file, named `example.Rmd`:

```
This is some text. Some of it is *italicized*, and some is in **bold**.
```{r}
x <- c(5, 12, 103)
y <- x ^ 2
```

The mean of `x` is `r mean(x)`, and the min value of `y` is `r min(y)`.
```

This example contains one R *chunk*. This is the portion of R code between the opening ```` ```{r} ```` and the closing ```` ``` ````. It also has two pieces of inline R code. These are the code segments in the last line between the opening `` `r `` and closing `` ` ``. The remainder of the code in this example is plain Markdown code.

As we will see, we could open this file in the RStudio editor and then *knit* it to, for example, a PDF document. This can be accomplished by clicking on the small arrow to the right of the ⚙ icon on the RMarkdown file editor, and choosing `Knit to PDF`. Alternatively, in the console, we could do the following, assuming that `example.Rmd` is in the current working directory.

A PDF document `example.pdf` will be produced and its contents will be as follows:

This is some text. Some of it is *italicized*, and some is in **bold.**

```
x <- c(5, 12, 103)
y <- x ^ 2
```

The mean of x is 40, and the min value of y is 25.

The key features to notice here are that the Markdown code within the RMarkdown file is formatted according to its instructions. For example, the appropriate words are italicized and emboldened. Also, the R code in the chunk is appropriately formatted as code, using a monospaced font, and is syntax highlighted. Finally, and most interestingly in this example, the *values* returned by the R commands in the two pieces of inline code are inserted at the locations of, and thus replace, the original two pieces of inline code. In other words, in the final document, the values of 40 and 25 replace `` `r mean(x)` `` and `` `r min(y)` ``, respectively.

Although this is a very simple example, a lot has happened to produce the final PDF output. The procedure is roughly as follows:

- First, `knitr` extracts the R code from `example.Rmd` and runs it in a separate R session. The code is run in the order in which it appears in the document. So, first, the R chunk is run, which creates two vectors, x and y. Then, the R commands `mean(x)` and then `min(y)` are executed.
- Next, all the Markdown code in `example.Rmd` is extracted and inserted into a new temporary file `example.md`. Likewise, by default, copies of the R code in the chunk, though not the inline code, are inserted into this `example.md` Markdown file. Any R code that is inserted into `example.md` is marked up as R code so that it will be properly rendered, including with syntax highlighting, in the final output document.
- Next, any *output* from the R code, whether the R chunk or the R inline code, is inserted into the `example.md` file. In the example above, there is no output from the R chunk. However, obviously the commands `mean(x)` and `min(y)` both return numbers, and so these two numbers are inserted into the `example.md` Markdown file at the exact locations of where the two pieces of inline R code occurred.
- Now, `knitr` calls pandoc. The latter first converts the `example.md` Markdown into a LaTeX source code file named `example.tex`. This file is essentially just another script whose contents would be easily understandable to anyone who knows LaTeX.
- Next, pandoc calls a LaTeX rendering engine, such as PDFLaTeX, and converts the LaTeX source code file `example.tex` into the PDF document `example.pdf`.
- Finally, the intermediate files, including `example.md` and `example.tex` are, by default, removed so that the only remaining files are the original RMarkdown source file `example.Rmd` and the final output document `example.pdf`.

An extended RMarkdown example

```
---
title: "Data Analysis: A Report"
author: "Mark Andrews"
date: "October 25, 2019"
output: pdf_document
---

```{r setup, echo=FALSE}
knitr::opts_chunk$set(message = F,
                      warning = F,
                      out.width = "45%",
                      fig.align='center')
```

Introduction

First, we will load the `tidyverse` packages, and read
in the the from a `.csv` file.
```{r load_packages_data}
library(tidyverse)
data_df <- read_csv('example.csv')
```

Analysis

Here, we do a Pearson's correlation analysis.
```{r analysis}
(corr_model <- cor.test(~ x + y, data = data_df))
```

The correlation coefficient is
`r round(corr_model$estimate, 3)`.

Visualization

The scatterplot between x and y is shown
in Figure \ref{fig:vis}.

```{r vis, echo=F, fig.cap='A scatterplot.'}
ggplot(data_df, aes(x, y)) +
  geom_point() +
  theme_classic()
```
```

Data Analysis: A Report

Mark Andrews

October 25, 2019

Introduction

First, we will load the tidyverse packages, and read in the the from a .csv file.

```
library(tidyverse)
data_df <- read_csv('example.csv')
```

Analysis

Here, we do a Pearson's correlation analysis.

```
(corr_model <- cor.test(~ x + y, data = data_df))
##
## 	Pearson's product-moment correlation
##
## data:  x and y
## t = 2.1583, df = 48, p-value = 0.03593
## alternative hypothesis: true correlation is not equal to 0
## 95 percent confidence interval:
##  0.02080268 0.53175304
## sample estimates:
##       cor
## 0.2974284
```

The correlation coefficient is 0.297.

Visualization

The scatterplot between x and y is shown in Figure 1.

Figure 7.1 An example of an RMarkdown file on the left, and its corresponding PDF output on the right. The PDF output is generated by knitting the RMarkdown file. In RStudio, this can be accomplished by `rmarkdown::render("example-2.Rmd")`, where `example-2.Rmd` is the RMarkdown file

In Figure 7.1, we show the code of an RMarkdown file on the left and its corresponding PDF output on the right. This example shows many of the features of a typical RMarkdown document. We will discuss these features by looking through each section of the RMarkdown code.

The YAML header

The first few lines of the document, specifically those lines that are delimited by the lines with the three dashes (---), constitute its *YAML* header.

```
---
title: "Data Analysis: A Report"
author: "Mark Andrews"
date: "October 25, 2019"
output: pdf_document
---
```

YAML (a recursive acronym for *YAML Ain't a Markup Language*) is itself a minimal markup language that is now often used for software configuration files. As is perhaps clear from this example, in this header we specify the title, author, date, and output format of the document. This information is used when rendering the output document. At its simplest, YAML consists of *key–value* mappings where the term on the left of the : is the key, and the term or statement on the right is the value. Thus, author: "Mark Andrews" indicates that the author is "Mark Andrews", and when the final document is being generated, "Mark Andrews" will be inserted as the value of the author in the output document's template. Note that although we use double quotation marks as the values of the title, author and date keys, neither single nor double quotation marks are always necessary. In this example, we would only require the quotation marks for the value of title. This is to ensure that the colon within Data Analysis: A Report is not mistakenly parsed by the YAML parser as indicating a key–value mapping.

We specify the document output type in the header by output: pdf_document. As mentioned above, when writing manuscripts, we recommend always using the PDF-based output document option as this will be generated by LaTeX. However, had we preferred to create an MS Word output document, we would state output: word_document. Likewise, had we preferred an HTML output document, which can obviously be viewed in any browser or used to create a webpage, we would put output: html_document.

The setup R chunk

It is common, though not necessary, to have a setup R chunk like the following at the beginning of our RMarkdown file:

```
```{r setup, echo=FALSE}
knitr::opts_chunk$set(message = F,
                      warning = F,
                      out.width = "45%",
                      fig.align='center')
```
```

In addition to including a common configuration statement, this example also has some important general RMarkdown features. First, in the minimal RMarkdown example in the previous subsection, the R chunk was defined by starting with ```{r} and ending with ```. Here, the chunk statement begins with

```
```{r setup, echo=FALSE}
```

The term setup after the initial r is simply a label for this chunk. It is not necessary to have a label for chunks, but it can be used for file navigation purposes in the RStudio editor, and is used for cross-referencing purposes, especially for so-called *floating* figures and tables, as we will see. As such, it is probably a good habit to always use a (unique) label for each R chunk.

After the chunk label, we have the chunk configuration option echo=FALSE. This indicates the R code in this chunk should not be displayed in the output document. Next, we have the following R statement:
```

```
knitr::opts_chunk$set(message = F,
                      warning = F,
                      out.width = "45%",
                      fig.align='center')
```

Here, we set the values of the `opts_chunk` list of global options used by `knitr`. For example, in this case, we start by indicating that, by default, all subsequent chunks in the RMarkdown document should have the options `message = FALSE` and `warning = FALSE` (because these are R statements, we can use `F` for `FALSE`). Setting `message = FALSE` entails that the messages, which can be verbose, produced by R commands are not shown. As an example of this, consider the usual output when we load a package, in this case using `lme4`:

```
library(lme4)
## Loading required package: Matrix
##
## Attaching package: 'Matrix'
## The following objects are masked from 'package:tidyr':
##
##      expand, pack, unpack
```

Therefore, globally setting `message = FALSE` can considerably reduce clutter in the output document. Likewise, it is often preferable to globally suppress R warnings to avoid clutter in the final document. Although not used in this example, another commonly set global option at this point is `echo=FALSE`. Often, especially in manuscripts for peer-reviewed articles, we do not wish to display all, or even any, of the R code used in the analysis. Rather, we just want to display the results of the analysis in tables, figures, and so on, and so globally setting `echo=FALSE` avoids having to set `echo=FALSE` on each subsequent chunk.

The next two settings, `out.width = "45%"` and `fig.align='center'`, pertain to how figures should be displayed by default. The `out.width = "45%"` indicates that the figure should occupy 45% of the width of the page, and `fig.align='center'` indicates that it should be centred on the page.

Markdown sections

The use of # followed by some text at the start of a line in the Markdown language indicates a section header. Thus, in our case, the following line indicates we should have a section entitled *Introduction* in our document:

```
# Introduction
```

While the single # is for a section, subsections are indicated by ##, and subsubsections are indicated by ###. Here is an example with three levels of sections.

```
# This is a section
```

```
## This is a subsection
```

```
# This is another section

## This is a subsection

### This is a subsubsection
```

In principle, further nested subsections (e.g. subsubsubsections) are possible. However, this does depend on both the output document type and the templates for this document that are used by `knitr` or pandoc.

R chunk outputs

Just as we see the output of R commands when those commands are run in the console, the output of R commands will appear in the output document unless we specifically request otherwise. Consider the following lines from our example RMarkdown file:

```
```{r analysis}
(corr_model <- cor.test(~ x + y, data = data_df))
```
```

In this case, the assignment statement is in parentheses, and in R this generally causes the output of the expression in this statement to be shown. In other words, the output that will be shown will be identical to what would be shown had we just typed

`cor.test(~ x + y, data = data_df)`

By default, this output will have each line beginning with ## (because they are part of the R chunk output they are not interpreted as subsection headers). Should we wish use alternative symbols at the beginning of the output, we can indicate this by setting the value of the `comment` chunk option. For example, if we wanted all R output to start with '>', we would set `comment = '>'`, as in the following code:

```
```{r, echo=T, comment='>'}
rnorm(5) %>% round(2)
```
```

This code would then be rendered as follows:

`rnorm(5) %>% round(2)`
```
> [1] 0.47 -1.66  0.11 -0.26 -0.79
```

LaTeX mathematical typesetting

On the line

```
The scatterplot between $x$ and $y$ is shown
```

we have the terms x and y. The dollar symbols indicate that x and y should be parsed by LaTeX's "math mode" and typeset according. In this example, this will simply cause the x and y to be shown in a different and italicized font compared to normal letters. However, in general, there are a vast number of mathematical notations, formulae and symbols that can be used here. For example, consider the following Markdown code:

```
If $\Phi = \phi_1, \phi_2, \ldots, \phi_k, \ldots, \phi_k$, where each $0 \leq \phi_k
\leq 1$, and $\sum_{k=1}^K \phi_k = 1$, then $\Phi$ is a probability mass function.
```

This code would then be rendered as follows:

If $\Phi = \phi_1, \phi_2, \ldots, \phi_k, \ldots, \phi_k$, where each $0 \leq \phi_k \leq 1$ and $\sum_{k=1}^K \phi_k = 1$, then Φ is a probability mass function.

In these examples, all the LaTeX code occurs in its *inline mode,* and this is obtained by using $ delimiters. In addition to inline mode, there is LaTeX *display* mode. This is obtained by using $$ delimiters. LaTeX display mode is used to display mathematical formulae and other notation on new lines. Consider the following example:

```
The probability of the observed data is as follows:
$$
\mathrm{P}(x_i, \ldots, x_n \vert \mu, \sigma^2)
= \prod_{i=1}^n \mathrm{P}(x_i \vert \mu, \sigma^2),
$$
where $\mu$ and $\sigma$ are parameters.
```

This would then be rendered as follows:

The probability of the observed data is as follows:

$$P(x_i,\ldots,x_n \mid \mu,\sigma^2) = \prod_{i=1}^n P(x_i \mid \mu,\sigma^2),$$

where μ and σ are parameters.

LaTeX provides a very large number of mathematical symbols, notations and formulae. It is beyond the scope of this chapter to even provide an overview of all of these features. However, we will provide an overview of some of the more widely used examples in a later section of this chapter.

Figures

If the R code in the R chunk generates a figure, for example by using `ggplot`, then that figure is inserted into the document immediately after the location of the chunk. These figures can optionally have figure captions by setting the value of `fig.cap` in the chunk header. When the `fig.cap` is set, at least when using the `pdf_document` output, the figure then *floats.* A floating figure is one whose placement location in the final document is determined by an algorithm that attempts to minimize a large number of constraints, such as the amount of white space on the page, the number of figures on one page, and so on.

In our example file, we have the following lines:

```
```{r vis, echo=F, fig.cap='A scatterplot.'}
ggplot(data_df, aes(x, y)) +
  geom_point() +
  theme_classic()
```
```

This chunk will create a `ggplot` figure that will float. Because of the global settings of `out.width = 40%` and `fig.align = 'center'`, the figure will be relatively small and centred on the page. Because there is sufficient space, the figure will be placed at the bottom of the page. However, were we to increase the width of the figure to even `out.width = 50%`, the default settings of the float placement algorithm would place the figure alone on the following page. Often, the choices made by LaTeX's float placement algorithm are initially unappealing. The recommendation, however, is not to attempt any fine control until the document is complete. As each new text block, figure or table is added to the document, the floats are relocated. When the document is complete, it is possible to influence float placement by changing parameter settings on the float placement algorithm.

It should be noted that if figures do not float, they are placed exactly where the chunk's output would otherwise occur. In some cases, especially if the figures are relatively small, this can be satisfactory.

An additional RMarkdown example

In Figure 7.2, we provide the code of another RMarkdown file. This example provides some additional important RMarkdown features that were not covered in the previous example. The PDF output document corresponding to this document is shown in Figure 7.3.

```
---
title: "Data Analysis: Report II"
author: "Mark Andrews"
date: "October 26, 2019"
output:
  pdf_document:
    keep_tex: yes
header-includes:
- \usepackage{booktabs}
bibliography: refs.bib
biblio-style: apalike
---

```{r setup, echo=FALSE}
knitr::opts_chunk$set(warning = FALSE, message = FALSE)
```

```{r load_packages, echo = FALSE}
library(tidyverse)
library(knitr)
library(kableExtra)
```

weight_df <- read_csv('weight.csv')
weight_df_grouped <- group_by(weight_df, gender)

sample_size <- weight_df_grouped %>%
  summarise(n=n()) %>%
  deframe()

weight_df_summary <- weight_df_grouped %>%
  summarise_at(vars(weight, height),
    list(avg=mean, stdev=sd))

Descriptive statistics

In this data set, we have measured the weight (in kg)
and height (in cm) of `r sum(sample_size)` participants
(`r sample_size['Male']` males, `r sample_size['Female']`
females). In the following table, we show the mean and
```

```
separately for males and females.

```{r descriptives_table, echo=F}
weight_df_summary %>%
  kable(format = "latex",
    booktabs = TRUE,
    digits = 2,
    align = 'c') %>%
  kable_styling(position = "center")
---

# Statistical model

We will model the relationship between weight and height
as a varying intercepts normal linear model as follows.
For each $i \in 1 \ldots n$,
$$
\begin{aligned}
y_i &\sim N(\mu_i, \sigma^2),\\
\mu_i &= \beta_0 + \beta_1 x_i + \beta_2 z_i,
\end{aligned}
$$
where $y_i$, $x_i$, $z_i$ are the weight, height,
and gender of participant $i$.

In R, this analysis can be easily performed as follows.
```{r stat_model}
model <- lm(weight ~ height + gender, data = weight_df)
---

```{r model_results, echo=F}
R_sq <- summary(model)$r.sq
f_stat <- summary(model)$fstatistic
p_value <- pf(f_stat[1], f_stat[2], f_stat[3], lower.tail = F)
```

The R^2 for this model is `r round(R_sq, 2)`,
$F(`r round(f_stat[2])`, `r round(f_stat[3])`) =
`r round(f_stat[1],2)`$,
$p `r format.pval(p_value, eps = 0.01)`$.

More information about varying intecept models can be
found in @GelmanHill:2007.

References
```

Figure 7.2 An additional RMarkdown file example. The rendered PDF output document is shown in Figure 7.3

Additional YAML header options

In this example file, we have set some additional settings in the YAML header. For example, we have the following lines:

```
output:
  pdf_document:
    keep_tex: yes
header-includes:
- \usepackage{booktabs}
```

The latter two lines relate to the bibliography, and we will return to these below. The first two lines indicate that the LaTeX command `\usepackage{booktabs}` should be included in the header of the resulting `.tex` file prior to being rendered to PDF by the LaTeX engine. Recall that, as mentioned above, the rendering process to produce the final `.pdf` document is that `knitr` takes the `.Rmd` file and creates a `.md` file, with R code and R code output inserted into it. If the final output is to be PDF, pandoc converts the `.md` file to a `.tex` file, and that is then rendered to `.pdf` by a LaTeX engine such as PDFLaTeX. When pandoc creates the `.tex` file from the `.md`, it uses `.tex` file templates that load some of the more widely used LaTeX packages. However, if any other LaTeX packages are required to create the final PDF document, they may be listed as we have done here in the YAML header using the `header-includes` option. It should be noted that there are many thousands of additional LaTeX packages that can be installed.

Another option to include additional functionality in your RMarkdown document is to include a block of code in the header. For example, we might have a file named `include.tex` with the following command:

```
\newcommand{\Prob}[1]{\mathrm{P}( #1 )}
```

If we had the following YAML header in our RMarkdown document, the commands in `include.tex` would be available to use in the body of the RMarkdown file:

```
output:
  pdf_document:
    includes:
      in_header: include.tex
```

For example, in this case, we could now write `\Prob{X = x}` = `0.25` in our RMarkdown file, and this would eventually be rendered as $P(X = x) = 0.25$. The file `include.tex` can have an extensive number of custom commands, including numerous `\usepackage{}` statements.

Formatted tables

When writing reports, we often wish to present the results of statistical analyses in tables. Naturally, we would ideally like these tables to be formatted to a high standard. As we've seen, we can always simply display the standard output of R commands that produce tables and data frames, but the resulting unformatted monospaced font text is not of an acceptable

Data Analysis: Report II

Mark Andrews

October 25, 2019

Descriptive statistics

In this data set, we have measured the weight (in kg) and height (in cm) of 6068 participants (4082 males, 1986 females). In the following table, we show the mean and the standard deviations of the weights and heights, separately for males and females.

gender	weight_avg	height_avg	weight_stdev	height_stdev
Female	67.76	162.85	10.98	6.42
Male	85.52	175.62	14.22	6.86

Statistical model

We will model the relationship between weight and height as a varying intercepts normal linear model as follows. For each $i \in 1 \ldots n$,

$$y_i \sim N(\mu_i, \sigma^2),$$
$$\mu_i = \beta_0 + \beta_1 x_i + \beta_2 z_i,$$

where y_i, x_i, z_i are the weight, height, and gender of participant i.

In R, this analysis can be easily performed as follows.

```
model <- lm(weight - height + gender, data = weight_df)
```

The R^2 for this model is 0.45, $F(2, 6065) = 2495.83$, $p < 0.01$.

More information about varying intecept models can be found in Gelman and Hill (2007).

References

Gelman, Andrew, and Jennifer Hill. 2007. *Data Analysis Using Regression and Multilevel/Hierarchical Models*. New York: Cambridge University Press.

Figure 7.3 The PDF document output corresponding to the RMarkdown code shown in Figure 7.2

standard for most manuscripts and reports, especially those that are intended for eventual publication. As an example, consider the table produced by the following R commands that use the built-in `swiss` data set:

```
(swiss_df <- swiss %>%
  select(Fertility:Examination) %>%
  slice(1:5))
##              Fertility Agriculture Examination
## Courtelary        80.2        17.0          15
## Delemont          83.1        45.1           6
## Franches-Mnt      92.5        39.7           5
## Moutier           85.8        36.5          12
## Neuveville        76.9        43.5          17
```

Clearly, this output is not sufficient for all but informal reports.

Fortunately, we have a number of options for formatting tables. For example, to use `kable` to create a table specifically for use in the `pdf_document` output, we can do the following:

```
library(knitr)
swiss_df %>%
  kable(format = 'latex',
        booktabs = TRUE,
        align = 'c')
```

This code will produce a nicely formatted table that looks like the following:

	Fertility	Agriculture	Examination
Courtelary	80.2	17.0	15
Delemont	83.1	45.1	6
Franches-Mnt	92.5	39.7	5
Moutier	85.8	36.5	12
Neuveville	76.9	43.5	17

Here, we use `booktabs = TRUE` and in the YAML header, as mentioned, we ensure that the `booktabs` LaTeX package is loaded. By loading the `booktabs` package, the typesetting of the tables in LaTeX is often improved over the default options. The `align = 'c'` option ensures that the values in each column in the table are centred. If we want to centre the table produced by the above `kable` command, we can use the `kable_styling` function in the `kableExtra` package as follows:

```
library(kableExtra)
swiss_df %>%
  kable(format = 'latex',
        booktabs = TRUE,
        align = 'c') %>%
  kable_styling(position = 'center')
```

Display maths

In this example, we provide some examples of *display*-mode mathematics. As mentioned, this is where the mathematical statements are on separate lines. In this example, we use the `aligned` environment in LaTeX, which allows us to align multiple mathematical statements. Specifically, the example we use is as follows:

```
$$
\begin{aligned}
```

```
y_i &\sim N(\mu_i, \sigma^2),\\
\mu_i &= \beta_0 + \beta_1 x_i + \beta_2 z_i,
\end{aligned}
$$
```

This is rendered as follows:

$$
\begin{aligned}
y_i &\sim N\left(\mu_i, \sigma^2\right), \\
\mu_i &= \beta_0 + \beta_1 x_i + \beta_2 z_i,
\end{aligned}
$$

The & symbol on each line is used to align the lines, so that the ~ on the first line is aligned with the = on the second line. Here, we need to add \\ at the end of the first line to force a line break. The `aligned` environment is widely used in LaTeX, especially for showing algebraic derivations. For example,

```
$$
\begin{aligned}
y &= \frac{e^x}{1+e^x}\\
  &= \frac{e^x}{e^x (e^{-x} + 1)}\\
  &= \frac{1}{1 + e^{-x}}.
\end{aligned}
$$
```

is rendered as follows:

$$
\begin{aligned}
y &= \frac{e^x}{1+e^x} \\
&= \frac{e^x}{e^x\left(e^{-x}+1\right)} \\
&= \frac{1}{1+e^{-x}}.
\end{aligned}
$$

Formatted inline R output

In this RMarkdown example, we display the R^2 of the linear model as well as its accompanying F-statistic and p-value with the following code:

```
The $R^2$ for this model is `r round(R_sq, 2)`,
$F(`r round(f_stat[2])`, `r round(f_stat[3])`) =
`r round(f_stat[1],2)`$,
$p `r format.pval(p_value, eps = 0.01)`$.
```

Here, we make use of some quantities (i.e. `R_sq`, `f_stat`, `p_value`) created earlier in the file. In addition, we place some inline R code inside $ so that it will be formatted as mathematical notation. Placing inline R code inside other LaTeX mathematical environments is always possible. Consider the following example:

```
$$
\int_{-\infty}^1 \frac{1}{\sqrt{2\pi}} e^{-\frac{x^2}{2}} dx = `r round(pnorm(1), 3)`
$$
```

This will produce the following output:

$$\int_{-\infty}^1 \frac{1}{\sqrt{2\pi}} e^{-\frac{x^2}{2}} dx = 0.841$$

Note that in this example we also use the R function `format.pval`. This function can be used to return an inequality when the *p*-value is lower than a certain threshold named `eps`. Consider the following example:

```
p <- c(0.05, 0.02, 0.011, 0.005, 0.001)
format.pval(p, eps = 0.01)
## [1] "0.050" "0.020" "0.011" "<0.01" "<0.01"
```

Bibliography

In the YAML header, we have included the following statements:

```
bibliography: refs.bib
biblio-style: apalike
```

The first tells RMarkdown to use the bibliographic information contained in the file `refs.bib`, which is assumed to be present in the working directory. The second line tells RMarkdown to format the citations and the references in the bibliography using American Psychological Association (APA) style.

The `refs.bib` file is just a plain text file, and can be named anything. In this example, its content is minimal and consists just of the following:

```
@book{GelmanHill:2007,
  address = {New York},
  author = {Gelman, Andrew and Hill, Jennifer},
  title = {Data Analysis Using Regression and Multilevel/Hierarchical Models},
  publisher = {Cambridge University Press},
  year = 2007
}
```

The `@book{ }` content is a BibTeX bibliographic entry for a book, with BibTeX being the primary bibliography manager used with LaTeX. As this is a simple text file, these bibliographic entries can be relatively easily created. However, because BibTeX is such a widely used bibliographic manager, BibTeX bibliographic entries are provided in many scholarly article databases, including Google Scholar. It is therefore very easy to build up a personal bibliography file, which can then be reused in all of one's reports.

Having defined a bibliography in the YAML header as we have done, we can now use the BibTeX *keys* to perform citations. The *key* for BibTeX entry is the text after the first brace and before the first comma. Consider the following three BibTeX entries:

```
@book{xie2017dynamic,
  title={Dynamic Documents with R and knitr},
  author={Xie, Yihui},
  year={2017},
  publisher={Chapman and Hall/CRC}
}


@article{knuth1984literate,
  title={Literate programming},
  author={Knuth, Donald Ervin},
  journal={The Computer Journal},
  volume={27},
  number={2},
  pages={97--111},
  year={1984},
  publisher={Oxford University Press}
}

@book{wickham:2019,
  Author = {Hadley Wickham},
  Title = {Advanced R},
  Publisher = {Chapman and Hall/CRC},
  Year = {2019},
  edition = 2
}
```

The keys here are `xie2017dynamic`, `knuth1984literate` and `wickham:2019`. Should we wish to refer to, say, Wickham's book in our RMarkdown file, we would simply write `@wickham:2019`. For example, the following statement in RMarkdown

```
As is described in @wickham:2019, R is a functional programming language.
```

would result in 'As in described in Wickham (2019), R is a functional programming language.' in the output document. Alternatively, had we written

```
R is a functional programming language [@wickham:2019].
```

this would result in 'R is a functional programming language (Wickham 2019).' in the output document.

In either case, the following line would then be inserted at the end of the output document:

Wickham, Hadley. 2019. *Advanced R*. 2nd ed. Chapman and Hall/CRC

If we had multiple citations, they would all be listed at the end of the output document in alphabetical order. By default in RMarkdown, this list of bibliographic references is not given a section name. Therefore, as we have done in this example RMarkdown document, we simply end the document with a section named *References* by using the following line as the last line.

```
# References
```

All the references will now be inserted after this section header. Should we prefer the name *Bibliography*, or another other option here, we simply change the name of this section.

Brief guide to Markdown

As a minimal markup language, there are not too many Markdown commands to learn. Here, we provide an overview of the main ones.

Headers

We have already seen section headers above. Section headers begin with a # at the start of a new line followed by the section title. These lines are preceded and followed by a blank line. The number of # symbols indicates the level of the section: # indicates a section, ## is a subsection, ### is a subsubsection, and so on. Note that there should be a space after the # symbol or symbols at the start of the line. For example, `# Introduction` will create a section entitled *Introduction*, but `#Introduction` will produce a line with #Introduction on it. In Figure 7.4, on the left, we see a Markdown file with multiple sections and subsections. On the right, we see this file rendered as a PDF document.

Font style and weight

As we've seen above in a few examples, we can produce italicized text by surrounding the text with *, and we obtain bold text by surrounding it with **. Here are some examples:

- `*this is italicized text*` produces *this is italicized text*
- `**this is bold text**` produces **this is bold text**
- `***this is bold and italicized text***` produces ***this is bold and italicized text***

Underscores (_) have the same effect as *:

- `_this is italicized_` produces *this is italicized*
- `_ _this is in bold_ _` produces **this is in bold**
- `_ _ _this is in bold and in italics_ _ _` produces ***this is in bold and in italics***

We can also mix _ and *:

- `*_ _this is italicized bold text_ _*` produces ***this is italicized bold text***
- `_ _*this is italicized bold text*_ _` produces ***this is italicized bold text***
- `_**this is italicized bold text**_` produces ***this is italicized bold text***

```
# Introduction

This is a sentence in the Introduction.

## Objectives of study

This is a sentence in the first subsection
of the Introduction.

# Analysis

This is a sentence in the Analysis section.

## Exploratory analysis

This is a sentence of the first subsection
of the Analysis section.

## Statistical model

This is a sentence of the second subsection
of the Analysis.

# Conclusion

This is a sentence in the last section
of the document.
```

Introduction

This is a sentence in the Introduction.

Objectives of study

This is a sentence in the first subsection of the Introduction.

Analysis

This is a sentence in the Analysis section.

Exploratory analysis

This is a sentence of the first subsection of the Analysis section.

Statistical model

This is a sentence of the second subsection of the Analysis.

Conclusion

This is a sentence in the last section of the document.

Figure 7.4 An example of a Markdown file on the left, and its corresponding PDF output on the right. The Markdown file has sections, indicated by lines beginning with #, and subsections, indicated by lines beginning with ##

In Markdown, there is no general way of producing underlined text. However, if we are using `pdf_document` output, we can use the LaTeX `\underline` command. For example, `\underline{this text is underlined}` gives <u>this text is underlined</u>.

Code

Often in technical documents, we need to display computer code. If we simply surround the code block by ` ``` `, we will obtain monospace typed text. For example, the following Markdown code shows Python code:

```
```
for x_i in x:
y.append(x_i)
```
```

This is rendered as follows:

```
for x_i in x:
  y.append(x_i)
```

However, ideally we would prefer the code to be syntax highlighted. We can do so by indicating the code's language after the initial ` ``` `. In the following Markdown code, we state that the code is Python:

```
```python
for x_i in x:
y.append(x_i)
```
```

This is then rendered as follows:

```
for x_i in x:
    y.append(x_i)
```

When we wish to display R code, we have another option. We can use a normal R code chunk, but set the chunk parameter eval to FALSE, and set echo to TRUE, assuming it is not globally set to TRUE:

```
```{r, echo=TRUE, eval=FALSE}
n <- 10
x <- rnorm(n)
y <- 2.25 * x + rnorm(n)
M <- lm(y ~ x)
```
```

This is then rendered as follows:

```
n <- 10
x <- rnorm(n)
y <- 2.25 * x + rnorm(n)

M <- lm(y ~ x)
```

Lists

There are three types of lists that are possible with the PDF document output: itemized lists, enumerated lists, and definition lists.

Itemized lists In itemized lists, also known as unordered lists or even bullet-point lists, each item begins on a new line that begins with * followed by a space. The list has to be both preceded and followed by a blank line. For example, we have Markdown code with an itemized list on the left, and its rendered output on the right.

`* Apple`	• Apple
`* Orange`	• Orange
`* Blueberry`	• Blueberry

Items in a list do not need to be written using only one line of Markdown code. A single item may be spread over multiple lines as in the following example:

`* If we start our item on one line, and continue to another line with no break, It will still appear as one item.`	• If we start our item on one line, and continue to another line with no break, it will still appear as one item.
`* The same thing happens if you continue on the next line after and indention.`	• The same thing happens if you continue on the next line after and indention.

We can also create nested lists by using indented lines that themselves begin with *, as in the following example:

```
*  Farm animal                    • Farm animal
     *  Cow                          - Cow
     *  Pig                          - Pig
     *  Sheep                        - Sheep

*  Wild animal                    • Wild animal
     *  Fox                          - Fox
     *  Wolf                         - Wolf
```

In general in Markdown, the indentation should be made with four spaces or a tab. In some cases, fewer spaces than four will suffice, but it is generally better to use four spaces. Also, beware that some editors, including the RStudio editor, map the Tab key to two spaces.

Enumerated lists Enumerated lists are defined and behave just like itemized lists except that instead of an item or sub-item being defined by a line beginning with a * (followed by a space), it is defined by a line beginning with a number followed by a . and then a space. In the following example, our items begin with 1. followed by a space:

```
1. Potato                         1.  Potato
1. Broccoli                       2.  Broccoli
1. Cabbage                        3.  Cabbage
```

We do not need to always use 1. to obtain an enumerated list. Any other numbers will suffice, as in the following example:

```
1.  Potato                        1.  Potato
4.  Broccoli                      2.  Broccoli
10. Cabbage                       3.  Cabbage
```

However, if we use a number greater than 1 as the first item, then that will be used as the starting value of the numbering of the list, as in the following example:

```
12. Potato                        12.  Potato
4.  Broccoli                      13.  Broccoli
10. Cabbage                       14.  Cabbage
```

Enumerated lists can be nested just like itemized lists:

```
1. Tree                           1.  Tree
     1. Fir                         1.  Fir
     1. Pine                        2.  Pine
     1. Oak                         3.  Oak

1. Flower                         1.  Flower
     1. Rose                        1.  Rose
     1. Tulip                       2.  Tulip
     1. Daffodil                    3.  Daffodil
```

We may also mix enumerated and itemized lists when using nestings as in the following example:

``
* Tree
    1. Fir
    1. Pine
    1. Oak
 	
* Flower
    1. Rose
    1. Tulip
    1. Daffodil
``
	• Tree
	   1. Fir
	   2. Pine
	   3. Oak
	
	• Flower
	   1. Rose
	   2. Tulip
	   3. Daffodil

Definition lists Definition lists, when rendered, begin with an emboldened term followed by a definition or description. This can be useful for definitions *per se*, but also when we need to elaborate on or describe certain terms. For example, they could be used to describe the meaning of different variables in a data set. We create a definition list by beginning a new line with some text, which is usually brief, such as a name. The subsequent line then begins with a : followed by the definition or description. For example, in the following code, we provide a definition list elaborating upon the variables in a data set.

``` participant-id : An integer that uniquely codes each participant. gender : A binary variable with values 'female' and 'male'. age : A numeric variable giving the participant's age in years. ```	**participant-id** An integer that uniquely codes each participant. **gender** A binary variable with values `female` and `male`. **age** A numeric variable giving the participant's age in years.

Brief guide to mathematical typesetting with LaTeX

RMarkdown provides an extensive set of commands for typesetting mathematical formulae, symbols and other notation. These commands are in fact LaTeX commands, but are available regardless of the output document format. In other words, even if we are not using the `pdf_document` output format, which is ultimately rendered by a LaTeX typesetting engine, we may still avail of these LaTeX commands for mathematical typesetting.

As we have seen above, there are two *modes* in which mathematical formulae and notation can appear: *inline* mode and *display* mode. Inline model is where the mathematical notation appears within a line of normal text. It is obtained by surrounding the code with $ symbols. For example, the code

```
Einstein's famous formula for mass-energy equivalence is $E = mc^2$.
```

is rendered as follows:

Einstein's famous formula for mass-energy equivalence is $E = mc^2$.

On the other hand, display mode is where the mathematical formulae or notation appear on a line on their own. It is obtained by surrounding the code by $$ symbols. For example, the code

```
Einstein's famous formula for mass-energy equivalence is
$$
```

```
E = mc^2.
$$
```

is rendered as follows:

> Einstein's famous formula for mass-energy equivalence is
>
> $E = mc^2$.

In what follows, we provide a brief and minimal introduction to the main mathematical typesetting commands that are available in RMarkdown. To be able to appreciate all of the mathematical typesetting options in RMarkdown, we would have to provide a thorough introduction to mathematical typesetting in LaTeX. This is well beyond the scope of this book, but there are many books that provide extensive details about mathematical typesetting in LaTeX. For example, one highly recommended, comprehensive and up-to-date book is Grätzer (2016).

Symbols for variables

In mathematical formulae and notation, there are a large number of symbols that are commonly used as variables. These include the upper- and lowercase letters of the English alphabet, which can be typed directly. For example, x becomes x, A becomes A. It also very common to use the upper- and lowercase letters of the Greek alphabet. The lowercase Greek symbols are in the following table:

\alpha	α	\iota	ι	\sigma	σ		
\beta	β	\kappa	κ	\tau	τ		
\gamma	γ	\lambda	λ	\upsilon	υ		
\delta	δ	\mu	μ	\phi	ϕ		
\epsilon	ε	\nu	ν	\chi	χ		
\zeta	ζ	\xi	ξ	\psi	ψ		
\eta	η	\pi	π	\omega	ω		
\theta	θ	\rho	ρ				

Given that some uppercase Greek letters are identical to uppercase letters in English, only those that are different from English letters have commands or even LaTeX to render them. These are shown in the following table.

\Gamma	Γ	\Lambda	Λ	\Sigma	Σ	\Psi	Ψ
\Delta	Δ	\Xi	Ξ	\Upsilon	Υ	\Omega	Ω
\Theta	Θ	\Pi	Π	\Phi	Φ		

Calligraphic and **blackboard bold** fonts of English uppercase letters commonly appear too. The following calligraphic uppercase English letters are often used in mathematical formulae and notation:

\mathcal{A}	$\mathcal{A}$	\mathcal{G}	$\mathcal{G}$	\mathcal{M}	$\mathcal{M}$	\mathcal{S}	$\mathcal{S}$	\mathcal{Y}	$\mathcal{Y}$
\mathcal{B}	$\mathcal{B}$	\mathcal{H}	$\mathcal{H}$	\mathcal{N}	$\mathcal{N}$	\mathcal{T}	$\mathcal{T}$	\mathcal{Z}	$\mathcal{Z}$
\mathcal{C}	$\mathcal{C}$	\mathcal{I}	$\mathcal{I}$	\mathcal{O}	$\mathcal{O}$	\mathcal{U}	$\mathcal{U}$		
\mathcal{D}	$\mathcal{D}$	\mathcal{J}	$\mathcal{J}$	\mathcal{P}	$\mathcal{P}$	\mathcal{V}	$\mathcal{V}$		
\mathcal{E}	$\mathcal{E}$	\mathcal{K}	$\mathcal{K}$	\mathcal{Q}	$\mathcal{Q}$	\mathcal{W}	$\mathcal{W}$		
\mathcal{F}	$\mathcal{F}$	\mathcal{L}	$\mathcal{L}$	\mathcal{R}	$\mathcal{R}$	\mathcal{X}	$\mathcal{X}$		

Likewise, the following blackboard bold fonts are widely used:

\mathbb{A}	$\mathbb{A}$	\mathbb{G}	$\mathbb{G}$	\mathbb{M}	$\mathbb{M}$	\mathbb{S}	$\mathbb{S}$	\mathbb{Y}	$\mathbb{Y}$
\mathbb{B}	$\mathbb{B}$	\mathbb{H}	$\mathbb{H}$	\mathbb{N}	$\mathbb{N}$	\mathbb{T}	$\mathbb{T}$	\mathbb{Z}	$\mathbb{Z}$
\mathbb{C}	$\mathbb{C}$	\mathbb{I}	$\mathbb{I}$	\mathbb{O}	$\mathbb{O}$	\mathbb{U}	$\mathbb{U}$		
\mathbb{D}	$\mathbb{D}$	\mathbb{J}	$\mathbb{J}$	\mathbb{P}	$\mathbb{P}$	\mathbb{V}	$\mathbb{V}$		
\mathbb{E}	$\mathbb{E}$	\mathbb{K}	$\mathbb{K}$	\mathbb{Q}	$\mathbb{Q}$	\mathbb{W}	$\mathbb{W}$		
\mathbb{F}	$\mathbb{F}$	\mathbb{L}	$\mathbb{L}$	\mathbb{R}	$\mathbb{R}$	\mathbb{X}	$\mathbb{X}$		

As examples of where these fonts are used, $\mathbb{N}, \mathbb{Z}, \mathbb{Q}, \mathbb{R}, \mathbb{C}$ are used to denote the natural numbers, integers, rational, real and complex numbers, respectively.

Subscripts and superscripts

Subscripts and superscripts are widely used in mathematical notation. For example, all symbols for variables commonly occur with subscripts and superscripts. In addition, subscripts and superscripts occur in mathematical operators and functions, as we will see below. As we've seen in passing in many examples above, we obtain a subscript by using _ and a superscript using ^. For example, x_1 is x_1 and x^2 is x^2. When we need to use more than just a single character or command for the subscript or superscript, we need to surround it with braces. For example, if want 10^{100}, we need to write 10^{100}. Writing 10^100 will lead to 10^100. Likewise with subscripts. For example, for x_{ijk}, we write x_{ijk} and not x_ijk, which would give xjk.

We may also use braces to nest sub- and superscripts, as in the following example:

```
2^{2^2}, 2_{i_j}
```

This is rendered as follows:

$$2^{2^2}, 2_{i_j}$$

It should be noted that not using the brace here would simply lead to a ! Double superscript or ! Double subscript error.

It is also possible to mix sub- and superscripts. For example, 2^i_j gives 2^i_j; 2_j^i also gives 2^i_j.

Arithmetic operations and fractions

For arithmetic, plus and minus are obtained by + and -, respectively. For example, $x + y$ gives $x + y$, $x - y$ gives $x - y$, and so on. The command \pm is used to produce the *plus or minus* symbol ±. For exponents, we use superscripts just as we saw above. For multiplication, it is conventional that the absence of any operator implies multiplication. For example, x times y is conventionally often written simply as xy. However, if we prefer to use a symbol to explicitly mark multiplication, we may use \cdot or \times. For example, $a \cdot b$ gives $a \cdot b$, and $a \times b$ gives $a \times b$.

For division, if we are simply dividing one symbol by another, we can use / or \div. For example, a / b gives a/b, and $a \div b$ gives $a \div b$. However, for formulae that involve ratios of sets of symbols or larger statements, we need to used \frac{}{}, as we see in the following example:

```
$$
\frac{1}{2} + \frac{3}{4} = \frac{4 + 6}{8} = \frac{5}{4}
$$
```

This is rendered as follows:

$$\frac{1}{2} + \frac{3}{4} = \frac{4+6}{8} = \frac{5}{4}$$

While it is perhaps more common to use \frac{}{} in display mode, it may be used in inline mode as well, as in the following example:

```
The result is $x = \frac{a + b}{c + d}$.
```

This is rendered as follows:

The result is $x = \frac{a+b}{c+d}$.

We may also nest fractions using \frac{}{}, as in the following example:

```
$$
\frac{a}{b + \frac{1}{c}}
$$
```

This is rendered as follows:

$$\frac{a}{b+\frac{1}{c}}$$

Sums, products, integrals, etc.

Summation over multiple variables is denoted using a variant of the uppercase Sigma symbol. However, for this, we use \sum and not \sigma. For example, to denote the sum over a set of numbers $x_1, x_2, ..., x_n$, we would write

```
$$
\sum_{i=1}^n x_i
$$
```

This is rendered as follows:

$$\sum_{i=1}^n x_i$$

The limits of the sum are not strictly necessary. Thus, we could omit them as follows:

```
$$
\sum x_i
$$
```

This appears as follows:

$$\sum x_i$$

However, this summation notation is ambiguous at best, and so including the limits of the sum is highly recommended at all times.

We write products using the uppercase Pi symbol, but again, we should not use \Pi but \prod instead. Just like \sum, \prod should always be used with limits, as in the following example:

```
$$
\prod_{i=1}^n x_i
$$
```

This appears as follows:

$$\prod_{i=1}^n x_i$$

Note that when sums or products are used in inline mode, they appear in a more compact form. For example, $\sum_{i=1}^n x_i$ appears as $\sum_{i=1}^n x_i$, and $\prod_{i=1}^n x_i$ appears as $\prod_{i=1}^n x_i$.

Integrals are written using the \int command. Like \sum and \prod, they may include limits, as in the following example, which gives the area under the curve defined by the function $f(x)$ between the values of $x = 0$ and $x = 1$:

```
$$
\int_{0}^1 f(x) dx
$$
```

This appears as follows:

$$\int_0^1 f(x)\,dx$$

When limits on the integral are given, it is known as a *definite integral*. In the absence of limits, we have an *indefinite integral* and this is the integral over all values of the integrand.

Roots

We obtain the square root symbol by the `\sqrt` command. To use this properly, unless the argument is a single digit, we must include the argument within {} after the command. In other words, to obtain $\sqrt{2}$, we can use $\sqrt{2}$, but to obtain $\sqrt{42}$, we must write $\sqrt{42}$. Had we written $\sqrt 42$ or even $\sqrt(42)$, we would have obtained $\sqrt{4}2$ or $\sqrt{(42)}$, which is not the desired result. Note that `\sqrt` produces a character that stretches to enclose the expression to which it applies, as we see in the following example that gives the formula for a sample standard deviation:

```
$$
s = \sqrt{\frac{\sum^n_{i=1} (x_i - \bar{x})^2}{n-1}}
$$
```

This will appear as follows:

$$
s = \sqrt{\frac{\sum_{i=1}^{n}(x_i - \bar{x})^2}{n-1}}
$$

To obtain the *n*th root, we place the value of *n* in square brackets after `\sqrt` and before the {}, as we see in the following example, which displays the cubed root:

```
$$
\sqrt[3]{125} = 5
$$
```

This will appear as follows:

$$
\sqrt[3]{125} = 5
$$

Equalities, inequalities and set operators

Equalities and inequalities can be denoted using = and < or >. For example, $x = y$ gives $x = y$, and $x < y$ gives $x < y$. However, there are many other symbols commonly used to denote equalities, equivalences or inequalities. Likewise, there are many symbols commonly used for set-theoretic operations. Some of the more widely used examples are shown in the following table:

=	=	\leq	≤	\gg	≫	\propto	∝	\doteq	≐	\subset	⊂	\supseteq	⊇
<	<	\geq	≥	\approx	↓	\equiv	≡	\in	∈	\supset	⊃	\cap	∩
>	>	\ll	≪	\sim	~	\triangleq	≜	\ni	∋	\subseteq	⊆	\cup	∪

Many of these operators can be negated using the `\not` command before the operator symbol or command. For example, `$x \not= y$` gives $x \neq y$, and `$x \not< y$` gives $x \not< y$.

Multiline and aligned formulae

We may create multiline formulae that are vertically aligned at designated points using `\begin{aligned}`, `\end{aligned}`, as in the following example:

```
$$
\begin{aligned}
f &= (x + y) (x + y),\\
&= x^2 + 2xy + y^2
\end{aligned}
$$
```

This appears as follows:

$$f = (x+y)(x+y)$$
$$= x^2 + 2xy + y^2$$

Note that, we use `&` for alignment and `\\` for new lines.

We may use the `aligned` environment even when we do not need alignment *per se*, but just require multiline equations, as in the following example:

```
$$
\begin{aligned}
x = a + b\\
y = c + d + e
\end{aligned}
$$
```

This appears as follows:

$$x = a + b$$
$$y = c + d + e$$

  Git

Version control software (VCS) is an essential tool for the efficient management and organization of source code. In the case of data analysis using R, the relevant source code files will primarily include `.R` and `.Rmd` scripts, but even in small and routine projects, there are many other possibilities too. VCS allows us to keep track of all the versions or revisions to a set of files in an efficient and orderly manner. As a simple example to motivate the use of a VCS system, let us say that we are working on a relatively small data analysis project initially involving some `.R` and `.Rmd` scripts, with names like `preprocessing.R`, `exploration.R`, `analysis.R`, and `report.Rmd`. Let's say that we work with these files, adding new code, editing or deleting old code, etc., every few days in a normal R session. If we were to simply save the files after each session, we would obviously only ever have their most recent versions. All the previous versions would be lost. In order to avoid loss of previous versions, in case they are needed, we could periodically *save as*, creating versions like `preprocessing_v1.R`, `analysis_oct23.R`, and so on. As time goes by, it is highly likely too that new files will appear. Some of these may have been only intended to be temporary files, but others might be intended to be vital parts of the project. Some new files might be *branches* of other files, where we copy the original, and work on some new feature of the code in the copy with the intention of merging the changes back if and when necessary. By proceeding in this manner, there is usually an eventual proliferation of new files and different versions of files with sometimes ambiguous or inscrutable names like `analysis_v1_tmp.R`, `analysis_v1_tmp_new.R`, `preprocessing_tmp_foo.R`, and so on. If files are being copied between different devices or to cloud-based storage, and edited on different devices, the situation can get ever more disorganized, with files of similar names but perhaps slightly different contents or different time-stamps across different machines. At this point, especially if we return to this work after a period of time, it is usually not clear even what each file does, where the latest version of any file is, not to mention what all the previous or temporary versions contain and when and why they were made. If we collaborate with others, things usually become even worse. First, we must decide on a means of sharing files, with email attachments still probably being the default and most widely used method of doing so. Sending back and forth emails with modifications creates yet more versions to manage, and multiple people working independently on the same files introduces conflicts that need to be manually resolved. Eventually, we have multiple files and versions, on multiple devices, being edited independently by multiple different people. Knowing what each file and version is or does, and who did what and when and where, is usually lost as a result.

This level of disorganization is frustrating, wasteful of time and effort, and obviously bad for reproducibility. The authors themselves may find it difficult or impossible to pick through their files to recover and reproduce all the steps involved in any analyses. Moreover, even if they were only working on one file such as an RMarkdown file from which their final report was generated, the proliferation of versions across different devices and owners would still occur, making it difficult to pick up and resume their work after a period of inactivity. In addition, they may lose track of which version of the `.Rmd` produced which version of the rendered manuscript. It is all very well knowing that a manuscript was produced by knitting an `.Rmd`, and hence that all its reported results are reproducible in principle, but if we have lost track of the `.Rmd` that produced it, it is obviously no longer reproducible in practice.

VCS systems allow us to manage our source files in an orderly and efficient manner. There are many VCS systems available, both proprietary and open source, and while precise information on usage worldwide is hard to establish definitively, almost all surveys of VCS usage show that *Git* is now by far the most popular and widely used VCS system. Git is open source software and was originally developed in 2005 for version control of the development of the Linux operating system, something for which it is still used. It gradually became more widely used in the open source community and within a few years had become more popular than the previously very widely used open source *subversion* VCS system. With the growing popularity of Git hosting sites like GitHub, which currently hosts over 100 million Git-based projects, Git is now the most widely used VCS system worldwide.

In what follows, we aim to provide a brief introduction to some of the main features of Git. Obviously, it is beyond the scope of this section to provide a comprehensive introduction to Git. Here, we just provide an introduction to installing and configuring Git, initializing a Git repository, adding files and editing files in the repository, and using a remote repository such as GitHub. These are the *must-knows* to get up and running with Git at the start. We do not cover important topics such reverting or resetting changes, branching, merging, rebasing, and so on. These topics, and many others, can be found in books such as Chacon and Straub (2014), which is available in its entirety online at https://git-scm.com/book/en/v2.

Installation

Git is available for Windows, MacOS and Linux. Git is first and foremost command-driven software. There are graphical interfaces to Git, but we will not consider them here and do not recommend them either, given that there are only a small number of core commands to learn and they allow Git to be used both efficiently and identically across all different devices.

For Windows, we highly recommend installing and using the *Git Bash* shell available from https://gitforwindows.org/. This provides a Bash Unix shell[3] from which Git can be used just as it would be used on other Unix systems like Linux[4] and MacOS.

For MacOS, Git is already preinstalled on recent versions. While this may be perfectly adequate, the preinstalled Git on MacOS is based on a build of Git by Apple and is usually not up to date with the latest version of Git. More recent versions of Git for MacOS are available elsewhere, such as https://git-scm.com/download/mac.

For Linux, given the role of Git in the development of Linux, Git is seen as a vital Linux tool. It is easily installed using the package managers of any Linux distribution; see https://git-scm.com/download/linux.

Once Git is installed, it is available for use using the command `git` in an operating system terminal. For Windows, this means that it is available in the DOS shell. However, if Git is installed, as we recommended, as the Git Bash shell, then that Bash shell should be always used instead of the DOS shell. For MacOS and Linux, Git will be available in the system terminal, and will work identically in the Bash, sh, zsh, etc., shells.

For what follows, we will assume users are using a Unix shell, but all of this will be equally applicable to users of Linux, MacOS and Windows, assuming they use Git Bash.

To establish that Git has been successfully installed and is available for use, type the following:

```
git --version
```

---

[3] https://en.wikipedia.org/wiki/Bash_(Unix_shell)

[4] Strictly speaking, Linux is not Unix, but rather a *nix or Unix-like operating system. However, it is essentially a free and open source reimplementation of Unix, and so can be seen as Unix for all practical purposes.

The output of this command on a relatively up-to-date (as of August 2020) version could appear as follows:

```
git version 2.25.1
```

Configuration

Before we start using Git, we need to perform some minimal configuration. Specifically, we first need to set our name and email address. Git requires that each time we *commit* to the repository, as we will see below, we have the name and email address of the person doing the committing. This information could be set on a per commit basis. However, it is more common and easier to set this information as a global configuration setting and then it will be used whenever the user performs a commit. This can be done using `git config` as in the following code:

```
git config --global user.name 'Mark Andrews'
git config --global user.email 'mjandrews.org@gmail.com'
```

It is recommended that we also set the text editor that we will use for writing our commit messages, which is also something we will see below. By default, the text editor is the `vi` or `vim` editor. These editors are standard Unix editors. They are loved by some and loathed by others. To the uninitiated, these editors are likely to be seen as difficult and probably annoying to use. In any case, it is certainly not necessary to use them as any text editor can be used instead. If a user already has a preference, they should use this. If not, one recommended editor, which is open source and available across the Windows, MacOS and Linux platforms, is the *Atom* editor; see https://atom.io/. Atom can be set as the default editor to be used with Git as follows:

```
git config --global core.editor "atom --wait"
```

Once set, this configuration information is stored in a *dot file* named `.gitconfig` in the user's home directory. Dot files are a standard Unix file system feature. They are simply files, or possibly even directories, that begin with a dot. They are hidden by default in file listings, and are primarily intended to be used for configuration information. The `.gitconfig` file can be edited at any time to change global configuration settings.

Creating and initiating a Git repository

A Git repository is simply a directory (i.e. a folder) in which all the files, including those in subdirectories, are being tracked and managed, or potentially tracked and managed, by Git. Sometimes, as we will see, we obtain a Git repository by *cloning* it. However, we can always turn any directory on our computer into a Git repository using a single command, as we will see below.

Now let us create a Git repository from a newly created empty directory. There is no necessity for the directory to be newly created and empty, that's just what we use in this example. First, let us create a new empty directory `project101` inside the `Documents` directory in our home directory. We will assume that the directory Documents already exists in our home directory, but this is quite common across different platforms. We will use the standard Unix commands mkdir to make the project101 directory, and then cd to change directory so that we are inside it:

```
mkdir ~/Documents/project101
cd ~/Documents/project101
```

We may list the contents of project101 using the Unix ls command. Here, we use the -1aF option to ls. The -1 asks for the information to be shown with one file or directory per line. The -a option will show so-called 'hidden' files and directories. Hidden files and directories, also known as *dot* files or directories, begin with a dot. They are intended to contain configuration information and, by default, not shown in lists of files and directories. The -F option is used primarily to indicate whether the items in a directory are files or subdirectories. Directories are listed by ending their name with a '/':

```
ls -1aF
./
../
```

From this listing, we see that the directory is empty. The two items that are listed, ./ and ../, are always present in a listing where we show hidden files. They are merely references to the present (.) and parent (..) directory.

We now create a Git repository in project101 as follows:

```
git init
Initialized empty Git repository in /home/rstudio/Documents/project101/.git/
```

From this, we see that Git initializes a repository in project101, and creates a directory therein named .git. We may now look at the contents of project101 again:

```
ls -1aF
./
../
.git/
```

We see that there is a hidden or dot directory named .git. The presence of the .git subdirectory is a necessary and sufficient condition for the directory to be a Git repository.

We can now run the git status command to see what is the current state of the repository:

```
On branch master

No commits yet

nothing to commit (create/copy files and use "git add" to track)
```

From the output of this command, we see a number of important pieces of information. First, it tells us that we are on the master branch of the repository. What branches are and how to use them is something to which we will return in due course below. Suffice it to say for now that they are a major feature of Git repositories. Next, we see that there are `No commits yet`. This means that we have not yet *committed* anything to the repository and so nothing is being tracked or managed by Git yet. Finally, we also see that there is currently `nothing to commit`. In other words, there are no files in `project101` that could potentially be committed to the repository.

Now, let us put some files into `project101`. These files could be any type of file, but because Git is intended for the management of source code, ideally the files should be text files rather than binary files. For this example, we will put one R script, `script.R`, and one other text file, `readme.md`, into `project101`. These files could be simply moved or copied from some other directory or could be written in an editor, such as RStudio, and then saved into `project101`. For this example, we will assume that `script.R` contains the following:

```
library(tidyverse)

survivors <- Titanic %>%
  apply(c('Sex', 'Survived'), sum)
```

We will assume that the contents of `readme.md` are as follows:

```
The project contains an R script, `script.R`, for processing the `Titanic` data set.
```

After we have put these files in `project101`, we can do a file listing as we did above:

```
ls -1aF
./
../
.git/
readme.md
script.R
```

We see that `script.R` and `readme.md` are there. Next, we can run the `git status` command as above:

```
git status
On branch master

No commits yet

Untracked files:
   (use "git add <file>..." to include in what will be committed)
     readme.md
     script.R

nothing added to commit but untracked files present (use "git add" to track)
```

Much of the information here is as it was previously, but now we are told that there are two `Untracked files`, namely `readme.md` and `script.R`. Files listed as *untracked* mean that they are present in the directory but not as yet being tracked or managed by Git. As the output indicates, however, we can use the command `git add` to get Git to track them, as we do in the following command:

```
git add readme.md script.R
```

Now let us check the status of the repository again:

```
git status
On branch master

No commits yet

Changes to be committed:
  (use "git rm --cached <file>..." to unstage)
    new file:   readme.md
    new file:   script.R
```

We see from the output that there are new files, `readme.md` and `script.R`, that *can* be committed. This is an important point. The files are not yet committed to the repository, they are *staged* for commitment. When files are staged, they are in an intermediate area, a bit like a departure lounge in an airport. To commit them, we must run the `git commit` command as follows:

```
git commit
```

This will open your editor, and it will contain the following text exactly:

```
# Please enter the commit message for your changes. Lines starting
# with '#' will be ignored, and an empty message aborts the commit.
#
# On branch master
#
# Initial commit
#
# Changes to be committed:
#   new file: readme.md
#   new file: script.R
#
```

In other words, the lines beginning with # provide information to you as you write your commit message, but they will not be part of the message itself. You write your message above these # lines. It is conventional and recommended[5] that the first line of this message is no more than 50 characters long and is followed by a blank line and then followed by more elaboration. The first line is treated as a subject line. Its first character should be capitalized, and it should not end in a full stop/period. It is also recommended that this subject line be written in imperative mood and not past tense. For example, it is recommended that we write something like 'Add

---

[5] See https://tbaggery.com/2008/04/19/a-note-about-git-commit-messages.html

new function …' rather than 'Added new function …'. Admittedly, this is probably initially an unnatural way to write for most people. After the subject line, there must be a blank line. Without it, some features of Git can be affected. Then, a more elaborate message can be written. Here, the imperative mood is no longer necessary. In fact, it is not necessary to have a body at all, but it is highly recommended to provide a message body and to use it to provide details about what the code being committed does. It will be helpful for others, including your future self, to understand what was being added and why. A body text character width of 72 is recommended. Most Git-aware editors, like Atom, will indicate if the subject line is over 50 characters, and if there is not a blank line after the subject, and will wrap the body at 72 characters.

In this example, because this commit is our first commit, our subject line should acknowledge that this is the beginning of the project. As such, a message like the following can be used:

```
Initialize the repository

Two files are added.
* `script.R` is an R script summarizing the `Titanic` data-set
* `readme.md` is the project's readme file.
```

Let us assume, therefore, that this is what we have typed into the editor after we ran the `git commit` command. After we save this file and quit the editor, the commit is completed.

Before proceeding, we should note that it is also possible to write one-liner commit messages using the option -m as follows:

```
git commit -m 'Do something to something'
```

Here, no editor opens and there's no body to the message. For simplicity, we will sometimes use this method below. However, using this method is probably to be avoided as it will, by necessity, lead to minimal and probably poorly thought-out commit messages.

We can now view the Git log of the repository with the following command:

```
git log
```

The output of `git log` would be something like this:

```
commit 71498247035bbe17e053b7e8b434e2eb0a663204
Author: Mark Andrews <mjandrews.org@gmail.com>
Date:   Wed Aug 12 16:27:57 2020 +0000

    Initialize the repository

    Two files are added.
    * `script.R` is an R script summarizing the `Titanic` data-set
    * `readme.md` is the project's readme file.
```

As we can see, our commit message is there, as are our name, email address, and the date and time-stamp of the commit. A crucial additional piece of information is the *commit hash*, which in this case is

```
71498247035bbe17e053b7e8b434e2eb0a663204
```

The commit hash is a vital feature of Git. It is a 40 hexadecimal character (160-bit) crypto-graphic hash of the contents and other defining information about each commit. In other words, it can be seen as essentially a fingerprint of the commit: not just an arbitrarily assigned identifier, but one that is calculated using a hashing algorithm applied to the contents of the commit. It can therefore be used to uniquely identify the commit and to do a file integrity check of its contents.

Having performed the commit, we can now again check the status of the repository:

```
git status
On branch master
nothing to commit, working tree clean
```

As we can see, now the repository is in a clean state. All the original files have been commit-ted. There are as yet no new files in the directory, and no edits to the existing files yet either.

As an interim summary, thus far, we have seen a number of essential and regularly used Git commands:

`git init` Create a Git repository in the current working directory of the shell.

`git status` Report the current working status of the repository. Specifically, are there untracked files in the repository or files in the staging area that have not yet been committed?

`git add <file>` ... Add the files `<file>` ... to the staging area. The staging area is like the departure lounge of an airport. The files therein are going to be scheduled for committal, though they may be taken out of the staging area too.

`git commit` Commit the files in the staging area. This command opens an editor and a commit message is entered there.

Adding and editing files

As with any data analysis project, as it progresses, new files will be made and edits will be made to the existing ones. With Git, we can choose whether and when to add new files to the repository. In other words, for example, if new files are added to the directory pro-ject101, they will be treated as *untracked* files. They will never be automatically added to the repository unless we explicitly add them, using `git add`. Moreover, as we've seen above, adding files with `git add` only puts them in the staging area for committal. They are not committed until we explicitly commit them with `git commit`. Something similar occurs with edits to the existing files. After any edits, Git identifies that files have be modified. However, for these changes to be committed to the repository, they must first be added to the staging area with the `git add` command. Then they must be explicitly committed with a `git commit` command. This double-step process allows us to build up the staging area gradually as we work, and then to commit all its contents when we are ready. The intended purpose of this is that we can then commit a set of files and edits that are all related to one another and together effectively do one main thing, such as fix a bug or a new feature. These are known as *atomic commits*.

Continuing with our very simple example project, let us now add a new file named models.R whose contents are as follows:

```
model <- lm(Fertility ~ Catholic, data = swiss)

model_summary <- summary(model)
```

In addition, let us edit the script.R file by changing the function sum to mean in the apply function:

```
survivors <- Titanic %>%

  apply(c('Sex', 'Survived'), mean)
```

Now let us check the working state of the repository:

```
git status

On branch master
Changes not staged for commit:
  (use "git add <file>..." to update what will be committed)
  (use "git restore <file>..." to discard changes in working directory)
    modified:   script.R

Untracked files:
  (use "git add <file>..." to include in what will be committed)
    models.R

no changes added to commit (use "git add" and/or "git commit -a")
```

As expected, we have one untracked file, models.R, and one modified file, script.R.

We may now add both of these files, and then commit them both to the repository at the same time using a single commit. Alternatively, we could add and commit them individually. Whether we proceed one way or another should be based on whether the commit is atomic: that is, has one main unitary function or purpose. In this example, because the new file and the change to script.R are not related to one another, we will perform two separate commits. First, we will add the modified script.R to staging:

```
git add script.R
```

Before we proceed, let us check the working state of the repository:

```
git status
On branch master
Changes to be committed:
  (use "git restore --staged <file>..." to unstage)
    modified:   script.R

Untracked files:
  (use "git add <file>..." to include in what will be committed)
    models.R
```

As we can see, `script.R` is now in the staging area ready to be committed. We now can do the commit:

```
git commit
```

This will bring up our editor with the following contents:

```
# Please enter the commit message for your changes. Lines starting
# with '#' will be ignored, and an empty message aborts the commit.
#
# On branch master
# Changes to be committed:
#   modified: script.R
#
# Untracked files:
#   models.R
#
```

As before, we should write our commit message above the lines beginning with #, following the conventions and recommendations for good Git messages. We will add the following text to the commit message in the editor:

```
Change function used in the apply functional

The functional now calculates the mean number of men and women who survived the
Titanic, not the total number.
```

Then, as before, when we save and quit, the staged changes are committed. If we look at the logs, we will now see the following:

```
git log
commit 0bf8b056614fa084f5a43f8f771cbbf9f653c772
Author: Mark Andrews <mjandrews.org@gmail.com>
Date:   Wed Aug 12 17:27:57 2020 +0000

    Change function used in the apply functional
```

The functional now calculates the mean number of men and
women who survived the Titanic, not the total number.

```
commit 71498247035bbe17e053b7e8b434e2eb0a663204
Author: Mark Andrews <mjandrews.org@gmail.com>
Date:   Wed Aug 12 16:27:57 2020 +0000

    Initialize the repository

    Two files are added.
      * `script.R` is an R script summarizing the `Titanic` data-set
      * `readme.md` is the project's readme file.
```

Let us again check the repository's status:

```
On branch master
Untracked files:
  (use "git add <file>..." to include in what will be committed)
    models.R

nothing added to commit but untracked files present (use "git add" to track)
```

As expected, we now see that there is just one untracked file, models.R, in the directory. We
first add this file to put it in the staging area:

```
git add models.R
```

Then, we commit it with the following message:

```
Add new lm script named `models.R`

This script performs a linear regression analysis of the
built-in `swiss` data-set.
```

The status of the repository should confirm that everything is now clean:

```
git status
On branch master
nothing to commit, working tree clean
```

We can also check the logs:

```
git log
commit 278ac8d7515d361242b9c4c8458e6c9331adffa0
Author: Mark Andrews <mjandrews.org@gmail.com>
Date:   Wed Aug 12 17:27:57 2020 +0000

    Add new lm script named `models.R`
```

```
    This script performs a linear regression analysis of the
    built-in `swiss` data-set.

commit 0bf8b056614fa084f5a43f8f771cbbf9f653c772
Author: Mark Andrews <mjandrews.org@gmail.com>
Date:   Wed Aug 12 17:27:57 2020 +0000

    Change function used in the apply functional

    The functional now calculates the mean number of men and
    women who survived the Titanic, not the total number.

commit 71498247035bbe17e053b7e8b434e2eb0a663204
Author: Mark Andrews <mjandrews.org@gmail.com>
Date:   Wed Aug 12 16:27:57 2020 +0000

    Initialize the repository

    Two files are added.
      * `script.R` is an R script summarizing the `Titanic` data-set
      * `readme.md` is the project's readme file.
```

As expected, we now have three commits in the log.

Using remote repositories

Thus far, we have been using Git locally on one computer, and there has been only one user. However, one of the key reasons for using Git, or any other VCS system, is for sharing and collaborating on projects. For this, we need to use *remote* repositories. It is both inexpensive (or possibly even free) and not technically difficult to host your own private Git server, which can then be used either for private team work or for sharing projects with the public. The required software, including the operating system of the server (i.e. Linux), is open source and free, and so the only expense is hiring a server from a hosting company.[6] However, we will not consider this option further here. Instead, we will consider special-purpose Git hosting sites, particularly GitHub. GitHub is extremely popular, with around over 40 million users and 100 million repositories as of early 2020.

To share your Git repository, the first step is to create a new repository on GitHub. This assumes that you already have a GitHub account. GitHub provides free and paid-for accounts. For most purposes, the free accounts are more than sufficient.

Assuming we have a GitHub account and have logged in, we then can browse to the following URL:

```
https://github.com/new
```

---

[6]From companies such as https://www.digitalocean.com/. This may be between $5 and $10 per month.

This will bring up a webpage that will allow us to create a new empty repository (see Figure 7.5). When asked for the repository name, you can use any name. In Figure 7.5, we use `project101`, but it is not necessary to use the same name for the remote and local repository. The contents of the repository will define it, not its name. You can then add a description. This description is just something for the GitHub listing itself. It will not be part of the repository in general. Then, assuming you've already created a local repository that you wish to push to GitHub, leave everything else on this page at its default. Specifically, do *not* add a `readme`, or a licence, or a `.gitignore` file. As important as these are, we can add them later using Git commands.

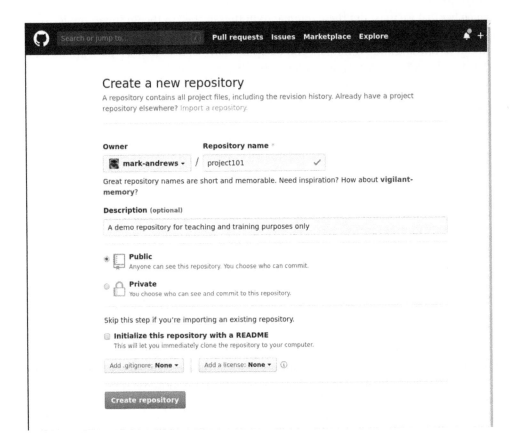

Figure 7.5 Screenshot of a GitHub page for creating a new repository

When we click on Create repository, we are brought to a page that provides some Git commands for different situations. We already have an existing repository, so we want the code listed under the heading *…or push an existing repository from the command line*, which is

```
git remote add origin git@github.com:mark-andrews/project101.git
git push -u origin master
```

There are two important commands here, and so we will look at them individually. The first command adds `github.com:mark-andrews/project101.git` as a remote host of the repository we have created. In this repository, this remote repository will be named `origin`. The name `origin` is the default name for remote repositories from which other repositories are *cloned*. However, we do not have to use this name, and in fact another name, such as `github`, might be more useful, especially if we have multiple remote repositories. The second command *pushes* the contents of the master branch of the local repository to the remote repository named `origin`. When you run this second command, you will be asked for your GitHub password, unless you have set up passwordless GitHub authentication using ssh keys, which is a very convenient feature when frequently using GitHub.

Remember that we must run these commands in the Git shell in the (in this example) `project101` repository that we have been using above. Having run them, if we then point a web browser to https://github.com/mark-andrews/project101 we will see that our repository and all its history and other vital information is now being hosted there.

Cloning remotes

If you create a public GitHub repository, as we did above, anyone can now *clone* your repository. For example, in a MacOS or Linux terminal or the Windows Git Bash shell, anyone can type the following command and clone `project101`:

```
git clone git@github.com:mark-andrews/project101.git
```

Alternatively, they could use this version of the `clone` command:

```
git clone https://github.com/mark-andrews/project101.git
```

The difference between these two versions is simply the internet protocol that is being used. Having cloned `project101`, they will have access to everything that you pushed to GitHub: the master branch and all the history and other vital features of the repository. They will be able to do everything you can do with the repository: view the logs, make changes, commit changes, undo changes, roll back history, etc. All the logs, commit messages, commit hashes, etc., will be the same in the clone as in the original. However, as is probably obvious, whatever actions they take, they will not be able to affect your local repository in any way. Moreover, they will not be able to affect your remote repository on GitHub either. They would only be able to `push` to your GitHub repository if they had a GitHub account and you explicitly gave them `push` permission.

PART II

STATISTICAL MODELLING

Part II Contents

8

Statistical Models and Statistical Inference

Introduction

As important as exploratory analysis is, it is a fundamentally different undertaking than statistical modelling and statistical inference. Exploratory data analysis aims to describe and visualize the data and to identify possible trends and patterns in it. Statistical models, by contrast, are mathematical models of the *population* from which the data originated. The term *population* is here used in a technical sense that is specific to statistics. In general, a population is the hypothetical set from which our actual data is assumed to be a random sample. From the perspective of statistical modelling, our ultimate interest lies not in the data itself but rather in the population, or more specifically in our mathematical models of the population.

Let us suppose that we have the data set $y_1, y_2, ..., y_n$, where each y_i is a single (scalar) value. From the perspective of statistical modelling, $y_1, y_2, ..., y_n$ is a random sample from a population. Ultimately, this population is described by a probability distribution. More specifically, we treat the values $y_1, y_2, ..., y_n$ as a *realization* of the random variables $Y_1, Y_2, ..., Y_n$. A random variable has a formal mathematical definition, but informally speaking, it is a variable that can take on different values according to some probability distribution. The probability distribution over the variables $Y_1, Y_2, ..., Y_n$ can be denoted generally by $P(Y_1, Y_2, ..., Y_n)$. This probability distribution is a function over an n-dimensional space that gives the probabilities of every possible combination of values of the n variables $Y_1, Y_2, ..., Y_n$. Our observed data $y_1, y_2, ..., y_n$ is but one realization of the random variables $Y_1, Y_2, ..., Y_n$, and every possible realization is a random sample from the probability distribution $P(Y_1, Y_2, ..., Y_n)$. Thus, the possible values that $Y_1, Y_2, ..., Y_n$ can take and their corresponding probabilities formally define the population.

In general, except in artificial scenarios, we do not know the nature of the population probability distribution $P(Y_1, Y_2, ..., Y_n)$. Our aim, therefore, is to first propose a model of this probability distribution, and then use statistical inference to infer the properties of this model. The model that we develop is a probabilistic model, which means that it defines a probability distribution over the variables $Y_1, Y_2, ..., Y_n$. This model is often referred to simply as the statistical model. In some contexts, it is also known as the *generative model*, the *probabilistic generative model*, or the *data generating model*. Almost always, as we will see, this statistical model is defined in terms of parameters and other variables that are assumed to have fixed but unknown values. We use statistical inference, which we will discuss at length below, to infer what the values of these variables are.

The process of developing a statistical model and inferring its parameters and other unknown variables is, in fact, an iterative process, and is illustrated in the following diagram.

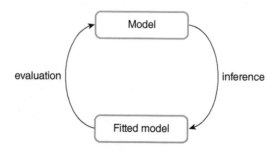

First, we propose or assume a statistical model. This may be done on the basis of some exploratory data analysis and visualization, as well as by using our scientific knowledge and understanding of the phenomenon being studied. Having assumed some model, we then infer its parameters and other unknowns. We are now in position to critically evaluate the resulting fitted model. Specifically, we evaluate whether or not the predictions of the model make sense and whether they are consistent with the data. On the basis of this elaboration, we may now need to elaborate or possibly simplify our originally proposed model, which leads to a new proposed model. The unknowns of this model are then inferred, and the new fitted model is evaluated. This process iterates until we are satisfied that the model is sufficient for practical purposes or that no major alternative models have been overlooked. The final fitted model is then used as the model of the population. As we will see through examples, this is then effectively a mathematical or probabilistic model of the phenomenon being studied. With this model, we can explain and reason about the phenomenon, make predictions about future data, and so on.

As a brief illustrative outline of this modelling process, consider the following `housing_df` data frame.

```
housing_df <- read_csv('data/housing.csv')
housing_df
## # A tibble: 546 x 1
##      price
##      <dbl>
##   1 42000
##   2 38500
##   3 49500
##   4 60500
##   5 61000
##   6 66000
##   7 66000
##   8 69000
##   9 83800
## 10 88500
## # ... with 536 more rows
```

This gives the prices (in Canadian dollars) of a set of 546 houses in the city of Windsor, Ontario in 1987. We can denote these values as $y_1, y_2, ..., y_n$ and treat them as a realization of the random variables $Y_1, Y_2, ..., Y_n$ whose probability distribution is $P(Y_1, Y_2, ..., Y_n)$. This defines the population. How best to conceive of this population in real-world terms is usually a matter of debate and discussion, rather than a simple matter of fact. For example, the population might be conceived of narrowly as the set of house prices in Windsor in 1987, or more widely as the set of house prices in mid-sized cities in Canada in the late 1980s, or more widely still as the set of house prices in North America during the time period, and so on.

Regardless of how we conceive of the population, we do not know the true nature of $P(Y_1, Y_2, ..., Y_n)$ and so begin by proposing a model of it. Among other things, this initial proposal could be based on exploratory data analysis and visualization, as shown in Figure 8.1. From the histograms and Q-Q plots shown here, we see that the logarithm of house prices appears to follow a normal distribution. This leads us to the following proposed model: for each $i \in 1,...,n$, $Y_i \sim \text{logN}(\mu, \sigma^2)$. Note that $\text{logN}(\mu, \sigma^2)$ is shorthand to denote a log-normal distribution whose parameters are μ and σ^2. A log-normal distribution is a distribution of a variable whose logarithm is normally distributed. In the model statement, the $\sim$ is read as *is distributed as*. This model therefore states that each random variable Y_i, for $i \in 1,...,n$, follows a log-normal distribution whose parameters are μ and σ^2. This model is an example of an *independent and identically distributed* model: the n random variables are modelled as independent of one another, and each has the same probability distribution.

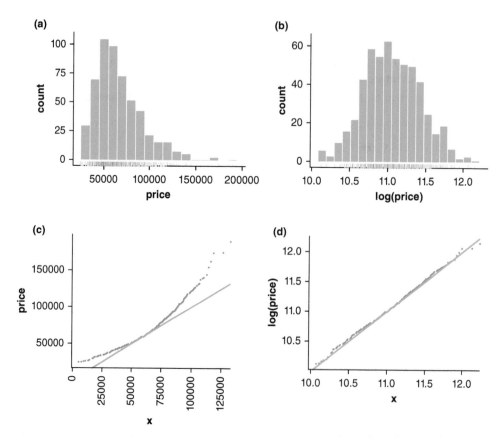

Figure 8.1 (a) Histogram of house prices (in Canadian dollars) from the city of Windsor, Ontario in 1987. (b) Histogram of the logarithm of the house prices. (c) Q-Q plot of the prices compared to a normal distribution whose mean and standard deviation are set to the median and median absolute deviation (MAD) of the prices. (d) Q-Q plot of log of the prices, again compared to a normal distribution whose mean and standard deviation are set to the median and MAD of the log prices

Having proposed an initial model, we must now infer the values of the unknown variables μ and σ. As we will discuss at length below, there are two major approaches to doing statistical inference, but in practical terms, both methods effectively lead to estimates of μ and σ as well as measures of the uncertainty of these estimates. If we denote the estimates of μ and σ by $\hat{\mu}$ and $\hat{\sigma}$, our fitted model is then the log-normal distribution $\log N(\hat{\mu}, \hat{\sigma}^2)$. At this point, we may evaluate this fitted model and determine if its assumptions or predictions are consistent with the observed data. If, on the basis of this evaluation, the assumed model is deemed satisfactory for present practical purposes, we can then use the fitted model, particularly taking into account the uncertainties in our estimates, to explain, reason about, or make predictions concerning house prices in cities like Windsor during this period.

Statistical inference

Statistical inference is the inference of the values of unknown variables in a statistical model. There are two major approaches to statistical inference. The first approach is variously referred to as the *classical, frequentist,* or *sampling theory based* approach. The second is the Bayesian approach. The classical approach is still the dominant one in practice, particularly for the more introductory or medium-level topics. It is also the principal, or even only, approach taught in most applied statistics courses. As such, it is the only approach that most working scientists will have been formally introduced to. The Bayesian approach, on the other hand, although having its origins in the eighteenth century and being used in practice throughout the nineteenth century, had a long hiatus in statistics until around the end of the 1980s. Since then, and as we will see, largely because of the growth in computing power, it has steadily grown in terms of its popularity and widespread usage throughout statistics and data science. Throughout the remainder of this book, we will attempt to pay adequate attention to both the classical and Bayesian approaches wherever we discuss statistical models. In this section, we aim to provide a brief general introduction to both approaches. For this, we will use a simple problem, propose a statistical model for it, and then infer the values of its unknown parameters using the classical and Bayesian approaches.

Example problem. The problem we will consider was described in the *Guardian* newspaper on 4 January 2002.[1] Polish mathematicians Tomasz Gliszczynski and Waclaw Zawadowski spun a Belgian 1 euro coin 250 times, and found it landed heads up 140 times. Here, the data is the observed number of heads, $m = 140$. The total number of spins, $n = 250$, is the sample size, and is a fixed and known quantity, and so is not modelled *per se*. From the perspective of statistical modelling, the observed number of heads is treated as a sample from a population. In this case, the population is the set of all possible observed number of heads, and their relative frequencies, that would be obtained if Gliszczynski and Zawadowski were to infinitely repeat their study under identical circumstances with the exact same Belgian 1 euro coin. The population is therefore a probability distribution over the set of possible values of the number of heads in a sample of $n = 250$ trials, which is a probability distribution over $0,1,\ldots,n$. Thus, m is a realization of a random variable Y whose possible values are $0,1,\ldots,n$ and whose probability distribution is $P(Y)$. We do not know $P(Y)$ and so we begin by proposing a model of it. In this case, the only viable option for this model is the binomial distribution: $Y \sim \text{Binomial}(\theta, n = 250)$. While more complex options are possible in principle, they would all go beyond what the data can tell us, and so simply cannot be evaluated.

[1]https://www.theguardian.com/world/2002/jan/04/euro.eu2

In general terms, a binomial distribution gives the probability of the number of so-called 'successes' in a fixed number n of 'trials' where the probability of a success on any trial is fixed quantity θ and all trials are independent of another. Translated into the terms of the current example, the binomial distribution is the probability distribution over the observed number of heads in $n = 250$ spins where the probability of a heads on any trial is θ, and where we assume the outcome on each trial is independent of every other trial. In this binomial model, the parameter θ has a fixed but unknown quantity. The value of θ is therefore the objective of our statistical inference.

Classical statistical inference

Classical statistical inference begins with an *estimator* of the value of θ, denoted by $\hat{\theta}$, and then considers the *sampling distribution* of $\hat{\theta}$ for any hypothetical true value of θ. Informally speaking, we can see the estimator $\hat{\theta}$ as an educated guess of what the true value of θ is. There are different methods of estimation available, and each one can be evaluated, as we will see, according to certain criteria, such as *bias* or *variance*. One widely used method of estimation, perhaps the most widely used method, is *maximum likelihood estimation*.

Maximum likelihood estimation

The maximum likelihood estimator of θ is the value of θ that maximizes the *likelihood function*. The likelihood function is an extremely important function in both classical and Bayesian approaches to statistical inference. It is a function over the set of all possible values of θ, which we will denote by Θ. It gives the probability of observing the data given any particular value of θ. In order to determine the likelihood function in the case of the binomial distribution model, we start with the definition of the binomial distribution itself. If Y is random variable following a binomial distribution with parameter θ and sample size n, which we can state succinctly as $Y \sim \text{Binomial}(\theta, n)$, then the probability that Y takes the value m is as follows:

$$P(Y = m \mid \theta, n) = \text{Binomial}(Y = m \mid \theta, n) = \binom{n}{m} \theta^m (1-\theta)^{n-m}.$$

Why the binomial distribution has the probability mass function shown on the far right-hand side is not something we will derive here, and we will just take it as given, but it is relatively straightforward to derive from the above definition of a binomial problem. Note that this probability mass function is a function that maps values of $m \in 0,1,\dots,n$ to the interval $[0,1]$ for fixed values for θ and n. The corresponding likelihood function takes the same formula, $\binom{n}{m} \theta^m (1-\theta)^{n-m}$, and treats it as a function of θ for fixed values of m and n. In other words, the likelihood function is

$$L(\theta \mid m, n) = \binom{n}{m} \theta^m (1-\theta)^{n-m},$$

where θ is assumed to take values in the interval $\Theta = [0,1]$ and where n and m are fixed. Thus, the likelihood function gives the probability of the observed data for every possible value of the unknown variable $\theta \in \Theta$.

Technically speaking, any likelihood function is defined up to a proportional constant. What this means is that multiplying, or dividing, any likelihood function by a fixed constant value results in the same likelihood function. In practice, therefore, when writing a likelihood function, we usually drop any constant multipliers. In the above likelihood function, the binomial coefficient $\binom{n}{m}$ is a constant term that does not change for any value of θ, and so it can be dropped, leading to the likelihood function being written as

$$L(\theta \mid m,n) = \theta^m (1-\theta)^{n-m}.$$

The likelihood function for $m = 140$ and $n = 250$ is shown in Figure 8.2(a). As we can see from this plot, the likelihood function is concentrated from around $\theta = 0.45$ to around $\theta = 0.65$. Outside of that range, the likelihood of any value of θ becomes negligible. In itself, this is very informative. It tells us that the probability of observing the data that we did, $m = 140$ heads in $n = 250$ spins, is negligible if θ is less than around 0.45 or greater than around 0.65. Therefore, only values in the range of approximately 0.45 to 0.65 have evidential support from the data.

The value of θ that maximizes the likelihood function is obtained by the usual procedure of optimizing functions, namely calculating the derivative of the function with respect to θ, setting the derivative equal to zero, and solving for the value of θ. We can do this more easily by using the logarithm of the likelihood function, rather than the likelihood function itself. The logarithm of the likelihood function is shown in Figure 8.2(b). Because the logarithm is a monotonic transformation, the value of θ that maximizes the logarithm of the likelihood also maximizes the likelihood function. The derivative of the log of the likelihood function with respect to θ is as follows:

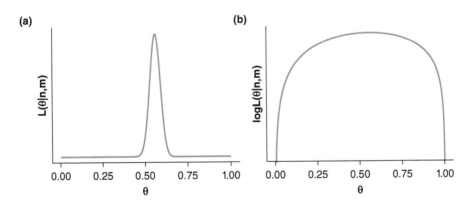

Figure 8.2 (a) The binomial likelihood function for θ when $m = 140$ and $n = 250$. (b) The logarithm of the likelihood function

$$\frac{d}{d\theta}\log\left(\theta^m(1-\theta)^{n-m}\right) = \frac{d}{d\theta}\left[m\log(\theta) + (n-m)\log(1-\theta)\right]$$

$$= \frac{m}{\theta} - \frac{n-m}{1-\theta}.$$

Setting this derivative equal to zero and solving for θ gives us the following:

$$\frac{m}{\theta} - \frac{n-m}{1-\theta} = 0$$

$$\theta = \frac{m}{n}.$$

Thus, the maximum likelihood estimator for θ is $\hat{\theta} = m/n = 140/250 = 0.56$. This is obviously a very simple and intuitive result. It tells us that the best guess for the value of θ, which is the probability of obtaining heads on any given spin, is simply the relative number of heads in the n spins so far.

Sampling distribution of $\hat{\theta}$

The maximum likelihood estimator can be seen as a random variable. It is a deterministic function of the observed data m, but m would vary were we repeat the experiment even under identical circumstances. For example, if we knew the true value of θ (let's call this true value θ_*) and we spun the coin n times, and did so *ad infinitum*, then we know that the distribution of m (the observed number of heads) would be the binomial distribution with sample size n and parameter value θ_*. Given that the maximum likelihood estimator is always $\hat{\theta} = m/n$, the probability that $\hat{\theta}$ takes the value of m/n for any given value of m if the true value of θ is θ_* is

$$\binom{n}{m}\theta_*^m(1-\theta_*)^{n-m}.$$

In general, the sampling distribution for $\hat{\theta}$ when the true value of θ is θ_* can be written as follows:

$$P(\hat{\theta}|\theta_*,n) = \binom{n}{\hat{\theta}n}\theta_*^{\hat{\theta}n}(1-\theta_*)^{n-\hat{\theta}n}.$$

The sampling distribution of $\hat{\theta}$ when $n = 250$ and for the arbitrarily chosen example value of $\theta_* = 0.64$ is shown in Figure 8.3.

The expected value of the sampling distribution of $\hat{\theta}$ is θ_*. In other words, on average, $\hat{\theta}$ is equal to θ_*. This tells us that the binomial maximum likelihood estimator is an *unbiased* estimator of the true value of θ, namely θ_*. The variance of the distribution of $\hat{\theta}$ is $\frac{1}{n}\theta_*(1-\theta_*)$. The lower the variance of the estimator, the less sampling variability there will be in the value of the estimators. Here, we see that the variance decreases as n increases, and so as sample size increases, there is less variability in the estimator's values. The standard deviation of the sampling distribution is $\sqrt{\frac{1}{n}\theta_*(1-\theta_*)}$. This is known as the *standard error*, and often plays an important role in classical statistical inference, as we will see in later examples.

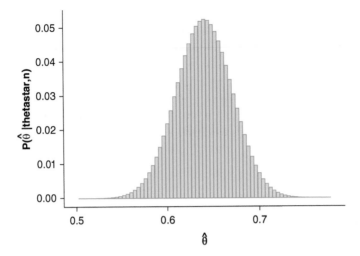

Figure 8.3 Sampling distribution of the binomial maximum likelihood estimator $\hat{\theta}$ when $n = 250$ and $\theta_* = 0.64$. Here, we limit the x-axis to just beyond those values of $\hat{\theta}$ that have non-trivial probabilities

p-values

Informally speaking, a p-value tells us whether the value of an estimator, or more generally, the value of any statistic or function of the observed data, is consistent with some hypothetical value of the unknown variable. If the p-value is low, the estimator's value is not consistent with the hypothesized value. The higher the p-value is, the more consistent the estimator's value is with the hypothesized value. If the p-value is sufficiently low, we can, practically speaking, rule out or reject the hypothesized value. In general, the p-value takes values from 0 to 1 and so is an inherently continuous measure of support for a hypothesis. Where we 'draw the line' on this continuum between low and not low is a matter of convention, but the almost universally held convention is that a p-value must be lower than at most 0.05 to be considered sufficiently low for the corresponding hypothesized value to be rejected. This threshold for rejection/non-rejection is usually denoted by α.

Technically speaking, p-values are tail areas of the sampling distribution of the estimator corresponding to a particular hypothesized value of the unknown variable. Once we have the sampling distribution, p-values are straightforward to calculate. In the current problem, the unknown variable is θ and we can in principle hypothesize that its true value is any value between 0 and 1. If, for example, we hypothesize that the true value of θ is $\theta_* = 0.64$, the sampling distribution of $\hat{\theta}$ is that shown in Figure 8.3. On the basis of this sampling distribution, we can see that some values for $\hat{\theta}$ are expected and others are not. For example, we see that the $\hat{\theta}$ values are mostly from around 0.58 to around 0.70, and values of $\hat{\theta}$ much below or above those extremes rarely occur. On the basis of the estimator's value that we did obtain, namely $\hat{\theta} = 140/250 = 0.56$, we can see that this result seems to be outside the range of values of $\hat{\theta}$ that we would expect if $\theta_* = 0.64$. In order to be precise in our statement of whether $\hat{\theta} = 0.56$ is beyond what we would expect if $\theta_* = 0.64$, we calculate the tail areas of the sampling distribution defined by values *as extreme as or more extreme than* $\hat{\theta} = 0.56$. These tail areas are shaded in Figure 8.4(a). The total area in these tails defines the *p*-value. In other words, the *p*-value is the probability of observing a value of the estimator *as extreme as or more extreme than* $\hat{\theta}$ = 0.56 if θ_* = 0.64. If the *p*-value is low, then we know that $\hat{\theta}$ = 0.56 is far into the tails of the sampling distribution when θ = 0.64. In this particular example, the area of these tails, and so therefore the *p*-value, is approximately 0.01. This is clearly low according to the conventional standards mentioned above, and so therefore we say that the result $\hat{\theta}$ = 0.56 is not consistent with the hypothesis that θ_* = 0.64, and so in practical terms, we can reject the hypothesis that the true value of θ is θ_* = 0.64.

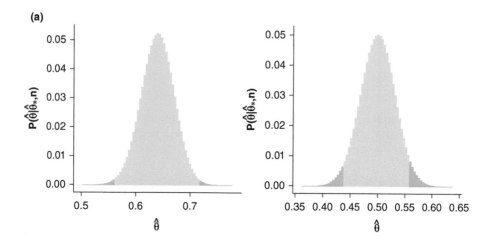

Figure 8.4 Sampling distribution of the binomial maximum likelihood estimator $\hat{\theta}$ when $n = 250$ and (a) $\theta_* = 0.64$, (b) $\theta_* = 0.5$. In both cases, as in Figure 8.3, we limit the *x*-axis to just beyond those values of $\hat{\theta}$ that have non-trivial probabilities. The shaded tail areas correspond to values of $\hat{\theta}$ that are as extreme as or more extreme, relative to the centre, than the value of the estimator we observed, which was $\hat{\theta}=140/250=0.56$

In more detail, the *p*-value is the sum of the two tails of the sampling distribution when $\theta_* = 0.64$. The lower tail is defined by all those values from $\hat{\theta} = 0$ up to and including the observed $\hat{\theta} = 0.56$. The upper tail is defined by all those values from $\hat{\theta} = 0.64 + |0.64 - 0.56| = 0.72$ up to 1. These are the values of $\hat{\theta}$ that are as extreme relative to $\theta_* = 0.64$ as is 0.56, but in the opposite direction. Thus, the *p*-value is calculated as follows:

$$p\text{-value} = \int_0^{0.56} \binom{n}{\hat{\theta}n} \theta^{\hat{\theta}n}(1-\theta)^{n-\hat{\theta}n} d\hat{\theta} + \int_{0.72}^1 \binom{n}{\hat{\theta}n} \theta^{\hat{\theta}n}(1-\theta)^{n-\hat{\theta}n} d\hat{\theta} \approx 0.01.$$

$$\underbrace{\phantom{\int_0^{0.56} \binom{n}{\hat{\theta}n} \theta^{\hat{\theta}n}(1-\theta)^{n-\hat{\theta}n} d\hat{\theta}}}_{\text{area of lower tail}} \quad \underbrace{\phantom{\int_{0.72}^1 \binom{n}{\hat{\theta}n} \theta^{\hat{\theta}n}(1-\theta)^{n-\hat{\theta}n} d\hat{\theta}}}_{\text{area of upper tail}}$$

More generally speaking, the precise definition of a *p*-value is as follows:

$$p\text{-value} = P(|\hat{\theta} = \theta_H| \geq |\hat{\theta}_{obs} = \theta_H|).$$

Here, for clarity, we distinguish between $\hat{\theta}_{obs}$, which is the actual value of the estimator calculated from the observed data, θ_H, which is the hypothesized value of θ, and $\hat{\theta}$, which is the estimator's random variable whose distribution is the sampling distribution when $\theta = \theta_H$.

We can calculate p-values for binomial problems like this using R with the `binom.test` command. We need to pass in the observed number of 'successes', which are heads in this case, as the value of the `x` parameter, and the sample size as the value of `n`. The hypothesized value of θ is passed in as the value of `p`:

```
binom_model <- binom.test(x = 140, n = 250, p = 0.64)
```

The value of the maximum likelihood estimator is given by the value of the `estimate` element of the output object:

```
binom_model$estimate
#> probability of success
#>                  0.56
```

The p-value is given by the value of `p.value` element:

```
binom_model$p.value
#> [1] 0.01004809
```

Null hypotheses and significance

In general, we can test any hypothetical value of the unknown variable. Often some hypothetical values have a special meaning in that they correspond to values that entail that there is no effect of any interesting kind. Hypotheses of this kind are known as *null* hypotheses. In the present example, the null hypothesis that $\theta = 0.5$ entails that the coin is completely unbiased; it is no more likely to come up heads than tails, and so any differences in the observed numbers of heads and tails in a set of spins or flips are just a matter of chance. The sampling distribution for $\hat{\theta}$ when $\theta_* = 0.5$ is shown in Figure 8.4(b). The total tail area, which is the p-value, is calculated similarly to the example above:

$$p\text{-value} = \underbrace{\int_0^{0.44} \binom{n}{\hat{\theta}n} \theta^{\hat{\theta}n}(1-\theta)^{n-\hat{\theta}n} d\hat{\theta}}_{\text{area of lower tail}} + \underbrace{\int_{0.56}^1 \binom{n}{\hat{\theta}n} \theta^{\hat{\theta}n}(1-\theta)^{n-\hat{\theta}n} d\hat{\theta}}_{\text{area of upper tail}} \approx 0.066.$$

Note that here the lower tail is defined up to $0.5 - |0.5 - 0.56| = 0.44$. From this p-value of 0.066, we see that this is not sufficiently low to reject the null hypothesis at the conventional $\alpha = 0.05$ threshold, though of course it is quite close to this threshold too. We can calculate this using `binom.test`:

```
null_binom_model <- binom.test(x = 140, n = 250, p = 0.5) # p = 0.5 is default
null_binom_model$p.value
## [1] 0.06642115
```

As a general point about null hypothesis testing, given that a null hypothesis is a hypothesis of no interesting effect, if we reject that hypothesis, we say the result is *significant*. Saying that a result is significant in this sense of the term, however, is not necessarily saying much. The estimated effect may be small or even negligible in practical terms, but may still be statistically significant. Moreover, even a highly significant p-value does not necessarily mean a large effect in practical terms. As an example, there were 731,213 live births in the United Kingdom in 2018. The p-value for the null hypothesis that there is equal probability of the birth being a male or a female is approximately 3.8×10^{-119}. This is a tiny p-value and so is an extremely significant result. However, the (maximum likelihood) estimator for the probability of a male birth is 0.514. Although certainly not practically meaningless, this is nonetheless quite a small effect: it corresponds to around 28 more males than females in every 1000 births. As such, an extremely statistically significant result corresponds to a small effect in practical terms. In general, because the p-value for a non-null true effect will always decrease as the sample size increases, we can always construct cases of arbitrarily small p-values for arbitrarily small effects, and so even practically trivial effects may be highly statistically significant.

Confidence intervals

Confidence intervals are counterparts to p-values. As we've seen, each p-value corresponds to a particular hypothesis about the true value of θ. If the p-value is sufficiently low, we will reject the corresponding hypothesis. If the p-value is not sufficiently low, we cannot reject the hypothesis. However, not rejecting a hypothesis does not entail that we should accept that hypothesis; it just simply means that we cannot rule it out. The set of hypothetical values of θ that we do *not* reject at the p-value threshold of α corresponds to the $1 - \alpha$ confidence interval. Practically speaking, we can treat all values in this range as the set of plausible values for θ.

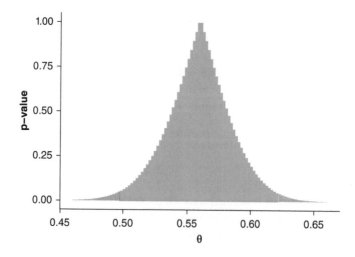

Figure 8.5 The p-value for each hypothetical value of θ from 0.46 to 0.66 in steps of 10^{-3}. Shaded in grey are all those values of θ that have p-values less than $\alpha = 0.05$. These values of θ would be rejected in a hypothesis test. All other values of θ have p-values greater than $\alpha = 0.05$ and so would not be rejected by a hypothesis test. These values of θ comprise the confidence interval

In Figure 8.5, we shade in red all those values of θ that would not be rejected by a hypothesis test at $\alpha = 0.05$. Therefore, these values of θ are in the $1 - \alpha = 0.95$ confidence interval. The lower and upper bounds of this interval as calculated in this figure, based on a discretization of the θ interval into steps of 10^{-3}, are $[0.498, 0.622]$. The interval can be calculated exactly by using a relationship between the cumulative binomial distribution and the cumulative beta distribution, a method known as the Clopper–Pearson method (Clopper and Pearson, 1934). Using R, we can calculate this Clopper–Pearson confidence interval as follows:

```
c(qbeta(0.025, 140, 250 - 140 + 1),
   qbeta(1-0.025, 140+1, 250 - 140))
#> [1] 0.4960662 0.6224941
```

This will also be returned by the `binom.test`:

```
M_binom <- binom.test(x = 140, n = 250)
M_binom$conf.int
#> [1] 0.4960662 0.6224941
#> attr(,"conf.level")
#> [1] 0.95
```

Confidence intervals have the following frequentist property. In an infinite repetition of an experiment,[2] the 95% confidence interval will contain the true value of the unknown variable 95% of the time. What this means in the case of the present problem is that if we were to repeat *ad infinitum* the original coin spinning experiment under identical conditions, so that the probability of a heads outcome is a fixed though unknown value of θ, and on each repetition calculate the 95% confidence interval, then 95% of these confidence intervals would contain the true value of θ. In Figure 8.6, we provide an illustration of this phenomenon. For 100 repetitions, we generate data from a binomial distribution with $n = 250$ and $\theta = 0.6$. From the data on each repetition, we calculate the 90% confidence interval. Those intervals that do not contain $\theta = 0.6$ are shaded in grey. In this set of 100 repetitions, there are 92 intervals out of 100 that contain $\theta = 0.6$.

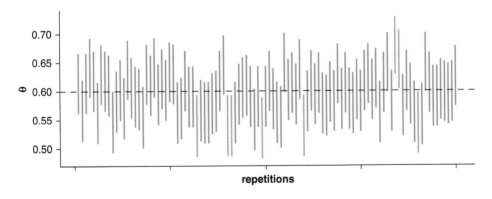

Figure 8.6 The 90% confidence intervals in 100 repetitions of a binomial experiment with $n = 250$ and $\theta = 0.6$. Shaded in grey are any confidence intervals that do not contain $\theta = 0.6$

---

[2]Here, we use the term 'experiment' in the sense that it is used in probability theory, which is of a well-defined procedure that generates data according to a specified probability distribution.

Bayesian statistical inference

Bayesian approaches to statistical inference ultimately aim to solve the same problem as classical approaches, namely the inference of the unknown values of variables in a statistical model. While the classical approach is based on calculation of estimators and their sampling distributions, Bayesian approaches rely on an eighteenth-century mathematical result known as *Bayes' rule* or *Bayes' theorem* to calculate a probability distribution over the possible values of the unknown variable. This probability distribution, known as the *posterior distribution*, gives us the probability that the unknown variable takes on any given value, contingent on the assumptions of the model. To introduce Bayesian inference, we will continue with the same example problem covered above.

It is important to emphasize that the choice of the statistical model is prior to and not dependent on whether a classical or Bayesian approach to inference is used. In other words, we first assume or propose a statistical model for the data at hand and then, in principle, we can choose to use a classical or Bayesian approach to inference of the unknown variables in the model. For the problem at hand, as described above, our statistical model is that Y is a random variable with a binomial probability distribution with unknown parameter θ and sample size $n = 250$. As we've seen, we can state this as follows:

$$Y \sim \text{Binomial}(\theta, n = 250).$$

The observed number of heads, $m = 140$, is a realization of the random variable Y, and the probability that Y takes the value m given fixed values of θ and n is given by the probability mass function

$$P(Y=m \mid \theta, n) = \text{Binomial}(Y=m \mid \theta, n) = \binom{n}{m} \theta^m (1-\theta)^{n-m}.$$

As we've also seen, the likelihood function corresponding to this probability distribution is

$$L(\theta \mid m, n) = \theta^m (1-\theta)^{n-m}.$$

As we'll see, the likelihood function plays a major role in Bayesian inference.

Priors

Having established our statistical model, to perform Bayesian inference on the value of θ, we must first provide a probability distribution for the possible values that θ can take in principle. This is known as the *prior* distribution. As an example, if we assume that θ can take on any possible value in the interval $[0,1]$ and each value has equal likelihood, our prior would be a uniform distribution over θ. On the other hand, if we assume that θ values are more likely to be equal to $\theta = 0.5$, but possibly be above or below $\theta = 0.5$ too, our prior might be a symmetrical unimodal distribution centred at $\theta = 0.5$. How wide this unimodal distribution is depends on what we think are the relative probabilities of values close to and far from $\theta = 0.5$. Likewise, if we assume that θ is likely to correspond to a bias towards heads, then the prior might be another symmetrical unimodal distribution but centred on some value of θ greater than 0.5. Examples of priors like this are shown in Figure 8.7.

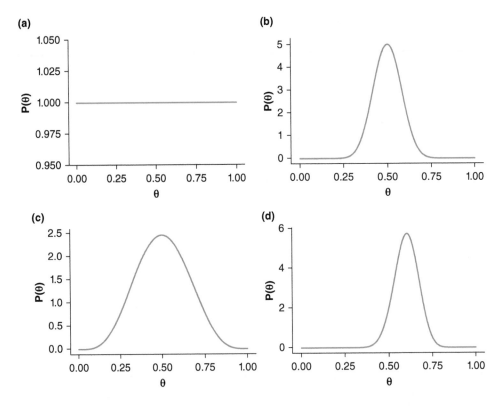

Figure 8.7 Examples of priors over θ. (a) A uniform prior. (b), (c) Priors where θ is more likely to be 0.5 than otherwise but values greater and less than 0.5 are probable too, and more so in the case of (c) whose variance is wider than the prior in (b). (d) A prior where θ is more likely to be $\theta = 0.6$ than any other value and more likely to be above rather than below 0.5

There is a vast literature on what priors are, how to choose them, and the relative merits of, for example, subjective, objective, informative, non-informative, weakly informative, reference, maximum entropy, and other kinds of priors. We will not even attempt a summary of this vast literature here. Our general advice on the topic is that the choice of a prior should not be automatic, but rather should be treated as a modelling assumption, just like the assumptions that lead to our choice of the original statistical model. When choosing the prior, just like when we choose the statistical model, we should follow a number of guiding principles: we should use our general understanding of the problem at hand, and also of the data itself; our choices should be reasonable and justifiable rather than arbitrary; our choices should be seen as tentative and subject to revision if the assumptions or reasoning on which they were based are found to be invalid or wrong. More specifically, following Gelman et al. (2017), we recommend that our choices of priors should be guided by whether the prior could generate the type of data that we expect to see in the problem at hand, that it covers the range of plausible values of the unknown parameter, and most of the prior mass should be in the parts of the parameter space that are likely to generate the type of data we are modelling.

It should be emphasized, however, that although in general the choice of priors is always important, it has more practical consequences in some problems than in others. In particular, in relatively simple models where the ratio of observed data to unknown variables is relatively high, as is the case with the present problem, most choices of priors, unless they are extreme, will lead to practically similar conclusions. In complex models, on the other hand, or models where the amount of data relative to the number of unknown variables is low, the priors play a much more important role in the final fitted model, and so choices of priors in these contexts need to be more careful and judicious.

For the present problem, the parameter θ is the probability that the coin lands heads up after a spin. The value of θ is a function of both the physical properties of the coin and the manner in which it is spun. It is arguably difficult to physically bias a coin so that one side is more likely in a flip (Gelman and Nolan, 2002a), but experimental results with different materials can lead to outcomes that are as much as 70–30 biased (Kerrich, 1946), and precise control over how the coin is flipped can lead to even 100% biased outcomes (Diaconis et al., 2007). Coin spins, as opposed to flips, can be easily biased to as much as 75–25 bias (Gelman and Nolan, 2002a). From this, it seems reasonable to have a unimodal and symmetrical prior centred at $\theta = 0.5$, but with a relatively wide spread to allow for relatively extreme possibilities. We will therefore use the prior displayed in Figure 8.7(c). Clearly, the most likely value of θ according to this prior is $\theta = 0.5$, but values of $\theta = 0.25$ or $\theta = 0.75$ have substantial prior mass in their vicinity, and even extreme values greater than $\theta = 0.9$ or less than $\theta = 0.1$ have non-trivial prior mass.

The prior that we have chosen (displayed in Figure 8.7(c)) is a beta distribution, which is a probability distribution over the interval from 0 to 1. There are two parameters in the beta distribution, which we call *hyper*parameters to distinguish them from the parameters of the statistical model, and these are conventionally denoted by α and β. In the particular beta distribution that we have chosen their values are $\alpha = 5$ and $\beta = 5$. The density function of any beta distribution is

$$P(\theta \mid \alpha, \beta) = \frac{\Gamma(\alpha + \beta)}{\Gamma(\alpha)\Gamma(\beta)} \theta^{\alpha-1}(1-\theta)^{\beta-1},$$

and its mean and variance are

$$\langle \theta \rangle = \frac{\alpha}{\alpha + \beta}, \quad \mathrm{Var}(\theta) = \frac{\alpha\beta}{(\alpha + \beta)^2 (\alpha + \beta + 1)}.$$

For our choice of prior therefore, the mean of the distribution is 0.5 and the variance is 0.023 (and so the standard deviation is 0.151).

Bayes' rule and the posterior distribution

Having specified our statistical model and our prior, we can now write out the full Bayesian model:

$$Y \sim \mathrm{Binom}(\theta, n = 250), \quad \theta \sim \mathrm{Beta}(\alpha = 5, \beta = 5).$$

We can view this model as an expanded generative model of the observed data. In other words, to generate hypothetical data sets, first we sample a value of θ from a beta distribution with hyperparameters $\alpha = \beta = 5$, and then we sample a value from a binomial distribution with parameter θ and sample size $n = 250$. This expanded model therefore defines a joint probability distribution over Y and θ, conditional on α, β and n, namely $P(Y, \theta \mid \alpha, \beta, n)$. We will use this joint probability distribution, coupled with the fact that we observe the value of Y, to calculate a probability distribution over the possible values of θ conditional on all the observed data and the assumptions of the model. This is known as the *posterior distribution*, and is the central result in Bayesian inference. To understand how the posterior distribution is calculated, we must introduce some elementary results from probability theory.

If we have two random variables A and B, elementary probability theory result shows how the joint probability distribution of A and B can be factored into products of *conditional* probability distributions and *marginal* probability distributions:

$$\underbrace{P(A, B)}_{\text{joint}} = \underbrace{P(A \mid B)}_{\text{conditional}} \underbrace{P(B)}_{\text{marginal}} = \underbrace{P(B \mid A)}_{\text{conditional}} \underbrace{P(A)}_{\text{marginal}} .$$

In other words, the joint probability of A and B is equal to the conditional probability of A given B times the probability of B, or equally, it is equal to the conditional probability of B given A times the probability of A. Another elementary result is how we calculate marginal probability distributions from summations over joint distributions:

$$P(A) = \sum_{\{B\}} P(A, B) = \sum_{\{B\}} P(A \mid B) P(B),$$
$$P(B) = \sum_{\{A\}} P(A, B) = \sum_{\{A\}} P(B \mid A) P(A),$$

where $\{A\}$ and $\{B\}$ in the summations indicate the set of all values of A and B, respectively.

We can illustrate these results easily using any joint probability distribution table. For example, we can use the following numbers, which give the number of males and females who survived or not on the RMS *Titanic*:

	Perished	Survived	
Male	1364	367	1731
Female	126	344	470
	1490	711	2201

There were 2201 people on board, and so we can divide the numbers in each category by 2201 to obtain a joint probability distribution table:

	Perished	Survived	
Male	0.620	0.167	0.786
Female	0.057	0.156	0.214
	0.677	0.323	1.000

Note that the column totals and row totals are provided here and these give the probabilities of a person on board *Titanic* being male or female, and surviving or not, respectively. From the joint probability distribution, we can get the two *conditional* probability distributions. The first tells us the probability of surviving or not given that we know that the person is male or a female:

Sex	Perished	Survived
Male	0.788	0.212
Female	0.268	0.732

The second conditional probability distribution table tells us the probability of being male or female given that the person survived or not:

Sex	Perished	Survived
Male	0.915	0.516
Female	0.085	0.484

Using the joint table, we can see that the probability of a person being both male and a survivor is

P(Sex = Male, Survival = Survived) = 0.167.

This is equal to the probability of being male given that the person survived times the probability of being a survivor:

P(Sex = Male|Survival = Survived)P(Survival = Survived) = 0.516 × 0.323 = 0.167.

It is also equal to the probability of being a survivor given that the person is a male:

P(Survival = Survived|Sex = Male)P(Sex = Male) = 0.212 × 0.786 = 0.167.

The same holds for any other element of the joint probability table. Using these tables we can also calculate marginal probabilities:

P(Sex = Male) = P(Sex = Male, Survival = Survived) + P(Sex = Male, Survival = Perished),

= P(Sex = Male|Survival = Survived)P(Survival = Survived) + P(Sex = Male| Survival = Perished)P(Survival = Perished)

= 0.516 × 0.323 + 0.915 × 0.677

= 0.786.

With these elementary results from probability theory, we end up with the following uncontroversial result known as *Bayes' rule*:

$$P(B|A) = \frac{P(A|B)P(B)}{\sum_{\{B\}} P(A|B)P(B)}.$$

This can be easily derived as follows:

$$P(B|A)P(A) = P(A|B)P(B)$$
$$P(B|A) = \frac{P(A|B)P(B)}{P(A)} = \frac{P(A|B)P(B)}{\sum_{\{B\}} P(A|B)P(B)}.$$

We can use this result to solve elementary probability puzzles like the following (Schiller et al., 2000, pp. 87–88). Box A has 10 light bulbs, of which 4 are defective. Box B has 6 light bulbs, of which 1 is defective. Box C has 8 light bulbs, of which 3 are defective. If we do choose a non-defective bulb, what is the probability it came from box C?

Here, we are being asked for P(Box = C|Bulb = Working). By Bayes' rule this is

$$P(\text{Box} = C\,|\,\text{Bulb} = \text{Working}) = \frac{P(\text{Bulb} = \text{Working}\,|\,\text{Box} = C)\,P(\text{Box} = C)}{P(\text{Bulb} = \text{Working})},$$

where the denominator is

$$\begin{aligned}
P(\text{Bulb} = \text{Working}) = \; & P(\text{Bulb} = \text{Working}\,|\,\text{Box} = A)\,P(\text{Box} = A) \\
& + P(\text{Bulb} = \text{Working}\,|\,\text{Box} = B)\,P(\text{Box} = B) \\
& + P(\text{Bulb} = \text{Working}\,|\,\text{Box} = C)\,P(\text{Box} = C).
\end{aligned}$$

The conditional probabilities of drawing a working bulb from each of box A, B, or C are given by knowing the number of bulbs in each box and the number of defective bulbs in each, and so are $\frac{6}{10}, \frac{5}{6}, \frac{5}{8}$ respectively. The marginal probabilities of box A, B, and C are $\frac{1}{3}, \frac{1}{3}$, and $\frac{1}{3}$. From this, we have

$$\begin{aligned}
P(\text{Box} = C|\text{Bulb} = \text{Working}) &= \frac{\frac{51}{83}}{\frac{6}{103} \cdot 1 + \frac{51}{63} + \frac{51}{83}}, \\
&= \frac{\frac{5}{8}}{\frac{6}{10} + \frac{5}{6} + \frac{5}{8}}, \\
&= 0.304.
\end{aligned}$$

Returning now to our joint distribution over Y and θ, $P(Y,\theta\,|\,\alpha,\beta,n)$, from this we have the following:

$$P(\theta\,|\,Y,\alpha,\beta,n) = \frac{P(Y\,|\,\theta,n)\,P(\theta\,|\,\alpha,\beta)}{\int P(Y\,|\,\theta,n)P(\theta\,|\,\alpha,\beta)d\theta}.$$

The left-hand side is the posterior distribution. There are three components on the right-hand side. First, there is $P(Y \mid \theta, n)$. Here, the values of Y and n are known and θ is a free variable, and so $P(Y \mid \theta, n)$ is a function over θ. This is the likelihood function over θ that we have already encountered, and which we can also write as $L(Y \mid \theta, n)$. Second, there is $P(\theta \mid \alpha, \beta)$, which is the prior. Like the likelihood function, this is also a function over the set of all possible values of θ. The third component is the denominator, which is the integral of the product of the likelihood function and the prior, integrated over all possible values of θ. This integral is known as the *marginal likelihood*, and is a single value that gives the area under the curve of the function that is the product of the likelihood function and the prior. We can write this as follows:

$$\underbrace{P(\theta \mid Y, \alpha, \beta, n)}_{\text{posterior}} = \frac{\overbrace{L(\theta \mid Y, n)}^{\text{likelihood}} \overbrace{P(\theta \mid \alpha, \beta)}^{\text{prior}}}{\underbrace{\int L(\theta \mid Y, n) P(\theta \mid \alpha, \beta) d\theta}_{\text{marginal likelihood}}}.$$

What this tells us is that, having observed the data, the probability distribution over the possible values of θ is the normalized product of the likelihood function and the prior over θ. The prior tells us what values θ could take in principle. The likelihood function effectively tells us the evidence in favour of any given value of θ according to the data. We multiply these two functions together (the numerator above) and then divide by the area under the curve of this product of functions (the marginal likelihood, which is the denominator). Dividing by the marginal likelihood ensures that the area under the curve of the posterior is *normalized* so that its integral is exactly 1.

Filling out the detail of this equation, we have the following:

$$P(\theta \mid Y, \alpha, \beta, n) \propto \frac{L(\theta \mid Y, n) P(\theta \mid \alpha, \beta)}{L(\theta \mid Y, n) P(\theta \mid \alpha, \beta) d\theta}$$

$$= \frac{\theta^m (1-\theta)^{n-m} \cdot \frac{\Gamma(\alpha+\beta)}{\Gamma(\alpha)\Gamma(\beta)} \theta^{\alpha-1}(1-\theta)^{\beta-1}}{\int \theta^m (1-\theta)^{n-m} \cdot \frac{\Gamma(\alpha+\beta)}{\Gamma(\alpha)\Gamma(\beta)} \theta^{\alpha-1}(1-\theta)^{\beta-1} d\theta}$$

$$= \frac{\theta^{m+\alpha-1}(1-\theta)^{n-m+\beta-1}}{\int \theta^{m+\alpha-1}(1-\theta)^{n-m+\beta-1} d\theta}.$$

The integral evaluates as follows:

$$\int \theta^{m+\alpha-1}(1-\theta)^{n-m+\beta-1} d\theta = \frac{\Gamma(m+\alpha)\Gamma(n-m+\beta)}{\Gamma(n+\alpha+\beta)}.$$

From this, we have

$$P(\theta \mid Y, \alpha, \beta, n) = \frac{\Gamma(n+\alpha+\beta)}{\Gamma(m+\alpha)\Gamma(n-m+\beta)} \theta^{m+\alpha-1}(1-\theta)^{n-m+\beta-1}.$$

For the case of our data and prior, where $m = 140$, $n = 250$, $\alpha = \beta = 5$, the posterior, likelihood, and prior are shown in Figure 8.8.

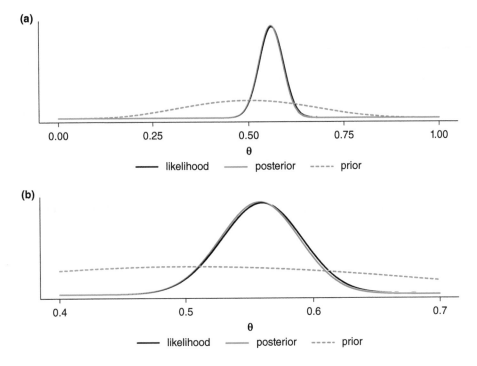

Figure 8.8 The posterior, likelihood, and prior in a binomial problem with $m = 140$ and $n = 250$ and where the prior is a beta distribution with $\alpha = 5$, $\beta = 5$. In (b) the same functions are plotted as in (a) but over a limited range of the x-axis in order to make the difference between the posterior and the likelihood more apparent. Note also that the likelihood function is scaled so that it integrates to 1. This is simply to make it easier to visualize on the same plot as the prior and posterior. Scaling the likelihood by an arbitrary positive quantity does not affect the calculations of the posterior

This formula for the posterior distribution is, in fact, a beta distribution with hyperparameters $m + \alpha$ and $n - m + \beta$, respectively. This situation where the posterior distribution is of the same parametric family as the prior is an example of a *conjugate prior*. A conjugate prior is a prior that when combined with a particular likelihood function yields a posterior distribution of the same probability distribution family. In this case, the beta distribution prior, when used with the binomial likelihood, always leads to a posterior distribution that is also a beta distribution.

Having a mathematical formula for the posterior distribution, as we do here, is an example of an *analytic solution* to the posterior distribution. This is not always possible. In other words, it is not always possible to have a mathematical expression with a finite number of terms and operations that describes the posterior distribution exactly. When an analytic solution is not possible, and in fact it is only possible in a relatively limited number of cases, we must rely on numerical methods to evaluate the posterior distribution, and in particular, *Monte Carlo* methods. We will return to this important topic in detail below.

Posterior summaries

The result of any Bayesian inference of any unknown variable is the posterior distribution. On the assumption that the statistical model and the prior are valid, the posterior distribution provides everything that is known about the true value of the variable. For the current problem, this is $P(\theta \mid Y = m = 140, \alpha = 5, \beta = 5, n = 250)$, which is a beta distribution with hyperparameters $m + \alpha$ and $n - m + \beta$. From the properties of the beta distribution mentioned above, the mean and standard deviation of this posterior are as follows:

$$\langle \theta \rangle = \frac{\alpha + m}{n + \alpha + \beta} = 0.558, \quad \text{SD}(\theta) = \sqrt{\frac{(\alpha + m)(\beta + n - m)}{(\alpha + \beta + n)^2 (\alpha + \beta + n + 1)}} = 0.031.$$

We can also use the cumulative distribution function of the beta distribution to determine the 2.5th and 97.5th percentiles of the posterior. Between these two bounds, there is 95% of the posterior probability mass. We can calculate this using R with the `qbeta` command, which is the inverse of the cumulative distribution function of the beta distribution:

```
n <- 250
m <- 140
alpha <- 5
beta <- 5
c(qbeta(0.025, m + alpha, n - m + beta),
  qbeta(0.975, m + alpha, n - m + beta))
#> [1] 0.4970679 0.6174758
```

This is a *posterior interval*, also known as a *credible interval*. More precisely, this interval is the *central* or *percentile* posterior interval.

Another posterior interval of interest is known as the *highest posterior density* (HPD) interval. The precise definition of the HPD is as follows: the φ interval for the posterior density function $f(\theta)$ is computed by finding a probability density value p^* such that

$$P\left(\{\theta : f(\theta) \geq p^*\}\right) = \varphi.$$

In other words, we find the value p^* such that the probability mass of the set of points whose density is greater than p^* is exactly φ. By this definition, no value of θ outside the HPD has a higher density than any value within the HPD. It will also be the shortest posterior interval containing φ. The HPD as precisely defined here is not easily calculated, and in general requires an optimization procedure to solve for p^*. In this model, using a numerical optimization technique, we calculate it to be $(0.4974, 0.6177)$. This is obviously very close to the quantile-based posterior interval defined above.

The posterior mean and the HPD interval can be compared to the maximum likelihood estimator and confidence interval in classical inference. Recall that the maximum likelihood estimator was 0.56 and the 95% confidence interval was $(0.496, 0.622)$. By contrast, the posterior mean and 95% central posterior interval are 0.558 and $(0.497, 0.617)$, respectively. While not identical, these are very close and for practical purposes are probably indistinguishable. This illustrates that classical and Bayesian methods can give very similar outcomes, especially in simple models.

Monte Carlo sampling

In the example problem that we have been discussing, the prior we chose was a beta distribution. As we've seen, when this prior is used with a binomial likelihood function, the posterior distribution is also a beta distribution. Thus, we have a relatively simple mathematical expression for the posterior distribution. Moreover, we can now use the properties of the beta distribution to determine the posterior mean, standard deviation, posterior intervals, etc. As mentioned, this is an example of an analytic solution to the posterior distribution. This is not always possible. Consider, for example, the posterior distribution when we change the prior to a *logit normal* distribution. This is a normal distribution over $\log(\theta/(1-\theta))$, which is the log odds of θ. A plot of this prior for the case of a zero-mean normal distribution with standard deviation $\tau = 0.5$ is shown in Figure 8.9(a). In Figure 8.9(b), we show a beta distribution over θ with parameters $\alpha = \beta = 8.42$, which is virtually identical to the $N(0,0.5^2)$ distribution over $\log(\theta/(1-\theta))$.

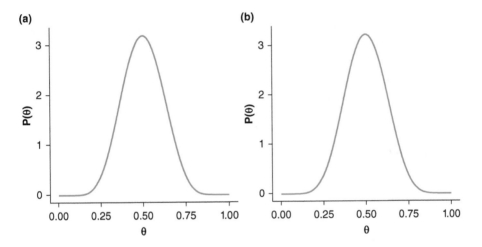

Figure 8.9 (a) A zero-mean normal distribution with standard deviation $\tau = 0.5$ over $\log(\theta/(1-\theta))$. (b) A beta distribution with parameters $\alpha = \beta = 8.42$

Despite the similarities of these two priors, if we use the normal distribution over the log odds, the posterior distribution is

$$P(\theta|m,n,\tau) = \frac{1}{Z}\,\theta^m(1-\theta)^{n-m}\,\frac{1}{\theta(1-\theta)}\,e^{-|\mathrm{logit}\,(\theta)|^2/2\tau^2},$$

where

$$Z = \int \theta^m(1-\theta)^{n-m}\,\frac{1}{\theta(1-\theta)}\,e^{-|\mathrm{logit}\,(\theta)|^2/2\tau^2}\,d\theta.$$

This does not simplify to an analytic expression, and it is not a known probability density function with well-documented properties. The problem here arises primarily because of the integral, which does not have an analytic solution. In cases like this, we need to resort to numerical alternatives to the analytic solution. For simple models such as this one, there are many options for how to do this. However, a general approach that applies to all Bayesian models, including and especially complex and high-dimensional models (i.e. with large numbers of unknown variables), is to use *Monte Carlo* sampling methods.

Monte Carlo methods, first introduced by Metropolis and Ulam (1949), can be generally defined as numerical methods for approximating mathematical *expectations* of random variables. If X is a random variable of dimensionality d whose probability distribution is P(X), and $\phi(X)$ is a function of X, then the expectation or expected value of $\phi(X)$ is

$$\langle \phi(X) \rangle = \int \phi(x) P(X = x) dx .$$

This can be approximated by

$$\langle \phi(X) \rangle = \frac{1}{n} \sum_{i=1}^{n} \phi(x_i),$$

where $x_1, x_2, \ldots, x_i, \ldots, x_n$ are n samples from P(X). Particularly important is the fact that the error of approximation decreases as a function of $\sqrt{n}$ and is independent of d, the dimensionality of X.

Quantities of interest related to the probability distribution P(X) such as the mean, variance, or probabilities of being above or below a certain value can all be expressed as expectations:

$$\langle X \rangle = \int x P(X = x) dx,$$

$$V(X) = \int (x - \langle X \rangle)^2 P(X = x) dx,$$

$$P(X > x_0) = \int I(x > x_0) P(X = x) dx.$$

They can, therefore, be approximated as follows:

$$\langle X \rangle \approx \bar{x} = \frac{1}{n} \sum_{i=1}^{n} x_i,$$

$$V(x) \approx \text{var}(x) = \frac{1}{n} \sum_{i=1}^{n} (x_i - \bar{x})^2,$$

$$P(X > x_0) \approx \frac{1}{n} \sum_{i=1}^{n} I(x_i > x_0).$$

What this entails for Bayesian inference is that if we can draw samples from the posterior distribution, Monte Carlo methods can be used to calculate all quantities of interest related to the posterior. Moreover, this can be done in high-dimensional problems without encountering the exponential rise in approximation error known as the *curse of dimensionality*.

There are many Monte Carlo methods for drawing samples from posterior probability distributions. Here, we will describe just two: the Metropolis sampler and the Hamiltonian Monte Carlo (HMC) sampler. Both of these are *Markov chain Monte Carlo* (MCMC) samplers, as we will see. The Metropolis sampler was one of the earliest MCMC samplers, introduced by Metropolis et al. (1953), and has traditionally been one of the most widely used samplers in Bayesian analysis. The HMC sampler is an extension of the Metropolis sampler. It is the main sampler that is used in the *Stan* probabilistic programming language that we will use extensively throughout the remainder of this book.

In order to discuss this topic generally, rather than just for a specific problem or model, we will assume that our observed data is $\mathcal{D}$ and that the unknown variable(s) that we are trying to infer is a d-dimensional variable θ. The posterior distribution is

$$P(\theta \mid \mathcal{D}) = \frac{L(\theta \mid \mathcal{D})P(\theta)}{\int L(\theta \mid \mathcal{D})P(\theta)d\theta},$$

where $L(\theta \mid \mathcal{D})$ is the likelihood function and $P(\theta)$ is the prior. We can rewrite the posterior distribution as

$$P(\theta \mid \mathcal{D}) = f(\theta)\frac{1}{Z}, \quad f(\theta) = L(\theta \mid \mathcal{D})g(\theta), \quad Z = \int L(\theta \mid \mathcal{D})g(\theta)d\theta.$$

Here, $f(\theta)$ is the unnormalized posterior distribution, where for notational simplicity we drop explicit reference to $\mathcal{D}$, Z is the normalization constant, and $g(\theta)$ is the prior distribution.

Metropolis sampler

For the Metropolis sampler, we need only be able to evaluate $f(\theta)$ at any given value of θ, and we do not need to know the value of Z. Evaluating $f(\theta)$ is often very straightforward, even in complex models. If we can evaluate the likelihood function at θ and the (normalized or unnormalized) prior at θ, we simply multiply their values together to obtain $f(\theta)$. To draw samples using the Metropolis sampler, we begin with an arbitrary initial value $\tilde{\theta}_0$, and then use a *proposal distribution* based around $\tilde{\theta}_0$ to propose a new point in the θ space, which we will call $\tilde{\theta}_.$. We can write this proposal distribution as $Q(\tilde{\theta} \mid \tilde{\theta}_0)$. In the standard implementation of the Metropolis sampler, the proposal distribution must be symmetric such that, for any two values $\tilde{\theta}_i$ and $\tilde{\theta}_j$, $Q(\tilde{\theta}_i \mid \tilde{\theta}_j) = Q(\tilde{\theta}_j \mid \tilde{\theta}_i)$. In the Metropolis–Hastings variant of the Metropolis sampler, as we will see, the proposal distribution need not be symmetric.

Having sampled $\theta_.$, if $f(\tilde{\theta}_.) \geq f(\tilde{\theta}_0)$, we accept that proposed new point and set $\tilde{\theta}_1 = \tilde{\theta}.$ We then propose a new point in θ space using our proposal distribution centred at $\tilde{\theta}_1$. If, on the other hand $f(\tilde{\theta}_.) < f(\tilde{\theta}_0)$, we accept $\tilde{\theta}.$ with probability

$$\frac{f(\tilde{\theta}_.)}{f(\tilde{\theta}_0)}.$$

If we accept it, then we set $\tilde{\theta}_1 = \tilde{\theta}.$ and propose a new point using our proposal distribution centred at $\tilde{\theta}_1$. If we reject $\tilde{\theta}_.$, we propose a new point using the proposal distribution centred at $\tilde{\theta}_0$, and repeat the above steps.

Continuing in this way, we produce a sequence of samples $\tilde{\theta}_0, \tilde{\theta}_1, \tilde{\theta}_2, \dots$ that are realizations of random variables $\theta_0, \theta_1, \theta_2 \dots$. Because each variable is dependent on the immediately preceding variable, and not dependent on any variable before that, these random variables form a first-order *Markov chain*. The marginal probability distributions of these variables are $\pi_0(\theta_0)$, $\pi_1(\theta_1)$, $\pi_2(\theta_2)$, $\dots$. The first distribution, $\pi_0(\theta_0)$, is an arbitrary starting distribution. The nature of the second distribution, $\pi_1(\theta_1)$, can be understood as follows: if $\tilde{\theta}_0 = \tilde{\theta}_a$, then the probability that $\tilde{\theta}_1 = \tilde{\theta}_b$ will be the $Q(\tilde{\theta} = \tilde{\theta}_b \mid \tilde{\theta}_a)$ if $f(\tilde{\theta}_b) > f(\tilde{\theta}_a)$ and will be $Q(\tilde{\theta} = \tilde{\theta}_b \mid \tilde{\theta}_b)$ otherwise. Thus, $\pi_1(\theta_1)$ is

$$\pi_1(\theta_1) = \int \underbrace{\min\left(\frac{f(\theta_1)}{f(\theta_0)}, 1\right) Q(\tilde{\theta}_1 \mid \tilde{\theta}_0)}_{T(\tilde{\theta}_1 \mid \tilde{\theta}_0)} \pi_0(\theta_0)d\theta_0.$$

By extension, for any i we have

$$\pi_i(\theta_i) = \int T(\theta_i \mid \theta_{i-1}) \pi_{i-1}(\theta_{i-1}) d\theta_i.$$

It can be shown that under some general and minimal conditions[3] of Markov chains, the sequence of probability distributions $\pi_0(\theta_0)$, $\pi_1(\theta_1)$, $\pi_2(\theta_2)$,... will converge upon a *unique* distribution that we will label $\pi(\theta)$. This is known as the *invariant* or *stationary* distribution of the Markov chain. Furthermore, if we have a function $\psi(\theta)$ that satisfies

$$T\left(\theta_i = \tilde{\theta}_b \mid \theta_{i-1} = \tilde{\theta}_a\right) \psi\left(\theta_{i-1} = \tilde{\theta}_a\right) = T\left(\theta_i = \tilde{\theta}_a \mid \theta_{i-1} = \tilde{\theta}_b\right) \psi\left(\theta_{i-1} = \tilde{\theta}_b\right)$$

for any two states $\tilde{\theta}_a$ and $\tilde{\theta}_b$, then $\psi(\theta)$ is this invariant distribution. We can see that $\psi(\theta)$ is the posterior distribution as follows. First, we will assume that $f(\tilde{\theta}_a) > f(\tilde{\theta}_b)$. If this is not the case, we simply reverse the labels of $\tilde{\theta}_a$ and $\tilde{\theta}_b$. Then we have

$$T\left(\tilde{\theta}_b \mid \tilde{\theta}_a\right) \psi\left(\tilde{\theta}_a\right) = T\left(\tilde{\theta}_a \mid \tilde{\theta}_b\right) \psi\left(\tilde{\theta}_b\right),$$

$$\frac{f(\theta_b)}{f(\theta_a)} Q\left(\tilde{\theta}_b \mid \tilde{\theta}_a\right) \psi\left(\tilde{\theta}_a\right) = Q\left(\tilde{\theta}_a \mid \tilde{\theta}_b\right) \psi\left(\tilde{\theta}_b\right).$$

Because of symmetry of the proposal distribution, we have

$$\frac{f(\theta_b)}{f(\theta_a)} Q\left(\tilde{\theta}_b \mid \tilde{\theta}_a\right) \psi\left(\tilde{\theta}_a\right) = Q\left(\tilde{\theta}_a \mid \tilde{\theta}_b\right) \psi\left(\tilde{\theta}_b\right)$$

$$\frac{f(\theta_b)}{f(\theta_a)} \psi\left(\tilde{\theta}_a\right) = \psi\left(\tilde{\theta}_b\right)$$

$$\frac{f(\theta_b)}{f(\theta_a)} = \frac{\psi\left(\tilde{\theta}_b\right)}{\psi\left(\tilde{\theta}_a\right)}.$$

From this we have

$$\psi(\theta) = \frac{1}{Z} f(\theta)$$

as the invariant distribution of the Markov chain.

In Figure 8.10, we show some of the sequence of distributions $\pi_0, \pi_1, \pi_2,...$ of a Metropolis sampler as it converges to the true posterior distribution, which is also shown. For this illustration, we use a binomial problem as above but where the data is $m = 14$ and $n = 25$, use a logit normal prior, and assume a uniform proposal distribution. From this illustration, we see a relatively quick convergence to the true posterior distribution.

The Metropolis–Hastings variant of the original Metropolis sampler allows for asymmetric proposal distributions. Given an initial sample $\tilde{\theta}_i$ and proposed new sample $\tilde{\theta}$, sampled from the proposal distribution $Q(\tilde{\theta} \mid \tilde{\theta}_i)$, we accept $\tilde{\theta}$ if

$$f(\tilde{\theta}) Q(\tilde{\theta}_i \mid \tilde{\theta}) \geq f(\tilde{\theta}_i) Q(\tilde{\theta} \mid \tilde{\theta}_i),$$

---

[3] These are *irreducibility*, which is the non-zero probability of eventually transitioning from any one state to any other, *aperiodicity*, which is having no perfectly cyclic state trajectories, and *non-transience*, which is the non-zero probability of returning to any given state.

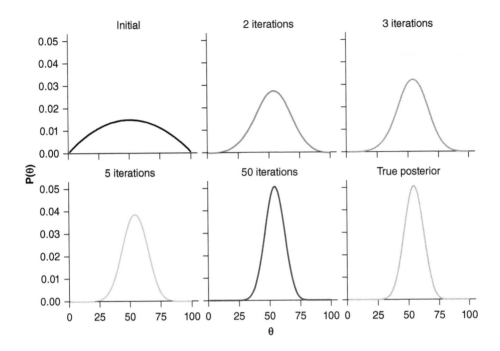

Figure 8.10 Convergence of a Metropolis sampler to the posterior distribution, having started at an arbitrary distribution

otherwise we accept it with probability

$$\frac{f(\tilde{\theta}_i)Q(\tilde{\theta}_i \mid \tilde{\theta}_i)}{f(\tilde{\theta}_i)Q(\tilde{\theta}_i \mid \tilde{\theta}_i)}.$$

Sampling in this way, as with the original Metropolis sampler, we converge upon an invariant probability distribution over θ that is the posterior distribution $(1/Z)f(\theta)$.

To illustrate the Metropolis algorithm, we will use our binomial problem with the logit normal distribution. The likelihood function at any value of θ is

$$L(\theta \mid m,n) = \theta^m (1-\theta)^{n-m}.$$

The unnormalized logit normal prior is

$$g(\theta) = \frac{1}{\theta(1-\theta)} e^{-|\text{logit}(\theta)|^2/2\tau^2}.$$

From this, we have

$$f(\theta) = \theta^{m-1}(1-\theta)^{n-m-1} e^{-|\text{logit}(\theta)|^2/2\tau^2}.$$

This can be easily implemented using R as follows:

```
logit <- function(x) log(x/(1-x))
f <- function(theta, m=140, n = 250, tau = 0.5){
  theta^(m-1) * (1-theta)^(n-m-1) * exp(-logit(theta)^2/(2*tau^2))
}
```

For the proposal distribution, for simplicity, we will use uniform distribution on (0, 1):

```
proposal <- function(theta_0){
  runif(1)
}
```

The following code implements a Metropolis sampler that draws 100 samples:

```
nsamples <- 100
i <- 1
theta <- numeric(length = nsamples)
theta[i] <- runif(1)  # initial sample from U(0,1)

while (i < nsamples) {
  theta_star <- proposal(theta[i])  # proposed sample
  p <- min(f(theta_star)/f(theta[i]), 1)  # prob. of acceptance
  if (runif(1) <= p){
    i <- i + 1
    theta[i] <- theta_star
  }
}
```

The trajectories of samples from two separate chains, each started at opposite ends of the θ space, are shown in Figure 8.11(a). These plots are known as *trace plots*. As can be seen, these trajectories both quickly converge upon the same area of θ space. The histogram of samples from one chain is shown in Figure 8.11(b).

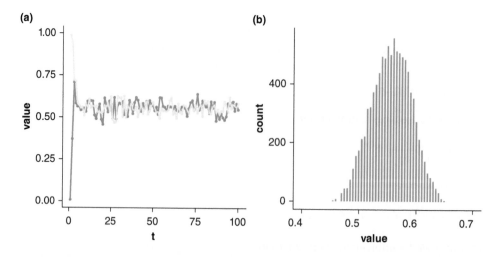

Figure 8.11 (a) Trajectory, or *trace plot*, of 100 samples from two separate chains of a Metropolis sampler for the binomial problem using a logit normal prior. (b) Histogram of 10,000 samples from one of the samplers

Hamiltonian Monte Carlo

The Metropolis algorithm suffers from the fact that its proposal distribution takes random steps in parameter space. *Hamiltonian Monte Carlo*, which was originally known as *hybrid Monte Carlo*, aims to overcome this limitation by taking account of the gradient of the posterior distribution when making its proposals. Both theoretically and in terms of its technical details, it is considerably more complex than the Metropolis method (see Neal, 2011; Betancourt, 2017). However, HMC is extremely efficient and is now widely used in Bayesian data analysis, and so any contemporary introduction of MCMC would be incomplete without covering it.

To appreciate HMC, we return to the fact that in any Bayesian analysis, our results are ultimately expectations of functions according to the posterior distribution. Thus, if the posterior distribution over our unknown variables is $P(\theta \mid \mathcal{D})$, the expected value of some function $\phi(\theta)$ according to the posterior is

$$\langle\phi(\theta)\rangle=\int\phi(\theta)P(\theta\mid\mathcal{D})d\theta.$$

The value of this integral is largely determined by where $P(\theta \mid \mathcal{D})$ is massed. In high-dimensional spaces, most of this mass is concentrated in a thin shell far from the mode of the distribution that is known as the *typical set* (see Betancourt, 2017). All methods ideally sample from this typical set. However, because the typical set is a thin shell, the random proposals made by the Metropolis sampler will be mostly in regions of low probability density outside of it, which will be rejected, leading to inefficiency. Likewise, those proposals that will be accepted will often be just those close to the current state of the sampler, and in this sense, the sampler becomes stuck in one region and does not explore the typical set.

HMC tries to overcome these problems with the random walk Metropolis by using the gradient of the posterior distribution to guide its proposals of new points to sample. For any given value of θ, the gradient of the posterior distribution is evaluated. This indicates the directions with higher or lower posterior density. Were we to simply follow the gradient, we would end up moving away from the typical set and towards the mode of the distribution. While the mode will have high density, it will have infinitesimally low volume in high-dimensional problems, and so is not part of the typical set as defined above. In order to remain within the typical set, therefore, each point in θ space is given a *momentum* value denoted by r, which gives a direction and velocity to each point. This momentum speeds up as the object approaches areas of high density, and slows and reverses in regions of low density.

In order to implement this system, HMC represents the value of θ as a point in a physical space that has *potential energy* and *kinetic energy*. The potential energy is determined by its position, and can seen as the effect of gravity. The kinetic energy is determined by the momentum of the point. Intuitively, we can imagine this as a smooth (frictionless) hilly landscape with a ball with a momentum moving over this landscape. If we kick the ball, we give it some momentum and it will move in a certain direction with a certain speed. If that direction is downwards, under the effect of gravity, it will speed up and then when it gets to the bottom of the hill, its momentum will allow it to continue moving and it will start to roll up the side of another hill. Eventually, the effect of gravity will start to slow it down, and it will then reverse and roll back down the hill, and so on. The movement of the ball is physically determined by its position and its momentum and their respective potential and kinetic energies.

In more detail, the *potential energy* at each point is given by

$$U(\theta) = -\log(f(\theta)),$$

where $f(\theta) \propto P(\theta \mid \mathcal{D})$ as defined above. This is equivalent to

$$P(\theta \mid \mathcal{D}) = \frac{1}{Z} e^{-U(\theta)}.$$

From this perspective, the HMC sampler can be seen as a physical system with an infinite number of states, each of which has a potential energy associated with it. The probability of the system being in any state is determined by the potential energy associated with that state.[4] The lower the energy, the more likely the system is to be in that state. The higher the energy, the less likely it is to be in that state. In addition to its potential energy, each state also has a *kinetic energy*, denoted by $K(r)$, which is determined by the momentum with value r. In one dimension, if the point has unit mass, the kinetic energy is $K(r) = r^2 / 2$, and in d dimensions it is

$$K(r) = \frac{1}{2} \sum_{k=1}^{d} r_k^2.$$

Given this energy function, the probability distribution corresponding to it is $P(r) \propto e^{-K(r)}$, which is a d-dimensional standard normal distribution. The total energy in this system is given by the *Hamiltonian* function:

$$H(\theta, r) = U(\theta) + K(r).$$

The change in the position and the momentum is now determined by classical mechanics and is given by the Hamiltonian equations:

$$\frac{d\theta_k}{dt} = \frac{\partial H}{\partial r_k} = \frac{\partial K(r)}{\partial r_k},$$

$$\frac{dr_k}{dt} = -\frac{\partial H}{\partial \theta_k} = -\frac{\partial U(\theta)}{\partial \theta_k},$$

where $d\theta_k/dt$ and dr_k/dt are the rate of change, at dimension k, of the position θ and momentum r, respectively, and $\partial H/\partial r_k$ and $\partial H/\partial \theta_k$ are the partial derivatives of the Hamiltonian function with respect to r_k and θ_k, respectively. Now, if we start at any point in θ space and give this point a momentum, the Hamiltonian equations will determine how the point will move through this space under the actions of both the potential and kinetic energy.

In order to simulate this continuous dynamical system, which is governed by differential equations, on a computer, we must use a discrete approximation to its dynamics. Widely used methods such as *Runge–Kutta methods* or *Euler's method* are possible, but a more

---

[4] In statistical mechanics, a physical system where the probability of being in any given state is proportional to e to the power of the negative of the energy at that state is said to have a *Boltzmann distribution*.

suitable method is the *leapfrog* algorithm, which involves taking steps, or half-steps, of size δ as follows:

$$r_k \leftarrow r_k - \frac{\delta}{2}\frac{\partial U(\theta)}{\partial \theta_k}, \quad \text{first half-step in } r \text{ space,}$$

$$\theta_k \leftarrow \theta_k + \delta \frac{\partial K(r)}{\partial r_k}, \quad \text{step in } \theta \text{ space,}$$

$$r_k \leftarrow r_k - \frac{\delta}{2}\frac{\partial U(\theta)}{\partial \theta_k}, \quad \text{second half-step in } r \text{ space.}$$

As a simple example of Hamiltonian dynamics, let us assume that the posterior distribution is a two-dimensional normal distribution with a mean μ and covariance matrix Σ. In this case, we have

$$U(\theta) = \frac{1}{2}(\theta - \mu)^{\mathsf{T}}\Sigma^{-1}(\theta - \mu),$$

and we will assume that $K(r) = \frac{1}{2}\sum_{k=1}^{d} r_k^2$. The partial derivatives are

$$\frac{\partial U(\theta)}{\partial \theta_k} = (\theta - \mu)^{\mathsf{T}}\Sigma^{-1}, \quad \frac{\partial K(r)}{\partial r_k} = r_k,$$

and so our leapfrog steps are

$$r_k \leftarrow r_k - \frac{\delta}{2}(\theta - \mu)^{\mathsf{T}}\Sigma^{-1}, \quad \theta_k \leftarrow \theta_k + \delta r_k.$$

Starting with an arbitrary point $\tilde{\theta} = (0, 1.5)$, and choosing r at random from a two-dimensional standard normal, we simulate the Hamiltonian dynamics for 45 leapfrog steps with $\delta = 0.1$. This is shown in Figure 8.12. As we can see, the trajectories move smoothly back and forth through the posterior distribution.

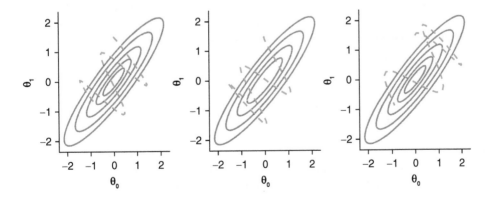

Figure 8.12 Three trajectories of a Hamiltonian dynamical system where the posterior distribution is a two-dimensional normal distribution, where each trajectory starts at $\tilde{\theta} = (0, 1.5)$, and where we choose the momentum r at random from a two-dimensional standard normal. The system is simulated for 45 leapfrog steps with $\delta = 0.1$

The key feature of HMC that differentiates it from random walk Metropolis is that it replaces the random proposal distribution with the deterministic dynamics of the Hamiltonian system. Specifically, a point in $\tilde{\theta}$ space is chosen at random, a value of the momentum variable r is chosen from the probability distribution corresponding to $K(r)$, that is $P(r) \propto e^{-K(r)}$, and the Hamiltonian system deterministically evolves for a period of time to arrive at a new point $\tilde{\theta}_.$ and new momentum $r_.$. The new point $\tilde{\theta}_.$ is then accepted if $H(\tilde{\theta}_.,r_.) > H(\tilde{\theta},r)$. Otherwise, $\tilde{\theta}_.$ is accepted with probability

$$e^{H(\tilde{\theta},r)-H(\tilde{\theta},r)} = \frac{P(\tilde{\theta}_. \mid \mathcal{D})\, P(r_.)}{P(\tilde{\theta} \mid \mathcal{D})\, P(r)}.$$

This acceptance step is essentially identical to the Metropolis–Hastings acceptance–rejection step.

One final issue to address concerns how long the trajectories of the deterministic Hamiltonian dynamics ought to be. If the trajectories are too short, the sampler will move slowly through the posterior distribution. If the trajectory is longer, as we can see in Figure 8.12, the trajectory may loop back upon itself. The extent to which the trajectories will loop around will depend on the curvature of the $U(\theta)$ space. In flat regions, the loop-arounds will not happen, but will happen sooner in curved regions. The *No-U-Turn Sampler* (NUTS) by Hoffman and Gelman (2014) optimally tunes the trajectory lengths according to the local curvature. This allows optimal trajectory lengths without manual tuning or without tuning runs of the sampler. The probabilistic programming language Stan, to which Chapter 17 is devoted, uses an HMC sampler that uses NUTS.

As an illustration of an HMC sampler, in fact based on the Stan language, we will use the brms package (Bürkner, 2018):

```
library(brms)
```

This package allows us to implement a very wide range of models using minimal and familiar R command syntax and creates, compiles and executes the Stan sampler. We will use brms-based models often in the remaining chapters. We can implement the logit normal prior based binomial model mentioned above as follows:

```
M_hmc <- brm(m | trials(n) ~ 1,
             data = tibble(n = n, m = m),
             prior = prior(normal(0, 0.5), class = Intercept),
             family = binomial)
```

By default, this will sample four independent chains, each with 1000 post-*warm up* samples. The warm up iterations are iterations prior to convergence on the typical set, and during this period, the HMC sampler is fine-tuned. The summary of this model is as follows:

```
summary(M_hmc)
#>   Family: binomial
#>    Links: mu = logit
#> Formula: m | trials(n) ~ 1
```

```
#>     Data: tibble(n = n, m = m) (Number of observations: 1)
#> Samples: 4 chains, each with iter = 2000; warmup = 1000; thin = 1;
#>          total post-warmup samples = 4000
#>
#> Population-Level Effects:
#>           Estimate Est.Error l-95% CI u-95% CI Rhat Bulk_ESS Tail_ESS
#> Intercept     0.23      0.13    -0.02     0.48 1.00     1539     2023
#>
#> Samples were drawn using sampling(NUTS). For each parameter, Bulk_ESS
#> and Tail_ESS are effective sample size measures, and Rhat is the potential
#> scale reduction factor on split chains (at convergence, Rhat = 1).
```

The histogram of the 4000 posterior samples of θ is shown in Figure 8.13.

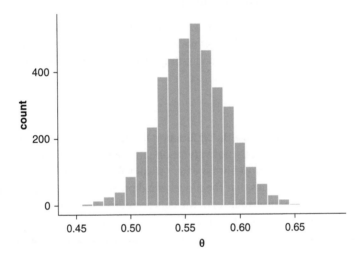

Figure 8.13 Histogram of the samples from the posterior distribution over θ from an HMC sampler of a logit normal prior based binomial model

8●5   Model evaluation

Let us return to the following diagram from the introduction to this chapter.

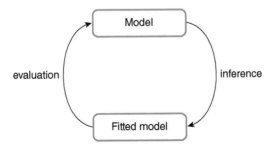

In our coverage of classical and then Bayesian methods of inference, we have dealt with the *inference* arc to right. This is where we begin with a statistical model that has variables or parameters whose values are unknown, and then use one general approach or another to effectively obtain estimates of these unknown variables, as well as measures of uncertainty of these estimates. The result is a model that it fitted to the data. However, whether it is a good fit, and, more importantly, whether the model is able to generalize to new data, remain to be seen. *Model evaluation* is the general term for this stage of the modelling process. Model evaluation is ultimately a large and multifaceted topic, involving various quantitative and graphical methods. Here, we will focus on the most common methods, and in particular on *model comparison*, which is where we directly compare two or more models against one another.

Deviance and log likelihood ratio tests

Let us first consider a widely used approach for model comparison for classical inference-based models. We will call the model that we are evaluating $\mathcal{M}_1$, whose vector of unknown parameters is θ_1, with maximum likelihood estimator $\hat{\theta}_1$ based on the observed data $\mathcal{D}$. The probability of $\mathcal{D}$ according to $\mathcal{M}_1$ and $\hat{\theta}_1$ is

$$P(\mathcal{D}|\mathcal{M}_1,\hat{\theta}_1).$$

Note that this is the value of the likelihood function for the model evaluated at its maximum value. In itself, this value is actually not very informative about how well $\mathcal{D}$ is predicted by $\mathcal{M}_1$ with parameters $\hat{\theta}_1$. It is almost always a very small value, based on the fact that there is a very large set of possible values that the model could predict. However, it is more informative to compare the relative probabilities of the data according to two models that we wish to compare. If we name the comparison model $\mathcal{M}_0$, and name its parameter vector θ_0 and its estimator of these parameters $\hat{\theta}_0$, then the ratio of the probabilities of $\mathcal{D}$ according to these two models is

$$\frac{P(\mathcal{D}|\mathcal{M}_0,\hat{\theta}_0)}{P(\mathcal{D}|\mathcal{M}_1,\theta_1)}.$$

This ratio is usually referred to as the *likelihood ratio*. Note that it is specifically the ratio of the maximum values of the likelihood functions of the two models. The logarithm of this likelihood ratio is

$$\log\left(\frac{P(\mathcal{D}|\mathcal{M}_0,\hat{\theta}_0)}{P(\mathcal{D}|\mathcal{M}_1,\hat{\theta}_1)}\right)=\log P(\mathcal{D}|\mathcal{M}_0,\hat{\theta}_0)-\log P(\mathcal{D}|\mathcal{M}_1,\hat{\theta}_1).$$

For reasons that will become clear, we usually multiple this logarithm by -2 to obtain the following:

$$-2\log\left(\frac{P(\mathcal{D}|\mathcal{M}_0,\hat{\theta}_0)}{P(\mathcal{D}|\mathcal{M}_1,\hat{\theta}_1)}\right)=-2\log P(\mathcal{D}|\mathcal{M}_0,\hat{\theta}_0)-(-2\log P(\mathcal{D}|\mathcal{M}_1,\hat{\theta}_1)),$$
$$=D_0-D_1.$$

Here, D_0 and D_1, which are simply -2 times the logarithm of the corresponding likelihoods, are known as the *deviance* of model $\mathcal{M}_0$ and $\mathcal{M}_1$, respectively. Note that because of the negative sign of the multiplier, the larger the deviance, the lower the likelihood of the model. Thus, if $D_0 > D_1$, model $\mathcal{M}_1$ is better able to predict the data than model $\mathcal{M}_0$.

Differences of deviances, and so the log likelihood ratio, are particularly widely used when comparing *nested models*. Nested models are where one model's parameter space is a subset of that of another. For example, if $\mathcal{M}_1$ is a normal distribution model with mean and variance parameters μ_1 and σ_1^2, both of which are unknown, and $\mathcal{M}_0$ is also a normal distribution but with fixed mean $\mu_0 = 0$ and only σ_0^2 being unknown, then $\mathcal{M}_0$ is nested in $\mathcal{M}_1$ because $\{\mu_0 = 0, \sigma_0^2\} \subseteq \{\mu_1, \sigma_1^2\}$. When comparing nested models, we can make use of *Wilks's theorem* which states that, if models $\mathcal{M}_0$ and $\mathcal{M}_1$ predict $\mathcal{D}$ equally well, then asymptotically (i.e. as sample size increases)

$$\Delta_D = D_0 - D_1 \sim \chi^2_{k_1 - k_0},$$

where k_1 and k_0 are the number of parameters in $\mathcal{M}_1$ and $\mathcal{M}_0$, respectively. In other words, if $\mathcal{M}_0$ and $\mathcal{M}_1$ predict the data equally well, then the difference of their deviances, which would be due to sampling variation alone, will be distributed as a χ^2 distribution whose degrees of freedom are equal to the difference of the number of parameters in the two models.

Wilks's theorem is widely used in regression models, as we will see in subsequent chapters. However, for now, we can illustrate with a simple example. Let us return to the house-prices_df data above. One model, $\mathcal{M}_1$, of the price variable could be that its logarithm is normally distributed with some mean μ_1 and variance σ_1^2, both of which are unknown. A nested model, $\mathcal{M}_0$, could be that the logarithm of price is normally distributed with a fixed mean $\mu_0 = \log(60{,}000)$ and unknown variance σ_0^2. Without providing too much details of the R commands, which we will cover in more detail in subsequent chapters, we can fit these two models as follows:

```
M_1 <- lm(log(price) ~ 1, data = housing_df)
mu_0 <- rep(log(60000), nrow(housing_df))
M_0 <- lm(log(price) ~ 0 + offset(mu_0), data = housing_df)
```

The logarithms of the likelihoods of M_1 and M_0 at the maximum values are as follows:

```
logLik(M_1)
#> 'log Lik.' -234.2995 (df=2)
logLik(M_0)
#> 'log Lik.' -240.6163 (df=1)
```

The corresponding deviances are -2 times these values, which we may also obtain as follows:

```
(d_1 <- -2 * logLik(M_1))
#> 'log Lik.' 468.599 (df=2)
(d_0 <- -2 * logLik(M_0))
#> 'log Lik.' 481.2327 (df=1)
```

The difference of the deviances Δ_D is as follows:

```
delta_d <- as.numeric(d_0 - d_1)
delta_d
#> [1] 12.6336
```

Assuming $\mathcal{M}_1$ and $\mathcal{M}_0$ predict the observed data equally well, this difference is distributed as a χ^2 distribution with 1 degree of freedom. This value for the degrees of freedom is based on the fact that one model has two parameters and the other has just one. We can calculate the p-value for Δ_D by calculating the probability of obtaining a result as extreme as or more extreme than Δ_D in a χ^2 distribution with 1 degree of freedom:

```
pchisq(delta_d, df = 1, lower.tail = F)
#> [1] 0.0003788739
```

Simply put, this result tells us that a value of $\Delta_D = 12.63$ is not an expected result if models $\mathcal{M}_0$ and $\mathcal{M}_1$ predict the data equal well, and so we can conclude that $\mathcal{M}_1$, which has the lower deviance, predicts the data significantly better than $\mathcal{M}_0$.

Cross-validation and out-of-sample predictive performance

Although widely used and very useful, the deviance-based model comparison just described is limited to both classical methods and nested models. It is also limited in that it examines how well any pair of models can predict the observed data on which the model was fitted. A more important question is how any model can generalize to new data that is from the same putative source as the original data. This is known as *out-of-sample* predictive performance. Any model may in fact predict the data on which it was fitted well, or even perfectly, and yet generalize poorly because it is too highly tuned to the peculiarities or essentially random element of the data. This is known as *overfitting* and it is a major problem, especially with complex models. To properly evaluate a model and identify any overfitting, we need to see how well the model can generalize to new data. Rather than waiting for new data to be collected, a simple solution is to remove part of the data that is used for model fitting, fit the model with the remaining data, and then test how well the fitted model predicts the reserved data. This is known as *cross-validation*.

One common approach to cross-validation is known as K-fold cross-validation. The original data set is divided randomly into K subsets. One of these subsets is randomly selected to be reserved for testing. The remaining $K - 1$ are used for fitting and the generalization to the reserved data set is evaluated. This process is repeated for all K subsets, and the overall cross-validation performance is the average of the K repetitions. One extreme version of K-fold cross-validation is where $K = n$ where n is the size of the data set. In this case, we remove each one of the observations, fit the model on the remaining set, and test on the held-out observation. This is known as *leave-one-out* cross-validation.

For leave-one-out cross-validation, the procedure is as follows, with the procedure for any K-fold cross-validation being similarly defined. Assuming our data is $\mathcal{D} = y_1, y_2, \ldots, y_n$, we divide the data into n sets:

$$(y_1, y_{-1}), (y_2, y_{-2}), \ldots, (y_i, y_{-i}), \ldots, (y_n, y_{-n}),$$

where y_i is data point i and y_{-i} is all the remaining data except for data point i. Then, for each i, we fit the model using y_{-i} and test how well the fitted model can predict y_i. We then calculate the sum of the predictive performance over all data points. In classical inference-based models, for each i, we calculate $\hat{\theta}^{-i}$, which is the maximum likelihood or other estimator of the parameter vector θ based on y_{-i}. We then calculate $P(y_i \mid \hat{\theta}^{-i})$, which is the logarithm of the predicted probability of y_i based on the model with parameters $\hat{\theta}^{-i}$. This then leads to

$$\text{ELPD} = \sum_{i=1}^{n} \log P(y_i \mid \hat{\theta}^{-i})$$

as the overall measure of the model's out-of-sample predictive performance, which we refer to as the *expected log predictive density* (ELPD). In Bayesian approaches, an analogous procedure is followed. For each i, we calculate the posterior distribution $P(\theta \mid y_{-i})$, and the model's overall out-of-sample predictive performance is

$$\text{ELPD} = \sum_{i=1}^{n} \log \int P(y_i \mid \theta) P(\theta \mid y_{-i}) d\theta.$$

This can be approximated by

$$\text{ELPD} \approx \sum_{i=1}^{n} \log \left(\frac{1}{s} \sum_{s=1}^{s} P(y_i \mid \hat{\theta}_s^{-i}) \right),$$

where $\tilde{\theta}_1^{-i}, \tilde{\theta}_2^{-i}, \dots, \tilde{\theta}_S^{-i}$ are S samples from $P(\theta \mid y_{-i})$.

In order to illustrate this, let us use the `price` variable in the `housing_df` data. One model for this data that we can consider, as described in the introduction to this chapter, is $y_i \sim \text{logN}(\mu, \sigma^2)$, for $i = 1, \dots, n$, where $\text{logN}(\mu, \sigma^2)$ is a log-normal distribution whose parameters are μ and σ^2. Using a classical inference-based model, this can be implemented in R as follows:

```
m1 <- lm(log(price) ~ 1, data = housing_df)
```

We can remove any $i = 1, \dots, n$ and fit the model with the remaining data as follows, using $i = 42$ as an example:

```
i <- 42
m1_not_i <- lm(log(price) ~ 1,
                data = slice(housing_df, -i)
)
```

The logarithm of the probability of y_i is the logarithm of the normal density for $\log y_i$ with the mean and standard deviation based on their maximum likelihood estimators in the fitted model. We can extract the maximum likelihood estimators of the mean and standard deviation from `m1_not_i` as follows:

```
mu <- coef(m1_not_i)
stdev <- sigma(m1_not_i)
```

Then the logarithm of normal density of $\log y_i$ based on these estimators is

```
y_i <- slice(housing_df, i) %>% pull(price)
dnorm(log(y_i), mean = mu, sd = stdev, log = T)
#> [1] 0.03483869
```

We can create a function to calculate the logarithm of the prediction for any $\log y_i$ as follows:

```
logprediction_m1 <- function(i){
  m1_not_i <- lm(log(price) ~ 1,
                 data = slice(housing_df, -i)
  )
  mu <- coef(m1_not_i)
  stdev <- sigma(m1_not_i)
  y_i <- slice(housing_df, i) %>% pull(price)
  dnorm(log(y_i), mean = mu, sd = stdev, log = T)

}
```

We can then apply this to all data points and sum the result:

```
n <- nrow(housing_df)
map_dbl(seq(n), logprediction_m1) %>%
  sum()
#> [1] -236.2388
```

Now let us compare this log-normal model's performance to a normal model, where we assume that $y_i \sim N(\mu, \sigma^2)$ for $i = 1, ..., n$. The log of the prediction of the held-out data point is calculated in an almost identical manner, except that we use the values of the price variable directly and not their logarithm:

```
logprediction_m0 <- function(i){
  m0_not_i <- lm(price ~ 1,
                 data = slice(housing_df, -i)
  )
  mu <- coef(m0_not_i)
  stdev <- sigma(m0_not_i)
  y_i <- slice(housing_df, i) %>% pull(price)
  dnorm(y_i, mean = mu, sd = stdev, log = T)

}
```

```
map_dbl(seq(n), logprediction_m0) %>%
  sum()
#> [1] -6342.375
```

It is common to multiply these sums of log predictions by −2 to put the values on a deviance scale. This is sometimes known as the leave-one-out information criterion (LOOIC). Thus, our measure of the out-of-sample predictive deviance of the log-normal model is 472.48, and for the normal model, it is 12,684.75. The log-normal model is clearly the better model with a much lower deviance score. In the next section, we will consider how best to interpret differences in LOOIC and related quantities.

To perform leave-one-out cross-validation using Stan models, we can make use of an efficient implementation of this based on *Pareto smoothed importance sampling* (Vehtari et al., 2017). This means that we do not have to manually divide the data set into subsets, as we did in the previous example. In fact, this efficient method allows us to effectively implement the leave-one-out cross-validation method without repeatedly rerunning the HMC models, which would be computationally extremely burdensome. All we need do is implement the Stan model, which we can do easily using brm as follows:

```
m1_bayes <- brm(log(price) ~ 1, data = housing_df)
m0_bayes <- brm(price ~ 1, data = housing_df
```

We may then get the ELPD and LOOIC using the command loo:

```
loo(m1_bayes)$estimates
#>                Estimate           SE
#> elpd_loo -236.234322  15.9135198
#> p_loo       1.888464   0.1616675
#> looic     472.468644  31.8270395
loo(m0_bayes)$estimates
#>                Estimate           SE
#> elpd_loo -6341.868732  23.4359160
#> p_loo        2.981645   0.6150526
#> looic     12683.737464  46.8718319
```

Leaving aside p_loo (a measure of effective number of parameters) and the standard errors (a measure of uncertainty of the estimates, as defined above), we see here that the elpd_loo and the looic estimates from the Bayesian models are very similar to those calculated using the classical inference-based models above.

Akaike information criterion

Cross-validation is an excellent method of model evaluation because it addresses the central issue of out-of-sample generalization, rather than fit to the data, and can be applied to any models, regardless of whether these models are based on classical or Bayesian methods of inference. On the other hand, cross-validation has traditionally been seen as too computationally demanding to be used in all data analysis situations. This is becoming less of a concern now, both because of the computational power and the development of efficient implementation such as the Pareto smoothed importance sampler method mentioned above. Nonetheless, one still widely used model evaluation model, the Akaike information criterion (AIC), originally proposed by Akaike (1973), can be justified as a very easily computed approximation to leave-one-out cross-validation (see Stone, 1977; Fang, 2011). The AIC is defined as follows:

$$AIC = 2k - 2\log P(\mathcal{D}|\hat{\theta})$$
$$= 2k + \text{deviance},$$

where k is the number of parameters in the model. Obviously, for models where the log of the likelihood is available, and where the number of parameters of the model is straightforward to count (which is not always the case in complex models), the AIC is simple to calculate. For example, for the log-normal and normal models that we evaluated above using cross-validation, both of which have $k = 2$ parameters, the AIC is calculated as follows:

```
m1 <- lm(log(price) ~ 1, data = housing_df)
m0 <- lm(price ~ 1, data = housing_df)
k <- 2
aic_1 <- as.numeric(2 * k - 2 * logLik(m1))
aic_0 <- as.numeric(2 * k - 2 * logLik(m0))

c(aic_1, aic_0)
#> [1]    472.599 12682.711
```

Clearly, these are very similar to the cross-validation ELPD for these two models.

Like the ELPD and other measures, a model's AIC value is of little value in itself, and so we only interpret differences in AIC between models. Conventional standards (see, for example, Burnham and Anderson, 2003, Chapter 2) hold that AIC differences greater than 4 or 7 indicate clear superiority of the predictive power of the model with the lower AIC, while differences of 10 or more indicate that the model with the higher value has essentially no predictive power relative to the model with the lower value. We can appreciate why these thresholds are followed by considering the concept of *Akaike weights* (see Burnham and Anderson, 2003, p. 75). Akaike weights provide probabilities for each of a set of K models that are being compared with one another. They are defined as follows:

$$p_k = \frac{e^{-\frac{1}{2}\Delta AIC_k}}{\sum_{k=1}^{K} e^{-\frac{1}{2}\Delta AIC_k}},$$

where ΔAIC_k is the difference between the AIC of model k and the lowest AIC value in the set of K models. These probabilities can be interpreted as the probabilities that any model has better predictive performance than the others. If we have just two models, with model $k = 1$ being the one with the lower AIC, then $\Delta AIC_1 = 0$ and ΔAIC_2 will be some value positive quantity δ. Using Akaike weights, the probability that the model with the lower AIC has the better predictive performance is

$$p = \frac{1}{1 + e^{-\delta/2}}.$$

For δ values of 4, 6, 9, the corresponding probabilities are 0.88, 0.95, 0.99. These values provide a justification for the thresholds proposed by Burnham and Anderson (2003).

Watanabe Akaike information criterion

The AIC is appealing because of its simplicity. As we have seen, despite its simplicity, it can be a highly accurate approximation to cross-validation ELPD. However, this approximation will not hold in all models, especially large and complex ones. In addition, in some situations calculating the maximum of the likelihood function is not straightforward, nor is defining the number of free parameters in the model. A more widely applicable version of the AIC is the *Watanabe Akaike information criterion* (WAIC). The WAIC was introduced in Watanabe (2010) under the name *widely applicable information criterion*. It has been shown that the WAIC is more generally or widely applicable than AIC, and is a close approximation to Bayesian leave-one-out cross-validation, yet can be calculated easily from a model's posterior samples. The WAIC is calculated as follows:

$$\text{WAIC} = -2\left(\sum_{i=1}^{n}\log\left(\frac{1}{S}\sum_{s=1}^{S}P(y_i \mid \theta^s)\right) - \sum_{i=1}^{n}V_{s=1}^{S}\left(\log P(y_i \mid \theta^s)\right)\right),$$

where y_i, θ^s, etc., are as they are defined above for the case of Bayesian ELPD. The term $V_{s=1}^{S}(\cdot)$ signifies the variance of its arguments.

Using Stan-based models, the WAIC is easily calculated using the loo package:

```
waic(m1_bayes)$estimates
#>              Estimate          SE
#> elpd_waic -236.232503 15.9133627
#> p_waic       1.886645  0.1614885
#> waic       472.465006 31.8267254
waic(m0_bayes)$estimates
#>              Estimate          SE
#> elpd_waic -6341.868701 23.4362820
#> p_waic        2.981614  0.6155333
#> waic      12683.737402 46.8725640
```

As we can see, this is very similar to the Bayesian cross-validation ELPD, but can be calculated directly from posterior samples.

9

Normal Linear Models

Introduction

Normal linear models play a foundational role in statistical modelling. In a sense, they can be seen as the backbone of most statistical modelling techniques. In themselves, they comprise such well-known and widely used models as simple and multiple linear regression, *t*-tests, ANOVA, ANCOVA, and related models, all of which we will cover in this chapter. They are the basis of all the classical and traditional approaches to path analysis, structural equation models, and factor analysis (see Chapter 14). They can be extended in relatively simple ways to lead to the *generalized* linear models that include the logistic regression models for categorical data, or the count models such as Poisson or negative binomial regression (see Chapters 10 and 11). Their standard form may be generalized further to lead to the multilevel, also known as the hierarchical or mixed effects, linear models (see Chapter 12). Even the *nonlinear* models are often based on linear models, being linear combinations of nonlinear *basis functions* (see Chapter 13).

The univariate normal linear model

In this chapter, we will deal exclusively with *univariate* normal linear models. In these models, we assume we have n independent observations, which can be represented as n pairs as follows:

$$(y_1, \vec{x}_1), (y_2, \vec{x}_2), \ldots, (y_i, \vec{x}_i), \ldots, (y_n, \vec{x}_n).$$

In each observation, y_i is the observed value of a univariate *outcome* variable. As we will see, the outcome variable is that which we are hoping to predict, explain or understand with the probabilistic model. On the other hand, the $\vec{x}_i = [x_{1i}, x_{2i}, \ldots, x_{ki}, \ldots, x_{Ki}]$ are a set of K values that are used in the model to predict or explain each value y_i. Thus, each $\vec{x}_i$ gives the observed values of a set of K *predictor* or *explanatory* variables. There is no upper bound to the number K of predictor variables we have. In terms of a lower bound, K can be 0, in fact, and this is an important special case that often arises.

The normal linear model of this data is as follows:

$$y_i \sim N(\mu_i, \sigma^2), \quad \mu_i = \beta_0 + \sum_{k=1}^{K} \beta_k x_{ki}, \quad \text{for } i \in 1, \ldots, n.$$

Here, $N(\mu_i, \sigma^2)$ denotes a univariate normal distribution with mean μ_i and variance σ^2. In other words, the normal linear model assumes that each observed value y_i is a sample from a normal distribution whose mean is μ_i, and whose standard deviation is σ, and the value of μ_i is a deterministic linear function of the values of the K predictor variables.

It is important to see that this model is a probabilistic model of $y_1, \ldots, y_n$. Specifically, it is a model of the probability of $y_1, \ldots, y_n$ conditional on $\vec{x}_1, \ldots, \vec{x}_n$, $\vec{\beta} = [\beta_0, \beta_1, \ldots, \beta_K]$, and σ. Furthermore, it factors this probability distribution into a set of n independent probability distributions. This can be written more formally as follows:

$$P(y_1 \ldots y_n \mid \vec{x}_1, \ldots, \vec{x}_n, \vec{\beta}, \sigma^2) = \prod_{i=1}^{n} P(y_i \mid \vec{x}, \vec{\beta}, \sigma^2) = \prod_{i=1}^{n} N\left(y_i \mid \beta_0 + \sum_{k=1}^{K} \beta_k x_{ki}, \sigma^2\right).$$

Here, $P(y_i \mid \vec{x}, \vec{\beta}, \sigma^2)$ is the probability distribution for y_i, which is $N(y_i \mid \beta_0 + \sum_k^K \beta_k x_{ki}, \sigma^2)$, a normal distribution with mean $\beta_0 + \sum_k^K \beta_k x_{ki}$ and standard deviation of σ.

Although we have observed $y_1, \dots, y_n$ and $\vec{x}_1, \dots, \vec{x}_n$, we do not know the values of $\vec{\beta} = [\beta_0, \beta_1, \dots, \beta_K]$ or σ, and so these must be inferred on the basis of the observed data. This can be done using classical or frequentist techniques or with Bayesian methods. We will consider both approaches in this chapter.

Having inferred the unknown variables, we then have a model of how the probability distribution of the outcome variable varies with changes of any or all of the predictor variables. Among other things, this allows us to predict values of the outcome variable for any possible combination of values of the predictor variables. It also allows us to see how the probability distribution of the outcome variables varies with changes in any of the predictor variables, assuming all other variables are held constant. This is a particularly powerful feature of regression models generally as it allows us to identify spurious correlations between predictors and the outcome variable.

As an example, let us consider a simple problem that we can analyse using a normal linear model. For this, we will use the `weight_df` data set that we already explored:

```
weight_df <- read_csv("data/weight.csv")
```

To simplify matters somewhat, we will initially just use data from males.

```
weight_male_df <- weight_df %>%
    filter(gender == 'male')
```

Let's say that our interest lies in understanding the distribution of the weights, which are measured in kilograms, of these men. A histogram of these weights is shown in Figure 9.1.

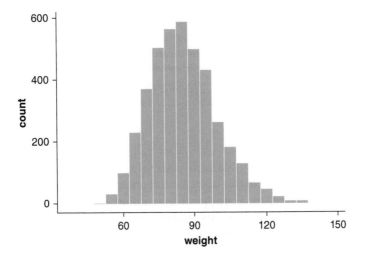

Figure 9.1 Histogram of the distribution of weights (kg) in a sample of men. The bin width is 5 kg

To begin with, let us imagine that we do not have any information concerning any other variable. In this case, our task is essentially to model the data that is being illustrated in the histogram in Figure 9.1. Although this data is somewhat positively skewed (skewness is 0.48), it is unimodal and roughly bell-shaped, and so, as a first approximation, we could model it as a normal distribution. In other words, we assume that all the observed weights, which we will denote by $y_1,...,y_n$, are samples from a normal distribution with a fixed and unknown mean μ and fixed and unknown standard deviation σ:

$$y_i \sim N(\mu,\sigma^2), \quad \text{for } i \in 1,...,n.$$

This turns out to be identical to a normal linear regression model with $K = 0$ predictor variables. Using our definition of this model just provided, when $K = 0$, the model is as follows:

$$y_i \sim N(\mu_i,\sigma^2), \quad \mu_i = \beta_0, \quad \text{for } i \in 1,...,n,$$
$$y_i \sim N(\beta_0,\sigma^2), \quad \text{for } i \in 1,...,n.$$

In other words, the intercept term of the linear model β_0 represents the mean of the normal distribution from which each of $y_1,...,y_n$ is assumed to have been drawn.

This model with no predictor variables essentially provides an *unconditional* probabilistic model of the weights $y_1,...,y_n$, and treats the probability distribution for each y_i as independent of the others. We can write this as follows:

$$P(y_1,...,y_n \,|\, \vec{\beta},\sigma^2) = \prod_{i=1}^{n} P(y_i \,|\, \vec{\beta},\sigma^2) = \prod_{i=1}^{n} N(y_i \,|\, \beta_0,\sigma^2).$$

Now let us consider what happens when we use an explanatory variable, such as the men's heights, to help us understand the distribution of men's weights. In Figure 9.2, we provide the histograms (a) and density plots (b) of weights subdivided by the quintile of the men's height. In each quintile-based group, we see that the distribution of heights is roughly normally distributed. We can also see that the means of these normal distributions increase as the height quintile increases. In fact, from (c), which plots the mean height against the mean weight in each quintile group, we see that the mean weight increases almost perfectly linearly with the increase in mean height.

Denoting the heights of the men by $x_1,...,x_n$, our new probabilistic model of their weights $y_1,...,y_n$ could be as follows:

$$y_i \sim N(\mu_i,\sigma^2), \quad \mu_i = \beta_0 + \beta_1 x_i, \quad \text{for } i \in 1,...,n.$$

In other words, we are assuming that each observed weight y_i is a sample drawn from a normal distribution. The mean of this normal distribution is determined by the corresponding observed height x_i according to the linear relationship $\mu_i = \beta_0 + \beta_1 x_i$. For simplicity and convenience, but not of necessity, we also usually assume that the standard deviations of these distributions are all identical and have the value σ. This is the *homogeneity of variance* assumption. While it is widely and sometimes unquestionably made, it is at least somewhat dubious in this case as it appears that the standard deviation of the weight may be increasing as height increases.

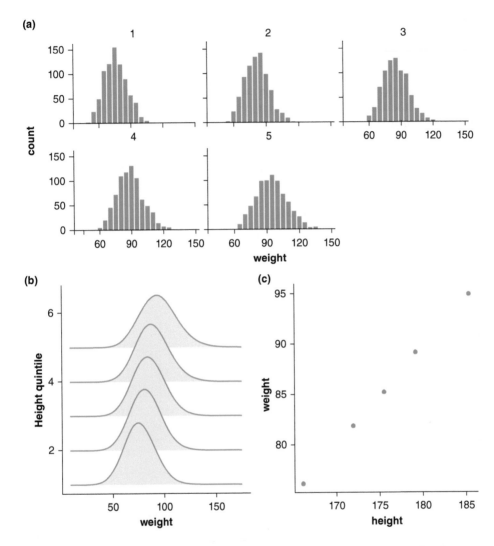

Figure 9.2 (a) Histograms and (b) density plots of the weights in a sample of men who are subdivided according to the quintile of their heights. In (c), we plot the mean weight against the mean height in each quintile

Although we have been referring specifically to the model above as being a model of the n weights $y_1,...,y_n$, it is in fact a model of men's weight generally, with $y_1,...,y_n$ being just a sample from a *population* of men's weights. In particular, it provides us with a model of the distribution of male weight conditional on their height. For example, according to the model, for any given male height x', the corresponding distribution of male weights is normally distributed with mean $\mu' = \beta_0 + \beta_1 x'$ and standard deviation σ. It also tells us that as height changes by any amount Δ_x, the mean of the corresponding normal distribution over weight changes by exactly $\beta_1 \Delta_x$. This fact entails that if height changes by exactly $\Delta_x = 1$, the mean of the corresponding normal distribution over weight changes by exactly β_1. From this, we have the general interpretation of the coefficient β_1 in a linear model with a single predictor as the change in the average of the distribution over the outcome variable for a *unit change* in the predictor variable.

We may use more explanatory variables to predict or explain the distribution of men's heights. For example, we also have a variable age that gives us the men's age in years. And so we can see how the distribution of weight varies with a change in either or both of the height and the age of men.

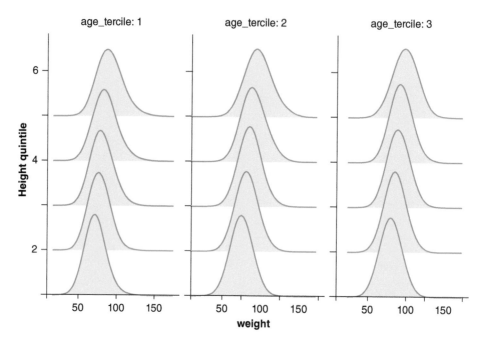

Figure 9.3 Density of male weight for the different quintiles of male height, and the different terciles of age. Although the changes by age are subtle, we see that for any given height, as age increases, so too does the average of the weight distribution

In Figure 9.3, we see the density plots of male weight for each height quintile and each age tercile. For any given combination of height and age, we have a distribution over weight that can be modelled as a normal distribution. For any given age tercile, as height increases, so too does the average of the distribution of weight. Likewise, for any given height quintile, as age increases, so too does the average distribution of weight.

Denoting the men's heights by $x_{11}, x_{12}, \ldots, x_{1i}, \ldots, x_{1n}$ and the men's ages by $x_{21}, x_{22}, \ldots, x_{2i}, \ldots, x_{2n}$, the model is now

$$y_i \sim N(\mu_i, \sigma^2), \quad \mu_i = \beta_0 + \beta_1 x_{1i} + \beta_2 x_{2i}.$$

If the height variable changes by Δ_{x_1}, when age is held constant, then the average value of the corresponding distribution of weight changes by $\beta_1 \Delta_{x_1}$. Conversely, if the age variable changes by Δ_{x_2}, when height is held constant, then the average value of the corresponding distribution of weight changes by $\beta_2\Delta_{x_2}$. The value of β_1 gives us the rate of change of the average of the distribution of men's weights for every unit change in height, assuming age is held constant. The value of β_2 gives us the rate of change of the average of the distribution of men's weights for every unit change in age, assuming height is held constant.

 ## Classical approaches to normal linear models

Given observed values of an outcome variable $y_1,...,y_n$, and given n corresponding vectors of K predictor variables $\vec{x}_1,...,\vec{x}_n$, and if we model $y_1,...,y_n$ using the normal linear model

$$y_i \sim N(\mu_i, \sigma^2), \quad \mu_i = \beta_0 + \sum_{k=1}^{K} \beta_k x_{ki}, \quad \text{for } i \in 1,...,n,$$

then we immediately face the problem of inferring the values of the unknown variables[1] $\beta_0, \beta_1,..., \beta_K$ and σ. As discussed in the previous chapter, there are two main approaches to the inference of the unknown variables: maximum likelihood estimation and Bayesian inference. Of these two approaches, maximum likelihood estimation is both the default and traditional approach, and we will consider it in this section. However, Bayesian methods have been steadily increasing in their popularity for decades and there is now powerful and flexible yet simple-to-use Bayesian regression modelling software available in R, and so this will be covered in a subsequent section.

Maximum likelihood estimation

As we have seen in the previous chapter, the maximum likelihood estimates are the values of the unknown variables in the model that maximize the model's likelihood function. The likelihood function is a function over the unknown variable space, which in this case is a $(K + 2)$-dimensional space (i.e. the $K + 1$ coefficients $\beta_0, \beta_1,..., \beta_K$ and σ). We will denote this space by Θ and a point in this space, which is a particular set of values for $\beta_0, \beta_1,..., \beta_K, \sigma$ by θ. The value of the likelihood function at the point θ gives the probability of the observed data when the unknown variables are equal to θ. If we denote the observed data, which in our case is $(y_1, \vec{x}_1),(y_2, \vec{x}_2),...,(y_i, \vec{x}_i),...,(y_n, \vec{x}_n)$, by $\mathcal{D}$, the likelihood function can be written as[2]

$$L(\theta \mid \mathcal{D}) = P(\mathcal{D} \mid \theta).$$

The maximum likelihood estimator, denoted by $\hat{\theta}$, is the value that maximizes this function and so is defined as follows:

$$\hat{\theta} = \underset{\theta}{\mathrm{argmax}}\, L(\theta \mid \mathcal{D}).$$

---

[1] It should be noted that some approaches to statistical inference insist on referring to these variables as *parameters* rather than variables *per se*, preferring to reserve the term 'variables' for observed or latent data variables. However, we will not insist upon this term here for reasons that will hopefully become clear as we proceed.

[2] More strictly speaking, we should define $L(\theta|\mathcal{D})$ as $L(\theta|\mathcal{D}) = c \cdot P(\mathcal{D}|\theta)$, where c is an arbitrary positive constant.

Note that because the logarithm is a monotonic function, maximizing the logarithm of $L(\theta \mid \mathcal{D})$ is the same as maximizing $L(\theta \mid \mathcal{D})$, which is the same as minimizing the negative of the logarithm of $L(\theta \mid \mathcal{D})$:

$$\hat{\theta} = \underset{\theta}{\mathrm{argmax}}\, L(\theta \mid \mathcal{D}) = \underset{\theta}{\mathrm{argmax}}\, \log L(\theta \mid \mathcal{D}) = \underset{\theta}{\mathrm{argmin}}\, (-L(\theta \mid \mathcal{D})).$$

The logarithm of $L(\theta \mid \mathcal{D})$ is as follows:

$$\log L(\theta \mid \mathcal{D}) = \log P(\mathcal{D} \mid \theta) = \log \prod_{i=1}^{n} P(y_i \mid x_i, \beta, \sigma)$$

$$= \sum_{i=1}^{n} \log P(y_i \mid x_i, \beta, \sigma)$$

$$= \sum_{i=1}^{n} \log \frac{1}{\sqrt{2\pi\sigma^2}} \exp\left(-\frac{|y_i - \mu_i|^2}{2\sigma^2} \right)$$

$$= -\frac{n}{2}\log(2\pi\sigma^2) - \frac{1}{2\sigma^2}\sum_{i=1}^{n}|y_i - \mu_i|^2,$$

where $\mu_i = \beta_0 + \sum_{k=1}^{K}\beta_k x_{ki}$.

The difference

$$y_i - \mu_i = y_i - \left(\beta_0 + \sum_{k=1}^{K}\beta_k x_{ki} \right)$$

is known as the *residual*. It is the difference between the observed value of the outcome variable y_i and the mean of the outcome variable according to the linear function of $\vec{x}_i$. In a simple linear model, with one predictor variable, we can easily visualize residuals. These are shown as the vertical grey line segments in Figure 9.4.

The sum of the squared residuals is

$$\mathrm{RSS} = \sum_{i=1}^{n}|y_i - \mu_i|^2.$$

RSS is obviously the summation term in $L(\theta \mid \mathcal{D})$. This will always be positive, and so the larger it is, the lower the likelihood. Thus, for any value of σ, maximizing the likelihood with respect to $\beta_0, \beta_1, ..., \beta_K$ will always be obtained by minimizing RSS. This is an important result; it tells us that maximum likelihood estimator for the coefficients $\beta_0, \beta_1, ..., \beta_K$ can be obtained by minimizing the sum of the squared residuals. In linear regression, the line that minimizes RSS is known as the *line of best fit*.

In order to find the values of $\vec{\beta}$ that minimize RSS, it is helpful to write RSS in matrix form. First note that

$$\mathrm{RSS} = \vec{\epsilon}^{\mathsf{T}} \vec{\epsilon},$$

where

$$\vec{\epsilon} = \left[\epsilon_1, \epsilon_2, ..., \epsilon_n \right]^{\mathsf{T}}$$

and

$$\epsilon_i = y_i - \mu_i.$$

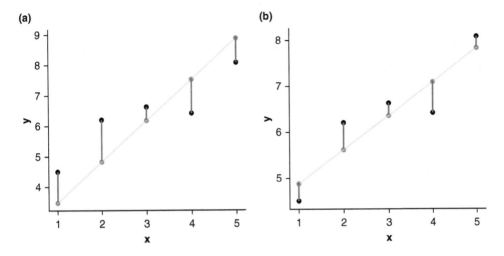

Figure 9.4 A set of five points $(y_1, x_1), \ldots, (y_5, x_5)$ are shown in black in both plots. Likewise, in each plot, a line $y = mx + c$ is shown in red, with different values of m and c in each case. The points in red are $(\hat{y}_1, x_1), \ldots, (\hat{y}_5, x_5)$ where each $\hat{y}_i = mx_i + c$. In other words, the points in red are the values of the linear function $y = mx + c$ that correspond to the sequence $x_1, \ldots, x_5$. The line segments shown in grey are the residuals. These are the vertical differences between the points $y_1, \ldots, y_5$ and the points $\hat{y}_1, \ldots, \hat{y}_5$. The sum of the squared residuals is less in (b) than in (a), and so we say that the line in (b) is a better fit to the data. In general, in normal linear regression, finding the line that minimizes the sum of the squared residuals gives us the maximum likelihood estimator of the regression coefficients. Usually, we call the line minimizing the sum of the squared residuals the line of best fit

We may then write $\vec{\epsilon}$ in matrix form as follows:

$$\vec{\epsilon} = \begin{bmatrix} \epsilon_1 \\ \epsilon_2 \\ \vdots \\ \epsilon_i \\ \vdots \\ \epsilon_n \end{bmatrix} = \begin{bmatrix} y_1 \\ y_2 \\ \vdots \\ y_i \\ \vdots \\ y_n \end{bmatrix} - \begin{bmatrix} \mu_1 \\ \mu_2 \\ \vdots \\ \mu_i \\ \vdots \\ \mu_n \end{bmatrix} = \begin{bmatrix} y_1 \\ y_2 \\ \vdots \\ y_i \\ \vdots \\ y_n \end{bmatrix} - \begin{bmatrix} 1 & x_{11} & x_{21} & \cdots & x_{K1} \\ 1 & x_{12} & x_{22} & \cdots & x_{K2} \\ \vdots & \vdots & \vdots & \cdots & \vdots \\ 1 & x_{1i} & x_{2i} & \cdots & x_{Ki} \\ \vdots & \vdots & \vdots & \cdots & \vdots \\ 1 & x_{1n} & x_{2n} & \cdots & x_{Kn} \end{bmatrix} \begin{bmatrix} \beta_0 \\ \beta_1 \\ \vdots \\ \beta_K \end{bmatrix} = \vec{y} - X\vec{\beta}.$$

The crucial part here is writing $\vec{\mu} = [\mu_1, \mu_2 \ldots \mu_i \ldots \mu_n]^{\mathsf{T}}$ as a matrix vector multiplication, $\vec{\mu} = X\vec{\beta}$. Here, X is an $n \times (K+1)$ matrix whose first column is all 1s, and each subsequent column is the n observations of each of the K predictor variables. This matrix X is usually known as the *design* matrix.

From this, we have

$$\text{RSS} = (\vec{y} - X\vec{\beta})^{\mathsf{T}} (\vec{y} - X\vec{\beta}).$$

This can be expanded as follows:

$$\text{RSS} = \vec{y}^{\mathsf{T}} \vec{y} - 2\vec{y} X\vec{\beta} + \vec{\beta}^{\mathsf{T}} X^{\mathsf{T}} X\vec{\beta}.$$

In order to find the minimum of RSS with respect to $\vec{\beta}$, we can calculate the gradient of RSS with respect to $\vec{\beta}$, set this to equal to zero, and solve for β. To simplify the calculation, we may instead calculate the gradient of $\frac{1}{2}$RSS with respect to $\vec{\beta}$, set this to equal to zero, and solve for β, and arrive at the same result. The gradient is as follows:

$$\nabla_\beta \frac{\text{RSS}}{2} = X^{\mathsf{T}} X \vec{\beta} - X^{\mathsf{T}} \vec{y}.$$

Setting this equal to zero, we get

$$X^{\mathsf{T}} X \vec{\beta} = X^{\mathsf{T}} \vec{y}.$$

Then solving[3] for $\vec{\beta}$, we get

$$\hat{\beta} = (X^{\mathsf{T}} X)^{-1} X^{\mathsf{T}} \vec{y}.$$

Thus, $\hat{\beta}$ is the maximum likelihood estimator for β.

To obtain the maximum likelihood for σ^2, we calculate the partial derivative of $\log L(\theta \mid \mathcal{D})$ with respect to σ^2 when $\vec{\beta}$ is set to $\hat{\beta}$. Then we set this derivative equal to zero and solve for σ^2. The log of the likelihood when $\vec{\beta} = \hat{\beta}$ can be written as follows:

$$-\frac{n}{2}\log(2\pi) - \frac{n}{2}\log(\sigma^2) = \frac{1}{2\sigma^2}(\vec{y} - X\hat{\beta})^{\mathsf{T}}(\vec{y} - X\hat{\beta}).$$

The derivative of this function with respect to σ^2 is

$$\frac{n}{2\sigma^2} - \frac{1}{2\sigma^4}(\vec{y} - X\hat{\beta})^{\mathsf{T}}(\vec{y} - X\hat{\beta}).$$

Setting this equal to zero, multiplying both sides by $2\sigma^2$ to simplify it, and then solving for σ^2, we obtain

$$\hat{\sigma}^2_{\text{mle}} = \frac{1}{n}(\vec{y} - X\hat{\beta})^{\mathsf{T}}(\vec{y} - X\hat{\beta})$$

$$= \frac{1}{n}\sum_{i=1}^{n}|v_i - \hat{\mu}_i|^2,$$

where $\hat{\mu}_i = \hat{\beta}_0 + \sum \hat{\beta}_k x_{ki}$ is the mean of the outcome variable corresponding to $\vec{x}_i$, assuming the coefficients are $\hat{\beta}$. Thus, the maximum likelihood estimate of σ^2 is the mean of the squared residuals, and the maximum likelihood estimator of σ is the square root of this mean.

It turns out that the maximum likelihood estimator $\hat{\sigma}^2$ is a biased estimator of the true value of σ^2. An unbiased estimator is as follows:

$$\hat{\sigma}^2 = \frac{1}{n - K - 1}\sum_{i=1}^{n}|v_i - \hat{\mu}_i|^2 = \frac{n}{n - K - 1}\hat{\sigma}^2_{\text{mle}}.$$

This version is used widely as the estimator of σ^2.

Having calculated the maximum likelihood estimators $\hat{\beta}$ and $\hat{\sigma}_{\text{mle}}$, we can now evaluate the log of the likelihood function at its maximum by substituting $\hat{\beta}$ and $\hat{\sigma}_{\text{mle}}$ for $\vec{\beta}$ and σ, respectively, in the log likelihood function:

$$L(\theta \mid \mathcal{D}) = -\frac{n}{2}\log(2\pi) - \frac{n}{2}\log(\sigma^2) - \frac{1}{2\sigma^2}(\vec{y} - X\hat{\beta})^{\mathsf{T}}(\vec{y} - X\hat{\beta}).$$

---

[3]This assumes that $X^{\mathsf{T}}X$ is invertible, which it will be if $K < n$.

This is

$$\log L\left(\theta = \left\{\hat{\beta}, \hat{\sigma}_{\text{mle}}\right\} | \mathcal{D}\right) = -\frac{n}{2}\log(2\pi) - \frac{n}{2}\log(\hat{\sigma}_{\text{mle}}^2) - \frac{1}{2\hat{\sigma}_{\text{mle}}^2}(\vec{y} - X\hat{\beta})^{\top}(\vec{y} - X\hat{\beta})$$

$$= -\frac{n}{2}\log(2\pi) - \frac{n}{2}\log(\hat{\sigma}_{\text{mle}}^2) - \frac{n}{2}$$

$$= -\frac{n}{2}(\log(2\pi) + \log(\hat{\sigma}_{\text{mle}}^2) + 1)$$

$$= -\frac{n}{2}(\log(2\pi) - \log(n) + \log(\text{RSS}) + 1).$$

Maximum likelihood estimation using `lm`

The main command for doing normal linear modelling in R is `lm`. This is probably the most widely used statistical modelling command in R.

As an example, we will model `weight` as a function of `height` and `age` in the sample of men in the `weight_male_df` data set:

```
M <- lm(weight ~ height + age, data = weight_male_df)
```

The first thing we usually do with the object returned by `lm` is to look at the output provided by the `summary` function:

```
summary(M)
#>
#> Call:
#> lm(formula = weight ~ height + age, data = weight_male_df)
#>
#> Residuals:
#>      Min      1Q  Median      3Q     Max
#> -40.860  -8.209  -1.006   7.355  47.819
#>
#> Coefficients:
#>               Estimate Std. Error t value Pr(>|t|)
#> (Intercept) -97.97157    4.90633  -19.97   <2e-16 ***
#> height        0.97875    0.02763   35.43   <2e-16 ***
#> age           0.38484    0.02150   17.90   <2e-16 ***
#> ---
#> Signif. codes:  0 '***' 0.001 '**' 0.01 '*' 0.05 '.' 0.1 ' ' 1
#>
#> Residual standard error: 12.1 on 4079 degrees of freedom
#> Multiple R-squared:  0.2767, Adjusted R-squared:  0.2764
#> F-statistic: 780.3 on 2 and 4079 DF,  p-value: < 2.2e-16
```

Although there is a lot of valuable information here, we will not pick it all apart immediately, preferring instead to concentrate on individual results one at a time through this and subsequent sections.

We will begin by focusing on the estimated values of the coefficients β_0 (the intercept), β_1 (coefficient for height), β_2 (coefficient for age). These are available in the `Coefficients` section of the summary output in the column labelled `Estimate`. They may also be returned directly using the `coef` (or equivalently, `coefficients`) function:

```
(estimates <- coef(M))
#> (Intercept)        height            age
#> -97.9715727    0.9787473     0.3848439
```

The meaning of these values is as follows. The coefficient for height, 0.9787473, gives the estimated change on average of the distribution of `weight` for every unit increase of `height`, assuming `age` is held constant. The coefficient for age, 0.3848439, gives the estimated change on average of the distribution of `weight` for every unit increase of `age`, assuming `height` is held constant. Because understanding the meaning of the coefficients in regression analyses is so important, let us go through these values carefully. First, assume that we have a very large group of men who have exactly the same age in years. It in fact does not matter what particular age they are, but for concreteness, let's just assume their age is 30 years. Then we find all the men in this group who have a particular height. Again, it does not matter which height we choose, but for concreteness, let's assume we look at those with height 175 cm. Now, we will look at the distribution of the weight of these men who are 30 years old and 175 cm. Our model assumes that it will be a normal distribution whose mean, which we will denote by $\hat{\mu}_{(175,30)}$, is estimated to be (rounding the coefficients to three decimal places) as follows:

$$\hat{\mu}_{(175,30)} = -97.972 + 0.979 \cdot 175 + 0.385 \cdot 30 = 84.85.$$

Now, let us assume we stay with the 30-year-old men, but find all the men in this age group whose heights are 176 cm rather than 175 cm. The corresponding mean of the distribution of weight would change by exactly 0.979 kg. We can see this as follows:

$$\hat{\mu}_{(176,30)} = -97.972 + 0.979 \cdot 176 + 0.385 \cdot 30$$
$$= -97.972 + 0.979 \cdot (175 + 1) + 0.385 \cdot 30$$
$$= -97.972 + 0.979 \cdot 175 + 0.385 \cdot 30 + 0.979,$$
$$= \hat{\mu}_{(176,30)} + 0.979$$
$$= 85.83.$$

Were we to choose 30-year-old men whose heights were 177 cm, then the corresponding mean of the distribution of weights would again increase by exactly 0.979 kg. This increase by 0.979 kg for every unit increase in `height` would occur regardless of what age group we were focusing on. For example, if instead of looking at 30-year-old men, we looked at 40-year-old men, and then looked at men in this age group who were 175, 176, 177 cm tall, we would see that the average of the corresponding distribution of weight would increase by 0.979 kg for each cm change in height:

$$\hat{\mu}_{(175,40)} = -97.972 + 0.979 \cdot 175 + 0.385 \cdot 40,$$
$$\hat{\mu}_{(176,40)} = -97.972 + 0.979 \cdot 176 + 0.385 \cdot 40$$
$$= -97.972 + 0.979 \cdot (175 + 1) + 0.385 \cdot 40$$
$$= -97.972 + 0.979 \cdot 175 + 0.385 \cdot 40 + 0.979$$
$$= \hat{\mu}_{(175,40)} + 0.979,$$
$$\hat{\mu}_{(177,40)} = -97.972 + 0.979 \cdot 176 + 0.385 \cdot 40$$
$$= -97.972 + 0.979 \cdot (176 + 1) + 0.385 \cdot 40$$
$$= -97.972 + 0.979 \cdot 176 + 0.385 \cdot 40 + 0.979$$
$$= \hat{\mu}_{(176,40)} + 0.979.$$

Reasoning along these lines, we can see that when we hold `age` constant at any value, and increase `height` by 1 cm from any starting value, the corresponding mean of the distribution of `weight` always increases by 0.979 kg. Similarly, and for identical reasons, if we hold `height` constant at any value, and increase `age` by 1 year from any starting value, the corresponding mean of the distribution of `weight` always increases by 0.385 kg.

The intercept term, by contrast, can sometimes be relatively meaningless. It is always exactly the average of the distribution of the outcome variable when the predictor variable(s) have values of zero. Given that having zero as the value of `height` and `age` is essentially meaningless, so too then is the value of the intercept term. However, when values of zero of the predictor are meaningful, then likewise the intercept is meaningful too. Consider the situation where we change `height` and `age` by subtracting their mean values. As a result, both have means of zero, and their values indicate the difference from the man's height or age from average. We can perform the same regression analysis as above with these zero-mean `height` and `age` variables:

```
weight_male_df %>%
  mutate(height = height - mean(height),
         age = age - mean(age)
  ) %>% lm(weight ~ height + age, data = .) %>%
  coef()
#> (Intercept)        height           age
#>   85.5239588     0.9787473     0.3848439
```

As we can see, the coefficients for `height` and `age` are as before. However, the intercept term is now 85.524 rather than –97.972 as in the original model. As the intercept is always the average of the distribution of the outcome variable when the predictors are zero, and because the predictors having a value of zero denote a person of average height and average age, then the intercept term of 85.524 is simply the mean of the distribution of weight for a man of average height and age.

Let us now verify that coefficients calculated above (in the original model) are the maximum likelihood estimators defined by $\hat{\beta} = (X^\mathsf{T}X)^{-1}X^\mathsf{T}\vec{y}$. For this, we will use some of R's matrix operations, particularly `t()` for the matrix transpose, `%*%` for matrix multiplication or inner product, and `solve` for the matrix inverse:

```
y <- weight_male_df %>% pull(weight)
n <- length(y)

# design matrix
X <- weight_male_df %>%
  mutate(intercept = 1) %>%
  select(intercept, height, age) %>%
  as.matrix()

# beta hat
solve(t(X) %*% X) %*% t(X) %*% y
#>                  [,1]
#> intercept -97.9715727
#> height      0.9787473
#> age         0.3848439
```

Clearly, these are the values returned by `coefficients(M)`.

While the design matrix above was simple to create, in general it is easier to use tools in R such as `modelr::model_matrix` or base R's `model.matrix`:

```
library(modelr)
```

```
X <- model_matrix(weight_male_df, weight ~ height + age) %>%
   as.matrix()
```

```
# beta hat
solve(t(X) %*% X) %*% t(X) %*% y
#>                    [,1]
#> (Intercept) -97.9715727
#> height        0.9787473
#> age           0.3848439
```

As mentioned, the unbiased estimator of σ in this model is

$$\hat{\sigma} = \sqrt{\frac{1}{n-K-1}\sum_{i=1}^{n}|y_i - \hat{\mu}_i|^2}.$$

This is returned by the command `sigma` applied to the model `M`:

```
sigma(M)
#> [1] 12.09717
```

We can verify that the value of `sigma(M)` is $\hat{\sigma}^2$ by using the vector of residuals, $\hat{\epsilon} = [y_1 - \hat{\mu}_1, y_2 - \hat{\mu}_2 \ldots y_n - \hat{\mu}_n]^T$, which can be obtained by `residuals(M)`:

```
n <- nrow(X)
K <- ncol(X) - 1
```

```
epsilon <- residuals(M)
```

```
sqrt(sum(epsilon^2)/(n - K - 1))
#> [1] 12.09717
```

We can also verify that $\hat{\sigma} = \sqrt{(n/(n-K-1))}\hat{\sigma}_{\text{mle}}$:

```
sigma2_mle <- mean(epsilon^2)
sqrt(n * sigma2_mle/(n - K - 1))
#> [1] 12.09717
```

The value of the log of the likelihood at its maximum can be obtained from the `logLik` function applied to `M`:

```
logLik(M)
#> 'log Lik.' -15966.92 (df=4)
```

We can verify that this gives us the following:

$$\log L\left(\theta = \left\{\hat{\beta}, \hat{\sigma}_{\text{mle}}\right\} \mid \mathcal{D}\right) = -\frac{n}{2}(\log(2\pi) - \log n + \log(\text{RSS}) + 1):$$

```
rss <- sum(epsilon^2)
- (n/2) * (log(2*pi) - log(n) + log(rss) + 1)
#> [1] -15966.92
```

Sampling distribution of $\hat{\beta}$

In general, in a normal linear model, we assume that $y_1, \ldots, y_n$ were generated as follows:

$$y_i \sim N(\mu_i, \sigma^2), \quad \mu_i = \beta_0 + \sum_{k=1}^{K} \beta_k x_{ki}, \quad \text{for } i \in 1, \ldots, n,$$

where $\beta_0, \beta_1, \ldots, \beta_K$ and σ have some fixed but unknown values. Let us denote the true, but unknown, values of $\beta_0, \beta_1, \ldots, \beta_K$ and σ by $\vec{\beta}_*$ and σ_*, respectively. Using the matrix notation from before, this means that we are assuming that

$$\vec{y} \sim N\left(X\vec{\beta}_*, I_{\sigma_*^2}\right),$$

where $I_{\sigma_*^2}$ is an $n \times n$ diagonal matrix with σ_*^2 at each value on the diagonal. This means that

$$\vec{y} = X\vec{\beta}_* + \vec{\epsilon}, \quad \vec{\epsilon} \sim N\left(0, I_{\sigma_*^2}\right).$$

We have established that $\hat{\beta}$ is

$$\hat{\beta} = (X^T X)^{-1} X^T \vec{y}.$$

Therefore, we have

$$\begin{aligned}
\hat{\beta} &= (X^T X)^{-1} X^T (X\vec{\beta}_* + \vec{\epsilon}) \\
&= (X^T X)^{-1} X^T X\vec{\beta}_* + (X^T X)^{-1} X^T \vec{\epsilon} \\
&= \vec{\beta}_* + (X^T X)^{-1} X^T \vec{\epsilon}.
\end{aligned}$$

Because $\vec{\epsilon}$ is a zero-mean (multivariate) normally distributed random variable, $(X^T X)^{-1} X^T \vec{\epsilon}$ is also a zero-mean normally distributed random variable, and its variance can be shown to be $\sigma_*^2 (X^T X)^{-1}$. From this, we obtain

$$\hat{\beta} \sim N(\vec{\beta}_*, \sigma_*^2 (X^T X)^{-1}).$$

This is the sampling distribution of the maximum likelihood estimator $\hat{\beta}$. From this, for any given element of $\hat{\beta}$, its sampling distribution is

$$\hat{\beta}_k \sim N(\beta_k^*, \sigma_*^2 (X^T X)_{kk}^{-1}).$$

This entails that

$$\frac{\hat{\beta}_k - \beta_k^*}{\sigma_* \sqrt{(X^T X)_{kk}^{-1}}} \sim N(0, 1).$$

For the unbiased estimator $\hat{\sigma}^2$, it can shown that

$$(n-K-1)\frac{\hat{\sigma}^2}{\sigma_*^2} \sim \chi_{n-K-1}^2.$$

For any variable Z following a standard normal distribution and any variable V following a χ^2 distribution with ν degrees of freedom, we have the following result:

$$Z\sqrt{\frac{\nu}{V}} \sim t_\nu,$$

where t_ν denotes a t-distribution with ν degrees of freedom. From this, we have the following result:

$$\frac{\hat{\beta}_k - \beta_k^*}{\sigma_*\sqrt{(X^\mathsf{T}X)_{kk}^{-1}}}\sqrt{\frac{n-K-1}{(n-K-1)\hat{\sigma}^2/\sigma_*^2}} = \frac{\hat{\beta}_k - \beta_k^*}{\hat{\sigma}\sqrt{(X^\mathsf{T}X)_{kk}^{-1}}} = \frac{\hat{\beta}_k - \beta_k^*}{\widehat{se}_k}.$$

We usually refer to $\hat{\sigma}\sqrt{(X^\mathsf{T}X)_{kk}^{-1}}$ as the *standard error* of the estimator $\hat{\beta}_k$, and so we denote it here by $\widehat{se}_k$. With this result, as we will see, we may use our estimator of $\hat{\beta}_k$ to test the hypothesis that β_k^* has any given value. Likewise, we may use this result to calculate confidence intervals for $\hat{\beta}_k$.

Hypothesis testing and confidence intervals using `lm`

The standard errors for all $K + 1$ estimators $\beta_0, \beta_1, ..., \beta_K$ can be obtained from the coefficients table that is given in the `summary(M)`. We extract this table as an attribute of the `summary` output as follows:

```
summary(M)$coefficients
#>                 Estimate Std. Error    t value        Pr(>|t|)
#> (Intercept) -97.9715727 4.90632557  -19.96842    1.025374e-84
#> height        0.9787473 0.02762615   35.42830   6.065526e-240
#> age           0.3848439 0.02149567   17.90332    4.586034e-69
```

The standard errors are obviously given by the second column, which we extract as a vector:

```
(std_err <- summary(M)$coefficients[,2])
#> (Intercept)       height          age
#>  4.90632557   0.02762615   0.02149567
```

Let us first verify that these are $\hat{\sigma}\sqrt{\text{diag}(X^\mathsf{T}X)^{-1})}$, where diag extracts the diagonal of a square matrix:

```
sigma(M) * sqrt(diag(solve(t(X) %*% X)))
#> (Intercept)       height          age
#>  4.90632557   0.02762615   0.02149567
```

Now, should we wish test the null hypothesis that the true value of the coefficient for the height predictor is zero, $H_0 : \beta_{\text{height}}^* = 0$, we know that under this hypothesis $\hat{\beta}_{\text{height}}/se_{\text{height}}$

follows a t-distribution with $n - K - 1$ degrees of freedom. The observed value of this t-statistic is as follows:

```
(t_stat <- estimates['height']/std_err['height'])
#>   height
#> 35.4283
```

Note that this value is available in the `t value` column in the coefficients table above. The p-value corresponding to this t-statistic gives the probability of a getting a result as extreme as or more extreme than this value in a t-distribution with $n - K - 1 = 4079$ degrees of freedom. In this case, this is the probability of having a value greater than 35.428297 *or less* than −35.428297 in this t-distribution. In other words, it is the sum of two tail areas in a t-distribution. Because this t-distribution is symmetrical and centred at zero, the two tail area probabilities are identical, and so their sum is any one of them multiplied by 2.

To calculate the tail areas in a t-distribution we need its cumulative distribution function. If we denote the density function of a t-distribution with v degrees of freedom by $t(x|v)$, the corresponding cumulative distribution function is

$$T_v(x) = \int_{-\infty}^{x} t(x'|v)dx'.$$

For any value x, $T_v(x)$ is the probability of getting a result less than or equal to x in a t-distribution with v degrees of freedom. This function is implemented in R using the `pt` function. For example, if $x = 1.5$ and $v = 5$, then $T_{v=5}(x = 1.5)$ is obtained as follows:

```
pt(1.5, df = 5)
#> [1] 0.9030482
```

If we wanted the complement, $1 - T_v(x) = \int_{-\infty}^{x} t(x'|v)dx'$, we could use the `lower.tail = FALSE` option in `pt`. For example, the probability of getting a value *greater* than $x = 1.5$ in a t-distribution with $v = 5$ is

```
pt(1.5, df = 5, lower.tail = F)
#> [1] 0.09695184
```

Therefore, to get the sum of the tail areas, we do the following:

```
pt(t_stat, df = n-K-1, lower.tail = F) * 2
#>          height
#> 6.065526e-240
```

As we can see, this (very small) number is what is also reported in the `Pr(>|t|)` column in the summary coefficients table.

For the calculation of confidence intervals, we need the inverse of the cumulative distribution function, defined as $T_v^{-1}(p)$ where $p \in (0,1)$. This returns the value x such that $T_v(x) = p$. If a variable x has a t-distribution with v degrees of freedom, we can make statements like

$$P(T_v^{-1}(0.05) \le x \le T_v^{-1}(0.95)) = 0.9,$$
$$P(T_v^{-1}(0.005) \le x \le T_v^{-1}(0.995)) = 0.99.$$

Or more generally

$$P(T_v^{-1}(\epsilon) \le x \le T_v^{-1}(1-\epsilon)) = 1 - 2\epsilon.$$

where $\epsilon \in (0, 0.5)$.

By the fact that $(\hat{\beta}_k - \beta_k^*)/\hat{se}_k$ has a t-distribution with $v = n - K - 1$ degrees of freedom, we can therefore state that

$$P\left(T_v^{-1}(\epsilon) \le \frac{\hat{\beta}_k - \beta_k^*}{\hat{se}_k} \le T_v^{-1}(1-\epsilon)\right) = 1 - 2\epsilon.$$

We can then rearrange this statement as follows:

$$P\left(\hat{\beta}_k - T_v^{-1}(\epsilon) \cdot \hat{se}_k \ge \beta_k^* \ge \hat{\beta}_k - T_v^{-1}(1-\epsilon) \cdot \hat{se}_k\right) = 1 - 2\epsilon.$$

If we denote $T_v^{-1}(1-\epsilon)$ by $\tau_{(1-\epsilon,v)}$, which is always a positive quantity, because the t-distribution is symmetric, $T_v^{-1}(\epsilon) = -\tau_{(1-\epsilon,v)}$. Substituting in, this leads to

$$P\left(\hat{\beta}_k - \tau_{(1-\epsilon,v)} \cdot \hat{se}_k \le \beta_k^* \le \hat{\beta}_k - \tau_{(1-\epsilon,v)} \cdot \hat{se}_k\right) = 1 - 2\epsilon.$$

This is the $1 - 2\epsilon$ confidence interval. Thus, for example, if want to obtain the 95% confidence intervals for the height coefficient, we first obtain $\tau_{(0.975, n-K-1)}$ as

```
tau <- qt(0.975, df = n-K-1)
```

and then obtain the confidence interval

```
estimates['height'] + c(-1, 1) * std_err['height'] * tau
#> [1] 0.924585 1.032910
```

This is also available using the confint function applied to the lm object M:

```
confint(M, parm = 'height', level = 0.95)
#>                2.5 %   97.5 %
#> height 0.924585 1.03291
```

We can use confint to obtain the confidence interval at any given level for any or all predictor variables or the intercept term by changing parm and level accordingly. Note that by default, confint gives the 95% confidence interval for all predictor variables:

```
confint(M)
#>                     2.5 %        97.5 %
#> (Intercept) -107.5906483 -88.3524970
#> height         0.9245850    1.0329096
#> age            0.3427007    0.4269872
```

Predictions

Given the definition of the normal linear model, if we knew the true values of $\beta_0, \beta_1, ..., \beta_K, \sigma^2$, which we will denote again by $\vec{\beta}_*$ and σ_*^2, then for any new vector of predictor variables $\vec{x}_i$, the corresponding y' is

$$y_i \sim N(\mu_i^*, \sigma_*^2), \quad \mu_i^* = \beta_0^* + \sum_{k=1}^{K} \beta_k^* x_{ik},$$

where the mean of this distribution, μ_i^*, is a linear function of $\vec{x}_i$, which we could also write as $\mu_i^* = \vec{x}_i \vec{\beta}_*$.

Of course, we do not know $\vec{\beta}_*$ and σ_*^2. On the other hand, we have estimates for them, which we have denoted by $\hat{\beta}$ and $\hat{\sigma}^2$, and in the previous section we saw their sampling distributions:

$$\hat{\beta} \sim N(\vec{\beta}_*, \sigma_*^2(X^\top X)^{-1}), \quad (n-K-1)\frac{\hat{\sigma}^2}{\sigma_*^2} \sim \chi_{n-K-1}^2.$$

Based on $\hat{\beta}$, the estimated value of μ_i is $\hat{\mu}_i = \vec{x}_i \hat{\beta}$, and its sampling distribution is

$$\hat{\mu}_i \sim N(\mu_i^*, \sigma_*^2 \vec{x}_i (X^\top X)^{-1} \vec{x}_i^\top).$$

For reasons identical to those used above when discussing the sampling distribution of $\hat{\beta}$, we have

$$\frac{\hat{\mu}_i - \mu_i^*}{\sigma_* \sqrt{\vec{x}_i (X^\top X)^{-1} \vec{x}_i^\top}} \sim N(0,1)$$

and then

$$\frac{\hat{\mu}_i - \mu_i^*}{\hat{\sigma} \sqrt{\vec{x}_i (X^\top X)^{-1} \vec{x}_i^\top}} = \frac{\hat{\mu}_i - \mu_i^*}{\widehat{se}_{\mu_i}} \sim t_{n-K-1}.$$

From this, again following the same reasoning as before, we obtain the *confidence interval* for μ_i^*:

$$P\left(\hat{\mu}_i - \tau_{(1-\epsilon, \nu)} \cdot \widehat{se}_{\mu_i} \le \mu_i^* \le \hat{\mu}_i - \tau_{(1-\epsilon, \nu)} \cdot \widehat{se}_{\mu_i} \right) = 1 - 2\epsilon.$$

There is a second interval that we can consider, that of y_i. Given that $y_i \sim N(\mu_i^*, \sigma_*^2)$, we can write this as $y_i = \mu_i^* + \epsilon_i$ where $\epsilon_i \sim N(0, \sigma_*^2)$. Using the $\hat{\mu}_i$ estimator for μ_i^* we have $\hat{y}_i = \hat{\mu}_i + \epsilon_i$. Given the distributions of $\hat{\mu}_i$ and ϵ_i, which are independent of one another, we then have

$$\hat{y}_i \sim N(\mu_i^*, \sigma_*^2(1 + \vec{x}_i(X^\top X)^{-1} \vec{x}_i^\top)).$$

Following the same reasoning as above, this leads to the following *prediction interval* for y_i:

$$P\left(\hat{\mu}_i - \tau_{(1-\epsilon, \nu)} \cdot \widehat{se}_{y_i} \le y_i \le \hat{\mu}_i - \tau_{(1-\epsilon, \nu)} \cdot \widehat{se}_{y_i} \right) = 1 - 2\epsilon,$$

where

$$\widehat{se}_y = \hat{\sigma} \sqrt{1 + \vec{x}_i(X^\top X)^{-1} \vec{x}_i^\top}.$$

Predictions with `lm`

We can calculate the confidence interval on μ_i and the prediction interval on y_i using the generic `predict` function applied to the `lm` object. When applied to `lm` objects, `predict` will return either the point estimator $\hat{\mu}_i$, or else the confidence interval on μ_i^*, or else the prediction interval on y_i depending whether we set `interval` option in `predict` to `none`, or `confidence`, or `prediction`. As an example, let us say we want to make predictions about a man's weight when his `height` is equal to 175 cm and `age` is equal to 35 years. First, regardless of the type of prediction we need to do, we have to set up a data frame with variables `height` and `age`:

```
weight_male_df_new <- tibble(height = 175,
                             age = 35)
```

Then we can do the following:

```
predict(M, newdata = weight_male_df_new)
#>        1
#> 86.77874
```

Here, we did not explicitly set the `interval` option and so it took its default value of `interval = 'none'`. This then gives us the estimate of $\hat{\mu}_i$, which is simply the linear function of `height` using the maximum likelihood estimates $\hat{\beta}_0$ and $\hat{\beta}_1$. We can easily verify this:

```
mu_hat <- (estimates['(Intercept)'] +
              estimates['height'] * 175 +
              estimates['age'] * 35) %>%
   unname()
mu_hat
#> [1] 86.77874
```

To obtain the confidence intervals on μ_i^* we use the option `interval = 'confidence'`:

```
predict(M,
        interval = 'confidence',
        newdata = weight_male_df_new)
#>        fit      lwr      upr
#> 1 86.77874 86.35402 87.20346
```

This is the 95% confidence interval, which is the default, but which we can change by using the `level` option. For example, the 99% confidence interval is obtained as follows:

```
predict(M,
        interval = 'confidence',
        level = 0.99,
        newdata = weight_male_df_new)
#>        fit      lwr      upr
#> 1 86.77874 86.22047 87.33701
```

Again, we can verify that this confidence interval is calculated as described above:

```
x_new <- c(1, 175, 35)
std_err_mu <- sigma(M) * sqrt(x_new %*% solve(t(X) %*% X) %*% matrix(x_new))
%>%
  as.numeric()
c(mu_hat,
  mu_hat + c(-1, 1) * std_err_mu * qt(0.995, df = n - K - 1)
) %>% set_names(nm = c('fit', 'lwr' ,'upr'))
#>      fit       lwr      upr
#> 86.77874 86.22047 87.33701
```

To obtain the prediction interval on y_i rather than the confidence interval on μ_i^* we use `interval = 'prediction'`. In the following, we calculate the 99% prediction interval for y_i:

```
predict(M,
        interval = 'prediction',
        level = 0.99,
        newdata = weight_male_df_new)
#>          fit      lwr      upr
#> 1 86.77874 55.5989 117.9586
```

Again, we can confirm that this value is calculated according to the description above:

```
std_err_y <- sigma(M) * sqrt(1 + x_new %*% solve(t(X) %*% X) %*% matrix(x_new))
%>%
  as.numeric()
c(mu_hat,
  mu_hat + c(-1, 1) * std_err_y * qt(0.995, df = n - K - 1)
) %>% set_names(nm = c('fit', 'lwr' ,'upr'))
#>      fit        lwr        upr
#> 86.77874  55.59890 117.95858
```

R^2 and Adjusted R^2

The observed values of the outcome variable are $y_1,...,y_n$. The mean and variance of these values are

$$\bar{y} = \frac{1}{n}\sum_{i=1}^{n} y_i, \quad \text{var}(y) = \frac{1}{n-1}\underbrace{\sum_{i=1}^{n}(y_i - \bar{y})^2}_{TSS}.$$

The TSS summation term in the variance stands for *total sum of squares*, and is the sum of the squared differences of each observation from the mean. It can be shown that in general

$$\underbrace{\sum_{i=1}^{n}(y_i - \bar{y})^2}_{TSS} = \underbrace{\sum_{i=1}^{n}(\hat{\mu}_i - \bar{y})^2}_{ESS} + \underbrace{\sum_{i=1}^{n}(y_i - \hat{\mu}_i)^2}_{RSS},$$

where ESS stands for *explained sum of squares*, and RSS stands for *residual sum of squares*. RSS is the sum of the squared residuals when the coefficients take their maximum likelihood values

$\hat{\beta}$. ESS, by contrast, measures the variability in the outcome variable due to changes in the predictor variables. Equivalently, because $\bar{y} = \bar{\mu}$, where $\bar{\mu} = 1 / n \sum_{i=1}^{n} \hat{\mu}_i$, ESS can also be written as

$$\text{ESS} = \sum_{i=1}^{n} (\hat{\mu}_i - \bar{\mu})^2 = (n-1) \cdot \text{var}\left(\hat{\mu}\right),$$

and so it is the variability of the predicted mean values of weight. The proportion of the variability in the outcome variable due to changes in predictors is referred to as R^2:

$$R^2 = \frac{\text{ESS}}{\text{TSS}} = \frac{\text{var}\left(\hat{\mu}\right)}{\text{var}(y)}.$$

This is equivalent to 1 minus the proportion of variability in the outcome variable that is residual variation:

$$R^2 = 1 - \frac{\text{RSS}}{\text{TSS}} = 1 - \frac{\hat{\sigma}^2}{\text{var}(y)}.$$

R^2 is routinely taken to be a measure of model fit in linear models. Given that it is a proportion, it varies between 0 and 1. When ESS = 0, TSS = RSS and so R^2 = 0. When RSS = 0, TSS = ESS, and so R^2 = 1. In other words, R^2 takes its maximum value of 1 when the observed values of the outcome variables can be predicted exactly as a linear function of the predictors, that is, for each i, $y_i = \hat{\mu}_i = \sum_{k=1}^{K} \hat{\beta}_{ki} x_{ki}$, or equivalently, for each i, $\epsilon_i = 0$. On the other hand, when TSS = RSS, it must be the case that $\beta_1 = \beta_2 = ... = \beta_K = 0$, and so no change in the outcome variable's value can be predicted as a function of any of the K predictors.

R^2, by definition, gives the proportion of total variation due to variation in the predictor variables. This is often stated as the *proportion of variation explained* by the model. While in one sense this is true by definition, it is misleading if we interpret it as measuring the extent to which the predictor variables explain, in a causal sense, the outcome variable.

The value of R^2, necessarily increases, or does not decrease, as we add more predictors to the model, even if the true values of the coefficients for these predictors are zero. To overcome this spurious increase in R^2, the following adjustment is applied:

$$R_{\text{Adj}}^2 = 1 - \frac{\text{RSS}}{\text{TSS}} \frac{n-1}{n - K - 1}$$
$$= 1 - \left(1 - R^2\right) \underbrace{\frac{n-1}{n - K - 1}}_{\text{penalty}}.$$

The value of R_{Adj}^2 is necessarily less than or equal to R^2. The amount of adjustment is determined by the penalty term. Note that this term is greater than 1 and it is multiplied by RSS/TSS, which measures the proportion of the total variation due to residual variation.

As n increases, R_{Adj}^2 and R^2 become closer in value, but for relatively small n and relatively large K, the adjustment can be considerable.

Unlike R^2, R_{Adj}^2 can have negative values. Moreover, it does not represent a proportion of the total variation in the outcome variable. For this reason, it is incorrect to state it as measuring, as R^2 does, the proportion of explained variation. On the other hand, both R^2 and R_{Adj}^2 can be seen as estimators of the true or population R^2, and R_{Adj}^2 can be seen as a less biased estimator of this than R^2.

R^2 and adjusted R^2 with `lm`

From the `lm` object, R^2 and R_{Adj}^2 are easily obtained using the `summary` function:

```
S <- summary(M)
S$r.squared
#> [1] 0.276709
S$adj.r.squared
#> [1] 0.2763543
```

We can verify that these values are calculated as described above:

```
tss <- sum((y - mean(y))^2)
# R^2
(rsq <- (1 - rss/tss))
#> [1] 0.276709
# Adj R^2
(adj_rsq <- 1 - rss/tss * (n-1)/(n-K-1))
#> [1] 0.2763543
```

Note than in this case, the adjustment is minimal because $n \gg K$ and so the penalty term is close to 1.0:

```
(n-1)/(n-K-1)
#> [1] 1.00049
```

Model comparison

Given that $R^2 = 0$ if and only if $\beta_1 = \beta_2 = ... = \beta_K = 0$, a null hypothesis test that $R^2 = 0$ is the hypothesis that all coefficients, except the intercept term, are simultaneously zero. When all coefficients are simultaneously zero, we are essentially saying that the following two models are identical:

$$\mathcal{M}_0 : y_i \sim N\left(\hat{\mu}_i, \sigma^2\right), \quad \hat{\mu}_i = \beta_0, \text{ for } i \in 1,...,n,$$

$$\mathcal{M}_1 : y_i \sim N\left(\hat{\mu}_i, \sigma^2\right), \quad \hat{\mu}_i = \beta_0 + \sum_{k=1}^{K}\beta_k x_{ki}, \text{ for } i \in 1,...,n.$$

In $\mathcal{M}_0$ and $\mathcal{M}_1$, we have estimators $\hat{\sigma}_{\mathcal{M}_0}^2$ and $\hat{\sigma}_{\mathcal{M}_1}^2$ respectively, which are both estimators of σ_*^2, and their respective relationships to σ^2 are as follows:

$$\frac{(n-1)\hat{\sigma}_{\mathcal{M}_0}^2}{\sigma^2} = \frac{RSS_0}{\sigma^2} \sim \chi_{n-1}^2, \quad \frac{(n-K-1)\hat{\sigma}_{\mathcal{M}_1}^2}{\sigma^2} = \frac{RSS_1}{\sigma^2} \sim \chi_{n-K-1}^2.$$

The ratio of the difference of RSS_0 and RSS_1 to σ^2 is also distributed as χ^2:

$$\frac{RSS_0 - RSS_1}{\sigma^2} \sim \chi_K^2.$$

Given that

$$\frac{RSS_0 - RSS_1}{\sigma^2}, \quad \frac{RSS_1}{\sigma^2}$$

are independent of one another and both are χ^2 distributed with K and $n - K - 1$ degrees of freedom respectively, then we have the following sampling distribution under the null hypothesis:

$$\frac{(RSS_0 - RSS_1)/K}{RSS_1/(n-K-1)} \sim F(K, n-K-1).$$

Note that above statistic can be rewritten as follows:

$$\frac{ESS/K}{RSS/(n-K-1)} = \frac{R^2}{1-R^2} \times \frac{n-K-1}{K} \sim F(K, n-K-1).$$

We can extend the above result to test whether any subset of the K predictors has coefficients that are simultaneously zero. In general, we can compare two models $\mathcal{M}_1$ and $\mathcal{M}_0$ that have K_1 and K_0 predictors, respectively, and where $K_0 < K$ and all the K_0 predictors in $\mathcal{M}_0$ are also present in $\mathcal{M}_1$. Following identical reasoning to the above, the null hypothesis that the $K_1 - K_0$ predictors in $\mathcal{M}_1$ and not in $\mathcal{M}_0$ are simultaneously zero is

$$\frac{(RSS_0 - RSS_1)/(K_1 - K_0)}{RSS_1/(n-K_1-1)} \sim F(K_1 - K_0, n - K_1 - 1).$$

Model comparison using `lm`

The results of the null hypothesis test that are $R^2 = 0$ can be obtained in numerous ways, but the easiest is to use the generic `anova` function where we compare model `M` against `M_null`:

```
M_null <- lm(weight ~ 1, data = weight_male_df)
A <- anova(M_null, M)
A
#> Analysis of Variance Table
#>
#> Model 1: weight ~ 1
#> Model 2: weight ~ height + age
#>    Res.Df    RSS Df Sum of Sq       F    Pr(>F)
#> 1    4081 825294
#> 2    4079 596927  2    228366 780.25 < 2.2e-16 ***
#> ---
#> Signif. codes:  0 '***' 0.001 '**' 0.01 '*' 0.05 '.' 0.1 ' ' 1
```

Note that the values in the `Sum Sq` column are TSS and RSS respectively, which we can verify as follows:

```
c(tss, rss)
#> [1] 825293.6 596927.5
```

The TSS is in fact the RSS of the null model with no predictors. The ESS is therefore as follows:

```
ess <- tss - rss
```

Likewise, the `Df` and the second value of the `Res.Df` column give us the degrees of freedom by which `ess` and `rss` are divided:

```
c(K, n - K - 1)
#> [1]    2 4079
```

The `F value` column gives the ratio of these two values:

```
f_stat <- (ess/K) / (rss/(n - K - 1))
f_stat
#> [1] 780.2501
```

Finally, the *p*-value gives us the probability of getting a result greater than this *F*-statistic in an *F*-distribution with K and $n - K - 1$ degrees of freedom. We can calculate this using the cumulative distribution function of the *F*-distribution, which is `pf`:

```
pf(f_stat, K, n-K-1, lower.tail = F)
#> [1] 1.172286e-287
```

This is identical to the value calculated by the `anova` function, which we may verify if we extract the value from the ANOVA table:

```
A[2,'Pr(>F)']
#> [1] 1.172286e-287
```

 ## Bayesian approaches to normal linear models

In the Bayesian approach to normal linear models, our starting point is identical to that of the classical approach. Specifically, we assume we have n independent observations that can be represented as

$$(y_1, \vec{x}_1), (y_2, \vec{x}_2), \ldots, (y_i, \vec{x}_i), \ldots, (y_n, \vec{x}_n),$$

and we assume the following model of $y_1, \ldots, y_n$:

$$y_i \sim \mathrm{N}(\mu_i, \sigma^2), \quad \mu_i = \beta_0 + \sum_{k=1}^{K} \beta_k x_{ki}, \text{ for } i \in 1, \ldots, n.$$

We also assume that $\vec{\beta} = [\beta_0, \beta_1, \ldots, \beta_K]$ and σ^2 have *fixed but unknown* values. Inference in Bayesian approaches, just like in classical approaches, aims to infer what these values are. The reasoning and procedure for doing this, however, differ markedly between the two approaches. Despite this, as we will see, the ultimate conclusions can nonetheless be remarkably similar to one another.

As we've seen in the previous chapter, the fundamental point of departure between the classical and the Bayesian approaches is that the Bayesian approach assumes that $\vec{\beta}$ and σ have been drawn from a *prior* distribution. The prior effectively extends the linear model above. Writing $\vec{x}_i \vec{\beta} = \beta_0 + \sum_{k=1}^{K} \beta_k x_{ki}$, the extended model is

$$y_i \sim \mathrm{N}(\vec{x}_i \vec{\beta}, \sigma^2), \quad \text{for } i \in 1, \ldots, n,$$
$$\vec{\beta}, \sigma \sim \mathrm{P}(\vec{\beta}, \sigma)$$

where $P(\vec{\beta}, \sigma)$ is an as yet unspecified probability distribution over $\vec{\beta}$ and σ, respectively. In other words, the Bayesian approach assumes, like the classical approach, that each y_i is drawn from a normal distribution centred at $\vec{x}_i\vec{\beta}$ and whose standard deviation is σ. However, the Bayesian approach, unlike the classical approach, also assumes that the values $\vec{\beta}$ and σ have been drawn from the probability distribution $P(\vec{\beta}, \sigma)$. Having made this assumption, it is now possible to use Bayes' theorem to calculate the *posterior* probability that $\vec{\beta}$ and σ have any given values conditional on the data we have observed. Writing $\vec{y}$ for the $n \times 1$ vector of outcome variable observations, and X for the $n \times (K + 1)$ matrix of predictors, the posterior distribution can be written as follows:

$$\overbrace{P(\beta, \sigma \mid \vec{y}, X)}^{\text{posterior}} = \frac{\overbrace{P(\vec{y} \mid X, \vec{\beta}, \sigma)}^{\text{likelihood}} \overbrace{P(\vec{\beta}, \sigma)}^{\text{prior}}}{\underbrace{\int P(\vec{y} \mid X, \vec{\beta}, \sigma) P(\vec{\beta}, \sigma) d\beta d\sigma}_{\text{marginal likelihood}}}.$$

In general across all Bayesian models, the posterior distribution is a probability distribution, that is a non-negative function over all possible values of a variable, which may be multivariate, that integrates to exactly 1.0. However, whether we have a *closed-form* or *analytic* expression for this function varies from model to model. As described in the previous chapter, a closed-form or analytic expression means that the function can be described, like all probability distributions we have seen so far, in a finite number of mathematical operations. Informally speaking, when there is a closed-form or analytic expression, we say we have a formula for the probability distribution and we can obtain the value of the function at any value of the variable by a small number of calculations, possibly even by hand. For most Bayesian models, we simply do not have closed-form expressions for the posterior distribution. This is primarily because the right-hand side of the formula above involves the evaluation of an integral, which is the product of two functions, and there may be no analytic expression for this integral. In situations where we have no closed-form expression for the posterior, we generally resort to Monte Carlo, specifically Markov chain Monte Carlo (MCMC), sampling methods whereby we draw samples from the posterior distribution. We provided an introduction to MCMC in Chapter 8, and throughout the remaining chapters we will often use MCMC, and in doing so it will become more apparent what these methods afford us in practice.

For normal linear models, with judicious choices of the types of priors we use, we can in fact obtain analytic expressions for the posterior distribution. It can be informative and useful to use these approaches. On the other hand, by using MCMC sampling methods, we are not limited to certain choices of priors. Moreover, the MCMC sampling methods we use for normal linear models are identical to those used for more general and more complex statistical models, and so using and understanding these sampling methods in the normal linear model, which are relatively simple, can be very helpful before using them in more complex models. As such, we will consider both the analytic and MCMC-based approaches here.

Closed-form solutions

The first term in the numerator on the right-hand side of Bayes' rule above is the likelihood function. The likelihood function is not a probability distribution, but is a function over the $\vec{\beta}$ and σ space. It is exactly the same function that was maximized to find the maximum likelihood estimators in the classical approach to inference in linear models. It can be written as follows:

$$P\left(\vec{y} \mid X,\hat{\beta},\sigma\right) = \prod_{i=1}^{n} P\left(y_i \mid \vec{x}_i, \beta, \sigma^2\right)$$

$$= \left(\frac{1}{\sqrt{2\pi}}\right)^n \sigma^{-n} \exp\left[-\frac{1}{2\sigma^2}(\vec{y} - X\vec{\beta})^{\top}(\vec{y} - X\vec{\beta})\right]$$

$$= \left(\frac{1}{\sqrt{2\pi}}\right)^n \sigma^{-n} \exp\left[-\frac{1}{2\sigma^2}\left[(n - K - 1)\hat{\sigma}^2 + (\hat{\beta} - \beta)^{\top} X^{\top} X(\hat{\beta} - \beta)\right]\right],$$

where $\hat{\beta}$ and $\hat{\sigma}^2$ have identical values to those defined above, namely

$$\hat{\beta} = (X^{\top} X)^{-1} X^{\top} \vec{y},$$

$$\hat{\sigma}^2 = \frac{1}{n - K - 1} \sum_{i=1}^{n} |y_i - \hat{\mu}_i|^2.$$

The second term in the numerator is the prior. Like the likelihood function, it is a function over the $\vec{\beta}$ and σ space, but of course it is also a probability distribution. In principle, this probability distribution can be from any parametric family that is defined on the $\vec{\beta}$ and σ space. However, as mentioned, in order to obtain an analytic expression for the posterior, we must restrict our choices of probability distributions. One common choice for normal linear models is to use an *uninformative prior*, specifically one that is uniform over $\vec{\beta}$ and $\log(\sigma)$. This turns out to be equivalent to

$$P\left(\vec{\beta}, \sigma^2\right) \propto \frac{1}{\sigma^2}.$$

This prior works well when n is relatively large and K is relatively small.[4]

The posterior $P\left(\vec{\beta}, \sigma \mid \vec{y}, X\right)$ is the product of the likelihood and the prior, divided by their integral. The resulting distribution is a normal-inverse-Gamma distribution, which can be written in the following factored form:

$$P\left(\vec{\beta}, \sigma \mid \vec{y}, X\right) = P\left(\vec{\beta} \mid \sigma, \vec{y}, X\right) P\left(\sigma \mid \vec{y}, X\right)$$

$$= N\left(\vec{\beta} \mid \hat{\beta}, \sigma^2 \left(X^{\top} X\right)^{-1}\right) \times \text{invGamma}\left(\sigma^2 \mid \frac{n - K - 1}{2}, \frac{(n - K - 1)\hat{\sigma}^2}{2}\right).$$

An interesting consequence of this distribution is when we marginalize over the σ^2, this leads to a multivariate t-distribution with location parameter $\hat{\beta}$, scale parameter $\hat{\sigma}^2(X^{\top} X)^{-1}$ and degrees of freedom $n - K - 1$:

$$P\left(\vec{\beta} \mid \vec{y}, X\right) \sim t_{n-K-1}\left(\vec{\beta} \mid \hat{\beta}, \hat{\sigma}^2 (X^{\top} X)^{-1}\right).$$

From this, for any β_k, we have

$$P\left(\beta_k \mid \vec{y}, X\right) \sim t_{n-K-1}\left(\beta_k \mid \hat{\beta}_k, \hat{\sigma}^2 (X^{\top} X)^{-1}_{kk}\right).$$

In other words, the posterior distribution of β_k is a (non standard) t-distribution with degrees of freedom $n - K - 1$, mean $\hat{\beta}_k$ and scale parameter $\hat{\sigma}^2 (X^{\top} X)^{-1}_{kk}$. This entails, among other things, that the probability, according to the posterior distribution, that β_k is in the range

---

[4] It should be noted that this is an *improper prior*, which means that it does not have a finite value for its integral.

$$\hat{\beta}_k \pm \tau_{(1-\epsilon,n-K-1)} \hat{\sigma} \sqrt{(X^\top X)^{-1}_{kk}},$$

is $1-2\epsilon$. Note that here, $\tau_{(1-\epsilon,n-K-1)}$ is the inverse cumulative distribution function of a standard t-distribution, as defined above. This gives us the *highest posterior density* (HPD) interval for β_k. Setting $\epsilon = 0.025$, for example, gives us the 95% HPD interval. In other words, according to the posterior distribution, there is a 95% probability that β_k is in the range $\hat{\beta}_k \pm \tau_{(0.975,n-K-1)} \hat{\sigma} \sqrt{(X^\top X)^{-1}_{kk}}$. What is particularly interesting about this result is that it is identical to the 95% confidence interval for β_k defined above.

In Bayesian approaches in general, as we will see repeatedly below, a common focus of interest is the *posterior predictive distribution*. In normal linear models, this is defined as follows:

$$P(y_i \,|\, x_i, \vec{y}, X) = \int P(y_i \,|\, x_i, \vec{\beta}, \sigma^2) \underbrace{P(\vec{\beta}, \sigma^2 \,|\, \vec{y}, X)}_{\text{posterior}} d\vec{\beta} d\sigma^2.$$

The first term in the integral is the probability distribution over the outcome variable given that the predictor takes the value x_i, and given known values of $\vec{\beta}$ and σ^2. This, of course, is a normal distribution centred at $x_i \vec{\beta}$ and whose standard deviation is σ. This integral simplifies to

$$P(y_i \,|\, x_i, \vec{y}, X) \sim t_{n-K-1}\left(x_i \vec{\beta} \vee \hat{\sigma}^2 (1 + x_i (X^\top X)^{-1} x_i^\top) \right).$$

This entails that the $1-2\epsilon$ density interval for predicted value of y_i is the following range:

$$x_i \vec{\beta} \pm \tau_{(1-\epsilon,n-K-1)} \hat{\sigma} \sqrt{1 + x_i (X^\top X)^{-1} x_i^\top}.$$

This interval is identical to prediction interval for y_i that we defined above.

Monte Carlo approaches

As mentioned, in situations where a closed-form expression for the posterior distribution is not available, we may use Monte Carlo methods to draw samples from this distribution. Even though, as we have seen, we can obtain a closed-form expression for the normal linear model, it is still useful and informative to use Monte Carlo methods, especially because there is excellent general-purpose software for doing so. In particular, here we will use the `brms` package, which we used already in Chapter 8.

The main command in the `brms` package is `brm`. When used for normal linear models, assuming we accept all the default settings, the usage of this command is identical to that of `lm`:

```
library(brms)
M_bayes <- brm(weight ~ height + age, data = weight_male_df)
```

We can view the results of this analysis using the generic `summary` function:

```
summary(M_bayes)
#>  Family: gaussian
#>   Links: mu = identity; sigma = identity
#> Formula: weight ~ height + age
```

```
#>     Data: weight_male_df (Number of observations: 4082)
#> Samples: 4 chains, each with iter = 2000; warmup = 1000; thin = 1;
#>          total post-warmup samples = 4000
#>
#> Population-Level Effects:
#>            Estimate Est.Error l-95% CI u-95% CI Rhat Bulk_ESS Tail_ESS
#> Intercept    -98.08      4.93  -108.17   -88.56 1.00     4960     3304
#> height         0.98      0.03     0.93     1.04 1.00     4914     3454
#> age            0.39      0.02     0.34     0.43 1.00     4512     3253
#>
#> Family Specific Parameters:
#>       Estimate Est.Error l-95% CI u-95% CI Rhat Bulk_ESS Tail_ESS
#> sigma    12.09      0.13    11.84    12.36 1.00     4636     3193
#>
#> Samples were drawn using sampling(NUTS). For each parameter, Bulk_ESS
#> and Tail_ESS are effective sample size measures, and Rhat is the potential
#> scale reduction factor on split chains (at convergence, Rhat = 1).
```

There is a lot information in this output, and we will not focus on all of it immediately. Let us begin by noting that it tells us that we drew 1000 samples from four independent chains, each one drawing samples from the same posterior distribution. Thus, for each of the three coefficients and for the standard deviation, we represent the posterior by a set of 4000 samples.

Let us now look at the first few columns of the coefficients table, which is listed in the summary output under Population-Level Effects:

```
summary(M_bayes)$fixed[,1:4] %>%
  print(digits = 2)
#>            Estimate Est.Error l-95% CI u-95% CI
#> Intercept    -98.08     4.928  -108.17   -88.56
#> height         0.98     0.028     0.93     1.04
#> age            0.39     0.021     0.34     0.43
```

The values listed under Estimate and Est.Error are the means and the standard deviations, respectively, of the posterior distributions for the three coefficients. The remaining two columns give us the lower and upper bounds, respectively, of the HPD interval.

Compare these results to the maximum likelihood estimates, standard errors, and 95% confidence intervals from the lm model:

```
cbind(summary(M)$coefficients[,1:2],
      confint(M)
) %>% print(digits = 2)
#>              Estimate Std. Error  2.5 % 97.5 %
#> (Intercept)    -97.97      4.906 -107.59 -88.35
#> height           0.98      0.028    0.92   1.03
#> age              0.38      0.021    0.34   0.43
```

Clearly, these results are remarkably similar, and any minor differences that there are may in fact be due to the sampling variation.

In Figure 9.5, we plot the density functions and trace plots of the samples for each of the four unknown variables. The density plots are essentially smoothed histograms of the samples. The trace plots plot the trajectory of the samples from each chain for each variable:

```
plot (M_bayes)
```

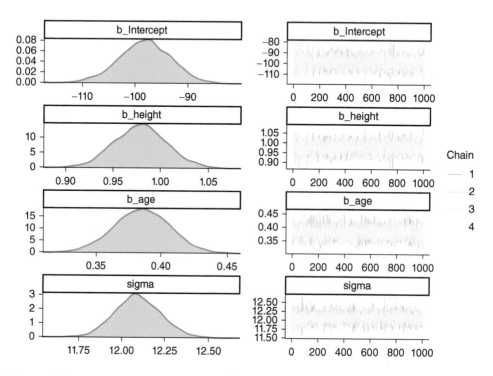

Figure 9.5 Density plots and trace plots of the posterior distribution of each of the three coefficients and σ

These trace plots can tell us whether the four chains are sampling over time from the same areas of space. If they are, then the trace plots should appear like a 'hairy caterpillar', with the traces of each chain being on top of one another.

When we represent a posterior distribution using samples, the posterior predictive distribution is calculated as follows:

$$\int P\left(y_i \mid x_i, \vec{\beta}, \sigma^2\right) P\left(\vec{\beta}, \sigma^2 \mid \vec{y}, X\right) d\vec{\beta}\sigma^2 \approx \frac{1}{J}\sum_{j=1}^{J} P\left(y_i \mid x_i, \tilde{\beta}_j, \tilde{\sigma}_j^2\right),$$

where $\{\tilde{\beta}_j, \tilde{\sigma}_j^2\}_{j=1}^{J}$ are the J samples from the posterior distribution.

Using the weight_male_df_new data that we also used above, with the brm object, we can calculate this posterior predictive distribution as follows:

```
predict(M_bayes, newdata = weight_male_df_new)
#>      Estimate Est.Error     Q2.5     Q97.5
#> [1,] 86.92183  12.16127  62.83207 110.4554
```

Note how this is almost identical to the prediction interval calculated using classical methods:

```
predict(M, newdata = weight_male_df_new, interval = 'prediction')
#>        fit       lwr      upr
#> 1 86.77874  63.05787 110.4996
```

Categorical predictor variables

Thus far, we have only considered predictor or explanatory variables that are continuous, like height or age. The important feature of these variables is that they are defined on a metric space, and we assume that the average of the outcome variable changes by a constant proportion of any change of each predictor. Of course, some potentially important explanatory variables are not continuous, or are not defined on a metric space, but have categorically distinct values. For these variables, we assume that changing from one of these categorically distinct values to another corresponds to a constant change in the average of the outcome variable.

As a simple example, again using `weight` as our outcome variable, we could have a single explanatory variable `gender`, which takes on two categorically distinct values: `male`, `female`. In Figure 9.6(a), we show the density plots for the weights of both males and females. When modelling weight in a normal linear model with `gender` as a explanatory variable, for each of its two discrete and categorically distinct values, we assume that weight is normally distributed. In other words, we assume the distribution of weight for males and also for females is a normal distribution. We assume that these distributions have different means, but that their standard deviations are identical. Using binary-valued categorical predictor variables in a normal linear model is, as we will see, easily accomplished by coding one of the two values as 0 and the other as 1, and then treating the resulting coding variable as a normal numerical predictor variable.

When using `lm`, we can simply use the categorical variable in the formula for `lm` just as we would any other variable. For example, in the following code, we model the distribution of weight as before, but now model how its distribution varies by `gender`:

```
M_gender <- lm(weight ~ gender, data = weight_df)
```

The variable `gender` has values `male` and `female`. When used in `lm`, one of these is recoded as 0 and the other as 1. Which one is coded as 0 or 1 is completely arbitrary and ultimately makes no difference to the model. Nonetheless, we do have to know which is coded as 0 and 1 in order to be able to interpret the model. In R, we can always control how categorical variables are coded, but by default, the value that is listed first alphabetically is coded by 0. In the case of `gender`, this means `female` is coded as 0 and `male` as 1. The model above then is equivalent to the following:

$$y_i \sim N(\mu_i, \sigma^2), \quad \mu_i = \beta_0 + \beta_1 x_i, \quad \text{for } i \in 1, \ldots, n,$$

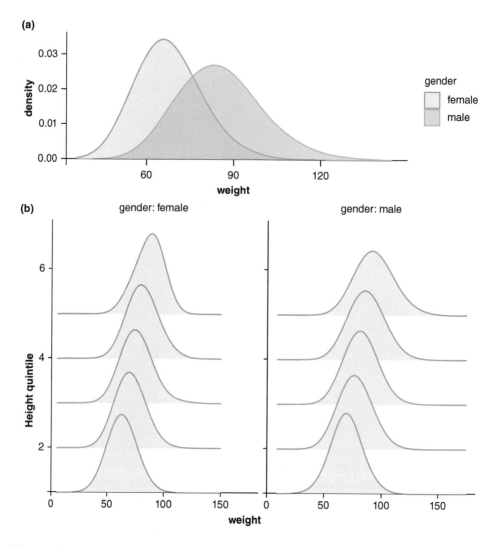

Figure 9.6 (a) Density plots of the weights of males and females. (b) Density plots of the weights of males and females for each of the different quintiles of height (across both males and females)

where $x_i = 0$ if person i is female and $x_i = 1$ if person i is male. Put another way, we create variables $x_1, \ldots, x_n$ defined as follows:

$$x_i = \begin{cases} 0, & \text{if gender}_i = \text{female} \\ 1, & \text{if gender}_i = \text{male} \end{cases}$$

Let us look at the coefficients:

```
coef (M_gender)
#> (Intercept)  gendermale
#>    67.75821    17.76575
```

As we can see, the intercept term has a value of 67.76, and the second coefficient is 17.77. The intercept term β_0 is, by definition, the average of the distribution of weight when the predictor variable takes a value of 0. In this case, x_i takes a value of 0 whenever $gender_i$ is female. As such, the intercept term is the average of the distribution of weights for females. On the other hand, the average of the distribution of weight for males is equal to the value of μ_i when $x_i = 1$, which is $\beta_0 + \beta_1 \cdot 1 = \beta_0 + \beta_1$. This entails that β_1 gives the *difference* in the average of the distribution of weight for females and males.

We can therefore also write this model as follows:

$$y_i \sim N(\mu_i, \sigma^2), \quad \mu_i = \begin{cases} \beta_0, & \text{if } gender_i = \text{female}, \\ \beta_0 + \beta_1, & \text{if } gender_i = \text{male}. \end{cases}$$

Note that this model is identical to an independent samples t-test. In that model, we assume we have two groups of independent observations. Each group is assumed to be drawn from a normal distribution, and the two distributions are assumed to have identical standard deviations. The null hypothesis in the t-test is that the means of these two distributions are identical. This is identical to a null hypothesis that $\beta_1 = 0$ in the above linear model. This is zero if and only if the mean of the males and the mean of the females are identical.

When we include gender as a explanatory variable in addition to a continuous predictor variable, such as height, we are dealing with a situation like that shown in Figure 9.6(b). Using a linear model for this situation, we assume that for both males and females, the average of the weight distribution changes as a constant proportion of height. More precisely, the model is as follows:

$$y_i \sim N(\mu_i, \sigma^2), \quad \mu_i = \beta_0 + \beta_1 x_{1i} + \beta_2 x_{2i}, \quad \text{for } i \in 1...n,$$

where x_{1i} is the height of person i, and

$$x_{2i} = \begin{cases} 0, & \text{if } gender_i = \text{male}, \\ 1, & \text{if } gender_i = \text{female}. \end{cases}$$

To implement this model using lm we would do the following:

```
M_gender_height <- lm(weight ~ height + gender, data = weight_df)
coef(M_gender_height)
#> (Intercept)       height   gendermale
#> -87.7293652    0.9548058    5.5689395
```

Using the same reasoning as above, given that x_{2i} takes that value of 0 when the gender is female and takes the value of 1 when gender is male, this model can be written as follows:

$$y_i \sim N(\mu_i, \sigma^2), \quad \mu_i = \begin{cases} \beta_0 + \beta_1 x_{1i}, & \text{if } gender_i = \text{female} \\ \beta_0 + \beta_1 x_{1i} + \beta_2, & \text{if } gender_i = \text{male}. \end{cases}$$

This is identical to a *varying intercept* model. In particular, we have two linear models, one for males and one for females. The slopes for these two models are the same, namely β_1, but the intercepts are different. The intercept for the females is β_0, and the intercept for the males is $\beta_0 + \beta_1$.

To make the values of the coefficients somewhat easier to interpret, let us subtract an arbitrary constant from the `height` variable and rerun the analysis:

```
weight_df %>%
  mutate(height = height - 150) %>%
  lm(weight ~ height + gender, data = .) %>%
  coef()
#> (Intercept)        height   gendermale
#>   55.4915013     0.9548058    5.5689395
```

This tells us that the distribution of weight of females with height exactly 150 cm has an average value of 55.49 kg. For males on the other hand, the distribution of their weights is centred at 55.49 + 5.57, which is 61.06 kg. For any given height, the average of the distribution of weights for males is greater than that of females by 5.57 kg. But for both males and females, according to this model, the average of the distribution of weight increases by 0.95 for every change by 1 cm in height.

In linear models, we can also use categorical predictor variables that have more than two levels. Consider, for example, the variable `race`. This has seven distinct values in the original `weight_df` data set. Some of these values have very few corresponding observations, so therefore, for simplicity, we will limit the observations to just those where the values of `race` are white, black, or hispanic:

```
weight_df_2 <- weight_df %>%
  filter(race %in% c('white', 'black', 'hispanic'))
```

We may easily include `race` as a predictor in an `lm` model. When used on its own, for example, this would effectively model the distribution of weight as a normal distribution for each of the white, black, and hispanic people. Unlike in the case of a variable with two values, however, we cannot use a single coding variable. For example, while we could code `female` and `male` by $x_i = 0$ and $x_i = 1$, respectively, we cannot code white, black, hispanic by $x_i = 0$, $x_i = 1$, $x_i = 2$. To do so would entail that `race` is variable on a metric space and that white, black, and hispanic are ordered and equidistant positions in this space. This would mean that, among other things, the difference in the average heights of white and black would be exactly the same as the average difference in height of black and hispanic.

To deal with categorical variables with more than two levels we use *dummy* codes. In a dummy code, one value of the variable is chosen as the *base* level. If this variable has three values, then the base level has the dummy code of 0, 0. One of the remaining values is dummy-coded as 0, 1, and the final one is coded as 1, 0. Which value is coded using which code is arbitrary, but by default in R the alphabetically first value is the base level.

Using `race` as our single categorical predictor variable, the linear model would be as follows:

$$y_i \sim N(\mu_i, \sigma^2), \quad \mu_i = \beta_0 + \beta_1 x_{1i} + \beta_2 x_{2i}, \quad \text{for } i \in 1, \ldots, n,$$

Where

$$x_{1i}, x_{2i} = \begin{cases} 0,0 & \text{if race}_i = \text{black}, \\ 1,0 & \text{if race}_i = \text{hispanic}, \\ 0,1 & \text{if race}_i = \text{white}. \end{cases}$$

Using `lm`, we would simply do as follows:

```
M_race <- lm(weight ~ race, data = weight_df_2)
coef(M_race)
#>  (Intercept) racehispanic    racewhite
#>    78.672958    -1.655727     2.464647
```

The intercept term is, as always, the predicted mean of the outcome variable when the predictors are equal to zero. In this case, both predictors are zero if and only if the `race` of the observation is `black`. Thus, the predicted average of the distribution of weight when `race` is `black` is 78.67 kg.

On the other hand, when the `race` of the observable is `hispanic`, then the dummy code is $x_{1i} = 1, x_{2i} = 0$. Therefore, the predicted mean of the weight distribution for Hispanics is

$$78.67 + -1.66 \times 1 + 2.46 \times 0 = 77.02.$$

From this, we see that –1.66 is the difference in the average of the distribution of weight between the `black` and the `hispanic` race categories.

Finally, when the `race` is `white`, then the dummy code is $x_{1i} = 0, x_{2i} = 1$. Therefore, the predicted mean of the weight distribution for whites is

$$78.67 + -1.66 \times 0 + 2.46 \times 1 = 81.14.$$

From this, we see that 2.46 is the difference in the average of the distribution of weight between the `black` and the `white` race categories.

This linear model is identical to a one-way ANOVA, in which we have J distinct groups and have independent observations from each one. We assume that these J groups can each be modelled as normal distributions, whose means differ, but which have a common standard deviation. This is precisely the model assumed when using `lm` as above. Moreover, the null hypothesis test that $\beta_1 = \beta_2 = 0$ in the model above is exactly the same as the null hypothesis, as in the one-way ANOVA, that the mean weights of all three race groups are the same. Using the `lm` model, the F-statistic for the null hypothesis that $\beta_1 = \beta_2 = 0$ is $F(2,5766) = 27.33$ (to two decimal places). The corresponding ANOVA table can be obtained as follows:

```
anova(M_race)
#> Analysis of Variance Table
#>
#> Response: weight
#>              Df  Sum Sq Mean Sq F value    Pr(>F)
#> race          2   13179  6589.4  27.327 1.541e-12 ***
#> Residuals  5766 1390348   241.1
#> ---
#> Signif. codes:  0 '***' 0.001 '**' 0.01 '*' 0.05 '.' 0.1 ' ' 1
```

If we use `aov` to perform a standard one-way ANOVA with this data set, we see that its null hypothesis test is identical to this:

```
aov(weight ~ race, data = weight_df_2) %>%
    summary()
```

```
#>                 Df   Sum Sq Mean Sq F value    Pr(>F)
#> race             2    13179    6589   27.33 1.54e-12 ***
#> Residuals     5766 1390348     241
#> ---
#> Signif. codes:  0 '***' 0.001 '**' 0.01 '*' 0.05 '.' 0.1 ' ' 1
1
```

10

Logistic Regression

1 Introduction

The normal linear model that we described in Chapter 9 models an outcome variable as a normal distribution whose mean varies as a linear function of a set of predictors. As useful and important as this model is, it is clearly limited in that it can only be applied to data that is both continuous and has a (conditionally) roughly normal distribution. That unquestionably excludes variables that are categorical, or other variables like count variables. We can, however, make relatively simple extensions to the normal linear model to produce a class of regression models that work in many respects just like the normal linear models but are applicable to data sets characterized by different types of outcome variables such as categorical or count variables. These are known as the *generalized linear models*. In this chapter, we will focus on a class of models known as the *logistic regression models*. These are some of the most of the widely used examples of the generalized linear models. In the next chapter, we will cover some of the other major types of generalized linear models.

Perhaps the single most common type of logistic regression is binary logistic regression, which we will cover here first. Other types of logistic regression, which are fundamentally related to binary logistic regression, include ordinal logistic regression and categorical (or multinomial) logistic regression, and we will also cover these models is this chapter.

2 Binary logistic regression

Let use assume, as we did with the normal linear model, that we have n independent observations, which can be represented as the n pairs

$$(y_1, \vec{x}_1), (y_2, \vec{x}_2), \ldots, (y_i, \vec{x}_i), \ldots, (y_n, \vec{x}_n).$$

Here, just as before, in each observation, y_i is the observed value of a univariate *outcome* variable, and this is the variable which we are hoping to predict or explain. Also as before, each $\vec{x}_i$ is a row vector of values of a set of K predictor or explanatory variables that can predict or explain the value of the outcome variable. Now consider the situation where the outcome variable is a binary variable. Any binary variable's values can be represented, without loss of generality, as {0, 1}. In other words, no matter what the actual values (e.g. {no, yes}, {false, true}), we can always represent these by {0, 1}. If the outcome variable is a binary variable, we simply cannot use the normal linear model here. To do so would make the highly implausible claim that each value of y_i, which is always either 0 or 1, was drawn from a normal distribution. Because the normal distribution is a unimodal, symmetric and continuous distribution, it cannot be used as a probability distribution over the discrete values {0, 1}.

A suitable distribution for a binary-valued random variable x is a Bernoulli distribution, an example of which we depict in Figure 10.1. A Bernoulli distribution is an extremely simple distribution. It has a single parameter, which we will denote by θ. This θ gives the probability that x takes the value 1. In other words,

$$P(x = 1) = \theta,$$

and so the probability that x takes the value 0, given that $P(x = 0) = 1 - P(x = 1)$, is $1 - \theta$.

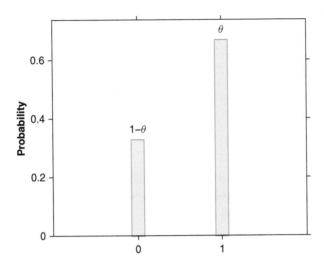

Figure 10.1 A Bernoulli distribution with parameter θ. The parameter θ gives the probability that the binary variable takes the value 1. In other words, if x is a binary variable, $P(x = 1) = \theta$, and so $P(x = 0) = 1 - P(x = 1) = 1 - \theta$

We can therefore begin to extend the normal linear model by exchanging the normal distribution of the outcome variable for a Bernoulli distribution:

$$y_i \sim \text{Bernoulli}(\theta_i), \quad \text{for } i \in 1,\dots,n.$$

In the case of the normal linear model, we had each $y_i \sim N(\mu_i, \sigma^2)$ with each μ_i being a linear function of $\vec{x}_i$, $\mu_i = \beta_0 + \sum_{k=1}^{K} \beta_k x_{ki}$. In the case of the Bernoulli distribution, however, we cannot have each θ_i being a linear function of $\vec{x}_i$ because each θ_i is constrained to take values between 0 and 1, and in general, if we allow θ_i to be a linear function of $\vec{x}_i$, we cannot guarantee that it will be constrained to the interval (0, 1). In order to deal with this issue, we can transform θ_i to another variable ϕ_i that can take on any value on the real line $\mathbb{R}$ between $-\infty$ and ∞ and then treat ϕ_i as the linear function of $\vec{x}_i$. For this, we need an invertible function $f : (0,1) \mapsto \mathbb{R}$ that can map any value of θ_i to a unique value of ϕ, and vice versa. This function f is known as a *link function*, and it is a defining feature of a generalized linear model.

Our extended model is now

$$y_i \sim \text{Bernoulli}(\theta_i), \quad \theta_i = f^{-1}(\phi_i), \quad \phi_i = \beta_0 + \sum_{k=1}^{K} \beta_k x_{ki}, \quad \text{for } i \in 1,\dots,n.$$

Compare this model to the original normal linear model,

$$y_i \sim N(\mu_i, \sigma^2), \quad \mu_i = \beta_0 + \sum_{k=1}^{K} \beta_k x_{ki}, \quad \text{for } i \in 1,\dots,n.$$

There are two key differences here. First, the outcome variable's distribution is the normal distribution in the normal linear model, while it is the Bernoulli distribution in the binary outcome variable model. Second, in the normal linear model, the location parameter μ_i is a linear function of $\bar{x}_i$, while in the case of the binary outcome variable model, it is a transformation of the location parameter θ_i, rather than θ_i itself, that is the linear function of $\bar{x}_i$.

There are endless possibilities for the link function f, but the default choice, and in fact the defining choice for the binary logistic regression model, is the *log odds*, otherwise known as the *logit*, function. The logit function is defined as

$$\phi = f(\theta) = \mathrm{logit}(\theta) = \log_e\left(\frac{\theta}{1-\theta}\right).$$

In other words, this function takes a value $\theta \in (0, 1)$ and divides it by $1 - \theta$, and then calculates the natural logarithm[1] of this function. The term $\theta/(1 - \theta)$, when θ is assumed to be a probability, is known as the *odds* of θ. Hence, the logit is simply the natural logarithm of the odds of θ. The logit function is invertible:

$$\theta = f^{-1}(\phi) = \mathrm{ilogit}(\phi) = \frac{1}{1+e^{-\phi}}.$$

This function is usually known as the inverse logit, hence ilogit, function. The logit and the inverse logit functions are shown in Figure 10.2(a) and Figure 10.2(b), respectively.

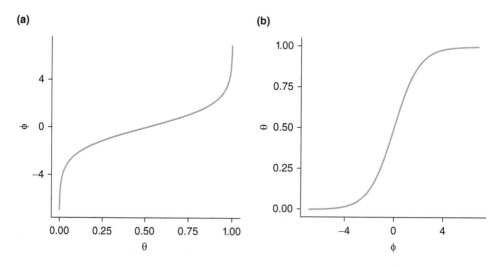

Figure 10.2 (a) The log odds, also known as the logit, function that maps the interval $(0,1)$ to $\mathbb{R}$. (b) The inverse of the log odds, also known as the inverse logit, function that maps $\mathbb{R}$ to the interval $(0,1)$

[1] Note that the natural logarithm is the logarithm to base $e \approx 2.7183$, hence we write it as $\log_e$. It is common to see this also written as ln. Because the natural logarithm is probably the most used logarithm base in statistics, we will usually denote it simply as log without explicitly stating the base.

The binary logistic regression model is therefore defined exactly as follows:

$$y_i \sim \text{Bernoulli}(\theta_i), \quad \theta_i = \text{ilogit}(\phi_i), \quad \phi_i = \beta_0 + \sum_{k=1}^{K} \beta_k x_{ki}, \quad \text{for } i \in 1,\dots,n.$$

This can be written identically but in a more succinct manner as follows:

$$y_i \sim \text{Bernoulli}(\theta_i), \quad \text{logit}(\theta_i) = \beta_0 + \sum_{k=1}^{K} \beta_k x_{ki}, \quad \text{for } i \in 1,\dots,n.$$

As an example of a binary logistic regression, let us look at a data set concerning extramarital affairs. This data set was collected by the magazine *Psychology Today* and described in its July 1969 issue, and is described in more detail in Fair (1978):

```
affairs_df <- read_csv('data/affairs.csv')
```

It has 601 observations for nine variables. One of these nine variables is `affairs`, which gives the number of times the respondent to the survey engaged in an extramarital act of sexual intercourse in the past year. The distribution of values of the `affairs` variable is as follows:

```
affairs_df %>%
  pull(affairs) %>%
  table()
#> .
#>   0   1   2   3   7  12
#> 451  34  17  19  42  38
```

Here, the values of 0, 1, 2, and 3 indicate exactly 0, 1, 2, and 3 times, while 7 indicates 4–10 times, and 12 indicates monthly or weekly or daily. To simplify matters, we will create a new variable `cheater` that takes the value TRUE if the respondent engaged in any amount of extramarital sexual intercourse, and FALSE otherwise:

```
library(magrittr)
affairs_df %<>% mutate(cheater = affairs > 0)
```

This variable, which is obviously binary, will be our outcome variable. Other variables, which can serve as explanatory variables, include `gender` and `rating`. The `rating` variable takes values 1 to 5 that mean the following: 1 = very unhappy, 2 = somewhat unhappy, 3 = average, 4 = happier than average, 5 = very happy. In Figure 10.3 we show the proportion of people who cheat by (a) gender, (b) marriage rating and (c) marriage rating and gender.

We can understand binary logistic regression in a manner directly analogous to normal linear regression. Recall from Chapter 9 that we said that normal linear regression models the outcome variable as a normal distribution whose mean varies as we change the values of the predictor variables. In binary logistic regression, we model the outcome variable as a Bernoulli distribution whose parameter, which gives the probability of one of the two outcomes, varies as we change the values of the predictor variables. For example, consider Figure 10.3(a). As we change `gender` from `female` to `male`, the proportion of those who

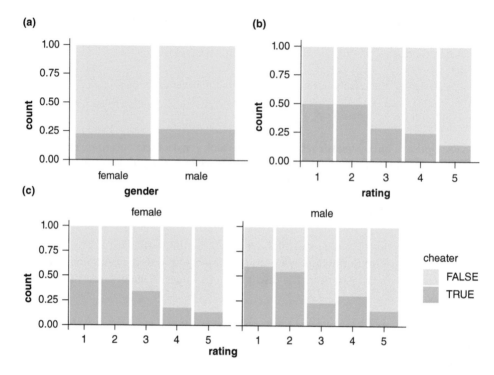

Figure 10.3 Each bar in each plot shows the proportion of people in the relevant group who have had an affair or not in the past year. (a) Proportions for females and males. (b) Proportions according to the rating of the happiness of the marriage. (c) Proportions according to the marriage rating for females and males

have had affairs increases from 0.23 to 0.27. Similarly, as we see in Figure 10.3(b), as `rating` increases, the proportion of people cheating declines. Likewise in Figure 10.3(c), for females and males separately, as `rating` increases, the proportion of people cheating declines, but for the most part, for any given value of `rating`, the proportion of males who cheat is greater than the number of females who cheat. As we will see, we can model these changes in the probability of cheating as a function of predictors using a binary logistic regression analogously to how we could model changes in a normally distributed outcome variable as a function of predictors using normal linear regression.

One of the key differences between normal linear and binary logistic regression models, as we have mentioned, is that while in normal linear models we model the location parameter of the outcome variable as a linear function of the predictors, in binary logistic regression we model the log odds of the location parameter of the outcome variable as a linear function of the predictors. In other words, in binary logistic regression, as predictor variable k changes by Δ_k, we assume the log odds of the probability of the outcome variable changes by $\beta_k \Delta_k$, where β_k is the coefficient for predictor k. In Figure 10.4(a) we plot the proportion of cheaters as a function of the marriage rating level, and in Figure 10.4(b) we plot the log odds of this proportion as a function of the marriage rating level.

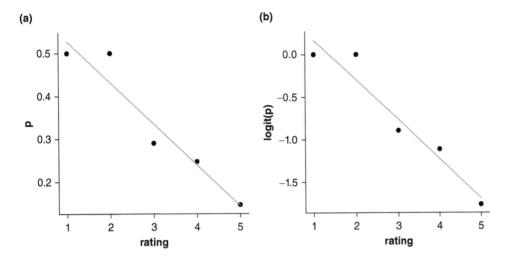

Figure 10.4 (a) Proportion of cheaters as a function of the marriage rating. (b) Log odds of the proportion of cheaters as a function of the marriage rating

Using the `affairs_df` data, we can model changes in the probability of cheating as a function of `gender` or `rating` or both `gender` and `rating` using a binary logistic regression as follows. When using `gender` as a predictor, our model would be

$$y_i \sim \text{Bernoulli}(\theta_i), \quad \theta_i = \text{ilogit}(\phi_i), \quad \phi_i = \beta_0 + \beta_1 x_{1i}, \quad \text{for } i \in 1,\ldots,n,$$

or equivalently,

$$y_i \sim \text{Bernoulli}(\theta_i), \quad \text{logit}(\theta_i) = \beta_0 + \beta_1 x_{1i}, \quad \text{for } i \in 1,\ldots,n,$$

where x_{1i} indicates if person i is a male or female by $x_{1i} = 1$ if gender$_i$ is male and $x_{1i} = 0$ if person gender$_i$ is female. Once we have inferred the value of β_0 and β_1 (we will describe how to do so below), $\text{ilogit}(\beta_0 + \beta_1 \times 0) = \text{ilogit}(\beta_0)$ will give us the estimate of the probability that a female will have an affair, while $\text{ilogit}(\beta_0 + \beta_1 \times 1) = \text{ilogit}(\beta_0 + \beta_1)$ will give us the estimate of the probability that a male will have an affair. Equivalently, β_0 is the estimate of the log odds that a female will have an affair, while $\beta_0 + \beta_1$ is the estimate of the log odds that a male will have an affair. This means that β_1 is the difference in the log odds of having an affair between males and females. As we will discuss in more detail below, this also entails that e^{β_1} is the *odds ratio* of having an affair between males and females.

If we wish to model how the probability of having an affair varies by the `rating` variable, our model could be the following:

$$y_i \sim \text{Bernoulli}(\theta_i), \quad \theta_i = \text{ilogit}(\phi_i), \quad \phi_i = \beta_0 + \beta_2 x_{2i}, \quad \text{for } i \in 1,\ldots,n,$$

which is equivalent to

$$y_i \sim \text{Bernoulli}(\theta_i), \quad \text{logit}(\theta_i) = \beta_0 + \beta_2 x_{2i}, \quad \text{for } i \in 1,\ldots,n,$$

where $x_{2i} \in \{1,2,3,4,5\}$ is the rating of the happiness of the marriage by person i. Here, we are explicitly assuming that the log odds of having an affair varies linearly with a change in the value of rating. In other words, we assume that the log odds of having an affair changes by β_2 whenever rating changes by one unit, regardless if it changes from 1 to 2, 2 to 3, 3 to 4, or 4 to 5. That the log odds changes by this constant amount whenever rating changes by one unit is not strictly necessary, nor is it beyond dispute in this data set as we can see from Figure 10.4(b). However, this assumption is a standard one, and to go beyond this assumption would require a nonlinear extension to the logistic regression, which is something we will not consider in this chapter.

Modelling how the probability of having an affair varies with gender and rating, assuming no interaction between these two variables, could be done with the following model:

$$y_i \sim \text{Bernoulli}(\theta_i), \quad \theta_i = \text{ilogit}(\phi_i), \quad \phi_i = \beta_0 + \beta_1 x_{1i} + \beta_2 x_{2i}, \text{ for } i \in 1,\dots,n,$$

which is equivalent to

$$y_i \sim \text{Bernoulli}(\theta_i), \quad \text{logit}(\theta_i) = \beta_0 + \beta_1 x_{1i} + \beta_2 x_{2i}, \text{ for } i \in 1,\dots,n,$$

where x_{1i} and x_{2i} are as above. We interpret this model similarly to the two previous ones, with the exception that now β_1 is the change in the log odds of having an affair as we go from females to males, assuming that the value of rating is held constant. In other words, assuming that rating has any given value, as the log odds of having an affair changes by β_1 as we go from females to males. Likewise, holding gender constant, if rating increases by one unit, then the log odds of having an affair changes by β_2.

Maximum likelihood estimation

As in normal linear regression, we can estimate the values of the unknown variables in the model, namely $\beta_0, \beta_1, \dots, \beta_K$, using maximum likelihood estimation. Unlike in the case of normal linear models, however, there is no closed-form solution giving the maximum likelihood estimates. In other words, we cannot simply solve for $\beta_0, \beta_1, \dots, \beta_K$ to find the values that maximize the likelihood function. Alternative, numerical methods to obtain the maximum likelihood estimates are therefore used.

The likelihood function can be written as

$$P(\vec{y} \mid X, \vec{\beta}) = \prod_{i=1}^{n} P(y_i \mid \vec{x}_i, \beta)$$

$$= \prod_{i=1}^{n} \theta_i^{y_i} (1-\theta_i)^{1-y_i},$$

where $\vec{y} = [y_0, y_1, \dots, y_n]^T$, $\vec{\beta} = [\beta_0, \beta_1, \dots, \beta_K]^T$, X is an n by $K+1$ matrix whose ith row is $[1, \vec{x}_i^\top]$ and $\theta_i = \text{ilogit}(X\vec{\beta})$. The logarithm of the likelihood is

$$\log L(\vec{\beta} \mid \vec{y}, X) = \log P(\vec{y} \mid X, \vec{\beta})$$

$$= \sum_{i=1}^{n} y_i \log(\theta_i) + (1-y_i)\log(1-\theta_i).$$

Although this is clearly a function of $\vec{\beta}$, we cannot, as we did in the case of normal linear models, simply calculate its gradient with respect to $\vec{\beta}$, set it to zero and solve for $\vec{\beta}$,

However, $\log L(\vec{\beta}|\vec{y}, X)$ is a convex function and has a global maximum, and hence we may use numerical optimization methods to find this global maximum. Relatively simple methods to maximize this function include gradient descent methods that choose an arbitrary starting value for $\vec{\beta}$, calculate the gradient of the function at this point, and then choose the next value of $\vec{\beta}$ by adding to it a constant times the gradient vector. More computationally efficient and effective methods include using Newton's method for root finding applied to the derivative of the log of the likelihood function. When applied to binary logistic regression, this is known as *iteratively reweighted least squares* (see Murphy, 2012, for details). Specifically, we start with an arbitrary starting value for $\vec{\beta}$, which we will call $\vec{\beta}_0$, and then for $t \in 0,1,2,...$, we update our estimate of $\vec{\beta}$ using the following update rule until the estimate converges:

$$\vec{\beta}_{t+1} = (X^\top S_t X)^{-1} X^\top (S_t X \vec{\beta}_t + \vec{y} - \vec{\theta}_t).$$

Here, S_t is an $n \times n$ diagonal matrix whose value at the ith element of the diagonal is $\theta_i^t (1 - \theta_i^t)$, where $\theta_i^t = \mathrm{ilogit}(X\vec{\beta}_t)$ and $\vec{\theta}_t = [\theta_1^t, \theta_2^t, ..., \theta_n^t]$.

As before, we will denote the maximum likelihood estimator of $\vec{\beta}$ by $\hat{\beta}$. It can be shown that the sampling distribution of $\hat{\beta}$ is distributed asymptotically as follows:

$$\hat{\beta} \sim N(\vec{\beta}, (X^\top S_t X)^{-1}).$$

This result is very similar, though not identical, to the sampling distribution of $\hat{\beta}$ in the case of the normal linear model. Using this result, the sampling distribution for any particular coefficient is

$$\hat{\beta}_k \sim N(\vec{\beta}_k, (X^\top S_t X)^{-1}_{kk}),$$

which entails that

$$\frac{\hat{\beta}_k - \beta_k}{\sqrt{(X^\top S_t X)^{-1}_{kk}}} \sim N(0,1),$$

where $\sqrt{(X^\top S_t X)^{-1}_{kk}}$ is the standard error term.

Binary logistic regression using R

Using R, we can implement binary logistic regression using the `glm` function. The `glm` function is used almost identically to how we used `lm`, but because it is for different types of generalized linear models and not just the binary logistic regression model, we must specify both the outcome variable probability distribution that we assume and the link function.

When applied to the `affairs_df` problem, using `gender` and `rating` as the predictor variables, we implement the binary logistic regression in R as follows:

```
affairs_m <- glm(cheater ~ gender + rating,
                 family = binomial(link = 'logit'),
                 data = affairs_df)
```

As we can see, the way we use `glm` is almost identical to how we used `lm`, but we have to use a new argument, `family`, to specify the outcome distribution and link function. Given that the outcome variable's probability distribution is a Bernoulli distribution, it may be unexpected that we state here that it is a binomial distribution. However, the binomial distribution is in fact a generalization of the Bernoulli distribution: a binomial distribution when the number of observations is 1 is exactly the Bernoulli distribution. As such, it is technically correct to say that a binary variable has a binomial distribution. Note that we state the link function `link = 'logit'` inside `binomial()`. The logit link function is the default, so we could simply write `family = binomial()`.

Just like with `lm`, we may see the maximum likelihood estimates of $\beta_0, \beta_1, \beta_2$ with the `coef()` function:

```
(estimates <- coef(affairs_m))
#> (Intercept)    gendermale         rating
#>   0.7093252     0.2547430     -0.5108324
```

From this, for example, we see that difference in the log odds of having an affair between males and females, assuming that `rating` is held constant at any value, is 0.255. Likewise, assuming `gender` is held constant, as we increase `rating` by one unit, the log odds of having an affair decreases by 0.511 (in other words, it increases by –0.511). The trouble with these statements about the coefficient is that they won't make much intuitive sense for those not used to thinking in terms of log odds. We will return to consider some alternative explanations of these coefficients below after we have considered predictions in logistic regression.

Let us now turn to hypothesis tests and confidence intervals for these coefficients. The relevant information is as follows:

```
summary(affairs_m)$coefficients
#>                    Estimate Std. Error   z value     Pr(>|z|)
#> (Intercept)       0.7093252 0.33745388  2.101992 3.555402e-02
#> gendermale        0.2547430 0.19540750  1.303650 1.923529e-01
#> rating           -0.5108324 0.08495009 -6.013324 1.817574e-09
```

The standard error for each coefficient k is, as described above, $\hat{se}_k = \sqrt{(X^{\mathsf{T}} S_t X)^{-1}_{kk}}$. We can easily confirm this similarly to how we did in the case of normal linear models:

```
library(modelr)

X <- model_matrix(affairs_df, cheater ~ gender + rating) %>%
    as.matrix()

p <- affairs_m$fitted.values
S <- diag(p * (1 - p))

(std_err <- solve(t(X) %*% S %*% X) %>% diag() %>% sqrt())
#> (Intercept)    gendermale         rating
#>   0.33745388    0.19540750    0.08495009
```

Note that `affairs_m$fitted.values` gives the values of $\vec{\theta}$ as defined above.

In the table above, the `z value` is the test statistic for the null hypothesis tests that the true value of each β_k is zero. In other words, it is $\hat{\beta}_k / se_k$, as can be easily verified. The accompanying p-value, listed as `Pr(>|z|)`, is the probability of getting a result more extreme than the test statistic in a standard normal distribution:

```
z <- summary(affairs_m)$coefficients[,'z value']
2 * pnorm(abs(z), lower.tail = F)
#>  (Intercept)    gendermale        rating
#> 3.555402e-02 1.923529e-01 1.817574e-09
```

The confidence intervals for the coefficients can be obtained as follows:

```
confint.default(affairs_m)
#>                    2.5 %       97.5 %
#> (Intercept)   0.04792776  1.3707227
#> gendermale   -0.12824866  0.6377347
#> rating       -0.67733153 -0.3443333
```

We can confirm that for each coefficient β_k, this is $\hat{\beta}_k \pm \widehat{se}_k \cdot \zeta_{(0.975)}$, where $\zeta_{(0.975)}$ is the value below which lies 97.5% of the probability mass in a standard normal distribution. For example, for the case of `gender`, we have

```
estimates['gendermale'] + c(-1, 1) * std_err['gendermale'] * qnorm(0.975)
#> [1] -0.1282487  0.6377347
```

Predictions in binary logistic regression

Given $\hat{\beta}$, we can easily make predictions based on any given values of our predictors. In general, if $\vec{x}_i$ is a vector of values of the predictor variables that we wish to make predictions about, the predicted log odds corresponding to $\vec{x}_i$ is simply

$$\phi_i = \vec{x}_i \hat{\beta},$$

and so the predicted probability of the outcome variable, which is the predicted values of the parameters of the Bernoulli distribution of the outcome variable, is

$$\theta_i = \frac{1}{1+e^{-\phi_i}}.$$

For example, the predicted log odds of having an affair for a male with a `rating` value of 4 is as follows:

```
predicted_logodds <-
   (estimates['(Intercept)'] + estimates['gendermale'] * 1 + estimates['rating']
 * 4) %>%
   unname()
predicted_logodds
#> [1] -1.079261
```

If we then want the predicted probability, we use the inverse logit function. While this function does exist in R as the `plogis` function, it is nonetheless instructive to implement it ourselves as it is a very simple function:

```
ilogit <- function(phi){
  1/(1 + exp(-phi))
}
```

Using this function, the predicted probability is as follows:

```
ilogit(predicted_logodds)
#> [1] 0.2536458
```

Doing predictions in logistic regression as we have just done is instructive but becomes tedious and error prone for all but very simple calculations. Instead, we should use the generic `predict` function as we did in the case of `lm`. For this, we must first set up a data frame with the same variables as are the predictors in the model and whose values are the values we want to make predictions about. For example, if we want to see the predictions for both females and males at all values of the `rating` variable, we can set up the data frame using `expand_grid`, which will give us all combinations of the values of the two variables:

```
affairs_df_new <- expand_grid(gender = c('female', 'male'),
                              rating = seq(5)
)
```

We can now make predictions as follows:

```
predict(affairs_m, newdata = affairs_df_new)
#>          1          2          3          4          5          6
#>  0.19849280 -0.31233961 -0.82317202 -1.33400444 -1.84483685  0.45323579
#>          7          8          9         10
#> -0.05759662 -0.56842903 -1.07926144 -1.59009385
```

By default, this gives us the predicted log odds. We can get the predicted probabilities easily in one of two ways. First, we can pipe the predicted log odds to `ilogit`:

```
predict(affairs_m, newdata = affairs_df_new) %>% ilogit()
#>         1         2         3         4         5         6         7         8
#> 0.5494609 0.4225438 0.3050907 0.2084978 0.1364803 0.6114083 0.4856048 0.3615994
#>         9        10
#> 0.2536458 0.1693707
```

Alternatively, we can use the `type = 'response'` argument with `predict`:

```
predict(affairs_m, newdata = affairs_df_new, type = 'response')
#>         1         2         3         4         5         6         7         8
#> 0.5494609 0.4225438 0.3050907 0.2084978 0.1364803 0.6114083 0.4856048 0.3615994
```

```
#>          9         10
#> 0.2536458 0.1693707
```

As we have seen elsewhere, it is useful to use the `modelr::add_predictions` function to return these predictions as new variables in the data frame we are making predictions with:

```
affairs_df_new %>%
  add_predictions(affairs_m, type='response')
#> # A tibble: 10 x 3
#>     gender rating  pred
#>     <chr>   <int> <dbl>
#>  1 female      1 0.549
#>  2 female      2 0.423
#>  3 female      3 0.305
#>  4 female      4 0.208
#>  5 female      5 0.136
#>  6 male        1 0.611
#>  7 male        2 0.486
#>  8 male        3 0.362
#>  9 male        4 0.254
#> 10 male        5 0.169
```

Above, we established that the estimator $\hat{\beta}$ has the following asymptotic sampling distribution:

$$\hat{\beta} \sim N(\vec{\beta},(X^{\mathsf{T}}SX)^{-1}) .$$

Given that the predicted log odds ϕ_i is $\vec{x}_i\hat{\beta}$, the sampling distribution of ϕ_i is as follows:

$$\phi_i \sim N(\vec{x}_i\,\hat{\beta},\underbrace{\vec{x}_i(X^{\mathsf{T}}SX)^{-1}\vec{x}_i^{\mathsf{T}}}_{\hat{se}_i^2}).$$

From this, the 95% confidence interval on the true value of ϕ_i will be

$$\phi_i \pm \widehat{se}_i \cdot \zeta_{(0.975)}.$$

Unlike in the case of `lm`, there is no option for the `predict` function to return this confidence interval directly. However, it will return the standard errors, and from this, we can calculate the confidence intervals easily.

```
predictions <- predict(affairs_m, newdata = affairs_df_new, se.fit = T)
cbind(
  predictions$fit - predictions$se.fit * qnorm(0.975),
  predictions$fit + predictions$se.fit * qnorm(0.975)
)
#>            [,1]        [,2]
#> 1  -0.31580817  0.71279377
#> 2  -0.69575622  0.07107699
#> 3  -1.11464246 -0.53170159
#> 4  -1.61390737 -1.05410150
```

```
#> 5    -2.20146018 -1.48821351
#> 6    -0.07157505  0.97804664
#> 7    -0.44875880  0.33356556
#> 8    -0.86174317 -0.27511488
#> 9    -1.35221279 -0.80631009
#> 10   -1.93420954 -1.24597816
```

The confidence intervals just given are on the log odds scale, but we can easily put them on the probability scale using the `ilogit` function:

```
cbind(
    predictions$fit - predictions$se.fit * qnorm(0.975),
    predictions$fit + predictions$se.fit * qnorm(0.975)
) %>% ilogit()
#>              [,1]       [,2]
#> 1    0.42169767 0.6710182
#> 2    0.33275380 0.5177618
#> 3    0.24700640 0.3701201
#> 4    0.16604683 0.2584383
#> 5    0.09961944 0.1841900
#> 6    0.48211387 0.7267205
#> 7    0.38965591 0.5826267
#> 8    0.29697528 0.4316518
#> 9    0.20550884 0.3086774
#> 10   0.12628538 0.2233971
```

Risk ratios and odds ratios

As mentioned above, the coefficients in a binary logistic regression give us differences in log odds. For example, we saw that the difference in the log odds of having an affair between males and females, assuming that `rating` is held constant at any value, is 0.255. We mentioned that these values are not easily interpreted in intuitive terms, and it is preferable to compare probabilities if possible.

Using the predicted probabilities we made above, we can `pivot_wider` the predictions for females and males to make them easier to compare:

```
predictions <- affairs_df_new %>%
    add_predictions(affairs_m, type='response') %>%
    pivot_wider(names_from = gender, values_from = pred)
predictions
#> # A tibble: 5 x 3
#>   rating female  male
#>    <int>  <dbl> <dbl>
#> 1      1  0.549 0.611
#> 2      2  0.423 0.486
#> 3      3  0.305 0.362
#> 4      4  0.208 0.254
#> 5      5  0.136 0.169
```

With this, we can now calculate the difference and ratios of the probabilities of males and females:

```
predictions %>%
    mutate(prob_diff = male - female,
           prob_ratio = male/female)
#> # A tibble: 5 x 5
#>    rating female  male prob_diff prob_ratio
#>    <int>  <dbl> <dbl>     <dbl>      <dbl>
#> 1      1  0.549 0.611    0.0619       1.11
#> 2      2  0.423 0.486    0.0631       1.15
#> 3      3  0.305 0.362    0.0565       1.19
#> 4      4  0.208 0.254    0.0451       1.22
#> 5      5  0.136 0.169    0.0329       1.24
```

The `prob_ratio` values are obviously the ratios of the probabilities of having an affair by males to the corresponding probabilities for females. These ratios are usually referred to as *risk ratios* or *relative risks*. Note, however, that these values are not constant across all values of `rating`. In other words, the relative risks of having an affair by men and women vary according to value of `rating`.

Instead of ratios of probabilities, we can also calculate ratios of odds. We saw above that the odds is simply the ratio of a probability p to $1 - p$.

```
predictions %>%
    mutate(odds_male = male/(1-male),
           odds_female = female/(1-female),
           odds_ratio = odds_male/odds_female)
#> # A tibble: 5 x 6
#>    rating female  male odds_male odds_female odds_ratio
#>    <int>  <dbl> <dbl>     <dbl>       <dbl>      <dbl>
#> 1      1  0.549 0.611      1.57        1.22       1.29
#> 2      2  0.423 0.486     0.944       0.732       1.29
#> 3      3  0.305 0.362     0.566       0.439       1.29
#> 4      4  0.208 0.254     0.340       0.263       1.29
#> 5      5  0.136 0.169     0.204       0.158       1.29
```

As we can see, the odds ratios comparing males and females are constant for all values of `rating`. Thus, we can say that for any value of `rating`, the odds of having an affair by a male are exactly 1.29 greater than the odds of having an affair by a female.

Let us look more closely at how we calculated these odds ratios. Let us assume that the value of `rating` is r. Then the log odds of having an affair by a female and a male are, respectively,

$$\log\left(\frac{\theta_{female}}{1-\theta_{female}}\right) = \beta_0 + \beta_2 \cdot r, \ \log\left(\frac{\theta_{male}}{1-\theta_{male}}\right) = \beta_0 + \beta_1 + \beta_2 \cdot r.$$

This means that the odds of having an affair by a female or a male are, respectively,

$$\frac{\theta_{female}}{1-\theta_{female}} = e^{\beta_0 + \beta_2 \cdot r}, \ \frac{\theta_{male}}{1-\theta_{male}} = e^{\beta_0 + \beta_1 + \beta_2 \cdot r}.$$

The odds ratio comparing males to females is therefore

$$\frac{\theta_{male}}{1-\theta_{male}} \Big/ \frac{\theta_{female}}{1-\theta_{female}} = \frac{e^{\beta_0 + \beta_1 + \beta_2 \cdot r}}{e^{\beta_0 + \beta_2 \cdot r}} = e^{(\beta_0 + \beta_1 + \beta_2 \cdot r) - (\beta_0 + \beta_2 \cdot r)} = e^{\beta_1}.$$

More generally, by the same reasoning, we can see that for any predictor k, e^{β_k} gives the odds ratio corresponding to a unit change in x_k. In other words, e^{β_k} is the factor by which the odds increases whenever x_k increases by one unit, assuming any other predictors are held constant.

Note that, as we saw above, we can obtain the 95% confidence intervals for the coefficients as follows:

```
confint.default(affairs_m, parm = c('gendermale', 'rating'))
#>                    2.5 %      97.5 %
#> gendermale -0.1282487   0.6377347
#> rating        -0.6773315 -0.3443333
```

To get the confidence intervals on the odds ratios corresponding to these predictors, we simply raise the confidence intervals to the power of e:

```
confint.default(affairs_m, parm = c('gendermale', 'rating')) %>%
  exp()
#>                   2.5 %     97.5 %
#> gendermale 0.8796346 1.8921896
#> rating        0.5079707 0.7086927
```

Model comparison

As we saw above, we obtain the p-values for the null hypothesis tests that the true values of the coefficients are zero from the z-statistic, which is the estimate of the coefficient divided by its standard error. A more general way of doing null hypothesis tests in logistic regression, and also in related models as we will see below, is to perform a log likelihood ratio test, which is in fact the deviance comparison test for nested model comparison that we saw in Chapter 8. This allows us to compare one model with K predictors to another model with $K' < K$ predictors, where the K' predictors are a subset of the K predictors. This is a type of *nested model comparison* because the model with the K' predictors is a subset of the model with the K predictors. For example, we could compare the model using the gender and the rating predictors to a model using either gender or rating alone, or to a model using no predictors. In each of these two comparisons, we are comparing a model with two predictors to a model with a subset of these two predictors.

Generally speaking, we can describe the problem of nested model comparison using binary logistic regressions as follows. We assume, as before, that our outcome variable is $y_1, y_2, ..., y_i, ..., y_n$, where each $y_i \in \{0, 1\}$, and that we have a set of predictors $\vec{x}_1, \vec{x}_2, ..., \vec{x}_i, ..., \vec{x}_n$, where each $\vec{x}_i$ is

$$\vec{x}_i = [x_{1i}, x_{2i}, ..., x_{ki}, ..., x_{K'i}, ..., x_{Ki}].$$

Obviously, $[x_{1i}, x_{2i}, ..., x_{ki}, ..., x_{Ki}] \subset [x_{1i}, x_{2i}, ..., x_{ki}, ..., x_{K'i}, ..., x_{Ki}]$.

From this, we can set up two models, one nested in the other. The first model, which we will call $\mathcal{M}_1$, uses all K predictors:

$$\mathcal{M}_1 : y_i \sim \text{Bernoulli}(\theta_i),\ \text{logit}(\theta_i) = \beta_0 + \sum_{k=1}^{K} \beta_k x_{ki}.$$

We will compare this to model $\mathcal{M}_0$ that uses K' predictors:

$$\mathcal{M}_0 : y_i \sim \text{Bernoulli}(\theta_i),\ \text{logit}(\theta_i) = \beta_0 + \sum_{k=1}^{K'} \beta_k x_{ki}.$$

The null hypothesis comparing $\mathcal{M}_1$ and $\mathcal{M}_0$ is that

$$\beta_{K'} = \beta_{K'+1} = \ldots = \beta_K = 0.$$

In other words, it is the hypothesis that all the coefficients corresponding to the predictors that are in $\mathcal{M}_1$ but not in $\mathcal{M}_0$ are simultaneously zero. We can test this null hypothesis using a *likelihood ratio test*.

We begin by inferring the maximum likelihood estimators of the coefficients in both $\mathcal{M}_0$ and $\mathcal{M}_1$. We will denote the estimators for $\mathcal{M}_0$ and $\mathcal{M}_1$, by $\hat{\beta}_{\mathcal{M}_0}$ and $\hat{\beta}_{\mathcal{M}_1}$. Having done so, we can obtain the value of the likelihood function in $\mathcal{M}_0$ and $\mathcal{M}_1$ evaluated at $\hat{\beta}_{\mathcal{M}_0}$ and $\hat{\beta}_{\mathcal{M}_1}$. We will denote these by $\mathcal{L}_0$ and $\mathcal{L}_1$, respectively. The likelihood ratio comparing $\mathcal{M}_0$ to $\mathcal{M}_1$ is simply

$$\text{likelihood ratio} = \frac{\mathcal{L}_0}{\mathcal{L}_1}.$$

The logarithm of this likelihood is

$$\text{loglikelihood ratio} = \log\left(\frac{\mathcal{L}_0}{\mathcal{L}_1}\right) = \log(\mathcal{L}_0) - \log(\mathcal{L}_1).$$

According to Wilks's theorem, when the null hypothesis is true, $-2 \times$ loglikelihood ratio asymptotically follows a χ^2 distribution with $K - K'$ degrees of freedom. Therefore, we calculate $-2 \times$ loglikelihood ratio and then calculate the p-value, which is simply the probability of a getting a result greater than $-2 \times$ loglikelihood ratio in a χ^2 distribution with $K - K'$ degrees of freedom. Because

$$\text{loglikelihood ratio} = \log(\mathcal{L}_0) - \log(\mathcal{L}_1),$$

we have

$$-2 \times \text{loglikelihood ratio} = \left(-2 \cdot \log(\mathcal{L}_0)\right) - \left(-2 \cdot \log(\mathcal{L}_1)\right).$$

We refer to -2 times the log of the likelihood of a model as its *deviance*, and we'll denote the deviances of models $\mathcal{M}_0$ and $\mathcal{M}_1$ by $\mathcal{D}_0$ and $\mathcal{D}_1$, respectively:

$$\mathcal{D}_0 = -2 \cdot \log(\mathcal{L}_0),\ \mathcal{D}_1 = -2 \cdot \log(\mathcal{L}_1).$$

Therefore, our likelihood-ratio-based null hypothesis test is based on the statistic

$$\mathcal{D}_0 - \mathcal{D}_1,$$

which we compare to a χ^2 distribution with $K - K'$ degrees of freedom.

We can perform this null hypothesis test in R easily in different ways. As an example, we will compare the model with the two predictors `gender` and `rating` to a model with neither. We already have the model with both predictors, and have named it `affairs_m`. We name the model with neither predictor `affairs_m0`:

```
affairs_m0 <- glm(cheater ~ 1,
                  family = binomial(link = 'logit'),
                  data = affairs_df)
```

The formula `cheater ~ 1` indicates that we have an intercept only in this model and so the model is

$$y_i \sim \text{Bernoulli}(\theta_i), \quad \text{logit}(\theta_i) = \beta_0,$$

which entails that we assume that, for each observation, there is a fixed probability, namely ilogit (β_0), that $y_i = 1$.

We can obtain the log of the likelihoods of `affairs_m` and `affairs_m0` with the `logLik` function:

```
logLik(affairs_m)
#> 'log Lik.' -318.2889 (df=3)
logLik(affairs_m0)
#> 'log Lik.' -337.6885 (df=1)
```

The corresponding deviances can be obtained with the `deviance` function.

```
deviance(affairs_m)
#> [1] 636.5778
deviance(affairs_m0)
#> [1] 675.377
```

These are easily verified as –2 times the log of the likelihoods:

```
logLik(affairs_m) * -2
#> 'log Lik.' 636.5778 (df=3)
logLik(affairs_m0) * -2
#> 'log Lik.' 675.377 (df=1)
```

The difference between the two deviances is as follows:

```
deviance(affairs_m0) - deviance(affairs_m)
#> [1] 38.79919
```

If the null hypothesis is true, this difference of the deviances will follow a χ^2 distribution with 2 degrees of freedom. The *p*-value for the null hypothesis is therefore

```
K <- affairs_m %>% coef() %>% length()
K_prime <- affairs_m0 %>% coef() %>% length()
pchisq(deviance(affairs_m0) - deviance(affairs_m),
       df = K - K_prime,
       lower.tail = F)
#> [1] 3.757193e-09
```

While it is instructive to go through the calculations in a step-by-step manner as we have just done, in practice it is much easier and less error prone to use the generic anova function for doing likelihood ratio tests. We perform the above analyses using anova as follows:

```
anova(affairs_m0, affairs_m, test='Chisq')
#> Analysis of Deviance Table
#>
#> Model 1: cheater ~ 1
#> Model 2: cheater ~ gender + rating
#>   Resid. Df Resid. Dev Df Deviance  Pr(>Chi)
#> 1       600     675.38
#> 2       598     636.58  2   38.799 3.757e-09 ***
#> ---
#> Signif. codes:  0 '***' 0.001 '**' 0.01 '*' 0.05 '.' 0.1 ' ' 1
```

As we can see from this output, we have the deviances, the differences of the deviance, the degrees of freedom for the χ^2 distribution, and the p-value.

Bayesian approaches to logistic regression

The Bayesian approach to binary logistic regression begins with an identical probabilistic model to that of the classical approach. In other words, we assume our data is

$$(y_1, \vec{x}_1), (y_2, \vec{x}_2), \ldots, (y_i, \vec{x}_i), \ldots, (y_n, \vec{x}_n),$$

where each $y_i \in \{0,1\}$ and each $\vec{x}_i$ is a vector of the values of K predictor or explanatory variables, and that

$$y_i \sim \text{Bernoulli}(\theta_i), \quad \text{logit}(\theta_i) = \beta_0 + \sum_{k=1}^{K} \beta_k x_{ki}, \quad \text{for } i \in 1,\ldots,n.$$

At this point, the classical approach and the Bayesian approach diverge. The classical approach obtains the maximum likelihood estimators $\hat{\beta}$ and uses these estimators and their sampling distribution for hypothesis testing, confidence intervals, and predictions, as we have seen above. On the other hand, the Bayesian approach begins with the essential step of inferring the posterior distribution:

$$\overbrace{P(\vec{\beta} \mid X, \vec{y})}^{\text{posterior}} = \frac{\overbrace{P(\vec{y} \mid X, \vec{\beta})}^{\text{likelihood}} \overbrace{P(\vec{\beta})}^{\text{prior}}}{\underbrace{\int P(\vec{y} \mid X, \vec{\beta}) P(\vec{\beta}) d\beta}_{\text{marginal likelihood}}} \propto \overbrace{P(\vec{y} \mid X, \vec{\beta})}^{\text{likelihood}} \overbrace{P(\vec{\beta})}^{\text{prior}},$$

where $\vec{y} = [y_1, y_2, \ldots, y_n]$, X is the matrix with rows $\vec{x}_1, \vec{x}_2, \ldots, \vec{x}_n$, and $\vec{\beta} = [\beta_0, \beta_1, \ldots, \beta_K]$. The likelihood function, which we have seen above, is a function over $\vec{\beta}$. Its value gives us the probability of observing our data given any value of $\vec{\beta}$. The prior, on the other hand, is also a function over $\vec{\beta}$, specifically a probability density function. It gives the probability distribution over the possible values that $\vec{\beta}$ could take in principle. These two functions are multiplied by one another to result in a new function over $\vec{\beta}$, which is then divided by its integral so that the resulting posterior distribution integrates to 1, and hence is a probability density function. We interpret the posterior distribution as follows. Assuming that the data is generated by the stated logistic regression model, and also that the possible values that $\vec{\beta}$ could take in principle are given by $P(\vec{\beta})$, then the posterior distribution gives the probability that the true value of $\vec{\beta}$ is any given value.

Unlike the case of Bayesian linear regression, there are no choices of prior that will lead to an analytic or closed-form solution to the posterior distribution. As such, we must use alternative numerical methods. One traditionally commonly used approach, described in Bishop (2006), Murphy (2012) and elsewhere, is to use a *Laplace approximation* to the posterior distribution, which approximates the posterior distribution in a multivariate normal distribution. However, given the current state of general-purpose software for MCMC sampling in Bayesian models, as we described in Chapter 8 and will described further in Chapter 17, it is now much easier in practice to use MCMC methods, particularly the Hamiltonian Monte Carlo methods available with the Stan probabilistic programming language. As we've seen, a very easy-to-use R-based interface to Stan is available through the `brms` package.

In the following code, we define and fit a Bayesian logistic regression model predicting `cheater` from both `gender` and `rating`, just as we did above:

```
affairs_m_bayes <- brm(cheater ~ gender + rating,
                       family = bernoulli(),
                       data = affairs_df)
```

This syntax is almost identical to the `glm` model. However, the `family` is specified as `bernoulli` rather than `binomial`. The link function will default to `logit`.

By using the default settings, we use four chains, each with 2000 iterations, and where the initial 1000 iterations are discarded, leading to 4000 total samples. The priors used by default are seen in the following table:

```
prior_summary(affairs_m_bayes)
#>                      prior    class      coef group resp dpar nlpar bound
#> 1                                 b
#> 2                                 b gendermale
#> 3                                 b     rating
#> 4 student_t(3, 0, 2.5) Intercept
```

The blanks in the `prior` column for the coefficients for `gender` and `rating` tell us that a uniform prior is being used, while a non-standard *t*-distribution with 3 degrees of freedom and a scale of 10 is on the `Intercept` coefficient.

We can view the summary of the inference of the coefficients as follows:

```
summary(affairs_m_bayes)$fixed
#>             Estimate Est.Error    1-95% CI     u-95% CI      Rhat Bulk_ESS Tail_ESS
#> Intercept  0.7089189 0.34298420  0.05357066  1.4032220 1.000832     4413     2981
#> gendermale 0.2613167 0.20020218 -0.13226492  0.6528835 1.000461     4097     3401
#> rating    -0.5130190 0.08648511 -0.68262469 -0.3473037 1.000304     3735     2830
```

First, the `Rhat` values are all almost exactly equal to 1.0, which indicates that the chains have converged. `Bulk_ESS`[2] is an estimate of the number of independent samples that are informationally equivalent to the samples from the sampler, which are necessarily non-independent. We see that for each coefficient these are close to the theoretical maximum of 4000. This indicates that the sampler is very efficient.

Notice how the posterior mean and its standard deviation, given by `Estimate` and `Est.Error` respectively, are almost identical to the maximum likelihood estimator and the standard error of the sampling distribution of the maximum likelihood estimator. Likewise, the 95% credible interval, given by `1-95% CI` and `u-95% CI`, also closely parallels the classical 95% confidence interval. We saw this close parallel between the classical and Bayesian models in the case of linear regression as well. It is to be expected in any situation where we have a relatively large amount of data, thus leading to a concentrated likelihood function, and a diffuse prior distribution.

In the following code, we calculate the 95% posterior interval on $\phi_i = \vec{x}_i \vec{\beta}$, where $\vec{x}_i$ is a vector of values of the predictor variables. We do this for each observation in the `affair_df_new` data frame that was used above:

```
posterior_linpred(affairs_m_bayes, newdata = affairs_df_new) %>%
  as_tibble() %>%
  map_df(~quantile(., probs=c(0.025, 0.5, 0.975))) %>%
  set_names(c('l-95% CI', 'prediction', 'u-95% CI')) %>%
  bind_cols(affairs_df_new, .)
#> # A tibble: 10 x 5
#>    gender rating `l-95% CI` prediction `u-95% CI`
#>    <chr>  <int>       <dbl>      <dbl>       <dbl>
#>  1 female     1     -0.314      0.194      0.733
#>  2 female     2     -0.706     -0.315      0.0825
#>  3 female     3     -1.12      -0.829     -0.531
#>  4 female     4     -1.64      -1.34      -1.05
#>  5 female     5     -2.23      -1.85      -1.49
#>  6 male       1     -0.0652     0.452      0.980
#>  7 male       2     -0.443     -0.0564     0.332
#>  8 male       3     -0.855     -0.570     -0.277
#>  9 male       4     -1.35      -1.08      -0.809
#> 10 male       5     -1.94      -1.59      -1.24
```

Again, we see a close parallel between these results and those of the 95% confidence interval on predictions obtained from the classical approach.

---

[2] `Bulk_ESS` and `Tail_ESS` are two separate measures of effective sample size, with one (`Bulk`) using samples from the centre of the distribution of the samples and the other (`Tail`) using samples from the tails. We will primarily focus on `Bulk_ESS` here, but if `Tail_ESS` is low when `Bulk_ESS` is not low, which may happen in heavy-tailed distributions, this may indicate convergence problems with the sampler.

Latent variable formulation

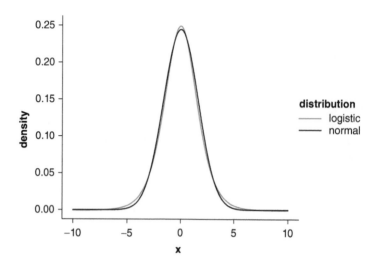

Figure 10.5 The standard logistic distribution whose mean is equal to 0 and whose scale parameter is 1. This is compared to a normal distribution centred at 0 and with standard deviation 1.63

Before we leave binary logistic regression, as we will see when considering other forms of logistic regression, it is useful to consider an alternative formulation of it. In this, y_i is a binary variable that takes the value 1 or 0 if a latent variable η_i is respectively above or below 0. More precisely, this latent variable formulation is as follows:

$$\text{for } i \in 1,\ldots,n, \ y_i = \begin{cases} 1, & \text{if } \eta_i \geq 0, \\ 0, & \text{if } \eta_i < 0, \end{cases}$$

$$\eta_i \sim \text{logistic}(\phi_i, 1).$$

Here, η_i is a latent or unobserved random variable that is distributed as a *logistic distribution* whose mean is $\phi_i = \beta_0 + \sum_{k=1}^{K} \beta_k x_{ki}$ and whose scale parameter is equal to 1. The logistic distribution, displayed in Figure 10.5, is a bell-shaped distribution. It is roughly similar to a normal distribution centred with a standard deviation of 1.63. The probability density of the logistic distribution with location parameter ϕ_i and scale parameter equal to 1 is as follows:

$$P(\eta_i \mid \phi_i) = \frac{e^{-(\eta_i - \phi_i)}}{(1 + e^{-(\eta_i - \phi_i)})^2}.$$

The cumulative distribution function of the logistic distribution is as follows:

$$P(\eta_i \leq \omega \mid \phi_i) = \int_{-\infty}^{\omega} \frac{e^{-(\eta_i - \phi_i)}}{(1 + e^{-(\eta_i - \phi_i)})^2} d\eta_i = \frac{1}{1 + e^{-(\omega - \phi_i)}}.$$

From this cumulative distribution function, we can see that the probability that y_i will take the value 1 is equal to the probability that η_i takes a value of greater than 0:

$$P(y_i=1)=1-P(\eta_i<0\mid\phi_i)=1-\frac{1}{1+e^{\phi_i}}=\frac{1}{1+e^{-\phi_i}}=\mathrm{ilogit}(\phi_i).$$

Hence, we see that the latent variable formulation is identical to original definitions of the logistic regression given above, where the probability that y_i takes the value 1 was equal to θ_i, which was equal to $1/(1+e^{-\phi_i})$.

From this formulation, we see the correspondence between the normal linear model and the binary logistic regression. In the normal linear model, the outcome variable y_i is modelled as a normal distribution whose mean increases or decreases as a linear function of a set of predictors. In the binary logistic regression, a latent variable η_i is modelled as a logistic distribution whose mean increases or decreases as a linear function of a set of predictors, and the binary outcome variable y_i takes the value 0 or 1 depending on whether this latent variable is, respectively, above or below 0. We can see the latent variable as an evidence variable, and so the distribution over it as a distribution over the evidence in favour of one outcome value, $y_i=1$, or another, $y_i=0$. In Figure 10.6 we show three logistic distributions over a latent variable η. We can view these as three different representations of the degree of evidence for the value of the outcome variable.

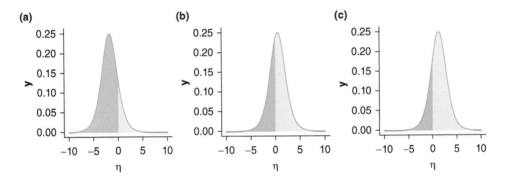

Figure 10.6 Three logistic distributions with means (a) −1.75, (b) 0.50, (c) 1.25. Each distribution can seen as a representation of the degree of evidence of the outcome variable y_i taking the value 1. As the distribution shifts to the right, there is more evidence in favour of the outcome variable taking the value 1. In these three distributions, the probabilities that the outcome is 1 correspond to 0.15, 0.62, and 0.78

Probit regression

Having seen the latent variable formulation of binary logistic regression, we are able to more easily understand *probit regression*, which is a regression model that is very closely related to binary logistic regression. In probit regression, each outcome variable y_i is binary. They are modelled as follows:

$$\text{for } i \in 1,\ldots,n,\ y_i=\begin{cases}1,\ \text{if } \eta_i\geq 0,\\ 0,\ \text{if } \eta_i<0,\end{cases}$$

$$\eta_i \sim N(\phi_i,1),$$

where $N(\phi_i, 1)$ is a normal distribution with mean ϕ_i and standard deviation 1, and where ϕ_i is a linear function of a set of predictors, just as above. By direct analogy with the latent variable formulation of the binary logistic model, in the probit model, the probability that y_i will take the value 1 is equal to the probability that η_i takes a value greater than 0, which is as follows:

$$P(y_i=1)=1-P(\eta_i<0\,|\,\phi_i)=1-\Phi(-\phi_i)=\Phi(\phi_i),$$

where Φ is the cumulative distribution function in a standard normal distribution. In other words, in binary logistic regression we have

$$P(y_i=1)=\text{logit}(\phi_i),$$

while in probit regression we have

$$P(y_i=1)=\Phi(\phi_i),$$

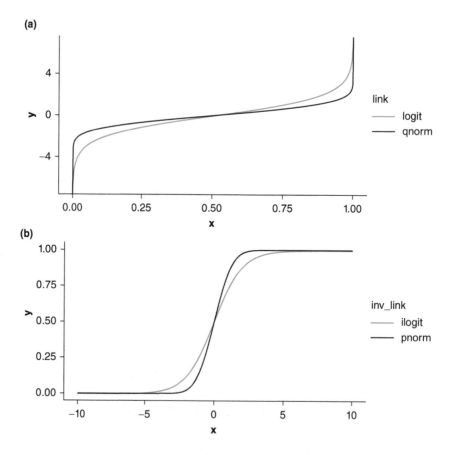

Figure 10.7 (a) Logit and quantile functions of the normal distribution, which are the link functions of binary logistic regression and probit regression, respectively. (b) Inverse logit and cumulative distribution functions of the normal distribution

Thus, binary logistic regression and probit differ by their *link* function. It is the log odds or logit function in the case of logistic regression, and it is the *quantile function* Φ^{-1}, which is the inverse of the cumulative distribution function Φ of the standard normal, in the case of probit regression. These functions are shown in Figure 10.7.

We can perform a probit regression in R using `glm` just as in the case of binary logistic regression, but using `link = 'probit'` instead of `link = 'logit'`. In the following, using the `affairs_df` data, we model how the probability of being a cheater varies as a function of the `rating` variable:

```
affairs_probit <- glm(cheater ~ rating,
                      family = binomial(link = 'probit'),
                      data = affairs_df)
```

In probit regression, statistical inference is identical to binary logistic regression: the maximum likelihood estimator of the regression coefficients is found by iteratively reweighted least squares, whose sampling distribution is asymptotically normal. The coefficients summary table for `affairs_probit` is as follows:

```
summary(affairs_probit)$coefficients
#>                Estimate Std. Error   z value     Pr(>|z|)
#> (Intercept)   0.4817451 0.19788927  2.434418 1.491577e-02
#> rating       -0.3031677 0.05023335 -6.035187 1.587786e-09
```

Comparing this to the set of coefficients for the binary logistic regression, we see that there are considerable differences in the scale of the coefficients and their standard errors, though with the z test statistics being very similar:

```
glm(cheater ~ rating, family = binomial(link = 'logit'), data = affairs_df) %>%
  summary() %>%
  extract2('coefficients')
#>                Estimate Std. Error   z value     Pr(>|z|)
#> (Intercept)   0.8253902 0.32548132  2.535907 1.121566e-02
#> rating       -0.5082193 0.08468845 -6.001046 1.960510e-09
```

Importantly, in the probit regression, we do not interpret the coefficients in terms of odds ratios. In probit regression, the coefficient gives the change in mean of the (unit-variance) normal distribution over the latent variable in the probit model for every unit change in the predictor. For example, in the `affairs_probit` model, the coefficient for `rating` is –0.303. This means that as `rating` increases by one unit, the mean of the normal distribution over the latent variable increases by –0.303 units. See Figure 10.8 for illustration.

Prediction in probit regression works like prediction in binary logistic regression, but we apply the inverse of the link function, which is the standard normal, to convert from the value of the linear predictor ϕ_i to the probability that $y_i = 1$. We can do this using the `predict` and `add_predictions` functions using `type = 'response'` as follows:

```
tibble(rating = seq(5)) %>%
  add_predictions(affairs_probit, type = 'response')
#> # A tibble: 5 x 2
#>   rating   pred
#>    <int>  <dbl>
#> 1      1  0.571
#> 2      2  0.450
#> 3      3  0.334
#> 4      4  0.232
#> 5      5  0.151
```

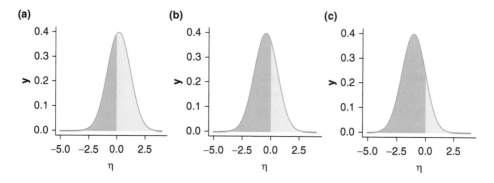

Figure 10.8 The distribution over the latent variable in the probit regression model that models the probability of being a cheater as a function of `rating`, for values of `rating` equal to (a) 1, (b) 3, and (c) 5. When `rating` increases by one unit, the mean of the normal distribution increases by –0.30, which is the value of the coefficient for `rating`. The areas shaded to the right are the corresponding probabilities that the outcome variable y_i takes the value 1, which in this case means the probability that the person has had an extramarital affair. These probabilities are 0.57, 0.33, and 0.15, respectively.

10.3 Ordinal logistic regression

In ordinal regression, the outcome variable y_i is an ordinal variable. An ordinal variable can be seen as a categorical variable where the values have an order. Alternatively, an ordinal variable can be seen as a numerical variable whose values can be ordered but not defined on a metric space. For example, the values of y_i could be low, medium, high. Here, there is a natural order: low < medium < high. However, we do not necessarily believe that difference between low and medium is the same as between medium and high. We may represent low, medium and high by {0,1,2}. We treat these values as essentially labels, just as we would do with a categorical variable, though with the understanding that $0 < 1 < 2$.

In a regression model with an ordinal outcome variable, we model the probability distribution over the outcome variable and how it changes with a set of predictor variables. For example, consider the World Values Survey data that is available in `carData` under the name `WVS`:

```
library(carData)
wvs_df <- as_tibble(WVS)
wvs_df
#> # A tibble: 5,381 x 6
#>    poverty      religion degree country   age gender
#>    <ord>        <fct>    <fct>  <fct>    <int> <fct>
#>  1 Too Little   yes      no     USA         44 male
#>  2 About Right  yes      no     USA         40 female
#>  3 Too Little   yes      no     USA         36 female
#>  4 Too Much     yes      yes    USA         25 female
#>  5 Too Little   yes      yes    USA         39 male
#>  6 About Right  yes      no     USA         80 female
#>  7 Too Much     yes      no     USA         48 female
#>  8 Too Little   yes      no     USA         32 male
#>  9 Too Little   yes      no     USA         74 female
#> 10 Too Little   yes      no     USA         30 male
#> # ... with 5,371 more rows
```

In this data set, we have a variable `poverty` that represents the responses to the survey question 'Do you think that what the government is doing for people in poverty in this country is about the right amount, too much, or too little?' This variable takes the values `Too Little`, `About Right`, and `Too Much`. Note that this variable is an ordered factor:

```
wvs_df %>% pull(poverty) %>% class()
#> [1] "ordered" "factor"
```

In other words, it is a factor variable whose levels have a defined order, namely the following:

```
wvs_df %>% pull(poverty) %>% levels()
#> [1] "Too Little"  "About Right" "Too Much"
```

In addition to `poverty`, we have predictor variables such as `religion`, `gender` and `age`. In Figure 10.9, we group the `age` variable into five quintiles, and plot the numbers of male and female respondents in these quintiles who choose each of the three responses to the `poverty` question. From this data, we can see that as age increases, the number of people responding `Too Little` declines, and the numbers of people responding either `About Right` or `Too Much` increase. We also see that more females than males respond `Too Little`, and usually more males than females respond `About Right` or `Too Much`.

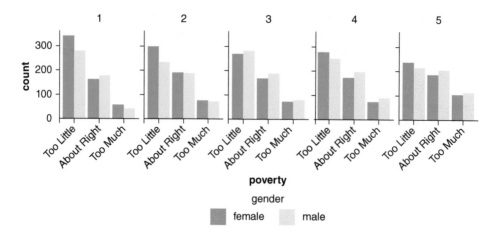

Figure 10.9 Frequencies of choosing each possible response to a survey question about what the government is doing about poverty, as a function of the respondent's age quintile (lower means younger) and gender

One of the most widely used regression models for ordinal outcome data is the *proportional odds* or *cumulative logit* logistic regression model. In the case of an ordinal outcome variable with three values, $y_i \in \{1,2,3\}$ this model is equivalent to the latent variable formulation of the binary logistic regression that we saw above, but with two thresholds rather than one, which are known as *cutpoints*, and denoted here by ζ_1 and ζ_2. In particular, the model is as follows:

$$\text{for } i \in 1,\ldots,n, \ y_i = \begin{cases} 3, & \text{if } \eta_i \geq \zeta_2, \\ 2, & \text{if } \zeta_1 \leq \eta_i < \zeta_2, \\ 1, & \text{if } \eta_i < \zeta_1, \end{cases}$$

$$\eta_i \sim \text{logistic}(\phi_i, 1).$$

From this we have

$$P(y_i \leq 2) = \int_{\infty}^{\zeta_1} P(\eta_i \mid \phi_i) d\eta_i = \frac{1}{1 + e^{-(\zeta_2 - \phi_i)}} = \text{ilogit}(\zeta_2 - \phi_i),$$

$$P(y_i \leq 1) = \int_{\infty}^{\zeta_0} P(\eta_i \mid \phi_i) d\eta_i = \frac{1}{1 + e^{-(\zeta_1 - \phi_i)}} = \text{ilogit}(\zeta_1 - \phi_i),$$

and so $P(y_i = 3) = 1 - P(y_i \leq 2) = 1 - \text{ilogit}(\zeta_2 - \phi_i)$. Stating these cumulative probabilities in terms of log odds, we have

$$\log\left(\frac{P(y_i \leq 2)}{1 - P(y_i \leq 2)}\right) = \zeta_2 - \phi_i,$$

$$\log\left(\frac{P(y_i \leq 1)}{1 - P(y_i \leq 1)}\right) = \zeta_1 - \phi_i.$$

In general, for an ordinal variable with J levels, $1,...,J$, for $j \in 1,...,J-1$, we have

$$\log\left(\frac{P(y_i \leq j)}{1-P(y_i \leq j)}\right) = \zeta_j - \phi_i,$$

where $\zeta_1 < \zeta_2 < ... < \zeta_{J-1}$.

The value of ϕ_i is, as it was used above, the linear sum of the predictors, $\phi_i = \beta_0 + \sum_{k=1}^{K}\beta_k x_{ki}$. Having the intercept term β_0 as well the cutpoints $\zeta_1, \zeta_2,...,\zeta_{J-1}$ means that neither are identifiable because we could add any constant value to β_0 and subtract this value from each of $\zeta_1, \zeta_2,...,\zeta_{J-1}$ to obtain an identical model. For this reason, we must constrain the values of either β_0 or the cutpoints. One possibility is to constrain ζ_1 to equal 0. Another, which is more common, is to constrain β_0 to equal to 0. In other words, $\phi_i = \sum_{k=1}^{K}\beta_k x_{ki}$.

The general model for the cumulative logit ordinal logistic regression is therefore the following:

$$\text{for } i \in 1,...,n, \; y_i = \begin{cases} J, & \text{if } \eta_i \geq \zeta_{J-1}, \\ J-1, & \text{if } \zeta_{J-2} \leq \eta_i < \zeta_{J-1}, \\ \cdots, \\ 2, & \text{if } \zeta_1 \leq \eta_i < \zeta_2, \\ 1, & \text{if } \eta_i < \zeta_1, \end{cases}$$

$$\eta_i \sim \text{logistic}(\phi_i, 1), \qquad \phi_i = \sum_{k=1}^{K}\beta_k x_{ki}.$$

For any $1 \leq j \leq J-1$ we have

$$P(y_i = j) = P(y_i \leq j) - P(y_i \leq j-1)$$
$$= \text{ilogit}(\zeta_j - \phi_i) - \text{ilogit}(\zeta_{j-1} - \phi_i).$$

Ordinal logistic regression in R

There are many options to perform ordinal logistic regression in R. For example, ordinal is an excellent package for many variants of the ordinal logistic model, including and especially mixed effects ordinal models. Here, however, we will use the polr function from the MASS package which is simple and easy to use and perfectly illustrates ordinal logistic regression as we have described it thus far. We will use it here to model how the poverty variable varies as a function of age and gender in the wvs_df data set:

```
library(MASS)
M_ord <- polr(poverty ~ age + gender, data = wvs_df)
summary(M_ord)
#> Call:
#> polr(formula = poverty ~ age + gender, data = wvs_df)
#>
#> Coefficients:
```

```
#>                    Value Std. Error t value
#> age              0.01308  0.001523    8.592
#> gendermale      0.15411   0.052139    2.956
#>
#> Intercepts:
#>                               Value    Std. Error t value
#> Too Little|About Right       0.6762    0.0779      8.6794
#> About Right|Too Much         2.4123    0.0850     28.3761
#>
#> Residual Deviance: 10656.41
#> AIC: 10664.41
```

In the summary, the values of the coefficients for the linear sum are listed under Coefficients, while the values of ζ_1 and ζ_2 are listed under Intercepts. The maximum likelihood estimates of the coefficients and the cutpoints are calculated using a general-purpose optimization based on the Broyden–Fletcher–Goldfarb–Shanno (BFGS) algorithm, and we estimate the standard error of these estimates using the Hessian matrix of the log likelihood function evaluated at its maximum. Note that the summary output does not contain p-values for either the coefficients or the cutpoints. The authors of MASS (Venables and Ripley, 2002) state that the exact distribution of the estimates is not known and so exact p-values cannot be calculated. Alternative methods for evaluating coefficients, based on likelihood ratio tests, are recommended instead. However, as an approximation, albeit one to be used cautiously, we can treat the sampling distribution for these estimates as normally distributed and so treat the t value as a standard normal statistic and calculate the p-value using the cumulative normal distribution.

Although, as we will see, we can use R's generic predict function to calculate the probabilities for the poverty outcome variable for any given set of values for the predictor variables, it

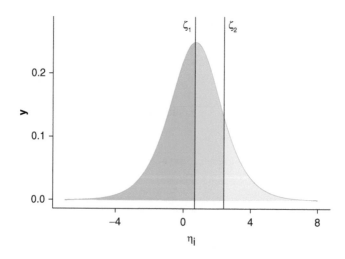

Figure 10.10 The partitioning of the area under the logistic distribution whose mean is $\phi_i = 0.73$, which is the value of the linear predictor for a median-aged male. The two cutpoints are $\zeta_1 = 0.68$ and $\zeta_2 = 2.41$

is instructive to do this manually. For example, for a male of median age (for men), which is 44 years in this data set, the value of ϕ_i is

$$\phi_i = 0.0131 \times 44 + 0.1541 \times 1$$
$$= 0.73.$$

The log odds that this median-aged male responds that poverty is 'Too Little' and poverty is 'Too Little' or 'About Right' are, respectively, $\zeta_1 - \phi_i = 0.676 - 0.73 = -0.05$ and $\zeta_2 - \phi_i = 2.412 - 0.73 = 1.68$. These correspond to cumulative probabilities of $\mathrm{ilogit}(\zeta_1 - \phi_i) = 0.49$ and $\mathrm{ilogit}(\zeta_2 - \phi_i) = 0.84$. Thus, the probability that the median-aged male responds 'Too Much', 'About Right', or 'Too Little' is, respectively, $1 - \mathrm{ilogit}(\zeta_2 - \phi_i) = 0.16$, $\mathrm{ilogit}(\zeta_2 - \phi_i) - \mathrm{ilogit}(\zeta_1 - \phi_i) = 0.36$, or $\mathrm{ilogit}(\zeta_1 - \phi_i) = 0.49$. The logistic distribution corresponding to $\phi = 0.73$ is shown in Figure 8.10.

Using the predict or add_predictions functions, we can easily calculate the probabilities over the outcome variable's values for any given set of values of the predictor variables. To do so, we must use the type = 'probs' argument when calling these functions:

```
new_data <- expand_grid(age = c(25, 50, 75),
                        gender = c('male', 'female'))
add_predictions(new_data, M_ord, type='probs')
#> # A tibble: 6 x 3
#>   age gender pred[,"Too Little"] [,"About Right"] [,"Too Much"]
#>   <dbl> <chr>              <dbl>            <dbl>         <dbl>
#> 1  25 male               0.549            0.325         0.127
#> 2  25 female             0.586            0.303         0.111
#> 3  50 male               0.467            0.366         0.167
#> 4  50 female             0.505            0.347         0.147
#> 5  75 male               0.387            0.395         0.218
#> 6  75 female             0.424            0.383         0.193
```

Odds ratios

We can interpret the values of the cutpoints and regression coefficients in terms of odds ratios. We saw above that, for all $j \in 1,\ldots,J$,

$$\log\left(\frac{P(y_i \le j)}{1 - P(y_i \le j)}\right) = \zeta_j - \phi_i.$$

From this, for any two cutpoints $j' > j$, we have

$$\log\left(\frac{P(y_i \le j')}{1 - P(y_i \le j')}\right) - \log\left(\frac{P(y_i \le j)}{1 - P(y_i \le j)}\right) = (\zeta_{j'} - \phi_i) - (\zeta_j - \phi_i)$$

$$\log\left(\frac{P(y_i \le j')}{1 - P(y_i \le j')} \middle/ \frac{P(y_i \le j)}{1 - P(y_i \le j)}\right) = \zeta_{j'} - \zeta_j$$

$$\frac{P(y_i \le j')}{1 - P(y_i \le j')} \middle/ \frac{P(y_i \le j)}{1 - P(y_i \le j)} = e^{\zeta_{j'} - \zeta_j}.$$

From this, we see that $e^{j'-j}$ is the odds ratio corresponding to the probabilities $P(y_i < j')$ and $P(y_i < j)$. In other words, the ratio of the odds that $y_i < j'$ to the odds that $y_i < j$, for any j'

and j, is $e^{j'-j}$. Note that this will hold for any value of ϕ and so holds for any set of values of the predictors.

To interpret the coefficients, consider increasing the value of any predictor k by one unit. If $\phi_i = \sum_{k=1}^{K} \beta_k x_{ki}$, if we increase x_{ki} by one unit, we have $\phi_i' = \sum_{k}^{K} \beta_k x_{ki} + \beta_k = \phi + \beta_k$. For any value j of the ordinal outcome variable, we have

$$\log\left(\frac{P(y_i \le j \mid \phi')}{1-P(y_i \le j \mid \phi')}\right) - \log\left(\frac{P(y_i \le j \mid \phi)}{1-P(y_i \le j \mid \phi)}\right) = (\zeta_j - \phi_i') - (\zeta_j - \phi_i) = \beta_k$$

$$\log\left(\frac{P(y_i \le j \mid \phi')}{1-P(y_i \le j \mid \phi')} \middle/ \frac{P(y_i \le j \mid \phi)}{1-P(y_i \le j \mid \phi)}\right) = e^{\beta_k}.$$

In other words, e^{β_k} is the factor by which the odds that $y_i \le j$, for any $j \in 1,...,J-1$, increases for every one-unit increase in predictor variable k.

Bayesian ordinal logistic regression

We can perform a Bayesian counterpart of the cumulative logit ordinal logistic regression model as follows:

```
M_ord_bayes <- brm(poverty ~ age + gender,
                   family = cumulative(link = 'logit'),
                   data = wvs_df)
```

As we can see, all we need specify is that the family is `cumulative` and the link is `logit`, and these are in fact the defaults. By using all the other default settings, we use four chains, each with 2000 iterations, and where the initial 1000 iterations are discarded, leading to 4000 total samples. The default priors in this model are seen in the following table:

```
prior_summary(M_ord_bayes)
#>                            prior       class        coef group resp dpar nlpar bound
#> 1                                          b
#> 2                                          b         age
#> 3                                          b  gendermale
#> 4       student_t(3, 0, 2.5)     Intercept
#> 5                                  Intercept                1
#> 6                                  Intercept                2
```

This tells us that the cutpoints have non-standard Student t-distributions and the coefficients have uniform distributions as priors.

The summary of the posterior distribution of the regression coefficients and the cutpoints is as follows:

```
summary(M_ord_bayes)$fixed
#>                  Estimate    Est.Error   l-95% CI    u-95% CI     Rhat Bulk_ESS Tail_ESS
#> Intercept[1]  0.67727898  0.079030844  0.51950236  0.83619957  0.9996931     4446     2906
```

```
#> Intercept[2]  2.41520856 0.086665885 2.24881906 2.58807770 1.0001916    4349    2911
#> age          0.01311032 0.001544013 0.01007376 0.01612692 0.9995239     4880    2799
#> gendermale   0.15377660 0.050522945 0.05841022 0.25147234 1.0018276     3474    2918
```

Clearly, the means of these estimates are very similar to those estimated using maximum likelihood estimation above.

 ## Categorical (multinomial) logistic regression

Thus far, we have considered regression models where the outcome variable is either a binary variable or an ordinal variable. If the outcome variable is a categorical variable with more than two values, we can use an extension of logistic regression that we will refer to here as *categorical logistic regression*, but which is more also commonly referred to as *multinomial logistic regression*. We prefer the term 'categorical' for this model, given that the outcome variable is a categorical variable. We prefer to reserve the term 'multinomial logistic regression' for models where the outcome variable is a vector of counts of the number of observations of each of a set of categorically distinct outcomes.

In categorical logistic regression, for each observation, our outcome variable can be represented as $y_i \in 1,...,J$, where $1,...,J$ are J categorically distinct values. For example, in a hypothetical pre-election voting preference poll in the UK, people might be asked if they will vote Conservative, Labour, Liberal Democrat, Green, Other. We might then model how the probability distribution over these choices varies by UK region, age, gender, etc.

In categorical logistic regression, we model the log of the probability of each category relative to an arbitrarily chosen baseline category as a linear function of the predictors. Setting the baseline category to $j = 1$, then for each $j = 2,...,J$, we have

$$\log\left(\frac{P(y_i=j)}{P(y_i=1)}\right) = \phi_{ji} = \beta_{j0} + \sum_{k=1}^{K} \beta_{jk}x_{ki},$$

and, by necessity, we have

$$\log\left(\frac{P(y_i=1)}{P(y_i=1)}\right) = \phi_{1i} = 0.$$

In other words, we model the log of the probability that $y_i = j$ relative to $y_i = 1$ as a linear function of the predictors. Note that we have a separate linear model with different coefficients for each $j > 2$. We can interpret the log ratio

$$\log\left(\frac{P(y_i=j)}{P(y_i=1)}\right) = \phi_{ji}$$

in one of two ways: either directly as simply the log of a relative probabilities, or as the log odds of the conditional probability that $y_i = j$ given that we know that $y_i = j$ or $y_i = 1$.

From this model, we have

$$P(y_i=j) = e^{\phi_{ji}} P(y_i=1),$$

and given that, by definition, we have

$$\sum_{j=1}^{J} P(y_i = j) = 1,$$

we therefore have the following:

$$P(y_i = 1) \sum_{j=1}^{J} e^{\phi_{ji}} = 1$$

$$P(y_i = 1) = \frac{1}{\sum_{j=1}^{J} e^{\phi_{ji}}}.$$

This leads to the following model of the probabilities of each of the J values of the outcome variable:

$$P(y_i = j) = \frac{e^{\phi_{ji}}}{\sum_{j=1}^{J} e^{\phi_{ji}}}.$$

Given that $e^{\phi_{1i}} = 1$, it is more common to write this as

$$P(y_i = j) = \frac{e^{\phi_{ji}}}{1 + \sum_{j=2}^{J} e^{\phi_{ji}}}.$$

Categorical logistic regression using R

We have many options for doing categorical logistic regression in R. One simple option is to use `multinom` from the `nnet` package.

To illustrate this model, we will use a data set based on a subset of the `weather_check` data set in the `fivethirtyeight` package:

```
weather_df <- read_csv('data/weather.csv')
weather_df
#> # A tibble: 916 x 2
#>      weather             age
#>      <chr>               <chr>
#>  1 app                 30 - 44
#>  2 app                 18 - 29
#>  3 app                 30 - 44
#>  4 app                 30 - 44
#>  5 app                 30 - 44
#>  6 app                 18 - 29
#>  7 weather_channel 30 - 44
#>  8 weather_channel 30 - 44
#>  9 app                 30 - 44
#> 10 internet            18 - 29
#> # ... with 906 more rows
```

In this data, people were asked what was their source of information about the weather (`weather`). This had values `app` for a mobile device app, `internet` for general internet search, `tv` for local television, `weather_channel` for the weather channel, and `other` for other sources such as newspapers. The respondents' ages were listed as the age groups 18 - 29, 30 - 44, 45 - 59, 60+. The frequency of each response for each age group is as follows:

```
weather_df %>%
  group_by(age, weather) %>%
  tally() %>%
  pivot_wider(id_cols = age, names_from = 'weather', values_from = n)
#> # A tibble: 4 x 6
#> # Groups:   age [4]
#>   age          app internet other    tv weather_channel
#>   <chr>      <int>    <int> <int> <int>           <int>
#> 1 18 - 29       92       35     9    14              26
#> 2 30 - 44      108       26     8    34              28
#> 3 45 - 59      108       33    21    67              49
#> 4 60+           80       36    33    74              35
```

From this, we see a relative increase with age for television, particularly local television, and a relative decline with age for mobile apps.

The following code models the probability distribution of the different weather news sources. First, we will set the age and source variables as factors, which will order the results to make them easier to interpret:

```
weather_df %<>%
  mutate(age = factor(age, levels = c('18 - 29', '30 - 44', '45 - 59', '60+')),
         weather = factor(weather, levels = c('other', 'app', 'internet', 'tv',
  'weather_channel'))
  )
```

For simplicity, we will begin with a model that has a single constant term:

```
M_cat <- multinom(weather ~ 1, data = weather_df)
```

The values of coefficients are estimated using a BFGS-based optimization of the log of the likelihood, as was also done above in the case of ordinal logistic regression. Note that weather == 'other' is the baseline against which all other weather news sources are compared.

```
summary(M_cat)
#> Call:
#> multinom(formula = weather ~ 1, data = weather_df)
#>
#> Coefficients:
#>                 (Intercept)
#> app               1.6981849
#> internet          0.6047535
#> tv                0.9789591
#> weather_channel   0.6644412
#>
```

```
#> Std. Errors:
#>                       (Intercept)
#> app                    0.1290746
#> internet               0.1475638
#> tv                     0.1391899
#> weather_channel        0.1460458
#>
#> Residual Deviance: 2656.368
#> AIC: 2664.368
```

In order to appreciate the meaning of the coefficients, it helps to calculate the probability distribution over the five options using the formula

$$P(y_i = j) = \frac{e^{\phi_{ji}}}{1 + \sum_{j=2}^{J} e^{\phi_{ji}}}.$$

For $j \in 2,3,4,5$, for all i, $\phi_{ji} = \beta_j$, while $\phi_{1i} = 0$.

```
phi <- rbind(other = 0, coef(M_cat)) %>% as_tibble(rownames = 'id') %>%
deframe()
phi
#>            other            app         internet            tv weather_channel
#>        0.0000000      1.6981849        0.6047535     0.9789591       0.6644412
```

From this, the corresponding probabilities are as follows:

```
exp(phi)/sum(exp(phi))
#>            other            app         internet            tv weather_channel
#>       0.07751992     0.42357044       0.14192354    0.20633355      0.15065255
```

We can now use `age` as a predictor as follows:

```
M_cat_2 <- multinom(weather ~ age, data = weather_df)
summary(M_cat_2)
#> Call:
#> multinom(formula = weather ~ age, data = weather_df)
#>
#> Coefficients:
#>                        (Intercept) age30 - 44 age45 - 59     age60+
#> app                      2.3244935  0.2782843 -0.6867980 -1.4389520
#> internet                 1.3580627 -0.1793077 -0.9059785 -1.2710166
#> tv                       0.4417131  1.0052996  0.7185451  0.3658706
#> weather_channel          1.0607799  0.1920954 -0.2133944 -1.0019129
#>
#> Std. Errors:
#>                        (Intercept) age30 - 44 age45 - 59     age60+
```

```
#> app                 0.3492458   0.5062047   0.4229123 0.4059266
#> internet            0.3737301   0.5505876   0.4664758 0.4446970
#> tv                  0.4272412   0.5804809   0.4950589 0.4757649
#> weather_channel     0.3867369   0.5570370   0.4664723 0.4565528
#>
#> Residual Deviance: 2589.321
#> AIC: 2621.321
```

To calculate the probability distributions over weather, rather than doing so manually, we can use predict or add_predictions with type = 'probs':

```
tibble(age = c('18 - 29', '30 - 44', '45 - 59', '60+')) %>%
  add_predictions(M_cat_2, type='probs')
#> # A tibble: 4 x 2
#>     age     pred[,"other"] [,"app"] [,"internet"] [,"tv"] [,"weather_channel"]
#>     <chr>            <dbl>    <dbl>         <dbl>   <dbl>                 <dbl>
#> 1 18 - 29         0.0511    0.523        0.199   0.0795                0.148
#> 2 30 - 44         0.0392    0.529        0.127   0.167                 0.137
#> 3 45 - 59         0.0755    0.388        0.119   0.241                 0.176
#> 4 60+             0.128     0.310        0.140   0.287                 0.136
```

These predicted probabilities are shown in Figure 10.11. What is clear here is that we see that mobile device apps decline, and local television increases, as age increases.

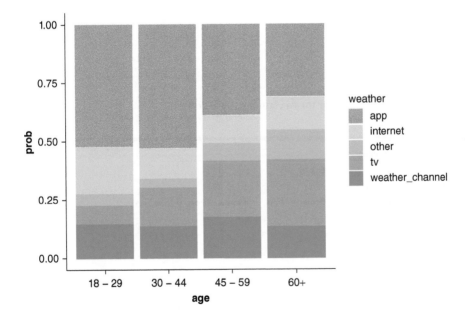

Figure 10.11 Probability distribution over different sources of weather news as a function of age group

Bayesian categorical logistic regression

We can perform a Bayesian version of the model in the previous section using `brm` with
`family = categorical(link = 'logit')`:

```
M_cat_bayes <- brm(weather ~ age,
                   family = categorical(link = 'logit'),
                   data = weather_df)
```

The summary output is formatted in long format, as opposed to the wide format seen above
with `multinom`:

```
summary(M_cat_bayes)$fixed
```

	Estimate	Est.Error	l-95% CI	u-95% CI	Rhat	Bulk_ESS	Tail_ESS
#> muapp_Intercept	2.3681937	0.3456028	1.7258611	3.07083399	1.001543	1189	1776
#> muinternet_Intercept	1.3900579	0.3663141	0.7067108	2.11194174	1.002289	1254	1776
#> mutv_Intercept	0.4512383	0.4309300	-0.3917491	1.27590583	1.002892	1354	2070
#> muweatherchannel_Intercept	1.0932604	0.3841146	0.3496441	1.84002398	1.001782	1270	1752
#> muapp_age30M44	0.2616396	0.5025598	-0.6793213	1.27311116	1.002277	1365	1775
#> muapp_age45M59	-0.7249908	0.4203623	-1.5574123	0.09504825	1.002130	1411	2088
#> muapp_age60P	-1.4856187	0.4025590	-2.2626366	-0.71451503	1.002007	1398	2053
#> muinternet_age30M44	-0.1979753	0.5396543	-1.2392054	0.87074519	1.001707	1514	1848
#> muinternet_age45M59	-0.9472343	0.4579603	-1.8520972	-0.05810783	1.002109	1548	2495
#> muinternet_age60P	-1.3162809	0.4376876	-2.1836292	-0.47309898	1.001769	1539	2293
#> mutv_age30M44	1.0099413	0.5791534	-0.1202443	2.16831825	1.001522	1398	2075
#> mutv_age45M59	0.7091732	0.4936254	-0.2720899	1.67957014	1.002489	1545	2207
#> mutv_age60P	0.3526576	0.4755895	-0.5502657	1.30851344	1.003199	1483	2250
#> muweatherchannel_age30M44	0.1734805	0.5555558	-0.9085286	1.27491266	1.000852	1411	1817
#> muweatherchannel_age45M59	-0.2450089	0.4601888	-1.1567660	0.64638359	1.002080	1476	2001
#> muweatherchannel_age60P	-1.0443862	0.4569367	-1.9499843	-0.17354991	1.001375	1584	2110

We can rearrange the posterior mean estimates as follows:

```
fixef(M_cat_bayes) %>%
  as_tibble(rownames = 'var') %>%
  dplyr::select(var, Estimate) %>%
  separate(var, into = c('var', 'age')) %>%
  pivot_wider(var, names_from = age, values_from = Estimate)
#> # A tibble: 4 x 5
#>   var               Intercept age30M44 age45M59 age60P
#>   <chr>                 <dbl>    <dbl>    <dbl>  <dbl>
#> 1 muapp                  2.37    0.262   -0.725  -1.49
#> 2 muinternet             1.39   -0.198   -0.947  -1.32
#> 3 mutv                   0.451   1.01     0.709   0.353
#> 4 muweatherchannel       1.09    0.173   -0.245  -1.04
```

Just as above, with the Bayesian model, we can perform predictions using `predict` or `add_
predictions`. Note that here we do not need to use `type = 'probs'`.

```
tibble(age = c('18 - 29', '30 - 44', '45 - 59', '60+')) %>%
  add_predictions(M_cat_bayes)
#> # A tibble: 4 x 2
#>   age     pred[,"P(Y = other)"] [,"P(Y = app)"] [,"P(Y = internet)"] [,"P(Y = tv)"] [,"P(Y = weather_channel)"]
#>   <chr>                  <dbl>           <dbl>                <dbl>          <dbl>                      <dbl>
#> 1 18 - 29               0.0455           0.535                0.193          0.082                      0.144
#> 2 30 - 44               0.0365           0.523                0.134          0.164                      0.144
#> 3 45 - 59               0.0707           0.394                0.124          0.235                      0.176
#> 4 60+                   0.135            0.309                0.138          0.283                      0.135
```

Generalized Linear Models for Count Data

Introduction

In the previous chapter, we covered logistic regression models, each of which are types of generalized linear model. Generalized linear models are regression models that extend the normal linear model so that it can model data that is not normally distributed around a mean that is a linear function of predictors. The general definition of a generalized linear model is as follows. Assuming that our data is

$$(y_1, \bar{x}_1), (y_2, \bar{x}_2), \ldots, (y_i, \bar{x}_i), \ldots, (y_n, \bar{x}_n),$$

where $y_1, \ldots, y_n$ are the observed values of an outcome variable and $\bar{x}_1, \ldots, \bar{x}_n$ are the corresponding vectors of predictors and each $\bar{x}_i = [x_{1i}, x_{2i}, \ldots, x_{ki}, \ldots, x_{Ki}]$, a generalized linear model of this data is

$$y_i \sim D(\theta_i, \psi), \quad f(\theta_i) = \beta_0 + \sum_{k=1}^{K} \beta_k x_{ki}, \quad \text{for } i \in 1, \ldots, n,$$

where $D(\theta_i, \psi)$ is some probability distribution centred at θ_i and with an optional parameter ψ that controls the scale or shape of the distribution, and f is a monotonic (and thus invertible) *link* function. As an example, we've already seen that the binary logistic regression is

$$y_i \sim \text{Bernoulli}(\theta_i), \quad \text{logit}(\theta_i) = \beta_0 + \sum_{k=1}^{K} \beta_k x_{ki}, \quad \text{for } i \in 1, \ldots, n.$$

Thus, in this case, $D(\theta_i, \psi)$ is Bernoulli(θ_i), so there is no optional ψ parameter, and the link function is the logit function.

In this chapter, we will cover some other generalized linear models, and ones that are specifically designed to model *count* data. Count data simply tells us the number of times something has happened. Examples of count data are widespread: the number of car accidents that occur in a region each day (or week, year, etc.); the number of extramarital affairs that a married person has in a year; the number of times a person visits a doctor in a year. Count data must be non-negative integers: they can take zero values, but not negative values, and they must be whole numbers. Although there are many models that could be considered under this general topic, we will cover just some of them, but ones that are very widely used or otherwise very useful. In particular, we will cover Poisson regression, negative binomial regression, and so-called zero-inflated count models, particularly zero-inflated Poisson regression.

 Poisson regression

In Poisson regression, our data is

$$(y_1, \bar{x}_1), (y_2, \bar{x}_2), \ldots, (y_i, \bar{x}_i), \ldots, (y_n, \bar{x}_n),$$

as described above, where each $y \in 0, 1, 2, \ldots$. In other words, y_i takes a non-negative integer value which specifically represents a *count*, or the number of times something happened a period of time.

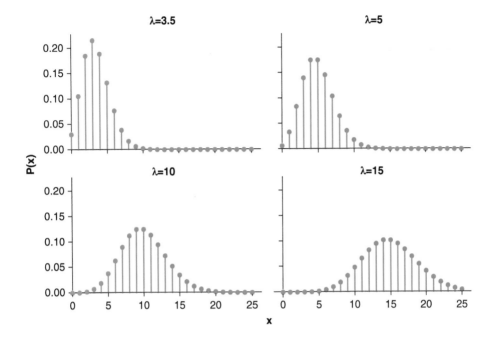

Figure 11.1 Poisson distributions with different values of the parameter λ

In order to deal with count outcome data in a regression framework, we must first use an appropriate probability distribution as a model of the outcome variable. A default choice here is the *Poisson distribution*. A Poisson distribution is a probability distribution over non-negative integers. If x is a Poisson random variable, it takes values $k \in 0,1,\ldots$, and the probability that $x = k$ is

$$\text{Poisson}(x = k|\lambda) = P(x = k|\lambda) = \frac{e^{-\lambda}\lambda^k}{k!}.$$

Here, λ is the Poisson distribution's single parameter, usually known as the *rate* or the *rate parameter*. It gives the average value of the random variable x. Unlike the values of x, which must be non-negative integers, λ is not constrained to be an integer, it is just constrained to be non-negative. In Figure 11.1, we plot four different Poisson distributions, which differ from one another by the value of λ.

The Poisson distribution can be understood as the limit of a binomial distribution. The binomial distribution is also a distribution over counts but where there are a fixed number of times, known as the number of *trials* and signified by n, an event can happen, known as a *success*, and where the probability of a success, denoted by θ, is independent and identical on each trial. As the number of trials in a binomial distributions tends to infinity, but $\theta \cdot n$ is held constant, the distribution tends to a Poisson distribution with parameter $\lambda = \theta \cdot n$. This phenomenon is illustrated in Figure 11.2.

This relationship between the binomial distribution and the Poisson distribution helps us to understand why the Poisson distribution commonly occurs in the natural and social world. In situations where events occur independently with fixed probability θ, when the number

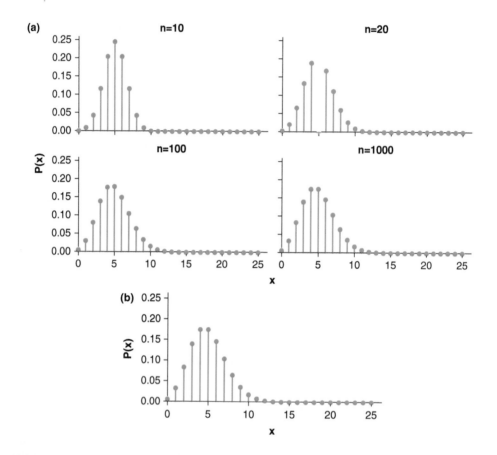

Figure 11.2 (a) Binomial distributions with increasing values of n, which denote the number of trials, but where $\theta \cdot n$ is held constant at $\theta \cdot n = 5$. (b) A Poisson distribution with $\lambda = 5$

of opportunities for these events to occur is very large but where θ is very low, the distribution of the number of times an event occurs tends to a Poisson distribution. As an example, the number of occasions when a car accident can occur on any given day is extremely high, yet the probability of an accident occurring on any one of these occasions is very low, and so the resulting distribution of the number of car accidents is well described by a Poisson distribution.

In Poisson regression, we assume that each y_i is distributed as a Poisson distribution with parameter λ_i and that λ_i is determined by a function of $\vec{x}_i$. For analogous reasons to what occurs in the case of logistic regression, we cannot have each λ_i being a linear function of $\vec{x}_i$ because each λ_i is constrained to take non-negative values only, and in general, if we allow λ_i to be a linear function of $\vec{x}_i$, we cannot guarantee that it will be constrained to be non-negative. For this reason, again analogously to what happened in the logistic regression, we can transform λ_i to another variable ϕ_i, which can take any value in $\mathbb{R}$, and then treat ϕ_i as the linear function of $\vec{x}_i$. For this, as before, we need an invertible *link function*

$f : \mathbb{R}^+ \mapsto \mathbb{R}$ that can map any value of λ_i to a unique value of ϕ, and vice versa. For this case, we have a number of options for f, but the default choice is simply the natural logarithm function:

$$\phi_i = f(\lambda_i) = \log(\lambda_i).$$

As such, our Poisson regression model is as follows:

$$y_i \sim \text{Poisson}(\lambda_i), \quad f(\lambda_i) = \log(\lambda_i) = \beta_0 + \sum_{k=1}^{K} \beta_k x_{ki}, \quad \text{for } i \in 1,\dots,n,$$

which is identical to

$$y_i \sim \text{Poisson}(\lambda_i), \quad \lambda_i = e^{\phi_i}, \quad \phi_i = \beta_0 + \sum_{k=1}^{K} \beta_k x_{ki}, \quad \text{for } i \in 1,\dots,n.$$

Returning to the general definition of generalized linear models:

$$y_i \sim D(\theta_i, \psi), \quad f(\theta_i) = \beta_0 + \sum_{k=1}^{K} \beta_k x_{ki}, \quad \text{for } i \in 1,\dots,n,$$

we see that in the case of Poisson regression, $D(\theta_i, \psi)$ is $\text{Poisson}(\lambda_i)$, where we follow conventions and use λ_i instead of θ_i as the location parameter, where there is no optional ψ parameter, and where the f link function is the log function.

As an example of a problem seemingly suited to a Poisson regression model, we will use the following data set:

```
lbw_df <- read_csv('data/lbw.csv')
lbw_df
#> # A tibble: 189 x 11
#>       X1     low smoke   race    age    lwt    ptl     ht     ui    ftv    bwt
#>    <dbl>   <dbl> <dbl>  <dbl>  <dbl>  <dbl>  <dbl>  <dbl>  <dbl>  <dbl>  <dbl>
#>  1     1       0     0      2     19    182      0      0      1      0   2523
#>  2     2       0     0      3     33    155      0      0      0      3   2551
#>  3     3       0     1      1     20    105      0      0      0      1   2557
#>  4     4       0     1      1     21    108      0      0      1      2   2594
#>  5     5       0     1      1     18    107      0      0      1      0   2600
#>  6     6       0     0      3     21    124      0      0      0      0   2622
#>  7     7       0     0      1     22    118      0      0      0      1   2637
#>  8     8       0     0      3     17    103      0      0      0      1   2637
#>  9     9       0     1      1     29    123      0      0      0      1   2663
#> 10    10       0     1      1     26    113      0      0      0      0   2665
#> # ... with 179 more rows
```

This gives us data relating to infants with low birth weight. One variable in this data set is ftv, which is the number of visits to the doctor by the mother in her first trimester of pregnancy. In Figure 11.3 we show the distribution of value of ftv as function of the age of the mother, which we have grouped by age tercile. There, we see that the distribution shifts upwards as we go from the first to the third age tercile. Thus, we could model ftv as a Poisson variable whose mean varies as a function of age, as well as other potentially interesting explanatory variables.

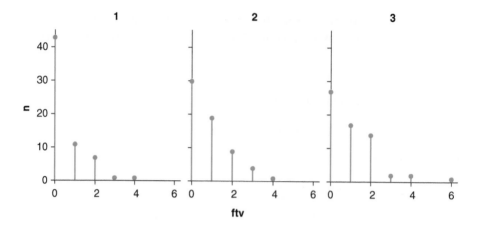

Figure 11.3 The number of visits to a doctor in the first trimester of pregnancy for each age tercile

In general, in Poisson regression, we model a count response variable as a Poisson distribution whose parameter λ varies by a set of explanatory variables. More precisely, we model the log of λ as a linear function of the explanatory variables.

Maximum likelihood estimation

Just as with linear and logistic regression, our estimate of the value of $\vec{\beta}$ is the maximum likelihood estimator. The likelihood function is

$$P(\vec{y} \mid X, \vec{\beta}) = \prod_{i=1}^{n} P(y_i \mid \vec{x}_i, \vec{\beta})$$

$$= \prod_{i=1}^{n} e^{-\lambda_i} \frac{\lambda_i^{y_i}}{y_i!},$$

where

$$\lambda_i = e^{\vec{x}_i \vec{\beta}} = e^{\beta_0 + \sum_{k=1}^{K} \beta_k x_{ki}},$$

$\vec{y} = [y_1, y_2, \ldots, y_n]^\top$, $\vec{\beta} = [\beta_0, \beta_1, \ldots, \beta_K]^\top$ and X is an n by $K + 1$ matrix whose ith row is $[1, \vec{x}_i^\top]$. The logarithm of the likelihood is then defined as

$$L(\vec{\beta} \mid \vec{y}, X) = \log P(\vec{y} \mid X, \vec{\beta})$$

$$= \sum_{i=1}^{n} (\lambda_i + y_i \log(\lambda_i) - \log(y_i!)).$$

The maximum likelihood estimator is the value of $\vec{\beta}$ that maximizes this function. We obtain this by calculating the gradient of $L(\vec{\beta} \mid \vec{y}, X)$ with respect to $\vec{\beta}$, setting this to equal zero, and solving for $\vec{\beta}$. As with the logistic regression, this is done using the Newton–Raphson method, and the resulting estimator is labelled $\hat{\beta}$. Similarly to the case of logistic regression, the asymptotic sampling distribution of $\hat{\beta}$ is

$$\hat{\beta} \sim N(\vec{\beta},(X^{\intercal}WX)^{-1}),$$

where W is an $n \times n$ diagonal matrix whose ith element is

$$\hat{\lambda_i} = e^{\vec{x_i}\hat{\beta}}.$$

This entails that

$$\frac{\hat{\beta_k} - \beta_k}{\sqrt{(X^{\intercal}WX)^{-1}_{kk}}} \sim N(0,1),$$

where $\sqrt{(X^{\intercal}WX)^{-1}_{kk}}$ is the standard error term $\hat{se}_k$. This is the basis for hypothesis testing and confidence intervals for the coefficients.

Poisson regression using R

Here, we will use the `lbw_df` data set and model `ftv` as a function of the mother's age:

```
lbw_m <- glm(ftv ~ age,
             data = lbw_df,
             family = poisson(link = 'log')
)
```

Note that we use `glm` just as we did with logistic regression, but use `family = poisson(link = 'log')`. It would have been sufficient to use `family = poisson()`, given that the `link = 'log'` is the default.

First, let us look at $\hat{\beta}$, the maximum likelihood estimators for $\vec{\beta}$, which we can do with `coef`:

```
(estimates <- coef(lbw_m))
#> (Intercept)          age
#> -1.41276618  0.04929373
```

From this, we see that the logarithm of the average number of visits increases by 0.049 for every extra year of age. This entails that the average number of visits increases by a factor of $e^{0.049} = 1.051$ with every extra year of marriage.

Now, let us turn to hypothesis tests and confidence intervals. We can begin by examining the coefficients table:

```
summary(lbw_m)$coefficients
#>                Estimate Std. Error   z value     Pr(>|z|)
#> (Intercept) -1.41276618 0.35717007 -3.955444 7.639269e-05
#> age          0.04929373 0.01404709  3.509178 4.494944e-04
```

Let us first confirm that this standard error is calculated as we have stated above:

```
library(modelr)
X <- model_matrix(lbw_df, ~ age) %>%
     as.matrix()
```

```
W <- diag(lbw_m$fitted.values)
```

```
std_err <- solve(t(X) %*% W %*% X) %>% diag() %>% sqrt()
std_err
#> (Intercept)             age
#>  0.35717008   0.01404709
```

The z value is the statistic for the hypothesis that each $\hat{\beta}_k$ is zero, which is easily verified as the maximum likelihood estimate divided by its corresponding standard error:

```
(z_stat <- estimates / std_err)
#> (Intercept)             age
#>   -3.955444       3.509178
```

The corresponding *p*-values are given by `Pr(>|z|)`, which is also easily verified as the probability of getting a value as extreme as or more extreme than z value in a standard normal distribution, as we see in the following:

```
2 * pnorm(abs(z_stat), lower.tail = F)
#>  (Intercept)             age
#> 7.639269e-05 4.494944e-04
```

The 95% confidence interval for age is as follows:

```
confint.default(lbw_m, parm='age')
#>            2.5 %       97.5 %
#> age 0.02176194 0.07682551
```

We can confirm that this is $\hat{\beta}_k \pm \hat{\text{se}}_k \cdot \zeta_{(0.975)}$:

```
estimates['age'] + c(-1, 1) * std_err['age'] * qnorm(0.975)
#> [1] 0.02176194 0.07682551
```

Prediction in Poisson regression

Given a vector of new values of the predictor variables $\bar{x}_i$, and given the estimates $\hat{\beta}$, the predicted value of the log of the rate is

$$\hat{\phi}_i = \bar{x}_i \hat{\beta},$$

and so the predicted value of the rate is obtained by applying the inverse of the log link function,

$$\hat{\lambda}_i = e^{\hat{\phi}_i} = e^{\bar{x}_i \hat{\beta}}.$$

For example, the predicted log of the rate for mothers aged 20, 25, 30 is easily calculated as follows:

```
estimates['(Intercept)'] + estimates['age'] * c(20, 25, 30)
#> [1] -0.42689167 -0.18042304   0.06604559
```

And so the predicted rate for these women is

```
exp(estimates['(Intercept)'] + estimates['age'] * c(20, 25, 30))
#> [1] 0.6525342 0.8349169 1.0682754
```

As we've seen above, these calculations are easier using the predict function. There, we have the option of obtaining these predictions on the linear scale, the default, or by using type = 'response' to give predictions after the inverse of the link function is applied:

```
lbw_df_new <- tibble(age = c(20, 25, 30))
predict(lbw_m, newdata = lbw_df_new)
#>           1            2            3
#> -0.42689167 -0.18042304   0.06604559
predict(lbw_m, newdata = lbw_df_new, type = 'response')
#>          1           2           3
#> 0.6525342 0.8349169 1.0682754
```

We also saw that these predictions can be even more easily performed using add_predictions:

```
lbw_df_new %>%
  add_predictions(lbw_m)
#> # A tibble: 3 x 2
#>     age     pred
#>   <dbl>    <dbl>
#> 1    20   -0.427
#> 2    25   -0.180
#> 3    30    0.0660
lbw_df_new %>%
  add_predictions(lbw_m, type='response')
#> # A tibble: 3 x 2
#>     age  pred
#>   <dbl> <dbl>
#> 1    20 0.653
#> 2    25 0.835
#> 3    30 1.07
```

Given that $\phi_i = \vec{x}_i \hat{\beta}$ and that $\hat{\beta}$ has the multivariate normal distribution stated above, ϕ_i will have the following sampling distribution:

$$\hat{\phi}_i \sim N(\vec{x}_i \vec{\beta}, \underbrace{\vec{x}_i (X^T W X)^{-1} \vec{x}_i^T})._{\widehat{se}_k^2}$$

From this, the 95% confidence interval on $\phi_i = \vec{x}_i \vec{\beta}$ is

$$\hat{\phi}_i \pm \widehat{se}_t \cdot \zeta_{(0.975)}.$$

Using the se.fit = TRUE option in predict, we can obtain the standard errors for prediction:

```
predict(lbw_m, newdata = lbw_df_new, se.fit = T)$se.fit
#>          1          2          3
#> 0.10547495 0.08172315 0.10999279
```

We can verify that these are calculated as stated above:

```
x_iota <- model_matrix(lbw_df_new, ~ age) %>%
  as.matrix()
```

```
x_iota %*% solve(t(X) %*% W %*% X) %*% t(x_iota) %>%
  diag() %>%
  sqrt()
#> [1] 0.10547495 0.08172315 0.10999279
```

We can use the standard errors to calculate the confidence intervals on the predicted log of the rates:

```
predictions <- predict(lbw_m, newdata = lbw_df_new, se.fit = T)
cbind(
  predictions$fit - predictions$se.fit * qnorm(0.975),
  predictions$fit + predictions$se.fit * qnorm(0.975)
)
#>            [,1]         [,2]
#> 1 -0.6336188 -0.22016457
#> 2 -0.3405975 -0.02024862
#> 3 -0.1495363  0.28162749
```

Applying the inverse of the link function, we can get confidence intervals on the predicted rates:

```
cbind(
  predictions$fit - predictions$se.fit * qnorm(0.975),
  predictions$fit + predictions$se.fit * qnorm(0.975)
) %>% exp()
#>           [,1]        [,2]
#> 1 0.5306680 0.8023867
#> 2 0.7113452 0.9799550
#> 3 0.8611072 1.3252849
```

Model comparison

Just as we did in the case of binary logistic regression, we can compare nested Poisson regression models using a likelihood ratio test. If we have one model with a set of K predictors and another model with $K' < K$ predictors, the null hypothesis when comparing these two models is that the coefficients of all the $K - K'$ predictors in the larger model but not in the smaller one are simultaneously zero. In other words, if the larger model $\mathcal{M}_1$ has K predictors whose coefficients are $\beta_0, \beta_1, ..., \beta_{K'}, ..., \beta_K$, and the smaller model $\mathcal{M}_0$ has K' predictors whose coefficients are $\beta_0, \beta_1, ..., \beta_{K'}$, then the null hypothesis is

$$\beta_{K'+1} = \beta_{K'+2} = ... = \beta_K = 0.$$

We can test this null hypothesis by comparing the maximum of the likelihood of the model with the K predictors to that of the model with the K' predictors. Under this null hypothesis, –2 times the log of the likelihood ratio of the models will be distributed as $\chi^2_{K-K'}$.

As an example, consider the model whose predictor variables are age, low, and smoke, where low is a binary variable that indicates if the birth weight of the newborn infant was low (low = 1) or not (low = 0), and smoke is a binary variable that indicates if the pregnant woman was a smoker (smoke = 1) or not (smoke = 0). We will denote this model with three predictors by $\mathcal{M}_1$. We can then compare this to the model with age alone, which we will denote by $\mathcal{M}_0$. The null hypothesis when comparing $\mathcal{M}_1$ and $\mathcal{M}_0$ is that the coefficients for low and smoke are both zero. To test this null hypothesis, we calculate $\mathcal{L}_1$ and $\mathcal{L}_0$, which are the likelihoods of $\mathcal{M}_1$ and $\mathcal{M}_1$ evaluated at their maximum. According to the null hypothesis,

$$-2\log\left(\frac{\mathcal{L}_0}{\mathcal{L}_1}\right) \sim \chi^2_2,$$

where the number of degrees of freedom, 2, is the difference between the number of predictors in $\mathcal{M}_1$ and $\mathcal{M}_0$. We can calculate –2 times the log of the likelihood by the difference of the deviances:

$$\Delta_{\mathcal{D}} = -2\log\left(\frac{\mathcal{L}_0}{\mathcal{L}_1}\right) = \mathcal{D}_0 - \mathcal{D}_1,$$

where $\mathcal{D}_0 = -2\log\mathcal{L}_0$ and $\mathcal{D}_1 = -2\log\mathcal{L}_1$.

Model $\mathcal{M}_1$ with age, low, and smoke as predictors is as follows:

```
lbw_m_1 <- glm(ftv ~ age + low + smoke,
                 family = poisson(link = 'log'),
                 data = lbw_df)
```

Model $\mathcal{M}_0$ with just age is lbw_m from above. The deviances $\mathcal{D}_1$ and $\mathcal{D}_0$ are as follows:

```
deviance(lbw_m_1)
#> [1] 252.5803
deviance(lbw_m)
#> [1] 252.9566
```

The difference of these two deviances is

```
(delta_deviance <- deviance(lbw_m) - deviance(lbw_m_1))
#> [1] 0.3762127
```

By the null hypothesis, this Δ_D will be distributed as χ_2^2, and so the p-value is the probability of getting a value greater than Δ_D in a χ_2^2 distribution:

```
pchisq(delta_deviance, df = 2, lower.tail = F)
#> [1] 0.8285266
```

This null hypothesis test can be performed more easily with the generic anova function:

```
anova(lbw_m_1, lbw_m, test='Chisq')
#> Analysis of Deviance Table
#>
#> Model 1: ftv ~ age + low + smoke
#> Model 2: ftv ~ age
#>    Resid. Df Resid. Dev Df Deviance Pr(>Chi)
#> 1       185     252.58
#> 2       187     252.96 -2 -0.37621   0.8285
```

From this result, we cannot reject the null hypothesis that coefficients for low and smoke are simultaneously zero. Put less formally, the model with age, low, and smoke is not significantly better at predicting the ftv outcome variable than the model with age alone, and so we can conclude that low and smoke are not significant predictors of ftv, at least when age is known.

Bayesian approaches to Poisson regression

As was the case with linear and binary logistic regression models, the Bayesian approach to Poisson regression begins with an identical probabilistic model of the data to the classical approach. In other words, we assume

$$y_i \sim \text{Poisson}(\lambda_i), \quad \log(\lambda_i) = \beta_0 + \sum_{k=1}^{K} \beta_k x_{ki}, \quad \text{for } i \in 1,\dots,n,$$

but now our aim is to infer the posterior distribution over $\vec{\beta} = [\beta_0, \beta_1,\dots,\beta_K]^\top$:

$$P(\vec{\beta}\,|\,\vec{y},X) \propto \overbrace{P(\vec{y}\,|\,X,\vec{\beta})}^{\text{likelihood}}\,\overbrace{P(\vec{\beta})}^{\text{prior}}.$$

Just as was the case with binary logistic regression, there is no analytic solution to the posterior distribution, and so numerical methods are necessary. As we explained already, a powerful and general numerical method for this purpose is Markov chain Monte Carlo. Practically, the most powerful general-purpose MCMC Bayesian modelling software is the probabilistic programming language Stan, for which we have the extremely easy-to-use R interface package brms.

We perform a Bayesian Poisson regression model of the lbw data with outcome variable ftv and predictor age using brms as follows:

```
lbw_m_bayes <- brm(ftv ~ age,
                   family = poisson(link = 'log'),
                   data = lbw_df)
```

The priors are very similar to the prior used by default by the logistic regression analysis above:

```
prior_summary(lbw_m_bayes)
#>                      prior     class coef group resp dpar nlpar bound
#> 1                               b
#> 2                               b   age
#> 3 student_t(3, -2.3, 2.5) Intercept
```

A uniform prior is on the coefficient for `age` and a non-standard *t*-distribution is on the intercept term. Using these priors, again, just as in the binary logistic regression, by using the default settings, we use four chains, each with 2000 iterations, and where the initial 1000 iterations are discarded, leading to 4000 total samples from the posterior.

We can view the summary of the posterior distribution as follows:

```
summary(lbw_m_bayes)$fixed
#>            Estimate   Est.Error    l-95% CI    u-95% CI     Rhat Bulk_ESS Tail_ESS
#> Intercept -1.40625739 0.37027631 -2.15780630 -0.68461735 0.9998967     2459     2172
#> age        0.04864108 0.01451812  0.01959422  0.07733883 1.0003260     2695     2536
```

As we can see, the `Rhat` values close to 1 and the relatively high `ESS` values indicate that this sampler has converged and mixed well. As was the case with binary logistic regression, the mean and standard deviation of the posterior distribution very closely match the maximum likelihood estimator and the standard error of the sampling distribution. Likewise, the 95% highest posterior density interval closely matches the 95% confidence interval.

The posterior distribution over the predicted value of $\phi_i = \vec{x}_i \vec{\beta}$, where $\vec{x}_i$ is a vector of values of the predictors, can be obtained similarly to the case of binary logistic regression:

```
posterior_linpred(lbw_m_bayes, newdata = lbw_df_new) %>%
  as_tibble() %>%
  map_df(~quantile(., probs=c(0.025, 0.5, 0.975))) %>%
  as.matrix() %>%
  t() %>%
  as_tibble() %>%
  set_names(c('l-95% CI', 'prediction', 'u-95% CI')) %>%
  bind_cols(lbw_df_new, .)
#> # A tibble: 3 x 4
#>       age `l-95% CI` prediction `u-95% CI`
#>     <dbl>      <dbl>      <dbl>      <dbl>
#> 1      20     -0.650     -0.353     -0.168
#> 2      25     -0.431     -0.188      0.0558
#> 3      30     -0.235     -0.0356     0.259
```

As we can see, these are very close to the confidence intervals for predictions in the classical approach.

In addition to the posterior distribution over $\phi_i = \vec{x}_i \vec{\beta}$, we can also calculate the *posterior predictive distribution*, which is defined as follows:

$$P(y_i \mid \vec{x}_i, \vec{y}, X) = \int P(y_i \mid \vec{x}_i \vec{\beta}) \underbrace{P(\vec{\beta} \mid \vec{y}, X)}_{\text{posterior}} d\vec{\beta},$$

where

$$P(y_i | \vec{x}_i, \vec{\beta}) = \frac{e^{-\lambda_i} \lambda_i^{y_i}}{y_i!}, \quad \text{where } \lambda_i = e^{\phi_i}, \quad \phi_i = \vec{x}_i, \vec{\beta}.$$

The posterior predictive distribution gives a probability distribution over the counts 0, 1, 2, ..., just like a Poisson distribution, but it essentially *averages* over all possible values of $\vec{\beta}$ according to the posterior distribution.

Using Stan/brms, the posterior_predict function can be used to draw samples from the posterior predictive distribution: for each sample from the posterior:

```
pp_samples <- posterior_predict(lbw_m_bayes, newdata = lbw_df_new)
```

This returns a matrix of 4000 rows and three columns, where each element of each column is a sample from $P(y_i | \vec{x}_i, \vec{\beta})$, and each column represents the different values of age that we are making predictions about. We plot the histograms of these samples for each value of age in Figure 11.4.

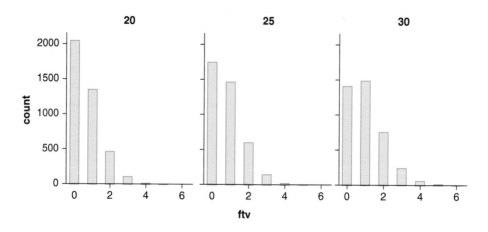

Figure 11.4 Posterior predictive distribution of the number of visits to the doctor by women of different ages

11.3 Negative binomial regression

We saw above that the mean of a Poisson distribution is equal to its rate parameter λ. As it happens, the variance of any Poisson distribution is also equal to λ. Therefore, in any Poisson distribution, as the mean increases, so too does the variance. We can see this in Figure 11.5. Likewise, if we draw samples from any Poisson distribution, the mean and variance should be approximately equal:

```
x <- rpois(25, lambda = 5)
c(mean(x), var(x), var(x)/mean(x))
```

```
#> [1] 5.4400000 5.4233333 0.9969363
x <- rpois(25, lambda = 3)
c(mean(x), var(x), var(x)/mean(x))
#> [1] 3.240000 3.440000 1.061728
```

Thus when modelling data as a Poisson distribution, the mean and the variance of the counts (conditional on the predictors) should be approximately equal. If the variance is much greater or much less than the mean, we say the data is *overdispersed* or *underdispersed*, respectively. Put more precisely, if the variance of a sample of values is greater or less than would be expected according to a given theoretical model, then we say the data is overdispersed or underdispersed, respectively.

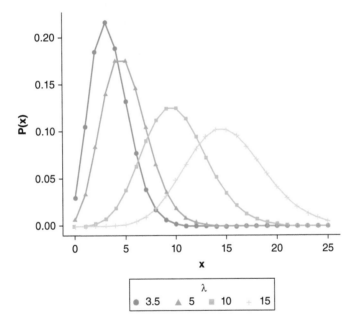

Figure 11.5 A series of Poisson distributions with increasing means. As the mean of the distribution increases, so too does the variance

Overdispersed data is quite a common phenomenon when using Poisson regression models. It occurs when the mean of the data being modelled by the Poisson distribution is relatively low, but the variance is not low. This is an example of model misspecification, and it will also usually lead to the underestimation of the standard errors in the regression model.

Let us consider the following data set:

```
biochemists_df <- read_csv('data/biochemist.csv')
biochemists_df
#> # A tibble: 915 x 6
#>    publications gender married children prestige mentor
#>           <dbl> <chr>  <chr>      <dbl>    <dbl>  <dbl>
```

```
#>  1           0 Men      Married       0    2.52      7
#>  2           0 Women    Single        0    2.05      6
#>  3           0 Women    Single        0    3.75      6
#>  4           0 Men      Married       1    1.18      3
#>  5           0 Women    Single        0    3.75     26
#>  6           0 Women    Married       2    3.59      2
#>  7           0 Women    Single        0    3.19      3
#>  8           0 Men      Married       2    2.96      4
#>  9           0 Men      Single        0    4.62      6
#> 10           0 Women    Married       0    1.25      0
#> # … with 905 more rows
```

In this data, we have counts of the number of articles published (`publications`) by PhD students in the field of biochemistry in the last three years. The distribution of these publications is shown in Figure 11.6. What is notable is that the variance of the counts is notably larger than the means, which we can see in the following:

```
publications <- biochemists_df %>% pull(publications)
var(publications)/mean(publications)
#> [1] 2.191358
```

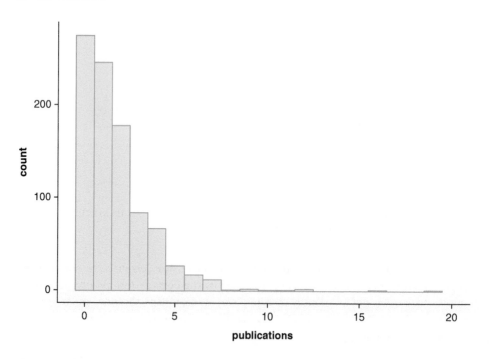

Figure 11.6 Histogram of the number of publications by PhD students in the field of biochemistry

Were we to model this data using a Poisson regression model, this would lead to the standard errors being underestimated. In the following, we use an intercept-only Poisson regression model with `publications` as the outcome variable. This effectively fits a Poisson distribution to the `publications` data:

```
Mp <- glm(publications ~ 1,
          family=poisson(link = 'log'),
          data = biochemists_df)
summary(Mp)$coefficients
#>             Estimate Std. Error  z value     Pr(>|z|)
#> (Intercept) 0.5264408 0.02540804 20.71945 2.312911e-95
```

The standard error, 0.025, is underestimated here.

One relatively easy solution to this problem is to use a so-called *quasi*-Poisson regression model. This is easily done with `glm` by setting the `family` to `quasipoisson` rather than `poisson`:

```
Mq <- glm(publications ~ 1,
          family=quasipoisson(link = 'log'),
          data = biochemists_df)
summary(Mq)$coefficients
#>             Estimate Std. Error  t value     Pr(>|t|)
#> (Intercept) 0.5264408 0.03761239 13.99647 1.791686e-40
```

Note that the standard error is now 0.038. The quasi-Poisson model calculates an *overdispersion parameter*, which is roughly the ratio of the variance to the mean, and multiplies the standard error by its square root. In this example, the overdispersion parameter is estimated to be 2.191. This value is returned in the summary output and can be obtained directly as follows:

```
summary(Mq)$dispersion
#> [1] 2.191389
```

We can see that this is very close to the ratio of the variance of `publications` to the `mean`:

```
var(publications)/mean(publications)
#> [1] 2.191358
```

The square root of this is 1.48. Multiplying this by the standard error of the Poisson model leads to 0.038.

An alternative and more principled approach to modelling overdispersed count data is to use a *negative binomial regression* model. As we will see, there are close links between the Poisson and negative binomial model, but for simplicity, we can see the negative binomial distribution as similar to a Poisson distribution, but with an additional dispersion parameter.

Negative binomial distribution

A negative binomial distribution is a distribution over non-negative integers. To understand the negative binomial distribution, we start with the binomial distribution, which we've encountered already. The binomial distribution gives the number of successes in a fixed number of trials, when the probability of a success on each trial is a fixed probability and all trials are independent. For example, if we have a coin whose probability of coming up heads is θ, then the number of heads in a sequence of n flips will follow a binomial distribution. In this example, an outcome of heads is regarded as a success and each flip is a trial. The probability mass function for a binomial random variable y is

$$\text{Binomial}(y=k\,|\,n,\theta) = P(y=m\,|\,n,\theta) = \binom{n}{m}\theta^m(1-\theta)^{n-m}.$$

In Figure 11.7, we show a binomial distribution where $n = 25$ and $\theta = 0.75$.

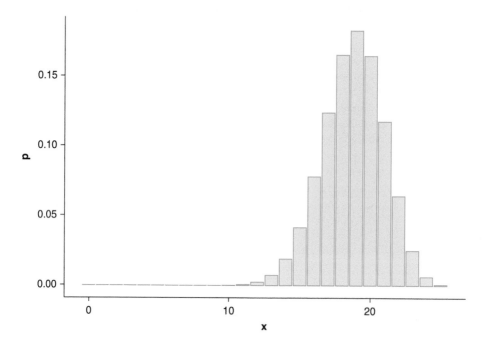

Figure 11.7 Binomial distribution with $n = 25$ and $\theta = 0.75$

By contrast to a binomial distribution, a *negative* binomial distribution gives the probability distribution over the number of *failures* before r successes in a set of independent binary outcome (success or failure) trials where the probability of a success is, as before, a fixed constant θ. Again consider the coin flipping scenario. The negative binomial distribution tells the probability of observing any number of tails (failures) before r heads (successes) occur. For example, in Figure 11.8, we show a set of binomial distributions, each giving the probability distribution over the number of failures (e.g. tails) that occur before we observe r successes (e.g. heads), when the probability of a success is θ, for different values of r and θ.

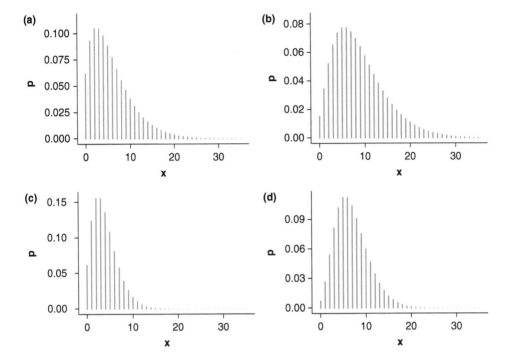

Figure 11.8 Negative binomial distributions with parameters (a) $r = 2$ and $\theta = 0.25$, (b) $r = 3$ and $\theta = 0.25$, (c) $r = 4$ and $\theta = 0.5$, and (d) $r = 7$ and $\theta = 0.5$

The probability mass function for a negative binomial random variable y, with parameters r and θ, is

$$\text{NegBinomial}(y = k \mid r, \theta) = P(y = k \mid r, \theta) = \binom{r+k-1}{k} \theta^r (1-\theta)^k,$$

or more generally

$$\text{NegBinomial}(y = k \mid r, \theta) = P(x = k \mid r, \theta) = \frac{\Gamma(r+k)}{\Gamma(r)k!} \theta^r (1-\theta)^k,$$

where $\Gamma()$ is a gamma function (note that $\Gamma(n) = (n-1)!$). In the negative binomial distribution, the mean of the distribution is

$$\mu = \frac{1-\theta}{\theta} \times r,$$

which we can rearrange as

$$\theta = \frac{r}{r+\mu},$$

and so we can generally parameterize the distribution by μ and r.

A negative binomial distribution is equivalent to a weighted sum of Poisson distributions. We illustrate this in Figure 11.9, where we show an average of four different Poisson distributions.

More precisely, the negative binomial distribution with parameters r and θ is an infinite mixture of Poisson distributions with all possible values of λ from 0 to ∞ and where the weighting distribution is a gamma distribution with shape parameter r and scale parameter $s = \theta/(1 - \theta)$:

$$\text{NegBinomial}(y = k * r, \theta) = \int_0^\infty \text{Poisson}(y = k * \lambda)\text{Gamma}\left(\lambda * \alpha = r, s = \frac{\theta}{1-\theta}\right)d\lambda.$$

We have seen that a Poisson distribution arises when there are a large number of opportunities for an event to happen but a low probability of it happening on any one of those opportunities. Given that the negative binomial is a weighted average of Poisson distributions, we can now see that it arises from a similar process to the Poisson distribution, but where there is a probability distribution (specifically a gamma distribution) over the probability of the event happening on any one opportunity.

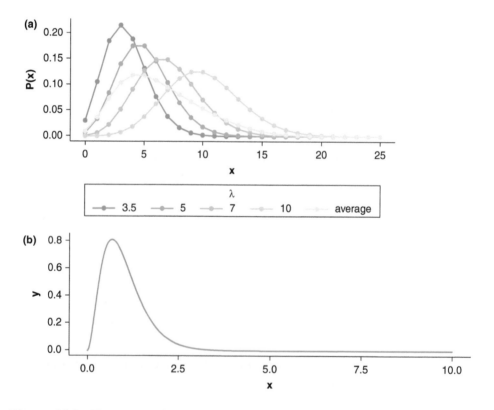

Figure 11.9 The negative binomial distribution is an infinite weighted sum of Poisson distributions, where the weighting distribution is a gamma distribution. (a) A set of four different Poisson distributions and their (unweighted) average. (b) A gamma distribution with shape parameter $r = 2$ and scale parameter $s = \theta/(1 - \theta)$, where $\theta = 0.25$

Negative binomial regression

In negative binomial regression, we have observed counts $y_1,...,y_n$, and a set of predictor variable vectors $\bar{x}_1,...,\bar{x}_n$, where $\bar{x}_i = [x_{1i}, x_{2i},..., x_{ki},..., x_{Ki}]$, and our model of this data is

$$y_i \sim \text{NegBinomial}(\mu_i, r), \quad \log(\mu_i) = \beta_0 + \sum_{k=1}^{K} \beta_k x_{ki}, \quad \text{for } i \in 1, \ldots, n.$$

In other words, our probability distribution for outcome variable y_i is a negative binomial distribution whose mean is μ_i, and which has an additional parameter r, whose value is a fixed but unknown constant. The link function is, as in the case of the Poisson model, the natural logarithm, and so we model the natural logarithm of μ_i as a linear function of the K predictors.

In R, we perform negative binomial regression using the `glm.nb` function from the MASS package, and we use `glm.nb` very similarly to how we have used other regression functions in R such as `lm` and `glm`. For example, we perform the intercept-only negative binomial regression on the `publication` data from `biochemists_df` as follows:

```
library(MASS)
Mnb <- glm.nb(publications ~ 1, data = biochemists_df)
```

Note that, unlike the case of `glm`, we do not need to specify a `family` in `glm.nb`. It is assumed that the distribution is a negative binomial. We can optionally change the link function, but its default value is `link = log`.

The inferred value of the parameter r, as it appeared in our formulae above, is obtained as the value of `theta` from the model:

```
r <- Mnb$theta
r
#> [1] 1.706205
```

The coefficients for the regression model are obtained as per usual:

```
summary(Mnb)$coefficients
#>              Estimate Std. Error  z value     Pr(>|z|)
#> (Intercept) 0.5264408 0.03586252 14.67942 8.734017e-49
```

From this, we can see that, for all i, μ_i is

$$\mu = e^{0.526} = 1.693.$$

Using the relationship between the probability θ and μ and r from above, we have

$$\theta = \frac{r}{r + \mu} = \frac{1.706}{1.706 + 1.693} = 0.502.$$

In other words, our model (using no predictor variables) of the distribution of the number of publications by PhD students in biochemistry is estimated to be a negative binomial distribution with parameters $\theta = 0.502$ and $r = 1.706$. This distribution is shown in Figure 11.10.

Now let us use the negative binomial regression model with predictors. Specifically, we will use `gender` as the predictor of the average of the distribution of the number of publications:

```
Mnb1 <- glm.nb(publications ~ gender, data=biochemists_df)
summary(Mnb1)$coefficients
#>                   Estimate Std. Error   z value      Pr(>|z|)
#> (Intercept)     0.6326491 0.04716825 13.412604 5.101555e-41
#> genderWomen    -0.2471766 0.07203652 -3.431268 6.007661e-04
```

Prediction in negative binomial regression works exactly as in Poisson regression. We can extract the estimates of the coefficients using `coef`:

```
estimates <- coef(Mnb1)
```

In this model, the two values for `gender` are `Men` and `Women`, with `Men` being the base level of the binary dummy code that corresponds to `gender` in the regression. Thus, the predicted log of the mean of number of publications for men is 0.633 and for women is 0.633 + (–0.247) = 0.386, and so the predicted means for men and women are $e^{0.633} = 1.883$ and $e^{0.633 - 0.247} = 1.47$, respectively. This prediction can be made more easily using the `predict` or `add_predictions` functions. For example, to get the predicted logs of the means, we do the following:

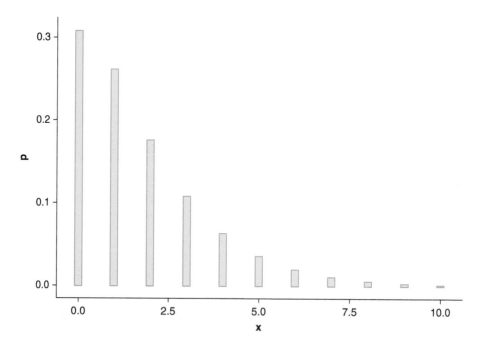

Figure 11.10 Negative binomial distribution with parameters $\theta = 0.502$ and $r = 1.706$. This is the estimated model of the distribution of the number of publications by PhD students in biochemistry

```
tibble(gender = c('Men', 'Women')) %>%
  add_predictions(Mnb1)
#> # A tibble: 2 x 2
#>    gender  pred
```

```
#>    <chr>  <dbl>
#> 1 Men     0.633
#> 2 Women   0.385
```

The predicted means can be obtained as follows:

```
tibble(gender = c('Men', 'Women')) %>%
  add_predictions(Mnb1, type= 'response')
#> # A tibble: 2 x 2
#>    gender   pred
#>    <chr>    <dbl>
#> 1 Men       1.88
#> 2 Women     1.47
```

The negative binomial distributions corresponding to these means are shown in Figure 11.11. In a negative binomial regression, for any predictor k, e^{β_k} has the same interpretation as it would have in a Poisson regression, namely the factor by which the mean of the outcome variable increases for a unit change in the predictor. The coefficient corresponding to gender is -0.247, and so $e^{-0.247} = 0.781$ is the factor by which the mean of the number of number of publications increases as we go from mean to women. Obviously, this is a value less than 1, and so we see that the mean decreases as we go from men to women.

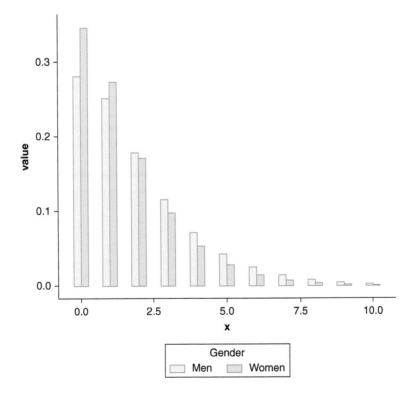

Figure 11.11 Estimated negative binomial distributions of the number of publications by male and female PhD students in biochemistry

As in the case of logistic and Poisson regression, we estimate the coefficients using maximum likelihood estimation. In addition, we estimate the value of *r* using maximum likelihood estimation. Once we have the maximum likelihood estimate for all the parameters, we can calculate the log of the likelihood function as its maximum, or the deviance, which is –2 times the log likelihood. In `glm.nb`, the value of log of the likelihood can be obtained with `logLik`:

```
logLik(Mnb1)
#> 'log Lik.' -1604.082 (df=3)
```

The deviance is not the value reported as `deviance` in the summary output, nor by using the function `deviance`. Instead, we multiply the log likelihood by –2, or equivalently use the negative of the value of the `twologlik` attribute of the model:

```
c(-2 * logLik(Mnb1), -Mnb1$twologlik)
#> [1] 3208.165 3208.165
```

We can compare nested negative binomial regressions using the generic `anova` function as we did with logistic regression or Poisson regression. For example, here we compare models Mnb and `Mnb1`:

```
anova(Mnb, Mnb1)
#> Likelihood ratio tests of Negative Binomial Models
#>
#> Response: publications
#>       Model      theta Resid. df    2 x log-lik.    Test    df LR stat.         Pr(Chi)
#> 1         1 1.706205       914        -3219.873
#> 2 gender 1.760904       913        -3208.165 1 vs 2     1 11.70892 0.0006220128
```

This layout is not the same as when we used `glm`-based models. However, it is easy to verify that the value of `LR stat.` is the difference of the deviance of the two models:

```
deviances <- -c(Mnb$twologlik, Mnb1$twologlik)
deviances
#> [1] 3219.873 3208.165
deviances[1] - deviances[2]
#> [1] 11.70892
```

Thus we have

$$\Delta_D = D_0 - D_1 = 3219.873 - 3208.165 = 11.709.$$

Under the null hypothesis of equal predictive power of the two models, Δ_D is distributed as a χ^2 distribution with degrees of freedom equal to the difference in the number of parameters between the two models, which is 1 in this case. Thus, the *p*-value for the null hypothesis is

```
pchisq(deviances[1] - deviances[2], df = 1, lower.tail = F)
#> [1] 0.0006220128
```

which is the value of `Pr(Chi)` reported in the `anova` table.

Bayesian negative binomial regression

Bayesian negative binomial regression can be done easily using `brms::brm`. We use it just like we used it above, and we need only indicate that the `family` is `negbinomial`. In the following model, we will use the predictors `gender`, `married`, `children`, `prestige` and `mentor` as predictors of `publications`. The variable `children` indicates the number of children the PhD student has, and so we will recode this as a binary variable indicating whether they have children or not. The variable `prestige` gives an estimate of the relative prestige of the department where the student is doing their PhD, and `mentor` indicates the number of publications by their PhD mentor in the past three years:

```
Mnb2_bayes <- brm(publications ~ gender + married + I(children > 0) + prestige
+ mentor,
                  data = biochemists_df,
                  family = negbinomial(link = "log"))
```

As we did above, we accepted all the defaults for this model. This means four chains, each of 2000 iterations, but with the first 1000 iterations from each chain being discarded. The priors are as follows:

```
prior_summary(Mnb2_bayes)
#>                      prior      class               coef group resp dpar nlpar bound
#> 1                                   b
#> 2                                   b       genderWomen
#> 3                                   b Ichildren>0TRUE
#> 4                                   b     marriedSingle
#> 5                                   b            mentor
#> 6                                   b          prestige
#> 7 student_t(3, 0, 2.5) Intercept
#> 8     gamma(0.01, 0.01)      shape
```

This tells us that we use a flat improper prior for coefficients for the predictors, a Student t-distribution for the intercept term, and a gamma distribution for the r parameter of the negative binomial distribution whose shape and rate (or inverse scale) parameters are 0.01 and 0.01. The gamma prior will have a mean of exactly 1, a variance of 100, and a positive skew of 20. The coefficients summary is as follows:

```
summary(Mnb2_bayes)$fixed
#>             Estimate    Est.Error    1-95% CI      u-95% CI   Rhat Bulk_ESS Tail_ESS
#> Intercept   0.38875785 0.128150414  0.13792671   0.64489299 1.000402  5282    3331
#> genderWomen -0.20490998 0.072479591 -0.34809029 -0.06308372 1.002637  5618    2871
```

```
#> marriedSingle      -0.14551425 0.084604551 -0.31343690  0.01636361 1.000203    4907    3214
#> Ichildren>0TRUE -0.22997153 0.088430409 -0.40120497 -0.05250130 1.000982    4837    2899
#> prestige           0.01547790 0.036156609 -0.05797008  0.08519567 1.001414    5503    2532
#> mentor             0.02945641 0.003444804  0.02256341  0.03632350 1.002656    5477    3157
```

Like the many cases we have seen above, these results are largely in line with those from classical maximum-likelihood-based methods, as we can see if we compare the results above to those of `glm.nb` applied to the same data:

```
Mnb2 <- glm.nb(publications ~ gender + married + I(children > 0) + prestige +
mentor,
                data = biochemists_df)
summary(Mnb2)$coefficients
#>                        Estimate   Std. Error    z value     Pr(>|z|)
#> (Intercept)          0.39147046 0.128450977  3.0476254 2.306573e-03
#> genderWomen         -0.20637739 0.072876028 -2.8318967 4.627279e-03
#> marriedSingle       -0.14384319 0.084788294 -1.6964983 8.979156e-02
#> I(children > 0)TRUE -0.22895331 0.085438163 -2.6797546 7.367614e-03
#> prestige             0.01547769 0.035978126  0.4301973 6.670521e-01
#> mentor               0.02927434 0.003229138  9.0656829 1.238261e-19
```

The posterior summary for the *r* parameter is as follows:

```
summary(Mnb2_bayes)$spec_pars
#>       Estimate Est.Error 1-95% CI u-95% CI     Rhat Bulk_ESS Tail_ESS
#> shape  2.22835 0.2645205 1.767754 2.812028 1.001407     5368     2577
```

We can see that this is very close to that estimated with `glm.nb`:

```
Mnb2$theta
#> [1] 2.239056
```

Zero-inflated count models

Zero-inflated models for count data are used when the outcome variable has an excessive number of zeros compared to what we would expect according to a probabilistic model such as the Poisson or negative binomial model. As an example of data of this kind, consider the following `smoking_df` data set:

```
smoking_df <- read_csv('data/smoking.csv')
smoking_df
#> # A tibble: 807 x 3
#>     educ   age  cigs
#>    <dbl> <dbl> <dbl>
#> 1   16    46     0
#> 2   16    40     0
```

```
#>  3  12       58    3
#>  4  13.5     30    0
#>  5  10       17    0
#>  6   6       86    0
#>  7  12       35    0
#>  8  15       48    0
#>  9  12       48    0
#> 10  12       31    0
#> # … with 797 more rows
```

In this, for each of 807 individuals, we have their number of years in formal education (educ), their age, and their reported number of cigarettes smoked per day (cigs). A barplot of cigs, shown in Figure 11.12, shows that there are an excessive number of zero values.

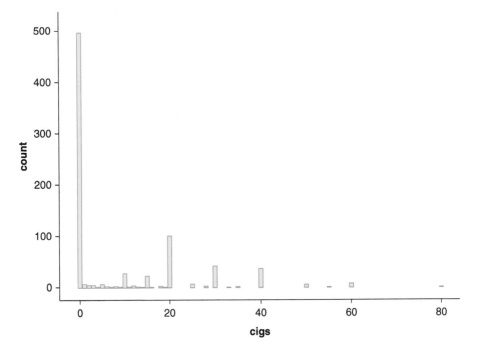

Figure 11.12 Barplot of frequency distribution of the cigs variable

To model count variables like cigs, we can use *zero-inflated* models, such as zero-inflated Poisson or zero-inflated negative binomial models. Here, we will just consider the example of zero-inflated Poisson regression, but all the principles apply equally to zero-inflated negative binomial and other count regression models.

Probabilistic mixture models

Zero-inflated Poisson regression is a type of *probabilistic mixture model*, specifically a probabilistic mixture of regression models. Let us first consider what mixture models are. Let us assume that our data consists of n observations $y_1,...,y_n$. A *non*-mixture normal distribution model of this data might be simply as follows:

$$y_i \sim N(\mu, \sigma^2), \quad \text{for } i \in 1,...,n.$$

By contrast, a $K = 3$ component mixture of normal distributions model assumes that there is a discrete latent variable $z_1,...,z_n$ corresponding to each of $y_1,...,y_n$, where each $z_i \in \{1,2,3\}$, and for for $i \in 1,...,n$,

$$y_i \sim \begin{cases} N(\mu_1, \sigma_1^2), & \text{if } z_i = 1, \\ N(\mu_2, \sigma_2^2), & \text{if } z_i = 2, \\ N(\mu_3, \sigma_3^2), & \text{if } z_i = 3, \end{cases}$$
$$z_i \sim P(\pi),$$

where $\pi = [\pi_1, \pi_2, \pi_3]$ is a probability distribution of $\{1,2,3\}$. More generally, for any value of K, we can write the K mixture of normals as follows:

$$y_i \sim N(\mu_{z_i}, \sigma_{z_i}^2), \quad z_i \sim P(\pi), \quad \text{for } i \in 1,2,...,n,$$

and $\pi = [\pi_1, \pi_2 \ldots \pi_K]$ is a probability distribution over $1,...,K$. In other words, each y_i is assumed to be drawn from one of K normal distributions whose mean and variance parameters are $(\mu_1, \sigma_1^2), (\mu_2, \sigma_2^2),...,(\mu_K, \sigma_K^2)$. Which of these K distributions each y_i is drawn from is determined by the value of the latent variable $z_i \in 1,...,K$, for each z_i, $P(z_i = k) = \pi_k$. In a model like this, we must infer the values of $(\mu_1, \sigma_1^2), (\mu_2, \sigma_2^2),...,(\mu_K, \sigma_K^2)$ and π and also the posterior probability that $z_i = k$ for each value of k; see Figure 11.13 for an illustration of the problem in the case of $K = 3$ normal distributions. Without delving into the details, the traditional maximum-likelihood-based approach to this inference is to use the expectation–maximization (EM) algorithm.

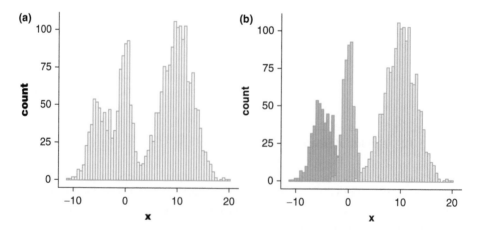

Figure 11.13 A probabilistic mixture of $K = 3$ normal distributions. A histogram of the observed data is shown in (a), and we model each observed value as drawn from one of three different normal distributions, as shown in (b). The parameters of the normal distributions, the relative probabilities of the three distributions, as well as the probability that any one observation came from each distribution, must be simultaneously inferred

The mixture models discussed so far were not regression models. However, we can easily extend their description to apply to regression models. For this, let us assume our data is $\{(y_1, \vec{x}_1), (y_2, \vec{x}_2), ..., (y_n, \vec{x}_n)\}$, just as we have described it repeatedly above. In a non-mixture normal linear regression model, we have seen that our model is as follows:

$$y_i \sim N(\mu_i, \sigma^2), \quad \mu_i = \beta_0 + \sum_{k=1}^{K} \beta_k x_{ki}, \quad \text{for } i \in 1, ..., n.$$

On the other hand, in a mixture of K normal linear models, we assume that there is a latent variable $z_1, ..., z_n$ corresponding to each observation, with each $z_i \in K$ and

$$y_i \sim N\left(\mu_i, \sigma_{z_i}^2\right), \quad \mu_i = \beta_{0[z_i]} + \sum_{k=1}^{K} \beta_{k[z_i]} x_{ki}, \quad z_i \in P(\pi) \text{ for } i \in 1, ..., n,$$

where $\pi = [\pi_1, ..., \pi_K]$ is a probability distribution over $1...K$. Note that, here, we have K sets of regression coefficients, $\left(\vec{\beta}_1, \sigma_1^2\right), \left(\vec{\beta}_2, \sigma_2^2\right), ..., \left(\vec{\beta}_K, \sigma_K^2\right)$, each defining a different linear model.

In the mixture of regressions just provided, the probability that z_i takes any value from $1, ..., K$ is determined by the fixed but unknown probability distribution π. We may, however, extend the mixture of regressions model to allow each z_i to also vary with the predictors $\vec{x}_i$. For example, each z_i could be modelled using a categorical logistic regression of the kind we saw in Chapter 10.

As interesting as these mixtures of normal linear regression models are, we will not explore them further here. However, we have described them in order to introduce zero-inflated Poisson models, which are a special type of mixture of regression model. Specifically, a zero-inflated Poisson regression is a $K = 2$ mixture regression model. There are two component models, and so each latent variable z_i is binary valued, $z_i \in \{0, 1\}$. Furthermore, the probability that $z_i = 1$ is a logistic regression function of the predictor $\vec{x}_i$. The two components of the zero-inflated Poisson model are a Poisson distribution and a zero-valued point mass distribution (a probability distribution with all its mass at zero).

More precisely, in a zero-Inflated Poisson regression, our data is

$$(y_1, \vec{x}_1), (y_2, \vec{x}_2), ..., (y_i, \vec{x}_i), ..., (y_n, \vec{x}_n),$$

where each $y_1 \in 0, 1, ...$ is a count variable. Our model is

$$y_i \sim \begin{cases} \text{Poisson}(\lambda_i), & \text{if } z_i = 0, \\ 0, & \text{if } z_i = 1, \end{cases}$$

$$z_i \sim \text{Bernoulli}(\theta_i),$$

where λ_i and θ_i are both functions of the predictors $\vec{x}_i$, specifically

$$\log(\lambda_i) = \beta_0 + \sum_{k=1}^{K} \beta_k x_{ki},$$

and

$$\log\left(\frac{\theta_i}{1 - \theta_i}\right) = \gamma_0 + \sum_{k=1}^{K} \gamma_k x_{ki}.$$

In other words, λ_i is modelled just as in ordinary Poisson regression and θ_i is modelled as in logistic regression. We are using $\vec{\beta}$ and $\vec{\gamma}$ to make it clear that these are two separate sets of regression coefficients.

Zero-inflated Poisson in R

We can perform zero-inflated Poisson regression, as well as other zero-inflated count regression models, using functions in the package `pscl`. Here, we model how `cigs` varies as a function of `educ`:

```
library(pscl)
Mzip <- zeroinfl(cigs ~ educ, data=smoking_df)
```

The two set of coefficients can be obtained as follows:

```
summary(Mzip)$coefficients
#> $count
#>              Estimate  Std. Error  z value     Pr(>|z|)
#> (Intercept) 2.69785404 0.056778696 47.515252 0.000000e+00
#> educ        0.03471929 0.004536397  7.653495 1.955885e-14
#>
#> $zero
#>              Estimate Std. Error   z value     Pr(>|z|)
#> (Intercept) -0.56273266 0.30605009 -1.838695 0.0659601142
#> educ         0.08356933 0.02417456  3.456912 0.0005464026
```

From this, we see that the logistic regression model for each observation is estimated to be

$$\log\left(\frac{\theta_i}{1-\theta_i}\right) = \gamma_0 + \gamma_1 x_i = -0.563 + 0.084 x_i,$$

and the Poisson model is estimated to be

$$\log(\lambda_i) = \beta_0 + \beta_1 x_i = 2.698 + 0.035 x_i,$$

where x_i is the value of `educ` on observation i.

Note that the logistic regression model gives the probability that the latent variable z_i takes the value 1, which means that y_i is assumed to be drawn from the zero model. The zero model means that the corresponding observation is *necessarily* zero. In this sense, $z_i = 1$ means that the person is a non-smoker. Obviously, a non-smoker will necessarily smoke zero cigarettes in a day, but it important to emphasize that the converse is not true. A smoker, albeit a light smoker, may smoke zero cigarettes on some days and some non-zero number on other days. Among other things, this means that knowing that $y_i = 0$ does *not* necessarily entail that $z_i = 1$.

Predictions in zero-inflated Poisson regression

There are at least three main types of prediction that can be performed in zero-inflated Poisson regression: predicting the probability that $z_i = 1$ from $\bar{x}_i$, predicting λ_i from $\bar{x}_i$ given that $z_i = 0$, and predicting λ_i from $\bar{x}_i$ generally.

To simplify matters, let us start by considering two values of `educ`: 6 and 18. For $x_i = 6$, the probability that $z_i = 1$, and so person i is a non-smoker, is

$$\theta_i = \frac{1}{1+e^{-(-0.563+0.504)}} = 0.485.$$

By contrast, for $x_i = 18$, the probability that $z_i = 1$, and so person i is a non-smoker, is

$$\theta_i = \frac{1}{1+e^{-(-0.563+1.512)}} = 0.719.$$

From this, we see that as the value of educ increases, the probability of being a non-smoker also increases.

For smokers, we can then use the Poisson model to provide the average of the number of cigarettes they smoke. For $x_i = 6$, the average number of cigarettes smoked is

$$\lambda_i = e^{2.698+0.21} = 18.287.$$

For $x_i = 18$, the average number of cigarettes smoked is

$$\lambda_i = e^{2.698+0.63} = 27.738.$$

From this we see that as educ increases, the average number of cigarettes smoked also increases. This is an interesting result. It shows that the effect of education on smoking behaviour is not a very simple one and that two opposing effects are happening at the same time. On the one hand, as education increases, it is more likely that a person does not smoke at all. This was revealed by the logistic regression model. On the other hand, if the person is a smoker, then the more educated they are, the more they smoke. This was revealed by the Poisson model.

These two predictions can be made more efficiently and with less error using predict or add_predictions. Let us consider the range of values for educ from 6 to 18 in steps of 2 years:

```
smoking_df_new <- tibble(educ = seq(6, 18, by = 2))
```

The predictions that $z_i = 1$, and hence that a person of that level of education is a non-smoker, can be made using type = 'zero' as follows:

```
smoking_df_new %>%
  add_predictions(Mzip, type = 'zero')
#> # A tibble: 7 x 2
#>     educ  pred
#>    <dbl> <dbl>
#> 1      6 0.485
#> 2      8 0.526
#> 3     10 0.568
#> 4     12 0.608
#> 5     14 0.647
#> 6     16 0.684
#> 7     18 0.719
```

The predicted average number of cigarettes smoked by a smoker is obtained by using type = 'count' as follows:

```
smoking_df_new %>%
  add_predictions(Mzip, type = 'count')
#> # A tibble: 7 x 2
#>    educ   pred
#>   <dbl>  <dbl>
#> 1     6   18.3
#> 2     8   19.6
#> 3    10   21.0
#> 4    12   22.5
#> 5    14   24.1
#> 6    16   25.9
#> 7    18   27.7
```

Now let us consider the average number of cigarettes smoked by a person, who might be smoker or a non-smoker, given that we know their level of education. Put more generally, what is the expected value of y_i given $\bar{x}_i$ in a zero-inflated Poisson model? This is the sum of two quantities. The first is the average value of y_i given $\bar{x}_i$ when $z_i = 0$ multiplied by the probability that $z_i = 0$. The second is the average value of y_i given $\bar{x}_i$ when $z_i = 1$ multiplied by the probability that $z_i = 1$. This second value is always zero: if $z_i = 1$ then $y_i = 0$ necessarily. The first value is

$$\lambda_i \times (1 - \theta_i).$$

We can obtain these predictions using type = 'response':

```
smoking_df_new %>%
  add_predictions(Mzip, type = 'response')
#> # A tibble: 7 x 2
#>    educ   pred
#>   <dbl>  <dbl>
#> 1     6   9.42
#> 2     8   9.28
#> 3    10   9.08
#> 4    12   8.82
#> 5    14   8.51
#> 6    16   8.17
#> 7    18   7.78
```

We can verify that these predictions are as defined above as follows. As we've seen, λ and θ are calculated using predict with type = 'count' and type = 'zero', respectively. Putting these in a data frame, we can then calculate $\lambda \times (1 - \theta)$:

```
smoking_df_new %>%
  mutate(lambda = predict(Mzip, newdata = ., type = 'count'),
         theta = predict(Mzip, newdata = ., type = 'zero'),
         response = lambda * (1-theta)
  )
#> # A tibble: 7 x 4
#>    educ lambda theta response
```

```
#>    <dbl>  <dbl> <dbl>    <dbl>
#> 1     6   18.3 0.485    9.42
#> 2     8   19.6 0.526    9.28
#> 3    10   21.0 0.568    9.08
#> 4    12   22.5 0.608    8.82
#> 5    14   24.1 0.647    8.51
#> 6    16   25.9 0.684    8.17
#> 7    18   27.7 0.719    7.78
```

Bayesian zero-inflated Poisson regression

We can easily perform a zero-inflated Poisson regression using `brms` as follows:

```
Mzip_bayes <- brm(cigs ~ educ,
                  family = zero_inflated_poisson(link = "log", link_zi = "logit"),
                  data = smoking_df)
```

As we can see, we use `zero_inflated_poisson` as the `family`. The default link functions for the Poisson and the logistic regression are, as we used them above, the log and the logit functions, respectively. From the summary, however, we can see that this model is not identical to the one we used above:

```
Mzip_bayes
#>  Family: zero_inflated_poisson
#>   Links: mu = log; zi = identity
#> Formula: cigs ~ educ
#>    Data: smoking_df (Number of observations: 807)
#> Samples: 4 chains, each with iter = 2000; warmup = 1000; thin = 1;
#>          total post-warmup samples = 4000
#>
#>
#> Population-Level Effects:
#>           Estimate Est.Error 1-95% CI u-95% CI Rhat Bulk_ESS Tail_ESS
#> Intercept     2.70      0.06     2.58     2.81 1.00     5081     3191
#> educ          0.03      0.00     0.03     0.04 1.00     4864     3108
#>
#> Family Specific Parameters:
#>    Estimate Est.Error 1-95% CI u-95% CI Rhat Bulk_ESS Tail_ESS
#> zi     0.62      0.02     0.58     0.65 1.00     3457     2693
#>
#> Samples were drawn using sampling(NUTS). For each parameter, Bulk_ESS
#> and Tail_ESS are effective sample size measures, and Rhat is the potential
#> scale reduction factor on split chains (at convergence, Rhat = 1).
```

As may be clear, this model is in fact the following:

$$y_i \sim \begin{cases} \text{Poisson}(\lambda_i), & \text{if } z_i = 0, \\ 0, & \text{if } z_i = 1, \end{cases}$$

$$z_i \sim \text{Bernoulli}(\theta),$$

where λ_i is a function of the predictors $\vec{x}_i$, specifically

$$\log(\lambda_i) = \beta_0 + \sum_{k=1}^{K} \beta_k x_{ki},$$

but θ is a fixed constant that does not vary with $\vec{x}_i$. To obtain the model, as we used it above in the classical inference-based example, where the log odds of θ_i is a linear function $\vec{x}_i$, we must define two regression formulae: one for the Poisson model and the other for the logistic regression model. We do so using the `brmsformula` function, which is also available as `bf`:

```
Mzip_bayes <- brm(bf(cigs ~ educ, zi ~ educ),
                  family = zero_inflated_poisson(link = "log", link_zi = "logit"),
                  data = smoking_df)
```

Note that inside `bf` there are two formulae. The first is as above, and second is the logistic regression model for the z_i latent variable.

Again, we have accepted all the defaults. Let us look at the priors that have been used:

```
prior_summary(Mzip_bayes)
#>                       prior     class coef group resp dpar nlpar bound
#> 1                                 b
#> 2                                 b educ
#> 3                                 b                          zi
#> 4                                 b educ                     zi
#> 5    student_t(3, -2.3, 2.5) Intercept
#> 6         logistic(0, 1) Intercept                          zi
```

Much of this is similar to previous examples. However, we note that the prior on the intercept term for the logistic regression model is a standard logistic distribution. We saw this distribution when discussing the latent variable formulation of the logistic regression in Chapter 10. It is close to a normal distribution with zero mean and standard deviation 1.63.

The coefficients for both the Poisson and logistic regression model can be obtained from the `fixed` attribute in the summary output, which we can see is very close to the estimates in the classical inference model above:

```
summary(Mzip_bayes)$fixed
#>                Estimate    Est.Error      l-95% CI     u-95% CI     Rhat Bulk_ESS Tail_ESS
#> Intercept     2.69858399 0.057104349  2.58963221 2.81069912 1.002627     5278     3240
#> zi_Intercept -0.56987666 0.305114497 -1.16609250 0.01653766 1.001369     4287     2929
#> educ          0.03463546 0.004544498  0.02561902 0.04345278 1.001924     5372     3358
#> zi_educ       0.08411914 0.024112174  0.03783867 0.13216619 1.001081     4147     2825
```

12

Multilevel Models

Introduction

Multilevel models are a broad class of models that are applied to data that consists of sub-groups or clusters, including when these clusters are hierarchically arranged. Although they have been in existence for decades, they have become very widely used within the last 10–20 years due to computational advances. They are now a major statistical modelling tool in the social sciences as well many other fields of research. A number of related terms are used to describe multilevel models: *hierarchical* models, *mixed effects* models, *random effects* models, and more. These terms are not strictly synonymous but do describe models that are all related to the general concept of a multilevel model. Here, we will prefer to use 'multilevel' as the main general term for these models. We will also use the term 'hierarchical model', at least a certain sense of the term, as essentially synonymous to multilevel model, and we'll use the term *mixed effect model*, or *mixed effect regression*, as the term for a particular widely used variant of the multilevel regression model.

As we will see, the defining feature of multilevel models is that they are *models of models*. In other words, for each cluster or subgroup in our data we create a statistical model, and then model how these statistical models vary across the clusters or subgroups. We will begin our coverage of multilevel models by exploring random effects models. These are some of the simplest types of multilevel models, yet they can make clear the key defining characteristics of multilevel models generally. We then proceed to cover multilevel linear models, which are often referred to as *linear mixed effects* models. We will also describe how to perform Bayesian versions of these models.

Random effects models

Let us consider the following data set, which is on rat tumours:

```
rats_df <- read_csv('data/rats.csv',
                    col_types = cols(batch = col_character())
)
rats_df
#> # A tibble: 71 x 3
#>    batch     m     n
#>    <chr> <dbl> <dbl>
#>  1 1         0    20
#>  2 2         0    20
#>  3 3         0    20
#>  4 4         0    20
#>  5 5         0    20
#>  6 6         0    20
#>  7 7         0    20
#>  8 8         0    19
#>  9 9         0    19
#> 10 10        0    19
#> # … with 61 more rows
```

This data set consists of data from $J = 71$ batches of rats. For each batch, we have the number of rats in it (n) and the number of rats in the batch that developed tumours (m). Let us begin by focusing on a single batch:

```
rats_df_42 <- filter(rats_df, batch == '42')
rats_df_42
#> # A tibble: 1 x 3
#>    batch     m     n
#>    <chr> <dbl> <dbl>
#> 1 42        2    13
```

In this batch, out of 13 rats, the recorded number of tumours was 2. With these numbers alone, we can provide a simple statistical model of the tumour rate in batch 42. In this model, we can say that there is a fixed but unknown probability of a tumour in this batch, which we will denote by θ. In other words, each rat in the batch of size $n = 13$ has probability θ of developing a tumour and so the recorded number of tumours, $m = 2$, is a draw from a binomial distribution with parameter θ and size $n = 13$. In other words, our model is a binomial model:

$$m \sim \text{Binom}(\theta, n).$$

This is identical to the following binomial logistic regression model:

$$m \sim \text{Binom}(\theta, n), \quad \log\left(\frac{\theta}{1-\theta}\right) = \beta.$$

This binomial model can be represented by the following diagram:

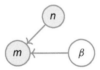

This kind of diagram is known as a *Bayesian network*. It is a directed acyclic graph showing each variable or parameter in the model. The shaded nodes indicate that the corresponding variable is observed. From this diagram we see that the variable m is conditionally dependent on n, which is observed, and β, which is not observed and so must be inferred. While this diagram is very simple, it is useful to use it here to compare it to other models that we will use below. We can implement this binomial logistic model in R using `glm`:

```
M <- glm(cbind(m, n-m) ~ 1,
         data = rats_df_42,
         family = binomial(link = 'logit')
)
```

Note that in this model, the left-hand side of the ~ operator is `cbind(m, n-m)`, where m gives the number of rats in the batch that have tumours and n-m gives the number of rats in the batch that do not have tumours. The command cbind is used to stack vectors side by side as columns, and so cbind(m, n-m) creates a matrix with two columns. From this model M, we can see that our estimate of θ is as follows:

```
ilogit <- function(x) 1/(1 + exp(-x))
coef(M) %>% ilogit() %>% unname()
#> [1] 0.1538462
```

This is expected, given that out of 13 rats in this batch, the recorded number of tumours was 2, and 2/13 = 0.1538462.

We can now easily extend this model to apply to all batches in our data set. In other words, for each of our J batches, where n_j is the batch size, θ_j is its fixed but unknown probability of developing a tumour, and m_j is its recorded number of tumours, we have the following model:

$$m_j \sim \text{Binom}\left(\theta_j, n_j\right), \quad \log\left(\frac{\theta_j}{1-\theta_j}\right) = \beta_j.$$

This is implemented using glm as follows:

```
library(broom) M <- glm(cbind(m, n-m) ~ 0 + batch,
          data = rats_df,
          family = binomial(link = 'logit')
)
```

Using broom::tidy and some dplyr and related tools, we can look at the estimates and confidence intervals for a random sample of 10 of the batches:

```
M_estimates <- tidy(M) %>%
  select(term, beta = estimate) %>%
  mutate(term = str_remove(term, 'batch'),
         theta = ilogit(beta)) %>%
  rename(batch = term)

M_estimates %>%
  sample_n(10) %>%
  arrange(beta) %>%
  mutate_at(vars(beta,theta), ~round(., 2))
#> # A tibble: 10 x 3
#>    batch    beta theta
#>    <chr>   <dbl> <dbl>
#> 1 5       -27.8   0
#> 2 13      -27.6   0
#> 3 29       -2.2   0.1
#> 4 23      -2.08   0.11
#> 5 37      -2.01   0.12
#> 6 48      -1.39   0.2
#> 7 58      -1.13   0.24
```

```
#>   8 59     -1.1    0.25
#>   9 64     -0.85   0.3
#> 10 70     -0.51   0.37
```

Although we have implemented a single glm model, this has effectively led to J separate binomial models. The Bayesian network diagram for these models is shown in the diagrams in Figure 12.1. In other words, we have a model of the tumour rate for batch 1, another for batch 2, and so on. From this, we do not have a model of the distribution of tumour rates across all batches. We do not, for example, have a model that gives us the mean or standard deviation, or any other information, about the tumour rate across all possible batches in this experiment, of which our set of 71 batches is a sample. In order to obtain this model, we must resort to a multilevel model.

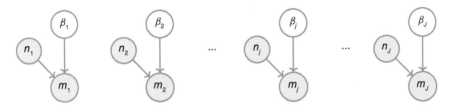

Figure 12.1   Inferring the log odds of a tumour β_j in each of the J batches is identical to J independent binomial models

A multilevel model extension of the binomial logistic regression model above is as follows:

$$\text{for } j \in 1,...,J, \quad m_j \sim \text{Binom}(\theta_j, n_j), \quad \log\left(\frac{\theta_j}{1-\theta_j}\right) = \beta_j, \quad \beta_j \sim \text{N}(b, \tau^2).$$

The crucial added feature here is that the log odds of the tumour probabilities is being modelled as normally distributed with a mean of b and a standard deviation of τ. These dependencies are shown in the Bayesian network diagram in Figure 12.2.

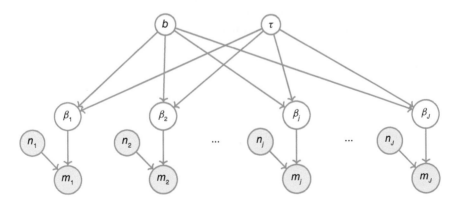

Figure 12.2   A multilevel binomial logistic regression.

In this multilevel model, just as in the previous non-multilevel model, $\beta_1, \beta_2, ..., \beta_j, ..., \beta_J$ have fixed but unknown values. However, in addition, these values are modelled as all drawn from the same normal distribution. The two important consequences of this are as follows. First, it provides a model of the *population* from which $\beta_1, \beta_2, ..., \beta_j, ..., \beta_J$ are a sample. Given that each β_j effectively defines a model for a batch of rats, the normal distribution from which $\beta_1, \beta_2, ..., \beta_j, ..., \beta_J$ are drawn is a model of models. Among other things, this population model of the βs allows us to predict the log odds, or probability, of a tumour for any future batch of rats, say, batch $J +$ 1. Second, because we are assuming that $\beta_1, \beta_2, ..., \beta_j, ..., \beta_J$ are all drawn from the same normal distribution, this introduces constraints on the inference of the values of each β_j. In other words, to infer the value of β_j, the observed values of m_j and n_j are not the only relevant pieces of information. Now, the values of b and τ are also relevant, and because b and τ are also unknown, they themselves must be inferred from $\beta_1, \beta_2, ..., \beta_j, ..., \beta_J$. This effectively means that the inferences concerning $\beta_1, \beta_2, ..., \beta_j, ..., \beta_J$ are interdependent and mutually constrain one another. We will explore both of these important general features of multilevel models below.

Given that we can rewrite $\beta_j \sim N(b, \tau^2)$ as $\beta_j = b + \xi_j$ where $\xi_j \sim N(0, \tau^2)$, we can rewrite the multilevel model as

$$\text{for } j \in 1...J, \quad m_j \sim \text{Binom}(\theta_j, n_j), \quad \log\left(\frac{\theta_j}{1 - \theta_j}\right) = b + \xi_j, \quad \xi_j \sim N(0, \tau^2).$$

We can then implement this model using the `glmer` model that is part of the `lme4` package:

```
library(lme4)
```

```
M_ml <- glmer(cbind(m, n-m) ~ 1 + (1|batch),
              data = rats_df,
              family = binomial(link = 'logit')
)
```

Before we proceed to examine the results of this model, let us first describe the formula syntax. The right-hand side of the formula is `1 + (1|batch)`. The first `1` indicates the intercept term of the model, which is b. This is identical to how we indicate an intercept-only model using `lm`, `glm`, etc. For example, if were modelling a set of n values $y_1, ..., y_n$ as $y_i \sim N(\mu, \sigma^2)$ we could write `lm(y ~ 1)`. The `(1|batch)` is a *random intercepts* statement. Specifically, in the case of `glmer`, it states that for each value of the `batch` variable we have a constant term, and that these constant terms are normally distributed from a zero-mean normal distribution. As such, `(1|batch)` gives us the $\xi_j \sim N(0, \tau^2)$ for each of the J batches.

Let us look at the summary of this model:

```
summary(M_ml)
#> Generalized linear mixed model fit by maximum likelihood (Laplace
#>   Approximation) [glmerMod]
#>  Family: binomial  ( logit )
#> Formula: cbind(m, n - m) ~ 1 + (1 | batch)
#>   Data: rats_df
#>
#>      AIC      BIC   logLik deviance df.resid
```

```
#>     319.9    324.4    -157.9    315.9        69
#>
#> Scaled residuals:
#>     Min      1Q  Median       3Q      Max
#> -1.2392 -0.6230 -0.1055   0.4795   1.0253
#>
#> Random effects:
#>   Groups Name            Variance Std.Dev.
#>   batch  (Intercept) 0.4417    0.6646
#> Number of obs: 71, groups:   batch, 71
#>
#> Fixed effects:
#>                 Estimate Std. Error z value Pr(>|z|)
#> (Intercept)    -1.9369      0.1211     -16   <2e-16 ***
#> ---
#> Signif. codes:   0 '***' 0.001 '**' 0.01 '*' 0.05 '.' 0.1 ' ' 1
```

The first thing to note is the estimated value of b, which is listed as the estimate of the intercept term in the Fixed effects section. We see that this has the value −1.937. The estimates of τ and τ^2, on the other hand, are given by the Std.Dev. and Variance terms for the (Intercept) for batch in the Random effects section. We see that the value of τ is 0.665. As such, our model of the distribution of the log odds of the tumours is a normal distribution whose mean and standard deviation are estimated to be −1.937 and 0.665, respectively. The translates into the probability distribution over the probabilities of tumours that we see in Figure 12.3.

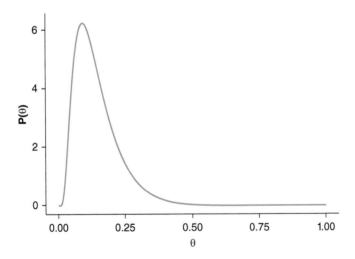

Figure 12.3 Estimate of the population distribution over θ for the rats tumour multilevel model

Given that this normal distribution with mean $b = -1.937$ and standard deviation $\tau = 0.665$ is a model of the population from which the β_1, β_2,..., β_j,..., β_J are drawn, we can make statements like the following. The expected value of the log odds of a tumour in a future batch of rats is –1.937, and with 95% probability this log odds is between –3.239 and –0.634. Equivalently, the expected value of the probability of a tumour in a future batch of rats is 0.126, and with 95% probability this probability is between 0.038 and 0.347.

From this model, we can also obtain the estimates of $\xi_1, \xi_2, ..., \xi_j, ..., \xi_J$ from the model by using the ranef command:

```
ranef (M_ml)$batch %>%
  head ()
#>     (Intercept)
#> 1    -0.6298720
#> 10   -0.6096908
#> 11   -0.6096908
#> 12   -0.5888596
#> 13   -0.5888596
#> 14   -0.5673326
```

We may obtain the estimates of b using the fixef command:

```
b <- fixef (M_ml)
```

We may then add on the estimates of b to get the estimates of $\beta_1, \beta_2, ..., \beta_j, ..., \beta_J$:

```
b + ranef (M_ml)$batch %>%
  head ()
#>     (Intercept)
#> 1    -2.566785
#> 10   -2.546604
#> 11   -2.546604
#> 12   -2.525773
#> 13   -2.525773
#> 14   -2.504246
```

We may obtain the estimates of $\beta_1, \beta_2, ..., \beta_j, ..., \beta_J$ more directly by using the coef command:

```
M_ml_estimates <- coef (M_ml)$batch
```

```
M_ml_estimates %>%
  head ()
#>     (Intercept)
#> 1    -2.566785
#> 10   -2.546604
#> 11   -2.546604
#> 12   -2.525773
#> 13   -2.525773
#> 14   -2.504246
```

Comparing these values to the corresponding values in the non-multilevel model, we can see how the estimates of $\beta_1, \beta_2, ..., \beta_j, ..., \beta_J$ mutually constrain one another. This phenomenon is an example of *shrinkage*. In this model, it is easier to visualize this effect if we look at $\theta_1, \theta_2, ...,$

$\theta_p, ..., \theta_J,$ which are simply the inverse logit transforms of $\beta_1, \beta_2, ..., \beta_p, ..., \beta_J$. In Figure 12.4, we compare the estimates of $\theta_1, \theta_2, ..., \theta_p, ..., \theta_J$ from the flat or non-multilevel model M against those of the multilevel model M_ml. As we can see, the estimates of $\theta_1, \theta_2, ..., \theta_p, ..., \theta_J$ and hence also of $\beta_1, \beta_2, ..., \beta_p, ..., \beta_J$, in the case of the multilevel model are brought closer together towards the centre compared to the non-multilevel model.

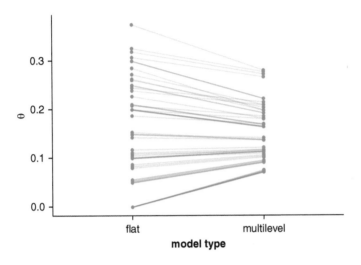

Figure 12.4 Estimates of $\theta_1, \theta_2, ..., \theta_p, ..., \theta_J$ from the flat or non-multilevel model (left) and the multilevel model (right)

To understand why this phenomenon occurs, let us compare the likelihood functions for the non-multilevel and the multilevel model. In the non-multilevel model, there are J unknowns, $\beta_1, \beta_2, ..., \beta_p, ..., \beta_J$, and, given the observed data, the likelihood function is

$$\prod_{j=1}^{J} P(m_j \mid n_j, \beta_j).$$

Maximizing this function with respect to β_j is equivalent to maximizing $P(m_j \mid n_j, \beta_j)$ with respect to β_j, which is $\hat{\beta}_j = \text{logit}(m_j / n_j)$. On the other hand, in the multilevel model, there are $J + 2$ unknowns, $\beta_1, \beta_2, ..., \beta_p, ..., \beta_J, b$ and τ, and the likelihood function is

$$\prod_{j=1}^{J} P(m_j \mid n_j, \beta_j) P(\beta_j \mid b, \tau).$$

Maximizing this function with respect to β_j is equivalent to maximizing $P(m_j \mid n_j, \beta_j) P(\beta_j \mid b, \tau)$, which is a compromise between maximizing $P(m_j \mid n_j, \beta_j)$ and maximizing $P(\beta_j \mid b, \tau)$, with the latter being maximized as β_j becomes closer to b. Maximizing the multilevel model's likelihood with respect to b is equivalent to maximizing $\prod_{j=1}^{J} P(\beta_j \mid b, \tau)$ with respect to b, which occurs at $\hat{b} = 1/J \sum_{j=1}^{J} \beta_j$. From this, we see that the estimate of each βj is based on the value of mj and n_p, but is also pulled towards the average of $\beta_1, \beta_2, ..., \beta_p, ..., \beta_J$.

Normal random effects models

Let us now consider a new data set:

```
alcohol_df <- read_csv ('data/alcohol.csv')
alcohol_df
#> # A tibble: 411 x 3
#>      country   year alcohol
#>      <chr>    <dbl>   <dbl>
#>  1 Russia     1985    13.3
#>  2 Russia     1986    10.8
#>  3 Russia     1987    11.0
#>  4 Russia     1988    11.6
#>  5 Russia     1989    12.0
#>  6 Chile      1990     9.43
#>  7 Ecuador    1990     8.4
#>  8 Greece     1990    12.5
#>  9 Russia     1990    12.3
#> 10 Russia     1991    12.7
#> # ... with 401 more rows
```

In this data set, we have the per capita average alcohol consumption in $J = 189$ countries in $K = 22$ different years, though we do not necessarily have data from each country in each year. Let us denote the per capita alcohol values by $y_1, y_2,..., y_i,..., y_n$. For each y_i, we have an indicator variable $x_i \in 1,...,J$, which indicates the country that y_i corresponds to. An initial model for $y_1, y_2,..., y_i,..., y_n$ could then be

$$y_i \sim N\left(\mu_{[x_i]}, \sigma^2\right), \text{ for } i \in 1,...,n,$$

where $\mu_1, \mu_2,..., \mu_j,..., \mu_J$ are the country alcohol per capita consumption averages for the J countries. This model can be represented by the Bayesian network diagram shown in Figure 12.5. This is a non-multilevel model because the alcohol consumption averages in each country are being modelled independently of those of other countries. In this model, however, we do assume that the standard deviations of the alcohol consumption values across all countries are the same, and given by σ, whose value is fixed but unknown. What this entails, therefore, is that this model is a one-way ANOVA model with the standard homogeneity of variance assumption. A multilevel counterpart to the above model would be as follows:

$$y_i \sim N\left(\mu_{[x_i]}, \sigma^2\right), \text{ for } i \in 1,...,n,$$
$$\mu_j \sim N\left(\phi, \tau^2\right), \text{ for } j \in 1,...,J.$$

This model, which is depicted by a Bayesian network diagram in Figure 12.6, extends the previous one by assuming that the $\mu_1, \mu_2,..., \mu_j,..., \mu_J$ are drawn from a normal distribution with mean ϕ and standard deviation τ. Given that y_i can be rewritten as $y_i = \mu_{[x_i]} + \epsilon_i$, where $\epsilon_i \sim N(0, \sigma^2)$, and that μ_j can be rewritten as $\mu_j = \phi + \xi_j$, where $\epsilon_i \sim N(0, \sigma^2)$, we can rewrite the above model as

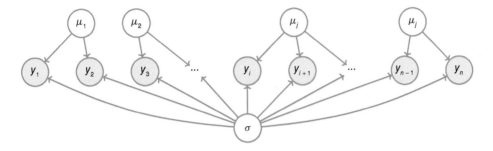

Figure 12.5   A non-multilevel model for average alcohol consumption across countries. The $y_1, ..., y_n$ variables are alcohol consumption averages for J different countries over different years. As depicted here, we are assuming that y_1 and y_2 represent averages for the same country, country $j = 1$, for two different years. The overall average for this country is given by μ_1, whose value is unknown. This non-multilevel model is identical to a one-way ANOVA model with J groups. The common standard deviation term σ is simply the homogeneity of variance assumption of the one-way ANOVA

$$y_i = \phi + \xi_{[x_i]} + \epsilon_i, \quad \text{for } i \in 1,...,n,$$

where each $\xi_j \sim N(0,\tau^2)$ and each $\epsilon_i \sim N(0,\sigma^2)$. Here, ϕ signifies the global average per capita alcohol consumption rate. Each ξ_j is the *random offset* of country j from ϕ, and each ϵ_i is the residual error for each observation. In this model, the residual error ϵ_i gives the random year-by-year deviation from country x_i's average consumption rate.

We can implement this model using lme4::lmer as follows:

```
M_ml <- lmer(alcohol ~ 1 + (1|country),
             data = alcohol_df)
summary(M_ml)
#> Linear mixed model fit by REML ['lmerMod']
#> Formula: alcohol ~ 1 + (1 | country)
#>    Data: alcohol_df
#>
#> REML criterion at convergence: 1918.2
#>
#> Scaled residuals:
#>     Min      1Q  Median      3Q     Max
#> -3.4661 -0.1582 -0.0719  0.1642  5.9576
#>
#> Random effects:
#>  Groups   Name        Variance Std.Dev.
#>  country  (Intercept) 22.208   4.713
#>  Residual              1.108   1.053
#> Number of obs: 411, groups:  country, 189
#>
#> Fixed effects:
#>             Estimate Std. Error t value
#> (Intercept)   6.6612     0.3469    19.2
```

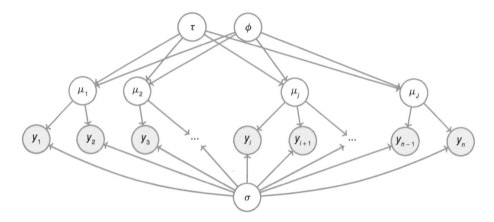

Figure 12.6 Multilevel model for average alcohol consumption across countries. This model is an extension of the non-multilevel model shown in Figure 12.5 by modelling the $\mu_1, \mu_2,..., \mu_j,..., \mu_J$ as samples from a normal distribution with mean ϕ and standard deviation τ

As we can see from the (Intercept) estimate in the Fixed effects and the Std.Dev. for country in the Random effects, the normal distribution of the μ values has mean $\phi = 6.661$ and standard deviation $\tau = 4.713$. The residual standard deviation σ is given by the Std.Dev. for Residual in the Random effects, and has the value $\sigma = 1.053$.

Given the nature of the random effects model, where each y_i is modelled as $y_i = \phi + \xi_{[x_i]} + \epsilon_i$, the variance of y is equal to $\tau^2 + \sigma^2$. The value

$$\frac{\tau^2}{\tau^2 + \sigma^2}$$

is known as the *intraclass correlation* (ICC), which takes values between 0 and 1. Obviously, it tells us how much of the total variance in the data is due to variation between the countries. If the ICC is relatively high, and so τ^2 / σ^2 is relatively high, the observed values *within* countries will be close together relative to the *between*-country averages, and thus there will be relatively high clustering of the data. In this data, the ICC is 0.95.

One consequence of a high ICC, and specifically a high value of τ^2 relative to σ^2, is that shrinkage effects will be less. This can be seen in Figure 12.7, where we compare the estimates of each μ_j from the non-multilevel and multilevel models. In more detail, in a normal random effects model, the estimate of μ_j will be approximately as follows (see Gelman and Hill, 2007, p. 253, for details):

$$\mu_j \approx \frac{\frac{n_j}{\sigma^2} \bar{y}_j + \frac{1}{\tau^2} \bar{y}}{\frac{n_j}{\sigma^2} + \frac{1}{\tau^2}},$$

where $\bar{y}_j$ is the average of the y_i values corresponding to country j, and $\bar{y}$ is the overall average of the y_i values. In general, when τ^2 is large relative to σ^2, the influence of the global average $\bar{y}$ on μ_j will be minimal. This will be especially the case as n_j grows larger.

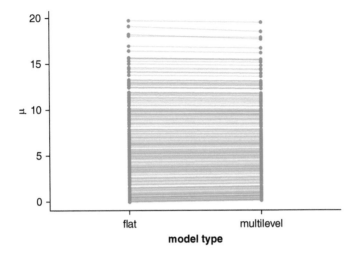

Figure 12.7 Estimates of $\mu_1, \mu_2, ..., \mu_j, ..., \mu_J$ from the flat or non-multilevel model (left) and the multilevel model (right). Shrinkage effects are minimal due to the high value τ^2 of relative to σ^2

12●4 Linear mixed effects models

We will now consider multilevel linear regression models. These are often referred to as *linear mixed effects models*, for reasons that will be clear after we describe them in more detail. As with random effects models, these models are best introduced by way of example. For this, we will use the `sleepstudy` data set from `lme4`, which provides the average reaction time for each person on each day of a sleep deprivation experiment that lasted 10 days:

```
sleepstudy <- lme4::sleepstudy %>%
  as_tibble()
sleepstudy
#> # A tibble: 180 x 3
#>     Reaction  Days Subject
#>        <dbl> <dbl> <fct>
#> 1      250.     0 308
#> 2      259.     1 308
#> 3      251.     2 308
#> 4      321.     3 308
#> 5      357.     4 308
#> 6      415.     5 308
#> 7      382.     6 308
#> 8      290.     7 308
#> 9      431.     8 308
#> 10     466.     9 308
#> # ... with 170 more rows
```

This data is displayed in Figure 12.8.

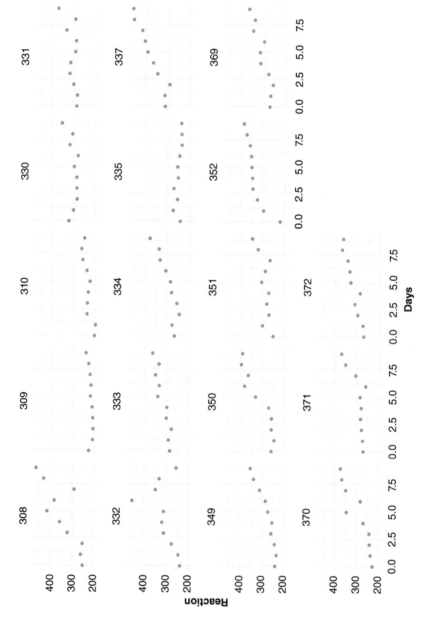

Figure 12.8 Each figure shows the average reaction time data from a subject in sleep deprivation on each day of the 10-day experiment

To begin our analysis, let us first focus on one arbitrarily chosen experimental subject, namely subject 350:

```
sleepstudy_350 <- sleepstudy %>%
  filter(Subject == 350)
sleepstudy_350
#> # A tibble: 10 x 3
#>    Reaction  Days Subject
#>       <dbl> <dbl> <fct>
#> 1     256.     0 350
#> 2     243.     1 350
#> 3     256.     2 350
#> 4     256.     3 350
#> 5     269.     4 350
#> 6     330.     5 350
#> 7     379.     6 350
#> 8     363.     7 350
#> 9     394.     8 350
#> 10    389.     9 350
```

The trend over time in this subject's average reaction time can be modelled using the following normal linear model:

$$y_d \sim \mathrm{N}\left(\mu_d, \sigma^2\right), \quad \mu_d = \beta_0 + \beta_1 x_d, \quad \text{for } d \in 1,\ldots,n,$$

where y_d represents the subject's reaction time on their dth observation, and $x_d \in \{0, 2, \ldots, n = 9\}$ denotes the day when this observation happened. Using $\vec{\beta} = [\beta_0, \beta_1]^{\mathsf{T}}$, we can represent this model using a Bayesian network diagram as in Figure 12.9. In that figure, we provide two equivalent diagrams, with Figure 12.9(b) using a plate notation that denotes a repetition of nodes within a bounding plate according to an index, which in this case is $d \in 1,\ldots,n$. This model is implemented in R as follows:

```
M_350 <- lm(Reaction ~ Days, data = sleepstudy_350)
```

The estimated values of the coefficients are as follows:

```
coef(M_350)
#> (Intercept)        Days
#>   225.83460    19.50402
```

Thus, we estimate that the average reaction time of subject 350 increases by 19.5 milliseconds on each day of the study. In addition, because the first day of the study was indicated by $x_i = 0$, this subject's average reaction prior to any sleep deprivation was 225.83 ms.

Were we to provide a similar model for each subject in the experiment, whom we will index by $j \in 1,\ldots,J$, this would lead to J independent normal linear models. If we denote

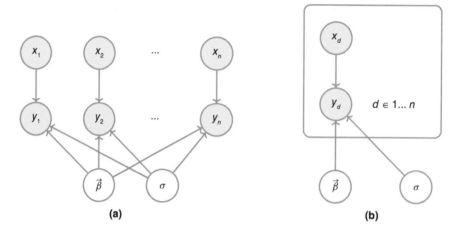

(a)   **(b)**

Figure 12.9 Two equivalent Bayesian network diagrams representing a normal linear model with one predictor variable. Diagram (b) uses a compact plate notation whereby all variables within the plate are repeated for all values of the index i, which takes values from 1 to n

the average reaction time on observation d for subject j by y_{jd}, this set of models is as follows:

$$y_{jd} \sim N\left(\mu_{jd}, \sigma_j^2\right), \quad \mu_{jd} = \beta_{j0} + \beta_{j1}x_{jd}, \text{ for } j \in 1...J, \text{ and } d \in 1,...,n_j.$$

Note that here we have J data sets, one for each subject in the experiment, and d is used to index the observations within each one. Thus, for the jth data set, d ranges from 1 to n_j. This model is represented in a Bayesian network diagram in Figure 12.10(a). If we assume that there is a common residual standard deviation term σ, rather than one for each of the J subjects, this model is identical to a varying intercept and varying slope linear model. These models are linear regression models whose intercepts and slopes vary according to a categorical variable, which in this case is the `Subject` variable. Using R, we can implement this model as follows:

```
M_flat <- lm(Reaction ~ 0 + Subject + Subject:Days, data = sleepstudy)
```

Note that the `0 + Subject` in the formula ensures that we obtain a separate intercept term for each subject, rather than one subject being the *base* level and all others being represented as offsets from this base. Likewise, the `Subject:Days` ensures that we obtain a separate slope for each subject. Formally, this model is equivalent to

$$y_{jd} \sim N\left(\mu_{jd}, \sigma^2\right), \quad \mu_{jd} = \beta_{j0} + \beta_{j1}x_{jd}, \text{ for } j \in 1...J, \text{ and } d \in 1,...,n_j.$$

We have provided a Bayesian network diagram of it in Figure 12.10(b). We can see that it is identical to that represented in Figure 12.10(a), with the exception of the shared standard deviation σ. In other words, a (non-multilevel) varying intercept and varying slope model, where the intercepts and slopes vary by subject, is identical to a set of independent linear models, one per subject, but with a single standard deviation term σ shared across all subjects.

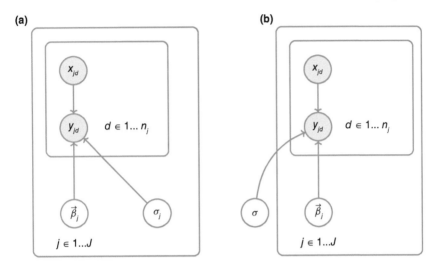

Figure 12.10 Bayesian network diagrams for (a) a set of J independent normal linear models, and (b) a varying slope and varying intercept linear model whereby the slope and intercept vary by a categorical variable with J levels

Let us now consider a multilevel variant of this non-multilevel varying intercept and slope model. In this, we assume that the vector of coefficients $\vec{\beta}_j = [\beta_{j0}, \beta_{j1}]^\intercal$ is drawn from a multivariate normal distribution with mean vector $\vec{b}$ and covariance matrix Σ. This model can be written as follows:

$$y_{jd} \sim N(\mu_{jd}, \sigma), \quad \mu_{jd} = \beta_{j0} + \beta_{j1}x_{jd}, \quad \text{for } j \in 1,\ldots,J, \text{ and } d \in 1,\ldots,n_j,$$
$$\vec{\beta}_j \sim N(\vec{b}, \Sigma), \quad \text{for } j \in 1,\ldots,J.$$

The Bayesian network diagram for this model is shown in Figure 12.11. As we can see, this is an extension of the Bayesian network diagram in Figure 12.10(b), with the extension being that each $\vec{\beta}_j$ is modelled as a function of $\vec{b}$ and Σ.

We can rewrite this multilevel model in the following manner.

$$\text{for } i \in 1,\ldots,n, \quad y_i \sim N(\mu_i, \sigma^2),$$
$$\mu_i = \beta_{[s_i]0} + \beta_{[s_i]1}x_i,$$
$$\text{for } j \in 1,\ldots,J, \quad \vec{\beta}_j \sim N(\vec{b}, \Sigma).$$

Note that here the index i ranges over all values in the entire data set, $i \in 1,\ldots,n$, and each $s_i \in 1,\ldots,J$ is an indicator variable that indicates the identity of the subject on observation i. This notation with a single subscript per observation and indicator variables is more extensible, especially for complex models. Using this new notation, given that $\vec{\beta}_j \sim N(\vec{b}, \Sigma)$, we can rewrite $\vec{\beta}_j$ as $\vec{\beta}_j = \vec{b} + \vec{\zeta}_j$ where $\vec{\zeta}_j \sim N(0, \Sigma)$. Substituting $\vec{b} + \vec{\zeta}_j$ for $\vec{\beta}$, and thus substituting $b_0 + \zeta_{j0}$ and $b_1 + \zeta_{j1}$ for β_{j0} and β_{j1}, respectively, we have the following model:

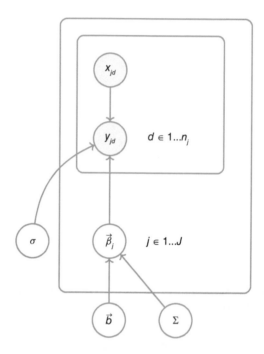

Figure 12.11 Bayesian network diagram for a multilevel varying slopes and intercepts linear model

for $i \in 1,\dots,n$, $\;y_i \sim N\left(\mu_i, \sigma^2\right)$,

$$\mu_i = \beta_{[s_i]0} + \beta_{[s_i]1}\, x_i$$
$$= b_0 + \zeta_{[s_i]0} + (b_1 + \zeta_{[s_i]1})\, x_i$$
$$= \underbrace{b_0 + b_1 x_i}_{\text{fixed effects}} + \underbrace{\zeta_{[s_i]0} + \zeta_{[s_i]1} x_i}_{\text{random effects}},$$

for $j \in 1,\dots,J$, $\;\vec{\zeta}_j \sim N(0, \Sigma)$.

As we can see from this, a multilevel normal linear model is equivalent to a simple linear model (the *fixed effects* model) plus a normally distributed random variation to the intercept and slope for each subject (the *random effects*). The fixed effects are sometimes known as *population-level* effects: they apply to all observations. The random effects, on the other hand, vary across each different value of the grouping variable, which in this example is an individual participant in the experiment. Put another way, the fixed effects give the average effects in the population. The extent to which each individual varies around this average is given by the random effects. That the multilevel linear model can be described in terms of fixed and random effects is why these models are known as a *linear mixed effects model*.

We can implement this model in R using `lme4::lmer`:

```
M_ml <- lmer(Reaction ~ Days + (Days|Subject),
             data = sleepstudy)
```

The syntax here matches the fixed and random effects description of the model. The `Reaction ~ Days` tells us that the fixed effects model is a simple linear regression model with one predictor, and so with one intercept and one slope term. The `(Days|Subject)` tells us that there is random variation to the slope for `Days` and implicitly there is also random variation to the intercept term. We could make the variation to the intercept term explicit by writing `(1 + Days|Subject)`, which is identical to `(Days|Subject)` because the `1 +` is included always by default, just as it is included by default in the fixed effects part, and just as it is in any R regression formula syntax.

The results of this model are obtained as follows:

```
summary(M_ml)
#> Linear mixed model fit by REML ['lmerMod']
#> Formula: Reaction ~ Days + (Days | Subject)
#>    Data: sleepstudy
#>
#> REML criterion at convergence: 1743.6
#>
#> Scaled residuals:
#>     Min      1Q  Median      3Q     Max
#> -3.9536 -0.4634  0.0231  0.4634  5.1793
#>
#> Random effects:
#>  Groups   Name        Variance Std.Dev. Corr
#>  Subject  (Intercept) 612.10   24.741
#>           Days         35.07    5.922   0.07
#>  Residual             654.94   25.592
#> Number of obs: 180, groups:  Subject, 18
#>
#> Fixed effects:
#>             Estimate Std. Error t value
#> (Intercept)  251.405      6.825  36.838
#> Days          10.467      1.546   6.771
#>
#> Correlation of Fixed Effects:
#>      (Intr)
#> Days -0.138
```

The value of $\bar{b}$ is available under `Estimate` in the `Fixed effects`, and we can get these directly as follows:

```
b <- fixef(M_ml)
b
#> (Intercept)        Days
#>   251.40510    10.46729
```

Thus, the average effect of sleep deprivation on reaction time across all individuals is that their reaction time increases by 10.47 ms each day. Also, the average individual has an average reaction time of 251.41 ms on day 0 of the experiment, which means that this is the average reaction time of the average person generally. The values in the covariance matrix Σ and of the residual standard deviation σ can be obtained from the values provided under Random effects. These are available more directly as follows:

```
VarCorr (M_ml)
#> Groups      Name         Std.Dev.  Corr
#> Subject     (Intercept)  24.7407
#>             Days          5.9221   0.066
#> Residual                 25.5918
```

Note that the covariance matrix is defined as follows:

$$\Sigma = \begin{bmatrix} \tau_0^2 & \tau_0\rho\tau_1 \\ \tau_0\rho\tau_1 & \tau_1^2 \end{bmatrix}.$$

We can obtain this directly as follows:

```
VarCorr (M_ml) $ Subject %>%
   Matrix::bdiag() %>%
   as.matrix()
#>               (Intercept)      Days
#> (Intercept)   612.100158   9.604409
#> Days            9.604409  35.071714
```

The values of the standard deviations τ_0 and τ_1 are also available as follows:

```
s <- VarCorr (M_ml) $ Subject %>% attr ('stddev')
s
#> (Intercept)        Days
#>   24.740658    5.922138
```

The correlation matrix corresponding to Σ is obtained as follows:

```
P <- VarCorr (M_ml) $ Subject %>% attr ('correlation')
P
#>               (Intercept)        Days
#> (Intercept)   1.00000000  0.06555124
#> Days          0.06555124  1.00000000
```

From this, we have $\rho = \Sigma_{12} = \Sigma_{21} = 0.066$. More generally, given that

$$\Sigma = \begin{bmatrix} \tau_0^2 & \tau_0\rho\tau_1 \\ \tau_0\rho\tau_1 & \tau_1^2 \end{bmatrix} = \begin{bmatrix} \tau_0 & 0 \\ 0 & \tau_1 \end{bmatrix} \underbrace{\begin{bmatrix} 1 & \rho \\ \rho & 1 \end{bmatrix}}_{\text{corr.matrix}} \begin{bmatrix} \tau_0 & 0 \\ 0 & \tau_1 \end{bmatrix},$$

we can also obtain Σ as follows:

```
# create a diagonal matrix of the stddev
s <- diag(s)

Sigma <- s %*% P %*% s
Sigma
#>                [,1]        [,2]
#> [1,] 612.100158    9.604409
#> [2,]   9.604409  35.071714
```

The contours of the two-dimensional normal distribution with mean vector $\vec{b}$ and covariance matrix Σ are shown in Figure 12.12.

The estimates of each $\vec{\beta}_j, j \in 1,...,J$, can be obtained using the `coef` function:

```
coef(M_ml)$Subject %>%
  head()
#>       (Intercept)       Days
#> 308      253.6637  19.666262
#> 309      211.0064   1.847605
#> 310      212.4447   5.018429
#> 330      275.0957   5.652936
#> 331      273.6654   7.397374
#> 332      260.4447  10.195109
```

These estimates are superimposed on the contours of the two-dimensional normal distribution in Figure 12.12. They are represented by the tip of the arrow corresponding to each subject. The base of the arrow, by contrast, represents the estimates of the coefficients in the non-multilevel varying intercept and varying slope model. As we can see, the estimates in the multilevel model are shrunk towards the centre of the $N(\vec{b}, \Sigma)$ distribution.

Inference

The multilevel model above, given by

$$\text{for } i \in 1,...,n, \quad y_i \sim N(\mu_i, \sigma^2),$$

$$\mu_i = \underbrace{b_0 + b_1 x_i}_{\text{fixed effects}} + \underbrace{\zeta_{[s_i]0} + \zeta_{[s_i]1} x_i}_{\text{random effects}},$$

$$\text{for } j \in 1,...,J, \quad \vec{\zeta}_j \sim N(0, \Sigma).$$

This can be rewritten in matrix notation as follows:

$$\vec{y} = X\vec{b} + Z\vec{\gamma} + \vec{\epsilon}, \quad \vec{\gamma} \sim N(0, \Omega), \quad \vec{\epsilon} \sim N(0, I_n \sigma^2).$$

Here, $\vec{y}$ is an $n \times 1$ (column) vector. X is an $n \times 2$ matrix whose first column is a vector where each value is 1 and whose second column is $\vec{x} = [x_1, x_2, ..., x_n]^\top$. Z is an $n \times 2J$ matrix.

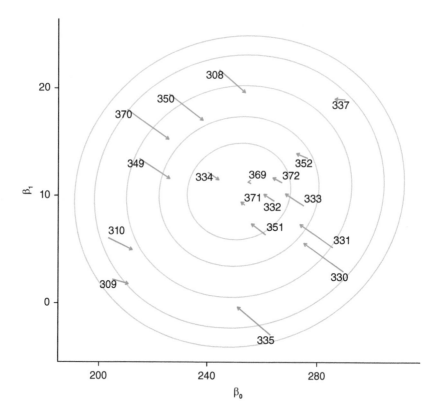

Figure 12.12 Contour plot showing the contours of the two-dimensional normal distribution centred at $\vec{b}$ and whose covariance matrix is Σ. Superimposed on this are the estimates of the coefficients of each subject, both in the non-multilevel model (base of arrow) and in the multilevel model (tip of arrow). As we can see, the estimates of the coefficients in the multilevel are all shrunk towards the overall mean $\vec{b}$

It is easiest to understand if viewed as the horizontal concatenation of two $n \times J$ matrices, Z^0 and Z^1:

$$Z = [Z^0, Z^1].$$

Row i and column j of Z^0 is Z^0_{ij}, which takes the value 1 if and only if $S_i = j$. In other words, each row i of Z^0 is a J-dimensional (row) vector whose values are all zero with the exception of one element, namely element S_i, whose value is 1. Likewise, in matrix Z^1, each row i is a J-dimensional (row) vector whose values are all zero with the exception of one element, namely element S_i, whose value is x_i. $\vec{\gamma}$ is a $2J \times 1$ vector, and is easiest to understand as the vertical concatenation of two $J \times 1$ vectors:

$$\vec{\gamma} = \begin{bmatrix} \vec{\gamma}_0 \\ \vec{\gamma}_1 \end{bmatrix}.$$

The vector $\vec{\gamma}_0 = \left[\varsigma_{1,0}, \varsigma_{2,0}, \ldots, \varsigma_{j,0}, \ldots, \varsigma_{J,0}\right]^T$, where $\varsigma_{j,0}$ is the first element of $\vec{\varsigma}_j$ from the original description of the model. Likewise, the vector $\vec{\gamma}_1 = \left[\varsigma_{1,1}, \varsigma_{2,1}, \ldots, \varsigma_{j,1}, \ldots, \varsigma_{J,1}\right]^T$, where $\varsigma_{j,1}$ is the second element of $\vec{\varsigma}_j$. $\vec{\gamma}$ is a random vector with a $2J$-dimensional multivariate normal distribution with a zero-mean vector and whose covariance matrix Ω has $\Sigma_{[1,1]}$ as its first J elements and $\Sigma_{2,2}$ as its remaining J elements. Its off-diagonal elements are zero except for elements $\Omega_{[j,\,J+j]}$ and $\Omega_{[J+j,\,j]}$, for each $j \in 1,...,J$, whose values are all $\Sigma_{[2,2]}$. The $n \times 1$ vector $\vec{\epsilon}$ is also a random vector distributed as an n-dimensional multivariate normal distribution with zero-mean vector and a covariance matrix $I_n \sigma^2$ where I_n is the n-dimensional identity matrix. In other words, this is a diagonal matrix whose diagonal elements are all equal to σ^2.

From this, we have that $\vec{y}$ has a multivariate normal distribution:

$$\vec{y} \sim \mathrm{N}(X\vec{b},V), \quad V = Z\Omega Z^{\mathsf{T}} + I_n \sigma^2,$$

where V is an $n \times n$ covariance matrix. The density function for $\vec{y}$ is

$$P\left(\vec{y} \mid X\vec{b},V\right) = \frac{1}{(2\pi)^{n/2} \mid V \mid^{1/2}} e^{-\frac{1}{2}(\vec{y}-X\vec{b})^{\mathsf{T}}V^{-1}(\vec{y}-X\vec{b})},$$

and so the log likelihood with respect to $\vec{b}$ and V is

$$L(\vec{b},V \mid \vec{y},X) \propto -\frac{1}{2}\left(\log \mid V^{-1} \mid + (\vec{y}-X\vec{b})^{\mathsf{T}}V^{-1}(\vec{y}-X\vec{b})\right).$$

If we know V, then the maximum likelihood estimator of $\vec{b}$, $\hat{b}$, is

$$\hat{b} = (X^{\mathsf{T}}V^{-1}X)^{-1}X^{\mathsf{T}}V^{-1}\vec{y}.$$

Setting $\vec{b}$ in the likelihood function equal to $\hat{b}$ gives the *profile likelihood* function, which may then be maximized with respect to the parameters of V, which are ultimately based on the parameters Σ and σ.

The maximum likelihood estimate for variance parameters is biased, however. As an alternative to the likelihood function, the *restricted* (also known as *residual*) maximum likelihood (REML) estimates are often used. These are obtained by maximizing the following variant of the likelihood function:

$$L_{\mathrm{reml}}(\vec{b},V \mid \vec{y},X) \propto -\frac{1}{2}\left(\log \mid V^{-1} \mid + (\vec{y}-X\vec{b})^{\mathsf{T}}V^{-1}(\vec{y}-X\vec{b}) + \log \mid X^{\mathsf{T}}V^{-1}X \mid\right).$$

Maximizing this with respect to $\vec{b}$ leads to the same solution as above, but the estimates of the variance parameters are unbiased.

Varying intercepts or varying slopes only models

The above model allowed for random variation in both the intercepts and slopes, but we can choose to have random variation in only one or the other. A varying intercept only multilevel model is defined as

$$\text{for } i \in 1,...,n, \quad y_i \sim \mathrm{N}\left(\mu_i,\sigma^2\right),$$
$$\mu_i = \beta_{[s_i]0} + b_1 x_i,$$
$$\text{for } j \in 1,...,J, \quad \beta_{j0} \sim \mathrm{N}\left(b_0,\tau_0^2\right),$$

which can be rewritten, using the same reasoning as above, as

$$\text{for } i \in 1,...,n, \quad y_i \sim N\left(\mu_i,\sigma^2\right),$$
$$\mu_i = b_0 + b_1 x_i + \zeta_{[si]0},$$
$$\text{for } j \in 1,...,J, \quad \zeta_{j0} \sim N\left(b_0,\tau_0^2\right).$$

Using `lmer`, we would implement this as follows:

```
M_ml_vi <- lmer(Reaction ~ Days + (1|Subject),
                data = sleepstudy)
```

The fixed effects give us an estimate of the slope and intercept as before:

```
fixef(M_ml_vi)
#> (Intercept)        Days
#>    251.40510    10.46729
```

The random effects just provide a measure of standard deviation τ_0 for the random intercepts as well as residual standard deviation σ:

```
VarCorr(M_ml_vi)
#>  Groups    Name        Std.Dev.
#>  Subject   (Intercept) 37.124
#>  Residual              30.991
```

Absent here, compared to the varying intercepts and varying slopes model, are the estimates for τ_1 and ρ. The estimates of the coefficients are obtained using `coef`, as before:

```
coef(M_ml_vi)$Subject %>%
   head()
#>      (Intercept)     Days
#> 308   292.1888 10.46729
#> 309   173.5556 10.46729
#> 310   188.2965 10.46729
#> 330   255.8115 10.46729
#> 331   261.6213 10.46729
#> 332   259.6263 10.46729
```

As we can see, all the subjects' slopes are identical and have the value of the estimate of b_1, which is 10.467. The lines corresponding to these coefficients are shown in Figure 12.13(a).

The varying slope only multilevel model allows only the slopes to vary across subjects and leaves the intercepts fixed. It is defined as

$$\text{for } i \in 1,...,n, \quad y_i \sim N\left(\mu_i,\sigma^2\right),$$
$$\mu_i = b_0 + \beta_{[si]1} + x_i,$$
$$\text{for } j \in 1,...,J, \quad \beta_{j1} \sim N\left(b_0,\tau_1^2\right),$$

which can be rewritten as

$$\text{for } i \in 1,\ldots,n, \quad y_i \sim N(\mu_i,\sigma^2),$$
$$\mu_i = b_0 + b_1 x_i + \zeta_{[s_i]1} x_i,$$
$$\text{for } j \in 1,\ldots,J, \quad \zeta_{j1} \sim N(0,\tau_1^2).$$

Using `lmer`, we would implement this as follows:

```
M_ml_vs <- lmer(Reaction ~ Days + (0+Days|Subject),
                data = sleepstudy)
```

The fixed effects give us an estimate of both the slope and intercept as with the previous models:

```
fixef(M_ml_vs)
#> (Intercept)          Days
#>    251.40510      10.46729
```

The random effects provide a measure of standard deviation τ_1 and σ:

```
VarCorr(M_ml_vs)
#>   Groups     Name Std.Dev.
#>   Subject    Days  7.260
#>   Residual         29.018
```

Absent here, compared to the full model, is the estimate for τ_0 and ρ. The estimates of the coefficients are obtained using `coef` as before:

```
coef(M_ml_vs)$Subject %>%
  head()
#>      (Intercept)        Days
#> 308    251.4051 20.0866918
#> 309    251.4051 -4.2326711
#> 310    251.4051 -0.8189202
#> 330    251.4051  9.1273878
#> 331    251.4051 10.6754843
#> 332    251.4051 11.5352979
```

Here, all the subjects' intercepts are identical and have the value of the estimate of b_0, which is 251.405. The lines corresponding to these coefficients are shown in Figure 12.13(b).

One final variant of the full model is where we allow for both varying slopes and intercepts but assume no correlation between each β_{j0} and β_{j1}. In other words, we assume that these are drawn from independent normal distributions:

$$\text{for } i \in 1,\ldots,n, \quad y_i \sim N(\mu_i,\sigma^2),$$
$$\mu_i = \beta_{[s_i]0} + \beta_{[s_i]1} x_i,$$
$$\text{for } j \in 1,\ldots,J, \quad \beta_{j0} \sim N(b_0,\tau_0^2),$$
$$\beta_{j1} \sim N(b_1,\tau_1^2),$$

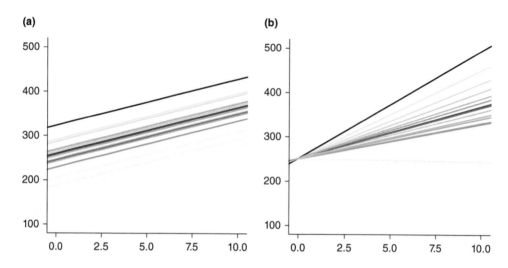

Figure 12.13 Lines of best fit for each data group in a varying intercepts only (a) or varying slopes only (b) multilevel linear model

which is identical to each β_j vector being drawn from a diagonal covariance matrix; that is, where $\rho = 0$.

Using lmer, we would implement this as follows:

```
M_ml_diag <- lmer(Reaction ~ Days + (1|Subject) + (0+Days|Subject),
                  data = sleepstudy)
```

We can obtain the same model using the following formula syntax:

```
M_ml_diag2 <- lmer(Reaction ~ Days + (Days||Subject),
                   data = sleepstudy)
```

The fixed effects give us an estimate of both the slope and intercept as with each of the previous models:

```
fixef(M_ml_diag2)
#> (Intercept)        Days
#>   251.40510    10.46729
```

The random effect provide a measure of the τ_0, τ_1 and σ standard deviations:

```
VarCorr(M_ml_diag2)
#> Groups      Name        Std.Dev.
#> Subject     (Intercept) 25.0513
#> Subject.1   Days         5.9882
#> Residual                25.5653
```

The only quantity that is absent here, compared to the full model, is the estimate for ρ. The estimates of the coefficients are obtained using coef as before:

```
coef (M_ml_diag2) $Subject %>%
  head()
#>      (Intercept)       Days
#> 308     252.9178 19.790783
#> 309     211.0312  1.868110
#> 310     212.2241  5.079492
#> 330     275.9240  5.498636
#> 331     274.3196  7.273348
#> 332     260.6271 10.158792
```

Here, both the intercepts and slopes vary across subjects.

Models for nested and crossed data

In all the examples considered thus far, our multilevel models had only two levels, which we can denote level 0 and level 1. For example, we had rats (level 0) within batches (level 1), observations of per capita alcohol consumption in different years (level 0) within different countries (level 1), individual observations of reaction times on different days (level 0) grouped by different experimental subjects (level 1). We can easily have groups within groups, and we usually refer to these models as *nested* multilevel models. Here, we will consider nested linear mixed effects models.

Let us consider the following data which is based on a subset of the classroom data made available in R package WWGbook:

```
classroom_df <- read_csv('data/classroom.csv')
classroom_df
#> # A tibble: 1,190 x 5
#>    mathscore   ses classid schoolid classid2
#>        <dbl> <dbl>   <dbl>    <dbl>    <dbl>
#> 1        480  0.46     160        1        1
#> 2        569 -0.27     160        1        1
#> 3        567 -0.03     160        1        1
#> 4        532 -0.38     217        1        2
#> 5        478 -0.03     217        1        2
#> 6        515  0.76     217        1        2
#> 7        503 -0.03     217        1        2
#> 8        509  0.2      217        1        2
#> 9        510  0.64     217        1        2
#> 10       473  0.13     217        1        2
#> # ... with 1,180 more rows
```

Each observation is of a child (level 0), and for each one we have their mathematics test score in their first grade (mathscore) and their home socioeconomic status (ses). There are n children in total, indexed by $i \in 1, ..., n$. Each child is in one of J classes (level 1, denoted by classid), and each class is within one of K schools (level 2, denoted by schoolid). This hierarchical arrangement of the data is shown in Figure 12.14.

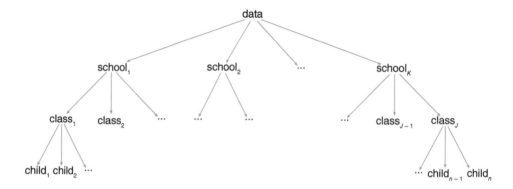

Figure 12.14 Hierarchical arrangement of the data in the `classroom_df` data set. Each one of the N children is in one of J classes and each one of the J classes is in one of K schools

The relationship between `ses` and `mathscore` can vary across different schools (see Figure 12.15(a)). Furthermore, *within* each school, there may be variation in the effect of `ses` on `mathscore` across different classes (see Figure 12.15(b)). Formally, a three-level multilevel varying intercepts and slopes linear model corresponding to the above problem may be presented as follows:

$$\text{for } i \in 1,\dots,n, \quad y_i \sim N\left(\mu_i, \sigma^2\right),$$

$$\mu_i = \gamma_{[c_i]0} + \gamma_{[c_i]1} x_i,$$

$$\text{for } j \in 1,\dots,J, \quad \vec{\gamma}_j \sim N\left(\vec{\beta}_{[s_j]}, \Sigma_c\right),$$

$$\text{for } k \in 1,\dots,K, \quad \vec{\beta}_k \sim N\left(\vec{b}, \Sigma_s\right),$$

For each of the *n* children, we have their `mathscore` variable y_i, their `ses` variable x_i, and an indicator variable $c_i \in 1,\dots,J$. The indicator variable indicates which of the J different classes the child is a member of. For each of one of these J classes, we have another indicator variable $s_j \in 1,\dots,K$. This indicates the school that class j is a member of. For example, if $s_j = k$, this means that class j is within school k. From this description, we see that there are J vectors of coefficients, $\vec{\gamma}_1, \vec{\gamma}_2,\dots,\vec{\gamma}_J$, and each one corresponds to one of the J different classes in the data set. Each vector $\vec{\gamma}_j$ is a sample from a multivariate normal distribution centred at $\vec{\beta}_{[s_j]}$, where S_j is the school that class j is a member of. The covariance matrix of this multivariate normal distribution is Σ_c. The K different vectors $\vec{\beta}_1, \vec{\beta}_2,\dots,\vec{\beta}_K$ are themselves drawn from another multivariate normal distribution whose centre is $\vec{b}$ and whose covariance matrix is Σ_s.

Using the same reasoning as above, we may rewrite $\vec{\gamma}_j \sim N(\vec{\beta}_{[s_j]}, \Sigma_c)$ as $\vec{\gamma}_j = \vec{\beta}_{[s_j]} + \vec{\xi}_j$, where $\vec{\xi}_j \sim N(0, \Sigma_c)$. Likewise, we may rewrite $\vec{\beta}_k \sim N(\vec{b}, \Sigma_s)$ as $\vec{\beta}_k = \vec{b} + \vec{\zeta}_k$, where $\vec{\zeta}_k \sim N(0, \Sigma_s)$. Thus, we have

$$\vec{\gamma}_j = \vec{\beta}_{[s_j]} + \vec{\xi}_j$$

$$= \vec{b} + \vec{\zeta}_{[s_j]} + \vec{\xi}_j.$$

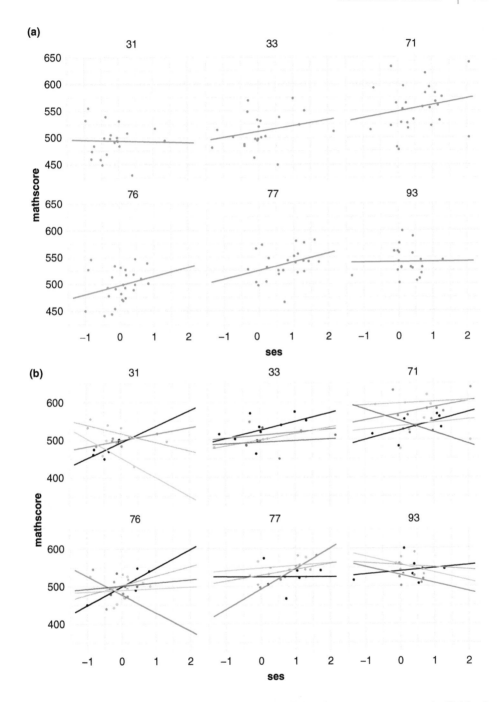

Figure 12.15 In each scatterplot in both (a) and (b), the points represent individual children, and for each one we have their mathematics test score plotted against their home socioeconomic status. Each scatterplot is from a different school. In (a) the line of best fit for the children in the school is shown. In (b), a separate line of best fit for each class within each school is shown

This allows us to rewrite the original model as follows:

$$\text{for } i \in 1,\dots,n, \quad y_i \sim N(\mu_i, \sigma^2),$$

$$\mu_i = \underbrace{b_0 + b_1 x_i}_{\text{fixed effects}} + \underbrace{\zeta_{[z_i]0} + \zeta_{[z_i]1} x_i}_{\text{school random effects}} + \underbrace{\xi_{[c_i]0} + \xi_{[c_i]1} x_i}_{\text{class random effects}},$$

$$\text{for } j \in 1,\dots,J, \quad \vec{\xi}_j \sim N(0, \Sigma_c),$$

$$\text{for } k \in 1,\dots,K, \quad \vec{\zeta}_k \sim N(0, \Sigma_s),$$

Here, for notational simplicity, we have used a new indicator variable $z_i = s_{[c_i]} \in 1,\dots,K$ that indicates the school that child i is a member of.

Using lmer, we can implement this model as follows:

```
M_classroom <- lmer(mathscore ~ ses + (ses|classid) + (ses|schoolid),
                    data = classroom_df)
```

As we can see, we simply use random effects terms, one for random variation by school and the other for random variation by class. Before we proceed, by examining the results of VarCorr, we see that there is a perfect correlation between the random slopes and random intercepts due to class:

```
VarCorr(M_classroom)
#> Groups    Name        Std.Dev.  Corr
#> classid   (Intercept) 8.33529
#>           ses         0.91453 1.000
#> schoolid  (Intercept) 15.44468
#>           ses         7.24255 0.443
#> Residual              32.90608
```

This indicates overparameterization in the model, and can be avoided by removing the possibility of a correlation between the slopes and intercepts for class:

```
M_classroom <- lmer(mathscore ~ ses + (ses||classid) + (ses|schoolid),
                    data = classroom_df)
```

Now, just like previous linear mixed effects models, our fixed effects will consist of a single slope and intercept term:

```
fixef(M_classroom)
#> (Intercept)           ses
#>    522.82481      11.20433
```

From this, we see that, at a population level, every unit increase in ses leads to an 11.2 increase in mathscore. Information concerning the random effects is available from VarCorr:

```
VarCorr(M_classroom)
#> Groups    Name        Std.Dev.  Corr
#> classid   (Intercept) 8.3964
```

```
#>   classid.1  ses            0.0000
#>   schoolid  (Intercept)  15.4398
#>              ses            7.3039  0.470
#>   Residual                 32.8950
```

From this, among other things, we see that there is a minimal random variation in the ses slopes across the different classes.

The variable classid unambiguously identified the class of children by giving each class in each school a unique identifier. In some cases, we do not have unique identifiers for nested groups. As an example, consider the classid2 variable in the classroom_df data sets. Let us draw a sample of observations from classroom_df:

```
classroom_df %>%
   sample_n(10)
#> # A tibble: 10 x 5
#>    mathscore    ses classid schoolid classid2
#>        <dbl>  <dbl>   <dbl>    <dbl>    <dbl>
#>  1       524  0.290      41       14        1
#>  2       519 -0.03      102       26        2
#>  3       552 -0.03      149       53        2
#>  4       552 -0.61       42       75        2
#>  5       499 -0.24      117       55        3
#>  6       522 -0.05      223       29        2
#>  7       473  0.13      217        1        2
#>  8       526  0.04       75       97        1
#>  9       557  0.8        29       72        1
#> 10       478 -0.03      217        1        2
```

Unlike classid, classid2 provides an identifier for each class that is *relative* to its school. Thus, we have class 1 in school 41, and class 1 in school 97. These are completely unrelated classes. In order to deal with variables like this, we must use an alternative formula syntax. For example, in order to have a varying intercepts only model, where the intercept varies by class and school, and assuming we are using the classid2 variable, we use the following syntax in the formula to indicate that the values of classid2 are relative to that of schoolid:

```
M_classroom_vi <- lmer(mathscore ~ ses + (1|schoolid/classid2),
                    data = classroom_df)
```

This is identical to the following model:

```
M_classroom_vi2 <- lmer(mathscore ~ ses + (1|schoolid) + (1|schoolid:classid2),
                    data = classroom_df)
```

The syntax in this second version makes it clear that we are effectively creating a unique identifier for the class by combining the values of schoolid and classid2. These two models, M_classroom_vi and M_classroom_vi2, are identical to that which would have been obtained had we used the unambiguous class identifier classid as in the following model:

```
M_classroom_vi3 <- lmer(mathscore ~ ses + (1|schoolid) + (1|classid),
                        data = classroom_df)
```

An alternative multilevel arrangement of data is known as a *crossed* structure. Again, this is easiest to illustrate by way of an example. Consider a type of cognitive psychology experiment known as a lexical decision task, which is used to understand the basic cognitive processes involved in reading words. In this experiment, multiple subjects are each shown multiple different letter strings (e.g. *dinosaur, morhet, children*), then they have to respond as to whether the string is a word or not, and their reaction times in doing so are also recorded. Thus, subjects $s_1, s_2,..., s_j,..., s_J$ are shown letter strings $w_1, w_2,..., w_k,..., w_K$, and from each subject for each string, we have a response (e.g. a yes/no binary response, a reaction, or both). Over the entire experiment, our total set of responses could be denoted $r_1, r_2,..., r_n$. These are our level 0 observations. Crucially, each response is cross-classified as belonging to a particular subject and a particular letter string. See Figure 12.16.

In general, when dealing with crossed multilevel structures, we simply consider the random variation of slopes or intercepts according to more than one grouping variable. As an example, consider the British Lexicon Project data that we also considered in Chapter 3. This provides us with data from a large lexical decision experiment, and a small fraction of this data is provided in the file data/blp-short2.csv:

```
blp_df <- read_csv('data/blp-short2.csv')
blp_df
#> # A tibble: 662 x 6
#>    spelling participant    rt old20 nletters   freq
#>    <chr>         <dbl> <dbl> <dbl>    <dbl>  <dbl>
#>  1 encode            4   470   2.2        6     93
#>  2 encode           46   599   2.2        6     93
#>  3 encode           78   403   2.2        6     93
#>  4 encode           72   975   2.2        6     93
#>  5 encode           32   504   2.2        6     93
#>  6 encode           52   588   2.2        6     93
#>  7 encode           68   418   2.2        6     93
#>  8 encode           10   718   2.2        6     93
#>  9 encode           54   742   2.2        6     93
#> 10 encode            6   776   2.2        6     93
#> # ... with 652 more rows
```

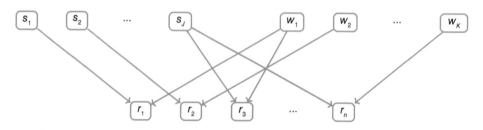

Figure 12.16 A *crossed* multilevel data arrangement, such as would arise in a lexical decision experiment. Each r_i is grouped under one of the $s_1, s_2,..., s_J$ and also one of the $w_1, w_2,..., w_K$

Here, each rt observation corresponds to a particular participant and a particular word (spelling). There are 58 distinct words and 78 distinct participants.

For simplicity, let us consider the multilevel linear model whereby average rt varies by both participant and spelling. This model is as follows:

$$\text{for } i \in 1,\ldots,n, \quad y_i \sim N(\mu_i, \sigma^2),$$
$$\mu_i = \beta_{[s_i]} + \gamma_{[w_i]},$$
$$\text{for } j \in 1,\ldots,J, \quad \beta_j \sim N(b_s, \tau_s^2),$$
$$\text{for } k \in 1,\ldots,K, \quad \gamma_k \sim N(b_w, \tau_w^2).$$

We can rewrite β_j as $\beta_j = b_s + \zeta_j$, where $\zeta_j \sim N(0, \tau_s^2)$, and rewrite γ_j as $\gamma_j = b_w + \xi_k$, where $\zeta_k \sim N(0, \tau_w^2)$. This leads to

$$\text{for } i \in 1,\ldots,n, \quad y_i \sim N(\mu_i, \sigma^2),$$
$$\mu_i = \nu + \zeta_{[s_i]} + \xi_{[w_i]},$$
$$\text{for } j \in 1,\ldots,J, \quad \beta_j \sim N(0, \tau_s^2),$$
$$\text{for } k \in 1,\ldots,K, \quad \gamma_k \sim N(0, \tau_w^2),$$

where $\nu = b_s + b_w$. This is implemented in lmer as follows:

```
M_blp <- lmer(rt ~ 1 + (1|participant) + (1|spelling),
              data = blp_df)
```

From this, we see the estimate of ν is as follows:

```
fixef(M_blp)
#> (Intercept)
#>    586.2724
```

The estimates of τ_s, τ_w and σ are as follows:

```
VarCorr(M_blp)
#> Groups       Name        Std.Dev.
#> participant  (Intercept) 77.738
#> spelling     (Intercept) 64.128
#> Residual                 137.229
```

Group-level predictors

In the examples thus far, the predictor variables were at the bottom level, level 0. For example, at level 0, we had children, and the values of the predictor variable ses were specific to each child. Consider the following two related data sets, which are based on the MathAchieve and MathAchSchool data sets, respectively, available in the nlme package:

```
mathachschool_df <- read_csv('data/mathachieveschool.csv')
mathach_df <- read_csv('data/mathachieve.csv')

mathach_df
#> # A tibble: 7,185 x 6
#>    pupil school minority sex        ses mathach
#>    <chr> <chr>  <chr>    <chr>    <dbl>   <dbl>
#>  1 p1    s1224  No       Female  -1.53    5.88
#>  2 p2    s1224  No       Female  -0.588  19.7
#>  3 p3    s1224  No       Male    -0.528  20.3
#>  4 p4    s1224  No       Male    -0.668   8.78
#>  5 p5    s1224  No       Male    -0.158  17.9
#>  6 p6    s1224  No       Male     0.022   4.58
#>  7 p7    s1224  No       Female  -0.618  -2.83
#>  8 p8    s1224  No       Male    -0.998   0.523
#>  9 p9    s1224  No       Female  -0.888   1.53
#> 10 p10   s1224  No       Male    -0.458  21.5
#> # ... with 7,175 more rows
mathachschool_df
#> # A tibble: 160 x 7
#>    school  size sector   pracad disclim himinty menses
#>    <chr>  <dbl> <chr>     <dbl>   <dbl>   <dbl>   <dbl>
#>  1 s1224    842 Public     0.35   1.60        0  -0.428
#>  2 s1288   1855 Public     0.27   0.174       0   0.128
#>  3 s1296   1719 Public     0.32  -0.137       1  -0.42
#>  4 s1308    716 Catholic   0.96  -0.622       0   0.534
#>  5 s1317    455 Catholic   0.95  -1.69        1   0.351
#>  6 s1358   1430 Public     0.25   1.54        0  -0.014
#>  7 s1374   2400 Public     0.5    2.02        0  -0.007
#>  8 s1433    899 Catholic   0.96  -0.321       0   0.718
#>  9 s1436    185 Catholic   1     -1.14        0   0.569
#> 10 s1461   1672 Public     0.78   2.10        0   0.683
#> # ... with 150 more rows
```

In the `mathach_df` data, for each pupil in a school, we have variables related to their ethnic minority status, sex, home socioeconomic background, and mathematical achievement score (`mathach`). Thus, in this data set, we have a level 1 grouping variable, `school`, but all predictors are at level 0. The `mathachschool_df` data set, on the other hand, provides us with predictors related to the schools. For example, we have the school's size, whether it is public or private, etc., the proportion of students in the school on an academic track (`pracad`), a measure of the discrimination climate in the school (`disclim`), whether there is a high proportion of minority students (`himinty`), and the mean socioeconomic status of the school (`meanses`). In order to use the school-level and pupil-level predictors together, we will join these two data frames by `school`:

```
mathach_df2 <- left_join(mathach_df,
                         mathachschool_df,
                         by = 'school')
```

Group-level predictors do not present special difficulty for linear mixed effects models but cannot be treated identically to individual observation-level predictors. For example, just as in similar examples above, we use a multilevel varying slope and varying intercept model to look at how `ses` affects `mathach` scores and how this effect varies by `school`. The `ses` variable is a pupil-level variable, and we would be able to treat other pupil-level variables in a similar way. We would not, however, be able to use group-level predictors (e.g. `pracad`, `disclim`) in a similar way. For example, we could not perform the following model:

```
# does not work
lmer (mathach ~ pracad + (pracad|school), data = mathach_df2)
```

This is simply because the effect of `pracad` on `mathach` cannot vary by school: each school has exactly one value of `pracad`.

We still can easily use `pracad` in a linear mixed effects model, for example as follows:

```
# does work
# glp: group level predictor
M_glp <- lmer (mathach ~ pracad + (1|school), data = mathach_df2)
```

In this case, our model is that a pupil's `mathach` varies by the school's `pracad`, and there is variation across schools in the terms of the average `mathach`, with the latter effect being due to the random intercepts term. In this model, the fixed effects coefficients are as follows:

```
fixef (M_glp)
#> (Intercept)        pracad
#>    8.384325      8.232278
```

We therefore see that a unit increase in `pracad` leads to an 8.23 point increase in `mathach`. The random effects are as follows:

```
VarCorr (M_glp)
#>  Groups    Name          Std.Dev.
#>  school    (Intercept)   2.0614
#>  Residual                6.2565
```

From this, we see that the standard deviation in the intercept terms across schools is 2.06.

A more interesting situation involving group-level predictors arises in the following situation. Assuming that our outcome variable is still `mathach`, we could model how this varies by the pupil's `ses`, and how this effect varies across schools, using a multilevel varying slopes and intercepts model. We could also use a school-level predictor, for example `himinty`, and model how the school-level slopes and intercepts for the `ses` effect vary by it. This is illustrated in Figure 12.17. Formally, this model would be as follows:

$$\text{for } i \in 1,\dots,n, \quad y_i \sim N\left(\mu_i, \sigma^2\right),$$
$$\mu_i = \beta_{[s_i]0} + \beta_{[s_i]1} x_i,$$
$$\text{for } j \in 1,\dots,J, \quad \vec{\beta}_j \sim N\left(\vec{b}_0 + \vec{b}_1 z_j, \Sigma\right),$$

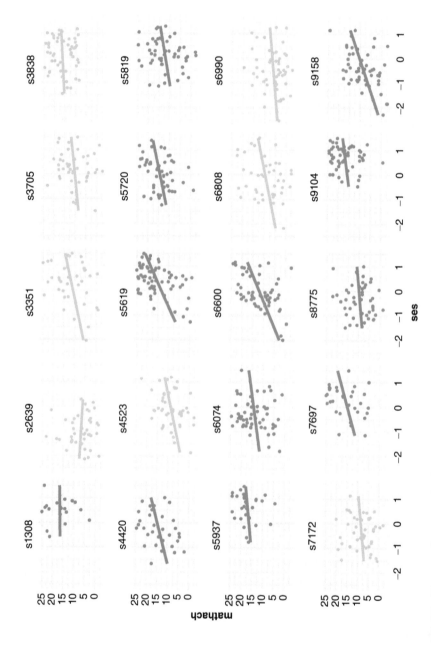

Figure 12.17 How mathematical achievement varies by a child's socioeconomic background across a sample of different schools. Schools are colour-coded to indicate whether they have high ethnic minority proportions (lighter colour) or not

where y_i is the `mathach` score and x_i is the `ses` score of pupil i, and z_j is the `himinty` score of school j. As before, we can rewrite $\vec{\beta}_j$ as follows:

$$\vec{\beta}_j = \vec{b}_0 + \vec{b}_1 z_j + \vec{\zeta}_j,$$

$$\begin{bmatrix} \beta_{j0} \\ \beta_{j1} \end{bmatrix} = \begin{bmatrix} b_{00} \\ b_{01} \end{bmatrix} + \begin{bmatrix} b_{10} \\ b_{11} \end{bmatrix} z_j + \begin{bmatrix} \zeta_{j0} \\ \zeta_{j1} \end{bmatrix},$$

where

$$\vec{\zeta}_j = \begin{bmatrix} \zeta_{j0} \\ \zeta_{j1} \end{bmatrix} \sim N(0, \Sigma).$$

From this, we have

$$\text{for } i \in 1, \ldots, n, \quad y_i \sim N(\mu_i, \sigma^2),$$

$$\mu_i = (b_{00} + b_{10} z_{[s_i]} + \zeta_{[s_i]0}) + (b_{01} + b_{11} z_{[s_i]} + \zeta_{[s_i]1}) x_i$$

$$= \underbrace{b_{00} + b_{01} x_i + b_{10} z_{[s_i]} + b_{11} z_{[s_i]} x_i}_{\text{fixed effects}} + \underbrace{\zeta_{[s_i]0} + \zeta_{[s_i]1} x_i}_{\text{random effects}},$$

$$\text{for } j \in 1, \ldots, J, \quad \vec{\zeta}_j \sim N(0, \Sigma).$$

We see that the role of the group-level predictor $z_{[s_i]}$ interacts with the pupil-level predictor x_i. To implement this model in R, we used the joined data set `mathach_df2`. Note that `himinty` is coded as binary variable where a value of 1 means that there is a high proportion of ethnic minorities in the school:

```
# glp: group level predictor
M_glp <- lmer(mathach ~ ses + himinty + ses:himinty + (ses|school),
              data = mathach_df2)
```

The standard deviations of variation in random intercepts and slopes, and their correlation, are as follows:

```
VarCorr(M_glp)
#>  Groups    Name         Std.Dev.  Corr
#>  school    (Intercept)  2.05931
#>            ses          0.60327   -0.285
#>  Residual               6.06828
```

The fixed effects coefficients are as follows:

```
fixef(M_glp)
#> (Intercept)         ses       himinty  ses:himinty
#>  13.1542443   2.5436697  -1.8593332   -0.5760956
```

From this, we see that as `himinty` changing its value from 0 to 1, the intercept decreases by 1.86 and the slope of the effect of `ses` decreases by 0.58.

Bayesian multilevel models

In practical terms, Bayesian approaches to multilevel modelling differ from their classical counterparts only by their method of inference. In both cases, we begin by specifying a probabilistic model of the observed data. For example, if our data were the sleep deprivation and reaction time data from above, regardless of whether a Bayesian or a classical approach is being taken, a reasonable model of this data would be the multilevel varying slopes and intercepts linear model that we have used already and that can be stated as follows:

$$\text{for } i \in 1,...,n, \quad y_i \sim \mathrm{N}\left(\mu_i, \sigma^2\right),$$
$$\mu_i = b_0 + b_1 x_i + \zeta_{[s_i]0} + \zeta_{[s_i]1} x_i,$$
$$\text{for } j \in 1,...,J, \quad \vec{\zeta}_j \sim \mathrm{N}(0, \Sigma),$$

where y_i, s_i, x_i are, respectively, the reaction time, subject index, and days of sleep deprivation corresponding to observation i. In general, how we specify this probabilistic model and the choices available to us are identical in both the Bayesian and classical approaches. Having specified the model, however, the Bayesian and classical approaches differ in terms of how they perform the inference of the unknown parameters. As we have seen in previous chapters, classical approaches infer estimators of these unknowns, for example by maximum likelihood estimation, and then consider the sampling distribution of these estimators for hypothetical true values of the parameters. From this, we obtain p-values for hypothesis tests, confidence intervals, and related concepts. Bayesian approaches, on the other hand, first posit a prior probability distribution over the unknown parameters. In the above model, for example, we can parameterize it in terms of six unknowns:

$$b_0, b_1, \sigma, \tau_0, \tau_1, \rho,$$

where τ_0^2, τ_1^2 are the diagonal elements of Σ, and ρ is its off-diagonal element. Bayesian methods will therefore posit a probability distribution $P(b_0, b_1, \sigma, \tau_0, \tau_1, \rho)$ over this six-dimensional space. This prior is then combined, via Bayes' rule, with the likelihood function over the parameters to result in the posterior distribution. The posterior distribution tells us the probability that the true values of the parameters are particular values, conditional on all the assumptions of the model.

If we accept default settings for priors and other quantities, performing a Bayesian multilevel linear model using `brms::brm` is identical to using `lme4::lmer`. For example, the following implements the Bayesian counterpart of the `lmer`-based model that we used on page 442, which clearly differs only by using the command `brm` instead of `lmer`:

```
M_bayes <- brm(Reaction ~ Days + (Days|Subject),
                data = sleepstudy)
```

The main results of this model may be obtained by `summary(M_bayes)`, or equivalently by just typing the name of the model `M_bayes`.

```
M_bayes
#>  Family: gaussian
#>   Links: mu = identity; sigma = identity
#> Formula: Reaction ~ Days + (Days | Subject)
#>    Data: sleepstudy (Number of observations: 180)
#> Samples: 4 chains, each with iter = 2000; warmup = 1000; thin = 1;
#>          total post-warmup samples = 4000
#>
#> Group-Level Effects:
#> ~Subject (Number of levels: 18)
#>                       Estimate Est.Error 1-95% CI u-95% CI Rhat Bulk_ESS Tail_ESS
#> sd(Intercept)            27.04      7.08    15.69    42.04 1.00     1750     2591
#> sd(Days)                  6.57      1.49     4.19     9.96 1.00     1701     2055
#> cor(Intercept,Days)       0.08      0.29    -0.48     0.64 1.00     1146     1907
#>
#> Population-Level Effects:
#>             Estimate Est.Error 1-95% CI u-95% CI Rhat Bulk_ESS Tail_ESS
#> Intercept     250.95      7.25   236.35   264.98 1.00     1626     2342
#> Days           10.46      1.66     7.24    13.83 1.00     1486     1985
#>
#> Family Specific Parameters:
#>        Estimate Est.Error 1-95% CI u-95% CI Rhat Bulk_ESS Tail_ESS
#> sigma     25.91      1.58    23.11    29.11 1.00     3568     2920
#>
#> Samples were drawn using sampling(NUTS). For each parameter, Bulk_ESS
#> and Tail_ESS are effective sample size measures, and Rhat is the potential
#> scale reduction factor on split chains (at convergence, Rhat = 1).
```

In this output, among other information, for each one of the six variables b_0, b_1, σ, τ_0, τ_1, ρ, we have the mean of the posterior distribution (Estimate), the standard deviation of the posterior distribution (Est.Error), and the upper and lower limits of the 95% highest posterior density interval (1-95% CI, u-95% CI).

The prior on M_bayes can be seen as follows:

```
M_bayes$prior
#>                            prior      class    coef    group resp dpar nlpar
bound
#> 1                                         b
#> 2                                         b      Days
#> 3     student_t(3, 288.7, 59.3) Intercept
#> 4         lkj_corr_cholesky(1)          L
#> 5                                         L          Subject
#> 6         student_t(3, 0, 59.3)         sd
#> 7                                        sd          Subject
#> 8                                        sd      Days Subject
#> 9                                        sd Intercept Subject
#> 10        student_t(3, 0, 59.3)      sigma
```

From this we see that an improper uniform prior was specified for the fixed effects slope parameter (b_1 in our formula above). For b_0, a non-standard Student t-distribution was used. This is centred at the overall median of the `Reaction` variable, and its scale is set to the median absolute deviation from the median (MAD). For the covariance matrix corresponding to Σ, the `lkj_corr_cholesky` prior with hyperparameter 1 is used. When the hyperparameter is set to 1, this effectively puts a uniform prior on the correlation matrix. For τ_0, τ_1, and σ a half-t-distribution, centred at 0, and with a scale equal to the MAD of `Reaction`, is used. Although it is not stated explicitly that a half-t-distribution is used, this is the case because of the nature of these variables, all being defined on the positive real line.

In general, we may use the command `brm` in place of `lmer` to produce a Bayesian counterpart of any `lme4`-based linear mixed effects model, assuming we accept the default priors set by `brm`. For example:

```
M_glp_bayes <- brm(mathach ~ ses + himinty + ses:himinty + (ses|school),
                   data = mathach_df2)
```

Very often, the results of the models in `brm` and `lmer` are very similar in terms of their practical conclusions. Consider, for example, the posterior means for the fixed effects from the Bayesian model, namely

```
M_glp_bayes %>%
  summary() %>%
  extract2('fixed') %>%
  extract(,'Estimate')
#>    Intercept            ses      himinty ses:himinty
#>   13.1445391      2.5461065   -1.8431743  -0.5778964
```

These are very similar to the maximum (restricted) likelihood estimates from `lmer`:

```
M_glp %>% fixef()
#> (Intercept)            ses      himinty ses:himinty
#>   13.1542443      2.5436697   -1.8593332  -0.5760956
```

Bayesian multilevel models, however, assuming we are implementing them using a probabilistic programming language like Stan, on which `brms` is based, become easier to extend. Exploring how to do this goes beyond the intended scope of this chapter, but we will cover examples in Chapter 17.

13

Nonlinear Regression

Introduction

In Chapters 10 (logistic regression), 11 (generalized linear models), and 12 (multilevel models), we saw how the basic or default regression model, which we referred to as the *normal linear model*, can be generalized and extended so that it can apply to a much wider range of problems than would otherwise be the case. In this chapter, we will consider another important generalization of the basic regression model. In order to introduce this generalization, let us again return to the normal linear model. In this normal linear model, we assume we have a set of n univariate observations:

$$y_1, y_2, \ldots, y_i, \ldots, y_n.$$

Corresponding to each y_i, we have a set of K predictor variables $\vec{x}_i = [x_{i1}, x_{i2}, \ldots, x_{ik} \ldots, x_{iK}]$. The normal linear model assumes that each y_i is a sample from a normal distribution with a mean μ_i and a variance σ^2, and the mean μ_i is a linear function of the predictors x_i. We can write that statement more formally as follows:

$$y_i \sim N(\mu_i, \sigma^2), \quad \mu_i = \beta_0 + \sum_{k=1}^{K} \beta_k x_{ik}, \quad \text{for } i \in 1, \ldots, n.$$

In other words, this model assumes that each y_i is a sample from a normal distribution whose mean μ_i is a (deterministic) linear function of the predictors.

The assumption of a linear relationship between the mean of the outcome variable and the predictor variables is a strong one. It means that we are assuming that the average value of the outcome variable will change as a constant proportion of a change in any predictor variable. For example, if were to change x_{ik} by $\Delta_{x_{ik}}$, we assume that μ_i will change by exactly $\beta_k \times \Delta_{x_{ik}}$. We assume that this holds for all predictor variables and for any value of the change $\Delta_{x_{ik}}$. Clearly, this is a restrictive assumption that will not generally hold. In Figure 13.1 we show some of the many ways in which this assumption can be violated. In each of these examples, the average value of the outcome variable does not change by a constant amount with any constant change in the predictor variable. Clearly, the average trends in each of these scatterplots are not adequately described by straight lines.

We can deal with these situations by no longer modelling the average value of the outcome variable as a linear function of the predictors. For example, we can define a normal *nonlinear* regression model as follows:

$$y_i \sim N(\mu_i, \sigma^2), \quad \mu_i = f(\vec{x}_i, \theta), \quad \text{for } i \in 1, \ldots, n,$$

where $\vec{x}_i$ is the vector of K predictors as before, f is some (deterministic) nonlinear function of $\vec{x}_i$, and θ is a set of parameters of f. More generally, of course, we do not have to assume our outcome variable is normally distributed. In fact it could be any parameterized probability distribution. Moreover, we do not have to assume that it is the mean of the outcome distribution that varies as the deterministic function of $\vec{x}_i$. This leads to the following more general nonlinear regression model:

$$y_i \sim D(\mu_i, \psi), \quad \mu_i = f(\vec{x}_i, \theta), \quad \text{for } i \in 1, \ldots, n$$

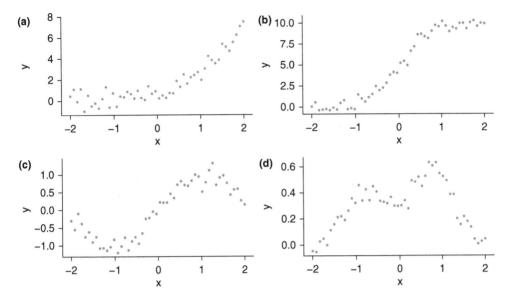

Figure 13.1 Examples of nonlinear regression models. In each case, the values of the outcome variables are sampled from normal distributions whose means are nonlinear functions of the predictor variable

where D is some probability distribution with parameters μ_i and ψ, and μ_i is the nonlinear function of $\vec{x}_i$, which is parameterized by θ.

Using a nonlinear regression model, whether the normal or the more general one, introduces considerable conceptual and practical difficulties. First, we must choose the nonlinear function, or functional form, f. There are indescribably many possibilities for f, and choosing between them or even choosing a plausible set of candidate functions can be very challenging, as we will see. Second, inference of the values of the unknown parameters of the model can also be very challenging. In the normal linear regression model, inference of, for example, the maximum likelihood estimator can be accomplished using algebra. Likewise, assuming appropriate choices of prior distributions for the parameters, the Bayesian posterior distribution over these parameters can be obtained through algebra. This is generally not the case when we use nonlinear functions, even if our outcome variable is normally distributed, and for arbitrary nonlinear functions f and arbitrary probability distributions for the outcome variable D, inference of the values of the unknown parameters in both f and D may lead to insurmountable computational challenges. Typically, different numerical algorithms are employed in different situations. Often these work well, but it is not at all uncommon to encounter computational problems or failures with these algorithms too. Finally, even assuming that inference was successful, the interpretation of parameters in nonlinear regression models may also be challenging or even impossible. In a linear model, each regression coefficient has a simple interpretation: it gives the rate of change of the outcome variable for any unit change of the predictor. In nonlinear models, it is not so simple. Certainly, in some cases of nonlinear regression, the parameters can have clear and meaningful interpretations. But in other cases, individual parameters cannot be understood independently of other parameters. This sometimes entails that it can be difficult to assess whether one predictor variable has any statistically meaningful relationship (e.g. a statistically significant relationship) with the outcome variable. More generally, it can be challenging to summarize and explain the relationship, if any, between the predictors and the outcome variable. Simply put, nonlinear regression models can be opaque, and as such it is sometimes preferable to treat them just as *black box* models, useful for the accuracy of their predictions rather than for any conceptual or explanatory insights.

For all of these reasons, nonlinear regression should be treated with some caution and as a relatively advanced statistical topic. That is emphatically not to say that it should be avoided. It is in general a very powerful tool that can allow us either to do more advanced analyses than were otherwise possible, or even to deal with problems that were otherwise impossible. It is just that we should also be clear that nonlinear regression raises additional conceptual and practical challenges compared to those we have encountered when using general or generalized linear models.

In this chapter, we'll discuss four topics related to nonlinear regression. First, we'll cover parametric nonlinear regression, which is where a certain parametric form of the nonlinear function is assumed. Next, we will cover polynomial and spline regression models, both of which can be seen as either semiparametric or nonparametric regression models. Finally, we will introduce the topic of generalized additive models (GAMs), a broad class of nonlinear regression models of which polynomial and spline models can be seen as subclasses.

Parametric nonlinear regression

In *parametric nonlinear regression* we choose a particular parametric functional form for the nonlinear function f and then infer the values of its unknown parameters from data. The other types of nonlinear regression that we will cover in this chapter also have parameters, which are inferred from data, and so can also be termed parametric models. However, in these cases, the functional form of the nonlinear function in the regression model is essentially unknown and is being approximated by a more flexible nonlinear model.

A sigmoidal regression

Let us start with an essentially arbitrarily chosen nonlinear function, such as the following nonlinear function of a single variable x:

$$f(x,b,\alpha,\beta) \triangleq b \tanh(\alpha + \beta x).$$

The hyperbolic tangent function (tanh) is defined as follows:

$$\tanh(x) = \frac{e^x - e^{-x}}{e^x + e^{-x}} = \frac{e^{2x} - 1}{e^{2x} + 1}.$$

It is a *sigmoidal* or S-shaped function that maps the real line to the interval $[-1,1]$ (see Figure 13.2(a)), and so $f(x,b,\alpha,\beta)$ is a linear function of a nonlinear function of another linear function of x. Functions of this type are widely used in artificial neural network models (see Bishop, 1995). With this nonlinear function, our nonlinear regression model would then be

$$y_i \sim N(\mu_i, \sigma^2), \quad \mu_i = b \tanh(\alpha + \beta x_i), \quad \text{for } i \in 1,\ldots,n.$$

In order to explore this regression model in practice, we will begin by simply generating data according to the model:

```
Df <- local({
  b <- 3.0
  alpha <- 0.75
  beta <- 0.25
  tibble(x = seq(-10, 10, length.out = 50),
         y = b * tanh(alpha + beta*x) + rnorm(length(x), sd = 0.5))
})
```

This data is shown in Figure 13.2(b).

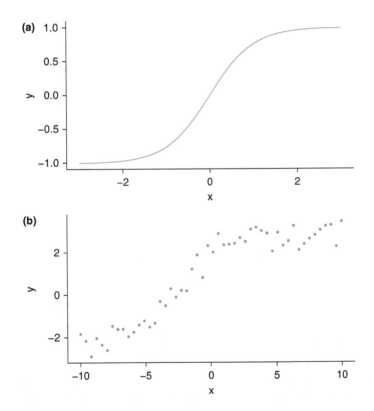

Figure 13.2 (a) The hyperbolic tangent function, tanh. (b) Data normally distributed around a linear function of a tanh function

To perform this regression analysis, we can use the nls function that is part of the base R stats package, which is always preloaded. With nls, in its R formula, we state the parametric form of the function we are assuming. In our case, this will be `y ~ b * tanh(alpha + beta * x)`. The `nls` function then attempts to find the *least squares* solution for `alpha` and `beta`. In other words, and more formally, it attempts to find the values of b, α and β that minimize the formula

$$\sum_{i=1}^{n}(y_i - b\tanh(\alpha + \beta x_i))^2$$

Usually, `nls` requires us to also provide an initial guess of the values of the unknown parameters. In the following example, we'll set `alpha` to 0 and `b` and `beta` to 1:

```
M <- nls (y ~ b * tanh (alpha + beta * x),
          start = list (b = 1, alpha = 0, beta = 1),
          data = Df)
```

We can view the results of this analysis using `summary` just as we did with `lm`, `glm`, `lmer` and other models:

```
summary (M)
#>
#> Formula: y ~ b * tanh (alpha + beta * x)
#>
#> Parameters:
#>        Estimate Std. Error t value Pr (>|t|)
#> b       2.84163    0.12458  22.809  < 2e-16 ***
#> alpha   0.77170    0.10205   7.562 1.15e-09 ***
#> beta    0.24426    0.02902   8.416 6.14e-11 ***
#> ---
#> Signif. codes:   0 '***' 0.001 '**' 0.01 '*' 0.05 '.' 0.1 ' ' 1
#>
#> Residual standard error: 0.4478 on 47 degrees of freedom
#>
#> Number of iterations to convergence: 9
#> Achieved convergence tolerance: 4.783e-06
```

As can we see, the least squares estimates of b, α and β, which we'll label as $\hat{b}$, $\hat{\alpha}$ and $\hat{\beta}$, are 2.842, 0.772 and 0.244. The estimate for σ, the standard deviation of the normal distribution around each μ_i, also known as the *residual standard error*, is 0.448. All of these values match well the parameters that we used to generate the data.

We may now view the predictions of the model using the `predict` function. Recall that, by default, `predict` will return the predicted values of the outcome variable for each value of the predictor variables using the estimated values of the parameters. In other words, it will calculate $\hat{y}_i = \hat{b}\tanh(\hat{\alpha} + \hat{\beta}x_i)$ for each x_i. We'll use the following code to perform this prediction and plot the results, as shown in Figure 13.3:

```
Df %>%
    mutate (y_pred = predict (M)) %>%
```

```
ggplot(aes(x = x)) +
geom_point(aes(y = y), size = 0.5) +
geom_line(aes(y = y_pred), colour = 'red')
```

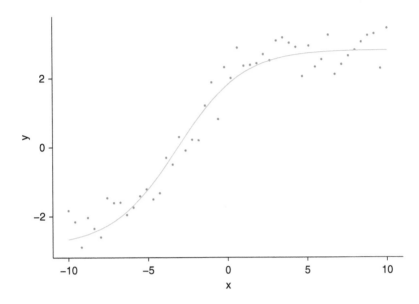

Figure 13.3 The fitted tanh regression model

One practical issue with `nls` is that choosing starting values may not always be a simple matter. Even in the above example, starting values relatively close to the true values, say 0 for all parameters, will lead to the algorithm failing:

```
M_tmp <- nls(y ~ b * tanh(alpha + beta * x),
             start = list(b = 0, alpha = 0, beta = 0),
             data = Df)
#> Error in nlsModel(formula, mf, start, wts) :
      singular gradient matrix at initial parameter estimates
```

In the case of some functions, however, the `stats` package provides functions that use heuristics to roughly estimate some reasonable starting values of parameters. These so-called `selfStart` functions only exist for a restricted set of functions. While it is possible to create new `selfStart` functions for new functions, creating the heuristics is itself not simple. For our function, no `selfStart` function exists. However, a `selfStart` function, `SSlogis`, does exist for a related function:

$$\text{SSlogis}\left(x, \text{Asym}, x_{\text{mid}}, \text{scal}\right) \triangleq \frac{\text{Asym}}{1 + e^{\frac{x_{\text{mid}} - x}{\text{scal}}}}$$

This is also a sigmoidal function, but it is bounded between 0 and a. Because it cannot take negative values, to use it with our data we must first subtract the minimum value of all the y_i

from each y_i. Having done so, we can use the getInitial function to return some plausible starting values for Asym, x_{mid} and scal:

```
inits <- getInitial(y ~ SSlogis(x, Asym, xmid, scal),
                     data = mutate(Df, y = y - min(y)))
)
inits
#>      Asym       xmid       scal
#>   5.850634  -3.055370   2.180384
```

With some algebra, we can then map the parameters of SSlogis to those of our tanh-based function as follows:

$$\alpha = \frac{Asym}{2scal}, \quad \beta = \frac{1}{2scal}, \quad b = \frac{Asym}{2}.$$

We may now use these starting values in our nls model:

```
starting_values <- within(list(),{
  alpha <- inits['Asym'] / (2 * inits['scal'])
  beta <- 1 / (2 * inits['scal'])
  b <- inits['Asym']/2
})

nls(y ~ b * tanh(alpha + beta * x),
    start = starting_values,
    data = Df) %>%
  summary()
#>
#> Formula: y ~ b * tanh(alpha + beta * x)
#>
#> Parameters:
#>        Estimate Std. Error t value Pr(>|t|)
#> b       2.84163    0.12458  22.809  < 2e-16 ***
#> beta    0.24426    0.02902   8.416 6.14e-11 ***
#> alpha   0.77170    0.10205   7.562 1.15e-09 ***
#> ---
#> Signif. codes:  0 '***' 0.001 '**' 0.01 '*' 0.05 '.' 0.1 ' ' 1
#>
#> Residual standard error: 0.4478 on 47 degrees of freedom
#>
#> Number of iterations to convergence: 10
#> Achieved convergence tolerance: 3.719e-06
```

Modelling golf putting successes

Thus far, our aim has simply been to introduce the basic principles of how to do nonlinear regression using nls, and for that we used a seemingly arbitrary nonlinear function and some data generated using this model. Let us now consider some real-world data, but also consider how the choice of the nonlinear function can be, and ideally ought to be, theoretically motivated. The data we will use concerns the relative frequencies with which professional golfers successfully putt a golf ball into the hole as a function of their distance from the hole. This data, which is available in the `golf_putts.csv` file, is taken from Berry (1995), and was discussed further in Gelman and Nolan (2002b).

```
golf_df <- read_csv('data/golf_putts.csv')
golf_df
#> # A tibble: 19 x 3
#>    distance attempts success
#>       <dbl>    <dbl>   <dbl>
#> 1         2     1443    1346
#> 2         3      694     577
#> 3         4      455     337
#> 4         5      353     208
#> 5         6      272     149
#> 6         7      256     136
#> 7         8      240     111
#> 8         9      217      69
#> 9        10      200      67
#> 10       11      237      75
#> 11       12      202      52
#> 12       13      192      46
#> 13       14      174      54
#> 14       15      167      28
#> 15       16      201      27
#> 16       17      195      31
#> 17       18      191      33
#> 18       19      147      20
#> 19       20      152      24
```

As we can see, this data provides the number of putting attempts and the number of successful putts at various distances (in feet) from the hole. For example, there were 1443 recorded putting attempts at a distance of 2 feet from the hole. Of these 1443 attempts, 1346, or around 93%, were successful. On the other hand, there were 200 recorded attempts at a distance of 10 feet, of which 67, or around 34%, were successful. The absolute number of attempts and successes at each distance is vital information and so ideally we should base our analysis on this data, using a binomial logistic regression or a related model. However, for simplicity here, we will just use the relative frequencies of successes at each distance. To do so, we will first create a new variable, `prob`, that is the ratio of successes to attempts at each distance. This is done in the following code, and the plot of these probabilities as a function of distance is shown in Figure 13.4:

```
golf_df %<>% mutate(prob = success/attempts)
```

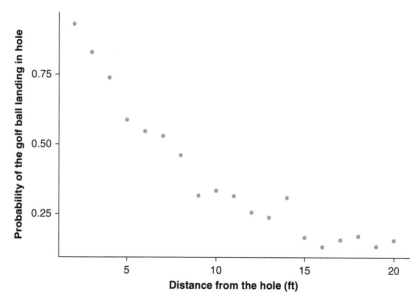

Figure 13.4 Relative frequencies of successful putts by professional golfers as a function of distance (in feet) from the hole

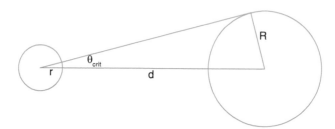

Figure 13.5 A golf ball of radius r (left) and the golf hole of radius R (right). The centres of these two circles are d apart. If the golf ball travels in a straight horizontal line to the hole, it will fall in. If its trajectory deviates, either to the right or to the left, greater than an angle of θ_{crit}, it will miss. The angle θ_{crit} is the angle between the horizontal line of length d and the tangent line from the centre of the ball to the hole. The line from the centre of the hole meets the tangent line at a right angle. As such, $\theta_{crit} = \sin^{-1}(R / d)$

In order to fit a parametric nonlinear regression model to this data, we must begin by choosing the nonlinear function. We could choose functions whose shape appears to roughly match the decaying pattern of the points. However, when this is possible, it is preferable to choose a function based on a principled model of the phenomenon. As an example, let us use the simple model described in Gelman and Nolan (2002b). We will treat the golf ball as a circle of radius r and the hole as a circle of radius R. In reality, the values of r and R are 21.33 mm and 53.975 mm, respectively. In Figure 13.5, we draw these two circles to scale, positioned a distance d apart. If the golf ball travels in a straight line along the line from its centre to the centre of the hole, it will fall into the hole. If it deviates slightly from this straight line, it will still fall in if the angle of the trajectory to the left or the right is no greater than $\theta_{crit}= \sin^{-1}(R/d)$, which is the angle between the vertical line of length d and the tangent line from the centre of the circle representing the ball to the circle representing the hole.[1] We can assume that deviation from a perfect straight line of a professional golfer's putt will be normally distributed with mean 0 and standard deviation σ, where the value of σ is unknown. Given this, the probability that the angle of their putt will be between 0 and θ_{crit} is

$$P(0 < \theta \le \theta_{crit}) = \Phi(\theta_{crit} \mid 0, \sigma^2) - \frac{1}{2},$$

where

$$\Phi(\theta_{crit} \mid 0, \sigma^2) \triangleq \int_{-\infty}^{\theta_{crit}} N(\theta \mid 0, \sigma^2),$$

which is the value at θ_{crit} of the cumulative distribution function of a normal distribution of mean 0 and standard deviation σ. We simply double the quantity $\Phi(\theta_{crit} * 0, \sigma^2) - \frac{1}{2}$ to get $P(\theta_{crit} < 0 \le \theta_{crit})$. Therefore, the probability of a successful putt is

$$2\Phi\left(\sin^{-1}\left(\frac{R}{d}\right) \mid 0, \sigma^2\right) - 1.$$

This is a nonlinear parametric function of distance d, where R is known to have a value of 53.975 mm, and σ is the single unknown parameter.

This nonlinear function is easily implemented as follows:

```
successful_putt_f <- function(d, sigma){
  R <- 0.17708333 # 53.975mm in feet
  2 * pnorm(asin(R/d), mean=0, sd=abs(sigma)) -1
}
```

The nls-based model using this successful_putt_f function is as follows:

```
M_putt <- nls(prob ~ successful_putt_f(distance, sigma),
              data = golf_df,
              start = list(sigma = 0.1)
)
summary(M_putt)
#>
#> Formula: prob ~ successful_putt_f(distance, sigma)
#>
#> Parameters:
#>        Estimate Std. Error t value Pr(>|t|)
#> sigma 0.041427   0.001289   32.15  <2e-16 ***
```

---

[1] The tangent line from the centre of the small circle intersects the line from the centre of the larger circle at a right angle. In the right-angled triangle that is formed (Figure 13.5), the side opposite θ_{crit} is length R, and the hypotenuse is of length d. The sine of θ_{crit} is $\sin(\theta_{crit}) = (R/d)$, and so $\theta_{crit} = \sin^{-1}(R/d)$.

```
#> ---
#> Signif. codes:   0 '***' 0.001 '**' 0.01 '*' 0.05 '.' 0.1 ' ' 1
#>
#> Residual standard error: 0.04233 on 18 degrees of freedom
#>
#> Number of iterations to convergence: 4
#> Achieved convergence tolerance: 9.886e-06
```

As we can see, the estimate for `sigma` is 0.041. This is the estimated standard deviation in the angle of errors in the golfer's putts. It is given in radians, and corresponds to 2.374 degrees. The nonlinear function with this estimated value for σ is plotted in Figure 13.6. This appears to be a good fit to the data, which is not necessarily expected given that the physical model that we used was a very simple one.

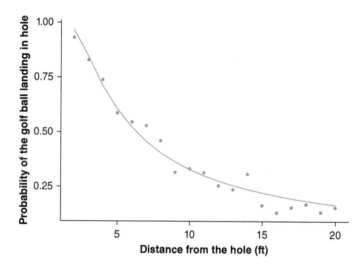

Figure 13.6 The predictions of the nonlinear regression model based on probabilities of errors in putting angles being normally distributed

13.3 Polynomial regression

Using `nls` required that we knew or could propose a specific functional form for the nonlinear function in our regression model. We saw the case of the golf putting data where, using some basic principles and knowledge of the domain, we could obtain a specific nonlinear function for our regression model. There are many other examples like this throughout science where theoretical descriptions of the phenomenon of interest, even if sometimes simplified ones, can lead to nonlinear functions that we can use in the regression model. When we are in these situations, `nls` and related tools are very useful. Often, however, we simply do not have theoretically motivated nonlinear functions that describe the phenomenon of interest. Certainly, it may be possible in principle to derive these functions, but this is essentially a type of scientific theory building, and so is not at all a simple matter, especially where the phenomenon and the related data are complex. In these situations, then, we often proceed by using a flexible class of nonlinear regression models that essentially attempt to approximate the nonlinear function in regression models. These models are sometimes termed *nonparametric* nonlinear regression models, although the validity of that term is debatable, and include spline and radial basis function regression models, generalized additive models, and Gaussian process regression models. We will cover some of these models in subsequent sections of this chapter. As a bridge to these topics, we will first cover polynomial regression models.

Polynomial regression models can be seen as just another parametric nonlinear regression model like those we used with nls in the previous section because we have a specific nonlinear function, namely a polynomial function of specified degree, that has parameters that we then infer from data. Indeed, it is perfectly possible to use a polynomial function in nls. However, polynomial functions are often chosen for their apparent ability to approximate other functions. In other words, in situations where we are modelling data whose trends are nonlinear but where there is no known parametric form to this nonlinearity, polynomial regression models are often the default choice. The reason why they are chosen is that, as we will see, they are particularly easy to use, being essentially a linear regression on transformed predictor variables. However, we will argue here that polynomial regression should be used with caution, and perhaps should not be a default choice when doing nonlinear regression, because they can often lead to poor fit to the data, either by underfitting or, more commonly, by *overfitting*, as we will see.

The nature of polynomial regression

For simplicity, let us begin with a regression model with a single outcome variable and a single predictor variable. As we've seen, a normal linear regression model in this case is defined as follows:

$$y_i \sim \mathrm{N}(\mu_i, \sigma^2), \quad \mu_i = \alpha + \beta x_i, \quad \text{for } i \in 1,\ldots,n.$$

The function $\mu_i = \alpha + \beta x_i$ is a *polynomial of degree 1*. In other words, we can write

$$\mu_i = \alpha + \beta x_i = \alpha x_i^0 + \beta x_i^1,$$

where the superscripts in x_i^0 and x_i^1 are exponents. In other words, x_i^0 is x_i raised to the power of 0, which is $x_i^0 = 1$, and x_i^1 is x_i raised to the power of 1, which is $x_i^1 = x_i$. The *degree* of the polynomial is the highest power in any of its terms. We can easily extend the linear model to become a polynomial of any degree. For example, a degree 2 polynomial regression version of the above model could be as follows:

$$y_i \sim \mathrm{N}\left(\mu_i, \sigma^2\right), \quad \mu_i = \alpha + \beta x_i + \gamma x_i^2, \quad \text{for } i \in 1,\ldots,n.$$

We could rewrite this as

$$y_i \sim \mathrm{N}\left(\mu_i, \sigma^2\right), \quad \mu_i = \alpha x_i^0 + \beta x_i^1 + \gamma x_i^2, \quad \text{for } i \in 1,\ldots,n,$$

or, to avoid proliferation of Greek letters for the coefficients, by

$$y_i \sim N\left(\mu_i, \sigma^2\right), \quad \mu_i = \beta_0 x_i^0 + \beta_1 x_i^1 + \beta_2 x_i^2, \text{ for } i \in 1,\dots,n,$$

where the subscripts in β_0, β_1, β_2 are simply indices. Continuing like this to any finite degree is easy. For example, here's a degree $K = 5$ polynomial of each x_i:

$$y_i \sim N\left(\mu_i, \sigma^2\right), \quad \mu_i = \beta_0 x_i^0 + \beta_1 x_i^1 + \beta_2 x_i^2 + \beta_3 x_i^3 + \beta_4 x_i^4 + \beta_5 x_i^5,$$

$$\mu_i = \sum_{k=0}^{K} \beta_k x_i^k, \text{ for } i \in 1,\dots,n.$$

Viewed in this way, a polynomial regression model of a single predictor is simply a linear regression model with multiple predictors, each being the predictor raised to a different power.

Raising a given predictor to successive powers 0, 1, ... leads to a different function of x. Some examples are shown in Figure 13.7. When the power is 0, the function is a flat line at 1 ($y = x^0 = 1$). When the power is 1, the function is a line with slope 1 ($y = x^1 = 1$). When the power is 2, the function is a parabolic, or quadratic, function, and so on. The polynomial function $\sum_{k=0}^{K} \beta_k x_i^k$ is a weighted sum of these functions, with the weightings of the sum being the coefficients β_0, β_1,..., β_K. These weighted sums can approximate different functions. For example, in Figure 13.8, we provide multiple plots, each with multiple functions of the form $y = \sum_{k=0}^{S} \beta_k x^k$ where β_0, β_1,..., β_{K_S} are random. In polynomial regression, therefore, we aim to infer a set of coefficients to essentially approximate the function that represents the curve from which our data was generated along with additive normally distributed noise. In other words, we assume that are data are generated as follows:

$$y_i \sim N(f(x_i), \sigma^2), \quad \text{for } i = 1,2,\dots,n,$$

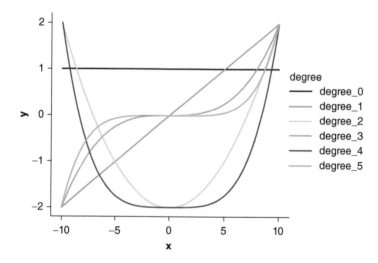

Figure 13.7 Plots of polynomial functions. For each degree $k \in 0,1,\dots,K$, we plot $y = x^k$. We have scaled the value of y in each case so that it occurs within the range $(-2,2)$, so as to aid the visualization of each function

where f is a nonlinear function that we will approximate with a polynomial of degree K; that is, for each x_i, we assume that $f(x_i)$ can be approximated by $\sum_{k=0}^{K} \beta_k x_i^k$ for some unknown values of $\beta_0, \beta_1, ..., \beta_K$.

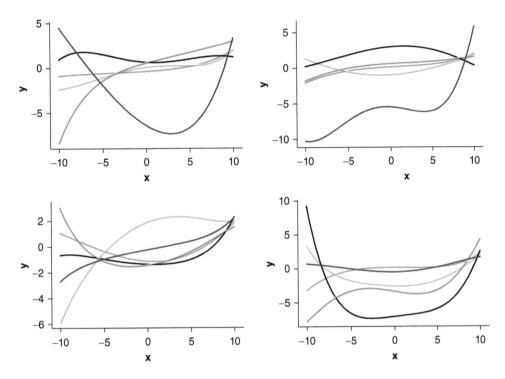

Figure 13.8 Examples of random polynomial functions. In each plot, we have five random polynomials of degree $K = 5$. In other words, each function shown in each plot is defined as $y = \sum_{k=0}^{5} \beta_k x^k$ for some random vector $\beta_0, \beta_1, ..., \beta_5$

Polynomial regression in practice

Let us use polynomial regression to model some eye-tracking data,[2] which is based on averaging data that was obtained from an eye-tracking-based cognitive psychology experiment, and is available in the file funct_theme_pts.csv:

```
eyefix_df <- read_csv('data/funct_theme_pts.csv')
```

The data provides the number of times over the duration of a few seconds that participants look at certain key objects in their visual scenes under different experimental conditions. To begin, we will look at the average number of eye fixations on one of the three different types of object in each (50 ms) time window, averaging over experimental subjects and experimental conditions. The fixation proportions for all three objects are shown in Figure 13.9. We will begin our analysis with just the data on the *Target* object:

[2]Data from D. Mirman and J. Magnussen. See https://github.com/dmirman/gazer for more details.

```
eyefix_df_avg <- eyefix_df %>%
  group_by(Time, Object) %>%
  summarize(mean_fix = mean(meanFix)) %>%
  ungroup()

eyefix_df_avg_targ <- filter(eyefix_df_avg, Object == 'Target')
```

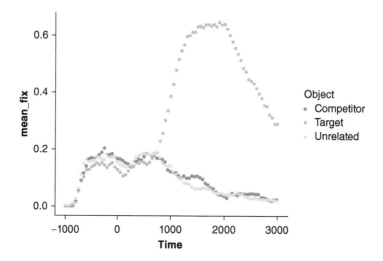

Figure 13.9 Average proportion of eye fixations on different types of objects (named *Competitor, Target, Unrelated*) in each time window in multisecond experimental trial

To perform a polynomial regression in R, we can use `lm`. All we need to do is to create new variables that are our original variable raised to different powers. For example, for a predictor variable `x` and outcome `y`, a degree 3 polynomial regression using `lm` could be written using the following `lm` formula:

```
y ~ x + I(x^2) + I(x^3)
```

Note that we must use `I()`, known as *as is*, here. This essentially transforms, for example, `x^2` to be a new variable in the regression. We can create the same formula more easily using `poly` as follows:

```
y ~ poly(x, degree=3, raw=T)
```

We will explain the meaning of `raw=T` in due course, but for now, we will note that by default `raw=F`.

In the following code, we perform polynomial regression on this data from degree 1 (which is a standard linear model) to degree 9. Note that we are using `purrr::map` here to rerun the same `lm` nine times. On the first iteration, the `degree` parameter in `poly` takes the value 1. On the second iteration, it takes the value 2, and so on for each value in the sequence 1 to 9. The nine resulting models are stored in the list `M_eyefix_targ`:

```
M_eyefix_targ <- map(seq(9),
                 ~lm(mean_fix ~ poly(Time, degree = ., raw = T),
                     data = eyefix_df_avg_targ)
)
```

The fitted models can be seen in Figure 13.10 and the model fit statistics are shown in Table 13.1. For the model fit statistics, we provide R^2, adjusted R^2, the log of the likelihood, and the AIC. We covered all four of these statistics in previous chapters. For example, R^2 and adjusted R^2 were covered in Chapter 9, and the log likelihood and AIC were covered in Chapter 8 and elsewhere. As we can see both in the figures and from the model summaries, we obtain better fits to the data as we increase the degree of the polynomial. This may seem to imply that higher-order polynomials are more flexible and so generally lead to better fits to data. This is an important point to which we will return later in this section.

Table 13.1 Model fit statistics for polynomial regression models

degree	Rsq	Adj Rsq	LL	AIC
1	0.57	0.56	44.35	-82.70
2	0.70	0.69	58.72	-109.44
3	0.89	0.89	100.49	-190.99
4	0.90	0.90	103.76	-195.53
5	0.98	0.97	161.26	-308.53
6	0.98	0.98	163.50	-311.01
7	0.99	0.99	202.69	-387.39
8	0.99	0.99	203.22	-386.43
9	0.99	0.99	207.39	-392.78

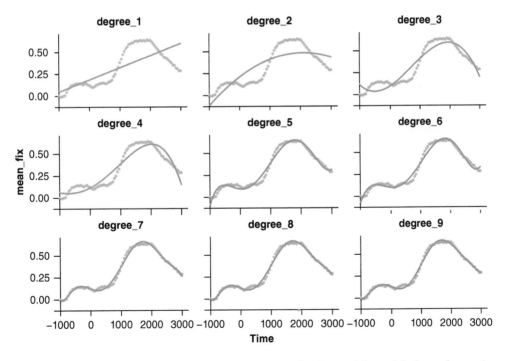

Figure 13.10 Predicted functions in a sequence of polynomial models from degree 1 to degree 9

Note that because the polynomial regression is essentially a linear model, everything that we know about linear models and `lm` applies to polynomial regression too. For example, the summary output of the model, which we show below for the case of degree $K = 3$, is interpreted identically to any other `lm` model summary:

```
summary(M_eyefix_targ[[3]])
#>
#> Call:
#> lm(formula = mean_fix ~ poly(Time, degree = ., raw = T), data = eyefix_df_
avg_targ)
#>
#> Residuals:
#>       Min        1Q     Median        3Q        Max
#> -0.140940 -0.053969  0.002774  0.062525  0.105314
#>
#> Coefficients:
#>                                   Estimate Std. Error t value Pr(>|t|)
#> (Intercept)                      1.043e-01  1.421e-02   7.336 1.91e-10 ***
#> poly(Time, degree = ., raw = T)1 2.220e-04  1.512e-05  14.681  < 2e-16 ***
#> poly(Time, degree = ., raw = T)2 1.623e-07  2.016e-08   8.051 8.13e-12 ***
#> poly(Time, degree = ., raw = T)3 -7.497e-11 6.359e-12 -11.790  < 2e-16 ***
#> ---
#> Signif. codes:  0 '***' 0.001 '**' 0.01 '*' 0.05 '.' 0.1 ' ' 1
#>
#> Residual standard error: 0.07177 on 77 degrees of freedom
#> Multiple R-squared:  0.8921, Adjusted R-squared:  0.8878
#> F-statistic: 212.1 on 3 and 77 DF,  p-value: < 2.2e-16
```

Thus, for example, the rate of change of the average value of the outcome variable for a unit change on $Time^2$ is given by the coefficient for this variable, which is 1.6231344×10^{-7}.

Orthogonal polynomials

In the polynomials we have just run, we used `poly` with `raw = T`. By setting `raw = F`, which is the default, we obtain *orthogonal polynomials*. This means that the predictor variables that represent the various powers of the predictor `Time` are uncorrelated with one another. To understand the basics of orthogonal versus raw polynomials, let us generate a set of $K = 5$ polynomial functions of both types as follows:

```
x <- seq(-1, 1, length.out = 100)
y <- poly(x, degree = 5) # orthogonal
y_raw <- poly(x, degree = 5, raw = T) # raw
```

Now let us look at the intercorrelation matrix of the five orthogonal vectors:

```
cor(y) %>%
  round(digits = 2)
#>    1 2 3 4 5
```

```
#> 1 1 0 0 0 0
#> 2 0 1 0 0 0
#> 3 0 0 1 0 0
#> 4 0 0 0 1 0
#> 5 0 0 0 0 1
```

As we can see, they all have zero correlation with one another. By contrast, the raw polynomials are highly intercorrelated:

```
cor(y_raw) %>%
  round(digits = 2)
#>      1    2    3    4    5
#> 1 1.00 0.00 0.92 0.00 0.82
#> 2 0.00 1.00 0.00 0.96 0.00
#> 3 0.92 0.00 1.00 0.00 0.98
#> 4 0.00 0.96 0.00 1.00 0.00
#> 5 0.82 0.00 0.98 0.00 1.00
```

Orthogonal polynomials are also usually rescaled so that each vector has a Euclidean length of exactly 1.0:

```
euclidean <- function(x) sqrt(sum(x^2))
apply(y, 2, euclidean)
#> 1 2 3 4 5
#> 1 1 1 1 1
apply(y_raw, 2, euclidean)
#>        1        2        3        4        5
#> 5.831529 4.562178 3.893977 3.467986 3.167594
```

We provide a plot of orthogonal polynomials from degree 1 to degree 5 in Figure 13.11.

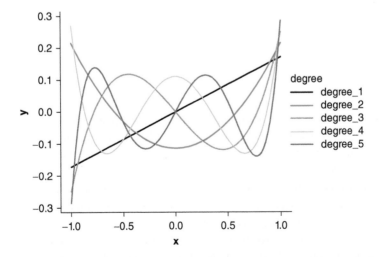

Figure 13.11 Plots of orthogonal polynomial functions of $x \in (-1,1)$ for degrees 1 to 5

Using orthogonal polynomials has computational and conceptual consequences. Computationally, it avoids any multicollinearity. Multicollinearity arises when any predictor variables can be predicted by some or all of the other predictors. In practice, there is almost always some multicollinearity because predictors in real-world data sets are often correlated, at least to a minimal extent. Extreme multicollinearity can lead to numerical instability in the inference algorithms. But more generally, multicollinearity leads to the variance of the estimates of the coefficients (i.e. the square of the standard error of the estimates) being inflated. Conceptually, on the other hand, orthogonal predictor variables entail that the coefficient for each predictor is the same regardless of which of the other predictors are present, or indeed whether any of the other predictors are present. In other words, the coefficient for the predictor corresponding to Time raised to the kth power will be the same in every regression that includes this term or if it is used as the only predictor. The coefficient for each predictor in the orthogonal polynomial regression gives the independent contribution of the various powers of the original predictors.

In the following, we rerun the above analysis using orthogonal predictors:

```
M_eyefix_targ_orth <- map(seq(9),
                          ~lm(mean_fix ~ poly(Time, degree = .),
                          data = eyefix_df_avg_targ)
)
```

Let us look, for example, at the coefficients in the first models from degree 1 to degree 4:

```
map(M_eyefix_targ_orth[1:4],
    ~coef(.) %>% unname())
#> [[1]]
#> [1] 0.3280476 1.4449036
#>
#> [[2]]
#> [1]  0.3280476  1.4449036 -0.6884575
#>
#> [[3]]
#> [1]  0.3280476  1.4449036 -0.6884575 -0.8461469
#>
#> [[4]]
#> [1]  0.3280476  1.4449036 -0.6884575 -0.8461469 -0.1753745
```

As we can see, the coefficient corresponding to any given particular power is the same in each model. Moreover, because the orthogonal polynomials are all normalized, they are on the same scale. As such, from the coefficient alone we can immediately see the effect size of each power of the original predictor.

It is important to remember, however, that the orthogonal predictors are no longer simply $x^0, x^1, x^2, ..., x^K$. They are based on a (relatively complex) transformation of this $(K + 1)$-dimensional vector space in a manner comparable to what is done in *principal components analysis*. In addition, it should also be noted that orthogonal polynomials of any given degree will still lead to an *identical* model fit to that obtained using the raw polynomials. Overall, then, the choice of orthogonal polynomials is motivated by the potential advantages in their interpretation, and also by their numerical properties.

Polynomial regression using other variables

Because we are using `poly` inside `lm` effectively to create a new set of predictors, how we use and interpret the model results in a polynomial regression is no different than when using `lm` generally. For example, in the following, we analyse how the average value of `mean_fix` varies as a polynomial function of time for each of the three different object categories, rather than just the `Target` category:

```
M_eyefix <- lm(mean_fix ~ poly(Time, 9)*Object, data=eyefix_df_avg)
```

We show the model fit for this in Figure 13.12.

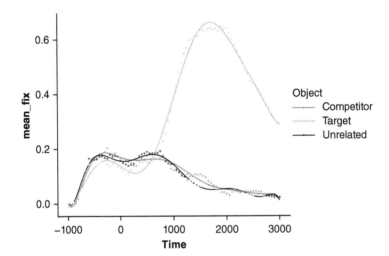

Figure 13.12 Predicted functions for proportion of looking times for each category using a polynomial of degree 9. In this case, we use the categorical predictor `Object` to vary coefficients for the polynomial regression for the three object categories

In this model, the `Object` variable is a categorical variable and so we are creating a different polynomial function for each `Object` category (`Target`, `Competitor`, `Unrelated`) by inferring polynomial coefficients for the base category (which is, by default, `Competitor`, based on the alphabetical order of the category names) and then differences in these coefficients corresponding to the `Target` and `Unrelated` categories. For example, in the following, we show the difference in the quadratic term, representing `Time` raised to the power of 2, between the `Competitor` and `Target` categories:

```
coef(M_eyefix) %>%
  extract('poly(Time, 9)2:ObjectTarget')
#> poly(Time, 9)2:ObjectTarget
#>                  -0.6477649
```

This tells us that that coefficient changes by approximately –0.648 from the `Competitor` to the `Target` category.

Although this analysis was as easy to perform as a varying slopes and varying intercept linear model, the interpretation of the model is more challenging. We can easily compare the M_eyefix model against a null alternative model, where `Object` is used as an intercept-only term:

```
M_eyefix_null <- lm(mean_fix ~ Object + poly(Time, 9), data=eyefix_df_avg)
anova(M_eyefix_null, M_eyefix)
#> Analysis of Variance Table
#>
#> Model 1: mean_fix ~ Object + poly(Time, 9)
#> Model 2: mean_fix ~ poly(Time, 9) * Object
#>   Res.Df    RSS Df Sum of Sq      F    Pr(>F)
#> 1    231 3.3021
#> 2    213 0.0470 18   3.2551 819.82 < 2.2e-16 ***
#> ---
#> Signif. codes:  0 '***' 0.001 '**' 0.01 '*' 0.05 '.' 0.1 ' ' 1
```

This shows that the polynomial functions for the Target, Competitor and Unrelated Object categories do not differ simply in terms of their intercept terms. However, beyond that, it is not a simple matter to say where and how the three different polynomial functions differ from one another, and so it is not a simple matter to explain the effect of Object on the time course of the eye fixation proportions in this experiment. This is a common issue with nonlinear regression models that we mentioned in the introduction to this chapter. Ultimately, the polynomial regression model, as with nonlinear regression more generally, provides us with a relatively complex probabilistic model of the phenomenon we are studying. However, key features of interest, such as the role played by one predictor variable, cannot be isolated as easily to role of individual parameters.

Overfitting in polynomial regression

Let us consider the following simple data set, which is also plotted in Figure 13.13:

```
set.seed(101)
Df <- tibble(x = seq(-2, 2, length.out = 20),
             y = 0.5 + 1.5 * x + rnorm(length(x))
)
```

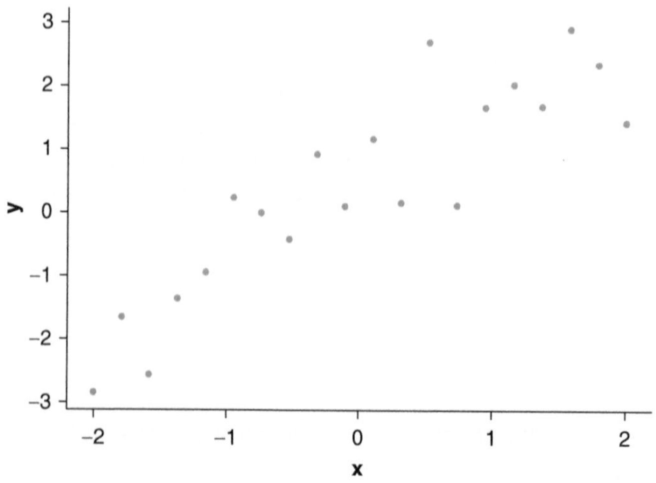

Figure 13.13 Data generated by a simple linear model, with intercept 0.5, slope 1.5, and noise standard deviation $\sigma = 1$

Although we know, because we have generated it, that this data is nothing more than data from a linear normal model, if this were real-world data, we simply would not know this. We could therefore see how well each in a sequence of increasingly complex polynomial regression models fits this data. These fits are shown Figure 13.14, where we also show the R^2 value for each polynomial.

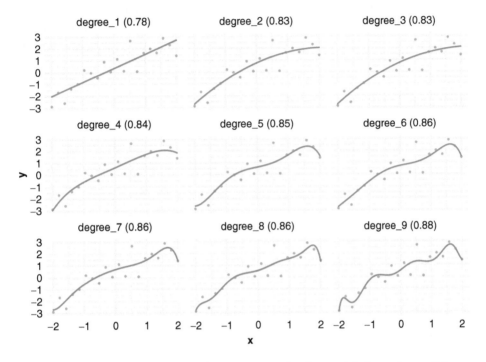

Figure 13.14 Fitting a data set with a sequence of polynomials from degree 1 to degree 9. Shown in the label for each model is its R^2 value. Clearly, the fit to the data is increasing but at a cost of *overfitting*

As the degree of the polynomial model increases, so too does its fit to the data. However, this fit to the data is essentially an *overfit*. There is no precise general definition of overfitting, but in this example it is clearly the case that the overfitted model is fitting the noise rather than the true underlying function, which we know in this case is just a linear model. We can see how the functions in higher-order polynomials are bending to fit individual data points. Overfitted models do not generalize well to new data. This is easy to observe in this example. We generate a new set of observations from the same true model that was used to generate the original data, and then see how well this new data is predicted by each of the nine previously fitted models. We can measure how the model predicts the new data sets by calculating R^2_{new} scores for each new data set as follows:

$$R^2_{new} = 1 - \frac{RSS_{new}}{TSS_{new}} = 1 - \frac{\sum_{i=1}^{n}(y_i^{new} - \hat{y}_i^{new})^2}{\sum_{i=1}^{n}(y_i^{new} - \bar{y}^{new})^2},$$

where $y_1^{\text{new}}, \ldots, y_n^{\text{new}}$ are the outcome variable values in the new data set, $\bar{y}^{\text{new}}$ is the mean of these values, and $\hat{y}_1^{\text{new}}, \ldots, \hat{y}_n^{\text{new}}$ are the predicted values of the outcome variable for the model. Obviously, the lower the value of R^2_{new}, the worse the model generalization performance. We will generate 1000 new data sets from the same data generating process as the original model, and for each data set calculate R^2_{new} for each of the nine polynomial models. The boxplot of the distribution of the R^2_{new} scores for each polynomial model is shown in Figure 13.15. Clearly, as the degree of the polynomial increases, its out-of-sample generalization performance decreases.

It should be noted that, as we discussed in Chapter 8, model evaluation methods such as the AIC are explicitly designed to measure out-of-sample generalization and hence help us to identify overfitted models. We may calculate the AIC value for each of the models above as follows:

```
map_dbl(M_overfits, AIC) %>%
  set_names(paste0('degree_', seq(M_overfits))) %>%
  round(2)
#> degree_1 degree_2 degree_3 degree_4 degree_5 degree_6 degree_7 degree_8
#>    51.40    48.41    50.40    51.73    51.79    53.49    55.31    56.51
#> degree_9
#>    56.25
```

As we can see, although the AIC model is lower for polynomials of degree 2 and 3 than for degree 1, the drop is not by much and after that, as the degree of the polynomial increases, so too does the AIC value.

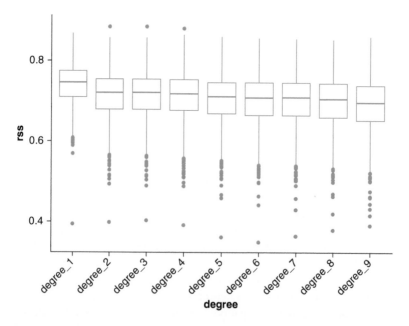

Figure 13.15 For each polynomial model, we show the boxplot of the distribution of R^2 scores of the predictions of new data sets generated from the same true data generating process as the original data, which was a normal linear model. The lower the value, the poorer the out-of-sample generalization of the model. As such, the more complex the polynomial model, the worse its generalization performance, despite the fact that the more complex models fit the original data better

Overfitting is a general problem in statistical modelling. However, polynomial regression is especially prone to overfitting. This is because higher-order polynomials are too unconstrained. The higher the order of the polynomial, the more it can twist and bend to fit the data. This is not always avoided by simply sticking to lower-order polynomials because lower-order polynomials *underfit* the data, having insufficient flexibility to fit the function. Thus a common problem with polynomial regression is that the lower-order polynomials are not flexible enough, and the higher-order ones are too unconstrained. Moreover, polynomial regression is also prone to a pathology related to *Runge's phenomenon*, which is where there is excessive oscillation in the polynomial function, particularly at its edges. We can see this easily by increasing the order of the polynomial to 16. This model is shown in Figure 13.16.

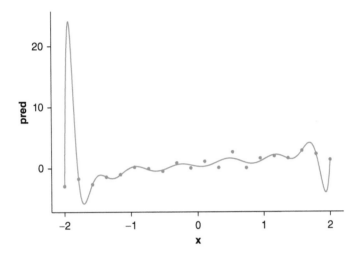

Figure 13.16 In higher-order polynomials, there is often excessive oscillation between fitted points, particularly at the edge of the function. Here, we plot a 16th-order polynomial. At the edges of the function, we see extreme oscillation between the fitted points

Spline and basis function regression

Polynomial regression can be seen as a type of *basis function* regression. In basis function regression, we model the nonlinear functions of the predictor variables using linear combinations of simpler functions that are known as basis functions. For example, in the case of a nonlinear regression with one predictor variable, and assuming normally distributed outcome variables, we would write our basis function regression model as follows:

$$y_i \sim N\left(\mu_i, \sigma^2\right), \quad \mu_i = f(x_i) = \sum_{k=1}^{K} \beta_k \phi_k(x_i), \quad \text{for } i \in 1,\ldots,n,$$

or, if we include an explicit intercept term,

$$\mu_i = f(x_i) = \beta_0 + \sum_{k=1}^{K} \beta_k \phi_k(x_i), \quad \text{for } i \in 1,\ldots,n.$$

Here, $\phi_1(x_i), \phi_2(x_i), \ldots, \phi_k(x_i), \ldots, \phi_k(x_i)$ are (usually) simple deterministic functions of x_i. In polynomial regression, our basis functions are defined as follows:

$$\phi_k(x_i) \triangleq x_i^k.$$

We saw in Figure 13.8 what weighted sums of these functions look like.

Cubic B-splines

Using basis functions for nonlinear regression is widely practised. There are many different types of basis functions that are possible to use, but one particularly widely used class of basis functions are *spline* functions. The term *spline* is widely used in mathematics, engineering and computer science, and may refer to many different types of related functions, but in the present context we are defining splines as piecewise polynomial functions that are designed in such a way that each piece or segment of the function joins to the next one without a discontinuity. As such, splines are smooth functions composed of multiple pieces, each of which is a polynomial. Even in the context of basis function regression, there are many types of spline functions that can be used, but one of the most commonly used types is *cubic B-splines*. The 'b' refers to *basis* and the *cubic* is the order of the polynomials that make up the pieces. Each cubic B-spline basis function is defined by four curve segments that join together smoothly. The breakpoints between the intervals on which these curves are defined are known as *knots*. If these knots are equally spaced apart, then we say that the spline is *uniform*. For basis function K, its knots can be stated as

$$t_0^k < t_1^k < t_2^k < t_3^k < t_4^k,$$

so that the curve segments are defined on the intervals $\left(t_0^k, t_1^k\right], \left(t_1^k, t_2^k\right], \left(t_2^k, t_3^k\right], \left(t_0^k, t_4^k\right)$. Spline basis function k takes the value 0 for values less than t_0^k or values greater than t_4^k. The cubic B-spline is then defined as follows:

$$\phi_k(x_i) = \begin{cases} \dfrac{1}{6}u^3, & \text{if } x_i \in (t_0^k, t_1^k], \text{ with } u=(x_i-t_0^k)/(t_1^k-t_0^k), \\[2mm] \dfrac{1}{6}(1+3u+3u^2-3u^3), & \text{if } x_i \in (t_1^k, t_2^k], \text{ with } u=(x_i-t_1^k)/(t_2^k-t_1^k), \\[2mm] \dfrac{1}{6}(4-6u^2+3u^3), & \text{if } x_i \in (t_2^k, t_3^k], \text{ with } u=(x_i-t_2^k)/(t_3^k-t_2^k), \\[2mm] \dfrac{1}{6}(1-3u+3u^2-u^3), & \text{if } x_i \in (t_3^k, t_4^k), \text{ with } u=(x_i-t_3^k)/(t_4^k-t_3^k), \\[2mm] 0, & \text{if } x_i < t_0^k \text{ or } x_i > t_4^k. \end{cases}$$

In Figure 13.17, we plot a single cubic B-spline basis function defined on the knots $\left\{-\frac{1}{2}, -\frac{1}{4}, 0, \frac{1}{4}, \frac{1}{2}\right\}$. In this figure, we have colour-coded the curve segments.

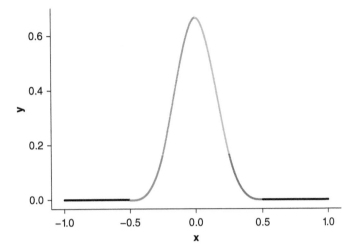

Figure 13.17 A single cubic B-spline basis function defined on the knots $\{-\frac{1}{2}, -\frac{1}{4}, 0, \frac{1}{4}, \frac{1}{2}\}$

In any basis function regression, including spline regression, we usually have many basis functions. In the case of spline regression, the number and location of the basis functions are defined by the position of the knots. In the case of any one basis function, as we've seen, only five knots are used. However, if there are many more knots, a basis function is defined on each set of five consecutive knots. In other words, if our knots are $t_0, t_1, t_2, \ldots, t_K$, one basis function is defined on knots t_0, t_1, t_2, t_3, t_4, the next is defined on knots t_1, t_2, t_3, t_4, t_5, and so on. In Figure 13.18(a), we provide examples of multiple basis functions defined on different consecutive sequences of a set of knots spaced 1/2 apart, from –2 to 2. In practice, sometimes lower-order splines are fitted to the sequences of less than knots at the start and end of the set of knots (e.g. the sequences t_0, t_1, t_3). The function bs available from the splines package creates B-spline basis functions in this way. In Figure 13.18(b), we provide the basis functions created by splines::bs for the same set of knots as were used in Figure 13.18(a). Examples of random sums of cubic B-spline basis functions are shown in Figure 13.19.

The simplest way to perform spline regression in R is to use splines::bs, or a related function from the splines package, just as we used poly for polynomial regression. For example, to perform a cubic B-spline regression on our eye fixation rates for the three object categories, we could do the following:

```
library(splines)
knots <- seq(-500, 2500, by = 500)
M_bs <- lm(mean_fix ~ bs(Time, knots = knots)*Object,
           data=eyefix_df_avg)
```

The model fit for this model is shown in Figure 13.20. Notice that we spaced the knots evenly from –500 to 2500 in steps of 500 ms. This gives us seven explicitly supplied knots,

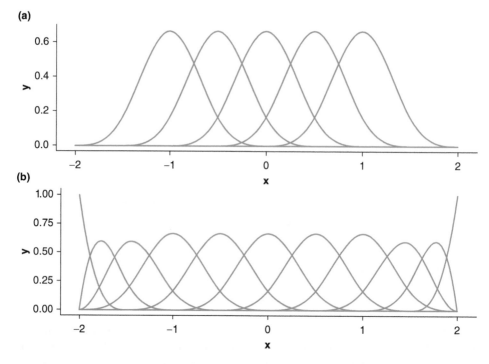

Figure 13.18 (a) A set of cubic B-spline basis functions defined on each consecutive set of five knots, spaced 1/2 apart, from –2 to 2. (b) The set of cubic B-spline basis functions defined on the same set of knots as in (a) generated by the `splines::bs` function, which includes lower-order B-splines at the edges of the set of knots

at which there will be a basis function. In addition, however, the `bs` function provides three (assuming `degree=3`, which is the default) extra lower-degree basis functions at the boundaries. From the model summary, we can see that we have an extremely high model fit, $R^2 = 0.994$. As before, the very high R^2 value must be treated with some initial caution, as it may indicate model overfit, a point to which we will return shortly.

An alternative approach to using `bs` with `lm` to perform B-spline regression is not to explicitly choose the location of the knots, but rather to let `bs` choose them at evenly spaced quantiles. We can accomplish this using the `df` parameter. If we set `df` to some K, then `bs` will find $K - 3$ knots. For example, the following code will perform a spline regression very similar to M_bs, and with the same number of basis function, but with the knot locations chosen based on quantiles:

```
M_bs_df10 <- lm(mean_fix ~ bs(Time, df = 10)*Object,
                data=eyefix_df_avg)
```

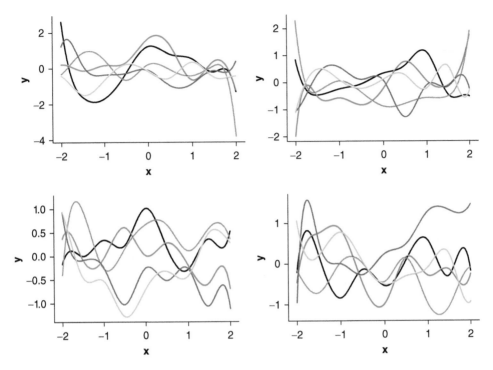

Figure 13.19 Examples of random sums of cubic B-spline basis functions. In each subplot, we have five random functions generated by different weightings of the same set of basis functions, which were defined on knots spaced 1/2 apart, from –2 to 2

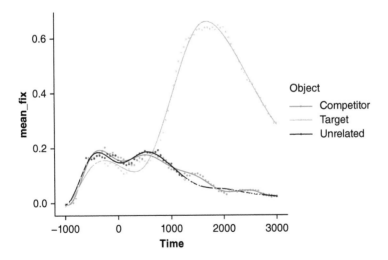

Figure 13.20 The fit of a cubic B-spline, with evenly spaced basis functions every 500 ms, to the average eye fixation rates on each `Object` category

We can see the location of the `df` - 3 knots by extracting the `knots` attribute from the object created by `bs` as follows:

```
with (eyefix_df_avg,
      attr (bs (Time, df = 10), 'knots')
)
#> 12.5%    25% 37.5%    50% 62.5%    75% 87.5%
#>  -500      0    500   1000   1500   2000   2500
```

In this case, the knots happen to be in the same location as when we explicitly made them.

Radial basis functions

An alternative class of basis functions are *radial basis functions* (RBFs). In these basis functions, which are related to spline basis functions, the value the function takes is defined by the distance of the input value from a fixed centre. As an example, one of the most commonly used models is the *Gaussian* or *squared exponential* defined as follows:

$$\phi(x) = e^{-\frac{|x-\mu|^2}{2\sigma^2}}.$$

An example of a Gaussian RBF, with $\mu = 0$ and $\sigma = 1$, is shown in Figure 13.21. These functions are identical to unnormalized normal distributions where the two parameters of the RBF play the same role as the mean and standard deviation of the normal distribution. Figure 13.22 shows random sums of nine RBF functions defined at the centres –2, –1.5, –1, –0.5, 0, 0.5, 1, 1.5, 2. In Figures 13.22(a)–(d) we set the σ parameter of the RBFs to 0.25, 0.5, 1.0, 2.0, respectively. As is clear from the figure, as the σ parameter increases, the resulting functions become smoother.

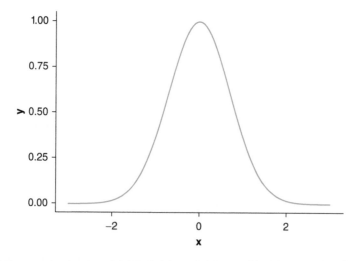

Figure 13.21 A Gaussian radial basis function is essentially an unnormalized normal distribution. In this figure, we display a Gaussian RBF that is centred at $\mu = 0$ and has width parameter $\sigma = 1.0$. This is identical to an unnormalized normal distribution with mean 0 and standard deviation 1

We can perform an RBF regression using `lm` similarly to how we used `lm` with `poly` or `splines:bs`. To do so, we will create a custom `rbf` function that returns the values of a set of Gaussian RBF functions defined at specified centres and with a common width parameter:

```
rbf <- function(x, centres, sigma = 1.0){
  map(centres,
        ~exp(-(x-.)^2/(2*sigma^2))
  ) %>% do.call(cbind, .)
}
```

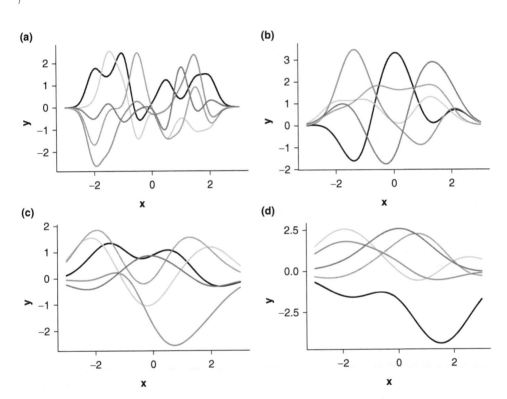

Figure 13.22 Examples of random sums of Gaussian RBFs. In each plot, we have five random functions generated by different weightings of the same set of RBFs, which were defined on centres spaced 1/2 apart, from −2 to 2. The width parameter σ of the RBFs, on the other hand, take the value (a) 0.25, (b) 0.5, (c) 0.75 and (d) 1.0. Clearly, as σ increases, the resulting functions become smoother

We may then use this `rbf` function inside `lm` by choosing the location of the centres, which we set to be at every 250 ms between −1000 and 3000 ms, and the width parameter, which we set to 500. We will use the `eyefix_df_avg` data set as before:

```
centres <- seq(-1000, 3000, by = 250)
M <-lm(mean_fix ~ rbf(Time, centres = centres, sigma = 500)*Object,
        data=eyefix_df_avg)
```

The predictions of this model are shown in Figure 13.23.

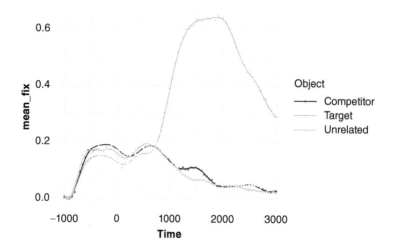

Figure 13.23   The fit of a Gaussian RBF, with centres at every 250 ms and $\sigma = 500$, to the average eye fixation rates on each `Object` category

Choosing basis function parameters

A persistent and major issue in basis function regression is choosing between or evaluating the different parameters of the basis functions. In the case of cubic B-splines, for example, this would primarily concern the choice of the number and location of the knots. Other basis functions, as we will see, have other parameters whose values must also be chosen. Although this issue can in principle be treated as just another type of parametric inference (i.e. where the basis function parameters are inferred along with the standard regression coefficients and the standard deviation of the outcome variable), doing so can often be technically very difficult. As a result, more commonly, this issue is treated as a model evaluation issue. In other words, evaluating or choosing between the number and location of knots in a spline regression can be seen as analogous, for example, to choosing between different parametric functions performing parametric nonlinear regression using `nls`. To do so, we typically employ a wide range of model evaluation methods including model fit statistics to guide our choices. Efficient methods for making these choices, as well as making other modelling choices with basis function regression, will be discussed in the next section on generalized additive models. For now, we will begin looking at this issue using some relatively simple general methods. For example, we evaluate choices concerning knots in spline regression by using the AIC values for each model in a sequence of spline models with increasing numbers of basis functions. Rather than using the standard AIC, however, we will use a correction for small sample sizes, AIC_c, defined as follows:

$$\mathrm{AIC}_c = \mathrm{AIC} + \frac{2k(k+1)}{n-k-1}.$$

This can be implemented as follows:

```
aic_c <- function(model){
  K <- length(coef(model))
  N <- nrow(model$model)
  AIC(model) + (2*K*(K+1))/(N-K-1)
}
```

This correction is generally advised when the ratio of sample size n to the number of parameters k is relatively low, as it would be in this case.

Here, we will consider a new data set GSSvocab, available from GSSvocab.csv, that provides scores on a vocabulary test for a relatively large number of people, collected over the course of a few decades. For simplicity, we will examine how vocabulary test scores vary with age, excluding the other variables in the data set. For this, we obtain the average vocabulary score for each year of age for a sequence of years from 18 to 89:

```
GSSvocab <- read_csv('data/GSSvocab.csv')
gssvocab <- GSSvocab %>%
  group_by(age) %>%
  summarize(vocab = mean(vocab, na.rm=T)) %>%
  ungroup() %>%
  drop_na()
```

This data is shown in Figure 13.24.

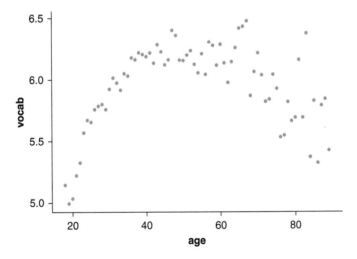

Figure 13.24 Average score on a vocabulary test for each year of age in a sequence of years from 18 to 89

Let us now fit a sequence of cubic B-spline regression model to this data, where we vary the number of knots from a minimum of 3 to 30. This is done in the following code where we use so-called *natural* cubic B-splines, using the `splines::ns` function. Cubic B-splines of this kind force the constraint that the function is linear beyond the knot boundaries:

```
df_seq <- seq(3, 30) %>%
    set_names(.,.)

M_gssvocab <- map(df_seq,
                      ~lm(vocab ~ ns(age, df = .),
                        data = gssvocab)
)


aic_results <- map_dbl(M_gssvocab, aic_c)%>%
    enframe(name = 'df',
          value = 'aic')
```

For comparison with the AIC$_c$ result, we will also perform a *leave-one-out cross-validation* (LOOCV). As discussed in Chapter 8 and elsewhere, this is where we remove one observation from the data, fit the model on the remaining data, and then see how well we can predict the outcome variable's value in the held-out data. In a data set with n observations, we leave each observation out and so it requires n repetitions of the model fitting process.

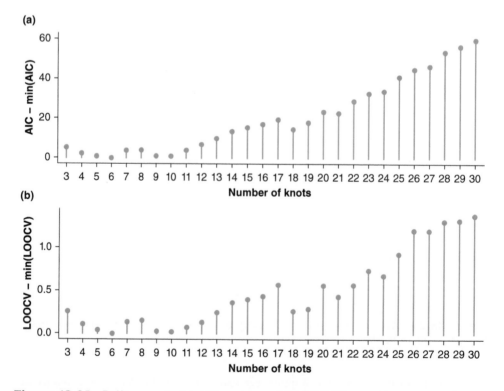

Figure 13.25 Differences in (a) AIC$_c$ scores and (b) LOOCV$_c$ scores between each model and the best-fitting model

```
loocv <- function(K){
  map_dbl(seq(nrow(gssvocab)),
          function(i){
            Df_train <- gssvocab %>% slice(-i)
            Df_test <- gssvocab %>% slice(i)
            M <- lm(vocab ~ ns(age, df = K), data = Df_train)
            Df_test %>%
              add_predictions(M) %>%
              summarize(rss = (vocab - pred)^2) %>%
              unlist()
          }
  ) %>% sum()
}


loocv_results <- map_dbl(df_seq, loocv) %>%
  enframe(name = 'df',
          value = 'loocv')
```

The minimum AIC$_c$ score is –38.35, which occurs at a df of 6. The minimum LOOCV score is 2.38, which also occurs at a df of 6.

In Figure 13.25(a) we show the difference between the AIC$_c$ scores at all df values and the minimum AIC$_c$ score, and in Figure 13.25(b) we show the differences between the LOOCV scores at all df values and the minimum AIC$_c$ score. As we can see, the best models have a low number of knots. High values of df tend to perform extremely poorly.

13●5 Generalized additive models

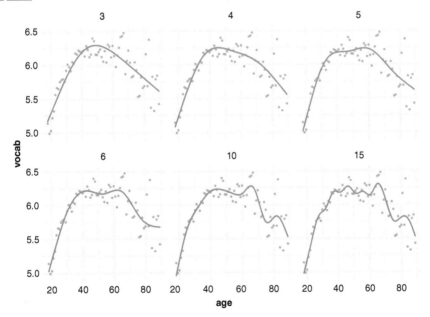

Figure 13.26 Cubic B-spline regression models of varying df values fitted to the vocabulary test data. The model with the df of 6 has the lowest AIC$_c$ and LOOCV score, but model 5 has a practically indistinguishable AIC$_c$ or LOOCV score

The polynomial and spline regression models that we have covered in the previous two sections can be regarded as special cases of a more general type of regression model known as the *generalized additive model* (GAM). GAMs are quite a general class of regression models, incorporating many special cases, and because of this, a single formal definition, while technically possible, may not be particularly clear. It is better, therefore, to define GAMs by a series of different definitions. We may begin our definition of GAMs as follows. Given n observations of a set of L predictor variables $x_1, x_2,..., x_l,..., x_L$ and outcome variable y, where $y, x_{1i}, x_{2i}...,$ $x_{li},..., x_{Li}$ are the values of the outcome and predictors on observation i, a GAM regression model of this data is given by

$$y_i \sim D(\mu_i, \psi), \quad \mu_i = f_1(x_{1i}) + f_2(x_{2i}) + ... + f_L(x_{Li}), \quad \text{for } i \in 1,...,n,$$

where D is some probability distribution with parameters ψ, and each predictor variable f_l is a *smooth function* of the predictor variable's values. Usually each smooth function f_l is a weighted sum of basis functions such as spline basis functions or other common types, some of which we describe below. In other words, the smooth function f_l might be defined as

$$f_l(x_{li}) = \beta_{l0} + \sum_{k=1}^{K} \beta_{lk} \phi_{lk}(x_{li}),$$

where ϕ_{lk} is a basis function of x_{li}. Although this definition is quite general in scope, we can in fact be more general. For example, instead of the outcome variable being described by a probability distribution D where the value of μ_i is the sum of smooth functions of the values of predictor variables at observation i, just as in the case of generalized linear models, we could transform μ_i by a deterministic *link function g* as follows:

$$y_i \sim D(g(\mu_i), \psi), \quad \mu_i = f_1(x_{1i}) + f_2(x_{2i}) + ... + f_L(x_{Li}), \quad \text{for } i \in 1,...,n.$$

More generally still, each smooth function may in fact be a multivariate function, that is a function of multiple predictor variables. Thus, for example, a more general GAM than above might be as follows:

$$y_i \sim D(g(\mu_i)), \quad \mu_i = f_1(x_{1i}) + f_2(x_{2i}, x_{3i}, x_{4i}) + ... + f_L(x_{Li}), \quad \text{for } i \in 1,...,n,$$

where in this case, f_2 is a three-dimensional smooth function.

From these definitions so far, we can view GAMs as extensions of the general and generalized linear models that are based on sums of smooth functions of predictors. However, multilevel GAMs are also possible. Recall that an example of a simple multilevel normal linear model can be defined as follows:

$$y_{ji} \sim N(\mu_{ji}, \sigma^2), \quad \mu_j = \alpha_j + \beta_j x_{ji}, \quad \text{for } i \in 1,...,n,$$
$$\text{with } \alpha_j \sim N(a, \tau_\alpha^2), \quad \beta_j \sim N(b, \tau_\beta^2), \quad \text{for } j \in 1,...,J.$$

This model can be rewritten as

$$y_{ji} \sim N\left(\mu_{ji}, \sigma^2\right),$$
$$\mu_{ji} = a + v_j + bx_{ji} + \xi_j x_{ji}, \text{ for } i \in 1,\dots,n, \text{ and } j \in 1,\dots,J,$$
with $v_j \sim N\left(0, \tau_\alpha^2\right),$ $\xi_j \sim N\left(0 \,|\, \tau_\beta^2\right),$ for $j \in 1,\dots,J.$

A GAM version of this model might be as follows:

$$y_{ji} \sim N\left(\mu_{ji}, \sigma^2\right),$$
$$\mu_{ji} = a + v_j + f_1(x_{ji}) + f_{2j}(x_{ji}), \text{ for } i \in 1,\dots,n, \text{ and } j \in 1,\dots,J,$$
with $v_j \sim N\left(0, \tau_\alpha^2\right),$ $f_{2j} \sim F(\Omega),$ for $j \in 1,\dots,J.$

Here, $f_{21}, f_{22}, \dots, f_{2j}, \dots, f_{2J}$ are *random smooth functions*, sampled from some function space $F(\Omega)$, where Ω specifies the parameters of that function space.

Using mgcv

The R package mgcv (Wood, 2017, 2019) is a powerful and versatile toolbox for using GAMs in R. Here, we will introduce some of the main features of mgcv. We will use a classic data set often used to illustrate nonlinear regression, namely the mcycle data set, available in the MASS package and elsewhere. This data set gives head acceleration measurements over time in a simulation of a motorcycle crash. We illustrate this data set in Figure 13.27.

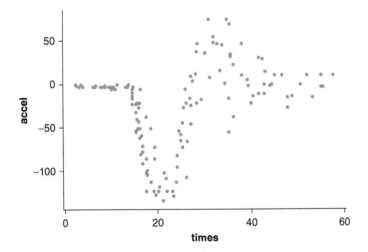

Figure 13.27 Head acceleration over time in a simulated motorcycle crash

The main function we will use from mgcv is gam. By default, gam behaves just like lm. In other words, to do a normal linear regression on the mcycle data, we could use gam as follows:

```
library(mgcv)
```

```
M_0 <- gam(accel ~ times, data = mcycle)
```

In order to use `gam` to do basis function regression, we must apply what `mgcv` calls *smooth terms*. There are many smooth terms to choose from in `mgcv` and there are many methods to specify them. Here, we will use the function simply named `s` to set up the basis functions. The default basis functions used with `s` are *thin-plate splines*. These are a type of radial basis function, not identical but similar to those we describe above. Therefore, to do thin-plate spline basis function regression using `gam`, we simply apply `s` to our predictor as follows:

```
M_1 <- gam(accel ~ s(times), data = mcycle)
```

The plot of the fit of this model can be accomplished using the base R `plot` function. This plot in shown in Figure 13.28.

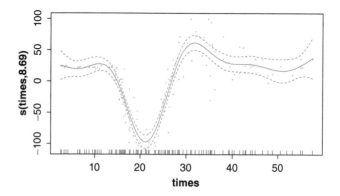

Figure 13.28 Thin-plate spline basis function regression model applied to the `mcycle` data set

The model summary output, using the generic `summary` function, gives us some different output than what we normally get from linear or generalized linear models, even when we use basis functions. In particular, it provides the following table for the basis functions:

```
summary(M_1)$s.table
#>                 edf    Ref.df        F      p-value
#> s(times) 8.693314 8.971642 53.51503 2.957613e-71
```

The `edf` is the effective degrees of freedom of the smooth term. We can interpret its values in terms of polynomial terms. In other words, an `edf` close to 1 means the smooth terms are effectively a linear function, while an `edf` close to 2, 3, etc., is effectively a quadratic, cubic, etc., model. The F-statistic and p-value that accompany this value tell us whether the function is significantly different from a horizontal line, which is a linear function with a zero slope. Even if the `edf` is greater than 1, the p-value may be not significant because there is too much uncertainty in the nature of the smooth function.

The number of basis functions used by s is reported by the `rank` attribute of the model. In our model, we see that it is 10:

```
M_1$rank
#> [1] 10
```

In general, `mgcv` will use a number of different methods and constraints, which differ depending on the details of the model, in order to optimize the value of `k`. We can always, however, explicitly control the number of basis functions used by setting the value of `k` in the s function. For example, in the following, we set the value of `k` to 5:

```
M_2 <- gam(accel ~ s(times, k = 5), data = mcycle)
M_2$rank
#> [1] 5
```

How models with different numbers of bases differ in terms of AIC can be easily determined using the `AIC` function. To illustrate this, we will fit the same model with a range of values of `k` from 3 to 30:

```
M_k_seq <- map(seq(3, 20),
               ~gam(accel ~ s(times, k = .), data = mcycle))
model_aic <- map_dbl(M_k_seq, AIC)
```

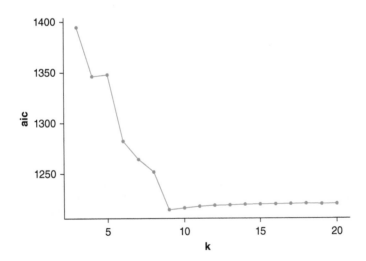

Figure 13.29 The AIC values of `gam` models of the `mcycle` data with different values of `k` from 3 to 20

We plot these AIC values in Figure 13.29. As we can see, the values drop to a minimum at 9, and then slowly increase after this minimum over the remaining values of `k` we have examined.

In addition to explicitly setting the number of basis functions, we can also explicitly set the *smoothing penalty* with the `sp` parameter used inside the s function. In general, the higher the smoothing penalty, the *less* flexibility in the nonlinear function. For example, very high values of the smoothing penalty effectively force the model to be a linear model. On the other hand, low values of the smoothing penalty may be overly flexible and overfit the data, as we saw above. In Figure 13.30, we display the model fits of gam models applied to mcycle data for three different values of sp.

From the figure, it is clear that values of sp greater than 1 tend to underfit the data. Therefore, it seems likely that much lower values of sp will be optimal in terms of AIC. In the following, we evaluate the AIC for a set of models whose sp ranges from 10^{-5} to 1 in powers of 10:

```
sp_seq <- 10^seq(-5, 0)
M_sp_seq <- map(sp_seq,
                ~gam(accel ~ s(times, sp = .), data = mcycle)
)
model_sp_aic <- map_dbl(M_sp_seq, AIC) %>%
  set_names(sp_seq)
```

We may then subtract the minimum value of the AIC to see the difference in AIC between each model and the optimal model:

```
model_sp_aic - min(model_sp_aic)
#>        1e-05        1e-04        0.001        0.01         0.1           1
#>    0.1529868    0.0656411    0.0000000   18.3651318  89.8999526 146.1496912
```

As we can see, the optimal model is at 0.001, with the AIC values for the lower orders of magnitude being very close, but rapidly increasing AIC values for higher orders of magnitude.

As with k, if sp is not explicitly set, mgcv uses different methods, including cross-validation, to optimize the value of sp for any given model. For example, for models M_1 and M_2 above, we can see that their sp values are as follows:

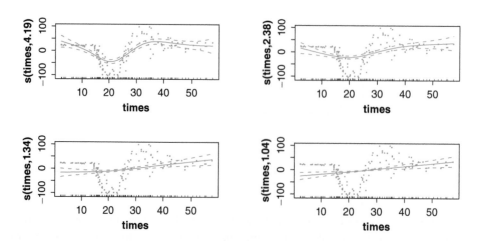

Figure 13.30 Plots of the fits of gam models to the mcycle data with different values of sp (from left to right and top to bottom, 10^{-1}, 1, 10, 100)

```
c(M_1$sp, M_2$sp)
#>      s(times)      s(times)
#> 0.0006195886 0.0213462068
```

These optimized sp values are close to the sp value we estimated using AIC above.

14

Structural Equation Modelling

Introduction

In practice, the term *structural equation modelling* (SEM) refers to a collection of related multivariate statistical techniques. These include factor analysis, path analysis, latent variable modelling, causal modelling, and combinations thereof. There is no one definitive definition of SEM. However, as we will see with examples, all structural equation models, certainly of the traditional kind, can be described by systems of linear regression models that usually, but not necessarily, involve latent, or unobserved, variables. In addition, these systems of regression models may, and from some perspectives always ought to (see Pearl, 2012), represent *causal hypotheses* about the variables being modelled.

Some structural equation models aim to discover a set of underlying unobserved variables that explain a set of intercorrelated observed variables. The classic example of this type of analysis is known as *factor analysis*. The seminal work on factor analysis, albeit more focused on psychometric theory than on statistics or mathematics, is said to be Spearman (1904). Other SEM methods include the classic path analysis work of Sewell Wright (1921, 1934). In this, causal relationships between a set of observed variables are represented using systems of linear regression models, and the magnitude of direct and indirect causal effects between them is then estimated. More recent major developments in SEM primarily include the introduction of the proprietary LISREL (*li*near *s*tructural *rel*ations) software (Jöreskog and Van Thillo, 1972) and the accompanying standardization of the structural equation model specification. In the LISREL model, there are observed outcome variables assumed to be functions of latent variables, as in factor analysis, and in addition, there are systems of the regression models, as in path analysis, between the latent variables and other observed variables.

In this chapter, we will cover classical factor analysis, a special case of path analysis known as mediation analysis, and then the more general classic structural equation model that includes elements of both factor analysis and path analysis. In this coverage, we will primarily use the `lavaan` R package.

Factor analysis

As a motivating example for introducing factor analysis, let us consider the following data set that is a subset of the `sat.act` data set in the `psych` package:

```
sat_act <- read_csv('data/sat_act.csv')
```

This provides us with scores from 700 students on three measures of academic ability: ACT (American College Testing), SAT-V (Scholastic Aptitude Test, Verbal) and SAT-Q (Scholastic Aptitude Test, Quantitative). The histograms and intercorrelation scatterplots of the three variables are shown in Figure 14.1. As we can see, there is a relatively high degree of positive intercorrelation between scores on these three tests. We could hypothesize, therefore, that students' scores on these three tests are all a result of some underlying ability, which we might refer to as general academic ability. Those individuals with higher values of this general academic ability are likely to have higher scores on ACT, SAT-V and SAT-Q. Individuals with lower values of general academic ability are likely to have lower scores on ACT, SAT-V and SAT-Q. From this perspective, general academic ability is a *latent* variable. It is not something directly unobserved, and possibly not even directly observable, but as its value changes, the values of the three test scores change too, albeit probabilistically rather than deterministically.

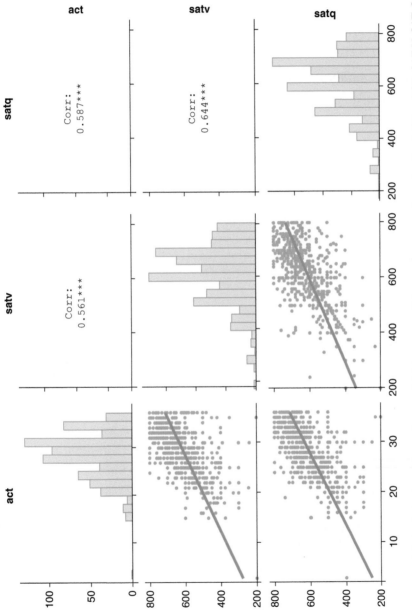

Figure 14.1 Pairwise scatterplots and histograms of three measures of academic ability: ACT, SAT-V, SAT-Q

A latent variable model is any statistical model of a phenomenon where we assume that observed variables are probabilistic functions of unobserved variables. There are many different types of latent variable models, but factor analysis is one very widely used one. Among other details, as we will see, it assumes that the observed variables are linear functions, plus normally distributed random errors, of one or more latent variables. It is, therefore, essentially a multivariate linear regression model where the predictor variables are unobserved.

The factor analysis model

In factor analysis, the observed variables are vectors. In general therefore, we can denote the observed variables by $\vec{y}_1, \vec{y}_2, ..., \vec{y}_i..., \vec{y}_n$, where each $\vec{y}_i$ is

$$\vec{y}_i = \left[y_{1i}, y_{2i}, ..., y_{di}..., y_{Di} \right]^\top .$$

Here, n is the number of independent observations we have, and D is the number of variables per each observation. For example, using our example above of the academic test scores, $D = 3$ and $n = 700$, and y_{di} is the score of student i on test d. We assume that each $\vec{y}_i \in \mathbb{R}^D$, where $\mathbb{R}^D$ denotes D-dimensional Euclidean space. In other words, each element of the vector $\vec{y}_i$ (i.e. each y_{di}) is assumed to be a random variable over the real line.

For each $\vec{y}_i$, there is a corresponding set of K latent variables, which we can denote by

$$\vec{x}_i = \left[x_{1i}, x_{2i}, ..., x_{Ki} \right]^\top .$$

Here, K can be said to denote the number of *factors*, or equivalently, the dimensionality of the latent space in the model. In principle, at least if we take a Bayesian perspective on factor analysis, K can be any positive integer. In practice, however, we have $1 \le K < D$. In fact, we often want K to be as small as possible, and certainly much smaller than D. In any case, we also assume each $\vec{x}_i \in \mathbb{R}^K$.

Each $\vec{y}_i$ is a linear function of $\vec{x}_i$ plus normally distributed errors. Given that $\vec{y}_i$ and $\vec{x}_i$ are vectors, the linear relationship between them is easiest to state using matrix notation as follows:

$$\vec{y}_i = A\vec{x}_i + \vec{b} + \vec{\epsilon}_i .$$

Here, A is a $D \times K$ matrix. This is known as the *factor loading matrix*. In addition, $\vec{b}$ and $\vec{\epsilon}_i$ are D-dimensional vectors. As such, $\vec{y}_i = A\vec{x}_i + \vec{b} + \vec{\epsilon}_i$ can be represented as

$$
\begin{bmatrix} y_{1i} \\ y_{2i} \\ \vdots \\ y_{di} \\ \vdots \\ y_{Di} \end{bmatrix}
=
\begin{bmatrix}
A_{11} & A_{12} & \cdots & A_{1K} \\
A_{21} & A_{22} & \cdots & A_{2K} \\
\vdots & \vdots & & \vdots \\
A_{d1} & A_{d2} & \cdots & A_{dK} \\
\vdots & \vdots & & \vdots \\
A_{D1} & A_{D2} & \cdots & A_{DK}
\end{bmatrix}
\begin{bmatrix} x_{1i} \\ x_{2i} \\ \vdots \\ x_{Ki} \end{bmatrix}
+
\begin{bmatrix} b_1 \\ b_2 \\ \vdots \\ b_d \\ \vdots \\ b_D \end{bmatrix}
+
\begin{bmatrix} \epsilon_{1i} \\ \epsilon_{2i} \\ \vdots \\ \epsilon_{di} \\ \vdots \\ \epsilon_{Di} \end{bmatrix} .
$$

Each $\vec{\epsilon}_i$ is assumed to be drawn from a D-dimensional multivariate normal distribution with zero-mean vector and a *diagonal* covariance matrix Φ, $\vec{\epsilon}_i \sim N(\vec{0}, \Phi)$, for each $i \in n$. As we have previously seen, this fact also entails that $\vec{y}_i$ itself has a D-dimensional multivariate normal distribution, specifically

$$\vec{y}_i \sim N(A\vec{x}_i + \vec{b}, \Phi).$$

From the description of the factor analysis model thus far, we gain two important perspectives. First, we see that each y_{di} is being modelled as a normal (in the sense of normal distribution) linear regression model of $\vec{x}_i$. Specifically, it is modelled as follows:

$$y_{di} = b_d + \sum_{k=1}^{K} A_{dk} x_{ki} + \epsilon_{di}, \quad \epsilon_{di} \sim N(0, \phi_d^2),$$

where ϕ_d^2 is the dth element of the main diagonal of the matrix Φ. Thus, factor analysis is a just a multivariate normal linear regression model, albeit with latent predictor variables. From this perspective, and particularly because Φ is a diagonal matrix, we also see that all of $y_{1i}, y_{2i}, \dots, y_{di}, \dots, y_{Di}$ are statistically independent of one another, conditional on $\vec{x}_i$. In other words, if we know the value of $\vec{x}_i$, then knowing any one or any subset of $y_{1i}, y_{2i}, \dots, y_{di}, \dots, y_{Di}$ provides no information about the values of any other. The importance of this result is that all the intercorrelations between the elements of the observed variables are explained entirely by the latent variables. This, in fact, is the purpose of factor analysis. It is a means to explain intercorrelations in observed data in terms of a smaller set of latent variables.

The final defining feature of the factor analysis model is that the probability distribution over each $\vec{x}_i$ is a K-dimensional multivariate standard normal distribution. A standard multivariate normal distribution has a mean vector of all zeros, and the identity matrix as its covariance matrix. In other words, we have

$$\vec{x}_i \sim N(\vec{0}, I),$$

where $\vec{0}$ is a vector of K zeros, and I is a $D \times D$ matrix with ones along the main diagonal and zeros elsewhere. It should be noted that there is no loss of generality in assuming a zero-mean vector and an identity covariance matrix. Any other choice for the mean vector and covariance matrix is equivalent to different choices of the A matrix and b vector.

From the above model, we obtain the conditional probability distribution of any $\vec{y}_i$ given $\vec{x}_i$, which we can write as $P(\vec{y}_i \mid \vec{x}_i, A, \vec{b}, \Phi)$. We also have the marginal distribution of $\vec{x}_i$, which we write as $P(\vec{x}_i \mid \vec{0}, I)$. Both of these are multivariate normal distributions. As such, we can calculate $P(\vec{y}_i \mid A, b, \Phi)$, which is the marginal distribution of $\vec{y}_i$ marginalizing over $\vec{x}_i$, as follows:

$$
\begin{aligned}
P(\vec{y}_i \mid A, b, \Phi) &= \int P(\vec{y}_i \mid \vec{x}_i, A, \vec{b}, \Phi) P(\vec{x}_i \mid \vec{0}, I) \\
&= \int N(\vec{y}_i \mid A\vec{x}_i + \vec{b}, \Phi) N(\vec{x}_i \mid \vec{0}, I) \\
&= N(\vec{y}_i \mid \vec{b}, AA^{\mathsf{T}} + \Phi).
\end{aligned}
$$

From this, we see that the unconditional or marginal probability distribution over any $\vec{y}_i$ is itself a multidimensional normal distribution with mean vector $\vec{b}$ and covariance matrix $AA^{\mathsf{T}} + \Phi$. That the covariance matrix of the elements of the observed vector can be stated as

$$\Sigma = AA^\mathsf{T} + \Phi$$

is sometimes known as the *fundamental theorem of factor analysis*. From this result, if we write σ_d^2 as the dth element of Σ and ϕ_d^2 as the dth element of Φ, then we can see that the variances of element d of the observed vector can be written as

$$\sigma_d^2 = \sum_{k=1}^{K} A_{dk}^2 + \phi_d^2.$$

The first term on the right-hand side, $\sum_{k=1}^{K} A_{dk}^2$, is known as the *communality*, or the part of the variance of the observed element d that is explained by the latent factors. The remaining term, ϕ_d^2, is known as the *uniqueness*, or the part of the variance of observed element d that is unique and not due to the latent factors.

Exploratory versus confirmatory factor analysis

In *exploratory* factor analysis the dimensionality of the latent variable space K is assumed to be unknown, and there are no specific hypotheses about how each factor relates to the elements of the observed vectors. In *confirmatory* factor analysis, by contrast, K is assumed to be known and the A matrix is assumed to have zero elements that reflect that certain factors are assumed to not relate to certain elements of the observed vector. As an example, in a confirmatory factor analysis with $D = 5$ elements to each observed vector, we might hypothesize that there are two latent factors, and that the first factor only relates to elements 1 and 2, while the second only relates to elements 3, 4 and 5. Given these hypotheses, the A matrix has zero elements as follows:

$$\begin{bmatrix} A_{11} & 0 \\ A_{21} & 0 \\ 0 & A_{32} \\ 0 & A_{42} \\ 0 & A_{52} \end{bmatrix}.$$

A major issue in exploratory factor analysis, as we can see, relates to both the number of factors and the optimal rotation of the A matrix. By contrast, neither of these issues arises in confirmatory factor analysis.

Parameter estimation

There are a variety of methods used to estimate the parameters of the factor analysis model. We will only consider maximum likelihood estimation here, but this is a major and widely used method in factor analysis.

As we've seen, the observed data in the factor analysis model is the n vectors $\vec{y}_1, \vec{y}_2, ..., \vec{y}_i ..., \vec{y}_n$. The parameters to be estimated are the $D \times K$ matrix A, the D-element vector $\vec{b}$, and the $D \times D$ diagonal matrix Φ. The log of the likelihood of the data given these parameters is as follows:

$$L(A,\vec{b},\Phi \mid \vec{y}_1,...,\vec{y}_n) = \sum_{i=1}^{n} \log P(\vec{y}_i \mid A,b,\Phi)$$

$$= -\frac{nD}{2}\log(2\pi) - \frac{n}{2}\log|\Sigma| - \frac{1}{2}\sum_{i=1}^{n}(\vec{y}_i - \vec{b})^{\mathsf{T}}\Sigma^{-1}(\vec{y}_i - \vec{b}).$$

The maximum of this function with respect to the vector $\vec{b}$ is obtained by setting $\vec{b}$ equal to the sample mean of the observed vectors:

$$\operatorname*{argmax}_{\vec{b}} L(A,\vec{b},\Phi \mid \vec{y}_1,...,\vec{y}_n) = \bar{y} = \frac{1}{n}\sum_{i=1}^{n}\vec{y}_i.$$

By substituting $\vec{b}$ with $\bar{y}$, the log likelihood function over A and Φ is

$$L(A,\Phi \mid \vec{y}_1,...,\vec{y}_n) = -\frac{n}{2}\Big(D\log(2\pi) + \log|\Sigma| + \mathrm{Tr}(\Sigma^{-1}S)\Big),$$

where S is the sample covariance matrix of the data,

$$S = \frac{1}{N}\sum_{i=1}^{N}(\vec{y}_i - \bar{y})(\vec{y}_i - \bar{y})^{\mathsf{T}}.$$

Maximizing $L(A,\Phi \mid \vec{y}_1,...,\vec{y}_n)$ with respect to A and Φ is complicated by the fact that if $\hat{A}$ maximizes this function, so too does any orthogonal rotation of $\hat{A}$, and so therefore there are an infinite number of solutions to this optimization problem. However, a common solution to this identifiability problem is to require the matrix $A^{\mathsf{T}}\Phi^{-1}A$ to be diagonal. With this constraint, Jöreskog (1967) introduced an iterative algorithm for maximum likelihood estimation. This algorithm is equivalent to positioning the latent factors on the *principal axes*: the first axis has the maximum variance, the second axis is orthogonal to the first and has the second greatest variance, and so on.

Axis rotation

In exploratory factor analysis, the estimated A matrix and, as a consequence, the axis of the latent space are initially not always ideally suited for interpretation. Ideally, we often require a so-called *simple structure* in A. This is where, for each element of the observed vector, a single factor alone primarily accounts for its variance, and each factor primarily accounts for the variance of only a subset of, rather than all, the observed elements.

To achieve this imprecisely defined goal of simple structure, a plethora of different rotation methods may be employed. Some of these rotations are orthogonal. The best known of these is *varimax*, which attempts to maximize the sum of variances on any given element of the observed vector. Other rotation methods are *oblique*, which means that the axes are no longer orthogonal. After an oblique rotation, values of the elements of the latent vectors are now correlated with one another. Some of the best known of the oblique rotations are *promax* and *oblimin*.

Examples

Here, we will consider exploratory factor analysis examples. Confirmatory factor analysis, by contrast, will be covered when we consider SEM more generally in a later section.

We will begin with the `sat_act` data set mentioned above. For simplicity, however, we will remove rows with NA elements first:

```
sat_act <- sat_act %>% na.omit()
```

We will perform a factor analysis with $K = 1$ (the default), using maximum likelihood as the estimation method, and, initially, with no rotation. For this, we will use the `factanal` function from the `stats` package. In this case, it is used as follows:

```
M <- factanal(~ act + satv + satq,
              data = sat_act,
              factors = 1,
              rotate = 'none')
```

It should be noted that `factanal` will normalize the data. In other words, it will subtract the mean of the three scores from all scores, and divide by the standard deviation. This is generally done for convenience, but does not affect the results. Among other things, this standardization makes the sample covariance matrix identical to the sample correlation matrix.

The *A* factor loading matrix is obtained as follows:

```
M$loadings
#>
#> Loadings:
#>      Factor1
#> act  0.715
#> satv 0.784
#> satq 0.822
#>
#>                 Factor1
#> SS loadings       1.801
#> Proportion Var    0.600
```

Because we have only one factor, the communality for each element of the observed vector is the square of the values of *A*. In other words, the communalities for the three elements are as follows:

```
M$loadings %>% as.vector() %>% raise_to_power(2)
#> [1] 0.5107335 0.6150754 0.6749130
```

The sum of the communalities for each factor is 1.801, and this is given as SS loadings. The uniquenesses, which are the diagonal elements of the diagonal covariance matrix Φ, are obtained as follows:

```
M$uniquenesses
#>       act       satv       satq
#> 0.4892665 0.3849246 0.3250870
```

These sum to 1.199. Given that the sum of the uniquenesses and communalities equals the sum of the variances, we can see that the communalities account for a proportion of 1.801/ (1.801 + 1.199) = 0.6 of the variance, as given by Proportion Var above.

Using the factor loadings and the uniquenesses, we can estimate the values of the latent vector corresponding to $\vec{y}$ as follows:

$$\hat{\vec{x}}_i = A^\mathsf{T}\Sigma^{-1}\vec{y}_i,$$

where $\Sigma = AA^\mathsf{T} + \Phi$ as above. These estimates of the latent vectors can be obtained if we set scores = "regression" in the call of factanal above:

```
M <- factanal(~ act + satv + satq,
              data = sat_act,
              factors = 1,
              rotate = 'none',
              scores = 'regression')
```

The estimates are then available as scores. For example, we can see the first few inferred values as follows:

```
x_est <- M$scores %>% head()
x_est
#>       Factor1
#> 1 -1.0151634
#> 2 -0.1189794
#> 3 -1.3513613
#> 4 -0.6757088
#> 5 -0.1393982
#> 6  0.1717458
```

In general, given the estimated values of each $\hat{\vec{x}}_i$, the predicted values of the corresponding $\vec{y}_i$, according to the model, can be obtained as follows:

$$\hat{\vec{y}}_i = A\hat{\vec{x}}_i + \vec{b}.$$

In the present example, the original data was standardized, as mentioned above. Therefore, we obtain predictions of $\vec{y}_i$ by $A\hat{\vec{x}}_i$, and then multiplying by the sample standard deviations and adding the sample means. In the following, we will do this for the predictions corresponding to the `x_est` above:

```r
y_bar <- apply(sat_act, 2, mean)
y_sd <- apply(sat_act, 2, sd)

y_pred <- M$loadings %*% t(x_est)

sweep(y_pred, 1, y_sd, `*`) %>%
  sweep(1, y_bar, `+`) %>%
  t()
#>          act      satv      satq
#> 1  25.04539  522.1341  513.7751
#> 2  28.13944  601.7631  598.9137
#> 3  23.88467  492.2617  481.8359
#> 4  26.21735  552.2958  546.0237
#> 5  28.06895  599.9488  596.9739
#> 6  29.14317  627.5950  626.5329
```

For comparison, we can compare these predictions with the corresponding values of the original data:

```r
head(sat_act)
#> # A tibble: 6 x 3
#>     act  satv  satq
#>   <dbl> <dbl> <dbl>
#> 1    24   500   500
#> 2    35   600   500
#> 3    21   480   470
#> 4    26   550   520
#> 5    31   600   550
#> 6    28   640   640
```

Let's now consider another example. For this, we will use the `bfi` data set from the `psych` package. This provides data on 25 personality variables from 2800 participants in a psychology study. In the following code, we select just the personality variables from `bfi`, and reverse-code selected items as required:

```r
data(bfi, package = 'psych')
bfi_df <- bfi %>%
  select(A1:O5) %>%
  # reverse code selected items
  mutate_at(c('A1', 'C4', 'C5', 'E1', 'E2', 'O2', 'O5'),
            ~ 7 - .)
```

In Figure 14.2, we show the correlation matrix heatmap of `bfi_df`. This is produced by calculating the correlation matrix use `stats::cor` and then using `geom_tile` to generate the heatmap, as in the following code:

```
bfi_df %>%
    as.matrix() %>%
    cor(use = 'complete.obs') %>%
    as_tibble(rownames = 'x') %>%
    pivot_longer(cols = -x, names_to = 'y', values_to = 'cor') %>%
    ggplot(mapping = aes(x = x, y = y, fill = cor)) +
    geom_tile(colour = 'white') +
    scale_fill_gradient(low = "white", high = "steelblue")
```

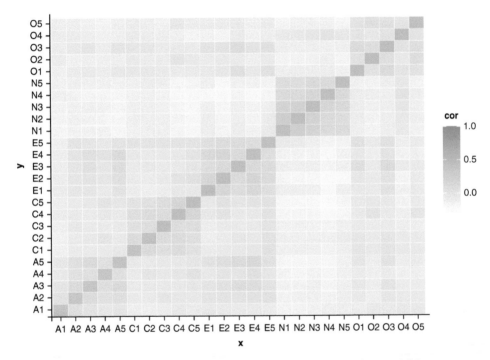

Figure 14.2 Heatmap of the correlation matrix of 25 personality variables

As can be seen on the diagonal from lower left to top right, there seem to be five clusters of five items, each of which have relatively high intercorrelation. However, this is not the only notable intercorrelation. There is also a relatively high intercorrelation between the 15 A, C, and E items. There are some negative correlations (shown by near-white colours) between some sets of items.

For factor analysis of this data, we will use the fa function from the psych package. This function is more powerful and versatile than the previously used factanal. In the following code, we perform a factor analysis with five factors (nfactors) using the factoring method of maximum likelihood (fm = "ml"), and also request no rotation:

```
M <- fa(bfi_df, nfactors = 5, fm="ml", rotate = 'none')
```

The factor loading matrix of a `psych::fa` model can viewed using the `print` function on `M$loadings` with a `cutoff` value to suppress relatively low values, as in the following example:

```
print(M$loadings, cutoff = 0.3)
```

We show the output of this `print` function on the left-hand side of Figure 14.3. As is clear, in this model, the first column of A, which corresponds to the factor labelled `ML1`, has the highest absolute values. This is confirmed by the `ss loadings`, listed at the bottom of this output, which provide the sum of the square of these values:

```
apply(M$loadings^2, 2, sum)
#>       ML1       ML2       ML3       ML4       ML5
#> 4.3669334 2.3428640 1.5051772 1.1850394 0.9530152
```

```
Loadings:                                        Loadings:
      ML1    ML2    ML3    ML4    ML5                    ML2    ML1    ML3    ML5    ML4
A1                                                A1                          0.364
A2   0.390  0.346               0.339             A2                          0.584
A3   0.460  0.391               0.328             A3                          0.648
A4   0.366                                        A4                          0.441
A5   0.540                                        A5                   0.340  0.585
C1                 0.463                          C1                          0.523
C2                 0.515                          C2                          0.621
C3                 0.407                          C3                          0.547
C4   0.438         0.491                          C4                          0.629
C5   0.484         0.345                          C5                          0.565
E1   0.358  0.310                                 E1                   0.587
E2   0.581                     -0.329             E2                   0.679
E3   0.455  0.430                                 E3                   0.482         0.336  0.301
E4   0.539  0.337                                 E4                   0.601         0.370
E5   0.414  0.421                                 E5                   0.486  0.314
N1  -0.593  0.560                                 N1   0.800
N2  -0.578  0.545                                 N2   0.782
N3  -0.529  0.487                                 N3   0.716
N4  -0.584                                        N4   0.558 -0.356
N5  -0.417  0.305                                 N5   0.522
O1                        0.402                   O1                                        0.521
O2                        0.368                   O2                                        0.434
O3   0.337  0.337         0.484                   O3                                        0.611
O4                        0.329                   O4                                        0.375
O5                        0.435                   O5                                        0.511

                ML1    ML2    ML3    ML4    ML5                        ML2    ML1    ML3    ML5    ML4
SS loadings    4.367  2.343  1.505  1.185  0.953  SS loadings        2.668  2.254  1.967  1.947  1.518
Proportion Var 0.175  0.094  0.060  0.047  0.038  Proportion Var     0.107  0.090  0.079  0.078  0.061
Cumulative Var 0.175  0.268  0.329  0.376  0.414  Cumulative Var     0.107  0.197  0.276  0.353  0.414
```

Figure 14.3 The A factor loading matrix for the factor analysis model with no rotation (left), and with *varimax* rotation (right). The rotated solution achieves a *simple structure*

Clearly, this unrotated solution does not have a *simple structure* whereby each element of the observed variable is accounted for by primarily one factor, and each factor primarily accounts for a small subset of the observed elements. In the following code, therefore, we request a *varimax* rotation:

```
Mv <- fa(bfi_df, nfactors = 5, fm="ml", rotate = 'varimax')
```

Again, we can print this loading matrix using the following code, and this is shown on the right-hand side of Figure 14.3:

```
print(Mv$loadings, cutoff = 0.3)
```

In this case, we can see that each variable is primarily accounted for by one factor and each factor accounts for a small number of items. Moreover, and not unexpectedly given our knowledge of this data set, each factor primarily accounts for all the items in one of the A, C, E, N, or O sets.

Model fit statistics

To evaluate model fits in factor analysis, we can in principle use methods that are standard throughout all of statistics for model evaluation. Nonetheless, in factor analysis and, as we will see, in SEM generally, a particular special set of model fit indices are widely used. There are, in fact, dozens of these *global fit indices*, but here we will concentrate on some of the more widely used ones.

The *model chi-square* is defined as

$$\chi^2_M = n'f_{mle},$$

where f_{mle} is the minimum value of the objective function that is being minimized to maximize the log of the likelihood. In other words, to maximize the log of the likelihood in a factor analysis, an alternative function that is the negative of the log of the likelihood, plus some constant terms, is minimized. The value of this objective function at its minimum, which is equivalent to the value of this objective function using the maximum likelihood estimates of the parameters, is f_{mle}. The value of n', on the other hand, is primarily based on the sample size. In some cases, n' is exactly the sample size (n, using our terminology above). In other cases, it is the sample size minus 1. In others, it is $n - 1 - (2D + 5) / 6 - 2K / 3$, and this is what is used in `psych::fa`.

In `psych::fa`, we can obtain the value of f_{mle} as follows:

```
Mv$objective
#> [1] 0.6279861
```

The value of χ^2_M is obtained as follows:

```
Mv$STATISTIC
#> [1] 1749.883
```

Given that χ^2_M is a function of f_{mle} scaled primarily by sample size, the *lower* the value of χ^2_M, the better the fit. Furthermore, for the hypothesis that the model is an exact fit of the observed data, χ^2_M will follow a χ^2 distribution whose degrees of freedom are so-called *model degrees of freedom*. The model degrees of freedom are the number of observed correlations in the data minus the number of parameters in the model:

$$\underbrace{\frac{D(D-1)}{2}}_{\text{correlations}} - \underbrace{\left(DK - \frac{K(K-1)}{2} \right)}_{\text{parameters}}.$$

Note that the number of parameters is less than $D \times K$, given the constraints that we impose on the A matrix. In `psych::fa`, the model degrees of freedom are obtained as follows:

```
Mv$dof
#> [1] 185
```

Thus, according to the hypothesis of exact fit, the expected value of χ_M^2 will be 185. If χ_M^2 were exactly 185, this would correspond to a p-value of close to 0.5. On the other hand, values of χ_M^2 much greater than the expected value of 185 will correspond to low p-values. In the case of model Mv, the value of χ_M^2 is much greater than 185 and so the corresponding p-value is very low. We can obtain this p-value as follows:

```
Mv$PVAL
#> [1] 1.394484e-252
```

In addition to χ_M^2, the *root mean square error of approximation* (RMSEA) is a widely used measure of model fit. It is defined as follows:

$$\text{RMSEA} = \sqrt{\frac{\chi_M^2 - df_M}{df_M(N-1)}},$$

where df_M is the model's degrees of freedom. However, if $\chi_M^2 < df_M$, then the RMSEA is defined as zero. In `psych::fa`, RMSEA is calculated by the following related formula:

$$\text{RMSEA} = \sqrt{\frac{f_{mle}}{df_M} - \frac{1}{df_M - 1}}.$$

We can obtain this, together with the 90% confidence interval, as follows:

```
Mv$RMSEA
#>       RMSEA        lower        upper confidence
#> 0.05496255 0.05263677 0.05734094 0.90000000
```

The RMSEA is usually interpreted as departure from close, as opposed to perfect, fit. Thus, the greater the value of $\chi_M^2 - df_M$, the further the departure from close fit. There is no consensus on what count as sufficiently low values of RMSEA to indicate a good fit, but traditionally, values less than 0.05 or 0.01 are usually taken to indicate good and very good fits, respectively.

Inferring the number of factors

Thus far we have assumed that the number of factors is known. This is often not the case. Ultimately, the problem of inferring or estimating the number of parameters is an example of the standard problem of model comparison that is a ubiquitous problem in statistics generally. However, in the context of (exploratory) factor analysis, a number of special procedures are usually followed to decide on the number of factors. Here, we will describe the method of *parallel analysis* implemented by Horn (1965), using `psych::fa.parallel`. This method is related to the widely used *scree* method whereby eigenvalues of a principal axis factoring in factor analysis are plotted in descending order. The eigenvalues will indicate the amount of variance accounted for by each of the principal axes. Usually, we simply look to try to identify where these eigenvalues begin to tail off. By contrast, the parallel analysis compares the scree plot to eigenvalues from principal axis factoring of random correlation matrices of the same size as that of the data.

In the following code, we perform the same factor analyses as we used previously, and compare the scree plot from these factor analyses to the average scree plot of the from `n.iter = 100` random matrices:

```
fa.parallel(bfi_df, fm = 'ml', fa = 'fa', n.iter = 100)
```

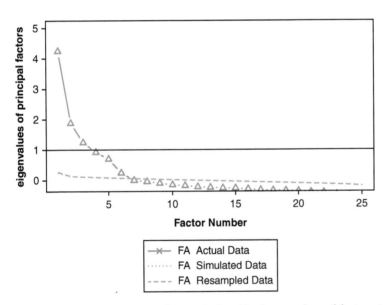

Figure 14.4 Parallel analysis scree plots to indentify the number of factors to use in the factor analysis

The resulting scree plots are shown in Figure 14.4. As we can see, six factors have eigenvalues greater than the corresponding average eigenvalues of the random matrices.

Mediation analysis

In a mediation model, the effect of one variable *x* on another *y* is due to its effect on a third variable *m*, which then affects *y*. Changes in the variable *x* lead to changes in *m* that then lead to changes in *y*. As an example of a mediation effect, it is widely appreciated that tobacco smoking x raises the probability of lung cancer y, and that this effect is due to tar (tobacco residue) produced by the burning of the tobacco accumulating in the lungs m. This tar contains the carcinogenic substances that cause the lung cancer.

In general, a mediation model describes a chain of effects. One possibility, known as the *pure* or *full* mediation model, assumes that the effect of x on y is entirely due to its effect on m. This can be depicted by the following path diagram:

Another possibility is a *partial mediation* model. In this case, we assume that x affects m and m affects y as before, but there is also a direct effect of x on y, as in the following diagram:

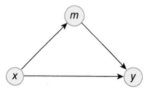

Assuming that we are dealing with a normal linear model,[1] we can write a pure mediation model as follows:

$$\text{for } i \in 1,\ldots,n, \quad y_i \sim N(\mu_i^y, \sigma_y^2), \quad \mu_i^y = \beta_{y0} + \beta_{ym} m_i,$$
$$m_i \sim N(\mu_i^m, \sigma_m^2), \quad \mu_i^m = \beta_{m0} + \beta_{mx} x_i,$$

which can also be written as

$$\text{for } i \in 1,\ldots,n, \quad y_i = \beta_{y0} + \beta_{ym} m_i + \epsilon_i^y, \quad \epsilon_i^y \sim N(0, \sigma_y^2),$$
$$m_i = \beta_{m0} + \beta_{mx} x_i + \epsilon_i^m, \quad \epsilon_i^m \sim N(0, \sigma_m^2).$$

By contrast, the partial mediation model can be written as follows:

$$\text{for } i \in 1,\ldots,n, \quad y_i \sim N(\mu_i^y, \sigma_y^2), \quad \mu_i^y = \beta_{y0} + \beta_{ym} m_i + \beta_{yx} x_i,$$
$$m_i \sim N(\mu_i^m, \sigma_m^2), \quad \mu_i^m = \beta_{m0} + \beta_{mx} x_i,$$

or equivalently as

$$\text{for } i \in 1,\ldots,n, \quad y_i = \beta_{y0} + \beta_{ym} m_i + \beta_{yx} x_i + \epsilon_i^y, \quad \epsilon_i^y \sim N(0, \sigma_y^2),$$
$$m_i = \beta_{m0} + \beta_{mx} x_i + \epsilon_i^m, \quad \epsilon_i^m \sim N(0, \sigma_m^2).$$

A note on nomenclature. In the mathematical descriptions of structural equation models and related models, there is an unavoidable proliferation of symbols, subscripts and superscripts.

---

[1]There is no necessary restriction to normal and linear models in mediation analysis or in SEM generally.

For the most part, we aim to keep the notation and symbols as consistent with other models as possible. For example, we will continue to use β for coefficients. We will use double subscripts for a coefficient to indicate that it is the coefficient to one node from another. For example, by β_{yx} we mean the coefficient to y from x, and by β_{mx}, we mean the coefficient to m from x. For intercept terms, which are not *from* anywhere, we will write, for example, β_{m0} or β_{y0}.

A partial mediation model

In order to explore mediation models, let us begin with data generated according to a specific model. While our aim is always to model real-world data, using generated data can be very useful when we are learning how and why the model works. The data we will generate is from a partial mediation model:

```
N <- 100
```

```
b_m0 <- 1.25; b_mx <- 1.25;
b_y0 <- -0.5; b_ym <- 1.75; b_yx <- 0.75;
sigma_m <- 1.5; sigma_y <- 2.0
```

```
mediation_df <- tibble(x = rnorm(N, sd = 2),
                    m = b_m0 + b_mx * x + rnorm(N, sd = sigma_m),
                    y = b_y0 + b_ym * m + b_yx * x + rnorm(N, sd = sigma_y)
)
```

Let us now set up this model using `lavaan`:

```
library(lavaan)
```

```
mediation_model_spec_1 <- '
y ~ m + x
m ~ x

'
```

Notice that what have done so far is simply to create a string `mediation_model_spec_1`. In this string, we write two R formulae, using the same syntax that we have used for formulae of all models so far, using the ~ symbol. This symbol has exactly the same interpretation as in, for example, `lm` and `glm`. Thus `m ~ x` means that m is regressed on x, or m is dependent on x, or m is a random variable that is a function of x, etc. As we will see, there are more model specification symbols in `lavaan` than are usually used in regression models in R, but for the present mediation model, we only need the ~ symbol. Thus, to specify the partial mediation model, we need only state that y is dependent on m and x, and m is dependent on x. Just as in, for example, linear regression using `lm`, the presence of an intercept term is assumed. In other words, by writing `y ~ m + x`, we are assuming that for each i, $y_i = \beta_{y0} + \beta_{ym}m_i + \beta_{yx}x_i + \epsilon_i^y$. However, by default, unless we explicitly state in the formula that we are using an intercept term, we will not get information about it. Therefore, we can rewrite `mediation_model_spec_1` as follows:

```
mediation_model_spec_1 <- '
y ~ 1 + m + x
m ~ 1 + x
'
```

Now that we have a model specification, we call `lavaan::sem` with reference to `mediation_model_spec_1`, and this fits the model using maximum likelihood estimation:

```
mediation_model_1 <- sem(mediation_model_spec_1,
                         data = mediation_df)
```

For now, let us just look at the parameter estimates of `mediation_model_1`:

```
parameterEstimates (mediation_model_1)
#>    lhs op rhs    est    se       z pvalue ci.lower ci.upper
#> 1    y ~1      -0.493 0.243 -2.030  0.042   -0.970   -0.017
#> 2    y  ~   m   1.843 0.118 15.648  0.000    1.612    2.073
#> 3    y  ~   x   0.639 0.180  3.558  0.000    0.287    0.991
#> 4    m ~1       1.256 0.164  7.665  0.000    0.935    1.577
#> 5    m  ~   x   1.280 0.083 15.471  0.000    1.118    1.443
#> 6    y ~~   y   3.633 0.514  7.071  0.000    2.626    4.640
#> 7    m ~~   m   2.620 0.371  7.071  0.000    1.894    3.347
#> 8    x ~~   x   3.826 0.000     NA     NA    3.826    3.826
#> 9    x ~1       0.305 0.000     NA     NA    0.305    0.305
```

The first thing to note about this output is that it gives us the estimates for all our coefficients, and also the variances σ_y^2 and σ_m^2. These variances are labelled in the output with `y ~~ y` and `m ~~ m`, which is `lavaan` syntax for specifying a variance or covariance, as we will see. It also provides estimates of the mean and variance of x. This is an important point in that it shows that it is creating a probabilistic model for all three variables in the model. In regression models, by contrast, variables like x are treated as given and their values are not modelled. Next, we note that, as expected, the estimated values of coefficients and variances are all close to the true values that we used to generate the data.

Model comparison

In mediation analysis, a major aim is evaluating first whether there is evidence of a mediation of the effect of x on y by m, and then whether this is pure or partial mediation. To do so, we first specify and then fit the full mediation model using similar syntax and commands to what we used for `mediation_model_spec_1` and `mediation_model_1`:

```
mediation_model_spec_0 <- '
  y ~ 1 + m
  m ~ 1 + x
'
```

```
mediation_model_0 <- sem(mediation_model_spec_0,
                         data = mediation_df)
```

Now, let us look at how well these two models fit the data using AIC:

```
mediation_models <- c(model_0 = mediation_model_0,
                      model_1 = mediation_model_1)

map_dbl(mediation_models, AIC)
#>   model_0   model_1
#> 816.8326 806.9121
```

As we can see, the AIC for `mediation_model_1` is lower than that of `mediation_model_0` by approximately 9.92. By the standards of AIC where differences of 10 or more indicate that the model with the lower value is overwhelmingly better able to generalize to new data, this indicates that the data is explained best by a partial rather than a pure mediation model.

Even if we just have three variables x, y, and m, and assume that there may be, or may not be, a directed arrow between x and m, m and y, and x and y, then there are exactly $2^3 = 8$ possible models to consider. These are shown in Figure 14.5. In the following code, we create a list with eight elements that are the specification strings for each of these eight model versions (using the same a–h labels as in Figure 14.5), explicitly stating the intercept terms for each one.

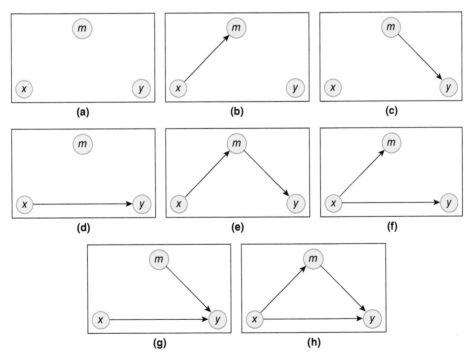

Figure 14.5 The $2^3 = 8$ possible versions of a simple mediation model with variables x, m, and y, assuming that there may or may not be a directed arrow between x and m, m and y, and x and y. In version (a), all three variables are independent. Version (e) is the pure mediation model. Version (g) is equivalent to a regression model, but where x and m have models. Version (h) is the partial mediation model

```
mediation_models_specs <- within(list(), {

    model_a <- '
      x ~ 1
      m ~ 1
      y ~ 1
    '
    model_b <- '
      x ~ 1
      m ~ 1 + x
      y ~ 1
    '
    model_c <- '
      x ~ 1
      m ~ 1
      y ~ 1 + m
    '
    model_d <- '
      x ~ 1
      m ~ 1
      y ~ 1 + x
    '
    model_e <- '
      x ~ 1
      m ~ 1 + x
      y ~ 1 + m
    '
    model_f <- '
      x ~ 1
      m ~ 1 + x
      y ~ 1 + x

      # Force independence of y and m
      y ~~ 0*m
    '
    model_g <- '
      x ~ 1
      m ~ 1
      y ~ 1 + x + m
    '
    model_h <- '
      x ~ 1
      m ~ 1 + x
      y ~ 1 + x + m
    '
})
```

Having each model specified as an element of a list, we now use `purrr::map` to fit each model and calculate its AIC score:

```
mediation_models <- map(mediation_models_specs,
                        ~sem(., data = mediation_df)
)
```

```
map_dbl(mediation_models, AIC) %>%
  sort()
#>   model_h  model_e  model_g  model_f  model_c  model_d  model_b  model_a
#> 1228.884 1238.804 1349.074 1350.682 1358.995 1470.873 1480.709 1600.900
```

These results are as we expect. The version with the lowest AIC is model_h, which is the partial mediation model. This is followed by model_e, which is the full mediation model.

Before we proceed, let us now generate some data, using a procedure similar to the above, from a pure mediation model:

```
mediation_df_new <- tibble(x = rnorm(N, sd = 2),
                           m = b_m0 + b_mx * x + rnorm(N, sd = sigma_m),
                           y = b_y0 + b_ym * m + rnorm(N, sd = sigma_y)
)
```

We used all the same settings to generate mediation_df_new as we used to generate mediation_df, but we removed the b_yx * x term, which is equivalent to setting b_yx to zero. Now, let us fit the eight models to mediation_df_new and evaluate the fit:

```
mediation_models_new <- map(mediation_models_specs,
                            ~sem(., data = mediation_df_new)
)
```

```
map_dbl(mediation_models_new, AIC) %>%
  sort()
#>   model_e  model_h  model_f  model_c  model_g  model_b  model_d  model_a
#> 1268.894 1270.717 1363.463 1401.127 1402.949 1466.873 1495.696 1599.106
```

Results here are close to what we would expect. The version with the lowest AIC is model_e, which is the pure mediation model. This is followed by model_h, which is the partial mediation model. Note, however, that the AIC value of the partial mediation model is 1270.72, while the AIC of the full model is 1268.89, which is only 1.82 less. By the standards of AIC, this is not a noteworthy difference and thus there is not much to distinguish between model_e and model_h. However, it is interesting to examine the parameter estimates of model_h:

```
mediation_models_new %>%
  extract2('model_h') %>%
  parameterEstimates()
#>   lhs op rhs    est    se       z pvalue ci.lower ci.upper
#> 1   x ~1      -0.186 0.209 -0.892  0.372   -0.596    0.223
#> 2   m ~1       1.049 0.161  6.501  0.000    0.733    1.365
#> 3   m  ~   x   1.293 0.077 16.816  0.000    1.143    1.444
#> 4   y ~1      -0.335 0.265 -1.263  0.207   -0.855    0.185
#> 5   y  ~   x   0.087 0.207  0.422  0.673   -0.319    0.494
```

```
#> 6    y   ~    m   1.732 0.138 12.567  0.000      1.462     2.002
#> 7    m ~~    m   2.583 0.365  7.071  0.000      1.867     3.299
#> 8    y ~~    y   4.906 0.694  7.071  0.000      3.546     6.266
#> 9    x ~~    x   4.367 0.618  7.071  0.000      3.156     5.577
```

As we can see, the parameter estimate for β_{yx} is close to zero, with an estimate of 0.087 and a confidence interval of (–0.391, 0.494). In that sense, model_h is essentially a pure mediation model.

Direct versus indirect effects

In a standard linear regression model given by

$$y_i \sim N(\mu_i, \sigma^2), \quad \mu_i = \beta_0 + \beta_1 x_i, \quad i \in 1,\ldots,n,$$

a change in any x_i by 1 unit (i.e. $x_i + 1$) would always lead to a change of β_1 in the expected (i.e. the average) value of the outcome variable. This is easy to see. Let $x_i' = x_i + 1$, and

$$\mu_i = \beta_0 + \beta_1 x_i, \quad \mu_i' = \beta_0 + \beta_1 x_i'$$
$$= \beta_0 + \beta_1(x_i + 1)$$
$$= \beta_0 + \beta_1 x_i + \beta_1$$
$$= \mu_i + \beta_1,$$

and so $\mu' - \mu = \beta_1$. Regardless of how many predictor variables there are in the linear regression, a change in predictor k by one unit always leads to a change β_k in the average value of the outcome variable. By contrast, in a mediation model, whether full or partial, the effect of a change in the predictor x on the outcome y is not as simple. First, let us consider a pure mediation model. In this case, as we have seen, we can write each y_i and m_i as follows:

$$y_i = \beta_{y0} + \beta_{ym} m_i + \epsilon_i^y, \quad \epsilon_i^y \sim N(0, \sigma_y^2),$$
$$m_i = \beta_{m0} + \beta_{mx} x_i + \epsilon_i^m, \quad \epsilon_i^m \sim N(0, \sigma_m^2).$$

From this, we have

$$y_i = \beta_{y0} + \beta_{ym}(\beta_{m0} + \beta_{mx} x_i + \epsilon_i^m) + \epsilon_i^y$$
$$= \beta_{y0} + \beta_{ym}\beta_{m0} + \beta_{ym}\beta_{mx} x_i + \beta_{ym}\epsilon_i^m + \epsilon_i^y,$$

and this entails

$$y_i \sim N(\mu_i, \beta_{ym}^2 \sigma_m^2 + \sigma_y^2), \quad \mu_i = \beta_{y0} + \beta_{ym}\beta_{m0} + \beta_{ym}\beta_{mx} x_i.$$

Following the same reasoning as above for the case of standard linear regression, this entails in turn that in a pure mediation model a unit change in x_i leads to a change of $\beta_{ym}\beta_{mx}$ in the expected value of y. In the case of the partial mediation model, we saw already that each y_i and m_i in the model can be defined as follows:

$$y_i = \beta_{y0} + \beta_{ym}m_i + \beta_{yx}x_i + \epsilon_i^y, \quad \epsilon_i^y \sim N\left(0, \sigma_y^2\right),$$
$$m_i = \beta_{m0} + \beta_{mx}x_i + \beta_{yx}x_i + \epsilon_i^m, \quad \epsilon_i^m \sim N\left(0, \sigma_m^2\right).$$

From this, we have

$$y_i = \beta_{y0} + \beta_{ym}(\beta_{m0} + \beta_{mx}x_i + \epsilon_i^m) + \beta_{yx}x_i + \epsilon_i^y,$$
$$y_i = \beta_{y0} + \beta_{ym}\beta_{m0} + \beta_{ym}\beta_{mx}x_i + \beta_{yx}x_i + \beta_{ym}\epsilon_i^m + \epsilon_i^y,$$

which entails

$$y_i \sim N\left(\mu_i, \beta_{ym}^2\sigma_m^2 + \sigma_y^2\right), \quad \mu_i = \beta_{y0} + \beta_{ym}\beta_{m0} + \left(\beta_{ym}\beta_{mx} + \beta_{yx}\right)x_i,$$

and following the reasoning above, this entails that a unit change in x_i leads to a change of $(\beta_{ym}\beta_{mx} + \beta_{yx})$ in the expected values of y_i. In general in a mediation model, we have the following:

$$\underbrace{\overbrace{\beta_{ym}\,\beta_{mx}}^{\text{indirect effect}} + \overbrace{\beta_{yx}}^{\text{direct effect}}}_{\text{total effect}}.$$

If there is no direct effect, as would be the case in a pure mediation model, then the total effect is equal to the indirect effect.

In a `lavaan` mediation model, we can create single variables that measure the direct, indirect and total effects. To do so, we must first use labels for our original parameters (i.e. the coefficients), and then use the `:=` operator to create new variables that are functions of the original parameters:

```
mediation_model_spec_1 <- '
y ~ 1 + b_ym * m + b_yx * x
m ~ 1 + b_mx * x

# Define effects
indirect := b_ym * b_mx
direct   := b_yx
total    := b_yx + (b_ym * b_mx)
'
```

We can fit this model as per usual:

```
mediation_model_1 <- sem(mediation_model_spec_1,
                         data = mediation_df)
```

In the usual parameter estimates output, we can use `dplyr::filter` to isolate these effects:

```
parameterEstimates (mediation_model_1) %>%
  filter (label %in% c('indirect', 'direct', 'total')) %>%
  select (label:ci.upper)
#>      label    est    se      z pvalue ci.lower ci.upper
#> 1 indirect 2.359 0.214 11.002      0    1.939    2.779
#> 2   direct 0.639 0.180  3.558      0    0.287    0.991
#> 3    total 2.998 0.181 16.566      0    2.643    3.353
```

As we can see, for example, the estimated effect for the total effect is 2.998, and the 95% confidence interval on this effect is (2.643, 3.353).

Modelling graduate school success

In the following gre_df data set, we have grade point average (GPA) scores for high school (hs), college (col), graduate school (grad), and Graduate Record Examination (GRE) scores (gre) from 200 individuals:

```
grad_df <- read_csv('data/grad.csv')
```

The scatterplot matrix, histograms, and intercorrelation matrix for these four variables are shown in Figure 14.6. As is clear from these plots, there is a high positive intercorrelation between all four variables.

To explore this data, we first perform a standard multiple linear regression predicting grad from all other variables:

```
coefs_summary <- function (model) summary (model)$coefficients

lm (grad ~ ., data = grad_df) %>%
  coefs_summary ()
#>               Estimate Std. Error  t value     Pr(>|t|)
#> (Intercept) 6.9711123 3.54114285 1.968605 5.040816e-02
#> hs          0.3723267 0.07617483 4.887792 2.116731e-06
#> gre         0.3694099 0.07848502 4.706756 4.749912e-06
#> col         0.1233100 0.08504079 1.450010 1.486539e-01
```

From this, we see that when hs and gre are known, col does not tell us much about variability in grad scores, and if we drop col, as we do in the following code, there is virtually no change in AIC scores:

```
lm (grad ~ ., data = grad_df) %>% drop1 ('col')
#> Single term deletions
#>
#> Model:
#> grad ~ hs + gre + col
#>        Df Sum of Sq   RSS    AIC
#> <none>             12000 826.86
#> col     1    128.72 12128 827.00
```

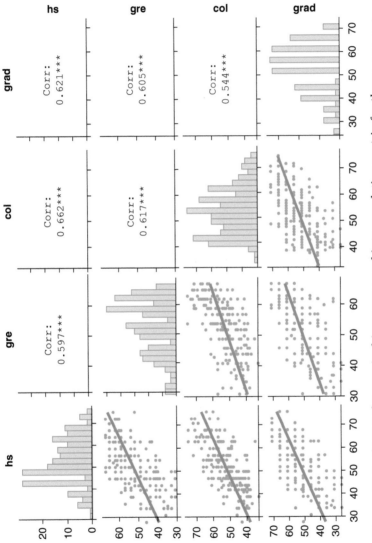

Figure 14.6 Scatterplot matrix, histograms, and intercorrelation matrix for the hs, gre, col, and grad scores

On the other hand, we see that `hs` and `col` together are predictors of `gre` scores:

```
lm(gre ~ hs + col, data = grad_df) %>%
    coefs_summary()
#>                 Estimate Std. Error   t value       Pr(>|t|)
#> (Intercept) 15.5338947 3.01804716 5.147002 6.382242e-07
#> hs           0.3093503 0.06554338 4.719779 4.471315e-06
#> col          0.4004889 0.07173143 5.583172 7.756667e-08
```

Dropping either `hs` or `col` from this model would lead to a substantial increase in AIC scores:

```
lm(gre ~ hs + col, data = grad_df) %>%
    drop1()
#> Single term deletions
#>
#> Model:
#> gre ~ hs + col
#>         Df Sum of Sq     RSS    AIC
#> <none>                9938.8 787.18
#> hs       1    1123.9 11062.7 806.60
#> col      1    1572.6 11511.5 814.56
```

From this, we may propose two hypothetical models that involve mediation of the effect of `col` on `grad` via its effect on `gre`. The two variants of this model are a pure (`model_0`) and a partial (`model_1`) mediation model:

```
grad_mediation_models_specs <- within(list(),{
  model_0 <- '
      grad ~ hs + gre
      gre ~ hs + col
  '

  model_1 <- '
      grad ~ hs + b_grad_gre*gre + b_grad_col*col
      gre ~ hs + b_gre_col*col

      # labels for indirect, direct, and total
      direct := b_grad_col
      indirect := b_gre_col*b_grad_gre
      total := b_grad_col + (b_gre_col*b_grad_gre)
  '
})
```

These models are depicted in Figure 14.7. Note that in these diagrams, we have a double-headed arrow from `col` to `hs`. This indicates that `col` and `hs` are correlated, or more precisely, that `col` and `hs` are assumed to be drawn from a two-dimensional normal distribution with a full covariance matrix (i.e. allowing for non-independence of `col` and `hs`):

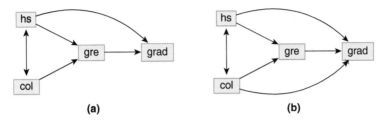

Figure 14.7 A full (a) and partial (b) mediation model of the effect of `col` on `grad` via its effect on `gre`

```
grad_mediation_models <- map(grad_mediation_models_specs,
                             ~sem(., data = grad_df)
)
```

In terms of AIC, these two models are practically identical:

```
map_dbl(grad_mediation_models, AIC)
#>   model_1   model_0
#> 2749.189 2749.323
```

Likewise, by performing a log likelihood ratio test, we find there is no significant difference between the two models:

```
grad_mediation_models %$%
  anova(model_0, model_1)
#> Chi-Squared Difference Test
#>
#>         Df    AIC    BIC Chisq Chisq diff Df diff Pr(>Chisq)
#> model_1  0 2749.2 2772.3 0.000
#> model_0  1 2749.3 2769.1 2.134      2.134       1     0.1441
```

These results imply that we cannot decide between the full and partial mediation models. However, similarly to the situation in an earlier example, the coefficient from `col` to `grad` in `model_1` is relatively close to zero and the 95% confidence interval is between –0.042 and 0.288:

```
grad_mediation_models[['model_1']] %>%
  parameterEstimates() %>%
  filter(label == 'direct') %>%
  select(est:ci.upper)
#>     est    se     z pvalue ci.lower ci.upper
#> 1 0.123 0.084 1.465  0.143   -0.042    0.288
```

In conclusion then, the effect of college GPA on graduate school GPA is largely, or completely, mediated by the effect of college GPA on GRE scores.

14●4 Structural equation modelling

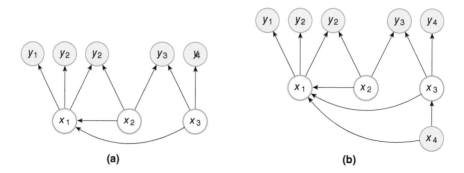

Figure 14.8   Two structural equation models. In (a), a set of observed variables are functions of a set of latent variables, which are functions of one another. In (b), a set observed variables are functions of both observed and latent variables, which are also functions on one another. We use the convention here of shading the nodes representing observed variables

The term SEM can be used as an umbrella term for a set of related techniques including factor analysis, path analysis, causal modelling, and even latent variable modelling generally. It is also used in a narrower sense to mean a kind of combination of factor analysis and path analysis models. In this more specific sense of the term, a structural equation model consists of a set of observed variables that are linear regression functions of latent variables, just as in factor analysis. Then, optionally, the latent variables themselves may be linear regression functions of one another, assuming that these relationships can be described by a directed acyclic graph, just as in a path analysis model. It may also be the case, however, that in addition to the latent variables, we may have further observed variables. For example, we may have observed variables that are predictors, or explanatory variables, of the latent variables. Two simple examples of these structural equation model scenarios are depicted in Figure 14.8.

In general, a structural equation model can be defined by a system of regression models some of whose outcome or predictor variables may be latent variables. This definition of a structural equation model treats observed variable path analysis models and confirmatory factor analysis as special cases. In the traditional structural equation model, all the regression models are normal linear ones. This was certainly the case in all the factor analysis and path analysis models we have looked at thus far. While there are in principle no restrictions on the regression models being normal and linear, these are still the default case and there are easy-to-use SEM software packages, including in R, that specifically assume these types of models.

In this section, we will explore using `lavaan` R package. We will explore some relatively simple models that illustrate the major features. For the models we consider, we will use the `PoliticalDemocracy` data set provided by `lavaan`. This is regarded as a classic data set for the illustration of models (Bollen, 1979, 1989). It includes the following variables:

y_1, expert ratings of the freedom of the press in 1960

y_2, the freedom of political opposition in 1960

y_3, the fairness of elections in 1960

y_4, the effectiveness of the elected legislature in 1960

y_5, expert ratings of the freedom of the press in 1965

y_6, the freedom of political opposition in 1965

y_7, the fairness of elections in 1965

y_8, the effectiveness of the elected legislature in 1965

x_1, gross national product (GNP) per capita in 1960

x_2, inanimate energy consumption per capita in 1960

x_3, the percentage of the labour force in industry in 1960.

The variables beginning with y_ are all measures of the democracy in a country at two points in time, 1960 and 1965. The variables y_1, y_2, y_3, and y_4 measure democracy variables in 1960. The variables y_5, y_6, y_7, and y_8 measure the same democracy variables but in 1965. The variables x_1, x_2, and x_3 are all measures of the economy in the represented countries in 1960.

A reasonable structural equation model is that variables y_1, y_2, y_3, and y_4 are all functions of a single underlying latent variable. This latent variable represents democracy in a country in 1960. Likewise, y_5, y_6, y_7, and y_8 are all functions of a single latent variable that represents democracy in 1965. Finally, x_1, x_2, and x_3 are all measures of a single latent variable representing industrialization in 1960. If we leave the model as such, this leads to a confirmatory factor analysis model. This can be specified using lavaan model syntax as follows:

```
sem_model_1_spec <- '
  ind60 =~ x1 + x2 + x3
  dem60 =~ y1 + y2 + y3 + y4
  dem65 =~ y5 + y6 + y7 + y8
'
```

A note on syntax. We have seen in the previous section that we can define regression and path analysis models easily in lavaan using the familiar R *formula* syntax. For example, to specify a regression model such as $y_i \sim \beta_0 + \beta_x x_i + \beta_z z_i + \epsilon_i$, we would write the following:

```
y ~ x + z
```

On the other hand, if we wish to specify a model where, for each i, a set of observed variables y_{1i}, y_{2i}, y_{3i} are functions of a latent variable x_i, we must code this as follows:

```
x =~ y_1 + y_2 + y_3
```

Here, the outcome variables are to the right, rather than to the left, of the formula operator, which in this case is =~ rather than ~.

We may now fit this model as follows:

```
sem_model_1 <- sem(sem_model_1_spec,
                data = PoliticalDemocracy)
```

As we did in the previous section, we may look at the parameter estimates of this model with the command `parameterEstimates`, and we will filter out the individual variance estimates for simplicity:

```
parameterEstimates (sem_model_1) %>%
   filter(op == '=~') %>%
   select(lhs, op, rhs, est, ci.lower, ci.upper)
#>        lhs op rhs    est ci.lower ci.upper
#> 1    ind60 =~  x1 1.000    1.000    1.000
#> 2    ind60 =~  x2 2.182    1.910    2.454
#> 3    ind60 =~  x3 1.819    1.521    2.117
#> 4    dem60 =~  y1 1.000    1.000    1.000
#> 5    dem60 =~  y2 1.354    1.012    1.696
#> 6    dem60 =~  y3 1.044    0.750    1.338
#> 7    dem60 =~  y4 1.300    1.029    1.570
#> 8    dem65 =~  y5 1.000    1.000    1.000
#> 9    dem65 =~  y6 1.258    0.936    1.581
#> 10   dem65 =~  y7 1.282    0.974    1.591
#> 11   dem65 =~  y8 1.310    1.009    1.611
```

Note that one of each of the factor loadings for each latent variable is exactly `1.000000`. This is because, by default, the latent variable variances are not set to 1 and so it is necessary to constrain the loading matrix values. This is done by setting one arbitrarily chosen value to 1. We may, however, set the variances of the latent variables to 1 as follows:

```
sem_model_1 <- sem(sem_model_1_spec, data = PoliticalDemocracy, std.lv = T)
```

In addition, we may force the latent factors to be orthogonal as follows:

```
sem_model_1 <- sem(sem_model_1_spec,
                        orthogonal = T,
                        std.lv = T,
                        data = PoliticalDemocracy)
```

We now see that the factor loadings are no longer constrained:

```
parameterEstimates (sem_model_1) %>%
   filter(op == '=~') %>%
   select(lhs, op, rhs, est, ci.lower, ci.upper)
#>        lhs op rhs    est ci.lower ci.upper
#> 1    ind60 =~  x1 0.667    0.540    0.795
#> 2    ind60 =~  x2 1.464    1.213    1.715
#> 3    ind60 =~  x3 1.217    0.965    1.469
#> 4    dem60 =~  y1 2.133    1.624    2.641
#> 5    dem60 =~  y2 2.993    2.206    3.780
#> 6    dem60 =~  y3 2.322    1.651    2.993
#> 7    dem60 =~  y4 2.922    2.294    3.551
```

```
#> 8   dem65 =~  y5 1.907    1.382    2.431
#> 9   dem65 =~  y6 2.703    2.052    3.354
#> 10  dem65 =~  y7 2.627    1.992    3.262
#> 11  dem65 =~  y8 2.891    2.296    3.486
```

We may assess the fit of this model using any of the many fit indices calculated by sem. For now, we will just look at those that we have defined above, namely AIC, χ^2_M, and RMSEA:

```
fitmeasures(sem_model_1,
            c("chisq", "df", "pvalue", "aic", "rmsea")
)
#>     chisq      df   pvalue       aic     rmsea
#>   197.210  44.000    0.000  3298.667     0.215
```

First, we see that the χ^2_M is well above its expected value and hence the corresponding p-value is very low. Hence, we confidently reject the hypothesis that this model provides a perfect fit to the data. The AIC value is 3298.667, which is essentially meaningless in itself, but will be valuable when we compare this model to comparable models later. The RMSEA value is 0.215, which is not low by conventional standards.

Let us now expand this model. The pairs of variables (y1, y5), (y2, y6), (y3, y7), (y4, y8), given that they each measure the same variable but in different years, ought to be correlated. We can implement this as follows:

```
sem_model_2_spec <- '
  ind60 =~ x1 + x2 + x3
  dem60 =~ y1 + y2 + y3 + y4
  dem65 =~ y5 + y6 + y7 + y8

  y1 ~~ y5
  y2 ~~ y6
  y3 ~~ y7
  y4 ~~ y8

'

sem_model_2 <- sem(sem_model_2_spec,
                   orthogonal = T,
                   std.lv = T,
                   data = PoliticalDemocracy)
```

Let us now consider the fit indices of this new model:

```
fitmeasures(sem_model_2,
            c("chisq", "df", "pvalue", "aic", "rmsea")
)
#>     chisq      df   pvalue       aic     rmsea
#>   171.295  40.000    0.000  3280.751     0.209
```

By comparison to `sem_model_1`, these indicate that modelling the residual covariances improves the model's fit, though clearly the fit is still not satisfactory.

As another example of how we can expand this model, we can model the covariances between some of the latent variables. For example, `dem65` and `dem60` are highly likely to be intercorrelated. We can specify this model as follows:

```
sem_model_3_spec <- '
  ind60 =~ x1 + x2 + x3
  dem60 =~ y1 + y2 + y3 + y4
  dem65 =~ y5 + y6 + y7 + y8

  y1 ~~ y5
  y2 ~~ y6
  y3 ~~ y7
  y4 ~~ y8

  dem60 ~~ dem65

'

sem_model_3 <- sem(sem_model_3_spec,
                   orthogonal = T,
                   std.lv = T,
                   data = PoliticalDemocracy)
```

We may again assess the model fit:

```
fitmeasures(sem_model_3,
            c("chisq", "df", "pvalue", "aic", "rmsea")
)
#>    chisq       df   pvalue         aic    rmsea
#>   74.218   39.000    0.001   3185.675    0.110
```

Clearly, this has improved the model fit.

As a final example, let us model `dem65` as a function of `dem60` and `ind60`, and `dem60` as a function of `ind60`. We can specify this model as follows:

```
sem_model_3_spec <- '
  ind60 =~ x1 + x2 + x3
  dem60 =~ y1 + y2 + y3 + y4
  dem65 =~ y5 + y6 + y7 + y8

  dem65 ~ dem60 + ind60
  dem60 ~ ind60

  y1 ~~ y5
  y2 ~~ y6
```

```
  y3 ~~ y7
  y4 ~~ y8
'

sem_model_3 <- sem(sem_model_3_spec,
                   orthogonal = T,
                   std.lv = T,
                   data = PoliticalDemocracy)
```

Let us consider the fit indices of this new model:

```
fitmeasures(sem_model_3,
           c("chisq", "df", "pvalue", "aic", "rmsea")
)
#>    chisq        df    pvalue       aic      rmsea
#>   50.835    37.000     0.064  3166.292      0.071
```

Again, this extension has further improved the fit of the model.

PART III

ADVANCED
OR SPECIAL
TOPICS IN DATA
ANALYSIS

Part III Contents

15

High-Performance
Computing with R

15.1 Introduction

R is a high-level programming language. Like most programming languages of this kind, R is designed for expressiveness – expressing complex statements and instructions in a simple, clear, and minimal syntax – rather than speed of execution. Often, R's relative lack of speed has no practical consequences for us. For example, if some task in R takes just a few hundred milliseconds to complete, even if we could speed it up by a few orders of magnitude, we might barely notice this in practice. Moreover, it might well be a waste of our time to reprogram the task in order to achieve this speed-up. Nonetheless, there are times when speed matters, and matters greatly. For example, many algorithms for statistical inference, both classical and Bayesian, use computationally intensive numerical methods such as numerical optimization, numerical integration or differentiation, and Monte Carlo methods. For these algorithms to be used for anything other than trivial problems, they must be implemented as computationally efficiently as possible. In these cases, implementing them using the set of R programming methods we explored in Chapter 6 might be highly inefficient. Fortunately, there are many ways in which we can continue using R, or at least using R as our computing environment, and achieve considerable improvement in computational speed and efficiencies. In this chapter, we will explore two of these approaches: interfacing with C++ code using Rcpp and coarse-grained parallel processing. We chose these two approaches over others because both are, in their own ways, very powerful, widely used in the R community, and relatively very straightforward to implement.

In addition to using C++ and parallel programming, in this chapter, we will also provide a very brief introduction to using Spark with R. Spark is a framework for big data analysis. It is usually used for analysing data sets that are too large for the RAM of one machine. A comprehensive introduction to Spark would require a book in itself. Here, we just provide a brief introduction to what Spark is and how it can be used in R with sparklyr.

15.2 Using C++ code with Rcpp

C++ is a general-purpose programming language. As the name implies, it is an extension of the C programming language, particularly by the inclusion of object-oriented programming. Since the 1990s, C++ has consistently been one of the most widely used programming languages of any kind, and its key strengths have been its power, flexibility, speed and efficiency. C++ is a low-level (relative to R, Python, etc.), statically typed, compiled language. By contrast, R is high-level, dynamically typed, interpreted language. What this means is that C++ code is more explicit, more detailed and less expressive than R. In addition, we must declare the data type of each variable in C++. For example, if x is an integer, we must explicitly declare that it is at the start of our code, and it cannot be changed to another type such as a string in the rest of the code. This contrasts with R, where we never need to declare variables' types in advance and can change them on the fly. Finally, C++ must be compiled into binary machine code by a compiler before it can be executed. By contrast, R code is executed one statement at a time by the R interpreter, which is another program (mostly written in C) that reads R code and converts it into machine instructions.

In practice, this makes C++ more difficult to master as a programming language, and leads to more verbose, lengthy, and syntactically precise and unforgiving code. Also, because of its write–compile–execute operation, we cannot use it interactively as we do with R. In return for this pain and inconvenience, however, C++ is much faster than R. As we will see, we can easily obtain orders-of-magnitude speed-ups if we rewrite computationally demanding R code in C++.

The Rcpp package (Eddelbuettel and Balamuta, 2017) has made the use of C++-based functions etc. from R particularly easy to accomplish. It allows us to focus on just writing the C++ code and not worry about the details of how C++ and R communicate. In most real-world cases, we put the C++ code in R packages, and use an R package builder command to compile it. We then load that R package just like any other, for example using library(), and then execute the compiled C++ code just like any other R function. We will demonstrate this procedure in this section. To begin, however, we show how Rcpp can be used interactively in the console to create C++ functions that are accessible in the R session. This is very helpful for learning more about how Rcpp works and for prototyping code.

We should be clear that our coverage of Rcpp here is just a brief introduction, aimed at illustrating the general principles and providing some illustrative examples. It is emphatically not intended to be a comprehensive introduction. For a lengthier introduction, consider Wickham (2019, Chapter 19), and for a comprehensive introduction, consider Eddelbuettel (2013), written by the author of Rcpp.

Using Rcpp interactively

The C++ function we will use as our first example, named average, calculates the arithmetic mean of a vector of values. Its code is as follows:

```cpp
double average(NumericVector x){

  // Declare loop variable
  int i;
  // Declare vector length variable
  int n = x.size();
  // Declare variable that accumulates values
  double total = 0;

  for (i = 0; i < n; i++){
    total += x[i];
  }

  return total/n;
}
```

Obviously, the arithmetic mean is already implemented in R as mean, and so we can compare average and mean. In addition, it is useful to compare average to the following pure R implementation:

```
averageR <- function (x) {

  total <- 0

  for (i in seq_along (x)) {
    total <- total + x[i]
  }

  total/length (x)
}
```

As we can see, there are a number of differences between the C++ and the pure R implementations of this function. One of the most obvious differences is that we must declare the data types of the variables in the C++ code. More specifically, in `average`, we declare the following:

- The return value of `average` is stated to be a `double`, which is a double-precision floating point number. A double is basically a single decimal number. Note that we make this declaration when we define the function: `double average (...)`.
- The input vector `x` is declared as a `NumericVector`, which is an `Rcpp`-specific, rather than C++ general, data type for using R numeric vectors in C++ functions. Note that we declare this data type in the function definition.
- The `for` loop variable `i` is declared as an integer using the key word `int`.
- The length of the input vector `x` is also declared as an integer with `int`. Note that we obtain the length of the `x` vector with `x.size()`.
- The variable `total`, which calculates a running sum of the elements of `x`, is declared as a `double`.

Other differences between `average` and `averageR` include that the syntax of the `for` loop in `average` follows the standard C/C++ syntax where we specify the starting value of the loop variable (`i = 0`), an expression that determines whether the loop continues on each iteration (`i < n`; therefore, it terminates when `i == n`), and the increment to `i` on each iteration (`i++`). Very importantly, notice that C++ starts the vector index at 0 rather than 1. Thus, for example, in C++, `x[1]` is the *second* element of the vector `x`, while `x[0]` is the first element. In R, `x[1]` is the first element of `x`, and `x[0]` returns an empty vector. Also in the `for` loop, we use the expression `i++`. This is shorthand for `i += 1`, which is itself a shorthand for `i = i + 1`. The expression `total += 1` is therefore the same as `total = total + 1`.

Other differences between the C++ and pure R functions are that in the C++ function we must terminate statements with `;`, we must also have an explicit `return` statement, we use `=` and not `<-` for assignment, and we do not use the `function` keyword in function definitions.

Now, let us compile `average` using the `cppFunction` from `Rcpp`. To do so, we simply paste the above function into `cppFunction` as a string:

```
library (Rcpp)
cppFunction ('double average (NumericVector x) {

// Declare loop variable
int i;
```

```
// Declare vector length variable
int n = x.size();
// Declare variable that accumulates values
double total = 0;

for (i = 0; i < n; i++){
  total += x[i];
}

return total/n;
}')
```

With this, average is now available to use in our R session just like any other function in R:

```
x <- runif(1e4)
average(x)
#> [1] 0.5003048
```

We can verify that this is correct with mean or averageR:

```
mean(x)
#> [1] 0.5003048
averageR(x)
#> [1] 0.5003048
```

Now let us compare the performance of these functions using the microbenchmark tool:

```
library(tidyverse)
theme_set(theme_classic())
library(magrittr)
library(microbenchmark)
results <- microbenchmark(average(x),
                          mean(x),
                          averageR(x))
results
#> Unit: microseconds
#>         expr      min       lq      mean    median        uq     max neval
#>   average(x)   12.196   12.352  22.41144   12.4550   12.5730 1003.499   100
#>      mean(x)   18.252   18.360  18.59492   18.4365   18.5905   26.276   100
#>  averageR(x)  276.172  276.967 279.54952  277.3215  279.2305  309.041   100
```

We see that the average function is about 12 times faster than the base R averageR function in terms of its mean performance, and about 22 times faster in terms of its median performance, on 100 iterations. We also see that average is roughly comparable in speed to the built-in mean function. mean is faster in terms of its mean value over the 100 iterations, but average has a faster median. This is notable because the mean is a much more carefully designed and optimized function than average. These results show the substantial gains that can be achieved by rewriting our code in C++.

Using `Rcpp` code in R packages

Using `cppFunction` is very useful but is intended for interactive use. For C++ code intended to be used across multiple R sessions and projects, it is preferable to put the code in its own files, compile it once, and then load the compiled functions into R sessions, R scripts, RMarkdown scripts, etc., and use them like any R function. The ideal way of doing this is to include the C++ code as a part of an R package, and use standard package build tools to compile and document the resulting functions.

We will demonstrate this by making a package that calculates a simple moving or rolling average. We will name this `smra` (simple *moving/rolling average*). We will use the `create_package` function in the `usethis` package to create a bare package directory with some of the necessary files and directories. To do this, we first load the `usethis` and the `fs` packages:

```
library(usethis)
library(fs)
```

The `usethis` package is a package for automating the set up and building of R packages, while `fs` provides tools for creating, listing and manipulating files. We now create a directory called `smra` inside a temporary directory created by the `tempdir` command, and we save the path to this directory:

```
path_to_package <- path(tempdir(), 'smra')
```

Next, we create a list with all the information that we need to pass to the `create_package` command. This information is put in the DESCRIPTION file inside the `smra` package directory:

```
fields <- list(Title = "Simple Moving/Rolling Average",
               Version = "0.0.1",
               `Authors@R` = person(given = "Mark",
                                    family = "Andrews",
                                    role = c("aut", "cre"),
                                    email = "mark.andrews@ntu.ac.uk"),
               Description = "Calculate a simple moving/rolling average.",
               License = 'MIT Licence',
               LinkingTo = 'Rcpp',
               Imports = 'Rcpp'
)
```

Most of the fields here are self-explanatory. Note that the `Authors@R` field uses the function `person` to define the author of the package. This author is assigned the roles `aut` (author) and `cre` (creator). Note also that the `LinkingTo` and `Imports` fields, both with values `Rcpp`, are necessary to allow us to build and export the `Rcpp`-based functions.

We may now execute the `create_package` command:

```
create_package(path_to_package,
               fields = fields,
               rstudio = F,
               open = F)
```

```
#> Package: smra
#> Title: Simple Moving/Rolling Average
#> Version: 0.0.1
#> Authors@R (parsed):
#>     * Mark Andrews <mark.andrews@ntu.ac.uk> [aut, cre]
#> Description: Calculate a simple moving/rolling average.
#> License: MIT Licence
#> Imports:
#>     Rcpp
#> LinkingTo:
#>     Rcpp
#> Encoding: UTF-8
#> LazyData: true
#> Roxygen: list(markdown = TRUE)
#> RoxygenNote: 7.1.1
```

In `create_package`, by setting `rstudio = T`, we set the directory to be an RStudio project, although this is not strictly necessary. By setting `open = F`, we do not open the resulting RStudio project/package in a new RStudio session.

At this point, the `smra` directory has two files, `DESCRIPTION` and `NAMESPACE`, and one empty directory named `R`, which we can see with the `dir_tree` command:

```
dir_tree(path_to_package)
/tmp/Rtmp06CvwS/smra
├── DESCRIPTION
├── NAMESPACE
└── R
```

We now create an empty file `code.cpp` and put this in a new directory named `src` in the package, which we will do using the `file_create` function from the `fs` package:

```
src_dir <- dir_create(path(path_to_package, 'src'))
file_create(path(src_dir, 'code.cpp'))
```

We put the following C++ code in this `code.cpp` file:

```
// code.cpp
NumericVector rolling_mean(NumericVector x, int k = 1) {

  // Declare outer loop counter
  int i;
  // Declare inner loop counter
  int j;
  // Declare vector length
  int n = x.size();
  // Declare inner loop summation variable
  double total;
  // Declare output vector
  NumericVector y(n);
```

```
for (i = 0; i < n; i++) {
  if (i < k - 1) {
    y[i] = NumericVector::get_na();
  } else {
    total = 0;
    for (j = 0; j < k; j++) {
      total += x[i - j];
    }
    y[i] = total/k;
  }
}
return y;
}
```

This program calculates a length k moving or rolling mean of a vector. Specifically, given a vector whose values are $x_1, x_2, ..., x_i, ..., x_n$, the length k moving average is a vector $y_1, y_2, ..., y_i, ..., y_n$ whose values are

$$y_i = \frac{1}{k}\sum_{j=1}^{k}x_{i-(j-1)} = \frac{1}{k}\sum_{j=0}^{k-1}x_{i-j},$$

if $i \geq k$ and undefined otherwise. For example, if $k = 5$, for $i \geq k$,

$$y_i = \frac{x_i + x_{i-1} + x_{i-2} + x_{i-3} + x_{i-4}}{5}.$$

To do this, we loop over all values of i from 0 to $n - 1$ (remembering that C++ starts its index at 0), and for values of $i \leq k - 1$, we assign the NA value to y[i]. For all other values of i, we calculate the mean of x[i] and the $k - 1$ previous values. At the beginning, we declare the data types of all the variables in this program. Note that the output of the function is of type NumericVector. We declare that y is a NumericVector of length n, where n is the length of x, by the following statement:

```
// code.cpp
NumericVector y(n);
```

Before we compile this function, we add the following comments immediately before the function begins:

```
// code.cpp
//' Simple moving average of a numeric vector
//'
//'
//' @param x A numeric vector
//' @param k The window length of the moving average
//' @return A vector of the same length of x
//' @export
// [[Rcpp::export]]
```

These are, in fact, more than just normal code comments. Those preceded by `//'` will be parsed by `roxygen2` to make the documentation for the resulting `rolling_mean` function. In addition, the `//' @export` statement ensures that `rolling_mean` will be an exported function of the package we make. The `roxygen2` documentation functions will write `export(rolling_mean)` to the NAMESPACE file in the R package. In addition, the `// [[Rcpp::export]]` comment will ensure that the C++ function is exported to R.

In order to ensure that more necessary information is included in the NAMESPACE file, we create the following file and place it in the R directory in the R package:

```
// smra-package.R
#' @useDynLib smra, .registration = TRUE
#' @importFrom Rcpp sourceCpp
NULL
```

The file structure of the package is now as follows:

```
dir_tree(path_to_package)
/tmp/Rtmp06CvwS/smra
├── DESCRIPTION
├── NAMESPACE
├── R
│   └── smra-package.R
└── src
    └── code.cpp
```

We are now ready to build the package. First, we document the package, which also ensures that the necessary lines are added to NAMESPACE. We can do this with the `devtools` package's `document` function:

```
library(devtools)
document(path_to_package)
```

We can load the package with `load_all`, which is roughly equivalent to installing and loading with the normal `library` function:

```
load_all(path = path_to_package)
```

Now we can use the `rolling_mean` function:

```
x <- rnorm(20)
rolling_mean(x, k = 5)
#>  [1]          NA          NA          NA          NA  0.99988573  0.92298972
#>  [7]  0.49955783 -0.08995363 -0.03230148  0.17451006  0.38450327  0.69945225
#> [13]  0.99568605  1.06842425  0.62634885  0.38136451  0.55827531  0.16512014
#> [19] -0.20141630 -0.26458559
```

We can verify that this rolling mean calculation is correct by comparing it to the `rollmean` function from the `zoo` package:

```
zoo::rollmean(x, k = 5, na.pad = T, align = 'right')
#>  [1]          NA          NA          NA          NA  0.99988573  0.92298972
#>  [7]  0.49955783 -0.08995363 -0.03230148  0.17451006  0.38450327  0.69945225
#> [13]  0.99568605  1.06842425  0.62634885  0.38136451  0.55827531  0.16512014
#> [19] -0.20141630 -0.26458559
```

15●3 Parallel processing in R

Parallel processing is arguably *the* defining feature of high-performance computing. At the very least, it is one of its defining features and one of its most important topics. Simply put, parallel processing is the simultaneous execution of multiple programs to perform some task. To do this, we need more than one *computing unit* (*processing unit*) on our computer. In general, these units can be cores either on the central processing unit (CPU) or on the graphics processing unit (GPU). Modern supercomputing and high-performance computing almost always use a mixture of both CPUs and GPUs. However, although most modern desktops and laptop machines usually have multicore CPUs, most do not have general-purpose GPUs, and so we will not consider GPU computing here.

The topic of parallel computing generally is a highly technical one, often focusing on relatively low-level programming concepts, the details of the hardware, and the algorithmic details of the task be carried out. Here, we will avoid all of this complexity. We will focus exclusively on what are called *embarrassingly parallel* problems. These are computing problems that can be easily broken down into multiple independent parts. We will also assume that we are working on a single computer (i.e. node), such as a laptop or desktop machine, rather than on a cluster of multiple nodes. And we will focus on parallel computing using R itself, as opposed to the parallelism that we can obtain using libraries such as OpenMP (Open Multi-Processing) or MPI (Message Passing Interface) when programming with C/C++ and other fast low level languages.

The `parallel` package

R provides many packages related to parallel computing (see the webpage https://cran.r-project.org/web/views/HighPerformanceComputing.html for a curated list of relevant packages). Here, we will focus exclusively on the R `parallel` package. This package builds upon and incorporates two other packages: `multicore` and `snow` (simple *network of* workstations). The principal way that parallel processing is done using `parallel` is by using multiple new processes that are started by a command in R. These processes are known as *workers* and the R session that starts them is known as the *master*. The communication between the master and the workers can be done using *sockets* (the code for doing so was developed by `snow`) or *forks* (the code for doing so was developed by `multicore`). Forks create copies of the master process, including all its objects, and workers and the master processes share memory allocations. Sockets are independent processes to which information from and to the master must be explicitly copied. In both forks and sockets, tasks are farmed out to the workers from the master using parallel versions of 'map' functionals, such as `lapply` and `purrr::map`, which we explored in Chapter 6. While there are many advantages to using forks, their key disadvantage is that they are not available on Windows. For that reason, we will only consider sockets here.

The `parallel` package is pre installed in R and is loaded with the usual `library` command:

```
library(parallel)
```

We can use the `detectCores` function from `parallel` to list the number of available cores on our computer. The option `logical = FALSE` will list only physical, rather than virtual, cores. It is advisable to always set `logical = FALSE` and so report only physical cores as this in general lists the maximum number of separate processes that can be executed simultaneously. The machine on which I am currently working has two Xeon Gold 6154 CPUs, each with 18 physical cores, and so there are 36 physical cores:

```
detectCores(logical = F)
#> [1] 36
```

Using `clusterCall`, `clusterApply`, etc.

The `parallel` package provides many functions for socket-based execution of parallel tasks or farming out tasks to workers. We will consider `clusterCall` and `clusterApply`, and related functions such as `parLapply` and `parSapply`. These are similar to one another, and are representative of how other socket-based parallel functions in `parallel` work.

The `clusterCall` function calls the same function on each worker. As a very simple example, let us create a function that returns the square of a given number:

```
square <- function(x) x^2
```

To apply this in parallel, first, we start with a set of workers. We can specify as many workers as we wish. Specifying more workers than there are cores will obviously not allow for all workers to occupy one whole core. Usually, if specifying the maximum number of workers, we set it to the total number of cores minus 1. Assuming that the workers are involved in computationally intensive tasks, this allows one core free for other tasks, like R or RStudio, running on your computer. For now, we will use just four cores. We do this using the `makeCluster` command:

```
the_cluster <- makeCluster(4)
```

This command returns an object, which we name `the_cluster` here, and which we need to use in subsequent commands. Now we call `square` with input argument `10` on each worker.

```
clusterCall(cl = the_cluster, square, 10)
#> [[1]]
#> [1] 100
#>
#> [[2]]
#> [1] 100
#>
#> [[3]]
#> [1] 100
```

```
#>
#> [[4]]
#> [1] 100
```

The `clusterCall` returns a list with four elements. Each element is the value returned by the function `square` with argument `10` that was executed on each worker. We could also use `clusterCall` with anonymous functions, as in the following example, where we calculate the cube of 10:

```
clusterCall(cl = the_cluster, function(x) x^3, 10)
#> [[1]]
#> [1] 1000
#>
#> [[2]]
#> [1] 1000
#>
#> [[3]]
#> [1] 1000
#>
#> [[4]]
#> [1] 1000
```

As another example, here we call `rnorm` with input argument `5`, which determines the number of random values:

```
clusterCall(cl = the_cluster, rnorm, 5)
#> [[1]]
#> [1]  0.89175353  0.58230920 -0.04553604 -0.46020684 -0.29019827
#>
#> [[2]]
#> [1]  1.11598121  0.06759077 -1.72311710  0.96135403  0.95410483
#>
#> [[3]]
#> [1]  1.0080573  0.1259768  0.7326909 -1.1768816  1.8536536
#>
#> [[4]]
#> [1]  1.0282337 0.3469490  0.8843403  1.4634417 -0.2920458
```

Usually, we need the workers to perform different tasks, and so calling the same function with the same arguments is not usually what we want to do. To call the same function with different arguments, we can use `clusterApply` and related functions. In the following, we apply `square` to each element of vector of four elements:

```
clusterApply(cl = the_cluster, x = c(2, 3, 5, 10), square)
#> [[1]]
#> [1] 4
#>
#> [[2]]
```

```
#> [1] 9
#>
#> [[3]]
#> [1] 25
#>
#> [[4]]
#> [1] 100
```

With `clusterApply`, we can still use anonymous functions and we can also supply optional input arguments:

```
clusterApply(cl = the_cluster, x = c(2, 3, 5, 10), function(x, k) x^k, 3)
#> [[1]]
#> [1] 8
#>
#> [[2]]
#> [1] 27
#>
#> [[3]]
#> [1] 125
#>
#> [[4]]
#> [1] 1000
```

Very similar to `clusterApply` is `parLapply`, which is the parallel counterpart to base R's `lapply`. In `lapply`, we supply a list, each element of which is applied to a function, and the result is returned as a new list:

```
lapply(list(x = 1, y = 2, z = 3), function(x) x^2)
#> $x
#> [1] 1
#>
#> $y
#> [1] 4
#>
#> $z
#> [1] 9
```

For `parLapply` we use an identical syntax but with the cluster being the first argument:

```
parLapply(cl = the_cluster, list(x = 1, y = 2, z = 3), function(x) x^2)
#> $x
#> [1] 1
#>
#> $y
#> [1] 4
#>
#> $z
#> [1] 9
```

Just as `sapply` can be used to simplify the output from `lapply`, we can use `parSapply` to simplify the output of `parLapply`. For example, in the following, the returned list is simplified as a vector:

```
parSapply(cl = the_cluster, list(x = 1, y = 2, z = 3), function(x) x^2)
#> x y z
#> 1 4 9
```

When we are finished with the parallel processing, we must shut down the cluster:

```
stopCluster(the_cluster)
```

Bootstrapping

Bootstrapping, which we have not covered in this book, is a way to obtain a sampling distribution for an estimator. We sample with replacement from the observed data, and draw a sample that is the same size as the original. With each sample, we calculate the estimator. We repeat this process a large number of times to obtain a distribution of the estimators. As an example, let us consider the `housing_df` data set that we considered in Chapter 8:

```
housing_df <- read_csv('data/housing.csv')
housing_df
#> # A tibble: 546 x 1
#>      price
#>      <dbl>
#>  1 42000
#>  2 38500
#>  3 49500
#>  4 60500
#>  5 61000
#>  6 66000
#>  7 66000
#>  8 69000
#>  9 83800
#> 10 88500
#> # ... with 536 more rows
```

This contains the prices of 546 houses in the city of Windsor, Ontario, in 1987. We can sample the rows of `housing_df` with replacement 546 times using the `sample` function as follows:

```
n <- nrow(housing_df)
housing_df[sample(seq(n), n, replace = T),]
#> # A tibble: 546 x 1
#>      price
#>      <dbl>
#>  1   64500
#>  2   77500
```

```
#>   3    56000
#>   4    66000
#>   5    73000
#>   6   123500
#>   7    65000
#>   8    64500
#>   9    73500
#>  10    65000
#> # … with 536 more rows
```

A function that can be used with any `lm` model is as follows:

```
bootstrap_lm <- function(formula, data){
  n <- nrow(data)
  resampled_data <- data[sample(seq(n), n, replace = T), ]
  lm(formula, data = resampled_data) %>%
    coef()
}
```

We can apply this to the `housing_df` data as follows:

```
bootstrap_lm(price ~ 1, data = housing_df)
#> (Intercept)
#>    69189.93
```

Note that this will produce just one bootstrap estimate. We need to reapply this a large number of times to obtain our distribution of bootstrapped estimates. This can be done in parallel. For that, we first start a new cluster of four workers:

```
the_cluster <- makeCluster(4)
```

Then, for code reuse, we create a function to perform a parallel distributed `bootstrap_lm(price ~ 1, data = housing_df)` call a specified number of times, denoted by n:

```
parallel_bootstrap <- function(n){
  parLapply(the_cluster,
            seq(n),
            function(x) {bootstrap_lm(price ~ 1, data = housing_df)}
  )
}
```

Were we to immediately try `parallel_bootstrap`, it would fail because the workers do not have the function `bootstrap_lm` or `housing_df`, which are both defined in the master process's R environment. To send `bootstrap_lm` and `housing_df` to the workers we must do the following:

```
clusterExport(cl = the_cluster, varlist = c('bootstrap_lm', 'housing_df'))
```

Note that `varlist` is a vector of names, rather than the objects themselves. This is still not sufficient, however, because `bootstrap_lm` also uses the pipe `%>%`, which must be loaded by a `library` call such as `library("tidyverse")`. We can execute this package load function on all workers with `clusterEvalQ` as follows:

```
clusterEvalQ(cl = the_cluster, library("tidyverse"))
```

We may now execute the parallel bootstrapping:

```
estimates <- parallel_bootstrap(10000)
```

The resulting `estimates` will be a list, which we can easily convert to a vector and then plot their histogram. We could also have used `parSapply` instead `parLapply` to directly return a vector. The histogram of these bootstrapped estimates is shown in Figure 15.1.

```
tibble(estimates = unlist(estimates)) %>%
    ggplot(aes(x = estimates)) + geom_histogram(bins = 100, col = 'white')
```

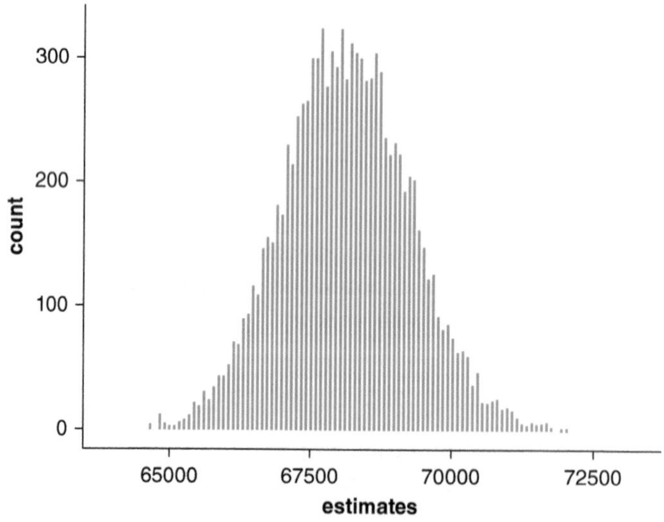

Figure 15.1 Bootstrap estimates of the mean of the prices in the `housing_df` data

Let us now compare the time taken by `parLapply` to sample 10,000 estimates and compare that to the time taken by `lapply` to do the same thing. For this timing, we will use the relatively crude timing procedure of using `Sys.time()`:

```
sequential_bootstrap <- function(n){
    lapply(seq(n),
             function(x) {bootstrap_lm(price ~ 1, data = housing_df)}
    )
}


# parallel version with 4 workers
start_time <- Sys.time()
```

```
estimates <- parallel_bootstrap (10000)
parallel_version <- Sys.time () - start_time


# sequential version
start_time <- Sys.time ()
estimates <- sequential_bootstrap (10000)
sequential_version <- Sys.time () - start_time
```

The times are as follows:

```
parallel_version
#> Time difference of 2.352102 secs
sequential_version
#> Time difference of 8.188133 secs
```

and so the parallel version is 3.48 times as fast. However, it is interesting to note that this roughly linear speed-up, which is the ideal speed-up in parallel processing, is not always going to happen. Consider, for example, the case of obtaining just 10 bootstrap estimates:

```
# parallel version with 4 workers
start_time <- Sys.time ()
estimates <- parallel_bootstrap (10)
parallel_version <- Sys.time () - start_time


# sequential version
start_time <- Sys.time ()
estimates <- sequential_bootstrap (10)
sequential_version <- Sys.time () - start_time
```

The times are now as follows:

```
parallel_version
#> Time difference of 0.03383422 secs
sequential_version
#> Time difference of 0.0380199 secs
```

and so the two versions are roughly the same speed. This occurs because there is overhead in farming out the tasks and communicating between the master and workers. For this reason, in general, it is always possible for a parallel processing task to be slower than its sequential counterpart.

```
stopCluster (the_cluster)
```

Parallel execution of MCMC models

Throughout this book, we have used MCMC-based Bayesian models, mostly using brms, and in Chapter 17 we cover Stan directly. In general, MCMC is computationally very intensive.

Although `brms` and Stan allow us to easily execute the chains within each model in parallel, we often need to run multiple separate `brms` or Stan models. When working on a high-end workstation or cluster, we would like to take advantage of all the cores available to us to do this. As an example, let us reconsider the `affairs_df` data set that we covered in Chapter 10:

```
affairs_df <- read_csv('data/affairs.csv')
affairs_df
#> # A tibble: 601 x 9
#>     affairs gender  age yearsmarried children religiousness education occupation
#>       <dbl> <chr> <dbl>        <dbl> <chr>            <dbl>     <dbl>      <dbl>
#>  1        0 male     37        10    no                   3        18          7
#>  2        0 female   27         4    no                   4        14          6
#>  3        0 female   32        15    yes                  1        12          1
#>  4        0 male     57        15    yes                  5        18          6
#>  5        0 male     22         0.75 no                   2        17          6
#>  6        0 female   32         1.5  no                   2        17          5
#>  7        0 female   22         0.75 no                   2        12          1
#>  8        0 male     57        15    yes                  2        14          4
#>  9        0 female   32        15    yes                  4        16          1
#> 10        0 male     22         1.5  no                   4        14          4
#> # … with 591 more rows, and 1 more variable: rating <dbl>
```

This gives us the number of extramarital affairs (`affairs`) in the last 12 months by each of `nrows(affairs_df)` 601 people. We could model this variable using, among other things, a Poisson, or negative binomial, or by the zero-inflated counterparts of these models. Likewise, we could use any combination of the eight predictor variables that we have available to us. Each one of these models could take at least a minute to complete. For many `brms` or Stan models, however, the running time could be many hours or even days. Even though each model can use up to four cores, with one core per chain, if we were working on a workstation or cluster, we could execute many of these models simultaneously. With the 36 cores on my workstation I could comfortably execute up to eight models simultaneously, leaving a few cores free for other tasks. This could be accomplished by opening eight different RStudio sessions and running a different model in each one, or running eight different R scripts using `Rscript` on eight different DOS or Unix terminals. It is, however, much more convenient and manageable to have a single R script that creates eight workers and farms out one of the eight models to each one.

Let us consider the following Poisson regression as a prototypical model:

```
M <- brm(affairs ~ gender + age + yearsmarried,
         data = affairs_df,
         cores   4,
         iter = 25000,
         family = poisson(link = 'log'))
```

Although not at all necessary for this model, we will use 25,000 iterations per chain in order to resemble a larger and hence slower model. The running time, including the C++ compilation, for this model is approximately 43 seconds. Variants of this model might use a different formula, a different `family` or both. We can make a function that accepts different formulae and families. We do this, for reasons that will be soon clear, by creating a function that accepts one input argument that is a list with elements named `formula` and `family`:

```r
affairs_model <- function(input){
  brm(input[['formula']],
      data = affairs_df,
      cores = 4,
      iter = 25000,
      family = input[['family']])
}
```

We now create a list of model specifications. Each element of this list is itself a list with two elements: `formula` and `family`. The `formula` is a `brmsformula` specifying the outcome variable and predictors. The `family` is one of the probability distribution families that `brms` accepts. Here, we specify six models, which are each a combination of two sets of predictors and three different families:

```r
model_specs <- list(

  # Poisson model with 3 predictors
  v1 = list(formula = brmsformula(affairs ~ gender + age + yearsmarried),
            family = poisson(link = 'log')),

  # Poisson model with 5 predictors
  v2 = list(formula = brmsformula(affairs ~ gender + age + yearsmarried +
            religiousness + rating), family = poisson(link = 'log')),

  # Negative binomial with 3 predictors
  v3 = list(formula = brmsformula(affairs ~ gender + age + yearsmarried),
            family = negbinomial(link = "log", link_shape = "log")),

  # Negative binomial with 5 predictors
  v4 = list(formula = brmsformula(affairs ~ gender + age + yearsmarried +
            religiousness + rating), family = negbinomial(link = "log",
            link_shape = "log")),

  # Zero-inflated Poisson with 3 predictors
  v5 = list(formula = brmsformula(affairs ~ gender + age + yearsmarried),
            family = zero_inflated_poisson(link = "log", link_zi = "logit")),

  # Zero-inflated Poisson with 3 predictors
  v6 = list(formula = brmsformula(affairs ~ gender + age + yearsmarried +
            religiousness + rating), family = zero_inflated_poisson
            (link = "log", link_zi = "logit"))

)
```

Using `parLapply` or a related function, we can farm each one of these model specifications out to a worker. That worker will then compile the model and sample from it using four chains, with each chain on its own core. Thus, when sampling, 6 × 4 cores will be in use. The six resulting models are then passed back to a list named `results`. First, we start the cluster of six workers, and to each we export the `affairs_df` data frame and load the `brms` package:

```
the_cluster <- makeCluster(6)

clusterExport(cl = the_cluster, varlist = 'affairs_df')
clusterEvalQ(cl = the_cluster, library("brms"))
```

We then run `parLapply` using `model_specs` as the list and `affairs_model` as the function to which each element of the list will be applied. For comparison with the sequential model, we will time it:

```
start_time <- Sys.time()

results <- parLapply(cl = the_cluster,
                     model_specs,
                     affairs_model)

parallel_version <- Sys.time() - start_time
```

The running time is 73 seconds. For comparison, executing these models in a sequential functional like `lapply` could be done as follows:

```
start_time <- Sys.time()

sequential_results <- lapply(model_specs, affairs_model)

sequential_version <- Sys.time() - start_time
```

The running time in this case is 245 seconds, and so it is about 3.4 times slower than the parallel version.

Now, all the results of these models are in the list `results` with names `v1`, `v2`, etc. We can use these models completely as normal. For example, to extract the WAIC value of each model, we could create a helper function `get_waic` and apply it to each element in `results`:

```
get_waic <- function(model) {
  waic(model)$estimates['waic', 'Estimate']
}
```

We will apply `get_waic` to `results` using a parallel functional like `parLapply` or `parSapply`, etc., but for these models it could also be done using, for example, `lapply` or `purrr::map`:

```
waic_results <- parSapply(cl = the_cluster,
                          results,
                          get_waic)
```

```
waic_results
#>        v1       v2       v3       v4       v5       v6
#> 3262.216 2910.343 1495.641 1471.287 1646.572 1617.744
stopCluster(the_cluster)
```

 Spark

Apache Spark is a very popular framework for big data analysis. Put very simply, it is used for doing data processing and data analysis where both the data and the processing are distributed across multiple nodes on a cluster. Spark is not an R-based tool. It is written in the programming language Scala, which is derived from Java. However, Spark can be used from R via packages like `sparklyr`. In this chapter, we will provide a brief introduction to using `sparklyr`.

Installing `sparklyr` and Spark

The usual way of working with Spark is on a remote Spark cluster. When learning about Spark, especially when using `sparklyr`, it is easier to use a local Spark installation on the computer on which you are working. Using Spark locally often defeats the whole purpose of using Spark, which is to perform parallel and distributed computing on large data sets that do not fit in the RAM of a single node. Nonetheless, the basics of Spark and `sparklyr` can be learned more easily this way.

We install `sparklyr` just as we would any R package using `install.packages`, and load it with `library`:

```
library(sparklyr)
```

Once installed and loaded, we can install Spark locally as follows:

```
spark_install()
```

Note that this requires Java to be installed on your machine. Now that we've installed Spark, we can create a connection to it as follows:

```
connection <- spark_connect(master = 'local')
```

Were we to connect to a remote Spark cluster, we would still use `spark_connect` but with different arguments. We can now verify the version of Spark we are using:

```
spark_version(connection)
#> [1] '2.4.3'
```

Copying data to Spark

We now need to get data to our local Spark cluster. Again, in practice, the data would be very large and would reside on the cluster, and so we would not copy it from our local device or R session to the cluster. For the present example, our Spark installation begins empty and so we have no choice but to copy data there in order to use Spark. There are no restrictions on the kind of data frame we can use. We will arbitrarily choose the HI data frame from the Ecdat package. This gives the health insurance and hours worked by married women:

```
data(HI, package = 'Ecdat')
HI %>% as_tibble()
#> # A tibble: 22,272 x 13
#>    whrswk hhi   whi   hhi2  education race  hispanic experience kidslt6 kids618
#>    <int> <fct> <fct> <fct> <ord>     <fct> <fct>        <dbl>     <int>  <int>
#> 1      0 no    no    no    13-15yea~ white no              13         2      1
#> 2     50 no    yes   no    13-15yea~ white no              24         0      1
#> 3     40 yes   no    yes   12years   white no              43         0      0
#> 4     40 no    yes   yes   13-15yea~ white no              17         0      1
#> 5      0 yes   no    yes   9-11years white no            44.5         0      0
#> 6     40 yes   yes   yes   12years   white no              32         0      0
#> 7     40 yes   no    yes   16years   white no              14         0      0
#> 8     25 no    no    no    12years   white no               1         1      0
#> 9     45 no    yes   no    16years   white no               4         0      0
#> 10    30 no    no    yes   13-15yea~ white no               7         1      0
#> # ... with 22,262 more rows, and 3 more variables: husby <dbl>, region <fct>,
#> #    wght <int>
```

We can copy HI to our Spark cluster with dplyr::copy_to as follows:

```
hi_df <- copy_to(connection, HI)
```

We can verify that it was copied to the cluster by listing the tables there:

```
src_tbls(connection)
#> [1] "hi"
```

The major class of hi_df is now tbl_spark, or a Spark-based tibble or data frame:

```
class(hi_df)
#> [1] "tbl_spark" "tbl_sql"   "tbl_lazy"  "tbl"
```

Although this appears just like a tibble in our local R session, this is just essentially a link to a data frame stored on our cluster. By typing the name hi_df, we see the first few rows:

```
hi_df
#> # Source: spark<HI> [?? x 13]
#>    whrswk hhi   whi   hhi2  education race  hispanic experience kidslt6 kids618
#>    <int> <chr> <chr> <chr> <chr>     <chr> <chr>        <dbl>     <int>  <int>
#> 1      0 no    no    no    13-15yea~ white no              13         2      1
#> 2     50 no    yes   no    13-15yea~ white no              24         0      1
#> 3     40 yes   no    yes   12years   white no              43         0      0
#> 4     40 no    yes   yes   13-15yea~ white no              17         0      1
```

```
#>  5     0 yes    no     yes    9-11years  white no              44.5      0          0
#>  6    40 yes    yes    yes    12years    white no              32        0          0
#>  7    40 yes    no     yes    16years    white no              14        0          0
#>  8    25 no     no     no     12years    white no               1        1          0
#>  9    45 no     yes    no     16years    white no               4        0          0
#> 10    30 no     no     yes    13-15yea~  white no               7        1          0
#> # … with more rows, and 3 more variables: husby <dbl>, region <chr>, wght <int>
```

Note that it does not list the number of rows, because it has not read them all, and just read the top. We can, however, see more rows with the print function. For example, to see the first 100 rows, we would do the following (we omit the results):

```
print(hi_df, n = 100)
```

Data wrangling with Spark

We can do exploratory analysis of Spark-based data frames using the dplyr verbs just like we would normally. For example, we can select with select:

```
hi_df %>% select(whrswk, hhi, starts_with('kids'))
#> # Source: spark<?> [?? x 4]
#>    whrswk hhi    kidslt6 kids618
#>     <int> <chr>    <int>   <int>
#> 1       0 no          2       1
#> 2      50 no          0       1
#> 3      40 yes         0       0
#> 4      40 no          0       1
#> 5       0 yes         0       0
#> 6      40 yes         0       0
#> 7      40 yes         0       0
#> 8      25 no          1       0
#> 9      45 no          0       0
#> 10     30 no          1       0
#> # … with more rows
```

We can filter with filter:

```
hi_df %>% filter(education == '13-15years', hispanic == 'no')
#> # Source: spark<?> [?? x 13]
#>    whrswk hhi   whi   hhi2  education  race  hispanic experience kidslt6 kids618
#>     <int> <chr> <chr> <chr> <chr>      <chr> <chr>         <dbl>   <int>   <int>
#> 1       0 no    no    no    13-15yea~  white no               13       2       1
#> 2      50 no    yes   no    13-15yea~  white no               24       0       1
#> 3      40 no    yes   yes   13-15yea~  white no               17       0       1
#> 4      30 no    no    yes   13-15yea~  white no                7       1       0
#> 5      45 no    yes   yes   13-15yea~  white no               16       0       2
#> 6      20 yes   no    yes   13-15yea~  white no               13       1       1
#> 7      10 yes   no    yes   13-15yea~  white no               24       0       3
```

```
#>  8    0 no     no    no    13-15yea~ white no              14         2        1
#>  9   40 no     yes   no    13-15yea~ white no              10         0        5
#> 10   22 yes    no    yes   13-15yea~ white no              15         2        0
#> # ... with more rows, and 3 more variables: husby <dbl>, region <chr>, wght <int>
```

We can modify the data frame with `mutate`. For example, here we select sum `kidslt6` and `kids618` as `kids`:

```
hi_df %>% mutate(kids = kidslt6 + kids618) %>% select(starts_with('kids'))
#> # Source: spark<?> [?? x 3]
#>    kidslt6 kids618  kids
#>      <int>   <int> <int>
#> 1        2       1     3
#> 2        0       1     1
#> 3        0       0     0
#> 4        0       1     1
#> 5        0       0     0
#> 6        0       0     0
#> 7        0       0     0
#> 8        1       0     1
#> 9        0       0     0
#> 10       1       0     1
#> # ... with more rows
```

Other `dplyr` verbs can also be used, but not all the verbs work. For example, trying `slice` will raise the error `Slice is not supported in this version of sparklyr`.

When dealing with large data frames, we often want to reduce them. For this, `summarize` and `group_by` are vital:

```
hi_df %>%
  group_by(education) %>%
  summarise(whrswk = mean(whrswk, na.rm = T))
#> # Source: spark<?> [?? x 2]
#>   education    whrswk
#>   <chr>         <dbl>
#> 1 9-11years      16.9
#> 2 <9years        12.5
#> 3 >16years       34.9
#> 4 13-15years     27.4
#> 5 12years        24.4
#> 6 16years        30.3
```

If we wish to save the results of an analysis, such as the `summarise`-based results above, we can pipe them to the function `compute` as follows:

```
hi_df %>%
  group_by(education) %>%
  summarise(whrswk = mean(whrswk, na.rm = T)) %>%
  compute('whrswk_summary')
```

```
#> # Source: spark<whrswk_summary> [?? x 2]
#>   education  whrswk
#>   <chr>      <dbl>
#> 1 9-11years   16.9
#> 2 <9years     12.5
#> 3 >16years    34.9
#> 4 13-15years  27.4
#> 5 12years     24.4
#> 6 16years     30.3
```

Now whrswk_summary is another table on the Spark cluster.

```
src_tbls(connection)
#> [1] "hi"              "whrswk_summary"
```

On the other hand, if we wanted to return this intermediate data frame to R, we'd use collect as in the following example:

```
whrswk_summary_df <-  hi_df %>%
  group_by(education) %>%
  summarise(whrswk = mean(whrswk, na.rm = T)) %>%
  collect()
```

We see that whrswk is just a regular tibble:

```
class(whrswk_summary_df)
#> [1] "tbl_df"      "tbl"        "data.frame"
```

In sparklyr, there are a number of functions that are similar to mutate in that they can be used to create new variables. These are primarily intended to produce data for use with machine learning methods. In the context of machine learning, predictor variables for use in predictive models are often referred to as 'features'. Hence, these variable creation or transformation functions are often named ft_<verb>, with ft standing for feature. For example, if we want to discretize a continuous variable according to the range of values it is in, similar to R's cut function, we could use ft_bucketizer as in the following example:

```
hi_df %>%
  ft_bucketizer("whrswk", "whrswk_cat", splits = c(0, 10, 30, 50, 70, Inf)) %>%
  select(starts_with('whrs'))
#> # Source: spark<?> [?? x 2]
#>   whrswk whrswk_cat
#>    <int>      <dbl>
#> 1      0          0
#> 2     50          3
#> 3     40          2
#> 4     40          2
#> 5      0          0
#> 6     40          2
```

```
#>  7      40          2
#>  8      25          1
#>  9      45          2
#> 10      30          2
#> # … with more rows
```

Note that the `ft_bucketizer` function, like all `ft_` functions, requires the name of the variable to which the transformation is applied, and the name of the variable created, to be character strings.

As another example, if we want to convert a categorical variable into a type of dummy code known as a one-hot code, where each value of the variable is represented by a 1 in a vector of 0s, we can use `ft_one_hot_encoder`. This only applies to numerical variables, so to apply it to a character vector, we'd first transform the character vector:

```
hi_df %>%
   ft_string_indexer('region', 'iregion') %>%
   ft_one_hot_encoder('iregion', 'one_hot_region') %>%
   select(region, one_hot_region)
#> # Source: spark<?> [?? x 2]
#>    region        one_hot_region
#>    <chr>         <list>
#>  1 northcentral  <dbl [3]>
#>  2 northcentral  <dbl [3]>
#>  3 northcentral  <dbl [3]>
#>  4 northcentral  <dbl [3]>
#>  5 northcentral  <dbl [3]>
#>  6 northcentral  <dbl [3]>
#>  7 northcentral  <dbl [3]>
#>  8 northcentral  <dbl [3]>
#>  9 northcentral  <dbl [3]>
#> 10 northcentral  <dbl [3]>
#> # … with more rows
```

Clearly, the `one_hot_region` is a list column. To see what has been done, we can collect the results using `collect`, and use `unnest_wider` (not available on Spark) to unnest the list column into new variables:

```
regions_df <- hi_df %>%
   ft_string_indexer('region', 'iregion') %>%
   ft_one_hot_encoder('iregion', 'one_hot_region') %>%
   select(region, one_hot_region) %>%
   collect()
regions_df %>% unnest_wider(one_hot_region) %>% distinct()
#> # A tibble: 4 x 4
#>    region         ...1  ...2  ...3
#>    <chr>         <dbl> <dbl> <dbl>
#> 1 northcentral      0     1     0
#> 2 other             0     0     1
```

```
#> 3 south              1       0      0
#> 4 west               0       0      0
```

Machine learning using Spark

Spark provides many machine learning tools. As mentioned in Chapter 1, machine learning is related to statistical modelling, which is the major topic of this book, though it is not something that we have directly addressed. However, some tools and methods used in machine learning are identical to widely used traditional statistical modelling methods, even if there is sometimes some change in terminology. One example of this is logistic regression, which we covered in Chapter 10. Logistic regression is also widely used in machine learning, particularly for predictive modelling.

In R, a logistic regression predicting whi, whether a married woman has health insurance through her job, from husby, husband's income, in the HI data set is accomplished as follows:

```
M <- glm(whi ~ husby, data = HI, family = binomial(link = 'logit'))
```

Using sparklyr, we can do the following:

```
M_spark <- ml_logistic_regression(hi_df, whi ~ husby)
```

What is returned by the ml_logistic_regression output are the coefficients:

```
M_spark
#> Formula: whi ~ husby
#>
#> Coefficients:
#>    (Intercept)            husby
#> -0.437475437 -0.003021714
```

We can verify that these match those returned by glm:

```
coefficients(M)
#>    (Intercept)            husby
#> -0.437475397 -0.003021715
```

Spark will not provide measures of uncertainty in the estimators, such as standard errors, from which we can obtain *p*-values and confidence intervals on coefficients. Likewise, other quantities like the log of the likelihood function or deviance are not provided, so that we cannot easily do model comparison based on log likelihood ratio tests. However, it is standard in machine learning to asses model fit using out-of-sample predictive performance by dividing the data into so-called 'training' and 'test' tests, fitting the model with the training set, and testing its performance on the test set. In the following, we split the data into a training set, which is 90%, and a test set, which is 10%:

```
partitions <- hi_df %>%
  sdf_random_split(training = 0.9, test = 0.1)
```

```
M_spark <- partitions$training %>%
  ml_logistic_regression(whi ~ husby)
```

We can now test how well the model predicts the test set using `ml_binary_classification_evaluator`:

```
predictions <- ml_predict(M_spark, partitions$test)
```

```
ml_binary_classification_evaluator(predictions)
#> [1] 0.5248326
```

The value that is returned here is the area under the ROC (Receiver Operating Characteristic) curve. This has multiple interpretations, but ultimately is based on the model's true positive rate (correct classification of positive instances, i.e. where the outcome variable is equal to 1) versus false positive rate (misclassification of a negative instance). A value of 0.5 indicates that the logistic regression is at chance level.

16

Interactive Web Apps
with Shiny

Introduction

Throughout this book we have performed data visualizations. In all cases, the graphic that was produced was static: we could not interact with it directly, nor did it change or update dynamically if the data or other variables changed. To change any graphic, we needed to modify the code or data and re-execute the code to produce a new plot. Having gained proficiency and experience with R and `ggplot2`, modifying code and re-executing it will usually be very quick and easy. However, sometimes we want to create a graphic that others, who may have no experience or proficiency with R, can interact with and change by simply selecting options or changing parameters in a graphical interface. Moreover, ideally we would like for this graphic and its interface to not even require the user to install R or RStudio, and for it be available instead on a webpage. Web-based graphics apps like this may often be just as valuable and useful to experienced R users who would immediately be able to use and interact with the graphic without having to download data, code, or install extra R packages.

The R package `shiny` is a powerful framework for creating interactive graphics in a web-based app. In fact, `shiny` allows us to create more than just interactive graphics. We may also use it to create dashboards, interactive tutorials, and so on. In general, Shiny is a framework for web apps that run R — for data analysis, statistical modelling, graphics, and so on — on the back end.

Shiny is a major topic. In this chapter, we aim to provide just a brief introduction. To learn more, the (as of August 2020) forthcoming book *Mastering Shiny* (Wickham, 2021) will be a thorough introduction (the preprint of the book is available at https://mastering-shiny.org/). Another excellent resource for learning more about Shiny is the gallery at https://shiny.rstudio.com/gallery/, which provides both the apps themselves and the accompanying source code.

 Getting started with Shiny

RStudio makes is easy to get started with Shiny. The necessary `shiny` R package is preinstalled, and RStudio also provides a minimal demo app, which may be studied to understand some of the core principles behind Shiny, or may then be modified to create a new app. To use this demo, go to the File menu, choose *New File* and then *Shiny Web App ...*, as in Figure 16.1(a). This brings up a dialog box, as in Figure 16.1(b). There, you choose a folder to put the Shiny app, and provide a name for the app. For the name, you can choose anything, but it is probably best to use a lowercase name with no spaces. In Figure 16.1(b), we choose `shinydemo` inside our `Documents` folder. You must also choose whether you want to use a single R script named `app.R` for the app, or to use two separate files named `ui.R` and `server.R`. The single `app.R` option is the default, which we will choose. You create the app by clicking the Create button. The folder `shinydemo` is created, and inside that an R script named `app.R` is created. The `app.R` script will then open in the RStudio file editor. In the upper right of the tab of this file in the editor there is a Run App button. Clicking this button launches a new RStudio window that runs the web app (see Figure 16.1(c)). From the RStudio console, we can see that clicking this button is equivalent to running the following command:

```
shiny::runApp('Document/shinydemo')
```

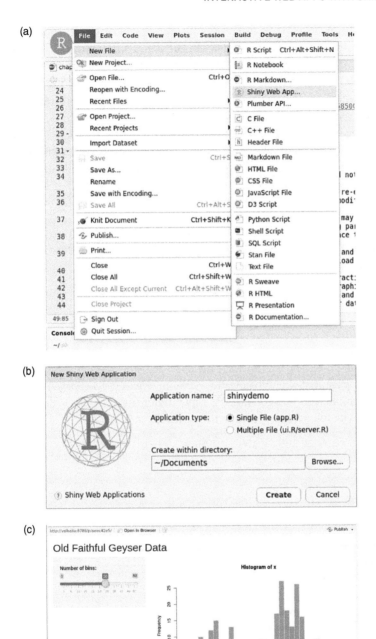

Figure 16.1 (a) We can create a Shiny app by selecting an option from the menu. This opens a dialog box, shown in (b), where we choose the name and folder for the app. The demo app that is produced is the histogram app shown in (c)

As we can see, this web app is an interactive histogram where we can choose the number of bins in the histogram by using a slider. On the bar at the top of the window, there is another button, Open in Browser. Clicking this will run the web app inside your default web browser.

The entirety of this demo is contained in the file app.R that is within the folder Documents/ shinydemo. This file contains only three statements in addition to the library call that loads the shiny package itself. The first statement calls the function fluidPage and assigns the name ui to the resulting object. The next defines a function that is assigned the name server. The final statement calls the function shinyApp with input arguments ui and server as defined in the previous statements:

```
shinyApp(ui = ui, server = server)
```

As we saw above, the whole app.R script is then called by supplying the folder in which it exists as the first input argument (which is named appDir) to the runApp function. Let us examine each of these parts in more detail.

fluidPage

The fluidPage function essentially creates a webpage object. In other words, it is an object that will determine the webpage in which the app occurs. As the name implies, fluidPage creates a flexible page that will dynamically rescale in size as the webpage is resized. It contains a set of invisible rows and columns. As input arguments, fluidPage takes a number of Shiny elements. The full fluidApp code in the demo app.R is as follows:

```
ui <- fluidPage(

    # Application title
    titlePanel("Old Faithful Geyser Data"),

    # Sidebar with a slider input for number of bins
    sidebarLayout(
        sidebarPanel(
            sliderInput("bins",
                        "Number of bins:",
                        min = 1,
                        max = 50,
                        value = 30)
        ),

        # Show a plot of the generated distribution
        mainPanel(
            plotOutput("distPlot")
        )
    )
)
```

As we can see, therefore, there are two elements as inputs to fluidPage: titlePanel and sidebarLayout. The titlePanel simply provides the title of the web app page. The sidebar-Layout creates a web app page with a sidebar and a main section. The sidebar contents are determined by the element sidebarPanel that is supplied as the first input to sidebarLayout, while the contents of the main panel are determined by the mainPanel element, which is the second element to sidebarLayout. By default, the side and main panels respectively occupy one-third and two-thirds of the width of the web app page. This can be controlled by changing the width parameters in sidebarPanel and mainPanel, respectively. By default, they take the values 4 and 8, respectively. Both can be changed, but the total width must be 12 or less.

As we can see, the sidebar contains a slider graphical user interface widget, created by sliderInput. GUI widgets like this play a major role in Shiny apps. They are what allow us to dynamically and interactively supply the different parameters to the graphic object. We will explore some other important Shiny GUI widgets below. In sliderInput there are five required input arguments: inputID, label, min, max, value. The inputID is a name that can then be used within the code that creates the graphic. In this example, it is bins. Thus, as we will see, in the code for the histogram, we can refer to the variable bins, which gives us the numerical value of the slider, to determine the number of bins in the histogram. The label argument to sliderInput is simply the title of the slider widget. The min and max define the starting and ending values of the slider. Thus, in this example, the slider ranges from 1 to 50. The value determines the initial position of the slider.

The mainPanel element of sidebarLayout contains plotOutput("distPlot"). This is a plot output element. As we will see, when we call renderPlot, it produces a plot output element that we can name. We can then access that element by its name, which in this example is distPlot, by calling plotOutput.

server

The contents of the second statement in app.R are as follows:

```
server <- function(input, output) {

    output$distPlot <- renderPlot({
        # generate bins based on input$bins from ui.R
        x    <- faithful[, 2]
        bins <- seq(min(x), max(x), length.out = input$bins + 1)

        # draw the histogram with the specified number of bins
        hist(x, breaks = bins, col = 'darkgrey', border = 'white')
    })

}
```

As we can see, this creates a function with two input arguments, input and output, and which we name server. This function is used internally by Shiny. The input argument allows us to access the values returned by the GUI widgets. For example, the value of bins that contains the value of the sliderInput is accessible by the bins attribute of the input argument. The output argument will contain the graphics or other objects that are produced by normal R code, but which may then be accessible in, usually, the main panel of the web app page. In this example, a base R histogram is created in the code block inside the `renderPlot` function. This code could be run in any R script or in the console with very little modification. Specifically, the only thing we would need to modify is `length.out = input$bins`, which obviously requires an object named `input` with an attribute named `bins`. The value of `input$bins` will be an integer. Replacing `input$bins` with an arbitrarily chosen integer like 20 will produce the histogram we see in Figure 16.2:

```
x <- faithful[, 2]
bins <- seq(min(x), max(x), length.out = 21)
hist(x, breaks = bins, col = 'darkgrey', border = 'white')
```

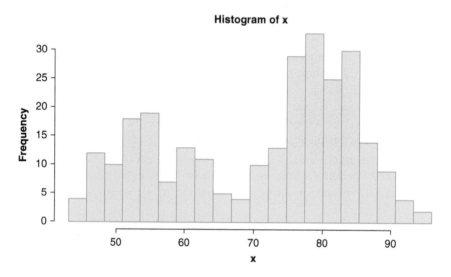

Figure 16.2 The static version of the histogram that is in the web app that we created

This is an important point to emphasize. Once you have a static graphic, produced for example by `ggplot`, this is the main code that makes up the dynamic and interactive Shiny app. The rest of the code is ultimately producing a wrapper around this code so that it appears in the web app page, and also creating widgets that allow you to control parameters and other properties of the graphic.

shinyApp

The final statement in our `app.R`, as seen above, is a simple function call to `shinyApp`. We supply two arguments named `ui` and `server`. In this example, their values are also `ui` and `server`, respectively, but this is not necessary. This function call is then used internally by the Shiny server.

runApp

The Shiny server that runs our app is run by `runApp` where we supply the directory that contains `app.R`. In general, this directory usually contains either a file named `app.R` that ends with an expression returning a Shiny app object (i.e. by a call to `shinyApp`), or else two separate files named `ui.R` and `server.R`.

The app that is run will contain, as shown in Figure 16.1(c), a side panel with a GUI slider and a main panel with a histogram. This app is *reactive*: whenever we move the slider, the histogram is redrawn using the new value of the slider, which is available to it through `input$bins`, as we've just seen.

Modifying the demo app

Let us now modify the demo in a few simple ways. We will make the histogram using `ggplot`, rather than base R. We will also use another data set, which we will read in using `read_csv`, and we will use a slider to modify the `binwidth` of the histogram, rather than the number of bins.

As a first step, we will make the static version of the plot (Figure 16.3):

```r
library(tidyverse)

housing_df <- read_csv('data/housing.csv')

ggplot(housing_df, aes(x = price)) +
  geom_histogram(binwidth = 10000, colour = 'white') +
  theme_classic()
```

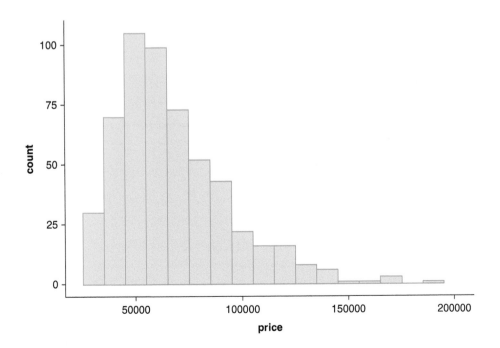

Figure 16.3 A static version of the graphic we will put in a Shiny app

This code, mostly as is, will go inside the new `app.R` that we create. All that we will change is that instead of `binwidth = 10000`, we will put `binwidth = input$binwidth`, where `binwidth` is the value returned by our slider.

At the start of the app, we load the necessary packages and the data:

```
library(shiny)
library(tidyverse)

houseprices_df <- read_csv("housing.csv")
```

Next, we modify the `fluidPage` as follows:

```
ui <- fluidPage(
    titlePanel("Histogram of house prices (Canadian dollars)."),

    sidebarLayout(
        sidebarPanel(
            sliderInput("binwidth",
                        "Width of bins (Canadian dollars):",
                        min = 1000,
                        max = 12000,
                        step = 1000,
                        value = 5000)
        ),
        mainPanel(
            plotOutput("houseprices_hist")
        )
    )
)
```

This is very similar to the original. The main difference is that the `inputId` of `sliderInput` is now `binwidth` and the slider takes values from 1000 to 12,000 is steps of 1000, with its initial position being 5000.

The `server` is as follows:

```
server <- function(input, output) {

    output$houseprices_hist <- renderPlot({

        ggplot(houseprices_df, aes(x = price)) +
            geom_histogram(binwidth = input$binwidth, colour = 'white') +
            theme_classic()

    })
}
```

Note that the rendered plot object is stored as `output$houseprices_hist`, which is then accessible in the main panel of the `ui` via the `plotOutput` function call. The resulting web app is shown in Figure 16.4.

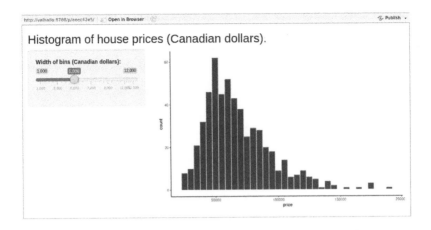

Figure 16.4 Screenshot of a Shiny webpage with a `ggplot` histogram

Extending the demo app

RStudio's demo app with a side panel and main panel is a prototypical, albeit minimal, Shiny web app. Here, we will consider a few different ways in which it can be easily extended to create new apps.

Using multiple widgets

In the demo app, there was one widget and one graphic. We may have multiple widgets each controlling parameters of one or more plots. To see examples of these, let us first consider a variant of the Shiny app available at https://lawsofthought.shinyapps.io/binomial_likelihood, whose source code is available at https://github.com/lawsofthought/psypag-kent-2017. A screenshot of this app is shown in Figure 16.5. This app has three widgets – two sliders and one set of radio buttons – that control the one graphic. Interestingly, the two sliders are not independent. As the first changes, the range of values of the second changes too. In addition to these widgets, there is a block of explanatory text.

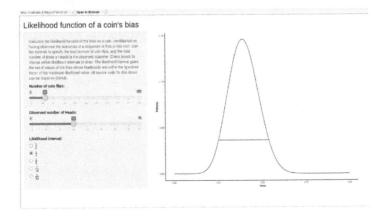

Figure 16.5 A web app with multiple widgets in the left-hand panel

Using multiple widgets and text blocks is very straightforward. For example, in the sidebarPanel, we may include as many GUI widgets as needed, as in the following partial code (ellipses indicate removed code):

```
ui <- fluidPage(
  ...

  sidebarLayout(

    sidebarPanel(
      helpText(...),
      sliderInput(...),
      sliderInput(...),
      radioButtons(...)
    ),

    mainPanel(...)
  )
)
```

Note that the helpText widget creates the explanatory text box. This may include multiple text strings and also HTML elements. For example, for the app linked above, the contents of helpText are partially as follows (the ellipses indicate removed text):

```
helpText("Calculate the likelihood function of the bias on a coin,
         conditioned on having observed the outcomes of a sequence of flips of
this coin.
         ...
         of the maximum likelihood value.",
         "All source code for this demo can be found on",
         a("GitHub.", href="https://github.com/lawsofthought/psypag-kent-2017",
target='_blank'))
```

Here, the a function is from htmltools and allows us to make URL hyperlinks.

The radioButtons widget is a commonly used GUI widget. It allows us to select exactly one of multiple different options. For example, to provide radio buttons for choosing one of five colours from a list, we may use the following:

```
radioButtons("colour_pick",
             label="Pick a colour:",
             choices=c("red", "green", "blue", "white", "yellow")
)
```

We could also use a variant like the following:

```
radioButtons("colour_pick",
             label="Pick a colour:",
```

```
        choices=c("red" = 1, "green" = 2, "blue" = 3, "white" = 4,
"yellow" = 5)
)
```

In this case, the colour names are shown as the radio button options but the value associated with the `colour_pick` variable is the value associated with the name in the named vector `choices`. In other words, the user will be presented with the names *red, green, blue, white, yellow* in the radio button's GUI widget. Their choice will be stored as the value of `colour_pick`, which will be 1, 2, 3, 4, or 5. This use of a named vector for the `choice` argument allows us to use LaTeX code such as $\tfrac{1}{2}$ as the labels of the radio buttons, as in the app linked above, and shown in Figure 16.5.

We may also have widgets that themselves are modified by other widgets. In the app linked above, the `sidebarPanel` contains the element `uiOutput("n.obs.slider")`. This is an element that is available as an element of the `output` argument of the `server` function. Inside that function, the relevant code is as follows:

```
output$n.obs.slider <- renderUI({
  sliderInput("n.obs",
              "Observed number of Heads: ",
              min=0,
              max=input$N,
              step=1,
              value=max(1, 0.4*input$N))
})
```

This `renderUI` function acts like a `renderPlot` function in that it takes values specified in the `input` argument and returns an object that will be displayed on the web app page. In this case, that object is a `sliderInput`. As we can see from the code above, this object uses the value of `input$N`, which is from another slider, whose code within `sidebarPanel` is as follows:

```
sliderInput("N",
            "Number of coin flips:",
            min = 1,
            max = 250,
            value = 130,
            step = 1)
```

Thus, this slider ranges from 1 to 250, and the value it selects is recorded as `N`, which is available in the `server` function as `input$N`. In the dynamically rendered slider, this value is used to set `max` and initial values of the slider. Examples of the dynamic interaction of widgets are shown in Figure 16.6.

Dynamic text

Consider the app available at https://lawsofthought.shinyapps.io/false_discovery/, whose source code is at https://github.com/lawsofthought/replication-crisis-demos. A screenshot of this app is provided in Figure 16.7. In it there are three sliders that control three

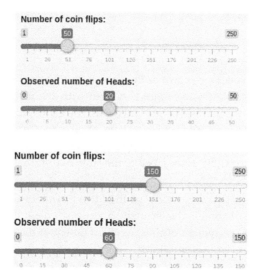

Figure 16.6 Examples of interacting widgets. When the upper widget changes, it changes the endpoint and initial condition of the middle widget

graphics. In addition, these sliders control the text shown in the bottom text block in the left side panel. The code to accomplish this is partially as follows (ellipses indicate omitted text or code):

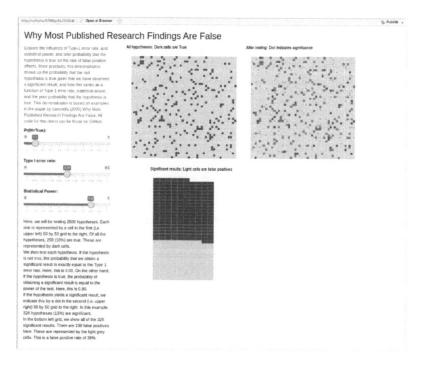

Figure 16.7 A web app with multiple graphics being controlled by multiple widgets

```
output$text <- renderUI({

  stmt.1 <- sprintf(...)

  stmt.2 <- sprintf(...)

  stmt.3 <- sprintf(...)

  stmt.4 <- sprintf(...)

  HTML(paste(stmt.1, stmt.2, stmt.3, stmt.4, sep = '<br/>'))
})
```

From this, we see that `renderUI` returns an `HTML` object whose input is text generated by multiple `sprintf` statements. This object is saved as the `text` attribute of the `output` object. It is then accessible inside the `ui` object using `htmlOutput("text")`, which is an element in the side panel. Examples of the `sprintf` statements are as follows:

```
stmt.1 <- sprintf("Here, we will be testing %d hypotheses.
                   Each one is represented by a cell in the first
                   (i.e. upper left) %d by %d grid to the right.
                   Of all the hypotheses, %d (%d%%) are true.
                   These are represented by dark cells.",
                   N*M,
                   N,
                   M,
                   as.integer(input$prior*N*M),
                   as.integer(100*input$prior))

stmt.2 <- sprintf("We then test each hypothesis. If the hypothesis is not true,
                   the probability that we obtain a
                   significant result is exactly equal to the Type 1 error rate.
                   Here, this is %2.2f.
                   On the other hand, if the hypothesis is true,
                   the probability of obtaining a significant
                   result is equal to the power of the test.
                   Here, this is %2.2f.",
                   input$alpha,
                   input$power)
```

The first argument to the `sprintf` statements is a text block with placeholders like `%d` (for integers) and `%2.2f` (for floats). The values of these are taken from variables in the code, such as `N` or `M`, and also from the values of the sliders, such as `input$prior`, `input$alpha`, `input$power`.

Multiple graphics

In the app shown in Figure 16.7, there are three graphics. There are different ways to present multiple graphics, but perhaps the easiest is to use a plot grid as we would in a figure panel in an article. In the code used to produce the app shown in Figure 16.7, three `ggplot` graphics were produced. These were given names and then `gridExtra::grid.arrange()` was used to put them in a grid. The relevant code is partially as follows (ellipses indicate removed code):

```
p0 <- ggplot(z, ...) + ... + ggtitle('All hypotheses: Dark cells are True')

p1 <- p0 + ... + ggtitle('After testing: Dot indicates significance')

p2 <- ggplot(...) + ggtitle("Significant results: Light cells are false positives")

grid.arrange(p0, p1, p2, nrow=2, ncol=2)
```

Interactive graphics

Thus far, the plots all dynamically update in reaction to a change in the widgets. After each update, we nonetheless have a static graphic as we would had we used `ggplot` in RStudio directly. It is possible, however, to directly interact with Shiny graphics in ways not possible with normal plots in R.

Selecting points

The `nearPoints` and `brushedPoints` functions allow us to select points on a plot and show the corresponding rows in a data frame. Consider the scatterplot shown in Figure 16.8 that is produced by the following code:

```
ggplot(swiss,
       mapping = aes(x = Examination, y = Fertility)
) + geom_point()
```

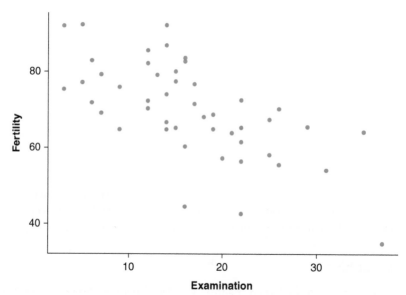

Figure 16.8 Scatterplot of a measure of fertility rates in Swiss regions in the 1880s plotted against the percentage of army draftees receiving highest scores on an entrance exam

Each point represents two of the variables – Fertility and Examination – in the R built-in swiss data set:

```
head(swiss)
#>                 Fertility Agriculture Examination Education Catholic Infant.Mortality
#> Courtelary         80.2        17.0           15        12     9.96             22.2
#> Delemont           83.1        45.1            6         9    84.84             22.2
#> Franches-Mnt       92.5        39.7            5         5    93.40             20.2
#> Moutier            85.8        36.5           12         7    33.77             20.3
#> Neuveville         76.9        43.5           17        15     5.16             20.6
#> Porrentruy         76.1        35.3            9         7    90.57             26.6
```

Using brushedPoints, we can select a region of the scatterplot and the corresponding rows in the swiss data frame are shown. An example of an app that does this is shown in Figure 16.9.

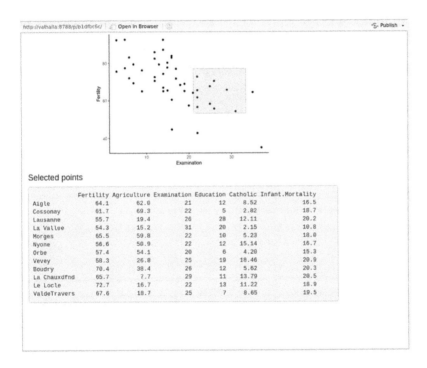

Figure 16.9 The brushedPoints function allows us to select regions of a scatterplot, for example, and the corresponding rows of the data frame used by the plot are then shown in a table

The app.R code that produces the app shown in Figure 16.9 has ui and server statements as before. The ui statement is as follows:

```
ui <- fluidPage(
  fluidRow(
    column(width = 10,
           align="center",
```

```
    plotOutput("scatterplot",
                    height = 300,
                    width = 400,
                    brush = brushOpts(id = "selected_region")))
  ),
  fluidRow(
    column(width = 10,
           h4("Selected points"),
           verbatimTextOutput("selected_region_info")
    )
  )
)
```

Here, we see two `fluidRow` elements in `fluidPage`. As is obvious, a `fluidRow` is a row of a `fluidPage`, and each `fluidRow` is divided into columns using the `column` element. In this case, the first row has one column of width 10, and this has a `plotOutput` element in it, which will show a plot named `scatterplot` that is rendered by the server function. This `plotOutput` element has `brush = brushOpts(id = "selected_region")` as an input argument. This allows the user to *brush* or select a rectangular region of the graphic. The properties of this rectangular region are then saved using the id `selected_region`. The second row of the page has a `verbatimTextOutput` element, which is a fixed width text region.

The `server` code is as follows:

```
server <- function(input, output){

  output$scatterplot <- renderPlot({
    ggplot(swiss, aes(x = Examination, y = Fertility)) +
      geom_point() +
      theme_classic()
  })

  output$selected_region_info <- renderPrint({
    brushedPoints(swiss, input$selected_region)
  })
}
```

The first output element is the `ggplot` produced by `renderPlot`, just like we've seen before. The second output element is produced by `renderPrint` and uses the `brushPoints` function, which uses `input$selected_region`, defined in the `ui`, and selects the rows in `swiss` that are selected in the brushed region. The object returned by `renderPrint` is saved as `selected_region_info` to the `output` object. This is then accessible in `ui` using the function `verbatimTextOutput`.

Zooming

Using, for example, `brush = brushOpts` inside a `plotOutput` element in `ui`, we can select a region and then zoom into it. We could, for example, zoom into that region in the same graphic, or alternatively, zoom into that region in a second accompanying graphic. We will consider the second version here. For this, the graphic that we will zoom into regions of is the `swiss` scatterplot above but with labels on the points. For this, we will use the default `ggplot` labelling method of `geom_text`, which we already saw in Chapter 4:

```
swiss %>%
  as_tibble(rownames = 'region') %>%
  ggplot(aes(x = Examination, y = Fertility, label = region)) +
  geom_point() +
  geom_text()
```

Using the default sizes for points, labels and segments, the resulting labelled scatterplot (Figure 16.10) is a bit cluttered. Zooming into regions is therefore a useful option in this case. A screenshot of the app that accomplishes this is shown in Figure 16.11.

As before, this `app.R` primarily consists of the `ui` and the `server`. The `ui` is as follows:

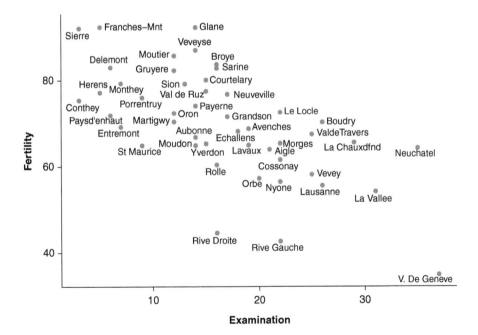

Figure 16.10 A labelled scatterplot using the `swiss` data set. Zooming into this plot allows us to see the otherwise cluttered points

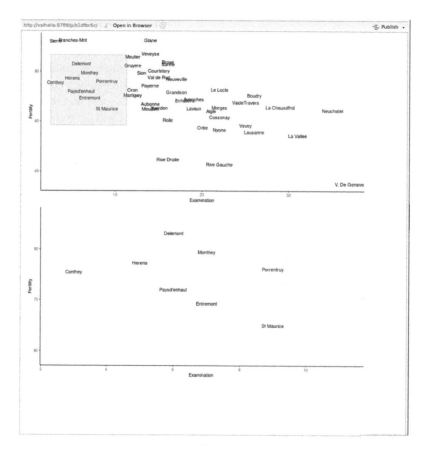

Figure 16.11 Using `brushedPoints` to select a region in the upper graphic that is zoomed into in the lower graphic

```r
ui <- fluidPage(
  fluidRow(
    column(width = 8,
           plotOutput("scatterplot", height = 400, width = 800,
                      brush = brushOpts(
                        id = "selected_region"
                      )
           )
    ),
    column(width = 8,
           plotOutput("scattersubplot", height = 400, width = 800)
    )
  )
)
```

Here, we have two `plotOutput` elements, the first of which has a `brush = brushOpts(...)` argument, which allows regions to be selected in it. The corresponding `server` code is as follows:

```r
server <- function(input, output) {

  xyrange <- reactiveValues(x = NULL, y = NULL)

  output$scatterplot <- renderPlot({
    ggplot(swiss_df,
           aes(x = Examination, y = Fertility, label = region)) +
      geom_text()
  })

  output$scattersubplot <- renderPlot({
    ggplot(swiss_df,
           aes(x = Examination, y = Fertility, label = region)) +
      geom_text() +
      coord_cartesian(xlim = xyrange$x, ylim = xyrange$y)
  })

  observe({
    sel_reg <- input$selected_region
    xyrange$x <- c(sel_reg$xmin, sel_reg$xmax)
    xyrange$y <- c(sel_reg$ymin, sel_reg$ymax)
  })

}
```

The principal new statement here is the `observe` function call. This is coupled to the `reactiveValues` statement that defines a dynamically updated object. In this case, this is named `xyrange`, which has attributes `x` and `y`. The `observe` function listens for changes in the brushed region, which is `input$selected_region`. When changes occur, `xyrange` updates its `x` and `y` values. The second plot, named `scattersubplot`, uses `xyrange$x` and `xyrange$y` as the limits of its axes, specified using `coord_cartesian`.

RMarkdown-based Shiny apps

In Chapter 7 we introduced RMarkdown. There, we primarily considered how RMarkdown can be used to create reproducible articles for publication and other communication purposes. RMarkdown is also widely used for creating webpages via the `html_document` output format. Normally, the resulting HTML documents are static documents. However, we may create dynamic webpages using `html_document` and Shiny. To host these webpages on the web, the web server must run the Shiny server. However, we may easily send this document to other RStudio users who may then use it immediately within RStudio itself.

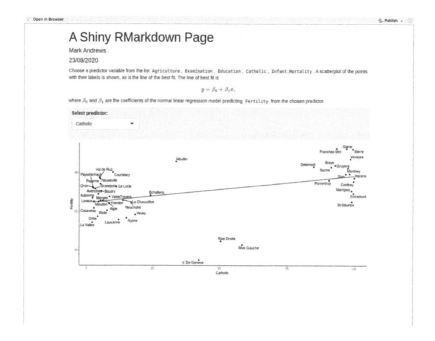

Figure 16.12 An HTML page made with RMarkdown that contains a Shiny app

An example of a Shiny-based RMarkdown webpage is shown in Figure 16.12. This contains some explanatory text, and then an app that shows a labelled scatterplot using one of five different predictor variables. The RMarkdown document that created this page has the following in its YAML header:

```
---
title: "A Shiny RMarkdown Page"
author: "Mark Andrews"
date: "23/08/2020"
output: html_document
runtime: shiny
---
```

Much of this information is standard. For example, we supply a `title`, `author` and `date` as usual, and we set the `output` to `html_document`. The only new field is `runtime`, which takes the value `shiny`.

The text in the document is typical of an Rmarkdown document, including some LaTeX maths, which is delimited by $ symbols. The Shiny app is all contained in the following R chunk in the document:

```
library(tidyverse)
library(ggrepel)
```

```
inputPanel(
  selectInput("predictor",
              label = "Select predictor:",
              choices = c("Agriculture",
                          "Examination",
                          "Education",
                          "Catholic",
                          "Infant.Mortality")
  )
)

renderPlot({
  swiss %>%
  as_tibble(rownames = 'region') %>%
  ggplot(aes_string(x = input$predictor, y = "Fertility", label = "region")) +
  stat_smooth(method = 'lm', se = F) +
  geom_point() +
  geom_text_repel() +
  theme_classic()
})
```

Here, we have two Shiny statements: `inputPanel` and `renderPlot`. Note that these are not separated into `ui` and `server` objects as in the previous examples. Nor do we have to call `shinyApp`. The `renderPlot` function is just as in the examples we have seen earlier. In the `inputPanel`, we create a dropdown selector widget that allows us to choose the value of the variable `predictor`. This is then accessed as `input$predictor` within the `renderPlot`.

Making `learnr` tutorials

A variant of the Shiny-based RMarkdown HTML document can be used to create interactive tutorials. This uses the `learnr` package. An example of a tutorial, albeit with no text, but with a quiz and code execution widgets, is shown in Figure 16.13.

The YAML header for this example tutorial is as follows:

```
---
title: "An Interactive Tutorial"
author: "Mark Andrews"
date: "Aug 23, 2020"
output: learnr::tutorial
runtime: shiny_prerendered
---
```

Note that the output is `learnr::tutorial` and the `runtime` is `shiny_prerendered`. Prerendered Shiny documents are rendered once prior to their deployment, rather than for each browser session.

Figure 16.13 An example of a `learnr` tutorial

To create the quiz items, we include the following code in a normal R chunk:

```
quiz(
    question("Which of the following models are used for modelling binary variables?",
        answer("Linear regression"),
        answer("Ordinal regression"),
        answer("Binary logistic regression", correct = TRUE),
        answer("Probit regression", correct = TRUE),
        answer("Poisson regression")
    ),
    question("Which of the following are continuous probability distributions?",
        answer("Normal distribution", correct = TRUE),
        answer("Binomial distribution"),
        answer("Poisson distribution"),
        answer("Negative binomial distribution")
    )
)
```

The first code execution widget contains the following code in a chunk with the options `exercise = TRUE`:

```
M <- lm(Fertility ~ Catholic, data = swiss)
```

The inclusion of `exercise = TRUE` as a chunk option will allow this code, or any modification of it, to be executed in the webpage. Any output from this executed code will also be shown in the page.

The second code execution widget contains a *blank* R chunk with `exercise = TRUE` as an option. The label for this R chunk is `swiss_lm_2`, and another R chunk labelled `swiss_lm_2-solution` contains the R code that is the solution to the exercise, and available via the Solution button.

 ## Deploying Shiny apps

Shiny apps and webpages, like those created by RMarkdown, that contain Shiny apps must be hosted by a Shiny server. There are two main options for doing this. The first is to use RStudio's Shiny server, which is available at https://www.shinyapps.io/. This is a paid-for service. However, there is a free tier that allows users to have five separate app projects and 25 user hours per month. The other options include up to 10,000 user hours per month and unlimited projects.

Alternatively, we may install the Shiny server, which is open source software, on our own server. The source code and precompilied binaries for major Linux distributions are available at https://rstudio.com/products/shiny/download-server/. This option, of course, requires that we have a server, such as a virtual private server, available to us. However, these may be rented from many providers for prices starting at around $10 per month. In addition, to install and configure the Shiny server, some (usually Linux) server admin knowledge and experience are required. Guidance on setting up a Shiny server on a Linux virtual private server can be found at https://www.digitalocean.com/community/tutorials/how-to-set-up-shiny-server-on-ubuntu-16-04.

17

Probabilistic Modelling with Stan

Introduction

In Chapter 8 and subsequent chapters, we described how the aim of Bayesian inference is to infer the posterior distribution of the assumed statistical model's parameters, which we can write as $P(\theta|D)$, where θ is the set of unknown parameters and D is the observed data. In general, in all but a small number of cases, this posterior distribution, which we can think of as simply as a function over an (often very high) dimensional space, does not have an analytical description. In other words, in general, there is no formula that will give quantities that we seek, such as the posterior's mean, standard deviation, highest posterior density interval and posterior predictive distribution. However, all of these quantities are *expectations* of the posterior distribution, which we can express as

$$\langle g(\theta) \rangle = \int g(\theta) P(\theta|D) d\theta,$$

where $g(\theta)$ is some function of the parameters θ. We can approximate these expectations using the *Monte Carlo integration* method, where we draw samples from $P(\theta|D)$ and then calculate the arithmetic mean of the function g applied to each one:

$$\langle g(\theta) \rangle \approx \frac{1}{n} \sum_{i=1}^{n} g(\tilde{\theta}_i),$$

where $\tilde{\theta}_1, \tilde{\theta}_2, ..., \tilde{\theta}_n$ are n samples drawn drawn from $P(\theta|D)$.

In Chapter 8 we also saw that Markov chain Monte Carlo methods, which include techniques such as the Metropolis (or, more generally, Metropolis–Hastings) sampler, the Gibbs sampler, and the Hamiltonian Monte Carlo variant of the Metropolis sampler, are algorithms for drawing samples from high-dimensional probability distributions that can be applied very generally. As useful and as general as these MCMC samplers are, they nonetheless can be relatively arduous to implement. Because samplers are computationally very intensive, they need to be implemented in lower-level programming languages such as C/C++ or Fortran. Even when we have knowledge of and experience with these languages, writing code in them is more difficult, time-consuming, and error prone than writing code in, say, R. In addition, there are often a lot of mathematical details about the models that we need to work out and then implement in code. For example, we must mathematically work out the likelihood function, which for large models may be relatively complex, and then we must implement this in code. For some samplers, such as Gibbs samplers or HMC, further mathematical details, such as conditional distributions or the derivative of the posterior distribution, must be worked out and implemented. We may then have to fine-tune the samplers to maximize their efficiency. In addition, every time we change major aspects of our model, we must often rewrite substantial portions of our code. Overall, compared to any code covered in this book, these are major programming tasks that require time and effort that we simply may not be able to afford.

The aim of a *probabilistic programming language* (PPL) is to automate the implementation of the MCMC sampler. With a PPL, all we need do is specify our probabilistic model, including the priors, in a high-level programming language. The sampler is then automatically derived and compiled and executed for us, and samples are then returned to us. The saving in terms of our time and effort can be remarkable. What might have taken days or even weeks of relatively tedious and error-prone programming in C++ or Fortran can now be accomplished in minutes by writing high-level code.

In this chapter, we cover the PPL Stan, which is named after the Polish American mathematician Stanislaw Ulam who was one of the inventors of Monte Carlo in the late 1940s. The first stable release of Stan was in 2012, and it has grown steadily in popularity since then. It is now arguably the dominant PPL for Bayesian data analysis in statistics. Here, we will attempt to provide a self-contained tutorial introduction to Stan and how it can be used in R by using `rstan`.

 ## Univariate models

Let us begin by considering some simple models, each one defined essentially by probability distributions over a single observed variable.

Loaded die model

Let us begin with a very simple one-parameter problem. Let us imagine that we have a die that is loaded to make an outcome of 6 more likely than other outcome. We throw this die $N = 250$ times and record the resulting face on each occasion. Simulated data of this kind is available in the following data set:

```
dice_df <- read_csv('data/loaded_dice.csv')
```

We can use `table` to count the number of outcomes of each face, and clearly there are more cases of 6 than other outcomes:

```
dice_df %>% table()
#> .
#>  1  2  3  4  5  6
#> 31 38 35 42 31 73
```

We can recode each outcome as a '6' or 'not-6' binary outcome:

```
dice_df %<>%
   mutate(is_six = ifelse(outcome == 6, 1, 0))
dice_df
#> # A tibble: 250 x 2
#>    outcome is_six
#>      <dbl>  <dbl>
#> 1        6      1
#> 2        1      0
#> 3        6      1
#> 4        2      0
#> 5        1      0
#> 6        4      0
```

```
#>  7        5        0
#>  8        6        1
#>  9        4        0
#> 10        1        0
#> # … with 240 more rows
```

Bernoulli model

If we denote these binary outcomes by $y_1, y_2,..., y_n$, with each $y_i \in \{0,1\}$, and assuming that there is a fixed probability θ that each $y_i = 1$, then our model of this data is as follows:

$$y_i \sim \text{Bernoulli}(\theta), \quad \text{for } i \in 1,2,...,n.$$

A Bayesian model places a prior probability distribution over θ. When using MCMC methods generally, especially with a PPL like Stan, we have practically endless choices for this prior. However, it must be a probability distribution over the real interval $[0,1]$, and so an easy choice would be a beta distribution with hyperparameters α and β, which we will assume are known. Thus, the complete Bayesian model is as follows:

$$y_i \sim \text{Bernoulli}(\theta), \quad \text{for } i \in 1,2,...,n,$$
$$\theta \sim \text{Beta}(\alpha,\beta).$$

To implement this model is Stan, we first extract the is_six variable as a standalone vector, which we will name y, and record the length of this vector as N:

```
y <- dice_df %>% pull(is_six)
N <- length(y)
```

Given that we've assumed the alpha and beta hyperparameters of the beta distribution are known, we will set them to be both equal to 1, which gives us a uniform prior distribution over θ:

```
alpha <- 1.0
beta <- 1.0
```

The four variables y, N, alpha, and beta are the data that we will send to Stan, and to do so we must put them into a list:

```
dice_data <- list(y = y,
                  N = N,
                  alpha = alpha,
                  beta = beta)
```

The Stan implementation of this model is written in an external file, namely loaded_dice.stan:

```
// loaded_dice.stan
data {
```

```
  int<lower=1> N;
  int<lower=0, upper=1> y[N];
  real<lower=0> alpha;
  real<lower=0> beta;
}


parameters {
  real<lower=0, upper=1> theta;
}
model {
  theta ~ beta(alpha, beta);
  y ~ bernoulli(theta);
}
```

We notice that in this Stan program, as with most Stan programs, we have multiple code blocks, specifically data, parameters and model. The data block defines the input data:

```
data {
  int<lower=1> N;
  int<lower=0, upper=1> y[N];
  real<lower=0> alpha;
  real<lower=0> beta;
}
```

Notice that we must declare not only the names of the variables that we will be passing to the program as data, but also their size and type. For example, we declare that N is a positive integer, that y is a vector of N integers which are bounded between 0 and 1, and so y is a binary vector, and alpha and beta are declared as non-negative real numbers. The parameters block declares the (free) parameters of the model:

```
parameters {
  real<lower=0, upper=1> theta;
}
```

In this example, we have just one parameter, theta, which corresponds to θ in the above mathematical description. This has a real value bounded between 0 and 1. The next block is model and is where we define the model itself:

```
model {
  theta ~ beta(alpha, beta);
  y ~ bernoulli(theta);
}
```

This code corresponds almost perfectly to the mathematical description of the model. First, we state that theta follows a beta distribution with hyperparameters alpha and beta. Next, we state that each element of y follows a Bernoulli distribution with parameter theta. Here, we are using vectorized notation. In other words, the statement

```
y ~ bernoulli(theta);
```

is equivalent to

```
for (i in 1:N) {
  y[i] ~ bernoulli(theta);
}
```

While the second form maps identically to the mathematical description, it is less concise notation and also less efficient.

We can execute this Stan program in R via commands provided by the rstan package:

```
library(rstan)
```

It should be noted, however, that Stan is a program that is completely independent of R, and can be interfaced with many other programming languages and environments such as Python, Matlab, Stata, Julia, Mathematica and Scala. The following command from the rstan package will compile a sampler based on the specifications in loaded_dice.stan and the data in dice_data, and then draw samples from it:

```
M_dice <- stan(file = 'loaded_dice.stan',
               data = dice_data)
```

Typing the name M_dice gives us the following output:

```
M_dice
#> Inference for Stan model: loaded_dice.
#> 4 chains, each with iter=2000; warmup=1000; thin=1;
#> post-warmup draws per chain=1000, total post-warmup draws=4000.
#>
#>           mean se_mean   sd    2.5%     25%      50%      75%    97.5% n_eff Rhat
#> theta     0.29    0.00 0.03    0.24    0.27     0.29     0.31     0.35  1397    1
#> lp__   -153.09    0.02 0.75 -155.30 -153.24 -152.80 -152.61 -152.56  1458    1
#>
#> Samples were drawn using NUTS(diag_e) at Wed Aug 19 00:01:33 2020.
#> For each parameter, n_eff is a crude measure of effective sample size,
#> and Rhat is the potential scale reduction factor on split chains (at
#> convergence, Rhat=1).
```

There we see output that is similar to that of a brm-based model, which of course is another interface to Stan. The number of chains, total number of iterations, and number of warm up iterations are all presented at the top of this output. In the summary of the samples themselves, we are given information concerning theta, which is our one unknown variable. From this, we have the mean, the standard deviation, and quantiles of the posterior distribution's samples. In addition, we have the Rhat convergence diagnostic, the effective number of samples n_eff. The se_mean is the standard deviation divided by the square root of the n_eff. As we can see, in addition to the information concerning theta, we have the same information for lp__. This is the logarithm of the (unnormalized) posterior density evaluated at the posterior samples of `theta`. This information is not often of direct interest in itself but is used in the calculation of various model fit statistics.

If we apply the generic `summary` command to `M_dice`, we obtain a list with two objects, `summary` and `c_summary`:

```
summary (M_dice) %>% class ()
#> [1] "list"
summary (M_dice) %>% names ()
#> [1] "summary"    "c_summary"
```

The `summary` object in this list is a matrix that summarizes the samples from all chains together. The `c_summary` object is a multidimensional array that gives a separate summary for each chain. With the main `summary` command, we can pass in a vector of parameters using the keyword `pars` and a vector of quantiles using the keyword `probs`. For example, to get the 2.5th and 97.5th percentile values of `theta`, and obtain these summaries for all chains together, we can do the following:

```
summary (M_dice, pars = 'theta', probs = c(0.025, 0.975))$summary
#>                mean       se_mean        sd      2.5%      97.5%     n_eff      Rhat
#> theta 0.2929358 0.0007865121 0.02939633 0.2359161 0.3541264 1396.933 1.002714
```

For convenience, we can create a custom function `stan_summary` to return the summary matrix as a tibble:

```
stan_summary <- function (stan_model, pars, probs = c(0.025, 0.975)){
    summary (stan_model, pars = pars, probs = probs)$summary %>%
      as_tibble (rownames = 'par')
}
```

```
stan_summary (M_dice, pars = 'theta')
#> # A tibble: 1 x 8
#>     par    mean   se_mean      sd  `2.5%`  `97.5%`  n_eff  Rhat
#>   <chr> <dbl>    <dbl> <dbl> <dbl>   <dbl> <dbl> <dbl>
#> 1 theta 0.293 0.000787 0.0294  0.236   0.354 1397.  1.00
```

Binomial model

Now let us consider a variant on the Bernoulli model for the loaded die. Because each of the n throws of the die and hence each 6 or not-6 binary outcome is independent of every other and dependent only on the value of θ, the mathematical model defined above is also identical to the following binomial model:

$$m \sim \text{Binomial}(n, \theta),$$
$$\theta \sim \text{Beta}(\alpha, \beta),$$

where *m* is the total number of observations where the outcome of the die throw was equal to 6. A Stan program for this model is in `loaded_dice_binomial.stan`:

```
// loaded_dice_binomial.stan
data {
    int<lower=1> N;
    int<lower=1, upper=N> m;
    real<lower=0> alpha;
    real<lower=0> beta;
}

parameters {
    real<lower=0, upper=1> theta;
}

model {
    theta ~ beta (alpha, beta);
    m ~ binomial (N, theta);
}
```

As we can see in the model block, we now have the line

```
m ~ binomial (N, theta);
```

rather than, from the previous Stan program,

```
y ~ bernoulli (theta);
```

As such, we no longer need to pass in `y` as data but need to pass in `m = sum(y)` instead. The value of `m` must be bounded between 1 and `N`, and hence we also include the following new line, which replaces the line declaring `y`:

```
int<lower=1, upper=N> m;
```

We then call the model as before:

```
M_dice_2 <- stan ('loaded_dice_binomial.stan',
                  data = list(m = sum(y),
                              N = length(y),
                              alpha = alpha,
                              beta = beta)
)
```

The summary results are almost identical to those of the Bernoulli model:

```
stan_summary (M_dice_2, pars = 'theta')
#> # A tibble: 1 x 8
```

```
#>    par      mean   se_mean       sd  `2.5%`  `97.5%`  n_eff   Rhat
#>    <chr> <dbl>      <dbl>  <dbl>   <dbl>   <dbl> <dbl> <dbl>
#> 1 theta 0.295 0.000741 0.0283   0.242   0.353 1457.   1.00
```

Logistic Bernoulli model

Another variant on the Bernoulli model above is the following logit model:

$$y_i \sim \text{Bernoulli}(\theta), \text{ for } i \in 1,2...n,$$

$$\log\left(\frac{\theta}{1-\theta}\right) = \mu, \ \mu \sim N(0,\sigma^2).$$

Here, the prior is a normal distribution, with mean 0 and variance σ^2, over the log odds of θ. This is simply an alternative prior over θ that is known as the *logit normal* distribution. Again, we will assume that σ is known. Setting $\sigma = 1.0$ gives a relatively diffuse prior over θ, albeit one that is unimodal and centred at $\theta = 0.5$. See Figure 17.1 for an illustration of this distribution.

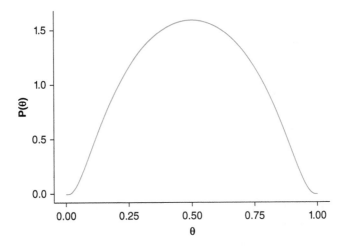

Figure 17.1 A logit normal prior over θ whose hyperparameters are $\mu = 0$ and $\sigma = 1$

The logit-normal-based model is defined in the `loaded_dice_logit.stan` file:

```
// loaded_dice_logit.stan
data {
  int<lower=1> N;
  int<lower=0, upper=1> y[N];
  real<lower=0> sigma;
}
parameters {
  real mu;
}
```

```
model {
  mu ~ normal(0, sigma);
  y ~ bernoulli_logit(mu);
}
generated quantities{
  real<lower=0, upper=1> theta;
  theta = inv_logit(mu);
}
```

In this program, we use the `bernoulli_logit` probability distribution that takes the normally distributed variable `mu` as a parameter. Given that we want to view samples from `theta` instead of, or at least in addition to, those of `mu`, we include the following `generated quan-tities` code block:

```
generated quantities{
  real<lower=0, upper=1> theta;
  theta = inv_logit(mu);
}
```

We can compile, execute and draw samples from this program using `rstan::stan` as usual. The summary results are almost identical to those of the Bernoulli model:

```
stan_summary(M_dice_3, pars = c('mu', 'theta'))
#> # A tibble: 2 x 8
#>   par      mean   se_mean        sd `2.5%`  `97.5%` n_eff  Rhat
#>   <chr>   <dbl>     <dbl>     <dbl>  <dbl>    <dbl> <dbl> <dbl>
#> 1 mu     -0.875   0.00344    0.135  -1.13   -0.616 1540.  1.00
#> 2 theta   0.295   0.000713   0.0280  0.244   0.351 1541.  1.00
```

Clearly, the posterior distribution over `theta` is practically identical in this model to that in the model with the beta prior.

Normal models

Now let us consider models where the observed variable is assumed to be normally distributed. In the following data set, we have data concerning mathematical achievement scores in a sample of US university students:

```
math_df <- read_csv('data/MathPlacement.csv')
```

A histogram for this data is shown in the mathematical Scholastic Aptitude Test (SAT) (SATM) scores shown in Figure 17.2:

```
math_df %>%
  ggplot(aes(x = SATM)) +
  geom_histogram(binwidth = 2, col='white')
```

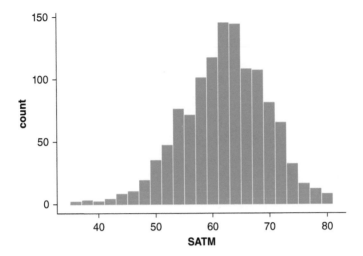

Figure 17.2 Histogram of mathematical SAT scores in a sample of students in a US university

Clearly, this data is unimodal and roughly bell-shaped, but also with a negative skew. Despite this lack of symmetry, a simple and almost default model of this data would be as follows:

$$y_i \sim N(\mu,\sigma^2), \quad \text{for } i \in 1,\dots,n,$$

where y_i is the maths SAT score of student i and where there are n students in total. Obviously, we have two unknowns, μ and σ, and so in a Bayesian model we first put priors over these two variables. As with the previous examples above, we have an almost endless variety of priors to use in this case. Given the simplicity of the model, and the fact that we have 1236 observations, excluding missing values, any prior that is not extremely precise will be dominated by the likelihood function when determining the posterior distribution, and thus most common choices are not likely to make much practical difference to the posterior distribution. A common choice for a prior on the μ parameter of the normal distribution is another normal distribution. This can be set to have a relatively high value for the variance (hyper)parameter to get a vague and hence weakly informative prior. For the prior over σ, Gelman (2006) generally recommends heavy-tailed distributions over the positive real values such as a half-Cauchy or half-t-distribution. Following these suggestions, our Bayesian model becomes, for example,

$$y_i \sim N\left(\mu,\sigma^2\right), \quad \text{for } i \in 1\dots n,$$
$$\mu \sim N\left(\nu,\tau^2\right), \quad \sigma \sim \text{Student}_+\left(\kappa,\phi,\omega\right),$$

where Student_+ is the upper half of the (non-standard) Student t-distribution centred at ϕ, with scale parameter ω, and with degrees of freedom κ. For this choice of prior, we therefore have in total five hyperparameters ν, τ, ϕ, ω and κ.

A Stan program implementing this model is in the file `normal.stan`:

```
// normal.stan
data {
```

```
    int<lower=0> N;
    real nu;
    real<lower=0> tau;
    real phi;
    real<lower=0> omega;
    int<lower=0> kappa;
    vector[N] y;
}
parameters {
    real mu;
    real<lower=0> sigma;
}
model {
    sigma ~ student_t(kappa, phi, omega);
    mu ~ normal(nu, tau);
    y ~ normal(mu, sigma);
}
```

This program is much the same as before with its three main code blocks. One important general feature of Stan not seen before is that the truncated Student t-distribution is defined by the general Student t-distribution. However, because `sigma` is defined as having only positive values, the resulting prior distribution over `sigma` is the half-t-distribution. In general, regardless of the prior distribution that we use, it will be truncated based on the variable's defined limits.

We can run this program with `rstan::stan` as follows:

```
math_data <- list(y = y, N = N, nu = 50, tau = 25, phi = 0, omega = 10, kappa = 5)
M_math <- stan('normal.stan', data = math_data)
```

As we can see, we have set the hyperparameters for the normal distribution on `mu` to `nu` = 50 and `tau` = 25. This places a relatively diffuse normal distribution over μ with its centre at 50 and with 95% of its mass from approximately 0 to 100. The half-t-distribution has its lower bound at 0, and with its scale being `omega` = 10, this entails that 95% of its mass extends as far as 30.

As before, we can view the summary of the results with `stan_summary`:

```
stan_summary(M_math, pars = c('mu', 'sigma'))
#> # A tibble: 2 x 8
#>    par     mean se_mean      sd `2.5%` `97.5%` n_eff  Rhat
#>    <chr>  <dbl>   <dbl>   <dbl>  <dbl>   <dbl> <dbl> <dbl>
#> 1 mu      62.6 0.00376  0.214   62.2    63.0  3229.  1.00
#> 2 sigma   7.50 0.00258  0.155    7.21    7.81 3609.  1.00
```

Clearly, this reveals very precise estimates of both the mean `mu` and standard deviation `sigma` of the normal distribution of maths SAT scores.

17.3 Regression models

Normal linear regression models are extensions of the normal-distribution-based model just described in the previous section.

Simple linear regression

As an example, using the `math_df` data, we will model how the score on a maths placement exam `PlcmtScore` varies as a function of `SATM`. A scatterplot of this data is shown in Figure 17.3.

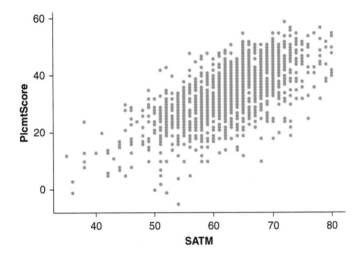

Figure 17.3 Scatterplot of scores on a mathematics placement exam against maths SAT scores

Denoting the `PlcmtScore` by y and `SATM` by x, the model can be written as follows:

$$\text{for } i \in 1,\ldots,n, \quad y_i \sim N(\mu_i, \sigma^2), \quad \mu_i = \beta_0 + \beta_1 x_i.$$

There are now three parameters in the model: β_0, β_1, σ. We will place normal priors on β_0 and β_1, and a half-t-distribution on σ. As such the full Bayesian model is as follows:

$$y_i \sim N(\mu_i, \sigma^2), \quad \mu_i = \beta_0 + \beta_1 x_i,$$
$$\beta_0 \sim N(v_0, \tau_0^2), \quad \beta_1 \sim N(v_1, \tau_1^2), \quad \sigma \sim \text{Student}_+(\kappa, \phi, \omega).$$

The Stan code for this model is in `normallinear.stan`:

```
// normlinear.stan
data {
  int<lower=0> N;
  vector[N] x;
  vector[N] y;
```

```
  // hyperparameters
  real<lower=0> tau;
  real<lower=0> omega;
  int<lower=0> kappa;
}

parameters {
  real beta_0;
  real beta_1;
  real<lower=0> sigma;
}

model {
  // priors
  sigma ~ student_t(kappa, 0, omega);
  beta_0 ~ normal(0, tau);
  beta_1 ~ normal(0, tau);
  // data model
  y ~ normal(beta_0 + beta_1 * x, sigma);
}
```

For this example, we will choose the hyperparameters to lead to effectively uninformative priors on β_0 and β_1. Specifically, the normal distributions will be centred on zero, $v_0 = v_1 = 0$, and will be sufficiently wide $\tau_0 = \tau_1 = 50$, so as to be effectively uniform over all practically possible values for β_0 and β_1. For the prior on σ, as above, we will use the upper half of the Student t-distribution centred at 0 with relatively low degrees of freedom and with a scale ω equal to the MAD of the outcome variable y. If we place the x and y data vectors and the values of the hyperparameters in the list `math_data_2`, we can call the Stan program using `rstan::stan` as we did above:

```
math_df_2 <- math_df %>%
  select(SATM, PlcmtScore) %>%
  na.omit()

x <- pull(math_df_2, SATM)
y <- pull(math_df_2, PlcmtScore)

math_data_2 <- list(
  x = x,
  y = y,
  N = length(x),
  tau = 50, omega = mad(y), kappa = 3
)

M_math_2 <- stan('normlinear.stan', data = math_data_2)
```

As before, we can view the results with `stan_summary`:

```
stan_summary (M_math_2, pars = c('beta_0', 'beta_1', 'sigma'))
#> # A tibble: 3 x 8
#>    par        mean   se_mean      sd   `2.5%`  `97.5%`  n_eff   Rhat
#>    <chr>     <dbl>     <dbl>   <dbl>    <dbl>    <dbl>  <dbl>  <dbl>
#> 1 beta_0   -23.6    0.0581    1.79    -27.3    -20.1    946.  1.00
#> 2 beta_1    0.913  0.000923  0.0284   0.858    0.970   945.  1.00
#> 3 sigma     7.62   0.00375   0.152    7.33     7.92    1642.  1.00
```

Multiple regression and categorical predictors

In general, we may have any number of predictors in a regression model. As we have seen previously, if any of these predictors are categorical variables, each one is recoded using a binary dummy code. For example, a categorical variable with L distinct levels can be recoded using $L - 1$ binary variables. The values of the predictors for all observations can be arranged as an $n \times (K + 1)$ matrix X, known as the design matrix, where n is the number of observations, K is the total final number of predictors after all categorical predictors have been recoded, and the first column of X is a vector of n ones. Therefore, in general, any normal linear model can be described as follows:

$$\vec{y} \sim N(\vec{\mu}, \sigma^2), \quad \vec{\mu} = X\vec{\beta},$$

where $\vec{y}$ is the n-dimensional vector of all observations of the outcome variable, $\vec{\beta}$ is a $(K + 1)$-dimensional vector of coefficients, and the first value of $\vec{\beta}$ is the intercept term. A full Bayesian version of this model is implemented in the program `mlreg.stan`:

```
// mlreg.stan
data {
    int<lower=0> N;
    int<lower=0> K;
    matrix [N, K+1] X;
    vector [N] y;

    // hyperparameters
    real<lower=0> tau;
    real<lower=0> omega;
    int<lower=0> kappa;
}

parameters {
    vector [K+1] beta;
    real<lower=0> sigma;
}
```

```
transformed parameters {
  vector[N] mu;
  mu = X * beta;
}


model {
  // priors
  beta ~ normal(0.0, tau);
  sigma ~ student_t(kappa, 0, omega);

  // data model
  y ~ normal(mu, sigma);
}
```

In this program, we have a normal prior on $\vec{\beta}$ and a half-t-distribution prior on σ as before. Note that the prior over $\vec{\beta}$ is specified in the Stan code as follows:

```
beta ~ normal(0.0, tau);
```

This places the same $N(0, \tau^2)$ prior over each element of $\vec{\beta}$. Note also that this program has a new command block that we have not used previously: transformed parameters. This is used to create parameters that are transformations of the original ones. Here, we have used it for the μ vector, which is a deterministic function of β and X.

To use this Stan program, the base R command model.matrix and the corresponding model_matrix command from the modelr package can used to create the design matrix X. As an example, in the following data set, we have the height, weight, gender, and race, among other variables, for a set of over 6000 individuals:

```
weight_df <- read_csv('data/weight.csv')
weight_df
#> # A tibble: 6,068 x 7
#>    subjectid gender height weight handedness   age race
#>        <dbl> <chr>   <dbl>  <dbl> <chr>       <dbl> <chr>
#>  1     10027 male     178.   81.5 right          41 white
#>  2     10032 male     170.   72.6 left           35 white
#>  3     10033 male     174.   92.9 left           42 black
#>  4     10092 male     166.   79.4 right          31 white
#>  5     10093 male     191.   94.6 right          21 black
#>  6     10115 male     172    80.2 right          39 white
#>  7     10117 male     181   116.  right          32 black
#>  8     10237 male     185    95.4 right          23 white
#>  9     10242 male     178.   99.5 right          36 white
#> 10     10244 male     181.   70.2 left           23 white
#> # ... with 6,058 more rows
```

The gender variable has two values, male and female. The race variable has seven values, of which white, black, hispanic make up around 95% of cases, and so we will limit our focus to them:

```
weight_df %<>% filter(race %in% c('black', 'white', 'hispanic'))
```

The design matrix to predict `weight` from `height`, `gender`, and `race` is as follows:

```
library(modelr)
model_matrix(weight_df, weight ~ height + gender + race)
#> # A tibble: 5,769 x 5
#>    `(Intercept)` height gendermale racehispanic racewhite
#>            <dbl>  <dbl>      <dbl>        <dbl>     <dbl>
#>  1             1   178.          1            0         1
#>  2             1   170.          1            0         1
#>  3             1   174.          1            0         0
#>  4             1   166.          1            0         1
#>  5             1   191.          1            0         0
#>  6             1   172           1            0         1
#>  7             1   181           1            0         0
#>  8             1   185           1            0         1
#>  9             1   178.          1            0         1
#> 10             1   181.          1            0         1
#> # ... with 5,759 more rows
```

Note that here, the `gender` variable has been coded with a single binary dummy code as follows:

female	0
male	1

On the other hand, the `race` variable has been coded by the following dummy code with two binary variables:

black	0	0
hispanic	1	0
white	0	1

The design matrix X and outcome vector $\bar{y}$ can now be obtained simply as follows:

```
X <- model_matrix(weight_df, weight ~ height + gender + race) %>%
  as.matrix()
y <- pull(weight_df, weight)
```

With this, the data list can be set up as follows:

```
weight_data <- list(
  X = X,
  y = y,
  N = length(y),
  K = ncol(X) - 1,
  tau = 100, kappa = 3, omega = mad(y)
)
```

We may then execute the Stan program with `stan`:

```
M_weight <- stan('mlreg.stan', data = weight_data)
```

We may view the summary of the posterior samples for $\vec{\beta}$ and σ using `stan_summary`:

```
stan_summary (M_weight, pars = c('beta', 'sigma'))
#> # A tibble: 6 x 8
#>    par          mean   se_mean      sd    `2.5%`  `97.5%`  n_eff  Rhat
#>    <chr>        <dbl>     <dbl>   <dbl>    <dbl>    <dbl>  <dbl> <dbl>
#> 1 beta[1]      -85.6    0.106     3.89    -93.1    -78.1  1348.  1.00
#> 2 beta[2]     0.950 0.000652  0.0237     0.904    0.996  1328.  1.00
#> 3 beta[3]      6.11    0.0117   0.456      5.20     7.00  1528.  1.00
#> 4 beta[4]    -0.446    0.0128   0.561     -1.54    0.654  1925.  1.00
#> 5 beta[5]     -2.30    0.00885  0.392     -3.06    -1.53  1962.  1.00
#> 6 sigma        11.6    0.00182  0.105     11.4     11.8   3356.  1.00
```

Generalized linear models

Extending the multiple linear regression example just described to a generalized linear model is very straightforward. Just as in the case of linear models, in generalized linear models, our predictor variables, including categorical predictor variables that have been recoded using a dummy binary code, can be represented as a $K + 1$ design matrix X. If our outcome variable vector $\vec{y}$ is a binary vector, a binary logistic regression model of this data would be as follows:

$$\vec{y} \sim \text{Bernoulli}\left(\vec{\theta}\right), \quad \text{logit}\left(\vec{\theta}\right) = X\beta.$$

On the other hand, if $\vec{y}$ is a vector of counts, we could use the following Poisson regression model for this data:

$$\vec{y} \sim \text{Poisson}\left(\vec{\lambda}\right), \quad \log\left(\vec{\lambda}\right) = X\beta.$$

Alternatively, our model for the count outcome variable could be a negative binomial regression model as follows:

$$\vec{y} \sim \text{NegBinomial}\left(\vec{\lambda}, \phi\right), \quad \log\left(\vec{\lambda}\right) = X\beta,$$

where ϕ is the inverse dispersion parameter.

Fully Bayesian versions of all of these models would be straightforward extensions of the multiple linear regression model in the previous section. For example, a Bayesian binary logistic regression with multiple predictors can be found in the `logitreg.stan`:

```
// logitreg.stan
data {
  int<lower=0> N;
  int<lower=0> K;
  matrix[N, K+1] X;
  int<lower=0, upper=1> y[N];
```

```stan
  // hyperparameters
  real<lower=0> tau;
}

parameters {
  vector[K+1] beta;
}

transformed parameters {
  vector[N] mu;
  mu = X * beta;
}

model {
  // priors
  beta ~ normal(0.0, tau);

  // data model
  y ~ bernoulli_logit(mu);
}
generated quantities{
  vector[N] theta;
  theta = inv_logit(mu);
}
```

This program is obviously similar to the normal linear regression model. The principal difference comes down to the model of the outcome variables, specified in the following line:

```stan
y ~ bernoulli_logit(mu);
```

Although not strictly necessary, we also include the following `generated quantities` block to calculate $\vec{\theta} = \mathrm{ilogit}(\vec{\mu})$, where $\vec{\mu} = X\vec{\beta}$:

```stan
generated quantities{
  vector[N] theta;
  theta = inv_logit(mu);
}
```

We can use this model with the following data set:

```r
biochem_df <- read_csv('data/biochemist.csv')
```

This contains data from 915 PhD students. For each one, we have the number of peer-reviewed articles they have published (publications), as well their gender (gender), whether they are married or not (married), how many children they have (children), a measure of the prestige of their institution (prestige), and the number of publications of their research mentor (mentor). We can also create a new variable that indicates if the PhD student was published or not:

```r
biochem_df %<>% mutate(published = publications > 0)
```

This binary variable can be the outcome variable in a logistic regression analysis that analyses how the probability of being published or not varies as a function of a set of predictor variables. We will use `gender`, `married`, `prestige` and `mentor` as predictors, and we will create a binary variable that indicates whether the number of children that the PhD student has is greater than zero or not. As above, we will create the design matrix for these predictors using `modelr::model_matrix`:

```
X <- model_matrix(~ gender + married + I(children > 0) + prestige + mentor,
data = biochem_df) %>%
  as.matrix()
```

Here, `gender` will be coded such that `Women` is coded as 1 and `Men` is coded as 0. For the `married` variable, `Married` is coded as 0 and `Single` is coded as 1. We can now create the necessary data for the Stan model:

```
y <- biochem_df %>% pull(published)
```

```
biochem_data <- list(y = y,
                     X = X,
                     N = nrow(X),
                     K = ncol(X) - 1,
                     tau = 100)
```

Here, with `tau` = 100, we set the standard deviation τ for the normal prior distribution over $\beta_0, \beta_1, ..., \beta_k, ..., \beta_K$. We can now call the Stan model with `stan`:

```
M_biochem <- stan('logitreg.stan', data = biochem_data)
```

We may view the summary of the posterior samples for $\vec{\beta}$ using `stan_summary`:

```
stan_summary(M_biochem, pars = 'beta')
#> # A tibble: 6 x 8
#>    par        mean    se_mean       sd   `2.5%`  `97.5%` n_eff  Rhat
#>    <chr>     <dbl>      <dbl>    <dbl>    <dbl>    <dbl> <dbl> <dbl>
#> 1 beta[1]    0.568    0.00614    0.277   0.0410    1.10   2039.  1.00
#> 2 beta[2]   -0.241    0.00283    0.160  -0.555   0.0730   3211.  1.00
#> 3 beta[3]   -0.347    0.00362    0.189  -0.710   0.0253   2727.  1.00
#> 4 beta[4]   -0.440    0.00376    0.187  -0.805  -0.0797   2491.  1.00
#> 5 beta[5]   0.0228    0.00165   0.0790  -0.134    0.178   2295.  1.00
#> 6 beta[6]   0.0818   0.000217   0.0128   0.0579   0.108   3460.  1.00
```

A Bayesian Poisson regression model can be implemented as a relatively minor extension of the logistic regression model, as we see in the following program from the file `poisreg.stan`:

```
// poisreg.stan
data {
  int<lower=0> N;
  int<lower=0> K;
```

```
  matrix[N, K+1] X;
  int<lower=0> y[N];

  // hyperparameters
  real<lower=0> tau;
}

parameters {
  vector[K+1] beta;
}

transformed parameters {
  vector[N] mu;
  mu = X * beta;
}

model {
  // priors
  beta ~ normal(0.0, tau);
  // data model
  y ~ poisson_log(mu);
}
generated quantities{
  vector[N] lambda;
  lambda = exp(mu);
}
```

The difference between this program and the logistic regression program occurs in three places. First, in the following line in the data block, we indicate that the values of y are integers that are bounded by zero but have no upper limit:

```
int<lower=0> y[N];
```

Second, in the following line in the model block, we indicate that y is modelled as a Poisson distribution:

```
y ~ poisson_log(mu);
```

Note that, here, the distribution is poisson_log. This entails that the input argument vector, denoted by mu, is the logarithm of the rate of the Poisson distribution. In other words, mu is $\bar{\mu} = \log(\lambda)$ from the mathematical description above. Third, to obtain the rate itself, we use the following generated quantities block:

```
generated quantities{
  vector[N] lambda;
  lambda = exp(mu);
}
```

We will use the x design matrix as before, but set y to be `publications`, which gives the number of publications for each student. Therefore, our input data list is as follows:

```
y <- biochem_df %>% pull(publications)
biochem_data_count <- list(y = y,
                           X = X,
                           N = nrow(X),
                           K = ncol(X) - 1,
                           tau = 100)
```

We then execute the program as follows:

```
M_biochem_pois <- stan('poisreg.stan', data = biochem_data_count)
```

We may then view the summary of the posterior samples for $\vec{\beta}$ using `stan_summary` as before:

```
stan_summary(M_biochem_pois, pars = 'beta')
#> # A tibble: 6 x 8
#>    par       mean     se_mean      sd    `2.5%`  `97.5%` n_eff  Rhat
#>    <chr>     <dbl>     <dbl>      <dbl>   <dbl>    <dbl> <dbl> <dbl>
#> 1 beta[1]  0.459    0.00214    0.0916   0.282   0.641   1825.  1.00
#> 2 beta[2] -0.218    0.00106    0.0551  -0.324  -0.112   2700.  1.00
#> 3 beta[3] -0.151    0.00123    0.0629  -0.275  -0.0280  2627.  1.00
#> 4 beta[4] -0.248    0.00121    0.0627  -0.373  -0.128   2666.  1.00
#> 5 beta[5]  0.00941  0.000567   0.0259  -0.0409  0.0622  2086.  1.00
#> 6 beta[6]  0.0258   0.0000257  0.00200  0.0219  0.0297  6029.  1.00
```

As a final example of a generalized linear model, let us consider a negative binomial model, which is suitable for overdispersed count data. A Stan program implementing this is in `negbinreg.stan`:

```
// negbinreg.stan
data {
  int<lower=0> N;
  int<lower=0> K;
  matrix[N, K+1] X;
  int<lower=0> y[N];

  // hyperparameters
  real<lower=0> tau;
}
parameters {
  vector[K+1] beta;
  real<lower=0> phi;
}
```

```
transformed parameters {
  vector[N] mu;
  mu = X * beta;
}


model {
  // priors
  beta ~ normal(0.0, tau);
  phi ~ cauchy(0, 10);


  // data model
  y ~ neg_binomial_2_log(mu, phi);
}


generated quantities{
  vector[N] lambda;
  lambda = exp(mu);
}
```

The outcome variable is modelled as a negative binomial with the key line

```
y ~ neg_binomial_2_log(mu, phi);
```

Note that, as described above in the mathematical description, the mean of the negative binomial is given by λ where $\log(\lambda) = X\vec{\beta}$. Thus, in the Stan code, the mu corresponds to $X\vec{\beta}$. The negative binomial distribution also has an additional parameter, ϕ. The higher the inverse of ϕ, the greater the overdispersion in the distribution. Here, we put a Cauchy prior with a scale of 10 on ϕ:

```
phi ~ cauchy(0, 10);
```

We will use the same biochem_data_count as we used in the case of the Poisson distribution and then execute the program as follows:

```
M_biochem_nb <- stan('negbinreg.stan', data = biochem_data_count)
```

We may then view the summary of the posterior samples for $\vec{\beta}$ using stan_summary as before:

```
stan_summary(M_biochem_nb, pars = 'beta')
#> # A tibble: 6 x 8
#>     par         mean     se_mean         sd    `2.5%`    `97.5%`  n_eff   Rhat
#>     <chr>       <dbl>       <dbl>      <dbl>     <dbl>      <dbl>  <dbl>  <dbl>
#> 1 beta[1]    0.392    0.00287    0.129      0.143     0.646     2032.  1.00
#> 2 beta[2]   -0.206    0.00135    0.0739    -0.348    -0.0604    2998.  1.00
#> 3 beta[3]   -0.144    0.00166    0.0856    -0.314     0.0181    2652.  0.999
#> 4 beta[4]   -0.228    0.00162    0.0863    -0.397    -0.0606    2828.  1.00
#> 5 beta[5]    0.0146   0.000748   0.0359    -0.0563    0.0858    2301.  1.00
#> 6 beta[6]    0.0294   0.0000484  0.00340    0.0228    0.0363    4948.  1.00
```

17●4   Multilevel models

A multilevel linear regression model, also known as a linear mixed effects model, can be written as follows:

$$y_i \sim N(\mu_i, \sigma^2), \quad \mu_i = \vec{x}_i \vec{\beta}_{z_i}, \quad \text{for } i \in 1,\dots,n,$$

where each $z_i \in 1,\dots,J$ and each $\vec{\beta}_j \sim N(\vec{b}, \Sigma)$. In other words, as we explained in Chapter 11, each observation i is a member of subgroup or cluster z_i, each cluster has its own set of regression coefficients (e.g. cluster j has coefficients vector $\vec{\beta}_j$), and the set of J coefficients vectors are each drawn from a multivariate normal distribution with mean vector $\vec{b}$ and covariance matrix Σ.

For simplicity here, we will consider a linear mixed effects model with one predictor variable. This can be written as follows:

$$y_i \sim N(\mu_i, \sigma^2), \quad \mu_i = \beta_{0z_i} + \beta_{1z_i} x_i, \quad \text{for } i \in 1,\dots,n,$$

where each $z_i \in 1, 2,\dots,J$ and

$$\vec{\beta}_j = \begin{bmatrix} \beta_{0j} \\ \beta_{1j} \end{bmatrix} \sim N(\vec{b}, \Sigma),$$

where $\vec{b} = [b_0, b_1]^{\mathsf{T}}$. The covariance matrix Σ can be written

$$\Sigma = \begin{bmatrix} \tau_0^2 & \tau_0 \tau_1 \rho \\ \tau_0 \tau_1 \rho & \tau_1^2 \end{bmatrix},$$

where τ_0 and τ_1 are the standard deviations of the group-level intercepts and slopes respectively, and ρ is their correlation coefficient.

In this model, we must specify priors for $\vec{b}$, Σ and the residual standard deviation σ. Clearly, there are other parameters in the model, namely $\vec{\beta}_1, \vec{\beta}_2,\dots,\vec{\beta}_J$. However, the prior for these is determined by the values of $\vec{b}$ and Σ. A commonly used, even default, prior family for $\vec{b}$ is the normal distribution. If this is centred at zero and has a relatively wide variance, then this is effectively an uninformative prior. For Σ, on the other hand, we have more choices. One generally useful prior for Σ is the LJK (named after Lewandowski, Kurowicka and Joe, 2009) prior on its corresponding correlation matrix, and a separate prior on the variance terms. In this example, however, because there is only one correlation coefficient term in the matrix, namely ρ, we will put a prior on that and then separate priors on τ_0 and τ_1. Finally, we will put a similar prior on σ.

A Stan program for this model is in the file `lmm.stan`:

```
// lmm.stan
data {
  int<lower=1> N; // no. observations
  int<lower=1> J; // no. groups

  vector[N] y; // outcome
  vector[N] x; // predictor
  int<lower=0, upper=J> z[N]; // group index
}
```

```
parameters {
  vector[2] b;
  vector[2] beta[J];
  real<lower=-1, upper=1> rho;
  vector<lower=0>[2] tau;
  real<lower=0> sigma;
}
transformed parameters {
  cov_matrix[2] Sigma;
  corr_matrix[2] Omega;
  Omega[1, 1] = 1;
  Omega[1, 2] = rho;
  Omega[2, 1] = rho;
  Omega[2, 2] = 1;
  Sigma = quad_form_diag(Omega, tau);
}


model {
  rho ~ uniform(-1, 1);
  tau ~ cauchy(0, 10);
  sigma ~ cauchy(0, 10);
  b ~ normal(0, 100);

beta ~ multi_normal(b, Sigma);

for (i in 1:N)
  y[i] ~ normal(beta[z[i], 1] + x[i] * beta[z[i], 2], sigma);
}
```

In the `model` block, we specify Cauchy priors on `sigma` and `tau`, where the latter corresponds to the vector $[\tau_0, \tau_1]^T$, a uniform prior on ρ, and a very diffuse normal distribution prior on the `b` vector. We also see that `beta`, which corresponds to the set of J vectors $\vec{\beta}_1, \vec{\beta}_2, ..., \vec{\beta}_J$, follows a multivariate normal distribution. For each individual observation, for $i \in 1,...,n$, the model is $y_i \sim N(\mu_i, \sigma^2)$, $\mu_i = \beta_{0z_i} + \beta_{1z_i} x_i$. In the Stan program, this is implemented in the following lines:

```
for (i in 1:N)
  y[i] ~ normal(beta[z[i], 1] + x[i] * beta[z[i], 2], sigma);
```

This model can be tested using the `sleepstudy` data set from `lme4`, which we explored in Chapter 12:

```
sleepstudy <- lme4::sleepstudy

y <- sleepstudy$Reaction
x <- sleepstudy$Days
z <- sleepstudy$Subject %>% as.numeric()
```

```
sleep_data <- list(N = length(y),
                   J = length(unique(z)),
                   y = y,
                   x = x,
                   z = z)


M_lmm <- stan('lmm.stan', data = sleep_data)
```

The summary of the main parameters of this model is as follows, which are comparable to the results obtained from the non-Bayesian `lmer` analysis of the same model:

```
stan_summary(M_lmm, pars = c('b', 'tau', 'rho', 'sigma'))
#> # A tibble: 6 x 8
#>    par       mean se_mean     sd `2.5%` `97.5%` n_eff  Rhat
#>    <chr>    <dbl>   <dbl>  <dbl>  <dbl>   <dbl> <dbl> <dbl>
#> 1 b[1]    250.    0.123    7.13  236.    264.   3354.  1.00
#> 2 b[2]     10.5   0.0277   1.66    7.10   13.8  3594.  1.00
#> 3 tau[1]   24.4   0.150    6.25   13.6    38.2  1740.  1.00
#> 4 tau[2]    6.32  0.0272   1.39    4.08    9.46 2620.  1.00
#> 5 rho       0.123 0.00785  0.293  -0.442   0.703 1388. 1.00
#> 6 sigma    25.9   0.0267   1.59   23.1    29.2  3526.  1.00
```

17●5   Posterior expectations

As mentioned in the introduction to this chapter, quantities of interest from a Bayesian model can be expressed as *posterior expectations* that can be approximated using Monte Carlo integration:

$$\langle g(\theta) \rangle = \int g(\theta) P(\theta \mid \mathcal{D}) d\theta \approx \frac{1}{n} \sum_{i=1}^{n} g(\tilde{\theta}_i),$$

where $\tilde{\theta}_1, \tilde{\theta}_2, \ldots, \tilde{\theta}_n$ are posterior samples of the unknown variables in the model. In general, any quantity of interest from a Bayesian model can be expressed in this way. For this reason, when we have the posterior samples, any question of interest concerning the model may be addressed.

We can obtain each sample from each chain for any variables using `rstan::extract` as follows, where we used the `M_dice` model as an example:

```
rstan::extract(M_dice, pars='theta', permuted=F, inc_warmup=T) %>%
  magrittr::extract(,,1) %>%
  as_tibble()
#> # A tibble: 2,000 x 4
#>    `chain:1` `chain:2` `chain:3` `chain:4`
#>        <dbl>     <dbl>     <dbl>     <dbl>
#> 1     0.345     0.211    0.0784     0.233
#> 2     0.345     0.211    0.0784     0.233
#> 3     0.345     0.211    0.0784     0.233
```

```
#>  4      0.345      0.332      0.367        0.307
#>  5      0.342      0.332      0.341        0.307
#>  6      0.346      0.325      0.253        0.293
#>  7      0.276      0.332      0.277        0.311
#>  8      0.328      0.291      0.324        0.324
#>  9      0.295      0.291      0.288        0.312
#> 10      0.262      0.297      0.279        0.312
#> # … with 1,990 more rows
```

(In this command, we use the `extract` function from both `rstan` and `magrittr` and so we use their namespaces to distinguish between them.) With `rstan::extract`, by using `permute = F` we obtain an array for each parameter that we specify in `pars`, and get all samples including the warm up samples by `inc_warmup`. This function returns a multidimensional array whose first dimension indexes the samples, whose second indexes the chains, and whose third indexes the parameters.

The package `tidybayes` provides many useful functions from working with Stan-based models, including functions from extracting samples. For example, using the `M_math_2` regression model described above, the following extracts the (post-warm up) samples into a data frame with one row for each sample from each chain:

```
library(tidybayes)
spread_draws(M_math_2, beta_0, beta_1, sigma)
#> # A tibble: 4,000 x 6
#>    .chain .iteration .draw beta_0 beta_1 sigma
#>    <int>      <int> <int>  <dbl>  <dbl> <dbl>
#>  1      1          1     1  -24.4  0.925  7.69
#>  2      1          2     2  -25.1  0.936  7.43
#>  3      1          3     3  -23.8  0.920  7.72
#>  4      1          4     4  -24.7  0.933  7.59
#>  5      1          5     5  -23.6  0.910  7.48
#>  6      1          6     6  -24.4  0.926  7.68
#>  7      1          7     7  -28.0  0.983  7.92
#>  8      1          8     8  -28.1  0.983  7.93
#>  9      1          9     9  -28.0  0.984  8.15
#> 10      1         10    10  -26.2  0.955  7.21
#> # … with 3,990 more rows
```

With these samples in this format, we may now easily compute quantities of interest. For example, let us imagine we are interested in knowing the probability that someone could score greater than 50 on `PlcmtScore`, given that their SATM score was exactly 75. If we knew the true values of β_0, β_1 and σ, we would calculate this as follows:

$$P(y > 50 \mid x = 75, \beta_0, \beta_1, \sigma) = \int_{50}^{\infty} N(y \mid \mu = \beta_0 + \beta_1 \times 75, \sigma) dy.$$

Integration over the posterior distribution of β_0, β_1 and σ is as follows:

$$P(y > 50 \mid x = 75) = \int P(y > 50 \mid x = 75, \beta_0, \beta_1, \sigma) P(\beta_0, \beta_1, \sigma \mid D) d\beta_0 d\beta_1 d\sigma.$$

Using Monte Carlo integration, this integral is approximated as follows:

$$P(y > 50 \mid x = 75) \approx \frac{1}{S}\sum_{i=1}^{S} P\left(y > 50 \mid x = 75, \tilde{\beta}_{0,s}, \tilde{\beta}_{1,s}, \tilde{\sigma}_s\right),$$

where $\tilde{\beta}_{0,s}$, $\tilde{\beta}_{1,s}$, $\tilde{\sigma}_s$, for $s \in 1,\ldots,S$, are S samples from the posterior distribution. This calculation can be easily performed using R. First, we write a function to calculate $P(y>50 \mid x=75, \beta_0, \beta_1, \sigma)$:

```
f <- function (beta_0, beta_1, sigma) {
  pnorm (50,
        mean = beta_0 + beta_1 * 75,
        sd = sigma,
        lower.tail = F
  )
}
```

We then compute this function for each sample from the posterior and calculate the average:

```
spread_draws (M_math_2, beta_0, beta_1, sigma) %>%
  mutate (p = f (beta_0, beta_1, sigma)) %>%
  summarise (prob = mean (p))
#> # A tibble: 1 x 1
#>     prob
#>    <dbl>
#> 1 0.251
```

REFERENCES

Akaike, H. (1973) Information theory and an extension of the maximum likelihood principle. In B. N. Petrov and F. Csáki (eds), *Proceedings of the Second International Symposium on Information Theory*. Budapest: Akadémiai Kiadó, pp. 267–281.

Anscombe, F. J. (1973) Graphs in statistical analysis. *The American Statistician*, 27(1), 17–21.

Berry, D. A. (1995) *Statistics: A Bayesian Perspective*. Belmont, CA: Duxbury Press.

Betancourt, M. (2017) A conceptual introduction to Hamiltonian Monte Carlo. Preprint, arXiv:1701.02434.

Bishop, C. M. (1995) *Neural Networks for Pattern Recognition*. Oxford: Oxford University Press.

Bishop, C. M. (2006) *Pattern Recognition and Machine Learning*. New York: Springer.

Bollen, K. A. (1979) Political democracy and the timing of development. *American Sociological Review*, 44(4), 572–587.

Bollen, K. A. (1989) *Structural Equations with Latent Variables*. New York: Wiley.

Breiman, L. (2001) Statistical modeling: The two cultures (with comments and a rejoinder by the author). *Statistical Science*, 16(3), 199–231.

Burnham, K. P. and Anderson, D. R. (2003) *Model Selection and Multimodel Inference: A Practical Information-Theoretic Approach*. New York: Springer.

Bürkner, P.-C. (2018) Advanced Bayesian multilevel modeling with the R package brms. *The R Journal*, 10(1), 395–411.

Chacon, S. and Straub, B. (2014) *Pro Git* (2nd edn). Berkeley, CA: Apress.

Cleveland, W. S. (2001) Data science: An action plan for expanding the technical areas of the field of statistics. *International Statistical Review*, 69(1), 21–26.

Clopper, C. J. and Pearson, E. S. (1934) The use of confidence or fiducial limits illustrated in the case of the binomial. *Biometrika*, 26(4), 404–413.

CrowdFlower (2016) CrowdFlower 2016 Data Science Report. https://visit.figure-eight.com/data-science-report.html

CrowdFlower (2017) CrowdFlower 2017 Data Scientist Report. https://www.figure-eight.com/download-2017-data-scientist-report

Diaconis, P., Holmes, S. and Montgomery, R. (2007) Dynamical bias in the coin toss. *SIAM Review*, 49(2), 211–235.

Eddelbuettel, D. (2013) *Seamless R and C++ Integration with Rcpp*. New York: Springer.

Eddelbuettel, D. and Balamuta, J. J. (2017) Extending *R* with *C++*: A Brief Introduction to *Rcpp*. *PeerJ Preprints*, 5, e3188v1.

Fair, R. C. (1978) A theory of extramarital affairs. *Journal of Political Economy*, 86(1), 45–61.

Fang, Y. (2011) Asymptotic equivalence between cross-validations and Akaike information criteria in mixed-effects models. *Journal of Data Science*, 9(1), 15–21.

Fecher, B., Friesike, S. and Hebing, M. (2015) What drives academic data sharing? *PLoS One*, 10(2), e0118053.

Fisher, R. A. (1925) *Statistical Methods for Research Workers*. Edinburgh: Oliver & Boyd.

Gelman, A. (2006) Prior distributions for variance parameters in hierarchical models (comment on article by Browne and Draper). *Bayesian Analysis*, 1(3), 515–534.

Gelman, A. and Hill, J. (2007) *Data Analysis Using Regression and Multilevel/Hierarchical Models*. Cambridge: Cambridge University Press.

Gelman, A. and Nolan, D. (2002a) You can load a die, but you can't bias a coin. *The American Statistician*, 56(4), 308–311.

Gelman, A. and Nolan, D. (2002b) *Teaching Statistics: A Bag of Tricks*. Oxford: Oxford University Press.

Gelman, A., Simpson, D. and Betancourt, M. (2017) The prior can often only be understood in the context of the likelihood. *Entropy*, 19(10), 555.

Gorgolewski, K. J. and Poldrack, R. A. (2016) A practical guide for improving transparency and reproducibility in neuroimaging research. *PLoS Biology*, 14(7), e1002506.

Grätzer, G. (2016) *Math into LaTeX* (5th edn). Cham: Springer.

Gruber, J. (2004) Markdown. https://daringfireball.net/projects/markdown/

Hartwig, F. and Dearing, B. E. (1979) *Exploratory Data Analysis*. Beverly Hills, CA: Sage.

Healy, K. (2019) *Data Visualization: A Practical Introduction*. Princeton, NJ: Princeton University Press.

Hern, A. (2013) Is Excel the most dangerous piece of software in the world? *New Statesman*, 11 February. https://www.newstatesman.com/technology/2013/02/excel-most-dangerous-piece-software-world

Hoffman, M. D. and Gelman, A. (2014) The No-U-Turn Sampler: Adaptively setting path lengths in Hamiltonian Monte Carlo. *Journal of Machine Learning Research*, 15(1), 1593–1623.

Horn, J. L. (1965) A rationale and test for the number of factors in factor analysis. *Psychometrika*, 30(2), 179–185.

Houtkoop, B. L., Chambers, C., Macleod, M., Bishop, D. V. M., Nichols, T. E. and Wagenmakers, E.-J. (2018) Data sharing in psychology: A survey on barriers and preconditions. *Advances in Methods and Practices in Psychological Science*, 1(1), 70–85.

Ioannidis, J. P. A. (2015) How to make more published research true. *Revista Cubana de Información en Ciencias de la Salud (ACIMED)*, 26(2), 187–200.

Iqbal, S. A., Wallach, J. D., Khoury, M. J., Schully, S. D. and Ioannidis, J. P. A. (2016) Reproducible research practices and transparency across the biomedical literature. *PLoS Biology*, 14(1), e1002333.

Jöreskog, K. G. (1967) Some contributions to maximum likelihood factor analysis. *Psychometrika*, 32(4), 443–482.

Jöreskog, K. G. and Van Thillo, M. (1972) *LISREL: A General Computer Program for Estimating a Linear Structural Equation System Involving Multiple Indicators of Unmeasured Variables*. Princeton, NJ: Educational Testing Service.

Kerrich, J. E. (1946) *An Experimental Introduction to the Theory of Probability*. Copenhagen: E. Munksgaard.

Knuth, D. E. (1984) Literate programming. *Computer Journal*, 27(2), 97–111.

Lamport, L. (1994) *LaTeX: A Document Preparation System*. Reading, MA: Addison-Wesley.

Landau, W. M. (2018) The drake R package: A pipeline toolkit for reproducibility and high-performance computing. *Journal of Open Source Software*, 3(21). https://doi.org/10.21105/joss.00550

Lewandowski, D., Kurowicka, D. and Joe, H. (2009) Generating random correlation matrices based on vines and extended onion method. *Journal of Multivariate Analysis*, 100(9), 1989–2001.

Lohr, S. (2014) For big-data scientists, 'janitor work' is key hurdle to insights. *New York Times*, 17 August. https://www.nytimes.com/2014/08/18/technology/for-big-data-scientists-hurdle-to-insights-is-janitor-work.html

MacFarlane, J. (2006) Pandoc: A Universal Document Converter. https://pandoc.org/

May, R. M. (1976) Simple mathematical models with very complicated dynamics. *Nature*, 261 (5560), 459–467.

Merton, R. K. (1973) *The Sociology of Science: Theoretical and Empirical Investigations*. Chicago: University of Chicago Press.

Metropolis, N., Rosenbluth, A. W., Rosenbluth, M. N., Teller, A. H. and Teller, E. (1953) Equation of state calculations by fast computing machines. *Journal of Chemical Physics*, 21(6), 1087–1092.

Metropolis, N. and Ulam, S. (1949) The Monte Carlo method. *Journal of the American Statistical Association*, 44(247), 335–341.

Mosteller, F. and Tukey, J. W. (1977) *Data Analysis and Regression: A Second Course in Statistics*. Reading, MA: Addison-Wesley.

Muenchen, R. A. (2019) The Popularity of Data Science Software. http://r4stats.com/articles/popularity

Munafò, M. R., Nosek, B. A., Bishop, D. V. M., Button, K. S., Chambers, C. D., Du Sert, N. P., Simonsohn, U., Wagenmakers, E.-J., Ware, J. J. and Ioannidis, J. P. A. (2017) A manifesto for reproducible science. *Nature Human Behaviour*, 1(1), 0021.

Murphy, K. P. (2012) *Machine Learning: A Probabilistic Perspective*. Cambridge, MA: MIT Press.

Neal, R. M. (2011) MCMC using Hamiltonian dynamics. In S. Brooks, A. Gelman, G. L. Jones and X.-L. Meng (eds), *Handbook of Markov Chain Monte Carlo*. Boca Raton, FL: CRC Press.

Nosek, B. A., Alter, G., Banks, G. C., Borsboom, D., Bowman, S. D., Breckler, S. J., Buck, S. et al. (2015) Promoting an open research culture. *Science*, 348(6242), 1422–1425.

Pearl, J. (2012) The causal foundations of structural equation modeling. In R. H. Hoyle (ed.), *Handbook of Structural Equation Modeling*. New York: Guilford Press.

Schiller, J. J., Srinivasan, R. and Spiegel, M. R. (2000) *Schaum's Outlines: Probability*. New York: McGraw-Hill.

Shamir, L., Wallin, J. F., Allen, A., Berriman, B., Teuben, P., Nemiroff, R. J., Mink, J., Hanisch, R. J. and DuPrie, K. (2013) Practices in source code sharing in astrophysics. *Astronomy and Computing*, 1, 54–58.

Spearman, C. (1904) 'General intelligence,' objectively determined and measured. *American Journal of Psychology*, 15(2), 201–292.

Stevens, S. S. (1946) On the theory of scales of measurement. *Science*, 103(2684), 677–680.

Stodden, V., Guo, P. and Ma, Z. (2013) Toward reproducible computational research: An empirical analysis of data and code policy adoption by journals. *PLoS One*, 8(6), e67111.

Stone, M. (1977) An asymptotic equivalence of choice of model by cross-validation and Akaike's criterion. *Journal of the Royal Statistical Society, Series B*, 39(1), 44–47.

Tenopir, C., Allard, S., Douglass, K., Aydinoglu, A. U., Wu, L., Read, E., Manoff, M. and Frame, M. (2011) Data sharing by scientists: Practices and perceptions. *PLoS One*, 6(6), e21101.

Tufte, E. R. (1983) *The Visual Display of Quantitative Information*. Cheshire, CT: Graphics Press.

Tukey, J. W. (1962) The future of data analysis. *Annals of Mathematical Statistics*, 33(1), 1–67.

Tukey, J. W. (1977) *Exploratory Data Analysis*. Reading, MA: Addison-Wesley.

Vehtari, A., Gelman, A. and Gabry, J. (2017) Practical Bayesian model evaluation using leave-one-out cross-validation and WAIC. *Statistics and Computing*, 27(5), 1413–1432.

Velleman, P. F. and Wilkinson, L. (1993) Nominal, ordinal, interval, and ratio typologies are misleading. *The American Statistician*, 47(1), 65–72.

Venables, W. N. and Ripley, B. D. (2002) *Modern Applied Statistics with S* (4th edn). New York: Springer.

Watanabe, S. (2010) Asymptotic equivalence of Bayes cross validation and widely applicable information criterion in singular learning theory. *Journal of Machine Learning Research*, 11, 3571–3594.

Weissgerber, T. L., Milic, N. M., Winham, S. J. and Garovic, V. D. (2015) Beyond bar and line graphs: Time for a new data presentation paradigm. *PLoS Biology*, 13(4), 1–10.

Westfall, P. H. (2014) Kurtosis as peakedness, 1905–2014. RIP. *The American Statistician*, 68(3), 191–195.

Wickham, H. (2010) A layered grammar of graphics. *Journal of Computational and Graphical Statistics*, 19(1), 3–28. https://doi.org/10.1198/jcgs.2009.07098

Wickham, H. (2016) *ggplot2: Elegant Graphics for Data Analysis*. New York: Springer. https://ggplot2.tidyverse.org

Wickham, H. (2019) *Advanced R* (2nd edn). Boca Raton, FL: Chapman and Hall/CRC.

Wickham, H. (2021) *Mastering Shiny*. Sebastopol, CA: O'Reilly.

Wilkinson, L. (2005) *The Grammar of Graphics*. Berlin: Springer.

Wood, S. (2019) Mgcv: Mixed GAM Computation Vehicle with Automatic Smoothness Estimation. https://CRAN.R-project.org/package=mgcv

Wood, S. N. (2017) *Generalized Additive Models: An Introduction with R* (2nd edn). Boca Raton, FL: Chapman and Hall/CRC.

Wright, S. (1921) Correlation and causation. *Journal of Agricultural Research*, 20(7), 557–585.

Wright, S. (1934) The method of path coefficients. *Annals of Mathematical Statistics*, 5(3), 161–215.

Xie, Y. (2017) *Dynamic Documents with R and Knitr*. Boca Raton, FL: Chapman and Hall/CRC.

INDEX